COMMENTARY ON
THE RULE OF ST. BENEDICT

The Rule of Saint Benedict

A COMMENTARY BY THE RIGHT REV.
DOM PAUL DELATTE, ABBOT OF SOLESMES
AND SUPERIOR-GENERAL OF THE CONGRE-
GATION OF BENEDICTINES OF FRANCE

TRANSLATED BY DOM JUSTIN McCANN

Wipf and Stock Publishers
EUGENE, OREGON

NIHIL OBSTAT:

D. CUTHBERTUS ALMOND.

IMPRIMATUR:

✠ EDUARDUS,
Archiep. Birmingamien.

die 14 Septembris, 1920.

First Published . . 1921
This Edition . . 1950

EX ACTIS CAPITULI GENERALIS XI CONGREGATIONIS
GALLICÆ O.S.B.

Unus e Capitularibus, nomine omnium adstantium, imo et totius Congregationis, gratias refert Rmo Præsidi quam maximas et meritissimas pro novo opere juris communis facto, nempe Commentario in Sanctam Regulam, ex quo omnes haurire possumus uberrimam æque ac profundissimam notitiam perfectionis status monastici et largiter accipere purissimum spiritum Sanctissimi Patris nostri Benedicti.

Wipf and Stock Publishers
199 West 8th Avenue, Suite 3
Eugene, Oregon 97401

Commentary on the Rule of St. Benedict
By Delatte, Paul
ISBN: 1-57910-460-6
Publication date: August, 2000
Previously published by The Archabbey Press, 1921.

THESE PAGES, WRITTEN WITH THE AIM OF DISCLOSING THE RICHES OF THE HOLY RULE, ARE DEDICATED, IN LOVE AND DEVOTEDNESS, TO ALL THOSE, WHETHER IN MONASTERIES OR IN THE WORLD, WHO BELONG TO THE GREAT FAMILY OF ST. BENEDICT.

QUARR ABBEY,
September 8th, 1913.

PREFACE

THE following translation was made at Ampleforth in 1917, and was not at first intended for publication. It has been published through the urgency of several friends, who persuaded the translator that some such commentary on the Rule, in English, was needed and would be welcomed.

The translation endeavours to be a faithful and accurate rendering of the original. In this endeavour the translator has received constant help from the Benedictines of Quarr, for which he is deeply grateful. He is aware that he has not entirely avoided the defects which are usual in translations, and for this he asks the indulgence of his readers.

The differences between the translation and the original are inconsiderable. A few modifications of the text have been rendered necessary by the publication of the *Codex Juris Canonici*. An index has been supplied, and an English version of the Rule set parallel with the Latin text. In constructing this version free use has been made of current versions, especially of the excellent *Rule of St. Benedict* of Abbot Hunter-Blair. Latin quotations in the text have generally been translated.

On one further point the translator feels that he owes a word of explanation, both to the general reader and to his own brethren. The Benedictine monasteries of the world are grouped in Congregations, generally on a national basis. Among these Congregations there is considerable diversity of discipline and custom; and this though all follow the same Rule. Such diversity has been characteristic of Benedictinism from the beginning. Now the translator is a member of the English Benedictine Congregation, a very ancient body with a unique tradition. It is natural therefore that there should be points of interpretation on which he would differ from the author of the Commentary. But he has not allowed his own opinions to affect the translation; he does not even think it necessary to mention them; he would only ask the reader to observe that such phrases as "our Congregation," "our Constitutions" etc., wherever they occur in the text, as indeed every word and sentence of the book, are uttered, not by the translator, but by the author, the very distinguished Superior-General of the Benedictines of France.

Finally, the translator desires to express his gratitude to the author for the privilege that has been allowed him. And he wishes to associate his work, in its degree, with the spirit and intention of the Dedication.

St. Benet's Hall,
   Oxford.
     1920.

INTRODUCTION

"THE man of God, Benedict, among the many wonderful works that made him famous in this world, was also conspicuous for his teaching: for he wrote a Rule for monks, remarkable for discretion and rich in instruction. If anyone desires to know more deeply the life and character of the man, he may find in the ordinances of that Rule the exact image of his whole government: for the holy man cannot possibly have taught otherwise than as he lived." To this judgement of St. Gregory the Great,[1] so complete for all its grace of form and sobriety of language, we may yet add two observations: first that the moral beauty of St. Benedict, his temperament and almost his characteristics, are reflected also in the pages, at once candid and profound, of his biographer; secondly, that the Rule itself came, in the middle of the sixth century, as the ripe fruit of a considerable monastic past and of the spiritual teaching of the Fathers.

St. Benedict was above all else a man of tradition. He was not the enthusiastic creator of an entirely new form of the religious life: neither nature nor grace disposed him to such a course. As may be seen from the last chapter of his Rule, he cared nothing for a reputation of originality, or for the glory of being a pioneer. He did not write till late, till he was on the threshold of eternity, after study and perhaps after experience of the principal monastic codes. Nearly every sentence reveals almost a fixed determination to base his ideas on those of the ancients, or at least to use their language and appropriate their terms. But even though the Rule were nothing but an intelligent compilation, even though it were merely put together with the study and spiritual insight of St. Benedict, with the spirit of orderliness, moderation, and lucidity of this Roman of old patrician stock, it would not for all that be a commonplace work: in actual fact, it stands as the complete and finished expression of the monastic ideal. Who can measure the extraordinary influence that these few pages have exercised, during fourteen centuries, over the general development of the Western world? Yet St. Benedict thought only of God and of souls desirous to go to God; in the tranquil simplicity of his faith he purposed only to establish a school of the Lord's service: *Dominici schola servitii*. But, just because of this singleminded pursuit of the one thing necessary, God has blessed the *Rule of Monks* with singular fruitfulness, and St. Benedict has taken his place in the line of the great patriarchs.

We may almost say of the Benedictine Rule—what is certainly true of the Law of God—that it bears in itself its own justification, that it is self-sufficient; "the judgements of the Lord are true, justified in themselves," and that it only needs to be read and loved and lived.

[1] *Dialogues*, bk. II., chap. xxxvi. This second book is devoted to the life of St. Benedict; there is a French translation by E. CARTIER. [An English translation, adapted from an earlier version, has been printed in the QUARTERLY SERIES.]

A practical commentary on words dictated by the Spirit of God has scarcely any other task than to spell them tenderly, to emphasize them wisely, and to put them in the clearest light. And, indeed, a long series of labours might very usefully converge on a literal explanation of the Rule: a study, for instance, of monastic institutions from the holy ventures of the Church of Jerusalem and the heroism of the Thebaid to St. Basil and to St. Benedict; a study of the life of St. Benedict; a critical history of the text of the Rule and a history of its diffusion; an account of the living interpretation furnished by the customaries and the Rules modelled on St. Benedict's; and finally a view of contemporary monachism. Without entirely neglecting any of these questions, especially those which are necessary for the understanding of the text, our Commentary remains, even in its printed form, what it originally was: an exposition of the Rule given in the Novitiate of the Abbey of Solesmes. It reproduces, in an abridged form, conferences introductory to the monastic life. Hence the absence of any scientific apparatus properly so called; hence sometimes the familiar and homely style; hence certain repetitions, provoked most often by the insistence of our Holy Father himself. Perhaps the publication of these notes will satisfy, in some measure, the interest of the many Christian souls who ask us every day for enlightenment on the mode of life, spirituality, and real usefulness of monks.

The text we explain is the one in current use in the Congregation of the Benedictines of France. But everyone may consult the critical editions of Schmidt and of Wölfflin, the labours of Traube, Plenkers, G. Morin, and other scholars, and especially the excellent edition brought out in 1912 by the Right Reverend Dom C. Butler.[1] We must indicate briefly the chief theories that have been propounded with regard to the history of the text. Dom Schmidt was the first to point out the existence of two very distinct families of manuscripts. According to him the most ancient manuscripts (*Oxoniensis*, of the end of the seventh century; *Veronensis* LII. (otherwise 50) and *Sangallensis* 916, of the eighth to ninth century) give the text of a first redaction of the Rule; all three seem to come from an immediate common source. D. Schmidt even thought that he had found in a Tegernsee manuscript (*Monacensis* 19408, ninth century) the representative of an autograph copy entrusted by St. Benedict to St. Maurus when the latter went to Gaul. The *Monte Cassino* autograph, of which Theodemar sent Charlemagne a faithful copy[2] that was spread widely, would then represent a second and final redaction. Wölfflin, in the preface to his edition of the Rule, puts forward the hypothesis of three or even four redactions.

[1] President of the English Benedictine Congregation.
[2] We may follow the history of this copy, if it be indeed the same one, in PAUL THE DEACON, *De gestis Langobardorum*, l. IV., c. xviii.; l. VI., c. xl. (*Patrologia Latina*, XCV., 547-548, 650-651), and in the *Chronicle of Monte-Cassino* by LEO OF OSTIA, l. I., 48 (*P.L.*, CLXXIII., 555). The latter relates that the autograph was destroyed in the burning of the monastery of Teano in 896.

Introduction

It is certain that St. Benedict did not compose his Rule at one stroke; Chapters LXVII.-LXXIII. are an addition; the Prologue was probably written last. But, according to the view that tends more and more to prevail, the manuscripts do not reveal the existence of several editions of the Rule issued by St. Benedict himself. Traube, Plenkers, and Butler have shown that the text of the most ancient codices that remain to us is really an emended and interpolated text. The genuine and standard text must be sought for in the twofold Carlovingian and Cassinese tradition: especially in *Sangallensis* 914, transcribed, in the early years of the ninth century, from the copy sent to Charlemagne.[1] D. Morin has issued a critical edition of this manuscript, and D. Butler has taken it as the basis of his labours. The text on which we comment is a vulgate, a text which has been worked up and improved, like that of the most ancient codices, and at about the same time; D. Butler finds traces of this *textus receptus* as early as the eighth century; and this is the text reproduced in the majority of the manuscripts of the tenth, eleventh, and twelfth centuries, and in the printed editions. Let us remember finally that St. Benedict wrote in the vulgar tongue as spoken in the neighbourhood of Cassinum in the sixth century: the grammar and spelling of our text are largely retouched. We have not yet got the definitive critical edition.

There is a very great interest in watching the genesis of the Rule, in examining in detail how much of it is old and how much new. To facilitate this task D. Butler has assembled and transcribed the chief sources at the foot of his text: we have thus been able to add some references to those which we had already collected. St. Benedict often quotes St. Augustine, and several times St. Jerome; he had read St. Cyprian, St. Leo, and Sulpicius Severus. The Rule is reminiscent continually of the *Institutes* and the *Conferences* of Cassian.[2] Much is borrowed from the two collections of the Rules of St. Basil, the *Regulæ fusius tractatæ*, and the *Regulae brevius tractatæ*, or rather from the summary and fusion of the two effected by Rufinus, their translator into Latin. St. Benedict reproduces many a passage of the Rule of St. Pachomius translated by St. Jerome. He quotes the Rules of St. Caesarius *Ad monachos* and *Ad virgines;* the Rule of St. Macarius of Alexandria; the first two of the so-called *Rules of the Holy Fathers;* the *Regula Orientalis;* the *Doctrina* of St. Orsiesius, etc.[3] He was

---

[1] *Cf.* Pauli Diaconi, *Epist.* I. (*P.L.*, XCV., 1585). This copy no longer exists.

[2] We shall cite Cassian after the edition of Michael Petschenig, vols. XIII. (*Conlationes*) and XVII. (*De institutis cænobiorum*) of the Vienna *Corpus scriptorum ecclesiasticorum latinorum.* But the reader will do well not to neglect the commentary of the old editor Dom Alard Gazet, *P.L.*, XLIX. These two works of Cassian have been translated into French by E. Cartier. [There is an English translation in vol. XI. of the *Select Library of Nicene and Post-Nicene Fathers.*]

[3] We shall cite all these Rules from the *Codex Regularum* of St. Benedict of Aniane, edited by Holstenius (Paris, 1663); likewise the Rules subsequent to St. Benedict, in particular the interesting anonymous Rule called the *Rule of the Master* (seventh century).

familiar also with various hagiographical collections since grouped under the general title of *Lives of the Fathers:* the *Life of St. Antony*, the *Lausiac History of Palladius*, the *History of the Monks of Egypt* translated by Rufinus, the *Verba seniorum;* etc.[1]

A word now on the principal commentaries. The oldest that has come down to us is probably that of Paul the Deacon, generally identified, though the point is not absolutely established,[2] with Paul Warnefrid, the historian of the Lombards, a monk of Monte Cassino towards the end of the eighth century. The commentary of the Frank Hildemar is scarcely more, according to Traube, than a slightly expanded copy of the preceding one. Like the commentary of Smaragdus, Abbot of St. Mihiel, Hildemar's was composed in the first half of the ninth century. Bernard of Monte Cassino in the thirteenth century, and Petrus Boherius in the fourteenth, also wrote explanations of the Rule.[3] In 1638 D. Hugh Ménard published, with copious and learned notes, the *Concordia Regularum* of St. Benedict of Aniane, the great monastic reformer of the beginning of the ninth century.[4] But the most complete commentaries are still those of D. Mège and D. Martène in the seventeenth century, and above all of D. Calmet in the century following. D. Mège and D. Calmet wrote in French; and the latter gives an "alphabetical list of authors who have written on the Rule of St. Benedict" with "critical observations on the rules of the monks and canons." The only French commentary of any size that has appeared since is the *Explication ascétique et historique de la Règle de saint Benoît, par un Bénédictin* (1901).

The Holy See having constituted the Congregation of France heir to Cluny and St. Maur, we have a special motive for paying regard to the customs of those two families. The most ancient collection that contains the use of Cluny is the customary of Guy of Farfa; next comes the *Ordo Cluniacensis* of Bernard; and finally the *Antiquiores consuetudines Cluniacenses* of Udalric, reproduced, with some modifications, in the *Constitutiones* of William of Hirschau: all works of the eleventh

---

[1] For simplicity we shall take passages that occur in the *Vitæ Patrum* from the edition of ROSWEYD (1615). The Greek text of the *Lausiac History of Palladius* should now be cited according to the edition of D. BUTLER (vol. VI. of *Texts and Studies*, Cambridge, 1904); it has been translated into French by A. LUCOT (Paris, 1912).

[2] *Cf.* D. BUTLER, *Sancti Benedicti Regula Monachorum*, Prolegom., p. xvii.

[3] The commentary of PAUL WARNEFRID was edited at Monte Cassino in 1880; that of HILDEMAR, by D. MITTERMÜLLER, being appended to bk. II. of the *Dialogues* of St. Gregory and SCHMIDT's edition of the Rule, and published by Pustet at Ratisbon, also in 1880; SMARAGDUS is printed in tome CII. of Migne's Latin Patrology (see L. BARBEAU, *Essai critique sur la vie et les œuvres de Smaragde*, thesis for the École des Chartes, 1906, pp. 1-6); BERNARD OF MONTE CASSINO was edited at Monte-Cassino by D. CAPLET, in 1894; BOHERIUS at Subiaco by D. L. ALLODI, in 1908.

[4] On the manuscripts of the two works of ST BENEDICT OF ANIANE, and on the edition of the ancient Latin monastic Rules which is being prepared by the Vienna Academy, see H. PLENKERS, *Untersuchungen zur Ueberlieferungsgeschichte der ältesten lateinischen Mönchsregeln*, Munich, 1906.

century.[1] Recourse may also be had to the *Disquisitiones monasticæ* of D. Haeften (1644), and to the *De antiquis monachorum ritibus* of D. Martène; as well as to the *Acta Sanctorum Ordinis S. Benedicti* and the *Annales* of D. Mabillon.[2]

The primary purpose of these studies is neither curiosity nor historical knowledge: our concern is with the soul and with the supernatural life. By constant communing with the master thought of St. Benedict and with the minds of his best disciples, will the sons of D. Guéranger be able to keep alive among them the true spirit of monasticism.

[1] The Customs of UDALRIC were edited by D. LUC D'ACHERY in his *Spicilegium*, and reprinted by Migne in tome CXLIX. of his *P.L.* The other customaries are to be found in the *Vetus disciplina monastica* of D. HERRGOTT; those of Farfa and Hirschau in tome CL. of the *P.L.*—Dom B. ALBERS re-edited the *Consuetudines Farfenses* (in 1900, at Monte Cassino) in the first volume of his *Consuetudines monasticæ*; in the second volume he gives *Consuetudines Cluniacenses antiquiores*, which, according to him, are in reality the oldest known, and of which part may date even from the time of St. Benedict of Aniane.

[2] We shall cite the *De ant. monach. rit.* after the Antwerp edition, 1738; the *De ant. Eccl. rit.* after the Antwerp edition, 1736; the *Annales* of MABILLON after the Lucca edition, 1739–1745; the Acta SS. O.S.B. according to the Venice edition, 1733.

CONTENTS

CHAPTER		PAGE
	INTRODUCTION	ix
	PROLOGUE	1
I.	OF THE VARIOUS KINDS OF MONKS	25
II.	WHAT KIND OF MAN THE ABBOT OUGHT TO BE	35
III.	OF CALLING THE BRETHREN TO COUNCIL	56
IV.	WHAT ARE THE INSTRUMENTS OF GOOD WORKS	61
V.	OF OBEDIENCE	83
VI.	THE SPIRIT OF SILENCE	92
VII.	OF HUMILITY	100
VIII.	OF THE DIVINE OFFICE AT NIGHT	131
IX.	HOW MANY PSALMS ARE TO BE SAID AT THE NIGHT HOURS	144
X.	HOW THE NIGHT OFFICE IS TO BE SAID IN SUMMER	153
XI.	HOW THE NIGHT OFFICE IS TO BE SAID ON SUNDAYS	154
XII.	HOW THE OFFICE OF LAUDS IS TO BE SAID	158
XIII.	HOW LAUDS ARE TO BE SAID ON WEEKDAYS	160
XIV.	HOW THE NIGHT OFFICE IS TO BE SAID ON SAINTS'-DAYS	164
XV.	AT WHAT TIMES OF THE YEAR "ALLELUIA" IS TO BE SAID	168
XVI.	HOW THE WORK OF GOD IS TO BE DONE IN THE DAY-TIME	170
XVII.	HOW MANY PSALMS ARE TO BE SAID AT THE DAY HOURS	174
XVIII.	IN WHAT ORDER THE PSALMS ARE TO BE SAID	177
XIX.	HOW TO SAY THE DIVINE OFFICE	185
XX.	OF REVERENCE AT PRAYER	189
XXI.	OF THE DEANS OF THE MONASTERY	194
XXII.	HOW THE MONKS ARE TO SLEEP	200
XXIII.	OF EXCOMMUNICATION FOR FAULTS	205
XXIV.	WHAT THE MEASURE OF EXCOMMUNICATION SHOULD BE	211
XXV.	OF GRAVER FAULTS	215
XXVI.	OF THOSE WHO CONSORT WITH THE EXCOMMUNICATE	218
XXVII.	HOW CAREFUL THE ABBOT SHOULD BE OF THE EXCOMMUNICATE	220
XXVIII.	OF THOSE WHO BEING OFTEN CORRECTED DO NOT AMEND	225
XXIX.	WHETHER THE BRETHREN WHO LEAVE THE MONASTERY ARE TO BE RECEIVED AGAIN	228
XXX.	HOW YOUNG BOYS ARE TO BE CORRECTED	231
XXXI.	OF THE CELLARER OF THE MONASTERY	233
XXXII.	OF THE TOOLS AND PROPERTY OF THE MONASTERY	243
XXXIII.	WHETHER MONKS OUGHT TO HAVE ANYTHING OF THEIR OWN	245
XXXIV.	WHETHER ALL OUGHT TO RECEIVE NECESSARY THINGS ALIKE	251
XXXV.	OF THE WEEKLY SERVERS IN THE KITCHEN	254
XXXVI.	OF THE SICK BRETHREN	258

CHAPTER		PAGE
XXXVII.	OF OLD MEN AND CHILDREN	263
XXXVIII.	THE WEEKLY READER	265
XXXIX.	OF THE MEASURE OF FOOD	270
XL.	OF THE MEASURE OF DRINK	275
XLI.	AT WHAT HOURS THE BRETHREN ARE TO TAKE THEIR MEALS	278
XLII.	THAT NO ONE MAY SPEAK AFTER COMPLINE	281
XLIII.	OF THOSE WHO COME LATE TO THE WORK OF GOD OR TO TABLE	286
XLIV.	OF THOSE WHO ARE EXCOMMUNICATED, HOW THEY ARE TO MAKE SATISFACTION	294
XLV.	OF THOSE WHO MAKE MISTAKES IN THE ORATORY	297
XLVI.	OF THOSE WHO OFFEND IN ANY OTHER MATTERS	299
XLVII.	OF SIGNIFYING THE HOUR FOR THE WORK OF GOD	302
XLVIII.	OF THE DAILY MANUAL LABOUR	304
XLIX.	OF THE OBSERVANCE OF LENT	317
L.	OF BRETHREN WHO ARE WORKING AT A DISTANCE FROM THE ORATORY OR ARE ON A JOURNEY	322
LI.	OF BRETHREN WHO DO NOT GO FAR AWAY	325
LII.	OF THE ORATORY OF THE MONASTERY	327
LIII.	OF THE RECEPTION OF GUESTS	330
LIV.	WHETHER A MONK OUGHT TO RECEIVE LETTERS OR TOKENS	343
LV.	OF THE CLOTHES AND SHOES OF THE BRETHREN	346
LVI.	OF THE ABBOT'S TABLE	358
LVII.	OF THE ARTIFICERS OF THE MONASTERY	361
LVIII.	OF THE DISCIPLINE OF RECEIVING BRETHREN INTO RELIGION	367
LIX.	OF THE SONS OF NOBLES OR THE POOR THAT ARE OFFERED	406
LX.	OF PRIESTS WHO MAY WISH TO DWELL IN THE MONASTERY	413
LXI.	OF PILGRIM MONKS, HOW THEY ARE TO BE RECEIVED	418
LXII.	OF THE PRIESTS OF THE MONASTERY	424
LXIII.	OF THE ORDER OF THE COMMUNITY	431
LXIV.	OF THE APPOINTMENT OF THE ABBOT	441
LXV.	OF THE PRIOR OF THE MONASTERY	456
LXVI.	OF THE PORTER OF THE MONASTERY	463
LXVII.	OF BRETHREN WHO ARE SENT ON A JOURNEY	468
LXVIII.	IF A BROTHER BE COMMANDED TO DO IMPOSSIBILITIES	472
LXIX.	THAT MONKS PRESUME NOT TO DEFEND ONE ANOTHER	476
LXX.	THAT NO ONE PRESUME RASHLY TO STRIKE OR EXCOMMUNICATE ANOTHER	479
LXXI.	THAT THE BRETHREN BE OBEDIENT ONE TO THE OTHER	482
LXXII.	OF THE GOOD ZEAL WHICH MONKS OUGHT TO HAVE	486
LXXIII.	THAT THE WHOLE OBSERVANCE OF JUSTICE IS NOT SET DOWN IN THIS RULE	491
	INDEX	497

COMMENTARY ON THE RULE OF ST. BENEDICT

PROLOGUE

Ausculta, o fili, præcepta magistri, et inclina aurem cordis tui, et admonitionem pii patris libenter excipe, et efficaciter comple; ut ad eum per obedientiæ laborem redeas, a quo per inobedientiæ desidiam recesseras.

Hearken, O my son, to the precept of your master, and incline the ear of your heart: willingly receive and faithfully fulfil the admonition of your loving father, that you may return by the labour of obedience to Him from whom you had departed through the sloth of disobedience.

OTHER Rules have a more impersonal character, a more concise and formal legislative air: St. Benedict in his first words puts himself in intimate contact with his followers, commencing the code of our monastic life with a loving address.

He who speaks is a master; for we cannot dispense with a master in the supernatural life, which is at once a science and an art. He gives precepts—that is to say, doctrinal and practical instruction. St. Benedict here speaks of himself, though many commentators have thought differently. It is no folly to call himself master, since he teaches not in his own name, nor things of his own devising. He wrote near the end of his life and in the fulness of his experience. Why should he not be a loving father—*pius pater*, as he expresses it?

"O my son": a title of endearment; softening whatever austerity there may be in the "precepts of the master," suggesting also that the highest form of fatherhood is that which transmits doctrine and enlightenment, having its ideal and source in God the "father of light" (Jas. i. 17). St. Thomas tells us that there is a true fatherhood among the angels;[1] and in the Old Testament, among the patriarchs for instance, if a man was a father he had to be a teacher as well, and while he gave life had to enlighten the soul and hand on the teachings of God and His promises; so is Noah called a "herald of justice" (2 Pet. ii. 5). Experience shows that no earthly fatherhood has ever so closely resembled the fatherhood of God as did St. Benedict's. The Church venerates him as the patriarch of the monks of the West; and God has so disposed the course of history that every religious Order is in some way indebted to him and has learnt from his fatherly wisdom.

Truly these first words of the prologue are attractive and reassuring. The master who addresses you, my child, is a father, a good and loving father. The precepts which he brings you are counsels dictated by

[1] St. Thomas Aquinas, *Summa Theol.*, P. I., q. xlv., a. 5, ad. 1.

his experience and his love—" the admonition of your loving father."
He does not dream of imposing them on you, but appeals to your good
will, to your delicacy of perception; there is no question of constraint,
but of a loving and glad acceptance, of supernatural docility.

This docility St. Benedict requires of every beginner; this same
docility, under the forms of humility and obedience, gives our monastic
life its authentic character; and, finally, by it is sanctity won: " Whoso
are led by the spirit of God, they are the sons of God " (Rom. viii. 14)
The sovereign importance of this simple, unaffected disposition comes
from the fact that it comprises in itself all virtue. To begin with,
docility means prudence, and in prudence are united all the moral
virtues. We cannot in our own persons have all experiences; but
others have had them, and we reap the benefit of these by our docility.
We make our own the wisdom of humanity supernaturalized, the
wisdom of St. Benedict, and faith makes us share the very wisdom of
God. Docility, and docility alone, establishes us in that state whence
all self-seeking has been driven, a state which is the condition and the
prelude of a living union with Our Lord. Its name then is charity.

We should note how St. Benedict analyzes and details the successive
stages of supernatural docility. " Hearken ": for we must listen; if
there be too much noise in the soul and the attention be scattered over
a multitude of objects, the voice of God which is generally quiet as
" the whistling of a gentle air " (3 Kings xix. 12) is not heard. That
silence which of itself is perfect praise, " To thee silence is praise,"[1]
is rare among beings so fickle and impressionable as we are.

But to hearken is not enough, and St. Benedict invites us in the
pretty phrase of the Book of Proverbs[2] and Psalm xliv. to " incline
the ear of our heart." We must have a receptive understanding, a
trustful attitude towards the truth that is proposed to us. If we begin
by putting obstacles, by establishing at the entry of our souls a strict
barrier, or still more, if we be filled with our own views to the point of
saying, " He cannot teach me anything new; I know all that and better
than he does ! . . ." then we are in the worst possible mental state,
not only for supernatural teaching, but even for purely human instruction. Claude Bernard[3] tells us that the scientist, while striving to
formulate and verify his hypothesis, must be careful not to be led captive

---

[1] Ps. lxiv. 2, according to the Hebrew.

[2] C. iv. *Audi, fili mi, et suscipe verba mea. . . . Fili mi ausculta sermones meos
et ad eloquia mea inclina aurem tuam. Ne recedant ab oculis tuis, custodi ea in medio
cordis tui.*

St. Jerome begins one of his letters *ad Eustochium* with the words of Ps. xliv.
(Ep. XXII. 1. *P.L.*, XXII., 394).

It would be inaccurate to set down as source of this beginning of the Prologue the
beginning of the *Admonitio ad filium spiritualem* which figures among the *spuria* of
St. Basil, and was inserted by HOLSTENIUS into the appendix of his *Codex regularum*.
This treatise is probably the work of ST. PAULINUS OF AQUILEIA; but the beginning and
other passages have been added later by some monk; *cf. P.L.*, XCIX., 212 *sq.* (See
also *P.L.*, XL., 1054 *sq.*)

[3] *Introduction à l'étude de la médecine expérimentale.*

by it, but must always remain accessible to any other better explanation. Our Holy Father asks us, then, to listen willingly, with free souls: "willingly receive." Let us ever accept at once the teaching which is given to us; if there be in it any elements which we cannot assimilate, these will be eliminated later of themselves.

"*Et efficaciter comple*." And faithfully fulfil. It is the property of truth to move us to action. We cannot "hold it captive in injustice" (Rom. i. 18). We shall have to answer to God for all the good we have seen and have not done. But therein too lies the difficulty; for sin has upset the balance of our being: seeing, willing, loving, performing, these are far from being one single operation.

So lest the work should frighten us, and to make clear at once its character and plan, our Holy Father, with the insight of genius, yet in the quiet classical style, sets down that which is the prize of our life, that which should be its single object, that which gives it its dignity, charm, and power, its merit and simplicity, that in which is contained the whole Rule: "that you may return to Him by the labour of obedience." For our business is not to live many years, and to become learned, or to make a name in the world, but to walk to God, to get near to Him, to unite ourselves to Him. This manner of conceiving the spiritual life as a fearless walking to God is a favourite one with St. Benedict; we shall meet it many times in the Rule. Our life is on an inclined plane: we may ascend or descend, and the latter is very easy. Since the Fall, man has only one way in which to separate himself from God, and that is the way of the old Adam, disobedience; and he has, too, but one way to return and that is by obedience, with the new Adam. "For as by the disobedience of one man, many were made sinners: so also by the obedience of one, many shall be made just" (Rom. v. 19). We pride ourselves on our disobedience, as giving proof of energy and vigorous personality; but St. Benedict declares that it is merely cowardice and sloth; and if he speaks of the contrary attitude of mind as "labour"[1] he will presently tell us of its solid fruitfulness and incomparable dignity.

Ad te ergo nunc meus[2] sermo dirigitur, quisquis abrenuntians propriis voluntatibus, Domino Christo vero regi militaturus, obedientiæ fortissima atque præclara arma assumis.

To you, therefore, my words are now addressed, whoever you are, that, renouncing your own will, you do take up the strong and bright weapons of obedience, in order to fight for the Lord Christ, our true King.

In these words St. Benedict indicates to whom his invitation is addressed, for whom is the scheme of life just sketched in rough outline. To you my words and my fatherly exhortation are now addressed, whoever you may be, provided you be docile and resolute. So that

---

[1] *Dicebant senes: quia nihil sic quærit Deus ab his qui primitias habent conversationis, quomodo obedientiæ laborem* (*Verba Seniorum: Vitæ Patrum*, V., xiv. 15. ROSWEYD, p. 619).

[2] The best reading is *mihi*. ST. JEROME likewise says, in Letter XXII. *ad Eustochium* (15): *Nunc ad te mihi omnis dirigatur oratio* (*P.L.*, XXII., 403).

if we except the incapable and those who are bound by the ties of other duty, no one is excluded. All that is required in the candidate is the intention to accept the conditions of the monastic life, which are reducible to three: renunciation of one's own will, the taking up of the weapons of obedience, and service of the Lord.

To renounce one's own will is a necessary preliminary. St. Benedict speaks of " wills " in the plural,[1] because self-will or egoism has many forms. Without pretending to classify them we may observe that states of will may be spontaneous, or systematic, or temperamental. The first of these are the least dangerous, because implying only the mistake of a moment, a temporary distraction or interruption of continuity. The systematic will is continually springing up in the course of the religious life. On the day of our profession we renounced all things, but we build up the old again later on. It may be a question of a person one likes or dislikes, or a question of doctrine, some detail perhaps on which we cannot yield. Still more difficult is it to rid ourselves of temperament, of that disagreeable, obstinate, wrangling temper which sets us everlastingly in opposition.

In proportion as we strip ourselves of the old secular vesture of egoism and cast off all its trappings, so shall we be ready to take and use the weapons of obedience. St. Paul regards the principal virtues as different pieces of the supernatural armour; but our Holy Father gives one general name to the arms which he gives to his monks,[2] and speaks of the " weapons of obedience." A soldier has to obey, to obey always and no matter what happens; and a soldier of Jesus Christ has to obey universally and without asking for reasons; it is the least he can do. We have heard a great deal on the immorality of the vow of obedience, and what are called the passive virtues have received plenty of abuse. But St. Benedict had other notions of human dignity; in his view the weapons of obedience were the strongest, the best tempered, the most splendid, the most glorious. We obey God, we obey a Rule which we have studied and chosen; we obey a man, but within the limits of our vow. And while we obey we are free, since it is of our own act that we unite our will to the will of God, which can hardly entail any loss of dignity. Moreover, we are bound to make the real motive of the act our own, and so we unite our thoughts with the Divine thought.

Once we are enrolled and armed we have but to fight under the standard of the true King, the Lord Christ: " to fight for the Lord Christ our true King."[3] We serve Him and His purpose, and we

---

[1] The same expression occurs in the *Verba Seniorum* (*Vitæ Patrum*, V., i. 9. ROSWEYD, p. 562) and in the *Historia monachorum* of RUFINUS (XXXI. ROSWEYD, p. 484). St. Benedict cites in Chapter VII. the verse of Ecclesiasticus, xviii. 30: *Et a voluntatibus tuis avertere.*

[2] *Cf. Exhortatio de panoplia ad monachos* (inter S. ÉPHREM. opp. græc. lat., t. III., p. 219).

[3] *Sum enim laboriosus, etiam nunc sub magno opere peccator; veteranus in numero peccatorum, sed æterno Regi novus incorporeæ tiro militiæ* (S. PAULINI NOLANI, Ep. IV. ad S. Augustinum. P.L., LXI., 165).

serve according to the example He has given. " In the head of the book it is written of me that I should do thy will. O my God, I have desired it, and thy law in the midst of my heart " (Ps. xxxix. 8, 9). " Being made obedient even unto death " (Phil. ii. 8). Let us have a full realization of the drama which is being enacted, and in which we have to play our part. This drama fills all time and all space. It began, with the very beginning of things, in the angelic world, by an act of disobedience. This brought another in its train here below, one which has been repaired by the obedience of Our Lord Jesus Christ. All intelligent beings are ranged in two camps, those who obey and those who obey not; and the struggle of the two forces knows no truce. Each has its king, and he who claims to withdraw himself from obedience passes by this very fact under the domination of the other King. God for god, I prefer my own. In the army of those who obey the Lord, religious form a picked body. Our Holy Father recognizes elsewhere that the monastic life is also a school, a workshop, and above all a family.

In primis,[1] ut quidquid agendum inchoas bonum, ab eo perfici instantissima oratione deposcas; ut, qui nos jam in filiorum dignatus est numero computare, non debeat aliquando de malis actibus nostris contristari.

In the first place, whatever good work you begin to do, beg of Him with most earnest prayer to perfect it; that He who has now vouchsafed to count us in the number of His children may not at any time be grieved by our evil deeds.

Our Holy Father's first piece of advice and his first care is that we should rest on God in order to go to Him. We need grace and we need the prayer which wins grace; for these two things are connected and go necessarily together. This clear statement, at the very beginning of the Rule, makes short work of any Pelagian or Semi-Pelagian corruption of the truth. Pelagius, a wandering monk, held that man was essentially good, that his good will was sufficient for right action. Besides this he needed, but only as external helps, the law, and the teaching and example of Our Lord. Cassian himself, in his thirteenth Conference, considers that our reason and will are sufficient for the first act by which we accept the faith and enter upon the life of grace. The words of St. Benedict are profoundly wise and are in agreement with the teaching of the Council of Orange:[2] " The assistance of God must ever be asked even by the baptized and the saints, that they may be able to reach a good end or to persevere in good."

We cannot do without God. God has part in each one of our acts, and influences their very origin. This is especially true of supernatural acts, because the created agent is there setting forces to work which are not his own. The first movement towards the faith and to baptism

[1] With recent editors (SCHMIDT, WÖLFFLIN), we might join *dirigitur* and *in primis*, treating *quisquis abrenuntians* . . . as a parenthetical clause. D. BUTLER rejects this punctuation as contrary to that of the best manuscripts and to the interpretation of the oldest commentators.

[2] Cap. x., MANSI, *Sacrorum Conciliorum nova et amplissima Collectio*, t. VIII., col. 714.

is due to an impulsion of His grace; so too a true religious vocation comes from Him and not from any course of reasoning or philosophic deduction. But the co-operation of God is as indispensable for the continuance of this supernatural work as for its commencement; for it is a long work, as long as life. And though our vocation be angelic, our natures are not so. The angel is steadfast in the one act of his will; we with our weaker natures, more open to attack and assailed by lower impulses, must ever be renewing our purpose, so ready are we to fail before difficulty. Therefore we must go to God and ask Him in fervent prayer, prayer instant and untiring, *instantissima oratione*, for the grace to "perfect," the grace of perseverance.

There can be no doubt that God yields to our prayer; He has already engaged to do so, He has tied His hands. The best answer to the natural question, Shall I have strength to persevere? is that God has anticipated us: "For he hath first loved us. . . . With an everlasting love have I loved thee, therefore I drew thee, having pity on thee." His love is eternal. He has drawn close to each one of us. As a mark of it He has in baptism given us unasked the supernatural and divine life. Now we are of the number of His children. Let us then be what He has made us. Let us not by misdeeds belie that dignity to which His mere love has raised us. Let us strive not to cheat His goodness, nor to give Him cause to repent of it. In words full of insight and filial love, St. Benedict regards the development of our perfection as a personal success of God, and its miscarriage as a disappointment of the Almighty.

Ita enim ei omni tempore de bonis suis in nobis parendum est: ut non solum, ut iratus pater, non aliquando filios suos exhæredet; sed nec ut metuendus Dominus, irritatus malis nostris, ut nequissimos servos perpetuam tradat ad pœnam, qui eum sequi noluerint ad gloriam.	For we must always so serve Him with the good things He has given us, that not only may He never, as an angry father, disinherit His children, but may never, as a dread Lord, incensed by our sins, deliver us to everlasting punishment, as most wicked servants who would not follow Him to glory.

These words develop what has just been said. Prayer and grace are necessary for us that we may obey God all our lives and at every moment of our lives, for that is really the task which has been set us and accepted by us. Nothing will be wanting to us that we may fulfil it well, if our prayers win us grace and our fidelity makes it fructify. The source and the measure of our supernatural riches are also the source and measure of our obligations and responsibilities, and we are become before God sons and servants.

We are children of God, not by any legal fiction, but by a deep and real assimilation to His only Son; because of that divine life which grace implants within us, we hold an unassailable title to the inheritance of that Son: "And if sons, heirs also, heirs indeed of God and joint heirs with Christ" (Rom. viii. 17). This supernatural life is endowed with faculties suitable to it: faith, hope, and charity. There are sanctifying grace, the theological virtues, the moral virtues, the gifts of the Holy Spirit, and all sorts of helps. These are the " good things He has given us " of which St. Benedict speaks. This is the treasure which He has entrusted to our charge and to which we have to add as much as possible. " Trade till I come " (Luke xix. 13).

Fidelity and success are asked of us not only because we love Our Lord and are anxious not to sadden Him, but also on grounds of honour and justice; and St. Benedict urges self-interest as well. Fundamentally God is nothing but goodness; it is we who make Him severe, when we provoke Him by our faults: " In Himself most good, in relation to us He is just," says Tertullian. If we betray God, as our Father He will disinherit us, as our master He will punish us; and this in exact proportion to the degree in which His love has been despised and His confidence abused. We must understand the words properly and not make St. Benedict say that God in His punishment makes two distinct grades, separable and capable of being superimposed one on the other, as though He sometimes merely disinherits, and at others, if infidelity be great, chastises with positive punishments; for there is no case in which a soul, which has been really disinherited by its own fault, does not suffer. Our Holy Father's purpose is to describe the two inseparable pains of eternity: not only the pain of loss, which deprives rebellious children of their heavenly heritage, that is of God; but also the pain of sense, whereby the fire torments those utterly evil servants " who have refused to follow Him to glory."

So man must either reign for ever with Christ or suffer for ever with the devils. St. Benedict puts this dread alternative before us several times in the course of the Prologue; and he sets forth the monastic life as the most direct and sure road to attain to God. In his eyes, to advance valiantly towards the full realization of one's baptism and the perfection of the supernatural life (he deals with nothing else in the Prologue) is both the most efficacious procedure for the escaping of everlasting death, and the most logical procedure, and that most glorious for God and for us. He makes no mistake; he knows that a man is free to enter or not to enter the monastic state, and that, for many of those whom his invitation will reach, the monastic life is not indispensable either for amendment of life or for perseverance in good; he does not confuse the precepts and the counsels; and yet we may say that he simplifies the problem. We can never sufficiently study the precise and clear terms in which the matter is stated.

Exsurgamus ergo tandem aliquando, excitante nos Scriptura, ac dicente: *Hora est jam nos de somno surgere.* Et apertis oculis nostris ad deificum lumen, attonitis auribus audiamus divina quotidie clamans quid nos admoneat vox, dicens: *Hodie si vocem ejus audieritis,*	Let us then at length arise, since the Scripture stirs us up, saying: " It is time now for us to rise from sleep." And our eyes being open to the deifying light, let us hear with wondering ears what the Divine Voice admonishes us, daily crying out: " To-day if ye shall

nolite obdurare corda vestra. Et iterum: *Qui habet aures audiendi, audiat quid Spiritus dicat Ecclesiis.* Et quid dicit ? *Venite, filii, audite me: timorem Domini docebo vos. Currite, dum lumen vitæ habetis, ne tenebræ mortis vos comprehendant.*

hear his voice, harden not your hearts." And again, " He that hath ears to hear, let him hear what the Spirit saith to the Churches." And what says He ? " Come, my children, hearken to me, I will teach you the fear of the Lord. Run while ye have the light of life, lest the darkness of death seize hold of you."

The preliminaries being settled, we must now begin, says St. Benedict, and put our hands resolutely to the work. Whatever may be our age, above all if we are past the prime of life and moving downwards towards the end, it is time, the appointed time, God's hour and the hour of grace. Too long have we been plunged in sleep,[1] in deep sleep, perhaps in a sleep troubled and crossed by painful dreams. Sleep is not death, but neither is it life; it is life in abeyance, latent and inactive. Want of consideration, or familiarity, have dulled the outlines of supernatural realities. We sleep, yet we are not happy. Let us rise then now, at the summons of the voice which wakens us, the voice of God Himself and not merely of our Holy Father St. Benedict. God invites us by His Scriptures; for there we have indeed the words of God, addressed individually to each of us; it is hard to see how the baptized soul can resist such teaching made especially for it. We shall find in the Rule that the sacred Scripture has always a decisive force. " It is now the hour to rise from sleep ": the liturgy of Advent uses this sentence of the Apostle (Rom. xiii. 11), nor is it ever unseasonable throughout the continual advent of our lives.

We must open our eyes; for it is thus that one begins to shake off sleep and recover consciousness. We must open them to " the deifying light," which phrase may be understood of the Scriptures, " Thy word is a lamp to my feet, and a light to my paths " (Ps. cxviii. 105), or of faith, or better of Our Lord Himself, the true Light who walks before us and guides us: " He that followeth me shall not walk in darkness but shall have the light of life " (John viii. 12). We must also hearken and give ear to a voice powerful at once and sweet " with wondering ears."[2] For inattention is the devil's strongest ally; and though we are ever enveloped by the divine light, and though God speaks to us every moment, we remain blind and deaf, sluggish and careless of the truth. Let us break through the shackles of habit, let us rouse our interest, stimulate our curiosity, for we are told by the wise men of old, and it is very true, that wonder or surprise is the origin of philosophical enquiry.

Every morning, at the beginning of the Office, the voice of Our Lord cries[3] appealingly to us: " To-day, if you should hear my call,

---

[1] *Cf.* Cass., *Conlat.,* III., iv.

[2] D. Butler compares Quintus Curtius, *History of Alexander,* bk. VIII., 4.

[3] In Chapter VII. also St. Benedict says, "the Scripture cries to us." The same expression is found in St. Cæsarius, *Sermon* CCLXIII., 4, in the appendix to the Sermons of St. Augustine (*P.L.,* XXXIX., 2233).

harden not your hearts" (Ps. xciv. 8). We are essentially laggards and loiterers. "To-day?" we say. "What you ask me to abandon is so attractive. Suppose I wait till to-morrow. Of course I shall be wise and mortified to-morrow. . . ." And so our evil habit grows stronger, for every act leaves its trace on our character, and we lose power every day that we delay. Will not conversion be harder to-morrow?

"He that hath ears to hear, let him hear what the Spirit saith to the Churches" (Matt. xi. 15; Apoc. ii. 7). The call is more emphatic: it is addressed to our understanding, to our self-esteem, to a certain legitimate pride. The Spirit of God bids the soul that He visits to come simply and learn in His school, for He is both Teacher and Father. He will teach the soul to fear God—that is to say, to live in God's sight with filial respect and love (Ps. xxxiii. 12). St. Benedict adds to this the solemn warning of Our Lord in St. John's gospel (xii. 35): "Hasten to come to God, while you have the light of life, lest the darkness of death seize hold of you."[1] The "to-day" of which he speaks does not extend beyond the present life, and who can tell whether to-morrow is yours? So while God speaks to you and gives you light, while He consents to walk before you, follow Him and accept His lead: otherwise the star that guides you will disappear.[2]

Et quærens Dominus in multitudine populi, cui hæc clamat, operarium suum, iterum dicit: *Quis est homo, qui vult vitam, et cupit videre dies bonos?* Quod si tu audiens respondeas: Ego, dicit tibi Deus: Si vis habere veram et perpetuam vitam, *prohibe linguam tuam a malo, et labia tua ne loquantur dolum. Diverte a malo, et fac bonum; inquire pacem et sequere eam.* Et cum hæc feceritis, oculi mei super vos, et aures meæ ad preces vestras. Et antequam me invocetis, dicam: *Ecce adsum.*

And the Lord, seeking His own workman in the multitude of the people to whom He thus cries out, says again: "Who is the man that will have life, and desires to see good days?" And if you, hearing Him, answer, "I am he," God says to you: "If thou wilt have true and everlasting life, keep thy tongue from evil and thy lips that they speak no guile. Turn from evil, and do good: seek peace and pursue it. And when you have done these things, my eyes will be upon you, and my ears will be open to your prayers; and before you call upon me, I will say unto you, Behold, I am here."

So far our souls have come into touch with our Holy Father; they have prayed with him, they have been moved by fear and roused by the

---

[1] St. Benedict does not always cite Scripture word for word, whether purposely or because he quotes from memory. Also he often uses a version other than our Vulgate. St. Cæsarius read the beginning of this text in much the same way as St. Benedict: *Curramus dum lucem vitæ habemus* (*P.L.*, XXXIX., 2230).

[2] Our Holy Father returns presently to Ps. xxxiii., from which he selects and comments on verses 12, 13, 14, 15, 16. He has in mind also St. Augustine's second *Enarratio* on this psalm; and from *audiamus divina . . .* to *quid dulcius . . .* he scarcely does more than quote it almost textually (nos. 16-20, 9. *P.L.*, XXXVI., 317-319, 313). See also the *Enarratio* on Ps. cxliii. (no. 9. *P.L.*, XXXVII., 1862); the combination of the two passages of Isaias, lxv. 24 and lviii. 9, that we meet presently in St. Benedict, is certainly inspired by St. Augustine.

We must abandon as a source of this passage the Pseudo-Chrysostom brought forward in the *Revue B n dictine*, 1894, pp. 385 *ff.*

divine words of the Scripture, but his call yet lacks something more personal, more decisive, and more dramatic. The householder, the owner of the vineyard (Matt. xx. 1-16), went down himself to the market-place to hire labourers, and the appeal which He makes to the whole Christian people is really addressed to each one, for He wishes to make a compact with each individual soul. In this we have a true picture of the relation of the soul to God: every soul is a labourer and God is one too. God, who has need of nothing, has yet willed the manifestation of His attributes by means of the natural order, but especially by means of the supernatural order. The Incarnation and Redemption represent God's great effort. To this He devoted Himself, but He did not consent to work alone. He willed to associate with Himself fellow-workers, and He deliberately left His work unfinished, knowing that it would be a joy to us to work after Him and with Him, and to spend our efforts there where He spent His blood (1 Cor. iii. 9; Col. i. 24).

Moreover, the invitation promises a reward: " Who is the man that will have life, and desires to see good days ?" (Ps. xxxiii. 13). God does not disdain to engage our self-interest, nor to use our primary and fundamental love of happiness. Of course His glory and our happiness are intimately connected. Now when a man is offered happiness and life, he never refuses: " Does not each one of you answer, ' I '?" says St. Augustine. " I am the man, O Lord, I wish it fervently." " But we must not have any misunderstanding," adds Our Lord, and for Him St. Benedict proceeds to state accurately the meaning and scope of His promise. Our ideal is not the Jewish one of temporal prosperity and length of days; we are concerned with the true and full life, the life of eternity. This life of eternity begins here below in the life of grace, and according to St. Benedict we shall know " good days." So if there were no life but the present, should we not be the happiest of men ? But without enlarging on the reward reserved for his labourer, St. Benedict, first briefly and then at greater length, indicates the conditions which he must accept.

Certain things have to be eliminated. " Keep thy tongue from evil . . ." (Ps. xxxiii. 14-15). Does this mean that we must avoid lying and deceit properly so called ? Certainly it does. But we may give the words of the Old Testament a value relative to the new dispensation and consequently a wider scope. There is sometimes a lie of act implied in our whole life, a practical negation of our faith, a secret duality: charity summons us, but egoism prevails; we are divided and drawn in opposite directions, and too often the lower attraction prevails. We receive Holy Communion every morning, but we remain ourselves. If we really wish for life, we must aim at unity of purpose and true loyalty.

" Turn from evil." Let us take our souls in our hands and resolutely separate ourselves from all that is evil. To avoid or turn aside from it is not enough; we must create between ourselves and evil a wide zone which neither we nor evil can cross; we must pronounce a sentence of eternal banishment against it. Let us not be like those men whom St. Francis de Sales compares to sick folk whose doctor has forbidden them melon under pain of death; they abstain indeed from the forbidden fruit, but they " brood on their deprivation and talk about melons and bargain for a little indulgence; they insist on smelling them at least and count those fortunate who may eat them."[1]

" And do good." This is the positive side of our programme. This is a simple thought, so simple that it seems childish, yet it is one which is frequently overlooked. Too many people spend all their intelligence and strength in avoiding the snares with which the path of life is strewn; some souls are always stuck, always worried by the difficulties they meet, always anxious about little flecks of dust; their energy is devoted to lamentation or exhausted in continual self-consideration. Undoubtedly a delicate conscience is a good thing, but it is dangerous to think too much of oneself, to magnify one's importance; of course we must know ourselves, but it is above all necessary to know God. At bottom, the purpose of our life is not merely to avoid sin and negation, but rather positively to exist, to do good, to reach God.

" Seek peace." The quotation of Psalm xxxiii. was not made by accident and is not continued mechanically. When unity, harmony, and order have been re-established in us, thanks to that loyalty of which we spoke above: when the disagreement with God, with our brethren, and with ourselves has ceased, and this much is finally won and settled, then we have peace, " the tranquillity of order." Peace is not sloth nor a false lack of interest; it is the attitude which is spontaneously assumed by the soul when it is united to God by charity. Peace, like joy, is not exactly a virtue, but is the fruit of the highest of virtues, for it is the daughter of charity.[2] Search for it in your house, says Our Lord, as for a hidden treasure; pursue it, if there be need. Sometimes it will appear to flee from us, but we must not be discouraged; we must not be irritated by its delay, for it may be that this itself is only our own delay with ourselves. And there is never any reason to leave this peace; no events, no sufferings, no faults even should cause us to do so; for anxiety does not correct mistakes and repentance does not imply trouble. St. Paul regards peace as a sort of cloister of the spirit, which keeps our soul near to God: " And may the peace of God which passeth all understanding keep your hearts and minds in Christ Jesus " (Phil. iv. 7). Let us remember that it is at once the recompense, fruit, measure, and cause of our virtue; and everyone knows that it has become the motto of the Benedictine Order.

The psalm is continued, but verse 16 is alluded to without being formally quoted. After our soul has been turned in this way towards God, and has attained peace, then the benevolent regard of Our Lord rests on it and His ear is always open to our prayers; He takes pleasure in this beauty which the light of His eyes has created. Then there is

---

[1] *Introduction to the Devout Life*, Part I., chap. vii.
[2] *Cf. S. Th.*, II.-II., q. xxix., *De Pace*.

the closest union: " He who is joined to the Lord is one spirit " (1 Cor. vi. 17). Our prayer will be still in the heart, we shall not have opened our lips, before the Lord will say: " Lo, I am here."

Quid dulcius nobis hac voce Domini invitántis nos, fratres charissimi ? Ecce pietate sua demonstrat nobis Dominus viam vitæ. Succinctis ergo fide vel observantia bonorum actuum lumbis nostris, per ducatum Evangelii pergamus itinera ejus, ut mereamur eum qui nos vocavit, in regno suo videre.

What can be sweeter to us, dearest brethren, than this voice of the Lord inviting us ? Behold in His lovingkindness the Lord shows unto us the way of life. Having our loins, therefore, girded with faith and the performance of good works, let us walk in His paths by the guidance of the Gospel, that we may deserve to see Him who has called us in His kingdom.

Our Holy Father allows an exclamation of joy to escape him. See, my beloved brethren, he cries, is there anything in the world could be more tender, more sweet, than this invitation of Our Lord, or couched in such terms ? It is God Himself, who in His loving-kindness calls to life and shows us the road. Up then, let us start our pilgrimage to God, let us walk quickly, with garment tucked up so that its folds may not beat round our legs and hinder us, but that we may have all our vigour: " Let your loins be girt and lamps burning in your hands " (Luke xxii. 35). Our girdle is faith, a practical faith which means the doing of good works and the habit of them. " And justice shall be the girdle of his loins, and faith the girdle of his reins " (Isa. xi. 5). Led and directed by the precepts of the Gospel,[1] let us pass every stage of the journey to God unto the end, so that we may deserve to see Him who has called us in His kingdom.[2]

In cujus regni tabernaculo si volumus habitare, nisi illuc bonis actibus currendo, minime pervenitur. Sed interrogemus cum Propheta Dominum, dicentes ei: *Domine, quis habitabit in tabernaculo tuo, aut quis requiescet in monte sancto tuo ?* Post hanc interrogationem, fratres, audiamus Dominum respondentem, et ostendentem nobis viam ipsius tabernaculi, ac dicentem: *Qui ingreditur sine macula, et operatur justitiam; qui loquitur veritatem in corde suo; qui non egit dolum in lingua sua; qui non fecit proximo suo malum, et opprobrium non accepit adversus proximum suum.*

And if we wish to dwell in the tabernacle of His kingdom, we shall by no means reach it unless we run thither by our good deeds. But let us ask the Lord with the prophet, saying to Him: " Lord, who shall dwell in thy tabernacle, or who shall rest upon thy holy hill ?" After this question, brethren, let us hear the Lord answering, and showing to us the way to His tabernacle, and saying: " He that walks without stain and works justice: he that speaks truth in his heart, that has not done guile with his tongue: he that has done no evil to his neighbour, and has not taken up a reproach against his neighbour."

---

[1] Instead of the expression *per ducatum Evangelii*, the meaning of which seemed rather vague, the most ancient manuscripts (we do not say the best, *cf.* Introduction) read: *et calceatis in præparatione Evangelii pacis pedibus, pergamus . . .*, a reminiscence of chap. vi. of Ephesians (verse 15; observe that in verse 14 the Apostle bids us have our loins girt: it has been thought that St. Benedict was quoting these two verses loosely).

[2] Perhaps the best reading is: *eum qui nos vocavit in regnum suum videre*, a quotation of 1 Thess. ii. 12.

Prologue

So you wish sincerely to walk to the sanctuary of God, our King, and to abide there with Him for all eternity? The society of God, of Our Lord Jesus Christ, of Our Lady, of the angels and saints, attracts you? Since then you know the end and have willed it, you must now learn the means which lead to it. "We shall by no means reach it unless we run thither by our good deeds." St. Benedict has said this before, but he insists on it and strives to put this point in the clearest possible light. A privileged state does not sanctify us, nor will grace secure our salvation of itself. It would be exceedingly rash to say to oneself: "I have made my profession, I am in healthy surroundings, I understand the supernatural life, I can speak of it on occasion with fluency and precision, I experience in my relations with God certain favours which tell me that I am in the higher ways. My toils therefore are over." No, there must be action, we must move unceasingly, we must run. Acts are the offspring of our life, they continue it, they develop it, and our life exists only for them: for an act is the ultimate term of all living energy. Let us recall the history of the fig-tree in the Gospel, which did not lack leaves, but was cursed and withered on the spot, because the fruit—that is to say, acts—was wanting. It may be objected that we are often told that our sanctification does not come from ourselves and that we have to let God work. Let us understand the matter: there is the preliminary work of clearing the ground, there is the constructive work, and there is the completion and perfection of the work, and in all of these is God's action exercised, especially in the last; but we are never dispensed from acting, and the two first stages are especially ours.

If we want further information, we should rather go to Our Lord and with the prophet put to Him the question with which the fourteenth psalm opens. For us Christians its subject is the New Jerusalem and the true temple of God: "Behold the tabernacle of God with men, and he will dwell with them" (Apoc. xxi. 3). God answers us in the same psalm and traces for us the way to His holy place. St. Benedict confines himself to quoting verses 2 and 3, of which the meaning is quite clear. All is embraced in this rapid summary: intention, word, fulfilment, interior and exterior work; so that we have a threefold preparation of soul in purity, uprightness, and justice.

| Qui malignum diabolum aliqua suadentem sibi, cum ipsa suasione sua a conspectibus cordis sui respuens, deduxit ad nihilum, et parvulos cogitatus ejus tenuit, et allisit ad Christum. | He that has brought the malignant evil one to naught, casting him out of his heart with all his suggestions, and has taken his bad thoughts, while they were yet young, and dashed them down upon Christ. |

Our Holy Father, from this on, paraphrases broadly the rest of the psalm, and first the first part of the fourth verse: "In his sight the malignant is brought to nothing." The literal sense refers to the attitude which the man who wishes to go to God must adopt in dealing with the good and the wicked: he disdains the wicked and

reserves all his esteem for the good: " He glorifies those who fear God."
But St. Benedict has understood the passage of the attitude which he
who seeks God must take up in the face of the malignant one, the devil,[1]
and all his teaching is full of a deep wisdom.

It is natural and prudent to examine rigorously and to look well in
the face the dispositions, emotions, and affections which follow one
another in us, and to question them: " What are you ? Whence do
you come ? What have you come to do with me ? What are the
ultimate consequences to which you will lead me ?" A wise man does
not open his door to every visitor, nor do we let the first comer into the
bosom of the family. If we can recognize the real source of certain
treacherous and misleading tendencies, the true author of certain secret
impulses, then we are safe.

Once the diabolical suggestion has been recognized and the suggestor
unmasked, St. Benedict wants us, at once and resolutely, to " drive
both one and the other from our hearts and to give them no consideration." Temptation takes various forms. We should always fight it
with humility and reliance on the help of God; but often the best way
to get rid of it is to neglect and despise it. There are temptations which
are merely silly, surprises or mere physiological effects: let us pass them
by. It is a case for the application of the precept: " Salute no one by
the way." For not only must one not worry about them, one must
not even resist or cramp oneself in a useless struggle, nor fight, nor protest
spasmodically, nor make any alteration in one's life.

However, there are cases when our Holy Father asks us to employ
different tactics; when, for example, the temptation is violent or prolonged, and above all when it is a question of our besetting temptation,
some peculiar habitual temptation which has a special affinity with our
character, a temptation which has assailed us in childhood, has followed
us like an ever-present menace or evil spirit, which has grown up with
us and grown old with us, and which we find still full of life. If we
do not wish to succumb inevitably, we must collect all the energy and
insight that we have, and vigorously grasping these hellish suggestions,
these children of Babylon, as though spontaneously and without
reflection, dash them at once on the rock, which is Christ (1 Cor. x. 4).
We must arm ourselves with faith, charity, and prayer, make an appeal
to Our Lord and so raise our souls into the region of peace. St. Benedict
quotes, in its allegorical sense like many of the Fathers,[2] the last verse

---

[1] CASSIODORUS, in his *Exposition* of this psalm (*P.L.*, LXX., 110), gives exactly the
same sense to verse 8 as St. Benedict. Farther on, after having spoken of the courageous
man *qui mundi vitia cum suo auctore prostravit*, he adds these words, which again recall
another passage of the end of the Prologue: *Sed precemur jugiter omnipotentiam ejus,
ut qui talia per nosmetipsos implere non possumus quæ jussa sunt, ejus ditati munere faciamus* (*ibid.*, 111). We notice the connection for the sake of those interested in the
question of the relation of Cassiodorus to St. Benedict.

[2] ORIGEN, *Contra Celsum*, l. VII., 22. *P.G.*, XI., 1453.
ST. HILARY, *Tract. in Ps.* cxxxvi. 14. *P.L.*, IX., 784.
ST. AMBROSE, *De pœnit.*, II., 106. *P.L.*, XVI., 523.

Prologue

of Psalm cxxxvi.: "Blessed is he that shall take and dash thy little ones against the rock."

Qui timentes Dominum, de bona observantia sua non se reddunt elatos, sed ipsa in se bona, non a se posse, sed a Domino fieri existimantes, operantem in se Dominum magnificant, illud cum Propheta dicentes: *Non nobis, Domine, non nobis, sed nomini tuo da gloriam.* Sicut nec Paulus Apostolus de prædicatione sua sibi aliquid imputavit, dicens: *Gratia Dei sum id, quod sum.* Et iterum ipse dicit: *Qui gloriatur, in Domino glorietur.*

These are they who, fearing the Lord, are not puffed up with their own good works, but, knowing that the good which is in them comes not from themselves but from the Lord, magnify the Lord who works in them, saying with the prophet: "Not unto us, O Lord, not unto us, but unto thy name give the glory." So the Apostle Paul imputed nothing of his preaching to himself, but said: "By the grace of God I am what I am." And again he says: "He that glorieth, let him glory in the Lord."

Though our text of Psalm xiv. means "the just man honours those who fear God," St. Benedict's had "*Timentes autem Dominum magnificant*"—i.e., "those who fear God give him glory," and these words furnish him with the application which follows.

We have to do good and repel evil; and when we have fulfilled these two duties, we must, under pain of spoiling all, guard against vain self-complacency. The true servants of God, those who fear the severity of His judgements on the proud, strive to attribute to Him the causality and so to speak the responsibility for their virtue. They glorify God in recognizing that nothing comes to them of their own power: neither the idea, nor the resolution, nor the accomplishment of good. Undoubtedly the act is both ours and His, indivisibly, and our merits are real; but the action of God has such priority, efficaciousness, and sovereignty, that He alone is to be credited with our sanctification: "But knowing that the good that is in them comes not from themselves but from the Lord, they magnify the Lord who works in them."[1] The hundred and thirteenth psalm proclaims this truth aloud; and that great worker St. Paul did not attribute to himself any of his apostolic success (I Cor. xv. 10), reminding us that every Christian could glory in naught but in the Lord (2 Cor. x. 17). We have already heard St. Benedict expressing his view on these nice questions of grace; here again his theology is sound and exact.

There would be danger in investigating with curiosity and contemplating unceasingly the good that is in us, but we must know how to recognize it tranquilly. Any serious examination of conscience should be arranged in two columns: the evil for which we alone are responsible and the good which is the work of God in us. God loves to be thanked,

---

St. Jerome, *Epist.* XXII. 6. *P.L.,* XXII., 398. *Commentariolum in Ps.* cxxxvi., apud *Anecdota Maredsolana,* vol. III., P. i., p. 94.
St. Augustine, *Enarr. in Ps.* cxxxvi. 21. *P.L.,* XXXVII., 1773-1774.
Cassian, *Inst.,* VI., xiii.
[1] *Cf.* Cass., *Inst.,* XII., xvi. *Conlat.,* III., xv.

and we can only give thanks for a benefit which we know and which we allow ourselves to contemplate.

Unde et Dominus in Evangelio ait: *Qui audit verba mea hæc, et facit ea, similabo eum viro sapienti, qui ædificavit domum suam supra petram: venerunt flumina, flaverunt venti, et impegerunt in domum illam, et non cecidit: fundata enim erat supra petram.*

Hence also the Lord says in the Gospel: "He that heareth these words of mine and doeth them, is like a wise man who built his house upon a rock; the floods came, the winds blew, and beat upon that house, and it fell not, because it was founded upon a rock."

Omitting some words of the psalm[1] St. Benedict passes at once to those which end it: "He that doth these things shall not be moved for ever." The just man shall not fall, he shall not be cheated of his hope, he shall reach the temple of God where he has longed to be. But, since this conclusion was somewhat abrupt, St. Benedict has thought fit to elucidate it with a text taken from the seventh chapter of St. Matthew, where Our Lord describes the security of the man who hears and fulfils His words, of the wise man who erects the edifice of his perfection upon a strong and unshakable foundation. Again Christ is the rock, and to attach ourselves to Him by faith, to love Him before all else, makes us partake of His strength and His eternal stability.

A house so built can withstand all assaults. They will not be wanting in a conscientious spiritual life, or in a community which wishes to keep its monastic faith pure and whole. Of all sorts they are, and from all directions; there is rain from heaven[2] and the winds of the air, and streams and torrents of the earth. So a community may experience trials from heaven, persecutions from the powers of this world, blasts which drive them over the seas, and yet take no harm. "And it fell not: because it was founded on a rock."

Hæc complens Dominus expectat quotidie his suis sanctis monitis factis nos respondere debere. Ideo nobis propter emendationem malorum, hujus dies vitæ ad inducias relaxantur, dicente Apostolo: *An nescis, quia patientia Dei ad pœnitentiam te adducit?* Nam pius Dominus dicit: *Nolo mortem peccatoris, sed ut convertatur, et vivat.* Cum ergo interrogassemus Dominum, fratres, de habitatore tabernaculi ejus, audivimus habitandi præceptum: sed si compleamus habitatoris officium, erimus hæredes regni cœlorum.

And the Lord in fulfilment of these His words is waiting daily for us to respond by our deeds to His holy admonitions. Therefore are the days of our life lengthened for the amendment of our evil ways, as says the Apostle: "Knowest thou not that the patience of God is leading thee to repentance?" For the merciful Lord says: "I will not the death of a sinner, but that he should be converted and live." Since then, brethren, we have asked of the Lord who is to inhabit His temple, we have heard His commands to those who are to dwell there: and if we fulfil those duties, we shall be heirs of the kingdom of heaven.

---

[1] St. Augustine (*Enarr. in Ps.* xiv. 4. *P.L.*, XXXVI., 144) also distinguishes this same portion of the psalm, and says that it is addressed to beginners in the spiritual life: *Sicut illa superiora pertinent ad perfectos, ita ea quæ nunc dicturus est, pertinent ad incipientes.*

[2] Mentioned by the Gospel, but omitted by St. Benedict.

Prologue

The words *hæc complens* have been variously translated, as to complete or to put the finishing touch to His kindness, or better perhaps thus:[1] Our Lord having invited us and having showed us the goal and marked out the path, and having answered the question we addressed to Him with the psalmist concerning the conditions of admission into His eternal tabernacle, now waits for our reply. He waits always, with divine patience, for us to set about the surrender of ourselves by our deeds to His sacred admonitions.

Ideo, "therefore," since God agrees to wait, our life on this earth has the character of a truce, of a delay; the duration of our life is a space of leisure contrived for us by God that we may at last amend. This is what St. Paul teaches; and in the prophecy of Ezechiel (xviii. 23) God proclaims His purpose of mercy and tenderness: He has no interest in our failure or damnation, and He desires our welfare more ardently than we do ourselves. Is it not then to be ignorant of the very meaning of life, if we spend it in endless delays, delays the more dangerous because the thread of life may be snapped suddenly?

So St. Benedict concludes thus: we have received from the mouth of God Himself a complete answer to all that it was to our interest to know; we have been told that we may some day dwell in His kingdom, whither we are called and where our coming is awaited, on condition that we fulfil, from this on, the duty of one who wishes to dwell there; for no one can enter into eternal life without doing the works and fulfilling the duties of a true citizen of eternity: "We have heard His commands to those who are to dwell there: but we must fulfil the duties of true dwellers." *Sed si compleamus habitatoris officium.*[2]

Ergo præparanda sunt corda et corpora nostra sanctæ præceptorum obedientiæ militatura; et quod minus habet in nobis natura possibile, rogemus Dominum, ut gratiæ suæ jubeat nobis adjutorium ministrare. Et si fugientes gehennæ pœnas ad vitam perpetuam volumus pervenire, dum adhuc vacat, et in hoc corpore sumus, et hæc omnia per hanc lucis viam vacat implere, currendum et agendum est modo, quod in perpetuum nobis expediat.

Our hearts, therefore, and our bodies must be made ready to fight under the holy obedience of His commands; and let us ask God to supply by the help of His grace what by nature is hardly possible to us. And if we would arrive at eternal life, escaping the pains of hell, then—while there is yet time, while we are still in the flesh, and are able to fulfil all these things by the light which is given us—we must hasten to do now what will profit us for all eternity.

This concluding portion of the Prologue seems directly designed to reassure and encourage souls who shrink from the holy demands of the

---

[1] Observe that immediately after the Sermon on the Mount, the conclusion of which St. Benedict has just cited, the evangelist added: *Cum consummasset Jesus verba hæc* ... (Matt. vii. 28).

[2] A scribe, doubtless surprised at this suspended and somewhat elliptical phrase, regarded it as the protasis of a conditional sentence and completed it with the somewhat frigid gloss: *erimus hæredes regni cælorum*. And with these words the Prologue ends in the three most ancient manuscripts; perhaps they had as their common source a codex in which the last page of the Prologue was lacking. (See the Introduction)

religious life, and who, when their first fervour has gone and the enthusiasm of their first days evaporated, are tempted to turn back towards the world. If it is true that our Holy Father wrote this page in the last days of his life, he had had time to receive a goodly number of postulants, and among them some of those soft natures, over-sensitive and lacking vitality, whose good will is real, but short-lived. St. Benedict appeals to them with the *sursum corda* which goes before sacrifice.[1]

The whole man has to take the field; first the heart, that is the secret dwelling and central source of all great thoughts and strong resolutions, and then the body itself, which must be trained by faithful observance. Otherwise monks will be in danger of resembling painted or stage soldiers, who ever threaten to strike or to march but never either strike or march. The monastic life is in fact a training camp, and before joining it it is better to be sure that you are determined. But, although no one can at his pleasure have literary genius or add an inch to his stature, in the moral order we may win any power or any stature that we wish. And we are not asked for muscular effort, but are simply told to submit to holy obedience and to exercise ourselves in the perfect fulfilment of a spiritual law. Can you not keep silence ? Why, women keep it, and well. Can you not love mortification ? Even children practise it. Can you not do what women and children do ?

Suppose there is some little discord of temperament, or even, it may be, of nature between you and the monastic law. Tell God about it. He will tell His grace and bid it come to your aid, and His grace will make possible for you what nature led you to regard as " hardly possible." St. Benedict's phrase here is touched with gentle humour.

Moreover, adds St. Benedict, we must be brave. You wish to avoid hell ? Yes. You wish to get to heaven ? Of course. Well, says he, let me tell you again that life is short, and that it is a truce. We were once enemies of God, and fortunately we were not then surprised by death. Let us make haste, while there is yet time, to do something for God; *currendum et agendum est ;* let us make haste to accomplish, by the light of this life,[2] all the good works that we shall in heaven congratulate ourselves on having done. What does St. Paul think now of his scourgings, or St. Lawrence of his gridiron, or St. Benedict of his rolling amid the thorns, or St. Benedict Labre of his poverty ? It is enough to cut short our procrastination, if we but ponder for an instant this weighty advice of our Holy Father.

| Constituenda est ergo a nobis Dominici schola servitii; in qua institutione nihil asperum nihilque grave nos constituturos speramus. | We have, therefore, to establish a school of the Lord's service, in the institution of which we hope to order nothing that is harsh or rigorous. |

At the same time as he strengthens and stimulates souls, St. Benedict is led to define the special form of the religious life which he has just

---

[1] These words echo the first paragraphs of the Prologue.
[2] We should read *vitam*, which is the only authoritative reading.

offered them in the Lord's name; hitherto he had limited himself to asking whether they were ready for the full Christian life. So he makes easy the transition to his enunciation of the monastic rule.

See then, he says, what I want to do, what I propose to establish with the help of your generosity: "a school of the Lord's service." We must always hold fast to this definition of our life. A monastery is not a club, nor a house of retreat, nor an appendage to the universities. Doubtless it is a place of leisure, of liberty, and of repose (and that is the original sense of the word "school," from the Greek $\sigma\chi o\lambda\acute{\eta}$); but this leisure has for its object the study of the things of God, and the training and education of His soldiers, His guard of honour. The ancients gave the name of "school," says Dom Calmet, to the places where were learnt literature, the sciences, the fine arts, and military exercises; also to the companies employed for the defence of the palace, or the person of a prince, and to the places in which they lodged and trained. It is now not unlikely that our Holy Father had in mind the *schola* or place of meeting of the Roman colleges or associations.[1]

So the monastic life is the "school of the Lord's service," the school where one learns to serve Him, where one is trained without cessation, in a novitiate which will last the whole of life. At bottom, St. Benedict has no other design than that of God Himself: "For the Father also seeketh such as will adore him in spirit and in truth." To serve God is to adore God. The service of God is made up of two elements: worship or the exercise of the virtue of religion, and—since the value of worship depends upon the value of the worshipper—personal sanctification by fidelity to the law of God and the union of our wills with His. This worship is "in spirit," since it comes from the interior man; it is "in truth," since no faculty of a man is excepted; no work of charity, no study may escape it; nor can there be any contrariety in act or intention. And, to conclude, this worship is collective, social, and public.

We have good hope, says St. Benedict, that this programme will contain nothing terrible. We need have no fear: the Rule is wise and therein is nothing disagreeable, harsh, or intolerable. It is to a marked degree gentler, both in its preliminary requirements and in its laws, than the monastic codes of the East; and our Holy Father, in his perfect discretion and in his love for souls, has allowed himself to appear somewhat relaxed. But the Benedictine life does not consist essentially in a dying, a merciless mortification, nor can it be adequately defined as a life of penance or violent asceticism. Perhaps St. Benedict here veils too much the austerity of his Rule. He does not want to frighten anyone, and that is a good intention enough; but will he not contradict himself in the fifty-eighth chapter: "Let there be set before him all the hard and rugged ways by which we walk towards God"? The

---

[1] *Cf.* G. Boissier, *La Religion romaine d'Auguste aux Antonins*, l. III., chap. iii. See on this comparison an interesting note by Dom Rothenhäusler, *Zur Aufnahmeordnung der Regula S. Benedicti* (Münster, 1912), p. 37, note 4.

contradiction is not a real one, and all will be explained to a nicety in the words which follow.

| Sed et si quid paululum restrictius, dictante æquitatis ratione, propter emendationem vitiorum, vel conservationem charitatis processerit, non illico pavore perterritus refugias viam salutis, quæ non est nisi angusto initio incipienda. Processu vero conversationis et fidei, dilatato corde, inenarrabili dilectionis dulcedine curritur via mandatorum Dei. . . . | But if anything be somewhat strictly laid down, according to the dictates of equity, for the amendment of vices or the preservation of charity, do not therefore fly in dismay from the way of salvation, whose beginning cannot but be strait. But as we go forward in our life and faith, we shall with hearts enlarged and unspeakable sweetness of love run in the way of God's commandments. |

We are first told affectionately and in measured terms not to be surprised if we meet a little mortification and pain on the road that leads to God. After all, there is something of both on the road to hell; we can even say that you may save your life with less suffering than you may lose it; and if we had remained in the world we should have learnt by experience, perhaps by cruel experience, that it is the true home of disappointment, constraint, servitude, ennui. And the suffering that is met in the world is often of bad quality, base, impure, degrading, though of course it may be both wholesome and profitable, such as that which is exacted by apprenticeship to any craft, or any sort of intellectual or practical training. Why should we wish to have less to suffer to become religious, than to become artisans, or soldiers, or explorers ? No great object can be achieved without sacrifice: " Everyone that striveth for the mastery refraineth himself from all things. And they indeed that they may receive a corruptible crown: but we an incorruptible one" (1 Cor. ix. 25).

There are, in the moral order, people who no longer suffer; they are those who belong without reserve to the good, whose life is become a foretaste of paradise. Our Holy Father describes, farther on, the blessed state of these perfect souls. Those who belong to evil, also unreservedly, and whose conscience is lulled to sleep and hardened, do not suffer any more either: but who would envy them that dreadful calm ? In the innumerable multitude of the suffering, there are those who do evil without being able to escape remorse, and who thus taste hell in this life; and there are those who do good habitually, but are still tempted by evil, and of this class the different degrees are as various as are souls.

It is true that we have said good-bye bravely to the world, and burnt our boats, but we have not yet reached the knowledge of God; we live as it were suspended between heaven and earth, and we feel the void, for does not Nature herself abhor a vacuum ? We must die, die that voluntary death which is precious in the sight of God; we must reset our type completely and issue, so to say, a new edition of ourselves. There can be no building up without this preliminary destroying, and that is why our Holy Father lays it down as a principle that the way of salvation "cannot but be strait" in its beginning. "How narrow is the gate and strait the way that leadeth to life!" said Our Lord (Matt. vii. 14). The gate is narrow and we are large; we suffer from moral obesity, from having accumulated habits, customs, likes, from having spread ourselves out exteriorly on all sorts of objects and drawn in our train a thousand hindrances; but the time has come to renounce them; we can only get through by reducing ourselves—let us remember the fable of the weasel—and this reduction must be accompanied with pain.

The cause of our suffering is single, it is self-will; but its occasions and instruments are manifold. In the first place there are the sufferings of the Rule, to which our Holy Father makes special allusion here, though his words may very well be understood of every monastic pain. Let us notice the terms in which he refers to this severity. There will be as little of it as possible, *paululum*. It will not consist of arbitrary restrictions and trials, whether left to the initiative of the religious, or even to the choice of the legislator or superior; but it will present itself spontaneously, *processerit*, it will only exist because the situation evokes it, it will be determined by the nature of things, it will spring from the very conditions of monastic life, where, as in every society, peace can only reign on condition of partial sacrifices freely consented to by every member. Sometimes, too, mortification will have as its end the safeguarding of our love of God or our moral life. "According to the dictates of equity"; everything is subjected to the law of a wise discipline.

Other sufferings will come from ourselves, from our sickly imagination. And there are those which we make for one another. The most formidable ones come from God. God loves souls as precious pearls bought by the blood of His Son: "O Lord who lovest souls" (Wis. xi. 27). But He does not love their dross and baseness. He wishes to be in our souls as a spiritual being in spiritual beings, as a force in a force which is submissive and receptive; and He wishes the mover and the moved to be fitly proportionate. So, since He intervenes specially and personally, immediately and directly, at each stage of our spiritual life, He takes on Himself the work of purifying us. He alone can penetrate into the depths of our being, and reach its most delicate fibres. This work he carries out thoroughly, but in a silent manner, interiorly and secretly, as befits our contemplative state. We are face to face with God; all distractions have vanished and we are alone in a solitude, abandoned in a desert. We win a piercing consciousness of the infinite purity of God and so of our unworthiness; the inexorable light of His divinity falls full on our defects, on all the wounds of our soul, and we feel without defence against God's punishment. "I am a man that see my poverty by the rod of his indignation" (Lam. iii. 1). We are in purgatory. We suffer the tortures of St. Bartholomew. Like **Prometheus** we are fastened to our rock, and God's vulture comes and opens our breast, and there, quietly and ceaselessly, eats away all that displeases Him. And so we are utterly sick, and the soul is sore all over, and we readily lay the blame on anyone or anything.

O blessed sufferings! These are the toils of the journey to God, and, like the real purgatory, these too lead to heaven. "Do not therefore fly in dismay from the way of salvation." We must not take fright, lose our heads, yield, and flee. Those who bravely accept these divine demands; those who, instead of driving away the physician of the soul and begging consolation on all sides, keep enough energy and self-possession to add some interior mortification and to weed their garden, as St. Teresa puts it, these have a future. Those who in tribulation speak tenderly to infinite Justice and through their tears bless Him for all, who say with Job: " Though he slay me, yet will I trust in him," who accept for years this burning severity, trusting that God will give Himself in the end, these are the candidates for sainthood, to these will God show Himself loving, both in time and in eternity. But for those who do none of these things we must surely weep; they will never know the deepest joy that the creature's heart may feel, the joy of Calvary, the joy of being God's unreservedly, as a thing with which He does what He will, as a trophy which He carries whither He pleases.

Whether suffering comes in single spies or in battalions, whether it comes from God or from men, it can always be borne, if we continue to pray and to be faithful to the duties of our state. Does not time, too, that wonderful invention of God's mercy, in some sort wear away and attenuate our pains, " that which is momentary and light of our tribulation " (2 Cor. iv. 17) ? Even in this world suffering will not last for ever. How long then ? So long as God wishes, so long as there remains in us something that must be burnt away. Therefore the duration of suffering depends in part on our generosity. In the end, we accept solitude and enjoy it, things which once seemed so necessary to us interest us no more, and we accomplish without effort that which at first appeared impossible. Our passions still at times pull at our lower nature, but their call becomes daily more and more remote. " Trifles of trifles and vanities of vanities, my old mistresses, held me back; they caught hold of the garment of my flesh and whispered in my ear, ' Can you let us go ?' . . . As I heard them, they seemed to have shrunk to half their former size. No longer did they meet me face to face with open contradiction, but muttered behind my back, and, when I moved away, plucked stealthily at my coat to make me look back."[1]

"But as we go forward in our life and faith "[2] . . . The habit of monastic observance, the habit of close union with God, the mental habit of seeing our life in its relation to God, all these empty us and free

---

[1] S. Aug., *Confess.*, l. VIII., c. xi. P.L., XXXII., 761.
[2] S. Pach., *Reg.* cxc.: . . . *Probatæ fratres conversationis et fidei.* But St. Benedict is thinking rather of Cassian, *Conlat.*, III., xv. Cassian, having recalled the fact after St. Paul (Phil. i. 29) that we must suffer with Christ, adds: *Hic quoque et initium conversationis ac fidei nostræ et passionum tolerantiam donari nobis a Domino declaravit.*

us of encumbrance. Our hearts expand and grow to the stature of God, and God is at home with us, free of our house and sovereign there. And our hearts, on their side, are at ease: " I have run the way of thy commandments, when thou didst enlarge my heart " (Ps. cxviii. 32). " Thy commandment is exceedingly broad " (*ibid.* 96). All conflict is over, naught is left but a glad docility, a sweet and holy confiscation of our will by Our Lord's will, a full surrender to His lead. A spring of tenderness has gushed forth from the depths of our desert, and its waters of sweetness unspeakable penetrate like a perfume to the very confines of its desolation. Such is the gentle touch of God and the effect of His substantial love. And so the soul sets out, and runs, and sings. *Dilatato corde, inenarrabili dilectionis dulcedine curritur via mandatorum Dei.*

ut ab ipsius nunquam magisterio discedentes, in ejus doctrina usque ad mortem in monasterio perseverantes, passionibus Christi per patientiam participemus, ut regni ejus mereamur esse consortes.	So that never departing from His guidance, but persevering in His teaching in the monastery until death, we may by patience share in the sufferings of Christ, that we may deserve to be partakers of His kingdom.

Some editors have thought that this last paragraph was connected logically with the word *speramus* above and have treated the passage between as a parenthesis. But there is no reason to take it thus, and this long parenthesis seems hardly in accordance with St. Benedict's manner of writing.

The monastery is a school where we learn to worship God; this school has one Master and only one: our Holy Father uttered His name when he spoke of the " way of the commandments of God." Our Lord Jesus Christ is the Master, since God has told us all by means of the Word. St. Augustine has pointed out many times the necessity of an interior master for either natural or supernatural knowledge. External teaching never gives intellectual illumination or grasp; its function is limited to throwing out a hint or setting an example, to analyzing, and to revealing the hidden connection that exists between premise and conclusion; apart from God we have only instructors. When Scripture, or the Fathers, or the Church speaks to us, then we have the teaching of God.

The Word of God knows not silence, and the monastic life is set before us as a constant attention and docility to this voice that is ever speaking. In monasteries more than anywhere else is God pleased to communicate His thought, His designs, His beauty. " Mary, sitting by the feet of the Lord, heard his word " (Luke x. 39). Every morning before receiving the Body and Blood of the Lord we say to Him: " Make me always cleave to Thy commandments and never suffer me to be separated from Thee " (*Dne. Jesu Xte, Fili Dei vivi* . . . before *Dne. non sum dignus*). This perseverance in His teaching will last till death, for no one ever deserts God who has once come to know Him. And it will pass beyond death, if it be true that the most perfect form of God's magisterium is found in the beatific vision.

In the next words there is introduced that essential element of the Benedictine Rule, stability: first negatively, "never departing," and then positively, "persevering in his teaching in the monastery until death."[1] Presented in this persuasive fashion it cannot frighten souls or seem to them a burden or a chain; it is simply fidelity to the blessed retreat where we are sure of finding the fulness of life. The first principle, the basis, the constituent, and the term of this supernatural life, is union with Our Lord Jesus Christ: union with His teaching, union with His sufferings, union with His blessedness. So that our Holy Father returns, at the end, to the idea of monastic suffering as being the prelude and price of our entry into the kingdom of God: "Heirs indeed of God, and joint-heirs of Christ; but if we suffer with him, so that we may be glorified with him" (Rom. viii. 17). Like stability, so is suffering transfigured: it is now no longer aught else than a glorious co-operation with " the sufferings of Christ," and the monk who suffers may say with the Apostle: "I now rejoice in my sufferings for you, and fill up those things that are wanting of the sufferings of Christ, in my flesh, for his body, which is the church " (Col. i. 24).

Even if the Office did not tell us that he was all wrapped in the divine brightness and as it were already beatified: *Tantaque circa eum claritas excreverat ut in terris positus in cælestibus habitaret*, we should still recognize in the frequency of these references to salvation, to heaven, and to God, the habitual trend of his thought: " The holy man could in no way teach otherwise than as he lived,"[2] His whole soul was fixed on eternity. This preoccupation has determined the organic conception of the religious life which he founded in the church; for with the most natural framework in the family, its pursuit is the highest that can be, union with God, and its goal, the utterly supernatural, eternity. This present life is only an apprenticeship, a trial or novitiate for eternity; and it is in view of eternity that we have to renounce, to learn, and to conquer.

[1] *In primis, si quis ad conversionem venerit, ea conditione excipiatur, ut usque ad mortem suam ibi perseveret* (S. Cæsar., *Reg. ad mon.*, i.).
[2] S. Greg. M., *Dial.*, l. II., c. xxxvi.

CHAPTER I

OF THE VARIOUS KINDS OF MONKS[1]

IT is possible to distribute the seventy-three chapters of the Rule logically into different groups, provided we note that these do not represent clear-cut divisions and that our Holy Father, like all ancient writers, even when he is dealing with legislative enactments, gives his thought a living and flexible form, careless of repetition or apparent disorder.

We may distinguish in every true association two elements: the constitutive and the legislative. St. Benedict describes briefly in the first three chapters the organic structure of monastic society, what it substantially is, and what it is not; its basis and its bond—viz., the authority of the Abbot; then its members and their part in its government. Next follows (IV.-VII.) what concerns the spiritual form of our life and the supernatural training of each member. It is in these seven chapters that is given, as it seems to us, the constitution of the monastery; what remains relates to its legislative aspect; the subdivisions of this we shall notice later.

De generibus Monachorum.—Monachorum quatuor esse genera manifestum est. Primum cœnobitarum, hoc est, monasteriale, militans sub regula vel Abbate.

It is plain that there are four kinds of monks. The first are the Cenobites—that is, those who do their service [*lit.* military service] in monasteries under a rule and an abbot.

The first word of the rule is the word "monk."[2] It comes from the Greek μοναχός, the original meaning of which is the same as that of μόνος: alone, unique, simple. In the early centuries of Christianity, when certain of the faithful separated themselves, though living in the world, from the conditions of ordinary life, and presently from society itself, so as to devote themselves, whether alone or in groups, to the practices of supernatural asceticism, they were sometimes called μοναχοί or μονάζοντες, separate, isolated, solitary;[3] the name was in vogue in the fourth century. A pagan poet at the commencement of the fifth century, Rutilius Namatianus, makes malicious play with the original meaning of the word:

> Squalet lucifugis insula plena viris:
> Ipsi se monachos graio cognomine dicunt,
> Quod soli nullo vivere teste volunt.[4]

---

[1] We translate the titles of the chapters. Though they are given by all the manuscripts, with some slight variations, the critics discuss whether they are really St. Benedict's. The reasons alleged against their attribution to him are not always very convincing; see, for example, W LFFLIN, *Benedicti Regula Monachorum*, Præf., p. x. We reproduce the Latin of the titles at the beginning of the first extract of each chapter.

[2] Haeft., l. III., tract. i., *De nomine monachorum*.   [3] *Cf.* Cass., *Conlat.*, XVIII., v.

[4] *Itinerarium*, l. I., 489 *sq*. The following may serve as a version of these lines:

> In truth the island's foul and swarms again
> With men that shun the open light of day;
> Who call them monks—that's Greek—because they'd fain
> Do ill alone where none may say them nay.

The idea of unity which is implied in their name has made it possible to define monks in various ways, each embracing a part of the truth. Thus they are men who live alone,[1] men who wish to introduce oneness and simplicity into their life, men who busy themselves with God only and seek nothing but union with Him. Paul Orosius says: "Monks are Christians who, setting aside the manifold activity of the world, devote themselves to the one work of their faith."[2] And St. Denis says: "Our pious masters have called these men, at one time *therapeutæ* because of the sincere service in which they adore the Divinity, at another monks, because of their single undivided life, which removes their spirit from the distraction of manifold interests and by which they are borne towards the oneness of God and the perfection of holy love."[3]

To these old writers the name monk denoted a genus, comprising all the faithful who renounced the world to give themselves to perfection. For a long period to be a religious and to be a monk were synonymous, and that is still the case in the East. But, with the appearance of forms of the religious life consecrated more directly to the service of souls, the term monk became specific. In actual fact it no longer belongs to any but the sons of St. Benedict and St. Bruno, though the custom has obtained in France of giving it to the followers of St. Francis and St. Dominic. However, St. Thomas and St. Bonaventure, in their controversy with the University of Paris, claimed for their brethren only the style of religious.

If we should wish at this time of day to map out the religious life and to classify it, we might divide religious with sufficient accuracy into five groups, according to the time of their historical appearance (I say nothing here of religious women, who are of innumerable types and of every variety): the five groups would be: monks, regular canons, friars or mendicants, regular clerks, and secular priests joined in congregation with or without vows.

In St. Benedict's time only four kinds of monks were recognized; and the division was so plain and so current that our Holy Father does not labour it. St. Jerome and Cassian[4] had noted, for Egypt, three

---

[1] St. Augustine explains how the cenobites themselves, though numerically many, may yet be called μονός, since they have only one heart and one soul (*Enarr. in Ps.* cxxxii. 6. *P.L.*, XXXVII., 1732-1733).

[2] *Histor.*, l. VII., c. xxxiii. *P.L.*, XXXI., 1145.

[3] *De Hierarchia ecclesiastica*, c. vi.

[4] *Tria sunt in Ægypto genera monachorum. Unum, Cœnobitæ, quod illi Sauses gentili lingua vocant, nos* in commune viventes *possumus appellare. Secundum, Anachoretæ, qui soli habitant per deserta. . . . Tertium, genus est quod Remoboth dicunt, deterrimum atque neglectum. . . . Hi bini vel terni, nec multo plures simul habitant, suo arbitrio ac ditione viventes* (S. Hieron., *Epist.* XXII., 34. *P.L.*, XXII., 419). Cassian reproduces and completes this list: *Tria sunt in Ægypto genera monachorum, quorum duo sunt optima, tertium tepidum atque omnimodis evitandum. Primum est cœnobitarum qui, scilicet in congregatione pariter consistentes unius senioris judicio gubernantur. . . . Secundum anachoretarum, qui prius in cœnobiis instituti jamque in actuali conversatione perfecti solitudinis elegere secreta. . . . Tertium reprehensibile Sarabaitarum est.—(Anachoretæ) in cœnobiis primum diutissime commorantes, omnem patientiæ ac discretionis*

kinds. St. Benedict reproduces their words in part, and mentions, as Cassian does,[1] a fourth category. But, while Cassian makes it consist of false anchorites, deserters from the cenobitical life, for St. Benedict[2] it comprises the class of vagrant, roving monks, the *gyrovagi*. Cassian and the Fathers of the East knew them well,[3] but the wretched species had made such increase that St. Benedict could give them a name for themselves; this name is first found in the Rule, but it may have existed already in common use.

St. Benedict first mentions the Cenobites (*i.e.*, those who live in common κοινός βίος) because, following in this many of the Fathers,[4] he gives them his preference. Cassian, who saw in the Christianity of Jerusalem a true religious family, considered them the first even historically.[5] Since he was to have full opportunity to talk about Cenobites in the course of this Rule which was destined for them, St. Benedict here confines himself to marking in a few words their chief characteristics. They have a common life, they dwell in a monastery, and this is the framework of their stability. They serve—that is, they strive together—in a common and convergent effort, towards one and the same end and victory: perfection, and that conventual perfection. They have a rule, so that the fundamental conditions of their life are fixed and in no way left to arbitrary arrangement; but the rule need not be written, it might be a collection of customs. *Vel Abbate.*—We may remark, once for all, that in St. Benedict's usage the disjunctive *vel* has often the force of the copula *et*; and that is the case in this passage. However precise may be the rule or customs, there are a thousand matters which will not be settled by them. So we have the living power of the Abbot to interpret the rule and fix its sense. Cenobites have an Abbot at their head—that is to say, a father; so they form a family.

Deinde secundum genus est anachoretarum, id est, eremitarum, horum qui non conversionis fervore novitio, sed monasterii probatione diuturna, didicerunt contra diabolum, multorum solatio jam docti, pugnare; et bene instructi fraterna ex acie ad singularem

The second are the Anchorites, Hermits—that is, those who, not in the first fervour of religious life, but after long probation in the monastery, have learned by the help and experience of others to fight against the devil; and going forth well armed from the ranks

---

regulam diligenter edocti, ... *dirissimis dæmonum prœliis congressuri penetrant heremi profunda secreta.—Emersit post hæc illud deterrimum et infidele monachorum genus* ... etc., ... *bini vel terni in cellulis commorantur, non contenti abbatis cura atque imperio gubernari*... etc.... (*Conlat.*, XVIII., iv., *Instit.*, V., xxxvi., [*cf.* also *Conlat.*, XVIII., vi.]; *Conlat.*, XVIII., vii.)

All the ancient forms of the monastic life, even the less reputable, are still represented to-day on Mt. Athos, the "holy mountain."

[1] *Conlat.*, XVIII., viii.
[2] St. Benedict puts with the sarabaites those monks who live alone, doing their own will: ... *aut certe singuli sine pastore.*
[3] *Cf.* D. Besse, *Les Moines d'Orient*, chap. ii.
[4] For example St. John Chrysost., *In Matt. Hom.* LXXII. *P.G.*, LVIII., 671-672. —St. Basil, *Reg. fus.*, vii.—St. Jerome, *Epist.* CXXV. 9. *P.L.*, XXII., 1077.
[5] *Conlat.*, XVIII., v.

pugnam eremi, securi jam sine consolatione alterius, sola manu vel brachio, contra vitia carnis vel cogitationum, Deo auxiliante, sufficiunt pugnare.

of their brethren to the single-handed combat of the desert, are now able to fight safely without the support of others, by their own strength under God's aid, against the vices of the flesh and their evil thoughts.

The second kind of monks are the anchorites (*i.e.*, those who live apart, in seclusion: ἀναχωρέω); St. Benedict does not distinguish them, as St. Isidore[1] did later, from hermits or dwellers in the desert (ἔρημος). The anachoretic life has always existed in the Church,[2] but it is no longer represented in our days, save in its mitigated form, among the Carthusians and Camaldolese . . . ; though there are as well, without doubt, a few hermits in solitudes and some recluses near certain monasteries. At the beginning of monasticism anchorites were innumerable, and we may even say that the religious life (in its special sense) took its origin among them, in the third century, with St. Paul of the Thebaid, St. Antony, and St. Hilarion, imitators of Elias and St. John the Baptist. Ecclesiastical law had not yet had time to regulate the religious state; so anyone who wished became an anchorite, with or without a master, in the dress and under the rule of his choice. And we know in what a very simple fashion St. Benedict himself became a hermit and made his profession.[3]

So he knew the anchorite's life by personal experience and had practised it with generous ardour. He was ignorant neither of its attractions nor of the terrible temptations and extraordinary illusions to which it readily lends itself.[4] Man is not sufficient for himself; we need support, and we find it in social intercourse, through intelligence and love. We need example, encouragement, and direction. In the desert there is no supernatural rivalry. We have there none of the supervision or example of others, which, as an external supplement to conscience, is at once so precious, so effective, and so sweet. We have no scope for the exercise of fraternal charity, which is, however, the plainest index of our love of God. In solitude the imagination runs wild, the senses are strained to exasperation; and, if perchance the devil interferes directly, there may come a complete upset of nature's balance, with vice or despair. Are not souls sometimes drawn into the desert by sloth, instability, pride, and hatred of their kind ? To escape from the tyranny of passion it is not enough to flee from men, as is proved by many a story in the Lives of the Fathers. Take the case of the monk plagued with an angry temper. He fled from the monastery so as to escape the occasions of sin, and soon found them again in the eccentricities of his pitcher.[5] On the subject of the dangers of the

---

[1] *De ecclesiasticis officiis*, l. II., c. xvi. *P.L.*, LXXXIII., 794-795.
[2] *Cf.* VACANT-MANGENOT, *Dictionnaire de Théologie*, art. "Anachorète."
[3] S. GREG. M., *Dial.*, l. II., c. i.
[4] Read the whole of *Conference* XIX. of Cassian.
[5] *Verba Seniorum: Vitæ Patrum*, III., 98. ROSWEYD, p. 515.

eremitical life St. Ephrem may be read, or, of a later period, St. Ivo of Chartres.[1]

Our Holy Father, however, is far from being blind to the sublimity of the anachoretical life. But he considers it too perfect to suit most souls, and he puts very high the conditions necessary for a prudent entry on such a way of life. With Cassian, St. Nilus,[2] and others of the old writers, he requires in the first place that the candidate be no longer in the first fervour of his conversion and religious life (*conversio* or *conversatio*). Monks, like wine, improve with age. The fervour and excitement of the novice are necessary, because it is by this fermentation that the soul gets rid of a multitude of minor impurities which make it heavy and sluggish. But this sort of fervour is transient; in proportion as the interior work of elimination is accomplished and the foreign elements are precipitated, it gives place to a fervour of charity which is purified and clear (*defæcata*). So the future hermit must try himself for long years in a monastery, learn the methods of the spiritual life, and become a past-master in the art of fighting the devil with the help and the consolation (παράκλησις) of all his brethren. It is only when he has been well drilled and trained in the ranks, and in such collective struggle, for the single combat of the desert, that he will be able to face the struggle against the vices of the flesh and the spirit, without help henceforth from others, with nothing more to count on but God and the strength of his own right arm. Finally, the permission of his Abbot will guarantee the monk from all danger of presumption.[3]

The conditions of religious life have been modified, but human nature remains the same, and the temptation to quit the community and become a hermit is of all time. This desire may appear at the earliest stage, whether because God is really calling the soul into solitude, or because our self-love, infatuated with the renunciation demanded by so novel a life, persuades us wrongly that we have made a mistake, that we have not enough silence, and that all sorts of tedious association with others disturb the even course of our prayer. The temptation may arise later on and spring from a sickly or misanthropic temperament, or from a debased mysticism. Under the pretext that pure contemplation is the ideal and that the life of the Carthusian has been recognized by the Church as the most perfect, a monk will plague

[1] S. EPHR., *De humilitate*, c. lviii. sq. (Opp. græc. lat., t. I., p. 315-317). *Parœn.* XXIII., XXIV., XXXVIII., XLII. (t. II., p. 102, 107, 136, 154).—YVON. CARNOT., *Epist.* CXCII. et CCLVI. *P.L.*, CLXII., 198, 260.

[2] *Tractatus ad Eulogium*, 32. *P.G.*, LXXIX., 1135.—*Epist.*, l. III., Ep. LXXII. *P.G.*, LXXIX., 422.

[3] *Cf.* SULP. SEVER., *Dial.* I., c. xvii. *P.L.*, XX., 195. The councils had often to concern themselves with anchorites, and that of Vannes, in particular, decreed in 465: *Servandum quoque de monachis, ne eis ad solitarias cellulas liceat a congregatione discedere, nisi forte probatis post emeritos labores, aut propter infirmitatis necessitatem asperior ab abbatibus regula remittatur. Quod ita demum fiet, ut intra eadem monasterii septa manentes, tamen sub abbatis potestate separatas habere cellulas permittantur* (MANSI, t. VII., col. 954). History shows that the anachoretical life was nearly always tempered by the cenobitical, and that the solitaries of the East were grouped in communities, or at least took companions, admitted disciples, and visited one another at long intervals.

his Abbot until he has consented to his departure, a departure which is often only the prelude to a sad series of wanderings. Or perhaps a man will try to make himself a sort of anchorite within the walls of his monastery. He constructs a little life of his own; he keeps himself at a distance from the Abbot and his brethren. The peaceful and leisured conditions secured by the monastic life no longer serve God, or charity, but self. Alas! such a monk will no longer have even the shadow of true happiness; he will never come near to God; he will die prosaically, a slave to his ease and to an old man's whimsies, hardened and swollen with his self-love. We must hold fast to the advice of the Apostle: "And let us consider one another, to provoke unto charity and good works; not forsaking our assembly, as some are accustomed; but comforting one another, and so much the more as you see the day approaching" (Heb. x. 24-25).

While maintaining our belief in extraordinary vocations, it is permissible to regard the cenobitical life as more natural than that of the anchorite. "It is not good for man to be alone." Absolute silence, says St. Hildegarde, is inhuman—that is to say, either above or below human nature.[1] Many things can only be well done in association; the stars themselves are grouped in constellations. So we, being all redeemed together by our Saviour, sanctify ourselves together in Him, so as to share with all fulness in the intimate union of the Divine Persons. As St. John says (1 Ep. i. 3), "That which we have seen and have heard, we declare unto you; that you also may have fellowship with us and our fellowship may be with the Father and with his Son Jesus Christ." So in eternity too our life will be cenobitical; and St. Thomas explains how even then the society of our friends will become an element of our happiness.[2] There is wisdom in not conceiving our earthly life on any different plan.

Tertium vero monachorum deterrimum genus est sarabaitarum, qui nulla regula approbati, experientia magistra, sicut aurum fornacis, sed in plumbi natura molliti, adhuc operibus servantes sæculo fidem, mentiri Deo per tonsuram noscuntur. Qui bini aut terni, aut certe singuli sine pastore, non Dominicis, sed suis inclusi ovilibus, pro lege eis est desideriorum voluptas: cum quicquid putaverint vel elegerint, hoc dicunt sanctum, et quod noluerint, hoc putant non licere.

A third and detestable kind of monks are the Sarabaites, who have been tried by no rule nor by experience the master, as gold by the furnace; but, being as soft as lead, still keep faith with the world in their works, while, as their tonsure shows, they lie to God. These in twos or threes, or even singly without a shepherd, shut up not in the Lord's sheepfolds but in their own, make a law to themselves of their own pleasures and desires: whatever they think fit or please to do, that they call holy; and what they like not, that they consider unlawful.

Our Holy Father strikes out the anachoretical life, because prudence forbids it to most men; for quite different motives he rejects the life

[1] *Regulæ S. Bened. Explanatio.* P.L., CXCVII., 1056.
[2] S. Th., I.-II., q. iv., a. 8.

of the Sarabaites, which is, as he says, detestable. Cassian attributes an Egyptian origin to the word Sarabaite: "From their sequestering themselves from the association of the monasteries and looking after their needs, each man for himself, they were called in the Egyptian idiom 'Sarabaites.'"[1] But perhaps, with more likelihood, it may be derived from the Aramaic term *sarab*, which means rebellious or refractory.[2] To understand how it is that monks such as St. Benedict here describes could be found in existence for several centuries, we must remember that the Church had not yet surrounded the approach to religion with a series of precautionary measures, designed for the elimination of the unworthy, the unsuitable, or the unstable. So a man had only to take a habit, or have one given him, and then cut his hair. Without previous novitiate, without becoming part of a regularly constituted community, he was a monk and in the language of the time "converted," provided that he showed by certain external acts that he had renounced the world and devoted himself to God. Such a one was bound to chastity and, in some degree, to poverty; but where was obedience?

The Sarabaites might say: "We recognize theoretically that obedience is implied in the concept of monasticism; more than that, we are quite prepared to obey; what then will the actual tendering of obedience add to the perfection of our interior dispositions?" St. Benedict foresees and discounts such sophisms. Only effective and practical obedience is any test of the reality of interior dispositions; and one only obeys where there are orders and a rule. Now the Sarabaites have no rule to test them, to prove them true religious: *nulla regula approbati*, "tried by no rule." Experience serves as a touchstone which teaches the monk and others his true value, *experientia magistra*,[3] "with experience as master." Far from being that true gold that readily stands the test of the furnace and emerges victorious, pure of all alloy, the man who refuses to pass through the crucible of a rule is convicted beforehand of being soft and base as lead. The life of the Sarabaites is an open lie. They lie at the same time to God and to the world: to the world, for they have put off its livery, yet their works are of the world worldly; to God, for they betray Him at the same time that they parade their consecration to His service. Their life is worldly, though their heads be shaven.

But perhaps, if they have not a written rule, at least they have a living rule in the person of an Abbot. No; they unite in parties of two or three, and none of them claims any sort of authority; or even, and this is still more agreeable, they live alone in hermitages. And so they form a fold without a shepherd, a fold which belongs to no master, not at all to God but entirely to themselves, "shut up, not in the

---

[1] *Conlat.*, XVIII., vii.

[2] *Cf.* Calmet, *in b. l.* Gazet, in his note on the passage of Cassian previously cited.

[3] This phrase is better supported from all points of view than the reading *experientia magistri*; it is borrowed from Cassian, *Conlat.*, XIX., vii.

Lord's sheepfolds but in their own." Their rule is what pleases them, their desire, or the whim of the moment. Not that they form any set purpose to themselves of belonging to their own will alone; perhaps they persuade themselves that they do obey a rule; but they make their rule of life for themselves. Whatever they think fit or determine to do, that they call holy;[1] and what they like not, that they consider unlawful.

We have here, expressed in singularly energetic language, a description of a psychological state which is only too common and which forms a most serious danger. If the Sarabaite of history is extinct, his spirit is by no means so. Man has the unfortunate facility of seeing things, not as they are, but as he is, of making the world after his own image and likeness. In the moral order, in the sphere of will, where a mistake is not palpable, betraying itself (as in a laboratory) by the tangible and instant punishment of failure or an explosion, we easily come to distort all our decisions, to canonize what we do, to adore that which pleases us. It is delusion.[2] Thanks to this tendency, a man may motive the most unjustifiable course of action by excellent principles, and set up as a dictate of conscience what is really inspired by the basest passions. What revolutionary ever proposes simply to upset social order ? What heretic is not persuaded that he is serving the Church ? And when the monks of Vicovaro tried to poison St. Benedict, their fierce good faith must have based itself on high considerations of public interest. It is nowhere more easy than in the religious life to deaden the conscience and distort its voice; the old axiom proves true: *Corruptio optimi pessima.* And this is the result of a whole course of interior diplomacy, of a chemical process of the mind: "I have vowed perfection. This imposes on me a yoke which I no longer have the courage to bear: must I then leave the monastery ? This petty obedience may be all right for the period of growth and formation; but I am a senior now. And, after all, are there not certain adjustments possible, certain legitimate interpretations of law ? And is not this also perfection ?" And so a man gently substitutes his own will for the law, until the fascination of self occupies the whole field of his interior vision; complete apostasy will not then be long in coming. Undoubtedly every tendency to isolate oneself from the community, all irregular fostering of an individual whim, does not end in such excess; but we should know the pitfalls that beset the way of the Sarabaite, and where it may lead, so that prudence may compel us to avoid it. Oh, if we could but profit by the fearful experiences of others ! There is no security save in the way of absolute obedience and in conventual life under the rule of an Abbot.

---

[1] A reminiscence of a Roman proverb, several times quoted by ST. AUGUSTINE; the latter relates that Tychonius made the Donatists say: *Quod volumus sanctum est* Epist. XCIII., 14, 43. *P.L.*, XXXIII., 328, 342.—*Contra Epist. Parmeniani*, l. II., c. xiii. *P.L.*, XLIII., 73.—*Contra Cresconium Donatistam*, l. IV., c. xxxvii. *P.L.*, XLIII., 572.

[2] Read Father Faber's *Spiritual Conference* on Self-deceit.

Quartum vero genus est monachorum, quod nominatur gyrovagum, qui tota vita sua per diversas provincias ternis aut quaternis diebus per diversorum cellas hospitantur, semper vagi et nunquam stabiles, et propriis voluptatibus et gulæ illecebris servientes, et per omnia deteriores sarabaitis; de quorum omnium miserrima conversatione melius est silere quam loqui.

The fourth kind of monks are those called Gyrovagues, who spend all their lives long wandering about divers provinces, staying in different cells for three or four days at a time, ever roaming, with no stability, given up to their own pleasures and to the snares of gluttony, and worse in all things than the Sarabaites. Of the most wretched life of all these it is better to say nothing than to speak.

It might have seemed difficult to find a more degraded form of the religious life than that of the Sarabaites; yet there is a worse still. After all the Sarabaites could work and pray; their fold was not the Lord's fold, but still they had one and so had an embryo of the monastic home; perhaps there were good souls to be met here and there among them; in any case the spectacle of their careless observance was not for many. But the Gyrovagues display their wretched state in the full light of day and in every place, without any reserve.

They made the vow of poverty only, and that with no intention of shutting themselves up in a cloister, but of living in the world at the expense of others. Their whole life was passed on the road; they saw the world and conversed with all men. They would knock devoutly at monastery or hermitage, and the excuse of fatigue or respect for the religious habit, besides the careful attention that is given to the passing guest, ensured them a pleasant life and good meals.[1] After three or four days the Gyrovague would take his leave, with wallet well stuffed with provisions. He took great care not to fix himself anywhere, for he would have had to adopt the customs of the monastery which entertained him. He vanished at the right moment and before he could be required to take his part in the common toil. He was the parasite of the monastic life, rather a tramp than a monk.[2] We can imagine the shamelessness, the vulgarity, the immorality, and general intractability of these men. They discredited the religious life, and St. Augustine, in a passage by which St. Benedict was inspired, depicts them as raised up by the devil for this very purpose. "He has scattered many hypocrites in the guise of monks in all directions, men who traverse the provinces with no work and no fixed dwelling, never quiet or at rest. Some go about selling bones of the martyrs; let us suppose they are those of martyrs."[3]

[1] *Cf.* S. Isidori Pelus., *Epist.*, l. I., *Ep.* XLI. *P.G.*, LXXVIII., 207. Instead of *voluptatibus* the best manuscripts have *voluntatibus;* which recalls this passage of the *Verba Seniorum*: *Oportet nos, . . . in congregatione manentes, non quæ nostra sunt quærere, neque servire propriæ voluntati* (*Vitæ Patrum*, V., xiv., 10. Rosweyd, p. 618). See also the *Historia monachorum* of Rufinus, c. xxxi. Rosweyd, p. 484.

[2] The *Regula Magistri*, xx., draws a far from flattering portrait of the gyrovague; read also the eighth chapter of the *Constitutiones monasticæ* which figure among the Works of St. Basil. *P.G.*, XXXI., 1367 sq.

[3] *De opere monachorum*, c. xxviii. *P.L.*, XL., 575.—In bk. X. of the *Institutions*, chap. vi., Cassian describes the idle monk in terms which recall those of St. Augustine.

To sum up: they have no recollection, no prayer, no work, no mortification, no stability, no obedience; and on all these heads the Gyrovagues are inferior to the Sarabaites: *et per omnia deteriores Sarabaitis*. St. Benedict, after a look at this picture, asks permission to insist no further[1] (*De quorum omnium* probably means the Sarabaites and Gyrovagues). Let us imitate him, and yet remember that the tendency to the life of the Gyrovague may always reappear. It is easy to grow fond of leaving the monastery, of good meals, of conversation with layfolk; to let oneself slip into taking little care with one's person and giving the name of " holy simplicity " to slovenliness or to gossip with externs.

| His ergo omissis, ad cœnobitarum fortissimum genus disponendum, adjuvante Domino, veniamus. | Leaving these alone, therefore, let us set to work, by the help of God, to lay down a rule for the Cenobites—that is, the strongest race of monks. |

St. Jerome expresses himself in nearly the same terms: " These then, like evil pests, being put away, let us come to those who are more numerous and dwell in community—that is, to those who are, as we said, called Cenobites."[2] So let us too leave on one side these caricatures of the monastic life; let us even, though for other reasons, leave aside the eremitical life, and now with God's help begin to organize by means of rule the sound and strong race of Cenobites. Already, even from the exclusions that form the theme of almost the whole of this first chapter, the great main lines of Benedictine life disengage themselves; that life will be conventual, ruled by obedience, vowed to stability.

---

[1] We read in RUFINUS also (*Hist. mon.*, c. vii.): *Unde silere de bis melius censeo, quam parum digne proloqui* (ROSWEYD, p. 464). An analogous formula occurs in SALLUST (*Jugurtha*, xix.); D. Butler observes that it strongly resembles a proverb.

[2] *Epist.* XXII., 35. *P.L.*, XXII., 419.

CHAPTER II

WHAT KIND OF MAN THE ABBOT OUGHT TO BE

IN order that our life may be truly cenobitical and conventual and not consist merely in the juxtaposition of men under the same roof, with the motto of the Abbey of Thelema, "Do as you like," it must be regulated by a rule; but this rule itself will be inadequate and inefficient without the intervention of a living authority. No society escapes this necessity; each must have a master. And St. Benedict speaks at once about the Abbot, because he looks upon him as the keystone in the arch of that edifice which he wishes to construct, as the foundation on which all rests, as the influence which co-ordinates the diverse members, as the head and the heart, from which flows all vitality. The queen-bee makes the hive, and it is matter of experience that a monastery takes after its Abbot. Therefore to show what the Abbot should be is at the same time to draw in advance the outlines of monastic society. No previous rule had given so complete an account of the duties of the Abbot, and although he borrows more than one idea from his predecessors[1]—as, for example, from St. Basil and St. Orsiesius—our Holy Father has in this chapter produced entirely original work.

QUALIS ESSE DEBEAT ABBAS.—Abbas, qui præesse dignus est monasterio, semper meminisse debet, quod dicitur, et nomen majoris factis implere. Christi enim agere vices in monasterio creditur, quando ipsius vocatur prænomine, dicente Apostolo: *Accepistis spiritum adoptionis filiorum, in quo clamamus: Abba, pater.*

An Abbot who is worthy to rule over the monastery ought always to remember what he is called, and correspond to his name by his works. For he is believed to hold the place of Christ in the monastery, since he is called by His name, as the Apostle says: "Ye have received the spirit of the adoption of sons, in which we cry: Abba, Father."

St. Benedict refuses to concern himself with him who would be Abbot for his own pleasure or for ostentation, but deals only with him who is worthy to rule the monastery. He is worthy in proportion as he realizes by constant consideration the meaning of the name which he bears, and compels himself to justify by his deeds this title of superior and head. It is a question of loyalty and moral concord; there must be this harmony between the thing and its name, between the man and his distinctive title, between the nature and the activity which is to express it. So if he understands his name aright the Abbot will find in it, not only the source, but the character and extent of his power and the measure of his responsibility.[2]

[1] *Cf.* HAEFT., l. III., tract. v.
[2] *Clericus qui Christi servit Ecclesiæ interpretatur primo vocabulum suum, et nominis definitione prolata, nitatur esse quod dicitur* (S. HIERON., *Epist.* LII., ad *Nepotianum,* 5. *P.L.,* XXII., 531).

The abbatial authority has its source in God: it does not come from the community, although the community designates its holder. It comes from God doubly, as authority and as spiritual authority. For all authority is from God. Those in our day who busy themselves in the thankless task of constructing a morality without obligation or sanction only expose the absolute impotence of men to create an ounce of authority. They may cajole, suggest, or compel; but authority they have not. A man is worth no more than his fellows; neither cleverness, nor force, nor even intellectual superiority is able to create a real right to power; and of this anarchists are not unaware. We must give up the supposition of a social contract, an original vote of the people on purpose to declare that society shall exist.[1] That was a blessed state formerly when civil authority was exercised by men consecrated by the kingly anointing and reigning " by the grace of God."

But here we are in the supernatural order, where power has no other end than to rule souls and sanctify them. Such power can only come from the special investiture of God: " Nor doth anyone take to himself honour, except he be called by God." Undoubtedly, according to the terms of Canon Law, the authority of the Abbot is " ordinary "; nevertheless, in respect of God it is only delegated. The Abbot is the deputy and understudy of the Lord. We may examine this divine delegation at close quarters, for the whole teaching of this chapter derives from it. To St. Benedict the monastery is in very truth the " house of God " (Chapter LIII.); first in this sense that Our Lord Jesus Christ dwells there and is its centre; for the joy of our conventual life consists in our all being grouped together round Him. But He does not dwell there as though in a hired house or in the rooms of an hotel; He is the sole true proprietor of the monastery, possessing both radical dominion and dominion of use. He is also the Abbot; and if Our Lord were to show Himself visibly, all obedience and all honour would go to Him; the crozier would have to be placed in His hands forthwith.[2]

Would it be very sweet and very easy to obey Our Lord directly ? Yet He has not willed it so, and for many reasons. In the first place, it would be to realize the conditions of eternity at once. And are we quite certain that we should never disobey Him ? His visible presence would give our faults a graver character, make them more worthy of condemnation. He has not even entrusted us to angels; perhaps they would have failed to be considerate for our weakness; or we might have obeyed because of their superiority of nature and God would not have been the motive of our submission. His procedure is always the same; He expresses Himself and comes to us under the humblest forms: in the Creation, in the Incarnation, in the Holy Eucharist, in His priests.

---

[1] Read Bossuet, *Cinquième avertissement sur les lettres du ministre Jurieu*, chap. xxxvi. ff.

[2] Read St. Gertrude's *Herald of Divine Love*, chap. ii. of bk. IV.: Our Lord presiding at chapter in the Office of Prime.

It is His mercy; the Son of God, as the Apostle says, "had in all things to be made like to his brethren, that he might become merciful. . . . For in that wherein he himself hath suffered and been tempted, he is able to succour them also that are tempted" (Heb. ii. 17-18). The Abbot is a human creature like us, frail like us, perhaps more weak than we. He has his own temperament and his own habits; but let us not stop at the exterior, recognizing as we should that God is in him, believing that he is Christ, understanding that our faith has to be exercised: "For he is believed to hold the place of Christ in the monastery." Be he pleasant or harsh, be he old or young, be he the Abbot we know or a new one, it makes no matter, for he is the Lord.

His name itself expresses this substitution: he is called, as Our Lord is called, Abbot—that is, Father. And to monks, who are Christians made perfect, we may apply the words which the Apostle St. Paul spoke of those who were regenerated in Christ. "You have received the spirit of the adoption of sons by which we cry: Abba, Father" (Rom. viii. 15). But a difficulty presents itself; the Christians' cry is to the First Person of the Holy Trinity and not to the Second; they say: "Abba, Father," to imitate the Son of God speaking to His Father (Mark xiv. 36). Does the text cited by St. Benedict really prove that the Abbot bears one of the names of Christ and that Christ may be called Father? We may reply that St. Benedict does not wish to give his quotation the character of rigorous demonstration; he merely notes that the Abbot has a "divine" name, and the sacred text which presents itself spontaneously to his thought appears to justify this teaching. Furthermore, theology teaches us that the title of Father may be given either to the First Person alone, when considered in relation to the Second, or to the Three Persons together, when regarded as a single essence *ad intra* and as a single principle of action *ad extra ;* for in God, according to the axiom formulated by the Council of Florence: "where there is no opposition of relation, all is one" (*Omnia sunt unum, ubi non obviat relationis oppositio*).

Ideoque Abbas nihil extra præceptum Domini (quod absit) debet aut docere, aut constituere, vel jubere: sed jussio ejus vel doctrina, fermentum divinæ justitiæ, in discipulorum mentibus conspergatur.	And therefore the Abbot ought not (God forbid) to teach, or ordain, or command anything contrary to the law of the Lord; but let his bidding and his doctrine be infused into the minds of his disciples like the leaven of divine justice.

The Abbot's authority is divine; it is paternal and absolute, and in this respect resembles the paternal authority of God more than the *patria potestas* of Roman law with which St. Benedict was familiar; but it is by no means an unlimited and arbitrary authority. No authority is lawful when exercised beyond its limits, and the limits of all authority are those fixed by God's grant. God does not support, and cannot be charged with, any exercise of authority for which He has given no grant, still less with any which militates against Himself;

for God cannot be divided against God. Now, precisely because the authority of the Abbot comes from God and shares in the force and extent of God's authority, the Abbot should use it only for the ends and for the interests of God and according to God's methods. For Our Lord is not dispossessed; though His authority be in the hands of the Abbot, it remains His still. Good sense teaches us this, and herein we have the basis of the simplicity, security, and perfect order of our life.

Consequently nothing in the teaching, nothing in the general arrangements or particular orders of the Abbot, shall be foreign or contrary to the law of the Lord; God forbid, *quod absit*,[1] for it would be a monstrous thing. But, so far from abusing his power to satisfy his passions and to cast into the souls of his disciples the evil leaven of false teachers (Matt. xvi. 6, 11-12), the Abbot must by his teaching and his orders infuse into them in abundance the leaven of divine justice (Matt. xiii. 33); by means of him does Our Lord wish to be born and grow in souls.[2]

St. Benedict's words are not an invitation to monks to scrutinize their Abbot narrowly, so as to make sure that he is a faithful steward and governs correctly. The filial spirit, in accord with the axiom of common law, will always give the superior the benefit of the doubt; the contrary attitude would tend to debase all authority and weaken all discipline. Men do not need to be encouraged to disobey. Of course exception is made of the case where misguided authority might prescribe what was bad or patently contrary to the Rule. Canonical visitations were instituted to prevent and correct abuses; St. Benedict suggests a different method.

Memor sit semper Abbas quia doctrinæ suæ vel discipulorum obedientiæ, utrarumque rerum, in tremendo judicio Dei facienda erit discussio, sciatque Abbas culpæ pastoris incumbere, quicquid in ovibus paterfamilias utilitatis minus potuerit invenire. Tantum iterum liber erit, si inquieto vel inobedienti gregi pastoris fuerit omnis diligentia attributa, et morbidis earum actibus universa fuerit cura exhibita: pastor earum in judicio Domini absolutus, dicat cum Propheta Domino: *Justitiam tuam non abscondi in corde*

Let the Abbot be ever mindful that at the dreadful judgement of God, an account will have to be given both of his own teaching and of the obedience of his disciples. And let him know that any lack of profit which the father of the household may find in his sheep, shall be imputed to the fault of the shepherd. Only then shall he be acquitted, if he shall have bestowed all pastoral diligence on his unquiet and disobedient flock, and employed all his care to amend their corrupt manner of life: then shall he be ab-

---

[1] D. BUTLER adopts, as better attested, the reading: *Nibil extra præceptum Domini quod sit.* . . .

[2] Our Holy Father remembered ST. BASIL, who reminds the superior that he is *minister Christi et dispensator mysteriorum Dei; timens ne præter voluntatem Dei, vel præter quod in sacris Scripturis evidenter præcipitur, vel dicat aliquid, vel imperet, ete inveniatur tanquam falsus testis Dei, aut sacrilegus, vel introducens aliquid alienum a doctrina Domini, vel certe subrclinquens et præteriens aliquid eorum quæ Deo placita sunt. Ad fratres autem esse debet tanquam si nutrix foveat parvulos suos*, etc. (Reg. contr., xv.). Cf. ibid., clxxxiv.

meo, veritatem tuam et salutare tuum dixi; ipsi autem contemnentes spreverunt me. Et tunc demum inobedientibus curæ suæ ovibus pœna sit eis prævalens ipsa mors.

solved in the judgement of the Lord, and may say to the Lord with the prophet: "I have not hidden thy justice in my heart, I have declared thy truth and thy salvation, but they contemned and despised me." So at the last to those disobedient sheep may their punishment come, overmastering death.

There is a problem of government which has not yet found a final solution—the problem, that is, of reconciling authority and liberty. It has been done, but at long intervals, and Tacitus noted in his *Life of Agricola* that the Emperor Nerva had had this chance: " Although . . . Nerva Cæsar combined things before incompatible, the principate and liberty. . . ." To-day men work at the problem incessantly; for this end they make constitutions and supplementary laws, they revise them, they proclaim the separation of offices, they balance them ingeniously, they parcel out authority so that its parts may counterpoise one another, they leave in the hands of him who presides over public affairs the smallest possible amount of initiative. But it very often happens that we escape the dictatorship of one only to become subject to an oligarchical dictatorship. And as for individual liberty and the pretence of securing its inviolability, well, we at least know what it comes to. So it is ascertained fact that the only truly effective curb on human activity is conscience, and to restrain and guide this activity you must reach men's souls.

St. Benedict is the wisest of legislators. He sets up an authority; he provides for the appointment of the holder of this authority by those concerned; he puts into the hands of the elect a power of enormous extent; and he simply makes this authority accountable to Our Lord. This is the only safeguard that he gives the monks. If the Abbot has faith and is anxious for his salvation, he can have no better incentive or curb; if the Abbot is unworthy of his position, nothing short of deposition will do any good; if he is merely weak and heedless, our Holy Father impresses on him, over and over again, the responsibility he is incurring, and he would have him remind himself of it continually: *Memor sit semper.* It would even seem that St. Benedict dreaded defect rather than excess in the exercise of authority.

The Abbot is responsible and will be judged for two matters: his own teaching and the observance of his disciples; " of both these things " as St. Benedict says emphatically.[1] Of course faults are personal matters; but, for all that, the Abbot will have to answer for the obedience of his monks, in the sense that he must maintain the yoke of obedience and in all discretion make his monks feel the salutary influence of his authority. He cannot be heedless. He will carry before the awful tribunal of God the load of community faults which he has known and

---

[1] *Cf.* S. ORSIESII, *Doctrina*, x., xi.

has not corrected. Between him and his monks there is set up a continuous current: his actions go out towards them as an influence, theirs seek him as their principle. The Father of the family has made him shepherd and entrusted His sheep to him; He expects to find them all when He comes, and to find them strong and prospering. If He be disappointed, if any harm have come to the flock, let the Abbot know for certainty that it will be imputed to him: " any lack of profit which He may find."

There is only one case,[1] when the shepherd will be relieved of responsibility, and that no pleasant case; it is when the loss God finds is not really the fault of the Abbot. His flock was unruly and turbulent. Yet he did not omit to spend his care on it and to administer all sorts of treatment for its moral ills. If such be the case the Abbot will be acquitted and absolved in the judgement, and he will be able to say to the Lord with the prophet David (Ps. xxxix. 11), with Ezechiel (xx. 27) and with Isaias (i. 2): " I have not hidden thy justice in my heart, I have declared thy truth and thy salvation, but they have contemned them and despised me." Then, says St. Benedict in conclusion, instead of the life which they would not, may death itself, for their punishment, take those sheep rebellious to his care and his treatment; may death overcome and have the final word: *pœna sit eis prævalens ipsa mors.*[2]

Ergo cum aliquis suscipit nomen Abbatis, duplici debet doctrina suis præesse discipulis; id est, omnia bona et sancta, factis amplius quam verbis ostendere, ut capacibus discipulis mandata Domini verbis proponat: duris vero corde et simplicioribus, factis suis divina præcepta demonstret. Omnia vero quæ discipulis docuerit esse contraria, in suis factis indicet non agenda; ne aliis prædicans, ipse reprobus inveniatur. Ne quando illi dicat Deus peccanti: *Quare tu enarras justitias meas, et assumis testamentum meum per os tuum? Tu vero odisti disciplinam, et projecisti sermones meos post te.* Et, *Qui in fratris tui oculo festucam videbas, in tuo trabem non vidisti?*

Therefore when anyone takes the name of Abbot, he ought to govern his disciples by a twofold doctrine: that is, he should show forth all that is good and holy by his deeds, rather than his words: declaring to the intelligent among his disciples the commandments of the Lord by words: but to the hard-hearted and the simple-minded setting forth the divine precepts by the example of his deeds. And let him show by his own actions that those things ought not to be done which he has taught his disciples to be against the law of God; lest, while preaching to others, he should himself become a castaway, and God should say to him in his sin: " Why dost thou declare my justice, and take my covenant in thy mouth? Thou hast hated discipline, and hast cast my words behind thee." And again, " Thou who sawest the mote in thy brother's eye, didst thou not see the beam in thine own?"

---

[1] D. BUTLER reads: *Tantundem iterum erit, ut, si,* etc.
[2] *Cf.* S. GREG. M., *Dial.,* l. II., c. iii.

So the Abbot has not received from God his dignity and his name in order to find in them the satisfaction of vanity or sloth: as the beginning of this chapter warned us, he is at the head of his monks to be useful to them and to lead them to God, " to profit rather than to preside," as our Holy Father tells us in Chapter LXIV. We learn also that the Abbot's responsibility holds in respect of two matters: his doctrine and the obedience of his disciples. St. Benedict now examines these two points more at leisure. He gives to the word doctrine the widest signification: it is at once teaching properly so called and the government of souls, all that goes to the making of " disciples," the whole policy of an Abbot who is at once a father and a master. In the course of the chapter the teaching of the Abbot and his government are dealt with successively; to conclude our Holy Father reminds him that he shall have to give an account to God for the obedience of all his monks, as for his own fidelity.

His first duty is to teach; consequently he must study and he must be learned.[1] Christians and monks are children of light. Sanctification is not a mechanical process but the development of supernatural understanding. If a love of doctrine reigns in a monastery, all goes well there. But though each religious can apply himself to the cultivation of his faith by his own study, it remains true that the life of the individual and the unity of the family need the Abbot's doctrine. Books, from the very fact that they speak to all men, speak to no one in particular; for this we need the living word of a master. And St. Benedict indicates in a phrase the subject-matter of the Abbot's teaching: *omnia bona et sancta*, " all that is good and holy," all that is apt to lead souls to God. For such is the knowledge that matters to us; other knowledge may be learnt in other schools; the purpose of this knowledge is moral and practical.

St. Benedict is thinking so little of human knowledge, or of dry theological or scriptural speculation, that he requires the Abbot to disseminate his doctrine by words and acts together, and even more by example than by word.[2] It is a matter of common experience that we teach more by our life than by our preaching, and example of whatever sort makes the deeper impression in proportion as it comes from a greater height. Therefore the motive which makes St. Benedict emphasize this twofold doctrine is precisely this, to make truth accessible to all the souls of which a community is ordinarily composed, including those whom mere didactic teaching of itself would fail to influence effectively.

There are open souls, *capaces*, whose intelligence is absolutely right, trustful, in harmony beforehand with the doctrine, whose will is resolute, active, and so yoked with their intelligence that it moves spontaneously in the direction of the light. To souls of this fine temper, lofty and

---

[1] *Cf.* MABILLON, *Traité des études monastiques*, P. I., chap. iii.
[2] The counsel is frequent in the old writers; *cf.* S. BASIL., *Reg. fus.* xliii. - S. NIL., *Epist.*, l. III., *Ep.* CCCXXXII. *P.G.*, LXXIX., 542.—CASS., *Conlat.*, XI., iv.

strong, it is enough to propose the good, to speak the mind of God, and they fall into line with ease and joy. They realize in some degree the perfect man of Plato, with whom Λόγος (reason) is supreme, understanding always effective, truth always decisive, who does evil only in spite of himself and by ignorance; they recall still more the angelic type. And without wishing to represent every monk as an angel, it is clear that in a modern community such receptive souls are the majority, because we benefit by a long Christian past, by education, and by the conditions of the sacerdotal life. But in the time of our Holy Father rough characters, souls of limited vision, *duri corde et simpliciores*, were to be met with. For such, supposing they still exist, the worthy life and regularity of the Abbot, the constant contact with his piety, will avail more than all exhortations. And we must add that the Abbot acts on his community not only by his spoken doctrine and by his example, but also by his tendency, by his spirit, by the deep motive of his actions. It is a sort of secret magnetism, an impulse which souls do not resist; and it is in this way that little by little a monastery takes the character of its Abbot. St. Benedict says nothing explicitly on the duty of residence, but it is plain that the Abbot could not teach and edify if he were always travelling.

The question whether the legislator comes under his own law does not arise here; for the Abbot is not a legislator, but the guardian of the Rule, and towards it he has a double obligation, to observe it in his capacity of monk, to see to its observance in his capacity of Abbot. What authority will his teaching have when his words are seen to be on one side and his deeds on the other? In such a flagrant contradiction there is not merely harm and danger for the community; as St. Benedict adds, there is grave peril for himself. While preaching salvation to others, is he not on the way to become a castaway? (1 Cor. ix. 27). When pronouncing judgement God will emphasize all the hatefulness of this deliberate contrast between severe moral teaching and scandalously relaxed practice (Ps. xlix. 16-17; Matt. vii. 3).

Non ab eo persona in monasterio discernatur. Non unus plus ametur quam alius, nisi quem in bonis actibus aut obedientia invenerit meliorem. Non convertenti ex servitio præponatur ingenuus, nisi alia rationabilis causa existat. Quod si ita, justitia dictante, Abbati visum fuerit, et de cujuslibet ordine id faciat; sin alias, propria teneant loca: quia sive servus, sive liber, omnes in Christo unum sumus, et sub uno Domino æqualem servitutis militiam bajulamus: *Quia non est personarum acceptio apud Deum.* Solummodo in hac parte apud ipsum discernimur, si meliores aliis in operibus bonis et

Let him make no distinction of persons in the monastery. Let not one be loved more than another, unless he be found to excel in good works or in obedience. Let not one of noble birth be put before him that was formerly a slave, unless some other reasonable cause exist for it. If upon just consideration it should so seem good to the Abbot, let him advance one of any rank whatever; but otherwise let them keep their own places; because, whether bond or free, we are all one in Christ, and bear an equal burden in the army of one Lord: for "with God there is no respect-

humiles inveniamur. Ergo æqualis sit omnibus ab eo charitas; una præbeatur omnibus, secundum merita, disciplina.

ing of persons." Only for one reason are we to be preferred in His sight, if we be found to surpass others in good works and in humility. Let the Abbot, then, show equal love to all, and let the same discipline be imposed upon all according to their deserts.

St. Benedict now deals with the Abbot's government. In this paragraph he settles that it must be equitable; in that which follows he shows that it must be moderate and discreet. The Abbot must not be an accepter of persons; which is a general principle. To accept persons is, in the application of distributive justice, to have regard to persons themselves and not to title and right and the facts of the case. Holy Scripture frequently warns us against this tendency to favouritism and unjustifiable preferences;[1] and St. Benedict had only to develop a thought familiar to the old monastic legislators.[2] Here too the rule of the Abbot must copy the rule of God, "for with God there is no respect of persons" (Rom. ii. 11; Col. iii. 25).[3] Nevertheless we must note that the resemblance is not complete. God gives each being its nature, and He remains entirely free as to the perfections which may be superadded to this nature; He gives as it pleases Him; and this sovereign right is plainer still in the supernatural order. Except for contract or promise God, when He gives, is independent of title or ground. But the same is not the case with the Abbot, who cannot, as God can, give the person preferred that which justifies the preference; all he can do is to recognize just titles to special treatment.

Equity in the Abbot will be concerned with these two points: internal and private preference, and that external and public preference which is manifested in the arrangements for the governance of the monastery or the appointment of officials. Motives drawn from natural sympathy, from relationship, from common origin, are insufficient grounds for any distinction of persons whatever. Also it is not enough that a man be agreeable, well brought up, of noble extraction, or have formerly been in high station, that he should therefore be summoned to an important charge; no more is age an adequate ground. In this matter the Abbot's responsibilities are far graver than when it is a matter of preferences which concern only individuals. To complete this subject we may add that the Abbot should never allow a foreign influence to be established at his side, whether in an individual or a group, to which he submits or with which he must count. There may be danger of this happening if the Abbot is by character impressionable, if he be somewhat weak, or is growing old. Such partial abdication of authority causes a vague sentiment of trouble and insecurity which

[1] Lev. xix. 15; Prov. xxiv. 23; James ii. 1 ff.—*Cf. S. Th.*, II.-II., *q*. lxiii.
[2] For example: *Reg.* I., SS. PATRUM, xvi.; *Reg. Orientalis*, I.; above all the letter of ST. CÆSARIUS, *ad Oratoriam Abbatissam* (HOLSTENIUS, *op. cit.*, P. III., p. 31-32).
[3] *Cf.* Deut. x. 17; Job xxxiv. 19.

souls are found to feel. We prefer, instinctively, to obey one man rather than several. The Abbot alone is responsible, and it is to him and him only, and not to any subsequent influence, that his children are entrusted. He must have his own ideas, he must know what he wants, and he must make for his end gently, yet without allowing himself to be turned aside by sympathy or foolish tenderness, by pusillanimity or fatigue.

St. Benedict borrows from St. Paul (1 Cor. xii. 13 ; Gal. iii. 28) the lofty motive in virtue of which all have the same radical right to the affection of the Abbot. It is still true that once—before baptism and in the life of the world—there were both Jew and Gentile, Greek and barbarian, freeman and slave, man and woman; but with baptism and faith in Our Lord Jesus Christ, all these distinctions vanish; and in spite of the diversity of our individual circumstances, in spite of the plurality of our natures, we are all one in Our Lord Jesus Christ. The same divine sonship is enjoyed by all, the same blood circulates in all veins, all have the same name, the same spirit, the same nourishment, the same life. This levelling is accomplished, not by the degradation of any, but by the elevation of all to the stature of Our Lord: "unto the measure of the age of the fulness of Christ" (Eph. iv. 13). All have the same freedom and the same nobility, all likewise have the same glorious servitude, which is worth more than all kingdoms (1 Cor. vii. 22). In natural society distinctions of caste still exist; but they disappear in the wholly supernatural society of the monastic family. We are all nothing but soldiers, performing the same service under the standard of the same Lord. So the Abbot must regard his monks only as God regards them.

The same principle, moreover, will allow the Abbot not to take literally and materially the precept: "let him make no distinction of persons in the monastery." It is not required of him that he should reduce all to a dead level, aim at a mathematical equality and apportion offices by chance. In this new world, where all are equal and one, God Himself makes use of discrimination and distinction; His tenderness goes out to those who more resemble His Son, who are more deeply grafted into Him; He does not give the same confidence to all, for there are manifold functions to be fulfilled in the great body of the Church and they need various aptitudes. So the Abbot may show greater affection for him whom he believes better—that is, as St. Benedict defines it, one who is more obedient, more humble, and richer in good works. Beauty is the cause of affection; where there is greater beauty, there is ground for more affection. Yet the Abbot must guard against delusion, though this is a matter for his own conscience. Likewise he shall appoint to offices at his pleasure, provided that he takes care that there is fitness, a real proportion between the office and its holder. A reasonable cause, merit, and justice, will allow him to make some exceptions to the law of order as defined in Chapter LXIII., where each holds the position that corresponds with his entry into religion. The freeman or noble, *ingenuus*, shall not have, as such, any advantage over him who comes from servitude, but other reasons may commend him to the choice of the Abbot, and his former nobility must not be reason for disgrace. No more may low birth be such a stigma. Whatever may be the social rank of a monk he may become the object of a justifiable distinction: "let him advance one of any rank whatever." But the general principle remains: there must be the same affection for all, the same line of conduct with respect to all, while at the same time account is taken of the merit of each. (The word *disciplina* has various meanings in the Rule.)[1]

In doctrina namque sua Abbas apostolicam debet illam semper formam servare, in qua dicitur: *Argue, obsecra, increpa*. Id est, miscens temporibus tempora, terroribus blandimenta, dirum magistri, pium patris ostendat affectum: id est, indisciplinatos et inquietos debet durius arguere; obedientes autem, et mites et patientes, ut melius proficiant, obsecrare; negligentes autem et contemnentes, ut increpet et corripiat, admonemus. Neque dissimulet peccata delinquentium, sed mox, ut coeperint oriri, radicitus ea, ut prævalet, amputet, memor periculi Heli sacerdotis de Silo.

For the Abbot in his doctrine ought always to observe the rule of the Apostle, wherein he says: "Reprove, entreat, rebuke": suiting his action to circumstances, mingling gentleness with severity; showing now the rigour of a master, now the loving affection of a father, so as sternly to rebuke the undisciplined and restless, and to exhort the obedient, mild, and patient to advance in virtue. And such as are negligent and haughty we charge him to reprove and correct. Let him not shut his eyes to the faults of offenders; but as soon as they appear, let him strive, as he has the authority for that, to root them out, remembering the fate of Heli, the priest of Silo.

The Abbot's government must be equitable; but it will only be so on condition that it is judicious. It is possible seriously to misunderstand the counsel of equity. There are people who have condensed their experience, which is often superficial and brief, into practical principles, formulas simple and easy of application. To resolve any concrete case that presents itself, they apply the formula, brutally. The method is one and invariable. It leaves the conscience at peace, sometimes even when the measures taken are devastating in their effect. We are all more or less imprisoned in our personality; we see all others through its medium; we are persuaded that measures which have succeeded with ourselves ought to suit all. Yet we cannot treat a living being as an abstraction; men are not the proper subject of experiments; each man is himself a little universe. Instead of

[1] This paragraph of the Rule recalls a passage in St. Jerome: *Nescit religio nostra personas accipere nec conditiones hominum, sed animos inspicit singulorum. Servum et nobilem de moribus pronuntiat. Sola apud Deum libertas est, non servire peccatis. Summa apud Deum est nobilitas, clarum esse virtutibus. . . . Frustra sibi aliquis de nobilitate generis applaudit, cum universi paris honoris et ejusdem apud Deum pretii sint, qui uno Christi sanguine sunt redempti; nec interest qua quis conditione natus sit, cum omnes in Christo æqualiter renascamur. Nam et si obliviscimur quia ex uno omnes generati sumus, saltem id semper meminisse debemus quia per unum omnes regeneramur.* (*Epist.* CXLVIII. *ad Celantiam*, 21. P.L., XXII., 1214).

making a man enter incontinent into our own system, and imprisoning him in our mental mould, it would be far better to try to know him, to see what he has in his heart, how he thinks and wills and suffers. Perhaps the true method here is to have no method. Since the Abbot is the depositary of the power of God, he ought to imitate the discretion and pliancy of Providence, which disposes all things with as much sweetness as force, and which, according to the words of theology, adapts itself wonderfully to the nature of the individual: *Unicuique providet Deus secundum modum suæ naturæ.*

"In his doctrine": that is, in general, practical teaching, the guidance and government of souls, but St. Benedict has especially in view the duty of correction. He alludes to the advice which St. Paul gave to Timothy: "Preach the word: be instant in season, out of season: reprove, entreat, rebuke in all patience and doctrine" (2 Tim. iv. 2). Reprove, entreat, rebuke: these are three different attitudes, necessitated by the very diversity of the characters to which the correction is addressed,[1] and corresponding to the three kinds of souls which our Holy Father enumerates a few lines farther on: for the first kind, reproof; for the second, exhortation; for the third, rebuke and punishment. But, before going into detail about this matter, St. Benedict reminds the Abbot of the variety and complexity of his rôle. *Miscens temporibus tempora.* The phrase is not easy to translate; it means that the Abbot ought to measure his action according to the circumstances of time, place, and person, to behave according to the conjuncture, to remember that there is a time for everything (Eccles. iii.), sometimes to use severity, sometimes gentleness: in one word, to model his mood according to the varying moods of each. The words which follow make St. Benedict's thought quite clear: the Abbot shall mingle caresses with threats, shall at one time display the severity of a master, at another the more loving attitude of a father.[2]

It is with the purpose of helping the Abbot in the discerning of spirits that our Holy Father divides them into three classes. "The undisciplined and restless: "[3] these are not so because they are formal rebels against discipline, but because they are like children, fickle and unquiet. They promise and do not perform; one has always to begin anew with them. Their intellect is not sufficiently developed, and they only obey impulses of sense; the intellect of another will come to their help, and they may be reached by their sensibility who are approachable in no other way. Such natures should feel the yoke, and they will be the less tempted to revolt the more they feel the weight of discipline. With them one must speak loud and clear, and sometimes not be content with exhortations, as shall be said presently.

[1] . . . *Dicente Apostolo : Argue, obsecra, increpa, cum omni patientia et doctrina.* . . . *Decernendum est ab illo qui præest, qualiter circa singulos debeat pietatis affectum monstrare, et qualiter tenere debeat disciplinam* (*Reg.* I., SS. PATRUM, V.).
[2] *Cf.* S. BASIL., *Reg. fus.*, xliii.; *Reg. contr.*, xxiii.
[3] Two of ST. BASIL'S words (*Reg. contr.*, xcviii.): *Tanquam inquietus et indisciplinatus confundatur.*

It is pleasanter to have to deal with the "obedient, mild, and patient"; and, thank God, these are the most numerous. It is only necessary to entreat them paternally, and to exhort them to the good and the better way. True monks have a quick ear, they understand half-sentences and obey at a mere sign, thus sparing the Abbot the disagreeableness of a reprimand.

This is necessary, however, when men are deliberately negligent, or resolutely contemptuous. These are dangerous folk, because they always have a bad influence, not on the monks who hold fast to God, but on temperaments which are rather changeable, distracted, of inferior mould; they are, besides, a source of irritation for all and a nuisance. "The negligent and haughty": their past has been spent in a long course of inobservance and to that their present remains fixed; if you try to attack this second nature, you will be startled to meet a fierce energy in characters whose essence you thought was softness. They expend more vigour in defence of their relaxation, against the efforts of the Abbot and the manifest disapproval of their brethren, than would be necessary for a resolute observance of the Rule. Or they become soured and discontented and give way to the spirit of contradiction; they have more than their share of spleen. Some minds are so made that they are always in love with the solution that has not won acceptance; it is fine, I know, to be the champion of the unsuccessful, but it is often embarrassing. In other cases there is a profound conviction that one has been misunderstood; no one in the community does justice to our worth or services. Undoubtedly it is the secret tendency of all men to value themselves much; but there are natures which value only themselves. They spend their lives in argument. They have a ready-made opinion on every subject and naïvely suppose that they are always right in every matter and against everybody. The idea never enters their heads that their opponent may have something to say for himself, and that their personal infallibility may be slightly at fault. So they summon the whole community to the bar of their minds and deliver a contemptuous and summary judgement, sometimes not without abusive terms. It is worth noting that they are often those who would have been incapable of steering a wise course in the world, for they lack judgement and their temperament leads them to all sorts of ineptitudes. They were gathered in with goodness and with pity; they came all broken and sick; the measure of indulgent kindness overflowed for them. And, suddenly, behold them endowed with the ability and power which they lacked: they become critics, authorities, reformers. St. Benedict warns the Abbot to deal with them resolutely and suppress them with vigour.

Yet our Holy Father is not blind to the painful side of this office. It is always a difficult thing to face the inobservant monk, to take him by the throat and say, as Nathan did to David, "Thou art that man." It is so pleasant not to make oneself trouble and to have a quiet life. And then one may say: It will do no good. I have spoken before.

To speak again is only to play the part of a Cassandra. There will be a scene, tears, a week of obstinate ill-humour, a violent ferment of rebellious thoughts, perhaps even the wish to break with a life which has become unbearable. Then is created this terrible situation: on one side timidity and reserve, on the other an attitude of defence and defiance and the disposition of the "deaf asp that stoppeth her ears" for fear of hearing. There is no worse misfortune for a soul than this of having forced truth to be silent, of having as it were discouraged God. Henceforth He keeps an awful silence and is provoked no more.

The Abbot will not fail of excuses to justify his saying nothing. Does not moral theology allow that there are circumstances in which it is better not to instruct, since the only result of knowledge would be to make a material sin into a formal one? Certainly it does; but it also recognizes that this privilege of silence no longer obtains when a community would suffer harm, scandal, and disgrace. The Abbot may not shut his eyes systematically: "let him not shut his eyes to the faults of offenders";[1] he is bound to speak and to do his duty, even when others refuse to do theirs. A word gracefully spoken and tempered with charity always does its work. Further, St. Benedict requires the Abbot not to delay, not to wait until he is absolutely constrained by the urgency of the danger; as soon as evil customs begin to appear he must cut them down vigorously, to the roots, *radicitus amputet:*[2] this is the only true mercifulness.[3] *Ut prævalet* is variously translated: sometimes "as is better," or "as it is in his power"; better, "since he has received authority for that purpose."

In order to convince the Abbot our Holy Father asks him to remember the tragic story of Heli (1 Kings ii.-iv.). The high-priest had not spared warnings to his wicked sons; but he had the power, and the Lord required him not only to reprimand but also to amputate and destroy. We know the results of his weakness: a bloody defeat of the Israelites, the death of the guilty, his solitary death, the profanation of the Ark of the Covenant, which fell into the hands of the enemy, the disgrace of the whole race. Faults which are tolerated have to be expiated just as much as others, but the whole family expiates them. Though the threat be a veiled one, the responsibility of the Abbot is clearly stated. Monastic houses rarely perish of hunger; they die of wounds which have not been cared for, where none has ministered strengthening wine or assuaging oil, of wounds which grow and fester. And if anything at all remains of such houses, it is but a mean and sorry plant, of which the Lord will not consent to make further use.[4]

[1] *Dissimulas peccata hominum* (Sap., xi. 24).
[2] . . . *Radicitus amputavit* (Cass., *Conlat.*, XVI., vi.).
[3] *Cf.* S. Basil., *Reg. fus.*, xxiv., xxv.; *Reg. contr.*, xvii., xxii.
[4] What St. Benedict says here about correction furnished the matter of the third book of St. Gregory the Great's *Regula Pastoralis;* the whole work is, moreover, only an extended commentary on the present chapter.

What Kind of Man the Abbot ought to be

Et honestiores quidem atque intelligibiles animos prima vel secunda admonitione verbis corripiat; improbos autem et duros ac superbos vel inobedientes, verberum vel corporis castigatione in ipso initio peccati coerceat, sciens scriptum: *Stultus verbis non corrigitur.* Et iterum: *Percute filium tuum virga, et liberabis animam ejus a morte.*

Those of good disposition and understanding let him correct, for the first or second time, with words only; but such as are froward and hard of heart, and proud, or disobedient, let him chastise with bodily stripes at the very first offence, knowing that it is written: "The fool is not corrected with words." And again: "Strike thy son with the rod, and thou shalt deliver his soul from death."

So the Abbot must resign himself to the duty of correction. Yet he must correct with wisdom, without suffering himself to be carried away by his temperament or zeal; St. Benedict repeats this advice, by explaining in detail what must be the nature of the correction, of which hitherto he has spoken only in a general manner. In this passage he indicates only two character groups, but the two coincide with the previous three. With refined and intelligent natures one should not resort to severity at once; a verbal reprimand will suffice for the first and second time. But as for those of coarse nature, hard of heart or rude, proud and refractory, they must be tamed by the rod or by some such bodily chastisement, and that as soon as their evil habit begins to show itself.

Our Holy Father furnishes us immediately with a reason for these vigorous measures of repression: "He who lacks intelligence cannot be corrected by words." He is thinking of Proverbs: "A slave will not be corrected by words" (xxix. 19. See also xviii. 2). Holy Scripture considers that the child has a right to correction, he must get it as he must get nourishment, and he will not die of it; on the contrary he will live the true life: "Withhold not correction from a child: for if thou strike him with the rod, he shall not die. Thou shalt beat him with the rod: and deliver his soul from hell." (Prov. xxiii. 13, 14). "He that spareth the rod, hateth his son" (Prov. xiii. 24). In his *De Institutione Oratoria* Quintilian, teacher of Domitian's great-nephews, lays it down that the child should be accustomed to virtue even before knowing what it is. He must be given certain associations of ideas. We know that for ourselves goodness first meant caresses and sweetmeats, while to be bad brought dry bread, the whip, or detention. And we need not blush at these humble beginnings of our moral life. It is not at all impossible that the general deterioration of character is due to a certain lack of virility in repression. When the child is not seven, we ask: "Why punish him? he is so young." When he is eight, "Why punish him? he is so big." And so it is always either too soon or too late to teach the child his duty and the function of mortification in the Christian life; thus are made tyrants and little monsters. Since St. Benedict's day characters and customs have changed. There are undoubtedly fewer children or barbarians in a modern monastery; and in any case the rod and the prison, which were much in vogue for long centuries of monasticism, have vanished from our midst. Yet one may still meet spoilt children, or wild and rebellious characters, for whom certain bodily punishments would be a sovereign remedy.

However, the Abbot must remember the precept of Chapter LXIV.: " Let him cut them off prudently and with charity, in the way he shall see best for each." Souls more often need carrying than driving. A monastery is not a sort of forge with the Abbot, like a cyclops, fanning the flame. Moral reform and spiritual development are not achieved by a succession of violent and rapid movements. There is with souls, as with God, a slowness which the Abbot must respect.

Meminisse debet semper Abbas, quod est, meminisse quod dicitur, et scire quia cui plus committitur, plus ab eo exigitur: sciatque quam difficilem et arduam rem suscepit, regere animas, et multorum servire moribus. Et alium quidem blandimentis, alium vero increpationibus, alium suasionibus, et secundum uniuscujusque qualitatem vel intelligentiam, ita se omnibus conformet et aptet, ut non solum detrimenta gregis sibi commissi non patiatur, verum etiam in augmentatione boni gregis gaudeat.	The Abbot ought always to remember what he is, and what he is called, and to know that to whom more is committed, from him more is required; and he must consider how difficult and arduous a task he has undertaken, of ruling souls and adapting himself to many dispositions. Let him so accommodate and suit himself to the character and intelligence of each, winning some by kindness, others by reproof, others by persuasion, that he may not only suffer no loss in the flock committed to him, but may even rejoice in their virtuous increase.

It is said of Moses, in the Book of Numbers (xii. 3), that he was meekest of all men that dwelt upon the earth; and yet it is plain that on some occasions his cup of wrath was full to overflowing. But he had the lofty good sense and supernatural spirit not to lose patience except in the presence of the Lord. That happened to him at the " graves of lust " (Num. xi. 34), when the people, weary of the manna, set themselves to lamentation and weeping, as they remembered the fish that they ate in Egypt. The Lord was angry, and to Moses also the thing seemed intolerable. So he said to the Lord: " Why hast thou laid the weight of all this people upon me ? Have I conceived all this multitude or begotten them, that thou shouldst say to me: Carry them in thy bosom, as the nurse is wont to carry the little infant . . . ? I am not able alone to bear all this people, because it is too heavy for me. But if it seem unto thee otherwise, I beseech thee to kill me " (Num. xi. 11-15). One might say that St. Benedict expected some secret protestation to take its rise in the Abbot's heart also, in view of the truly superhuman programme which he has just elaborated so calmly. And it seems too that at this point the Rule might have slipped in some word of encouragement, as is its wont, so as to lessen and calm the anxieties of the Abbot; but St. Benedict has no consideration for him, and all the concluding portion of the chapter has no other purpose than to hold him forcibly to the austere contemplation of his duty.

St. Benedict practically says: You have a heavy task. You must be always remembering what you are, and remembering the name that men give you: you are Abbot, men call you Father. You are not a prince, nor a great noble, nor a civil governor: you are a Father. This whole family is yours. God has entrusted it to you, as a deposit dear to His heart, and in His sight souls have an infinite value. The Master of our life makes use of it as He will: on some He showers His tenderness, to others He gives His confidences; there is the sweet and simple vocation of John, there is the vocation of Peter; and we do not choose. Let the Abbot also remember the judgement of God; His trusts have ever to be accounted for. God does not give His gifts to men to be their sport; authority, influence, wealth are talents entrusted to us, and He will demand from us interest on them in rigorous and judicial terms: more has been entrusted to you, from you more shall be required (Luke xii. 48).[1]

And the Abbot must know how difficult and arduous a task he has received of ruling souls and of making himself the servant of all by adapting himself to the character of each. Men often seem little concerned to lighten his burden; in a monastery all passions that are unmortified and therefore are sources of suffering, discharge themselves on the Abbot, as it were naturally. But St. Benedict has no thought of this irregular addition to his task; according to him the task is already a delicate one because it has to do with souls. In a material substance change may be foreseen and is not due to caprice; but a spiritual being does not act mechanically; there is need of light and patience to know it well and adjust oneself to it. Then how different are souls from one another! Manifold causes, and these of the sensible order, co-operate to make of each something very personal indeed; heredity, or a first vital pulsation given by the soul to the body, which starts with it, determining in some sort the whole trend of our lives, or a subjection, whether passive or deliberate, to animal tendencies—all these make our temperament. Each soul has to free itself, to redeem itself, from tendencies of sense, by education, by vigorous effort, by the supernatural life which devotes the whole activity to God. The authority of the Abbot is given us precisely in order to help us to win this self-possession. It is the Abbot's business to proportion his action to the moral dispositions of each. One man needs kind words and caresses, another rebuke and punishment, a third persuasion; in a word, each should be treated according to his temper and degree of intelligence. There is no clearer mark of the family character of the monastery than this insistence by St. Benedict that the Abbot should know his subjects and lead each of them individually.

It is this too that limits the size of a community: for if the monks are legion, the Abbot will only be a commander-in-chief, constructing a summary plan which his officials put into execution. Yet the Abbot

[1] St. Benedict may have taken his inspiration direct from the *Doctrina* S. Orsiesii, xv. (see D. Butler's note); or from St. Jerome, *Epist.* XIV. 9. *P.L.*, XXII., 353; or from St. Augustine, *Quæstiones in Heptat.*, l. III., xxxi. *P.L.*, XXXIV. (689-690).

is not forbidden to think about the increase of his flock. And it is certainly of increase in numbers that St. Benedict speaks in the word *augmentatio*, while at the same time suggesting the idea of increase in virtue: *boni gregis*. We should understand him well. When he recommends the Abbot to put himself aside and skilfully to condescend, so that he may suffer no loss in his sheep, he does not make any promise or put it forward as a sure effect; he is merely indicating the intentions which should guide his conduct. And how might the Abbot hope for such success as the Lord Himself has not obtained? There are souls whom neither patience nor tenderness nor severity can win, and for whom one can do nothing but pray and endure. St. Benedict would seem to say to the Abbot: Would you rejoice in the increase of a faithful flock? Well, take good care of the souls entrusted to you, busy yourself with what you have; so will you get what you have not yet. Fervent monasteries do their recruiting of themselves, and that much more by the good odour of their observance than by any human methods or indiscreet propaganda. God so disposes events and hearts, that His family grows unceasingly; and if at times recruitment languishes or stops, we must not lose confidence: as at the beginnings of Cîteaux, a St. Bernard will come with numerous companions.

Ante omnia, ne dissimulans aut parvipendens salutem animarum sibi commissarum, plus gerat sollicitudinem de rebus transitoriis, et terrenis atque caducis; sed semper cogitet quia animas suscepit regendas, de quibus et rationem redditurus est. Et ne causetur forte de minori substantia, meminerit scriptum: *Primum quærite regnum Dei et justitiam ejus, et hæc omnia adjicientur vobis.* Et iterum: *Nihil deest timentibus eum.*

Above all let him not, overlooking or undervaluing the salvation of the souls entrusted to him, be more solicitous for fleeting, earthly, and perishable things; but let him ever bear in mind that he has undertaken the government of souls, of which he shall have to give an account. And that he may not complain for want of worldly substance, let him remember what is written: " Seek first the kingdom of God and his justice, and all these things shall be added unto you." And again: " Nothing is wanting to them that fear him."

The Abbot's solicitude must not go astray on false tracks. It will not allow itself to be distracted by too great preoccupation with the matter of vocations, or by financial and material cares. In this last matter the temptation may be more insistent and treacherous, and it is for this reason that our Holy Father lays more stress on it. We must live, we must grow, we must pay our debts, we must build. And for these purposes we must make ourselves known, secure high and productive connections, write books and sell them, work the monastery lands profitably, purchase property and so on; we must, in a word, enter again on a mass of business affairs which it seemed that we had given up by the religious state.

It is obvious that the Abbot could not be careless of the finances of the monastery without imprudence and a sort of treason: his vigilance and effort in this matter are a duty to the community. To understand this point it is sufficient to reflect on the innumerable evils which are caused by negligence; it is not at all desirable for our good name that we should pass through the bankruptcy courts. And not only must we live, but a certain margin is indispensable, so that all may go well and the monks remain faithful to poverty. Disorder, excessive expenditure, dilapidation, carelessness of the morrow—these cannot be regarded as the true type of abbatial government.

Nevertheless, what St. Benedict insists on is that the care of material interests must never cause the Abbot to neglect or treat as a secondary matter, which he may readily throw off on to other shoulders, the formation and eternal salvation of the souls entrusted to him: " overlooking or undervaluing." The true wealth of a monastery is its souls; and compared with them how little worth are those " fleeting, earthly, and perishable things."[1] Undoubtedly the Abbot ought to be a wise administrator in temporals, because they have a sacred character from the fact of their belonging to the Lord; but souls belong to God more nearly still, and it is for these as well, and for these above all, that he will have to render an account: *semper cogitet quia animas suscepit regendas, de quibus et rationem redditurus est.*[2]

And, lest the Abbot should be tempted to allege the slenderness of the resources of the monastery, let him remember what is written in St. Matthew (vi. 33) and in the Psalm (xxxiii. 10). God has given His word. If the house be fervent, resources like vocations will come, in God's good time and according to His measure. The Lord gives what is necessary to monasteries which are faithful and which He loves; sometimes a little less, so that comfortable circumstances may not incline monks and Abbot to dispense with trust in God. Men of the world ask us: Is it not true that some phrases of the sixth chapter of St. Matthew seem to go beyond the laws of human prudence? What is their true sense? It is this: God wishes to lead us to be trustful and to the conviction that no anxiety should prevail over this trustfulness; for this end He makes use of various examples calculated to inspire it, but yet without telling us that we are dispensed from action: after all, the lilies and the birds are active. We may well believe that there are refinements which the world cannot grasp, evangelical counsels which cannot be realized save in the monastery, more enfranchised as it is from created conditions and belonging more to God. And it is because of the supreme jurisdiction exercised by Providence over those who belong to it, that trustfulness becomes a law, more immediately perhaps than prudence: for, when all is said, trust in God is a theological virtue, prudence a moral virtue; and, while I am not bound to keep the rules of prudence *semper et pro semper*, I am never dispensed from absolute trust.

[1] (*Prima causa*) *discidii, quæ nasci solet de rebus caducis atque terrenis* (Cass., *Conlat.*, XVI., ix.).
[2] *Semper cogitans* (*præposita*) *Deo se pro vobis reddituram esse rationem* (S. Aug., *Epist.* CCXI., 15. *P.L.*, XXXIII., 965).—*Doctr.* S. Orsiesii, xi.

Sciatque quia qui suscepit animas regendas, præparet se ad rationem reddendam. Et quantum sub cura sua fratrum se habere scierit numerum, agnoscat pro certo quia in die judicii ipsarum omnium animarum est redditurus Domino rationem, sine dubio addita et suæ animæ. Et ita timens semper futuram discussionem pastoris de creditis ovibus, cum de alienis ratiociniis cavet, redditur de suis sollicitus. Et cum de admonitionibus suis emendationem aliis subministrat, ipse efficitur a vitiis emendatus.

And let him know that he who has undertaken the government of souls, must prepare himself to render an account of them. And whatever may be the number of the brethren under his care, let him be certainly assured that on the Day of Judgement he will have to give an account to the Lord of all these souls, as well as of his own. And thus, being ever fearful of the coming judgement of the shepherd concerning the state of the flock committed to him, while he is careful on other men's accounts, he will be solicitous also on his own. And so, while correcting others by his admonitions, he will be himself cured of his own defects.

Our Holy Father is not afraid of repeating himself when he wants to remind the Abbot of the value of souls, of the delegated character of his power, and of the strict judgement which awaits him. At the tribunal of God every man will have to answer for himself, but the Abbot will have to answer for himself and for all the souls committed to his care, for each one in particular: this is incontestable, indubitable, *pro certo, sine dubio.* One would have to be senseless, or have lost the faith, not to be impressed by such a declaration. And likewise one would need a strong dose of delusion to want to take on one's shoulders such a burden, and to the problems of one's own soul superadd those of others.

Since the Abbot has consented, on the invitation of God, to make himself the servant of all; since his daily bread is work, anxiety, and suffering, he has assuredly some right to the prayers of his monks and to their compassion. It is on the ground of the responsibility assumed by priests and bishops that the Apostle St. Paul, in a text which our Holy Father doubtless remembered, begs Christians to repay by obedience and loving docility the devotion and benefits they have received: "Obey your prelates and be subject to them. For they watch as being to render an account of your souls: that they may do this with joy and not with grief. For this is not expedient for you" (Heb. xiii. 17). Make the exercise of their charge easy and sweet; cause them to fulfil it with joy and not with sadness, for that will in no way be advantageous to yourselves; the weariness caused in an Abbot by a difficult and discontented community issues always in serious detriment to the community.

If it is true that Abbots make their monks, it is certain that monks make their Abbot, and that the monastery is a school of mutual sanctification. The last two sentences of this chapter remind the Abbot of this point, if not to reassure him, for they are still austere, at least to strengthen his courage. The constant thought of the judgement which the shepherd[1] will one day have to face in respect of the sheep entrusted to him, the care which he takes in putting other people's accounts in order, will make him more attentive to his own account: so the first benefit of his charge will be his own growth in interior watchfulness. The very fact that he has to carry other souls naturally leads him to watch over himself. A man might give himself some freedom if he were independent of others; but he is more careful when he is the father of a family, and the deputy of God, when weaknesses such as were once his would now have a formidable effect and would find an echo in the lives of others. Being bound to seek the amendment of others by his instructions, the Abbot will at the same time set himself free of his own defects and redouble the fidelity of his life. Those for whom the duty of preaching is more than a vain amusement are always the first to reap the fruit of their words. We love harmony and moral unity; and influenced by this more than by the desire to avoid the sentence, "Physician, heal thyself," we labour little by little to put our actions in accord with our teaching.

The Abbot has a greater compensation of which St. Benedict does not speak: the profit which he wins from constant contact with good souls. This contact is the most wholesome that there is, and resembles a sacrament. It is partly that such souls are to the Abbot an encouragement and an example, but chiefly that they are for him a sort of anticipated vision of God. The greater the effect and the nearer to its cause, so much the more perfect is the knowledge we get of the cause; and here the effect is not only that work of God, a spiritual soul, but also all the means which God takes to transform it and unite it to His beauty. So may the Abbot find herein a true theology. And, until the day when he shall contemplate God face to face, he will nowhere see Him more clearly than in souls, in the living crystal of their purity. He will not find it hard then to keep very close to Our Lord, wherein is his sole safeguard and most sure consolation.

[1] The Abbot is meant here, rather than the Divine Pastor.

CHAPTER III

OF CALLING THE BRETHREN TO COUNCIL

DE ADHIBENDIS AD CONSILIUM FRATRIBUS.—Quoties aliqua præcipua agenda sunt in monasterio, convocet Abbas omnem congregationem, et dicat ipse unde agitur. Et audiens consilium fratrum, tractet apud se, et quod utilius judicaverit faciat. Ideo autem omnes ad consilium vocari diximus, quia sæpe juniori Dominus revelat quod melius est.

As often as any important matters have to be transacted in the monastery, let the Abbot call together the whole community, and himself declare what is the question to be settled. And, having heard the counsel of the brethren, let him weigh it within himself, and then do what he shall judge most expedient. We have said that all should be called to council, because it is often to the younger that the Lord reveals what is best.

THIS chapter fixes the constitution of the monastic body by defining the rôle which belongs to each member. Our Holy Father's purpose is not that of applying restrictions, limits, or counterpoises to the absolute power of the Abbot, for he never dreamt of introducing into his work the forms of democracy or parliamentary government; all the directions which we are just to read seem designed, on the contrary, to emphasize the sovereign character of abbatial authority, as interpreter and guardian of the authority of the Rule, and as a created form of the divine authority. But the depositary of this power remains a man, obliged to seek the truth laboriously, obliged to discover the best practical solutions, and liable to mistakes. Therefore, condescending to this weakness, St. Benedict gives him counsellors, whose function it is, not to share his power, to control, or on occasion to check him, but only to enlighten and support him, and so discreetly to prevent mistakes or abuses. One mind cannot exhaust every matter; what one man does not perceive another may discover, and affairs thus managed with the concert and wisdom of many are more certain of success. St. Benedict indicates this motive in concluding the chapter, when he cites the witness of Ecclesiasticus (xxxii. 24).

Our Holy Father distinguishes two classes of matters in which the Abbot shall take counsel: *præcipua* and *minora*, important and less important. For more serious matters he shall summon the whole community to council; for less serious matters, which are, however, important in their degree, he shall confine himself to consultation with the elders. There is a third class of questions which calls for no convoking of the brethren; such are, in the first place, matters of detail, and next, those which have a predetermined solution, or an evident one, or one reserved to the Abbot, or such that the community will not be competent to judge. According to our Holy Father it is for the Abbot to estimate if it be proper for him to seek advice. Whenever, for example, the good name of the community or its financial interests are seriously concerned, he should summon the whole community.

And in desiring the presence of all[1] St. Benedict obeys an inspiration of faith. God is actively interested in the affairs of a monastic house; He presides over it, and every wise decision should be imputed to Him (Matt. xviii. 20). Why, then, exclude the newly professed or the young oblates who are of an age to speak (see Chapter LIX.) ? Is it not matter of experience that the Lord loves to communicate His thought to us by the mouths of little children ?[2] The young are more natural, less individual, and God acts more freely through them. He made use of a Samuel and of a Daniel (see Chapter LXIII.); and at Monte Cassino He used St. Maurus and St. Placid. But the young monk would at once lose the benefit of this divine predilection, if he failed in moderation, courtesy, and humility in his judgements; if he gave his opinion on persons and things with solemnity and importance; if he did not stand on his guard against the tendency to formulate harsh and rigid decisions; for the outlook of such a one is often limited and narrow, and he does not always appreciate the complexity of the matters discussed.

At the same time it is the Abbot's place to sum up the case. He explains the matter clearly, so that all may understand what is discussed. He does this without passion and without attempting to extort support, since strictly speaking he does not need it. He listens with impartiality and patience to the advice of the brethren, which does not mean that he must let the long-winded talk indefinitely, or abstain from such correction as should be called for by right, by good order, or good sense. Then he takes counsel with himself, using the light that all have contributed, and decides sovereignly, not that which pleases him, nor always the contrary of the suggestions made, but what in God's sight he deems best.

Sic autem dent fratres consilium cum omni humilitatis subjectione, ut non præsumant procaciter defendere quod eis visum fuerit, sed magis in Abbatis pendeat arbitrio, ut quod salubrius esse judicaverit, ei cuncti obediant; sed sicut discipulis convenit obedire magistro, ita et ipsum provide et juste condecet cuncta disponere.

But let the brethren give their advice with all subjection of humility, and not presume stubbornly to defend their own opinion; but rather let the matter rest with the Abbot's discretion, that all may submit to whatever he shall consider best. Yet, even as it becomes disciples to obey their master, so does it behove him to order all things prudently and with justice.

If it be good for the Abbot to welcome advice and to practise self-abnegation, monks on their side have a strict duty to show themselves men of tact, and to be docile sons. The brethren shall give their advice, since it is for this that they were assembled; a sulky, cross, and sullen

---

[1] Novices, not yet belonging to the community (Chap. LVIII.), have no title to a part in its deliberations.
[2] *Cf.* S. CYPRIANI, *Epist.* IX., iv. *P.L.*, IV., 253.—CASS., *Conlat.*, XVI., xii.

attitude would be ridiculous and very far from monastic. They shall give their advice in turn, when they are asked or when they receive the sign. They shall speak with all the submission of humility: *cum omni humilitatis subjectione*, without taking a pompous, magisterial tone, without imagining themselves judges or members of Parliament, without regarding their opinion as decisive, or believing that the general welfare depends largely on them. We may add that it is necessary to keep within the scope of the matter in debate, and not to graft some motion or amendment on to the precise point that has been submitted for consideration.

It may be that the advice you give wins little acceptance; well, you should rejoice that a wiser course is followed, or at least have the good manners not to argue bitterly and obstinately for your notion. Thank God, men do not argue publicly with the Abbot; but there is more danger of a man defending his view against one or other of his brethren. A man may be tempted to take up the words of another in order to contradict them, sometimes in order to turn them to ridicule, and this either openly or in a treacherous and sly fashion. Such a way of acting is all the more misguided, as the brother who is attacked generally has his mouth closed by charity, or prudence, or official secrecy. A monastic assembly should never take the rowdy character of some of our parliamentary debates. And, according to the mind of our Holy Father, neither individuals, nor a majority, nor even the unanimous opinion of the brethren, has a right to make its view prevail; the decision is reserved exclusively to the Abbot;[1] he remains free to take that view which seems to him most opportune, and all shall hasten to submit to it. But, while it is proper that disciples should obey their master, it is fitting, too, that the master should dispose all things with foresight and equity. There is no parcelling of authority, but there are rights on both sides; those who obey are not handed over to arbitrary action, to the whims and caprices of passion; and the best guarantee that can be given them is this repeated declaration that the Abbot is accountable to God, and that, when all is said, he too and he especially must be obedient.

In omnibus igitur omnes magistram sequantur regulam, neque ab ea temere declinetur a quoquam. Nullus in monasterio sequatur cordis proprii voluntatem, neque præsumat quisquam cum Abbate suo proterve intus aut foris monasterium contendere. Quod si præsumpserit, regulari disciplinæ subjaceat. Ipse tamen Abbas cum timore Dei et observatione regulæ omnia faciat, sciens se procul dubio de

Let all, therefore, follow the Rule in all things as their guide, and from it let no man rashly turn aside. Let no one in the monastery follow the will of his own heart: nor let anyone presume insolently to contend with his Abbot, either within or without the monastery. But if he should dare to do so, let him be subjected to the discipline appointed by the Rule. The Abbot himself, however, must do

---

[1] *Per omnia ad nutum (Abbatis) potestatemque pendere* (SULP. SEVER., *Dial.* I., c. x *P.L.*, XX., 190.—*Cf.* CASS., *Conlat.*, XXIV., xxvi).

Of Calling the Brethren to Council

omnibus judiciis suis æquissimo judici Deo rationem redditurum.	everything with the fear of God, and in observance of the Rule: knowing that he will have without doubt to render to God, the most just Judge, an account of all his judgements.

The connection between this paragraph and the preceding one is close, as shown by the word *igitur*, "therefore." No one in the monastery may "follow the will of his own heart" and live as he likes. The form of our life is fixed by a Rule; the Rule is the standard to which all must conform, both the monks who give counsel and the Abbot who proposes and decides. In the discussion as well as in the decision of a matter each must seek inspiration in the Rule and its spirit; none may dispense with it without presumption. Supernatural prosperity and peace depend upon this submission of all to the same ideal and the same programme.

And since the written Rule needs to be interpreted, since debate would sometimes be interminable if a living authority did not intervene with decisive power, all discussion should cease when the Abbot has made up his mind. He alone is responsible, and he alone has the grace of state; he is without doubt better informed than any other, because he has the whole situation in his hands, and can envisage all the aspects and all the issues of a problem. No one shall be so rash as to contend insolently with him, whether within the monastery, or still less without it, a thing which would give rise to greater scandal;[1] and, both within and without, the brethren shall scrupulously abstain from criticizing his decisions. Baffled self-will does not always show itself in open resistance, but rather, and this especially with timid or refined or well-bred natures, in secret murmurings. A monk can be in no worse state than this. The Rule first mentions the "regular discipline" (which we shall describe later) for the repression by severe punishment of this refractory and censorious spirit.

But St. Benedict takes great care to remind the Abbot that he also has to face a judgement. All his decisions must be made in the fear of God, and in conformity with the Rule. He must know well, and without shadow of doubt, that he will give account of each one of them to the supremely just Judge. God reserves to Himself this business of weighing the Abbot's abuse of his independence of judgement, and the vista of a divine "regular discipline" will keep the Abbot from every slightest inclination to tyranny.

Si qua vero minora agenda sunt in monasterii utilitatibus,[2] seniorum tan-	If it happen that less important matters have to be transacted for the

---

[1] Without doubt the best reading is: *proterve aut foris monasterium contendere*. And D. BUTLER cites the interesting note of SMARAGDUS: *Non dixit intus aut foris, sicut aliqui codices habent, sed sicut in illo quem manibus suis scripsit, proterve aut foris monasterium reperitur. Unde intelligitur quia foris nullam, intus autem esse contentionem permisit amicam.* It is plain that some scribes and commentators have had difficulties with this passage. *Cf.* PAUL THE DEACON, *in h. l.*

[2] *Monasterii utilitas:* CASS., *Inst.*, VII., ix.

tum utatur consilio, sicut scriptum est: *Omnia fac cum consilio, et post factum non pænitebis.*

advantage of the monastery, let him take counsel with the seniors only, as it is written: "Do all things with counsel, and thou shall not afterwards repent it."

Here is the second case, affairs of less importance, of which we said a word at the beginning of the chapter. We should grasp well the meaning of the text from Ecclesiasticus (xxxii. 24). Undoubtedly the Abbot should beware of an unlimited confidence in his own competence and judgement; absolute power is dangerous, especially for him who wields it. Nevertheless we should not take the words "all things" too literally. Even when it is a question of important measures, experience shows that the Abbot will sometimes do better to consult only his own conscience. Moreover, we should note that failure does not prove that he has acted rashly. And when Holy Scripture tells him that if he takes counsel, he shall not afterwards repent it, it does not promise him success and infallibility. Nor does it declare that in case of failure he may throw the responsibility on to others and wash his hands of the issue.

Times have changed since St. Benedict. He wrote his Rule with a conception of the *patria potestas*, absolute paternal authority, such as was implied in Roman law. Both superiors and monks had a living faith, and men submitted very readily to practically absolute government. But, by slow process, the old framework has yielded a little under the pressure of changing custom. Democracy, if we would speak the truth, has no more been introduced into the monastery than it has into the Church; but it is undeniable that a greater importance has gradually been given to the individual. Undoubtedly, too, sad experience has shown to what imprudences a practically absolute power may lend itself. The abuse of *Commendam* forced monks to protect themselves against a power for life, without counterpoise and often very worldly. For this purpose were invented triennial Abbots and all the various means which tended to reduce, and sometimes even to weaken, the abbatial authority. The constitutions of each Congregation enumerate a certain number of cases in which the Abbot must obtain the consent of the Conventual Chapter, of the Council of Seniors, or even of General Chapter, and business is often decided by vote. We do not think an Abbot has anything to regret in the loss of the freedom and initiative of former times. It is enough that present legislative arrangements come from the Church for them to deserve to be well received; but, to repeat, we must recognize that they have their justification in the desire to banish arbitrary and dangerous measures. Yet, in communities which are wisely governed and which have a good spirit, things go on always much as they did in the days of St. Benedict: a feeling of filial trust causes matters which he knows better than anyone else to be left to the decision of the Abbot; conflicts between an Abbot and his council are unknown, and all is done in harmonious concord.

CHAPTER IV

WHAT ARE THE INSTRUMENTS OF GOOD WORKS

THE preceding chapters have given us the organic structure of monastic society. From this point to Chapter VIII. the subject is the individual and his means of supernatural perfection, so that we may say that this portion of the Rule is St. Benedict's spiritual doctrine and gives monks their spiritual constitution. We remember with what insistence our Holy Father declared in the Prologue that progress in the Christian life is effected by the practice of good works and the constant exercise of all the virtues; he now describes this well-regulated activity. This chapter gives a long list of the principal forms in which it is displayed; immediately after come separate chapters devoted to the fundamental dispositions of the soul, to obedience, recollection, and humility.

"The Instruments of Good Works." Commentators have exercised their sagacity in defining the exact meaning of these words. St. Paul the Apostle speaks twice of the armour of a Christian; does our Holy Father desire to indicate here the interior qualities with which we should be provided—*habitus activi quibus instruimur*—in order to accomplish all good works? Or does St. Benedict regard the Scripture texts, of which nearly all the sentences of this chapter are formed, as true instruments, as methods of proved efficaciousness, certain to make us practise good works? As though, for the realization of the good, we had but to listen to the appeal of God. In a less subtle way one might give to the word *instrumenta* its meaning of legal instruments, and translate, "rules of morals, practical principles of good." It means also tools, implements, apparatus, resources, and, in the present case, the tools with which good is wrought, all the methods and implements of virtue, concretely the virtues and good works themselves. This is, it would seem, the meaning most in harmony with St. Benedict's thought; for, in concluding the chapter, he speaks of the "tools of the spiritual craft," and represents the monastery as the "workshop" where a man learns to use them;[1] while it is because he is really dealing with good works that he can speak of them as *adimpleta*—*i.e.*, fulfilled.

A word on the sources of this fourth chapter. Almost the entire series of instruments is to be found in the second part of the first *Decretal Epistle* of St. Clement;[2] but it has long been recognized[3] that this second part is spurious and the work of Isidorus Mercator. There are

---

[1] Probably a reminiscence of CASSIAN, who says of fasts, vigils, etc., that they are *perfectionis instrumenta* (*Conlat.*, I., vii.). Elsewhere Cassian speaks of *instrumenta virtutum* (*Conlat.*, VI., x.); and St. Benedict reproduces this expression in the last chapter of his Rule. *Instrumenta* also means documents, records.

[2] *P.G.*, I., 480.

[3] MABILLON, *Vetera Analecta*, t. II., p. 94, note c. (1723 edition).

certainly analogies between St. Benedict's chapter and the beginning of the *Teaching of the Apostles* (reproduced in the seventh book of the *Apostolic Constitutions*); both, for example, commence with the statement of the twofold precept of charity; Dom Butler, however, holds that it is impossible to give certain proof of borrowing.[1] One may also compare the passage of the Holy Rule with the forty-nine sentences published by Cardinal Pitra under the title: *Doctrina Hosii episcopi* († A.D. 397);[2] or with the *Monita* of Porcarius, Abbot of Lerins (at the end of the fifth century);[3] or again with the *Doctrina* of a certain Bishop Severinus, who has not been identified yet so far as I know.[4] We find analogous collections of sentences in the pagan philosophers themselves; see, for example, the *Sentences* attributed to the Seven Sages of Greece,[5] the prose *Sentences* which precede the *Disticha Catonis*, and the *Sentences of Sextus*, a fragment of which St. Benedict cites in Chapter VII.[6] All civilizations have left us specimens of this gnomic literature; the Books of Proverbs and Ecclesiasticus belong to this class. We are naturally led to express our morality in mottoes, to embody it in practical axioms; it seems to us to make virtue much easier when we achieve a short, pithy, and well-turned phrase, which in its very perfection has a gracious charm. The old monastic rules were generally composed in this short, sententious style.[7] And it is from them, from Holy Scripture, and to some degree from all sources, that our Holy Father seems to have gleaned his seventy-two instruments of good works; it is not yet proved that he has only copied, with greater or less modifications, one or several previous collections.

It would be vain to attempt to reduce these instruments to a methodical series and to find in them the unfolding of one plan, for St. Benedict had nothing of the sort in his mind. He is content to put at the head the most important and fundamental, and to group together maxims which have the same end and are connected by some analogy. We shall notice that maxims of supernatural perfection lie close to essential Christian precepts. The reason is that the latter, in their simplicity, embrace all moral teaching, and that here, as in the Prologue and in the chapters which are to follow, St. Benedict conceives monastic sanctity under the form of a regular, normal, and tranquil development of the graces of baptism.

[1] " St. Benedict and the *duæ viæ*," in the *Journal of Theological Studies*, January, 1910, p. 282. See also in the same Review, January 1911, p. 261, an article in which D. BUTLER discusses the sources of Chapter IV.; he shows that the *Syntagma doctrinæ* ascribed to ST. ATHANASIUS (*P.G.*, XXVIII., 835) should not be ranked among St Benedict's sources.
[2] *Analecta sacra et classica*, p. 117.
[3] Reprinted in the *Revue bénédictine*, October 1909. See also an old translation of ST. BASIL's *Admonitio ad monachos*, reprinted in the same Review, April 1910.
[4] PEZ, *Thesaurus Anecdotorum novissimus*, t. IV., P. II., col. 1-4; or in FABRICIUS, *Bibliotheca latina mediæ et infimæ ætatis*, t. II. (*ad calcem*).
[5] MULLACH, *Fragmenta Philosophorum græcorum*, t. I., p. 212 *sq*.
[6] *Ibid.*, p. 523 *sq.*—*Cf.* WEYMAN, *Wochenschrift für klass. Philologie*, 1896, p. 209.
[7] See, for instance, the Rules of ST. MACARIUS, ST. PACHOMIUS (clix.), etc

Quæ sint instrumenta bonorum operum.—1. Primum Instrumentum:[1] In primis, Dominum Deum diligere ex toto corde, tota anima, tota virtute.	What are the Instruments of Good Works.—1. First Instrument: in the first place to love the Lord God with all one's heart, all one's soul, and all one's strength.

"In the first place": yes, from every point of view, this is certainly the first instrument. For, to begin with, it is a universal precept. It is found already in its entirety in the Mosaic Law (Deut. vi. 5); and Our Lord had only to recall it (Mark xii. 30). Nevertheless, we cannot but see that the New Testament has given it a place of greater honour. Under the New Law there came a larger and more intimate outpouring of the Spirit of God: "the charity of God is poured forth in our hearts, by the Holy Ghost who is given to us" (Rom. v. 5); and filial love, according to the teaching of the Apostle, is the characteristic mark of the New Covenant.

The precept is comprehensive and complete. It is satisfying to have all the duties of the Christian life comprised in one unique obligation. The mind is more attentive when it has but one thing to consider; the will is more determined when it has but one end to pursue; the soul is more serene and more joyously persevering when it has reduced all to unity. We are only required to love. In this is summed up all morality. "Love and do what you will," said St. Augustine; and before him the Apostle, attributing to charity the acts of all the particular virtues, established the truth that charity of itself is sufficient, while without it nothing suffices (1 Cor. xiii.).

It is an easy precept, whether we regard its act or its object. A man need not be great, or rich, or healthy, or clever, to love. It is the most spontaneous and simple of acts; it is an initial act for which we have been prepared from infancy, thanks to the smiles and tenderness which have enfolded our life; God has provoked it in such a way as to make sure of it. The act is easy on the side of its object; for it is as natural to love God as it is to know Him, and man's faculties are enough of themselves. Of course such a love, in so far as it has not a *supernatural* principle as its root, could not take us to God; yet God is naturally lovable. He is so supernaturally on many grounds; He has made Himself known to us by the general benefits of Christianity and by the revelation of His goodness which is implied in the existence of each one of us. He has given us what is needed so that we may love Him supernaturally, and render Him an affection equal to His own. And He adds the precept: "Thou shalt love"; which precept has its own power of making us know and love God, for He only who loves, He only who is good and beautiful, has the right to demand love, and He only who loves without reservation has the right to demand a love without reservation. Truly it is an easy and sweet thing to love God, to love Father, Son, and Holy Spirit, Tenderness and Beauty and Purity Infinite.

[1] The words *primum instrumentum* do not occur in the manuscripts; nor is there any numbering of the instruments.

The sole objection that a man might raise is this: "Granted that love is necessary and sufficient, is it easy to love? I have never encountered God. I have lived for long a stranger to Him and unheeding. I do not dispute the reality of His beauty or of His love for me; but all that belongs to too spiritual a sphere, to which I hardly have access. Moreover, my temperament is positive, rather dry and cold, so that the supernatural stirs no emotion in me." This objection is based on a false definition of charity. Charity, according to St. Thomas, is a friendship between man and God; and we are taught by a pagan that true friendship is to wish and to reject the same objects as one's friend: *Eadem velle, eadem nolle, ea demum firma amicitia est.* To love God is to wish what God wishes and to do what God demands, it is to unite our will practically with His. Is not this the teaching of Our Lord Himself in St. Matthew (vii. 20 *sq.*)?—" From their fruits you shall know them. Not everyone who saith to me: Lord, Lord, shall enter into the kingdom of heaven, but he that doth the will of my Father who is in heaven." Neither the fervour of our first days in the spiritual life, nor even the purified and very noble pleasure which is the effect of charity on the whole man, is necessary or constitutes an infallible indication of our intimacy with Our Lord. All these forms of joy are merely superadded to charity as an encouragement, or as an advance in our salary and inheritance. The fact is that to arrive, if not at sanctity, at least at a certain measure of genuine love, we must know how to be faithful without pleasure, in aridity, and in the very midst of interior disturbances which affect the whole sensitive nature.

We have only to read farther in the "first instrument" in order to appreciate the character and the measure of our charity. We must love "with the heart"—that is, not necessarily with a love of feeling and emotion, but with our inner being. That may seem easy enough. Yet there is always danger, in a regular and liturgical life, of loving God only with the lips, in the routine of duties fulfilled in a purely formal manner. This is the Jewish tendency, many times denounced and scourged by the prophets and Our Lord. It may spring from some too well loved occupation, which draws off to its own advantage the best of our attention and leaves God only the meagre homage of a compulsory ceremonial. To love "with all the heart" must be to make charity shine in our souls, to bow intelligence and will before God, and through them the lower powers; and it is precisely for the better embracing of the whole that love gathers itself to the centre, to the vital core: "O my God, I have desired it, and thy law in the midst of my heart" (Ps. xxxix. 9).

"With the whole soul." Without laying too great stress on such an interpretation or claiming for it an exclusive value, we might perhaps consider "soul" here as the principle of life and continued life; for when the soul departs life ceases. So that to love God with one's whole soul would suggest that law of continuity in our adhesion to Him which should rule all our supernatural activity. This continuity has its degrees. One meets with extraordinary graces, with graces of intellectual recollection in God, and of infused contemplation; but these are granted most often to those who use ordinary grace well. It is the normal thing that our thoughts should be turned with some assiduity towards Him to whom we have vowed to belong. Not of course that we could make an act of love each moment; but we can live habitually under the influence of charity. God is simple, and can permeate our whole life like a subtle odour. The best intellectual work is that which is done in His presence. With a little practice this contact with God becomes a habit. "Where the treasure is, there is the heart"; and our heart returns to Him expressly so soon as some alien interest no longer draws it away. Life is always a process of adaptation to environment: the supernatural life develops in the atmosphere of charity, of peaceful and continuous attention to Our Lord.

We must love " with all our strength "—that is, with all our powers, in such sort that they are employed without reservation for the advantage of love and of God. This is indeed the very condition of love; for all real loving must be absolute and without limits; so soon as one loves, deliberation ceases, one gives oneself entirely, and, if need be, attempts the impossible. Charity excepts nothing. It would possess all our time, direct all our steps, regulate all our affections. And when we have exhausted the long series of sacrifices, when we have bravely broken one after another of the idols that encumbered our souls, there remains generally one last idol, not the grossest, nor perhaps the best loved, an idol that is sometimes quite petty and ridiculous, but the last; and therein that self, which has been dislodged from every other stronghold, ensconces itself entire. If we do not wish to remain for ever stationary, we must arm ourselves with much resolve and delicacy of conscience, and cut the fastenings.

2. Deinde proximum tamquam seipsum (Mark xii. 31).

2. Then, one's neighbour as oneself.

With charity towards God goes charity towards one's neighbour: "On these two commandments dependeth the whole law and the prophets" (Matt. xxii. 40). So we may pause also at this precept of fraternal charity; it is a precept of continual application; half of the instruments of good works express different aspects of it, and are but its particular manifestations.

The object of this charity is our neighbour—that is, our brother, whoever he may be; and, according to Our Lord's definition, this means any man to whom we can do good, though he be a Samaritan. If we excommunicate our brethren, if we have someone or other whom we refuse to see, in whose presence we adopt an attitude of sulky and ill-tempered neutrality, or even of violent hostility, then we are renegades and heretics in charity. It is ourselves that we excommunicate. If you cherish enmity against one of your brethren, charity is no more in you, and what causes you to keep on good terms with the rest is self-love, natural attraction, human sympathy, sometimes even a lower feeling which may be purely animal. Why do Communions sometimes produce so little fruit? Because we put an obstacle in the way; and ordinarily this is the obstacle. Whence come some monastic apostasies? From the contempt of charity. It is certain that, among religious, faults against charity, whether by aversion or detraction, are those wherein grave matter is most easily met.

God is the motive of our charity. We love because God loves that we should love. We love because our neighbour belongs to God, and the love which we have for God naturally spreads to all that is connected with Him. We love because God loves, and we abase our personal repugnance before the sovereign judgement of God. We love because there is something of God in our neighbour: just as the Holy Eucharist is an extension of the Incarnation, so our neighbour is an extension of the Eucharist; God is jealous and would have us meet naught but Himself in all the avenues of our life. Our Lord regards Himself as the one really benefited by our charity: " As long as you did it to one of these my least brethren, you did it to me " (Matt. xxv. 40). For in truth the act of charity which embraces God, ourselves, and our neighbour, is but one: we love God for Himself, ourselves for His sake, our neighbour because he is His and in Him.

And, lest we should sometimes be undecided as to the range of our charity, we have been furnished with a ready standard—viz., the supernatural love which we have for ourselves: *tanquam seipsum*. Whatever good we desire for ourselves and labour to procure for ourselves, this we should contrive for our neighbour by our desires, prayers, and efforts. Whenever you deal with one of your brethren, as the ninth instrument tells us, and then above all when you ask some service of him, or exercise when required the duty of correction, make use of a loving self-extension: to use a commonplace but accurate expression, " put yourself in his place."

St. John continually speaks of charity. But, in the fourth chapter of his first Epistle, he expounds doctrinally what place it holds in the economy of the supernatural life. God, says he, is charity: He has proved it by the Incarnation and the Redemption; those who know Him truly, know Him only as such. And those who are really born of Him, who are His legitimate sons, cannot but have His character and cannot but be charity. Charity is an essence, a nature, a character. In this respect it is a universal law that those who are born of God cannot but love; and this affection must be spontaneously directed to the two objects of the divine affection, God and our neighbour. But our share in the divine life remains, like God Himself, a thing hidden from our sight. The proof that we are born of God can only be supplied there where the term of our charity is visible; our neighbour alone gives us the opportunity of showing that we love God, and are of His stock. When our charity is not exercised towards our neighbour, it is legitimate to conclude that it is non-existent: " For he that loveth not his brother, whom he seeth, how can he love God whom he seeth not?" (1 John iv. 20.) St. John's profound theology is only the development of the words of Our Lord: "By this shall all men know that you are my disciples, if you have love one for another." (John xiii. 35).

3. Deinde non occidere (Exod. xx. 13–17; Matt. xix. 18; Rom. xiii. 9).	3. Then not to kill.
4. Non adulterari (*ibid.*).	4. Not to commit adultery.
5. Non facere furtum (*ibid.*).	5. Not to steal.
6. Non concupiscere (*ibid.*).	6. Not to covet.
7. Non falsum testimonium dicere (*ibid.*).	7. Not to bear false witness.
8. Honorare omnes homines (1 Pet. ii. 17).	8. To honour all men.
9. Et quod sibi quis fieri non vult, alii non faciat.	9. Not to do to another what one would not have done to oneself.

In the instruments from the third to the seventh we have a negative analysis of the precept of charity. To love one's neighbour is to respect him in his person, in his life, in his consort, in his property; the very desire to hurt him is forbidden, and it is still less lawful to set any social influence in motion against him by means of false witness. We might ask how such warnings as these concern religious. But we must remember that St. Benedict is simply enumerating the elementary points of Christian morality, that a monk is never dispensed from attention to them, that even in a monastery these odious vices may be met with on a smaller scale, and that, after all, monastic history records some crimes like that of which our Holy Father himself was nearly the victim at Vicovaro.

The eight and ninth instruments give us the positive analysis of the precept. But while the Mosaic Law and the Gospel, from which the five preceding instruments are taken, added the counsel of honouring father and mother, St. Benedict, addressing men separated from their parents, takes from St. Peter the most general rule of honouring all men. Then he reminds us what should be the measure of our charity, in that "Golden Rule," which he cites anew in Chapters LXI. and LXX., and always in its negative form. We find it expressed positively in St. Matthew (vii. 12) and in St. Luke (vi. 31); but it is given in the negative form in the Book of Tobias (iv. 16), in certain ancient manuscripts of the Acts (xv. 20 and 29), in the *Teaching of the Apostles*, and in many of the Fathers of the Church. It would seem that St. Benedict quotes it from the Acts or the Fathers rather than from Tobias—that is, if it be not simply a proverb, engraved in the memory of all and in current use.[1]

10. Abnegare semetipsum sibi, ut sequatur Christum (Matt. xvi. 24, xix. 16).	10. To deny oneself, in order to follow Christ.
11. Corpus castigare (1 Cor. ix. 27).	11. To chastise the body.

[1] See D. BUTLER's article in the *Journal of Theological Studies*, January, 1910.

12. Delicias non amplecti.[1]	12. Not to seek after delicate living.
13. Jejunium amare.	13. To love fasting.

After having spoken of charity towards God, and charity towards our neighbour, St. Benedict was free to say something on self-love. In the state of original justice man leant on God in a conscious and deliberate manner; a man's dignity and power consisted then in returning to God the whole of the divine likeness that was his being. When he separated himself from God in the vain hope of getting nearer to Him, and becoming His equal, man fell back first on himself and then soon below himself, even to the likeness of the brute. This is the teaching of St. Augustine.[2] We were profoundly affected in that first of ties, in that initial love which controls the whole life. Henceforth the worship of self prevails, self-love in all its forms, whether the worship of the body in luxury, gluttony, and vanity, or the worship of thought and will. And whatever is loved, whether person or thing, is loved only for self. Self-love is the one universal trace of the Fall; it is the one antagonist of our charity and our salvation.

Now we understand why Our Lord asks those who would return to Him to renounce external and personal things, to leave the created, and, according to the phrase of the Gospel as St. Benedict read it,[3] to deny oneself to oneself. This is the general principle, and the instruments which follow mark three special applications of it. They combat that animality which is at the bottom of all self-love. We must chastise the body and compel it to be no more than a docile servant; we must not greedily seek comfort and the sweets of a sensual life; we must have a practical love for fasting, that standard Christian mortification.

14. Pauperes recreare (Isa. lviii. 7; Matt. xxv. 35–36).[4]	14. To relieve the poor.
15. Nudum vestire (*ibid.*).[5]	15. To clothe the naked.

[1] We must not try to find a scriptural source at all costs; yet we shall generally conform to the custom of giving references to the Bible.

[2] ... *Incipiens a perverso appetitu similitudinis Dei, pervenit ad similitudinem pecorum. Inde est quod nudati stola prima, pelliceas tunicas mortalitate meruerunt. Honor enim hominis verus est imago et similitudo Dei, quæ non custoditur nisi ad ipsum a quo imprimitur. Tanto magis itaque inhæretur Deo, quanto minus diligitur proprium. Cupiditate vero experiendæ potestatis suæ, quodam nutu suo ad se ipsum tanquam ad medium proruit. Ita cum vult esse sicut ille sub nullo, et ab ipsa sui medietate pœnaliter ad ima propellitur, id est, ad ea quibus pecora lætantur* (De Trinitate, l. XII., c. xi., P.L., XLII., 1006-1007).

[3] The same is to be found in ST. AMBROSE, *De Pænit.*, l. II., 96, 97. *P.L.*, XVI., 520-521. *Epist.* II., 26. *P.L.*, XVI., 886. St. Benedict had in mind a passage in the *Historia monachorum* of RUFINUS, c. xxxi. (ROSWEYD, p. 484): *Docebat beatus Antonius quod si quis velit ad perfectionem velociter pervenire, non sibi ipse fieret magister, nec propriis voluntatibus obediret, etiamsi rectum videatur esse quod vellet; sed secundum mandatum Salvatoris observandum esse, ut ante omnia unusquisque abneget semetipsum sibi et renuntiet propriis voluntatibus, quia et Salvator ipse dixit: Ego veni non ut faciam voluntatem meam sed ejus qui misit me.*

[4] *Recreare* is not merely to give alms, but to give food to the poor, to refresh them, to "re-create" them.

[5] Instruments 15, 16, 22, 23, 25, 26, 27, 41, occur in a sermon printed among the *spuria* of ST. AMBROSE (*Sermo* XXIV., 11. *P.L.*, XVII., 654). The beginning and some other parts of the sermon belong probably to ST. CÆSARIUS, but the whole is a compilation including later elements.

16. Infirmum visitare (Eccli. vii. 39; Matt. xxv. 35-6).	16. To visit the sick.
17. Mortuum sepelire (Tob. i. 21; ii. 7–9).	17. To bury the dead.
18. In tribulatione subvenire (Isa. i. 17).	18. To help in affliction.
19. Dolentem consolari (Eccli. vii. 38; 1 Thess. v. 14).	19. To console the sorrowing.

In proportion as we conquer our selfish appetites, we shall be able to provide for the divers necessities of our neighbours. If occasion for exercising the first two works of mercy scarcely comes to any but the Abbot and the cellarer, yet monks will sometimes have to visit the sick and bury the dead; and all can help the afflicted and console the sorrowing.

20. A sæculi actibus se facere alienum.	20. To keep aloof from worldly actions.
21. Nihil amori Christi præponere.	21. To prefer nothing to the love of Christ.

Perhaps the juxtaposition of the twentieth instrument with those which immediately precede was suggested to St. Benedict by the text of St. James (i. 27): Religion clean and undefiled before God and the Father is this: to visit the fatherless and widows in their tribulation, and to keep oneself unspotted from this world." However this may be, it is certain that the twentieth and twenty-first instruments have a general reference, that they are closely connected and complete each other, and that their object is to orientate our life, by showing from what mark we should turn and to what direct our course. The Prologue set this choice before us, the world or Our Lord, as mutually exclusive alternatives; we cannot remain neutral, but must belong wholly to the one or wholly to the other.

St. Benedict's language here is vigorous; he bids us keep aloof from worldly actions. By worldly actions is meant evil in all its forms: *Corrumpere et corrumpi sæculum vocatur* (To corrupt and be corrupted is called the fashion of the world). After our entering into Christ by baptism and by the monastic profession, we should hold ourselves as far aloof from the world as possible and have no connection with it. There shall no longer be more intercourse between us than there is between two corpses: " The world is crucified to me and I to the world " (Gal. vi. 14). Let us be on our guard against thinking that it may sometimes be proper to soften the differences, to lessen the distance which separates us. The Apostle warns us that we can only please God by preserving the integrity of our true life: " No man being a soldier to God, entangleth himself with secular businesses: that he may please him to whom he hath engaged himself " (2 Tim. ii. 4). The world itself is scandalized by our condescending to it, and the words of the *Imitation* are always fulfilled: " Sometimes we think to please others by our company; whereas we begin rather to be displeasing to them by reason of the bad qualities they discover in us" (I. viii.).

We are not, however, vowed to solitude; our separation from the world is only that we may draw near to God. No natural love for natural beauty shall prevail over the love which binds us to Christ. St. Benedict was fond of this sentence and repeats it in Chapter LXXII. Commentators give St. Matthew (x. 37-38) as the source of the passage, but it is more probably inspired by the Fathers. It is said in the *Life of St. Antony:* "His conversation, which was seasoned with wit, consoled the sad, instructed the ignorant, reconciled enemies: he persuaded all that nothing should be preferred to the love of Christ."[1] And St. Cyprian had written before this: "To prefer nothing to Christ."[2]

22. Iram non perficere (Matt. v. 22).

23. Iracundiæ tempus non reservare.

24. Dolum in corde non tenere (Prov. xii. 20).[3]

25. Pacem falsam non dare (Ps. xxvii. 3).

26. Caritatem non derelinquere (1 Pet. iv. 8).

27. Non jurare, ne forte perjuret (Matt. v. 33 *sq*).[4]

28. Veritatem ex corde, et ore proferre (Ps. xiv. 3).

29. Malum pro malo non reddere (1 Pet iii. 9).

30. Injuriam non facere, sed factam patienter sufferre (1 Cor. vi. 7).[5]

22. Not to gratify anger.

23. Not to harbour a desire of revenge.

24. Not to foster guile in one's heart.

25. Not to make a feigned peace.

26. Not to forsake charity.

27. Not to swear, lest perchance one forswear oneself.

28. To utter truth from heart and mouth.

29. Not to render evil for evil.

30. To do no wrong to anyone, yea, to bear patiently wrong done to oneself.

---

[1] *Versio Evagrii*, 14. P.G., XXVI., 865.

[2] Here is the whole passage of ST. CYPRIAN; St. Benedict seems to have known it well: *Humilitas in conversatione, stabilitas in fide, verecundia in verbis, in factis justitia, in operibus misericordia, in moribus disciplina, injuriam facere non nosse, et factam posse tolerare* (the thirtieth instrument), *cum fratribus pacem tenere; Deum toto corde diligere, amare in illo quod pater est, timere quod Deus est; Christo omnino nihil præponere, quia nec nobis quicquam ille præposuit, caritati ejus inseparabiliter adhærere* (De Oratione Dominica, xv. P.L., IV., 529).

[3] Instruments 22-28 recall Prov. xii. 16-20.

[4] This maxim occurs several times in ST. AUGUSTINE, for instance *Epist.*, CLVII., 40. P.L., XXXIII., 693. JOSEPHUS cites it (with a slight variation) as familiar to the Essenes: *De Bello Jud.*, l. II., c. viii. (*al*. vii.). It is interesting to note that a portion of the list of Essene virtues given by Josephus corresponds quite closely with the series of the instruments of good works from 13 to 28: sobriety, works of mercy, abstention from angry acts, true peace, fidelity to promises, abstention from oaths. We do not put forward Josephus as one of St. Benedict's sources, although he might very well have known the *Jewish War* by means of the Latin translation which was current in his time and which, according to CASSIODORUS (*De Institut. div. litt.*, c. xvii. P.L., LXX., 1133), was attributed to St. Ambrose, or St. Jerome, or Rufinus.

[5] St. Benedict's words come rather from ST. CYPRIAN or the *Rule* of ST. MACARIUS (xxi.).

31. Inimicos diligere (Matt. v. 44).	31. To love one's enemies.
32. Maledicentes se non remaledicere, sed magis benedicere (1 Pet. iii. 9).	32. Not to render cursing for cursing, but rather blessing.
33. Persecutiones pro justitia sustinere (Matt. v. 10).	33. To bear persecution for justice' sake.

The subject is still charity towards our neighbour; but charity exercised under difficult circumstances, when our neighbour is a trial to us or even becomes our enemy and persecutor. There are cases where simple interior benevolence will not do, where charity must be backed by courage and magnanimity. Our Lord sometimes requires heroism. Not only must we never abandon serenity of mind or seek revenge; every Christian must have in his heart this divine disposition of returning good for evil. For children of God, to suffer persecution for justice' sake is the highest happiness.

This group of counsels is interesting also for the fact that it adds the virtue of uprightness to that of charity. It is the glory of the monastic life to be founded in loyalty and absolute sincerity, to be delivered from all the diplomacy and shiftiness of the world. Happy those who have nothing to hide, who know nothing of tortuous or subterranean manœuvres, who live full in the day. Happy those who have brought all their being to a perfect simplicity, and who, before God and before men, are what they are, without duality, stiffness, or effort, but with flexibility and ease.

34. Non esse superbum (Tit. i. 7).	34. Not to be proud.
35. Non vinolentum (*ibid.*).	35. Not given to wine.
36. Non multum edacem (Eccli. xxxvii. 32).	36. Not a glutton.
37. Non somnolentum (Prov. xx. 13).	37. Not drowsy.
38. Non pigrum (Rom. xii. 11; Prov. xxiv. 30 *sq.*).	38. Not slothful.
39. Non murmurosum (Sap. i. 11).	39. Not a murmurer.
40. Non detractorem (*ibid.*).	40. Not a detractor.

From the thirty-fourth to the sixty-third, the instruments seem designed to regulate morally, not our life in relation to others, but our separate personal life. First comes a series of negative counsels. The preceding ones had put us on our guard against the ways of the world which foment discord among men; these warn the monk to abstain from other "worldly actions" which are incompatible with Christian dignity. Anger and all its train of vices having been banished already, it remained to denounce pride, gluttony, and sloth; lust is dealt with in the fifty-ninth and sixty-third instruments, and envy in the sixty-fifth. St. Benedict singles out for special condemnation the spirit of murmuring, a spirit habitual with the idle and lazy; the cantankerous, critical, and malicious spirit.

41. Spem suam Deo committere (Ps. lxxii. 28).	41. To put one's hope in God.
42. Bonum aliquod in se cum viderit, Deo applicet, non sibi.	42. To attribute any good that one sees in oneself to God and not to oneself.
43. Malum vero semper a se factum sciat, et sibi reputet.	43. But to recognize and always impute to oneself the evil that one does.

These counsels are designed to fortify us against the secret pride that rises in us when we have done good or avoided evil. We must know to whom we should ultimately attribute the glory of our virtues and the shame of our faults. It is too common a tendency to assume responsibility for the good alone and to give the glory of it to oneself; moreover, at an epoch which lay close to Pelagianism or Semi-Pelagianism, it was not superfluous briefly to recall the doctrines of grace and freewill; St. Benedict has done this already in the Prologue. In this place he proclaims that all man's strength and trust are in God and not in himself: " But it is good for me to cling to my God, to put my hope in the Lord God " (Ps. lxxii. 28); fallen man must claim nothing as his own but evil and sin.[1]

44. Diem judicii timere (Luc. xii.).	44. To fear the Day of Judgement.
45. Gehennam expavescere (ibid.).	45. To be in dread of hell.
46. Vitam æternam omni concupiscentia spirituali desiderare (Phil. i. 23; Ps. lxxxiii.).	46. To desire with all spiritual longing everlasting life.
47. Mortem quotidie ante oculos suspectam habere.[2]	47. To keep death daily before one's eyes.[2]

If it be wise to distinguish the sources from which our actions come, it is indispensable also to recognize whither they lead us. In these four counsels our Holy Father warns us to think of our last end: of death, judgement, hell, and heaven. The whole of life takes a different aspect according as we regard it as a walk or a journey. In the first case our

---

[1] Our Holy Father is in agreement with ST. AUGUSTINE: *Non præsumat de se, sentiat se hominem, et respiciat dictum propheticum : Maledictus omnis qui spem suam ponit in homine. Subducat se sibi, sed non deorsum versus. Subducat se sibi, ut hæreat Deo. Quidquid boni habet, illi tribuat a quo factus est ; quidquid mali habet, ipse sibi feci Deus quod in illo malum est, non fecit* (Serm. XCVI., 2. *P.L.*, XXXVIII., 386). A similar formula occurs in the Neo-Platonic philosopher PORPHYRY: Πάντων ὧν πράττομεν ἀγαθῶν τὸν θεὸν αἴτιον ἡγώμεθα · τῶν δὲ κακῶν αἴτιοι ἡμεῖς ἐσμέν οἱ ἑλόμενοι (*Epist. ad Marcellam*, xii.). We may also compare with St. Benedict's teaching that of the Council of Orange in 529: *Nemo habet de suo nisi mendacium et peccatum. Si quid autem habet homo veritatis atque justitiæ, ab illo fonte est, quem debemus sitire in hac eremo, ut ex eo quasi guttis quibusdam irrorati, non deficiamus in via* (Can. xxii., MANSI, t. VIII., col. 716). [The words of PORPHYRY echo a famous passage in PLATO's *Republic*.]

[2] Being recommended by Holy Scripture (Ecclus. vii. 40; Matt. xxiv. 42 ff.), this practice was familiar to the ancient monks: *Cogita apud temetipsum et dicito : utique non manebo in hoc mundo, nisi præsenti hac die, et non peccabis Deo. . . . Ponatque sibi mortem ante oculos* (*Reg.* S. ANTONII, xli., xlv.).—*Oportet monachum ut semper lugeat, semper suorum sit memor peccatorum et omni hora ponat sibi mortem ante oculos suos* (*Verba Seniorum : Vitæ Patrum*, III., 196. ROSWEYD, p. 529).

movements are free, and we may choose our own pace. But if it be a journey with a fixed end, and if the conditions of this journey be such that it must end soon, perhaps in an unexpected fashion, and that it would be simply terrible not to reach our goal, would it not be folly to travel at a venture? We have no right to forget the judgement of God which awaits us. We have no right to put aside the terrors of hell, as though hell did not concern us. There are not two Christianities. And since Satan could fall from the steps of God's throne to the depths of the abyss, there is no security for us but in the continual consideration of our destiny. We are moving towards it. Our Lord calls Himself "He that cometh," ὁ ἐρχόμενος. And those whose souls are turned to Him in faith and hope and charity may make their own the words of the Spirit and the Bride: "Come, Lord Jesus."

For there is a something better still than the fear of God's judgement, and it is the desire of eternity, the burning thirst to see Our Lord and to be with Him for ever. St. Benedict indicates the true character of this desire in a word: it should be supernatural. With the young sometimes, just after conversion and in the exaltation of their first fervour, the longing for eternity is but an emotional yearning, a curiosity legitimate in itself, yet mixed with imperfection. Some have this desire through a delicacy of conscience which shows them in how many ways they may offend God every day. With other souls it springs from weariness and cowardice, from the wish to be done with the toils of the spiritual life. But the desire of heaven is of purest metal when it awakes towards the end of our days, for we are never more attached to the charms of the present life than when it is passing from us; and few are they who, when the thread of their life is worn thin, ask God to come and sever it forthwith.

We must think upon death. Death has no terrors for a monk. Paganism, our imagination, and our feelings have taught us to envelop this last moment in dread. The idea, or rather the imagination, of death always suggests to us farewell scenes, tears, mournful chants, the horrors of corpses and tombs; our childish eyes pictured death as a skeleton holding a huge scythe, or under the symbol of a skull and crossbones. Certainly death is the proof of sin and its punishment. But Our Lord Himself tasted this bitter cup, and so delivered us from the terror which death inspired in the ancients. "Therefore because the children are partakers of flesh and blood, he also himself in like manner hath been partaker of the same: that, through death, he might destroy him who had the empire of death, that is to say, the devil: and might deliver them who through the fear of death were all their lifetime subject to servitude" (Heb. ii. 14–15). And if we regard death as the final meeting with Him whom we have sought and loved so long in faith, it is no longer possible to feel an indefinable superstitious fear at its approach. It is the true communion, and solemn profession, the veritable beginning of all things. "Yes," you will say, "but what about my failings?" You must labour to overcome them, and to expiate them. And it is right that we should love all that comes from God; we must love His justice, and we must love purgatory. From now on we must accept the reprisals which He has to take on us and abandon ourselves blindly to His infinite mercy. Do we not go towards it with souls bathed in the Blood of Our Saviour and all penetrated with His beauty ? Will not God refuse to see in us aught but His own Son ?

Very easy too is it to meditate on death in general or on the death of another, and such meditations are not without their usefulness. But our own death, the death of this individual concrete being—that above all is good for us to consider, if not for the purpose of imagining its form, at least to accept in advance all its bitterness, all its conditions, all its particular circumstances. "To keep death daily before one's eyes." There is an act of perfect charity embodied in this rehearsal of death. And, as experience shows well, we cannot extemporize our dying; when death has not been prepared and practised, the piece is a failure. Not that we must "make-up" beforehand, practise poses, and prepare fine speeches and pathetic farewells: for death should be natural; but precisely that it may be natural, and since it only happens once—" it is appointed unto men once to die "—let us fix ourselves in the dispositions which may make it " precious in the sight of God." St. Benedict would like this thought and this effort to be a daily practice: so that we may accustom ourselves to it the more, and prevent all surprise, and perhaps also that we may repress in ourselves a certain excessive enjoyment of life.

48. Actus vitæ suæ omni hora custodire (Deut. iv. 9).

49. In omni loco Deum se respicere, pro certo scire (Prov. v. 21).

48. To keep guard at all times over the actions of one's life.

49. To know for certain that God sees one everywhere.

We know our goal. St. Benedict now indicates some practices which help us to reach it. The constant thought of death makes us use life well. There is a close and necessary relation between what we are and what we shall be, for with the works of the present life do we construct our eternity. " To keep guard at all times over the actions of one's life " is to live thoughtfully, to be a person and not a puppet, a being that rules itself and not an animal deprived of reason; it is to weigh one's actions and make them conform to law, to have empty and void of fruit not even one of those days which Our Lord has given us for His service: " Defraud not thyself of the good day: and let not the part of a good day overpass thee" (Ecclus. xiv. 14; compare the prayers of Prime: *Domine Deus* . . . and *Dirigere* . . .). It is to set ourselves to accomplish our supernatural education by a resolute acceptance of all that God asks of us. The two first educations, the education of the family and the education of the school, even though without defects, even though they had always helped and never thwarted each other, would still not be enough to shape the whole man. For man has not only to ratify this work, he has to pursue it without ceasing. Grace is a principle of action, and it is given us abundantly only that our activity may be raised higher from day to day and secured from all the counter-attacks of self-love.

"To know for certain that God sees one everywhere." This advice must be very important since St. Benedict is constantly repeating it. He gives it in the Prologue, in the first and last degrees of humility, in the chapter "Of the discipline of saying the Divine Office." We find it in the Liturgy of the Church:

> Speculator adstat desuper,
> Qui nos diebus omnibus,
> Actusque nostros prospicit
> A luce prima in vesperum.[1]

The warning is so natural that it may be addressed to all: to the Christian as to the monk, to the child as to the mature man: "God sees you." It would seem that those prodigies of sanctity, the Patriarchs, walked towards perfection with no other principle. Holy Scripture considers that all has been said about their greatness when it is described in these few words: "He walked with God," "He walked before God"; and God gives Abraham no other rule but this: "Walk before me and be perfect."

The precept has a sovereign efficacy. The imperative of the moral law is only categorical when we see in it something more than an æsthetic rule, when we realize that God is not only the author of this law, but also its surety and its guardian. Our moral life requires a witness, a function assigned to friendship by pagans and lay directors of conscience. Making his own a maxim of Epicurus and Plato, Seneca wrote thus in his eleventh letter to Lucilius: "We must choose some good man and keep him ever before our eyes, so that we may live as though he were looking on and do all as though he saw us. . . . Many sins are prevented if there be a witness by the sinner." For us this is no fiction of the imagination, but a living reality; nor have we a mere witness, but a Being who is at once spectator and actor, no man but God. And we Christians say: *Nemo peccat videns Deum*, "No one seeing God sins." The impeccability of the elect is due to their being for ever rooted in good by the uninterrupted contemplation of beauty. Now we by faith may share in this privilege of vision, and the "exercise of the presence of God" may become something assiduous and constant, like our consciousness of ourselves.

50. Cogitationes malas cordi suo advenientes mox ad Christum allidere.	50. To dash down at the feet of Christ one's evil thoughts, the instant that they come into the heart.
51. Et seniori spirituali patefacere.	51. And to lay them open to one's spiritual father.

[1] *Feria V., ad Laudes.*

> The Watcher ever from on high
> Marks our days as they go by,
> And every act discerneth done
> From early dawn to setting sun.

52. Os suum a malo, vel pravo eloquio custodire (Ps. xxxiii. 14).[1]

52. To keep one's mouth from evil and wicked words.

53. Multum loqui non amare (Prov. x. 19).

53. Not to love much speaking.

54. Verba vana aut risui apta non loqui (Matt. xii. 36; 2 Tim. ii. 16).

54. Not to speak vain words or such as move to laughter.

55. Risum multum aut excussum non amare (Eccli. xxi. 23).

55. Not to love much or excessive laughter.

The forty-eighth and forty-ninth instruments were of a general character, inviting us to keep watch over our actions and giving us the motive for this watchfulness—namely, the watchfulness of God. From this point the Holy Rule descends to detail. In the first place our acts are interior ones, thoughts and tendencies. We observed in the Prologue, in dealing with a text of similar import to the fiftieth instrument, that we should exercise a rigorous control over the feelings and thoughts which present themselves to us. When recognized as evil or dangerous, they must be dashed at once on the Rock, which is Christ. There is great security in thus seizing every irregular motion in its beginnings, while it has not yet got all its strength and while our strength remains intact; for it is easier to extinguish a spark than a fire. And the author of the *Imitation* (I. xiii.) recalls in this connection the verses of Ovid:

Principiis obsta; sero medicina paratur,
Cum mala per longas invaluere moras.[2]

Another condition of security, equally absolute, is to drag Cacus from his cave, and to go simply and open one's soul, not only to one's confessor, but to one's Abbot, or Master of Novices, or to the superior against whom one is tempted. Our Holy Father makes of this course of action a special degree of humility,[3] and we may reserve our commentary for the seventh chapter.

But our actions are not only thoughts and secret movements of the soul; there are also the words and external signs which manifest them. St. Benedict counsels us to guard them equally and keep watch over them. Conversation should be monastic; we should banish from it all that would be out of place or of doubtful character. And since there is danger, when one speaks much, of saying many things that had far better not be said, and danger always of dissipation, we should agree to avoid wordiness. Our Holy Father adds: "Not to speak vain words or such as move to laughter." He does not mean to proscribe spiritual joy,

---

[1] D. BUTLER indicates as sources: *Ingenio malo pravoque* (SALLUST., *Catil.*, v.). *Malo pravoque consilio* (LUCIFER CALIG., *Mor. esse pro Dei fil.*, vi. *P.L.*, XIII., 1019).

[2] Resist beginnings; all too late the cure
When ills have gathered strength by long delay.

[3] CASSIAN had already written these words of gold: *Nullas penitus cogitationes prurientes in corde perniciosa confusione celare, sed confestim ut exortæ fuerint eas suo patefacere seniori, nec super earum judicio quicquam suæ discretioni committere, sed illud credere malum esse vel bonum, quod discusserit ac pronuntiaverit senioris examen. . . . Generale et evidens indicium diabolicæ cogitationis esse pronuntiant, si eam seniori confundamur aperire* (*Inst.*, IV., ix.).

nor that happiness which is sometimes an indication and an instrument of perfection,[1] but only gross gaiety, the unbridled noisy spirit, coarse and violent laughter. St. Benedict formulates the same restriction later on at greater length.

56. Lectiones sanctas libenter audire.

57. Orationi frequenter incumbere (Luc. xviii. 1; Col. iv. 2).

58. Mala sua præterita cum lacrimis vel gemitu quotidie in oratione Deo confiteri, et de ipsis malis de cetero emendare (Ps. vi. 7).

59. Desideria carnis non perficere. Voluntatem propriam odire (Gal. v. 16; Eccli. xviii. 30).

60. Præceptis Abbatis in omnibus obedire, etiam si ipse aliter (quod absit) agat, memor illius Dominici præcepti: *Quæ dicunt, facite, quæ autem faciunt facere nolite* (Matt. xxiii. 3).

61. Non velle dici sanctum, antequam sit, sed prius esse, quo verius dicatur.

62. Præcepta Dei factis quotidie adimplere (Eccli. vi. 37).

56. To listen willingly to holy reading.

57. To apply oneself frequently to prayer.

58. Daily to confess in prayer one's past sins with tears and sighs to God, and to amend them for the time to come.

59. Not to fulfil the desires of the flesh: to hate one's own will.

60. To obey in all things the commands of the Abbot, even though he himself (which God forbid) should act otherwise: being mindful of that precept of the Lord: "What they say, do ye; but what they do, do ye not."

61. Not to wish to be called holy before one is so; but first to be holy, that one may be truly so called.

62. Daily to fulfil by one's deeds the commandments of God.

The first two instruments mark the practical means which most effectively repress every evil habit and ensure to the monastic life its character of seriousness. Instead of letting himself slip into dissipation or gossip, a monk devotes himself to the study of spiritual things and to prayer. He is recommended to love holy reading and to have a taste for God's word: "Blessed are they that hear the word of God and keep it" (Luke xi. 28). It is by hearing that faith comes to us: "faith is from hearing" (Rom. x. 17); and it may be that the Rule speaks designedly of hearing and not of reading. Moreover, thanks to the word *audire* (hear) the fifty-sixth instrument was put within reach of all, including monks who could not read. Prayer is easy for souls who live in constant communion with the teaching of Scripture and the saints. We may believe that our Holy Father remembered what Sulpicius Severus wrote of St. Martin: "He never let any hour or moment pass by, but he applied himself to prayer or reading; though even while reading, or whatever else he was doing, he never relaxed his mind from prayer."[2]

To meditation and prayer the monk shall join the spirit of compunction. His intimacy with God does not dispense him from remembering ever that he is a sinner. So he shall replace worldly joy by tears and

---

[1] *Cf.* S. BASIL., *Reg. fus.*, xvii.
[2] *Vita B. Martini*, xxvi. P.L., XX., 175-176.

heartfelt lamentation; and, in proportion as this compunction is sincere, he shall watch that he commits his former faults no more, and shall undertake a serious reform of his life.[1]

Our watchfulness should be directed to the two sources of evil which are in us: the spirit and the flesh; for the whole man suffers if either is affected. The passions of the flesh are far from being the more formidable; for those of the spirit are more treacherous and merit well the hatred which St. Benedict requires. "Go not after thy desires and turn away from thine own will," says Ecclesiasticus.

To help us to triumph over all the forms of self-love, Our Lord has substituted for our wills His Divine Will, manifesting itself by the medium of a created authority. So our Holy Father traces for us a whole scheme of perfection and security when he writes: "To obey in all things the commands of the Abbot, even though he himself (which God forbid) should act otherwise: being mindful of that precept of the Lord: 'What they say, do ye; but what they do, do ye not.'"

St. Benedict next warns us wittily against a rather subtle temptation which may arise in religious souls. It is not wise to believe too soon that one has reached the "transforming union." When a monk admires himself and aims at being canonized by his brethren, it is a certain sign that he is still far from sanctity. The author of the letter *ad Celantiam matronam*, which appears among the letters of St. Jerome, gives the same warning to his correspondent: "Beware lest beginning to fast or abstain you think yourself already a saint."[2] Let us first become saints, if we would like to be justly called such; and with this purpose let us strive each day to establish absolute agreement between our actions and the commandments of God.

63. Castitatem amare (Judith xv. 11).	63. To love chastity.
64. Nullum odire (Lev. xix. 17; Matt. v. 43 *sq.*).	64. To hate no man.
65. Zelum et invidiam non habere (Jac. iii. 14; Gal. v. 19 *sq.*).	65. Not to be jealous, nor to give way to envy.
66. Contentionem non amare (2 Tim. ii. 14).	66. Not to love strife.
67. Elationem fugere.	67. To fly from vainglory.
68. Seniores venerari (Lev. xix. 32).	68. To reverence seniors.
69. Juniores diligere (1 Tim. v. 1).[3]	68. To love juniors.
70. In Christi amore pro inimicis orare (Matt. v. 44).	70. To pray for one's enemies in the love of Christ.
71. Cum discordantibus ante solis occasum in pacem redire (Eph. iv. 26).	71. To make peace with an adversary before the setting of the sun.

[1] The same advice occurs in the Rule ascribed to St. Antony (xxv., xxx., xliv.).
[2] *Epist.* CXLVIII., 22. *P.L.*, XXII., 1214.
[3] Weyman has noted that instruments 68 and 69 are found in the *Florilegium* of the Greek compiler John of Stobi or Stobæus (III., Περὶ φρονήσεως, 80. Σωσιάδου τῶν ἑπτὰ σοφῶν ὑποθῆκαι): Πρεσβύτερον αἰδοῦ· νεώτερον διδάσκε. Weyman proposes to read in St. Benedict *dirigere* instead of *diligere*; but Traube and Butler maintain the reading. Stobæus, a pagan, was probably contemporaneous with St. Benedict (about 550). As to Sosiades, who collected the maxims of the Sages, this is all that is known of him.

"To love chastity." This is the sole passage of the Rule where formal mention is made of chastity; doubtless because this virtue is so involved in the concept of the religious life that it was unnecessary to insist on it. Ancient monastic legislators are, however, more explicit, and while St. Benedict in the course of his Rule limits himself to putting us on our guard against bad thoughts and the desires of the flesh, his predecessors did not disdain to enter into detail concerning the occasions which must be avoided and the vices which must be punished.[1] St. Benedict simply says "to love chastity," as he said above "to love fasting." But while we are asked to love fasting only with a love of appreciation and as a useful tool, we must love chastity for itself and with a true affection. For priest and for monk chastity is a part of charity, its fine flower and perfection. With it the holocaust is complete and our body contributes its share to the work of the adoration of God and union with Him. "I beseech you . . . that you present your bodies a living sacrifice, holy, pleasing unto God" (Rom. xii. 1). And St. Paul recommends the state of chastity because it is beautiful and good, and because it secures leisure for the holding of a continuous converse with the Divine Purity, "for that which is seemly and which may give you power to attend upon the Lord without impediment" (1 Cor. vii. 35). In the enumeration of the fruits of the Spirit, where charity is first, chastity ends the list and seems to sum all up in itself: "Charity, joy, peace . . . continency, chastity" (Gal. v. 22-23). The exercise of charity, says St. Thomas, is most spontaneous, because, more than any other habit, charity has a powerful inclination towards its act; and the rest of the virtues borrow their facility from it. The preservation of chastity becomes an easy and delightful task so soon as it is subsumed into charity. And does it always require an heroic struggle to remain pure when one is far from the world, in touch with God, using prayer and study, and employing a detailed prudence, proportionate to the value of that which we wish to safeguard?

The instruments from the sixty-fourth to the seventy-first revert to the subject of fraternal charity. We have no right to indulge in estrangement or aversion from anyone whatsoever. Animosity, envy, and jealousy are proscribed. Even argument is rarely opportune: "Not to love strife. To fly from vainglory." In dispute or argument of a somewhat lively character, there constantly emerges some inordinate esteem of our own ideas and a tendency towards display. The discussion is often interminable and pure loss, since it is much less a question of principles than of mere accidentals.

Fraternal charity is wise even in the nuances of life. In every community old and young are side by side. The first have the experience of age, the second have vigour and spirit; the former love calm, the latter are restless; and it is not a very rare thing to find them forming two groups with opposing tendencies. Our Holy Father's design is to prevent rivalry and petty troubles, to unite the two ages in mutual

[1] *Cf.* MARTÈNE, *in h. loc.*

affection, to gather all souls together round the Abbot, and so by him close to God. So there will be respect and reverence for the old, and these in their turn will show affection and condescension towards the young. The same formula is repeated in Chapter LXIII.[1]

If, despite all the efforts of our charity, there be brethren who make themselves our enemies, there remains to us the last resource of praying for them, in union with Christ who taught this counsel of evangelical perfection and Himself practised it on the cross. We must also know how to effect a reconciliation with those who may have had some disagreement with us. Virtual reconciliation—that is, a reconciliation which is not formal but is implied in our attitude—is often sufficient and is the best. We should make peace quickly, or at least " before the setting of the sun," which should be the limit. It were even better to make Our Lord wait than to postpone reconciliation: " Go first and be reconciled with thy brother, and then come and offer thy gift " (Matt. v. 24).

72. Et de Dei misericordia nunquam desperare.	72. And never to despair of God's mercy.

This last recommendation has in the Christian life almost the value of the first, of which it seems an echo: for to be confident always of God's love no matter what may happen is to love Him truly: " I have hoped in the mercy of God for ever, yea for ever and ever " (Ps. li. 10). In making this instrument the last of the whole series our Holy Father seems to say to us: " Even though you should have neglected the others, grasp your soul again and set yourself face to face with duty." Every fault and every error of detail should stir in us a twofold movement, of regret and of confidence. The first is indispensable, but it should be expeditious and should never be alone. Perhaps the most formidable thing in our daily failings is not the fault itself, but the weariness, heaviness, discouragement, and disillusionment that it leaves after it. We promised perfect fidelity, and lo, how we have failed of its perfection! The spell is broken, done with, shattered, like the glass-drop that goes to dust when we break its point. And till next confession, or till some strong movement of grace, the soul will remain in the gloomy contemplation of its weakness.

True, it is a painful thing to be always running on the same rock, or always cleaning up the same dirt; it would be far sweeter to unite oneself to Our Lord for ever by a single act, like the angels. However, there is a good side even to these perpetual jerks and oscillations. For when all is said, to return to God when one has been misled, to make it up with Him, to put our whole soul back at His feet, this is an act of perfect charity. It is not impossible that these falls have contributed much to

---

[1] The *Rule of* SS. PAUL *and* STEPHEN says in gracious terms: *Seniores junioribus affectum paternum impendant et cum imperandi necessarium fuerit, non tumenti animositate et clamosis vocibus, sed fiducialiter, tranquilla simplicitate et auctoritate bonæ vitæ ad peragendam communem utilitatem quæ fuerint opportuna injungant* (c. ii.).

our progress. In any case they invite us to greater watchfulness and teach us the little or nothing that we are. Whatever our weakness may have been God has not changed, His arms are always open. Let us remember the father of the Prodigal Son, and the Good Samaritan, and other gospel parables, in which is enshrined for ever the form of divine mercy.

Ecce hæc sunt instrumenta artis spiritualis: quæ cum fuerint a nobis die noctuque incessabiliter adimpleta, et in die judicii reconsignata, illa merces nobis a Domino recompensabitur, quam ipse promisit: *Quod oculus non vidit, nec auris audivit, nec in cor hominis ascendit, quæ præparavit Deus his qui diligunt eum.* Officina vero ubi hæc omnia diligenter operemur, claustra sunt monasterii, et stabilitas in congregatione.

Behold, these are the tools of the spiritual craft, which, if they be constantly employed day and night, and duly given back on the Day of Judgement, will gain for us from the Lord that reward which He Himself has promised—"which eye hath not seen, nor ear heard; nor hath it entered into the heart of man to conceive what God hath prepared for them that love him." And the workshop where we are to labour diligently at all these things is the cloister of the monastery, and stability in the community.

This conclusion contains conditions and a promise. The promise is that Our Lord will give His workman the wage agreed on: a recompense that the eye of man has not seen, that his ear has never heard described, whose worth the secret presentiments of his heart have never led him to suspect (Isa. lxiv. 4; 1 Cor. ii. 9). This will be God Himself. We purchase God, we win Eternal Beauty, by means of these few good works; surely we shall not have laboured in vain. But we must employ and use properly the tools of the spiritual craft.[1] The Father of the household has entrusted them to us, all in good condition; He keeps a list of them in His infallible memory; He knows what each of them can achieve; He will demand an exact account of them from us on the Day of Judgement when we return them to Him: "duly given back on the Day of Judgement." St. Benedict perhaps alludes to the practice on the great Roman estates where the farmer would receive all the tools necessary to work the land profitably, the owner keeping an exact inventory of them.[2] The labour demanded of us must be persevering and free from negligence: "constantly employed night and day—labour diligently at all these things"; for the spiritual craft is the most delicate of all and does not tolerate slothful or capricious workmen.

Like every trade and every craft, it is only practised well in a special workshop, in appointed and appropriate surroundings. The best tools become useless if the farmer is a gadabout. "For the farmer should not be a lounger, nor go beyond his estate, except it be to learn some method of husbandry; and this if it be near enough for him to return

[1] *Cf.* CASSIAN, *Conlat.*, I., vii.
[2] VARRO, *De re rustica*, l. I., c. xxii.—COLUMELLA, *De re rust.*, l. I., c. viii. In Chapters XXXII. and XXXV. St. Benedict expresses himself in almost the same terms as these writers with regard to the implements and tools of the monastery.

quickly."[1] Similarly, in the eyes of our Holy Father, the work of religious perfection is only carried on successfully in the enclosure of a monastery where one abides, in the bosom of a family which one never quits: " the cloister of the monastery and stability in the community." Enclosure and stability realize our separation from the world: thanks to the enclosure, the world does not reach us; thanks to stability we do not go to it. Until the sixth century the great curse of monasticism was instability and contact with the world; and it is easy to see that St. Benedict is continually counteracting this perilous custom.[2]

Stability is a mark of Benedictinism, and we should hold to it as to a family possession. We are free and at home only in our cloister, and we should love it as the surety of our vocation itself. We may say that nuns enjoy the ideal monastic enclosure, the privilege in its entirety. We may envy them and instead of finding reasons for leaving enclosure, seek means not to leave it. Undoubtedly the interpretation of the law of enclosure, as of that of poverty, belongs to the Abbot, and filial obedience fixes the measure and the meaning of monastic duty; but we should in our hearts keep a love of enclosure, even though due obedience may cause us to break it in the letter. There are external works which remain compatible with the essential requirements of stability; but in proportion as these works withdraw us more from the normal conditions of our life, there is need of a more and more formal and explicit ruling of the Abbot to bind us to them. Save in cases of necessity—and superiors should strive prudently to reduce their number—we have no reason to meddle with apostolic works, social questions, or politics. St. Benedict has bidden us only employ the tools of the spiritual craft, and these in the cloister.

[1] COLUMELLA, *loc. cit.*
[2] Read the end of the Prologue, the protest against gyrovagues in Chapter I., the end of Chapter LIII., and Chapters LVIII., LXI., LXVI., LXVII.

CHAPTER V

OF OBEDIENCE

DE OBEDIENTIA DISCIPULORUM.—Primus humilitatis gradus est obedientia sine mora. Hæc convenit iis qui nihil sibi Christo carius existimant. Propter servitium sanctum quod professi sunt, seu propter metum gehennæ, vel gloriam vitæ æternæ, mox ut aliquid imperatum a majore fuerit, ac si divinitus imperetur, moram pati nesciunt in faciendo. De quibus Dominus dicit: *In auditu auris obedivit mihi.* Et item dicit doctoribus: *Qui vos audit, me audit.*

The first degree of humility is obedience without delay. This becomes those who hold nothing dearer to them than Christ, and who on account of the holy servitude which they have taken upon them, and for fear of hell, and for the glory of life everlasting, as soon as anything is ordered by the superior, just as if it had been commanded by God Himself, are unable to bear delay in doing it. It is of these that the Lord says: "At the hearing of the ear he hath obeyed me." And again, to teachers he saith: "He that heareth you heareth me."

THERE is no contradiction between the teaching with which this chapter begins and the teaching of Chapter VII., where obedience is represented as the third degree of humility; the point of view is different. The obedience which is spoken of here is not a special degree, with a second and a third to follow: St. Benedict insists on its sovereign value and declares that it is the summit, the "apex," the gist and most complete expression of humility. In fact, he is not treating of any sort of obedience, but of ready and loving obedience, which is the only true obedience, the only kind worthy of God and of ourselves; our Holy Father did not care to suppose that monks could be content with attenuated and lower forms of obedience. St. Benedict regards humility in the same way as in Chapter VII.; it is less a particular virtue, than a state, a temperament, a fixed moral disposition. Obedience and humility, conceived as St. Benedict conceives them, may be defined by each other; if they are distinct, it is as cause and effect, or as sign and reality: the acts of obedience prepare us and lead us to humility—that is to say, to being before God what we should be; and the perfection of this attitude, the attainment of humility, is prompt obedience.

We may recognize three divisions in this chapter: the motives of obedience, its external qualities, its interior perfection.

The mere fact of being creatures, and intelligent creatures, implies obedience. When God created, as theology tells us, He was not determined to the act or solicited by anything; but He had a design, and He has assigned an end, not for Himself and His action, but for things themselves. Creation has a moral end, a programme conceived externally by God and realizing itself in time under the hand of His omnipotence. The end of creatures ist he good; and the essential good of a creature is to be what God wishes it to be, to do what He wishes it to do, to move by its acts whither He wishes to lead it—that is to say, to the manifestation of the divine attributes. Everything co-operates after its kind, by means of the spontaneous activity of its being, in the execution of a vast general plan, the harmony of which we shall only appreciate in heaven; nothing may step aside and follow its own caprice; it is a harmony without discordant note. Ontologically every creature remains true and good: for it is from God and for God. All creation obeys and obeys well, with perfect pliancy, even miraculously; God may always expect from it what St. Benedict calls in Chapter LXXI. the "*obedientiæ bonum.*" And this universal subjection makes an imposing spectacle. But the material creation does the good without knowing it; *cæli enarrant gloriam Dei*, the heavens which sing the glory of God do not understand their song. Man alone is God's conscious and voluntary workman. His function and his happiness is to take part freely in the concord of creation, to be the loving fellow-worker of God. And every law which comes to us with authority tells us only how we may help God to realize His programme of good and beauty. Here we have the exact meaning of obedience.

The same is true and especially true of the supernatural sphere. And if our Holy Father gives us motives for our obedience more attractive and efficacious than that philosophical and rather stoic counsel: "Unite yourself with the universe," does he not, nevertheless, from the Prologue onwards, depict the monk as the favoured workman for whom God looks? Does he not here too invoke the "holy service" which the religious has vowed? And does he not describe obedience as the practical conformity of our aims with those of God?

All motives call upon us to give ready obedience: loyalty, prudence, hope, and charity. Some men regard obedience as fidelity to the promises of their profession: we have given our word; and certainly on that day we did not promise to disobey nor make any reservation. Others remember that hell was made to engulf the rebellious angels; to them obedience presents itself as the very condition of their security; and though this be not the highest of motives, still it is good and supernatural. Others, again, make obedience an exercise of the virtue of hope; for, knowing that the promised reward is eternal life, they turn to obedience as to the price of future glory.

But the deepest motive of obedience, the motive which precedes all the rest, and of which they are but partial expressions, is charity. Prompt obedience, says St. Benedict, befits those who hold nothing dearer to them than Christ (compare the twenty-first instrument of good works). Does it seem easy and ordinary to prefer nothing to Our Lord? It may be so; but practically, unknown perhaps to ourselves, there are often things which we love better than Him: some passion, idea, project, or desire. Hence come all our resistance, laziness, delay, difficulties. As long as we have our own personal programme, as long as we determine our own aim and the employment of our activity, so long we are not free and God is not free in us, perfect obedience is not yet ours. But from the day that we love nothing apart from God or more than God, we become in His hand a power which He can wield, a force He can utilize as He wills. How important it is not to build up again the edifice of our own will, which we threw down at the beginning of our monastic life! As we grow older there is this tendency, and sometimes our obedience itself becomes a snare. We should never unlearn the simplicity and unaffectedness of our first submission, since the thoroughness of our obedience will always be the true measure of our progress in the spiritual life.

Those who love Christ, says St. Benedict, cannot endure a delay in the execution of an order; delays are to them impossible: *moram pati nesciunt in faciendo*. They have recognized the beloved voice of their Lord.[1] The person of the superior, whatever his character and his faults, never furnishes them with an excuse for refusal. They make no distinction between what comes directly from God and what comes from Him through the medium of a man. They always obey God; as Our Lord Himself says to His representatives: " He that heareth you, heareth me" (Luke x. 16). To them, things have colour and savour only in so far as God wills them or loves them; they are indifferent until their relation to the will of God is clear: *mox ut aliquid imperatum a majore fuerit*.[2] The simple doctrinal fact that all our obedience has God for its end gives us the measure of its dignity and its merit; it also entails promptitude; and, with pride at being so well heard and understood, God commends it in the words: " At the hearing of the ear they have obeyed me " (Ps. xvii. 45).

It is only right that God should congratulate Himself on our obedience, since it is His work. We should understand this well. Our souls are sanctuaries, sanctuaries of the living God. The life of Our Lord has been poured out in us; and all the work of the Church has no other end than this, to ensure in each and in all the perfect growth of Christ. This is elementary and familiar doctrine. But perhaps it is a less familiar fact that in the supernatural order no work has real value or extent except such as proceeds from this treasure of the divine life which is given to us. Nor is our obedience perfect until it has become a profound and permanent deference towards Him who lives in our hearts. Surely the most finished form of obedience is to give oneself to every good work under the interior impulse of God and His Holy Spirit. Is not this the sense in which the Apostle says that to suffer oneself to be led by the Spirit of God is to be truly a child of God? And so God inclines us towards obedience, not merely by objective and external means, not only by suggesting to us motives of the natural or the supernatural order, but also by making us share within our souls in the life, the powers, the virtues of Him who became obedient unto death, even to the death of the cross.

It would be very easy to complete the praises of obedience and to

---

[1] A reminiscence of CASSIAN, *Inst.*, IV., x., xxiv.; XII., xxxii.
[2] *Statimque cum tibi a majore fuerit imperatum* (S. PACH., *Reg.*, xxx.).

show that while remaining, like the virtue of religion, a moral virtue, it is nevertheless in contact with the theological virtues, which have God directly for their object and which unite us to Him. Obedience prepares the way for these virtues and is in a way permeated by them; from the point of view of its positive content, it practically implies the exercise of them. It is *faith*, since we express our belief in the will of God who conceals Himself in the person of our superior. It is *hope*, since we make God's plan our own, for time and for eternity. It is *charity*, since filial obedience as much as friendship realizes the definition: *idem velle, idem nolle;* and especially because, according to St. John: " He that keepeth his word, in him in very deed the charity of God is perfected. And by this we know that we are in him " (1 John ii. 5). Furthermore, obedience implies the exercise of adoration in spirit and in truth, the essential homage which God asks from His redeemed creatures. We may say of obedience that it sums up Christianity: " He that doth the will of my Father who is in heaven, he shall enter into the kingdom of heaven " (Matt. vii. 21).

Ergo hi tales relinquentes statim quæ sua sunt, et voluntatem propriam deserentes, mox exoccupatis manibus, et quod agebant imperfectum relinquentes, vicino obedientiæ pede, jubentis vocem factis sequuntur; et veluti uno momento prædicta magistri jussio, et perfecta discipuli opera, in velocitate timoris Dei, ambæ res communiter citius explicantur, quibus ad vitam æternam gradiendi amor incumbit.

Such as these, therefore, leaving immediately all that is theirs, and forsaking their own will, with their hands disengaged and leaving unfinished what they were about, with the ready step of obedience, follow by their deeds the voice of him who commands; and so, as it were at the same instant, the bidding of the master and the perfect work of the disciple are together more perfectly fulfilled in the swiftness of the fear of God, by those upon whom presses the desire of attaining eternal life.

Here are given the qualities of obedience. The first is promptitude. St. Benedict has pointed to it already, but it seems to him so characteristic of true obedience that he takes pleasure in describing it, heaping up synonyms and most expressive images in what is perhaps the most elaborate passage in the whole of the Rule.

An obedient man does not hesitate. Not only does he not look for excuses in order to evade his duty, he even dispenses with all deliberation and reasoning before he acts. Whatever the order may be and whencesoever it may come, it always finds him ready. Nature has equipped us poorly for this spontaneous action, this resolute simplicity. All change puts us out. Only with effort do we modify the state of our bodies, whether towards rest or towards motion; and, even without appealing to purely material beings, we know quite well that when we apply ourselves to any work our activity converges on it in such a way, that if we are called to leave it in order to begin another, some internal shock is inevitable; there rises within us a secret protest, a sort of involuntary hesitation. But in the man who has attained true obedience, we no longer find any trace of this "first movement." He leaves his work at once, he abandons his own will—that is to say, his preference, his interest of the moment. His business falls from his hands and they are free. What matters it that his work is unfinished ?[1] It may be taken up again if there be a chance; but it is not right that God should wait. For God has spoken, and for the obedient man there are only two things in the world, God and God's will with him. His obedience, so to say, keeps step with his commander; the execution of an order follows the order at once and closely. Or, rather, there is no appreciable interval between the one and the other: for in some sort these two things, the logically prior order of the master and its fulfilment by the disciple, occur in the same rapid instant of time, indivisibly.

Obedience so described is a far different thing from the obedience that reproduces the passivity and inertia of a corpse, or the unthinking docility of the stick that we brandish in our hands.[2] It is said that a good commander ought to have his forces well in hand, so as to get from them with spirit and unity the maximum efficiency at the exact moment that it is needed. So is it with the obedient soul; true mastery, true interior sovereignty, is to have all one's vital forces in hand, well known and marshalled, so as to make them co-operate at the exact moment in the work which God asks from us. The soul is become an activity, but one which is always supple and always free, even in the act of its employment; it is perfectly intelligent and gives to things their real value; it applies itself or detaches itself at God's will, through God and for God. The extraordinary promptitude of its obedience comes solely from its fear of God: *in velocitate timoris Dei;* it fears to please Him less; it is afraid of losing or checking its intercourse with God. Such a soul loves, and has no other desire than that of mounting quickly the road to eternal life: *quibus ad vitam æternam gradiendi amor incumbit.*

Ideo angustam viam arripiunt; unde Dominus dicit: *Angusta via est, quæ ducit ad vitam;* ut non suo arbitrio viventes, vel desideriis suis, et voluptatibus obedientes, sed ambulantes alieno judicio et imperio, in cœnobiis degentes, Abbatem sibi præesse desiderant. Sine dubio hi tales illam Domini sententiam imitantur, qua dicit: *Non veni facere voluntatem meam, sed ejus qui misit me.*

These therefore choose the narrow way, of which the Lord says: "Narrow is the way which leadeth unto life"; so that living not by their own will, nor obeying their own desires and pleasures, but walking according to the judgement and command of another, they live in community, and desire to have an Abbot over them. Such as these without doubt fulfil that saying of the Lord: "I came not to do mine own will, but the will of him who sent me."

Shall we then calculate meanly and anxiously whether obedience has hardships, whether authority is sufficiently regulated, whether

[1] *Cf.* Cass., *Inst.*, IV., xii.
[2] When the masters of the spiritual life use these comparisons they merely wish to express the perfect pliancy of the obedient soul, dead to its own will. *Cf.* S. Nili *Liber de monastica exercitatione,* c. xli. *P.G.,* LXXIX., 769-772.—*Constitutiones Societatis Jesu,* P. VI., c. i. *Institutum Soc. J.* (Prague, 1757), vol. i., p. 408.

an order is easy or not? God and eternity are at stake; what matter, then, the difficulties of the road? It is the only one: *scientes se per hanc obedientiæ viam ituros ad Deum* (knowing that by this way of obedience they will go to God), as St. Benedict says towards the end of his Rule. Our Lord Himself says the same: " Narrow is the way which leadeth to life." Yet we must enter by it. And it is only narrow because our hearts are narrow; it becomes a royal and triumphal road so soon as we open them to God.

When they have once recognized that eternal life is only to be won by obedience, generous souls will choose their lot. We shall think no more of living as we will, of satisfying our desires and inclinations. We shall travel towards God, guided by the thought and the will of others; we shall live hidden in a monastery; like true cenobites, we shall willingly consent to have an Abbot over us, we shall readily accept this perpetual subjection: *Abbatem sibi præesse desiderant*.[1] How contrary is all this to the conception of obedience which worldly people have forged themselves! Monks do not submit through compulsion, or weakness, or incapacity, or lack of initiative.

When our obedience is such as St. Benedict wishes it to be, then the imitation of Our Lord is made perfect in us. " I am not come to do mine own will, but the will of him who sent me." All God's victories are won by obedience; it was so with that of which St. Michael was the instrument, it was so with the Incarnation, whether looked at from the side of Our Lord or of Our Lady; it was so with the Redemption, and in the Holy Eucharist Our Lord has found the means of being obedient unto the end. The obedient, therefore, are in good company. And in the face of such facts, the most elementary facts of our religion, what is all disobedience but disorder and folly?

Sed hæc ipsa obedientia tunc acceptabilis erit Deo, et dulcis hominibus, si quod jubetur, non trepide, non tarde, non tepide, aut cum murmure vel cum responso nolentis efficiatur; quia obedientia quæ majoribus præbetur, Deo exhibetur. Ipse enim dixit: *Qui vos audit, me audit.*

But this very obedience will then be acceptable to God and sweet to men, if what is commanded be done not fearfully, tardily, nor lukewarmly, nor with murmuring, nor with an answer showing unwillingness; for the obedience which is given to superiors is given to God, since He Himself has said: " He that heareth you, heareth me."

Truly St. Benedict is anxious to make sure of the perfection of our obedience; therefore he insists at the end of this chapter on its interior qualities. It should become, he first says, " acceptable to God and sweet to men." *Acceptabilis Deo.* We remarked above that God takes

---

[1] St. Benedict once more contrasts the ideal of the cenobite with that of the sarabaite or gyrovague. His words recall CASSIAN, *Conlat.*, XXIV., xxvi. (*cf. Conlat.*, XVIII., vii.), and SULPICIUS SEVERUS: *Summum jus est (cœnobitis), sub abbatis imperio vivere, nihil arbitrio suo agere, per omnia ad nutum illius potestatemque pendere. . . . Hæc illorum prima virtus est, parere alieno imperio* (*Dial.* I., c. x. P.L., XX., 190).

pride and pleasure in the obedience of His human creatures, even as He took pride in the fidelity of Job or the charity of St. Martin. Without any intention of making little of the obedience of the angels, we may be permitted to remark that it fulfils itself in a single act, which costs them no suffering, coming as it does from a nature which is perfectly balanced and not dislocated like ours; they have no martyrs, and no virgins.[1]

Perhaps, then, God's success is more apparent in us, where obedience is checked and thwarted by so many perverse solicitations; we are forced to repeat our acts of submission over and over again and to be recapturing incessantly our elusive nature. We are preparing a great triumph for God, " When he shall come to be glorified in his saints and to be made wonderful in all them who have believed " (2 Thess. i. 10).

The final end, then, of our obedience is to please God. But, while that is the essential point, St. Benedict requires something more: *et dulcis hominibus.* This is a spirituality far removed from some modern conceptions, where, on pretext of seeing only God and referring all to Him, it is alleged that pleasure should not intervene in questions of duty, and that we degrade our obedience if we seek in it a personal joy, and *a fortiori* doubtless if we seek the pleasure of others. Our Holy Father knows that happiness is the end of all life and that God has devoted thereto the first desire of our souls. And, in the monastic life, charity and obedience, which rule all our behaviour, have for their result and even for their end to make us all happy together. " All do all things and suffer all things that they may be glad and rejoice."[2] It is far from true that to seek to lighten the task of those who rule us and to be agreeable to them, is too human and too dangerous.

Obedience will be sweet to God and man, and earth will become heaven ("Thy will be done on earth as it is in heaven") if the order we have received is fulfilled under certain fixed conditions. *Non trepide*—that is, without hesitation or fear: for there are not two sides between which our soul may waver irresolute; there is only one, the side of God. *Non tarde*, without delay, as though there were in us a *vis inertiæ* which hinders obedience. *Non tepide*,[3] without lukewarmness, the soul lacking vigour and remaining as though weighed down by a secret affection which it keeps for some other object. *Aut cum murmure*, without any of that murmuring of which St. Benedict soon speaks explicitly; and finally and *a fortiori*, without protest or a bad grace: *vel cum responso nolentis*. And, after this exactly graduated description, St. Benedict repeats that the primary motive of obedience is that we obey God. We are uncompromising and proud enough to obey none but the Lord of heaven and earth.

[1] *Cf.* S. JOANN. CHRYS., *De virginitate*, x.-xi. P.G., XLVIII., 540.
[2] S. JOANN. CHRYS., *Adversus oppugnatores vitæ monasticæ*, l. III., 11. P.G., XLVII., 366.
[3] . . . *Trepidas et tepidas contradictiunculas* (S. AUG., *De consensu Evangel.*, l. I., 13. P.L., XXXIV., 1048). *De emissa tardius vel tepidius oratione deflemus* (CASS., *Conlat*, XXIII., vii.).

Et cum bono animo a discipulis præberi oportet, quia *hilarem datorem diligit Deus*. Nam cum malo animo si obedit discipulus, et non solum ore, sed etiam corde si murmuraverit: etsi impleat jussionem, tamen acceptus jam non erit Deo, qui cor respicit murmurantis; et pro tali facto nullam consequitur gratiam; immo murmurantium pœnam incurrit, si non cum satisfactione emendaverit.

And it ought to be given by disciples with a good will, because " God loves a cheerful giver." For if the disciple obey with ill-will, and not merely murmur with his lips but even in his heart, although he fulfil the command, yet he will not be accepted by God, who regards the heart of the murmurer. And for such an action he shall gain no reward; nay, rather, he shall incur the punishment due to murmurers, unless he amend and make satisfaction.

We may distinguish three kinds of obedience: of act, of will, and of thought. The first is necessary, who doubts it? But is it enough? It is—to make a Jew or a slave. That is true servitude, when our members reluctantly execute what our will disapproves; the harmony is only material and external. Unless the grace of God and education have made us supple beforehand, our obedience is apt to be, to start with, rough and mechanical, something like those angular characters which our childish hands traced when the teacher held them in his own. In a reasonable being it is necessary, for real obedience, that the will, ranging itself alongside the will of another, should adopt and make its own the order that is given. But to live " by the judgement and will of another " is in St. Benedict's eyes[1] a thing of still greater perfection.

We can well conceive this attitude: " My superior orders this. I shall do it, I wish to do it, and as well as I can. But it is absurd. It is obvious that there are better things to do." There we have no obedience of the understanding; there is rapine in the holocaust, it has lost its marrow. This may be military obedience, but it is not the obedience of a monk. " Very well," it may be answered, " perhaps your teaching is deduced from the text of the Rule; but it asks too much. In order to understand monastic obedience in that way, we shall have to believe in the universal infallibility of superiors. The Pope himself is only infallible in certain matters and under special conditions; but I must believe, according to this theory, that the first authority I meet is infallible, always and everywhere and in all circumstances. You ask me for too radical an abdication: I cannot go so far." It is a pity, I reply, for you are not, and you never will be an obedient man. And look what follows. Since we are all of one piece and since will must be guided by thought, you will not escape, even though you be a modernist, the psychological law of continuity and unity. Your obedience rests for a time on feeling alone or on habit; but little by little intellect must triumph over will. And then, because you would not give all, you will give nothing; you will attain, by degrees, the tranquil and obstinate exercise of your own will and contempt of obedience.

" Am I then bound to believe that the prescribed action is the best

---

[1] As for St. Ignatius in his celebrated letter *De virtute obedientiæ*.

possible?" There is no question at all of the absolutely good or the absolutely better. God is the absolute good. As soon as one enters the region of created things, the absolutely good no longer exists for practical purposes. It would be absurd to require it of a creature. God Himself does not achieve it outside Himself: the world is not the best of all possible worlds; and supernatural mysteries have their absolute grandeur only because they imply and contain God. You must require from your superiors only the good, and that a good which is fitted to a whole and will not disturb its harmony. Practically speaking, for each one of us, the absolute good is that which we are ordered in the name of God. Undoubtedly the Abbot is not infallible; but for all that he has his mission, he is given a grace of state, he is well and fully informed. And what matter if he is wrong? Provided that authority does not outstep its limits and does not command evil, we ordinary men cannot err and are infallible in always obeying.

With obedience of act, of will, and of thought, all is complete, but on condition that this full gift be offered with a good heart: *cum bono animo*. We give to God, not only without measure, but gladly and gracefully, with a smile and the regret that we cannot give more: "Everyone as he hath determined in his heart, not with sadness or of necessity, for God loveth a cheerful giver" (2 Cor. ix. 7).[1] If your heart is bitter and angry, *cum malo animo*, if there escape you words of protest or merely secret murmurings, your sacrifice is there, without doubt; but God does not accept such mere material sacrifices; in the Old Testament they were hateful to Him (Ps. xlix.); He wants the offering of a good will, and it is to such that His eyes are turned.[2] And what would be the result of a mere formal submission? Such a submission experiences all the small trials that obedience brings, but none of its recompense and its joy; more than this, it incurs the punishment reserved for murmurers by monastic discipline. St. Benedict alludes, in ending, to the penances of the rule, and to the humiliations which monks will spontaneously impose on themselves, when having caught themselves in a struggle with obedience, though but for a moment, they wish to destroy for ever so dangerous a tendency.

All the teaching of this chapter is, we may say, illustrated by the example of St. Maurus, and is admirably summarized in an antiphon of his office: *O beatum virum, qui spreto sæculo jugum sanctæ Regulæ a teneris annis amanter portavit; et factus obediens usque ad mortem, semetipsum abnegavit, ut Christo totus adhæreret.*[3]

---

[1] St. Paul alludes to a text of Ecclesiasticus of which St. Benedict also was thinking: *Bono animo gloriam redde Deo et non minuas primitias manuum tuarum; in omni dato hilarem fac vultum tuum* (xxxv., 10-11).

[2] We should read: *cor ejus respicit murmurantem.*

[3] O blessed man, who despising the world did lovingly bear the yoke of the Holy Rule from early youth; and, being made obedient unto death, denied himself that he might cleave wholly to Christ.

CHAPTER VI

THE SPIRIT OF SILENCE

OUR activity expresses itself in two ways, in work and in word: obedience determines the first, the law of silence rules the second. Our Holy Father obviously attaches considerable importance to silence; he devotes an entire chapter to it, and this he places among the chapters which describe the fundamental dispositions of the monastic character; he returns to it in Chapters VII., XXXVIII., XLII., XLVIII., LII., and alludes to it elsewhere also.

We must not mistake the true meaning of the word *taciturnitas* which St. Benedict uses. To our ears " taciturnity " has an evil sound. A taciturn man is for us a self-centred, almost a crafty or cunning man; but St. Benedict had no thought of introducing such a character among his disciples. The Latin word means neither taciturnity nor simply silence, but rather the disposition to keep silence, the habit and the love of silence, the spirit of silence.

Does this chapter institute perpetual silence? St. Hildegard condemns absolute silence in the words which we quoted in the first chapter: *Inhumanum est hominem in taciturnitate semper esse et non loqui.*[1] Speech has been given to us as the normal method of our intercourse with our kind; and when men are grouped together in community it seems natural *a priori* that they should use it, at least for that intercourse which is indispensable to the life of body and soul. Nor has anyone ventured to condemn the tongue to perpetual silence; for all rules make it lawful to speak to one's superior and to praise God with the lips. With these exceptions, because of the innumerable evils which spring from the tongue, it has sometimes been held expedient to forbid all verbal intercourse. Such a measure is a bold one. It is the literal and material application of the gospel counsel: " If thy right eye scandalize thee, pluck it out and cast it from thee . . . if thy right hand scandalize thee, cut it off and cast it from thee " (Matt. v. 29–30). To repress temptation, this is plainly a sovereign remedy; and, if applied universally it would suppress at once both sin and the sinner. Not to speak that we may not transgress in word, is then a possible method. Without trying to determine whether it is the most perfect method we may at least ask ourselves if it effects its purpose. Alas! it does not. In the first place because strained and exasperated nature often contrives ingenious escapes from so rigorous a law; and, above all, because the régime of signs and symbols, which must replace speech, presents the same dangers of dissipation along with new perils. Jealousy and misunderstanding are not banished; nay, they may even take a more formidable character than among people who converse, for these

[1] *Reg. S. Bened. Explanatio. P.L.*, CXCVII., 1056.

know one another better, and can exchange explanations. Experience proves, too, that the true silence of the soul may be obtained in another manner.

But what is the thought of our Holy Father on this point? It is enough to read without prejudice, not only this present chapter, but also many other passages which may easily be found. The Rule provides for good and useful conversation; it orders silence more or less strict according to time and place; it proclaims it sometimes more insistently, sometimes more gently; it requires us to abstain at all times from scurrility, and in Lent to have fewer and more serious conversations. The intention of Chapter VI. is less to legislate on the subject of silence than to remind us of principles, to remind us that every real monastic life should be a life of recollection. *Omni tempore silentio debent studere monachi* (Chapter XLII).

But let us say a few words on the traditional practice. Absolute or quasi-absolute silence has always been the exception, even in the East, and in the times of primitive fervour.[1] Certainly the ancient monks spoke much less than we do, and worldly conversation was banned. Yet they did speak. The Rule of St. Basil, for instance, allows the breaking of silence for good reasons, in moderation and at fitting times.[2] We see, too, from the Lives of the Fathers, and from Cassian, that spiritual conversations were frequent among religious; the Rule of St. Pachomius prescribes such conversation every morning.[3] St. Benedict having made no such rule as to regular conversation, it fell to superiors and customaries to supply it. At Cluny, in the time of Udalric,[4] there were every day (with the exception of Sundays and certain feast days or days of penance) two set times when the brethren could speak in the cloister: in summer after chapter and after None, in winter after chapter and after Sext. The morning conversation scarcely exceeded half an hour, that of the afternoon lasted sometimes less than a quarter of an hour; and even this was suppressed by Peter the Venerable. The monks took advantage of these moments of leisure to renew their stocks of pens, or paper, or books, to wash their refectory cups, to sharpen their knives, etc. In some monasteries all had to be present at the talk, which began with the word *Benedicite*. Even at Cîteaux, where a rigorous silence was practised from the outset, the brethren could converse on edifying topics, if not every day, at least from time to time;[5] and many passages of St. Bernard,[6] though directly

---

[1] *Cf.* D. Besse, *Les Moines d'Orient*, p. 489-495.

[2] *Reg. contr.*, xl., cxxxiv.; *Reg. brev.*, ccviii.

[3] C. xx. *Cf.* Ladeuze, *Etude sur le cénobitisme pakhomien pendant le IV*^{e} *siècle et la premi.re moitié du V*^{e}, p. 291.

[4] Udalr., *Consuet. Clun.*, l. I., c. xviii., xl.

[5] *Silentium autem per totum fere diem observantes mutuis collocutionibus et collationibus spiritualibus unam sibi horam reservant, invicem consolantes et invicem instruentes* (Jacques de Vitry, *Historia Occidentalis*, c. xiv.).

[6] *Tractatus de duodecim gradibus superbiæ*, c. xiii. *P.L.*, CLXXXII., 964. *Sermo* XVII., *de Diversis*. *P.L.*, CLXXXIII., 583 *sq.*

concerned with the abuse of speech, allow us to suppose that speaking was at times legitimate and that these conferences had the character of real recreation.

Our recreation, provided it remains conformable to the spirit of Chapter VI., is not, then, an innovation or relaxation. To absent oneself from it would be to commit a fault against the Rule, to lose an excellent opportunity of merit, and to deprive oneself of a rest which has become indispensable now that intellectual work has taken a large place in the monastic horarium. There are relaxations which are compatible with the gravity of the religious state and habitual union with Our Lord. Even for monks εὐτραπελία (a pleasant wit) may become a moral virtue.[1]

DE TACITURNATE.—Faciamus quod ait Propheta: *Dixi, Custodiam vias meas, ut non delinquam in lingua mea: posui ori meo custodiam: obmutui, et humiliatus sum, et silui a bonis.* Hic ostendit Propheta, si bonis eloquiis interdum propter taciturnitatem debet taceri, quanto magis a malis verbis propter pœnam peccati debet cessari?

Let us do as says the prophet: "I said, I will take heed to my ways, that I sin not with my tongue: I have placed a watch over my mouth; I became dumb, and was silent, and held my peace even from good things." Here the prophet shows that if we ought to refrain even from good words for the sake of silence, how much more ought we to abstain from evil words, on account of the punishment due to sin!

St. Benedict begins by laying down the principle of which the whole chapter is only the development. He borrows it, after the custom of the Fathers, from Sacred Scripture. In their literal sense these words of Psalm xxxviii. describe the silence of the just man under oppression, but St. Benedict gives them a general application; he sees in them the line of conduct suggested to all monks by prudence, wisdom, and humility. Since there is a danger of sinning with the tongue and of retarding our supernatural growth, we shall be attentive to all that passes our lips and guard them severely; we shall know how to be silent, even when good words are concerned.

The Prophet's meaning is plain. While recommending us to abstain, at times, from good discourses in the spirit of recollection, he assuredly means that we must at once suppress every evil word. Such words are positively sinful, and the fear of punishment at least should close our mouths. Certain conversations are no more permissible in the world than in the cloister; there are others which ill become religious. The spirit of the world, made up of pride, levity, and disregard of the supernatural, easily takes root in the mind of the talkative monk. Usually

---

[1] *Cf. S. Th.*, II.-II., *q.* clxviii., *a.* 2, *Utrum in ludis possit esse aliqua virtus.* The SALMANTICENSES discuss why St. Thomas has nowhere put silence among the virtues. The reason is, they say, because silence is not a special virtue: it only becomes " virtuous " by reason of the virtue which inspires it; it may imply the exercise of various virtues (*Cursus theologicus, Tract.* XII., *Arbor prædicamentalis virtutum*, ed Palmé, t. VI., pp. 503-504).

it is charity that suffers. Alas, how little remains of certain habitual conversations when all unkind criticism has been subtracted!

Ergo quamvis de bonis et sanctis ad ædificationem eloquiis, perfectis discipulis, propter taciturnitatis gravitatem, rara loquendi concedatur licentia, quia scriptum est: *In multiloquio non effugies peccatum.* Et alibi: *Mors et vita in manibus linguæ.* Nam loqui et docere magistrum condecet: tacere et audire discipulo convenit.

Therefore, on account of the importance of silence, let leave to speak be seldom granted even to perfect disciples, although their conversation be good and holy and tending to edification; because it is written: "In much speaking thou shalt not avoid sin;" and elsewhere: "Death and life are in the power of the tongue." For it becomes the master to speak and to teach, but it beseems the disciple to be silent and to listen.

Since we must avoid the faults of the tongue and their punishment, some reserve is imposed on us, even in the matter of good, pious, and edifying conversations, for not even these are without danger. St. Benedict, like the ancient monks, evidently admits the principle of spiritual conversations, but on condition that they are not multiplied, and that, under pretext of mutual assistance, the law of silence is not evaded. This law remains weighty, even for more advanced disciples, even for the perfect or those who think themselves such. And our Holy Father thus puts aside with a word the objection that these conversations can be dangerous only for novices. It is a general principle, and one enunciated by the Spirit of God, that where there is much talking it is hard to avoid sin (Prov. x. 19). And elsewhere it is written that "death and life are in the power of the tongue" (Prov. xviii. 21). "There is nothing better than the tongue and nothing worse," as the fable says. We should read in St. James the classical passage on the evils that spring from the tongue. Good conversations, then, are only good if they are authorized, short, and rare.

St. Benedict suggests one of the dangers of these spiritual conversations. Some speak, others listen; perhaps it is always the same persons who do the speaking: they are "spiritual," they have read a great deal, prayer has no more secrets for them, they are animated with a holy fervour. Or each offers advice, puts himself forward as teacher and director. But all this is often only pride and delusion; the hearers are bored and no one is profited. In a monastery all are pupils and disciples; divine instruction is given by proper authority. "It becomes the master to speak and to teach, but it beseems the disciples to be silent and to listen."[1]

Is, then, all spiritual conversation at times of recreation banned? God forbid that we should be ashamed to pronounce His Holy Name.

---

[1] The thought is CASSIAN'S: . . . *Ut indicas summum ori tuo silentium. Hic est enim primus disciplinæ actualis ingressus, ut omnium seniorum instituta atque sententias intento corde et quasi muto ore suscipias ac diligenter in pectore tuo condens ad perficienda ea potius quam ad docenda festines. Ex hoc enim cenodoxiæ perniciosa præsumptio, ex illo autem fructus spiritualis scientiæ pullulabunt* (Conlat., XIV., ix.).

But it is fitting that such subjects should be introduced quietly, and discussed with moderation, without any display. Those whose souls are habitually turned towards God do not think it necessary to proclaim the fact by eloquent protestations; their peace and happiness shine forth of themselves. We are not forbidden to speak of study in recreation time or to broach a serious subject, provided that we avoid a dogmatic tone, interminable discussions, and allusions that tend to cause dissension. We must not monopolize the conversation from beginning to finish, completely and in a very loud tone of voice, with stories which are not always very interesting and which people have often heard.

Apart from times of recreation a monk should be sparing of his words. Though the Constitutions allow him five minutes for the exchange of useful information, he will not think himself obliged to seek and multiply occasions; and when the conversation is to be longer he will obtain permission. He is able to meet his brethren without addressing them, without firing off some jest, without dissipating himself over many things. Our Holy Father says later that a wise man may be known by the sobriety of his speech; and the *Imitation*, which has some excellent pages on silence, warns us that only those can securely speak who love to be silent: *Nemo secure loquitur nisi qui libenter tacet.*

Et ideo, si quæ requirenda sunt a priore, cum omni humilitate et subjectione reverentiæ requirantur, ne plus videatur loqui quam expedit.[1]	And therefore, if anything has to be asked of a superior, let it be done with all humility and subjection of reverence, lest he seem to say more than is expedient.

The objection might be raised: Well, if spiritual conversations with one's brethren have their dangers and must be controlled, at least it is always lawful for us to talk to the Abbot and our elders. It *is* lawful, but with all humility, submission, and reverence, and without speaking more than is fitting.[2] Our Holy Father's idea is certainly not to require the disciple to lessen his intercourse with his superiors; he does not recommend him to be so restrained and formal as to weigh and prepare and count his words; but he knows that questions and objections are often put in a spirit of vainglory.

Direction of conscience itself should not become an idle chat. " I should say," wrote Bossuet to Sister Cornuau,[3] " that there seems to me a manifest defect in present-day piety: people talk too much about their prayer and their state. Instead of worrying about the degrees of prayer, they ought, without all this introspection, to pray simply

---

[1] St. Benedict continues to take his inspiration from CASSIAN, who wrote immediately after the words cited before: *Nihil itaque in conlatione seniorum proferre audeas; nisi quod interrogare te aut ignoratio nocitura aut ratio necessariæ cognitionis impulerit, ut quidam vanæ gloriæ amore distenti pro ostentatione doctrinæ ea quæ optime norunt interrogare se simulant.*

[2] *Hoc, quod dicit: ne videatur plus loqui quam expedit, non est in Regula, sed subauditio est* (HILDEMAR). As a matter of fact the manuscripts which best represent the Carlovingian and Cassinese traditions have not got this conclusion.

[3] September 17, 1690 (URBAIN et LEVESQUE, *Correspondance de Bossuet*, t. IV., p. 111).

as God gives them to pray, and not have so much to say about it." And St. John of the Cross says: "What is wanting, if there be anything wanting, is not writing or talking—there is more than enough of that—but silence and action. Moreover, talking distracts the soul, while silence joined to action produces recollection and gives the spirit a marvellous strength. Therefore, when one has made a soul know all that is necessary for its progress, it has no further need to listen to the words of others or to talk itself."[1]

We should note that even when we are speaking to God, the Gospel urges us not to be great talkers: "And when you are praying speak not much as the heathens do. For they think that in their much speaking they may be heard. Be you not therefore like to them" (Matt. vi. 7-8). And, except when divine grace calls us to prolong our prayer, St. Benedict tells us in a later chapter that prayer to be pure should be brief. Silence is one of the characteristics of God, *Non in commotione Dominus*. His greatest operations *ad extra* are achieved without noise, in mystery: "Truly thou art a hidden God, God of Israel, our Saviour" (Isa. xlv. 15). And the saints who have approached most nearly to God have become great votaries of silence.[2]

| Scurrilitates vero vel verba otiosa et risum moventia, æterna clausura in omnibus locis damnamus, et ad tale eloquium discipulum aperire os non permittimus.[3] | But as for buffoonery or silly words, such as move to laughter, we utterly condemn them in every place, nor do we allow the disciple to open his mouth in such discourse. |

Here we have a fourth and last class of conversations: buffoonery, idle words,[4] worldly talk, talk that has for sole end the causing of laughter (see the fifty-fourth and fifty-fifth instruments of good works); these are banned for ever, *æterna clausura*, and everywhere; a monk's lips shall not utter such talk. Our Holy Father interdicts it with vigour and with a certain solemnity.

He does not mean to forbid gaiety in recreation. There is wisdom in avoiding the prudery which is shocked and scandalized by everything; when we are good, the peace and innocence of childhood, its moral naïveté, return to us. Still it remains true that there are certain subjects, a certain coarseness, a certain worldly tone, which should never enter our conversation. These things are not such as to stir wholesome laughter; there are matters which one should not touch, which it is wholesome to avoid. Our own delicacy of feeling and the thought of Our Lord will save us from all imprudence.

When St. Benedict forbids frivolous conversation "in all places"

---

[1] *Letter* III., to the nuns of Veas.
[2] Read Bossuet, *Elévations sur les mystères*, XVIIIe semaine, 11e élév.
[3] *Si quis clericus aut monachus verba scurrilia, joculatoria, risumque moventia loquitur, acerrime corripiatur* (an ancient African Council, cited by the *Decree* of Gratian; *cf*. Mansi, t. III., col. 893). See also St. Jerome, *Ep.* LII., *ad Nepotianum. P.L.*, XXII., 527 sq.
[4] St. Basil thus defined idle words: *Generaliter omnis sermo qui non proficit ad aliquam gratiam fidei Christi* (*Reg. contr.*, xl.).

he leaves it to be understood that there are places where good conversation is lawful, and other places which are sacred to silence; in Chapter XLII. he speaks of sacred times. Monastic tradition determined very early that absolute silence should reign in the church and in the refectory, even outside of conventual acts. At Cluny and elsewhere the dormitory and the kitchen were added, and often the chapter room, the calefactory, the sacristy, and the cloister, especially in the part which was next the church. In order not to break silence in these privileged places a whole language of signs was adopted at Cluny[1] and Cîteaux. St. Benedict prescribes signs during meals, and before him St. Pachomius made use of the same method in certain cases.[2]

So far we have spoken of the silence of words, the only sort of silence of which our Holy Father speaks. But there is also a material silence, the absence of noise. A nun of the Visitation Order asked St. Francis de Sales what she should do to reach perfection. The holy Bishop, who doubtless knew whom he was addressing, replied: " Sister, I think Our Lord wants you to close doors quietly." A quite personal piece of advice not without its humorous sting, but one which in a large community and a sonorous house may become a general and ever appropriate recommendation. This external silence is favourable to prayer and study; one cannot pray easily in the midst of a bombardment. . . . It may not, then, be superfluous to watch one's manner of walking, of sneezing, of blowing one's nose. Need we mention the dread turmoil with which meals begin, or the cries that ring through the monastery in times of recreation?[3] All such things disappear with good taste and education, and when each remembers that he is not the only person in the world

Finally, there is interior silence. It is the very reason and end of all other sorts of silence. Though prepared and facilitated by them, yet it is very distinct from them in practice. Some souls do not care for external noise, nor take to endless conversations, and yet they are never in a state of silence. For behind the dumb lips there is a continuous hubbub of interior talk, in exact proportion to their unmortified passions. When Our Lord wished to declare the happiness and simplicity of contemplation, He said to Martha: " Martha, Martha, thou art anxious and troubled about many things." Is not this the reproach that He most often has need to address to us? Have we ever tried to review rapidly the infinite variety of objects and pictures which have just occupied the field of our interior vision? Memories, grudges, projects, regrets, vain quests, angry emotions, vexations, scruples—how many winds and waves buffet this world of our secret life! Some brother whom we see suddenly recalls a long series of experiences; and we abandon ourselves to following this foolish scent so far and so long that we do not recover ourselves. A mere detail is enough to suggest

---

[1] UDALR., *Consuet. Clun.*, l. II., c. vi.—BERNARD., *Ordo Clun.*, P. I., c. xvii.—*Constit Hirsaug.*, l. I., c. vi.-xxv.
[2] *Reg.*, cxvi.   [3] *Cf.* S. BASIL., *Reg. brev.*, cli.

a whole romance. Sometimes it is a pleasant little scene in which we review the past, or remember its joys and circumstances. Our soul becomes an entrance hall, a cinematograph, a phonograph, a kaleidoscope. The distractions of which we generally accuse ourselves are but rapid and unimportant parentheses in our lives; the serious distractions are those which control all our activity and lead it away from God.

The fundamental purpose of silence is to free the soul, to give it strength and leisure to adhere to God. It frees the soul, just as obedience gives the will its proper mastery. It has, like work, the twofold advantage of delivering us from the low tendencies of our nature and of fixing us in good. It sets us, little by little, in a serene region, *sapientum templa serena*, where we are able to speak to God and hear His voice. So silence in its turn is related to faith and charity. And just as in obedience we are not required to be slaves, so we are not to be silent in a mere access of vexation: all its protective limitations are something other than mortifications. Silence is a joyous work; and that is why, in the old Customaries, festivals were days of rigorous silence: *propter festivitatis reverentiam*. But, for the Christian soul, every day is a festival.

CHAPTER VII

OF HUMILITY

DE HUMILITATE.—Clamat nobis Scriptura divina, fratres, dicens: *Omnis qui se exaltat, humiliabitur, et qui se humiliat, exaltabitur.* Cum hæc ergo dicit, ostendit omnem exaltationem genus esse superbiæ: quod se cavere Propheta indicat, dicens: *Domine, non est exaltatum cor meum, neque elati sunt oculi mei; neque ambulavi in magnis, neque in mirabilibus super me.* Sed quid ? *Si non humiliter sentiebam, sed exaltavi animam meam; sicut ablactatus super matre sua, ita retributio in anima mea.*

The Holy Scripture cries out to us, brethren, saying: "Everyone that exalteth himself shall be humbled, and he that humbleth himself shall be exalted." In saying this, it teaches us that all exaltation is a kind of pride, against which the prophet shows himself to be on his guard when he says: "Lord, my heart is not exalted nor mine eyes lifted up; nor have I walked in great things, nor in wonders above me." And why ? "If I did not think humbly, but exalted my soul: like a child that is weaned from his mother, so wilt thou requite my soul."

THE teaching of this chapter is again based on a pronouncement of Holy Scripture, a solemn pronouncement and divine proclamation, delivered in terms so clear as to be understood even by those who are dull of hearing. "Everyone that exalteth himself shall be humbled, and he that humbleth himself shall be exalted" (Luke xiv. 11). Here is an axiom of faith, formulated by Our Lord Himself in His teaching and fulfilled first in His life; it admits of no contradiction. So we shall not consider the apparent paradox contained in the promise of glory to the humble and humiliation to the proud; it is a paradox familiar to Our Lord, and in proof we need only recall the eight beatitudes.

When Holy Scripture speaks thus and in such general terms, continues St. Benedict, it gives us to understand that every kind of personal exaltation is a form of the vice which is opposed to humility. Self-love and pride manifest themselves under the various species of exaltation, whether it be exaltation in thought—that is, arrogance; exaltation in words—that is, boastfulness; exaltation in deeds—that is, disobedience; exaltation in desire—that is, ambition; exaltation in aims—that is, presumption. The Prophet, according to his own testimony (Ps. cxxx.), was on his guard against this elation and these aims; in the depth of his heart as well as in his external action he would not so exalt himself. And why ? asks St. Benedict. Because, replies the Psalmist, if my thoughts were not humble, if I suffered my soul to be lifted up, Thou wouldst have treated it as the child that is weaned by its mother, and put away from her breast. The Psalmist had the fear of God and dreaded to lose the kindness and favour which are promised to the humble alone: "God resisteth the proud, but giveth grace to the humble" (James iv. 6).

Of Humility

Unde, fratres, si summæ humilitatis volumus culmen attingere, et ad exaltationem illam cælestem, ad quam per præsentis vitæ humilitatem ascenditur, volumus velociter pervenire, actibus nostris ascendentibus scala erigenda est, quæ in somno Jacob apparuit, per quam et descendentes et ascendentes Angeli monstrabantur. Non aliud sine dubio descensus ille et ascensus a nobis intelligitur, nisi exaltatione descendere, et humilitate ascendere. Scala vero ipsa erecta, nostra est vita in sæculo, quæ humiliato corde a Domino erigitur ad cælum. Latera enim hujus scalæ dicimus nostrum esse corpus et animam, in quibus lateribus diversos gradus humilitatis vel disciplinæ vocatio divina ascendendos inseruit.

Whence, brethren, if we wish to arrive at the highest point of humility and speedily to reach that heavenly exaltation to which we can only ascend by the humility of this present life, we must by our ever-ascending actions erect such a ladder as that which Jacob beheld in his dream, by which the angels appeared to him descending and ascending. This descent and ascent signify nothing else than that we descend by exaltation and ascend by humility. And the ladder thus erected is our life in the world, which, if the heart be humbled, is lifted up by the Lord to heaven. The sides of the same ladder we understand to be our body and soul, in which the call of God has placed various degrees of humility or discipline, which we must ascend.

The point is, then, that we must not lose God, as we shall do by exaltation, that we must remain attached to Him, as a child to its mother's breast, so as to live by Him and to grow in Him; and this is the work of humility. "Unless you be converted and become as little children, you shall not enter into the kingdom of heaven. Whosoever therefore shall humble himself as this little child, he is the greater in the kingdom of heaven" (Matt. xviii. 3-4). Do you really want God? Do you wish to go to Him rapidly and surely[1] and to attain the glorious exaltation of heaven? If so you must renounce the false exaltation of the present life and consent to be humble. Humility, it would seem, makes us descend to the confines of nothingness; and yet it is in its depths that we encounter the fulness of being. So it is more truly an ascension, for the final term of this abasement is really a lofty summit—*i.e.*, God. Therefore we must make of our lives and actions a sort of ladder of humility; we must erect the ladder of Jacob.

Let us recall the passage of Genesis (xxviii.). Jacob was in flight from the wrath of Esau. He went to sleep on a stone, and a mysterious dream showed him a ladder erected, by which angels were ascending and descending. Taken according to the literal sense this is a symbol of Divine Providence: angels go out from God as the executors of His orders and the bearers of His inspirations and graces; angels return to God as the messengers of creation, carrying to Him the prayers and works of rational creatures. Our Holy Father recalls this mission of the angels farther on; but in this place he takes the words of Genesis in an accommodated sense. "It is plain," he says, "that for us this descent and ascent signify nothing else than that we descend by exaltation and ascend by humility."

[1] *Si quis velit ad perfectionem velociter pervenire* . . . (RUFIN., *Hist. monach.* c. xxxi.—ROSWEYD, p. 484).

By humility the good angels ascended to God and were established in Him; by pride the bad angels fell from heaven. Humility alone made the difference; the same road pursued in opposite directions led the one kind to glory and the others to ruin. Now, with men as with the angels, the economy of salvation is simple, for all resolves itself into this twofold motion on the single ladder of humility. St. Benedict neglects the motion of illusory exaltation to deal only with the real exaltation, and he makes the meaning of his image clear by the details. The ladder erected to heaven is our life on this earth and all the acts that rise in a heart trained to humility. Since the ladder represents our life, we may regard body and soul, the two elements that go to the making of man, as the sides or the uprights of this ladder. In these uprights are inserted various steps of humility and moral perfection, which our vocation from God invites us to climb.[1] " In his heart he hath disposed to ascend by steps in the vale of tears " (Ps. lxxxiii. 6). We should note with what anxiety for sound doctrine St. Benedict determines the part played by God in our ascension towards Him: God calls, God provides the means to reach Him, and supplies the steps of the ladder: " the call of God hath placed various degrees "; and it is God who sets up the ladder and helps us to climb it by His grace: " is lifted up by the Lord to heaven."

The allegory of the heavenly ladder is a favourite with the old writers. It illumines with a pleasing touch the Passion of SS. Perpetua and Felicity; St. Basil, in a homily on the first psalm, compares the progressive exercise of the Christian virtues to the ascent of Jacob's ladder.[2] Shortly after St. Benedict, Cassiodorus also uses this comparison and with expressions which recall the text of the Rule.[3] Then St. John Climacus, in his treatise *The Scale of Paradise* which earned him his surname, describes the spiritual life under the figure of a ladder of thirty steps. Cassian does not speak explicitly of a ladder, but he shows how man arrives at perfection by attaining various degrees of humility;[4]

---

[1] St. Benedict's words recall this passage of a Paschal letter of THEOPHILUS OF ALEXANDRIA, translated by ST. JEROME: *Quod intelligens et patriarcha Jacob, scalam cernit in somnis, cujus caput pertingebat usque ad cælum, per quam diversis virtutum gradibus ad superna conscenditur, et homines provocantur, terrarum deserentes humilia, cum Ecclesia primitivorum dominicæ passionis festa celebrare* (S. HIERON., *Epist.* XCVIII., 3. *P.L.*, XXII., 793).

Quisquis igitur ad θεωρητικήν *voluerit pervenire. . . . Gradus quidam ita ordinati atque distincti sunt, ut humana humilitas possit ad sublime conscendere* . . . (CASS., *Conlat.*, XIV., ii.).

[2] *P.G.*, XXIX., 217 *sq.*

[3] *Expositio in Ps.* cxix. *P.L.*, LXX., 901-902. *De Institutione divin. Litter.,* præf. *P.L., ibid.,* 1107.

[4] *Principium nostræ salutis ejusdemque custodia timor Domini est. Per hunc enim et initium conversionis et vitiorum purgatio et virtutum custodia his qui inbuuntur ad viam perfectionis adquiritur. . . . Humilitas vero his indiciis conprobatur : primo si mortificatas in sese omnes habeat voluntates ; secundo si non solum suorum actuum, verum etiam cogitationum nihil suum celaverit seniorem ; tertio si nihil suæ discretioni, sed judicio ejus universa committat ac monita ejus sitiens ac libenter auscultet : quarto si in omnibus servet obedientiæ mansuetudinem patientiæque constantiam ; quinto si non solum injuriam inferat nulli, sed ne ab alio quidem sibimet inrogatam doleat atque tristetur ; sexto si nihil agat, nihil præsumat, quod non vel communis regula vel majorum cohortantur exempla ;*

and it is from him that St. Benedict has borrowed the whole framework of his chapter. The differences are small. Cassian enumerates only ten degrees, while St. Benedict gives twelve; but we may note that the fear of God which St. Benedict puts down as the first degree, is given by Cassian in the forefront of his treatment, but not in the series of the degrees: "The beginning of our salvation and its guard is the fear of God," says Cassian. So the twelfth degree alone belongs to St. Benedict. The order of the degrees is not always the same, and St. Benedict has much expanded the brief enumeration of Cassian.

St. Thomas Aquinas in an article of the *Summa Theologica*[1] shows the appropriateness of this division of humility into twelve degrees. He enumerates them in the reverse order, so that the twelfth becomes the first, the eleventh the second, and so on, and he tells us what led him to choose this inverted order, though St. Benedict had adopted the order of development. He explains that his enumeration proceeds from external to internal, while St. Benedict began with the internal. Without ignoring the theoretical and practical priority of interior dispositions, or the fundamental character and solidity of the fear of God: " Reverence for God is the principle and root," he notes that man obtains humility by the co-operation of two forces: " First and chiefly by the gift of grace: and in this respect the internal precedes the external. But it is otherwise with human effort: a man first puts a check on externals and later comes to eradicate the internal; and it is according to this order that the degrees of humility are here given." Have we not two methods of spirituality sketched in these words ? An opportunity to compare them will occur later. But we may remark at this point that a man's effort may just as well begin with the internal, and basing itself chiefly on the reality of the new life that has been created in him, so follow a line parallel to the expansion of grace.

There is besides a more considerable difference between St. Benedict's point of view and that of the angelic Doctor. St. Thomas regards humility as a particular virtue, designed to repress the immoderate love of greatness; it is a subdivision of moderation, which belongs to temperance as primary cardinal virtue. To St. Benedict, not only does humility imply the exercise of several other virtues, such as obedience or patience, which St. Thomas also recognizes, but it is as well a general virtue, mother and mistress of all virtue; it is the attitude which our soul habitually takes up in the sight of God, of herself, of everything and

---

septimo si omni vilitate contentus sit et ad omnia se quæ sibi præbentur velut operarium malum judicarit indignum ; octavo si semetipsum cunctis inferiorem non superficie pronuntiet labiorum, sed intimo cordis credat affectu ; nono si linguam cohibeat vel non sit clamosus in voce ; decimo si non sit facilis ac promptus in risu. Talibus namque indiciis et his similibus humilitas vera dinoscitur. Quæ cum fuerit in veritate possessa, confestim te ad caritatem, quæ timorem non habet, gradu excelsiore perducet, per quam universa, quæ prius non sine pœna formidinis observabas, absque ullo labore velut naturaliter incipies custodire, non jam contemplatione supplicii vel timoris ullius, sed amore ipsius boni et delectatione virtutum (Inst., IV., xxxix.).

[1] II.-II., *q.* clxi., *a.* 6.

everybody. St. Benedict shows in detail how it embraces all the forms of our activity and governs all our steps. The quotations from Scripture with which the chapter opened, and the very allegory of the ladder, have already indicated that St. Benedict takes humility in its widest acceptation. The seventh chapter is justly regarded as the finished expression of monastic spirituality.

Why are there twelve degrees, no more and no less? Such divisions are always somewhat arbitrary, but we only ask that they should fit the teaching and facilitate exposition. The commentators, as we might expect, find no difficulty in showing, each in his own way, the complete appropriateness of the number twelve, while observing, as does D. Mège after St. Bernard,[1] that it is more profitable to climb the degrees of humility than to count them. St. Benedict has not enumerated them at random, as we shall see; yet there is nothing to show that they correspond to distinct and successive stages of spiritual growth, and that one could compare them for example to the seven mansions of St. Teresa's *Interior Castle*. They describe the most characteristic dispositions of the humble soul towards the essential duties and principal circumstances of the supernatural and monastic life. Cassian calls them the indications or marks of humility. So we need not have attained one of these steps in order to ascend to the next; and although one or other mode of humility may belong more especially to a determined period in the spiritual life, it is wise to cultivate the whole of these dispositions at the same time, for it is their complete realization which constitutes perfection.

Primus itaque humilitatis gradus est, si timorem Dei sibi ante oculos semper ponens, oblivionem omnino fugiat, et semper sit memor omnium quæ præcepit Deus, qualiter contemnentes Deum in gehennam pro peccatis incidunt, et vitam æternam quæ timentibus Deum præparata est, animo suo semper revolvat.[2] Et custodiens se omni hora a peccatis et vitiis, id est cogitationum, linguæ, oculorum, manuum, pedum vel voluntatis propriæ, sed et desideria carnis amputare festinet.

The first degree of humility, then, is that a man always keep the fear of God before his eyes, avoiding all forgetfulness; and that he be ever mindful of all that God hath commanded, and that those who despise God will be consumed in hell for their sins; and that he ever reflect that life everlasting is prepared for them that fear Him.[2] And keeping himself at all times from sin and vice, whether of the thoughts, the tongue, the eyes, the hands, the feet, or his own will, let him thus hasten to cut off the desires of the flesh.

Christian humility is not a mere external and formal habit, attained by practice and exercise, nor is it a virtue of the lips, nor does it consist in the contempt of self. There are beings who are perfectly abject, who despise themselves sincerely, yet do not for this deserve to be called humble. It is not a virtue of the pure intellect, but resides in the will.

---

[1] *Tractatus de gradibus humilitatis et superbiæ*, c. i. *P.L.*, CLXXXII., 941.

[2] D. BUTLER reads : . . . *quæ præcepit Deus : ut qualiter et contemnentes Deum gehenna de peccatis incendat, et vita æterna, quæ timentibus Deum præparata est, animo suo semper evolvat.*

Nevertheless, it must be recognized that humility is based upon spiritual understanding and faith, and St. Benedict was not wrong on this point. According to him the whole edifice of humility is based upon an exact knowledge, so that humility may be defined as an attitude of " truth." First of all it regulates our relation to God. For this end we must know what God is in Himself and what He is in relation to us, and we must be aware of His presence. Our spiritual education is the fruit of a twofold looking: God's looking on us, our looking to Him. When our gaze meets God's and this state is prolonged and becomes habitual, then our souls possess the " fear of God." According to some Hebrew scholars we may establish a correspondence between the word which means to fear and that which means to look. When we were little children, we watched the looks of our mother so as to estimate the value of our actions, and this was the beginning of conscience. The look that we keep steadily fixed on God becomes the final form of our conscience as children of God: " To thee have I lifted up my eyes: who dwellest in heaven " (Ps. cxxii.).

There is hardly any disposition of soul that is so assiduously exacted in the Old Testament as the fear of God. It is given as the beginning of wisdom: " The fear of the Lord is the beginning of wisdom." It is presented as its attainment: " To fear God is the fulness of wisdom. . . . The fear of the Lord is the crown of wisdom " (Ecclus. i. 20, 22); and Holy Scripture likes to sum up the sanctity of its great men by saying that they " feared God." Finally it is offered as the best instrument of perfection, and the Psalmist asks God that He would deign to " pierce his flesh with his fear." We should also note that the fear of God is a variable quantity, that it takes diverse character and value according as it belongs to the old economy or the new, and in its expression in the individual life. There is the fear of the slave, of the son, of the spouse; there is temporal fear and eternal fear: " The fear of God is holy, enduring for ever and ever,"[1] for fear endures even among those who are with God.[2] It is among the gifts of the Holy Spirit, and without it there is no spiritual life. Our Holy Father would have it rooted in the hearts of his monks. We should read attentively these pregnant texts and understand all that is implied in this notion of the fear of God, whether for intellect or will or action.[3]

Our attitude towards God will be determined by the same appreciation of what He is to us and what we are to Him, of what He has ordained and under what penalties. We are creatures, which is to say

[1] *Cf.* S. Aug., *Enarr. in Ps.* cxxvii. 8-9. *P.L.*, XXXVII., 1681-1683.

[2] The Council of Sens recalled this fact when condemning Abelard's contrary error: Mansi, t. XXI., col. 569.

[3] We may compare with this paragraph of the Rule what St. Augustine wrote when expounding the seven degrees that lead to wisdom: *Ante omnia igitur opus est Dei timore converti ad cognoscendam ejus voluntatem, quid nobis appetendum fugiendumque præcipiat' Timor autem iste cogitationem de nostra mortalitate et de futura morte necesse est incutiat, et quasi clavatis carnibus omnes superbiæ motus ligno crucis affigat* (*De Doctrina christiana,* l. II., c. vii. *P.L.*, XXXIV., 39).

that we hold all from God: body, soul, life, continued existence, the influences that act on us, guidance, the day of death—in one word, all. Therefore God has over us an absolute right of ownership and authority. In all this there is nothing that need terrify us. It is the joy, the highest joy, of the creature, to recognize this divine sovereignty and to abandon itself to this absolute power. And God never does us more honour than when He disposes of us at His pleasure, without asking our leave, without appearing to suspect that there will be any hesitation in our will or reluctance in our flesh. So were treated Abraham, the prophets, St. John the Baptist, Our Lady, Our Lord Jesus Christ. The valiant soul knows what it means, for the cry of the crusader is of all time. Need we add that we too for our part have judged it well to extend and consecrate, by our profession, God's rights over us? Bound to God as His creatures, we are also bound as souls redeemed by His blood, as sinners who have perhaps many times been pardoned and snatched from hell; we are bound again on the ground of our adoptive sonship, and because, since we remain weak, we are in continual need of God. Besides, He has defined His purpose in our regard, and how we should co-operate with Him; He has given us precepts and fortified them with His sanction. Eternal life is prepared for them that fear Him; while for sinners, for those who neglect God and so make mockery of His infinite majesty, there is hell.

We recognize here the great teaching of the Prologue. Here, too, our Holy Father insists that the intellectual appreciation from which springs the fear of God must be continual, present every moment, always awake: *semper ponens, . . . semper sit memor, . . . animo suo semper revolvat . . . omni hora.* He knows that we long have need of an effort thus to preserve contact with God: *sibi ante oculos ponens;* faith alone makes us attentive to the presence of God and to supernatural realities, while it is fatally easy for us to be aware of ourselves and of the things of sense which surround us. *Oblivionem omnino fugiat:* inattentiveness is the great feeder of hell, and there is one whose whole interest it is to foster it in us. We may forget from inadvertence or distraction; our souls may be carried away by the influence of the sensible. We may forget from carelessness, cowardice, sleepiness: "I have never done it, I am too old; I cannot . . ." We may forget of set purpose, and then we have deliberate inattention, the sin against the Holy Spirit, the determination so to shut our souls that light and repentance can find no entry. And what is the good of this? When you forget thus, do you suppress your previous knowledge? Do you suppress the consciousness which you had, before you began to pervert it, of the ultimate consequences of your unfaithfulness? Do you suppress duty? As though, to extinguish a debt, it were enough to refuse to think of it. Do you suppress God? Do you really think that a petty ruse, some little internal diplomacy or wrongheadedness, is enough to get rid of God? We may do what we like, but we shall not change reality. God is master, we are creatures; and we have given our word. Not God Himself can change these facts.

There is heaven for those that fear Him, hell for those that despise Him; and when life is finished the time of probation is over. God would be a mockery, a sort of guy whom we might buffet and abuse indefinitely and with impunity, if He took no thought for the commands He has given, and if souls did not bear their responsibility and their burden before Him.

Et custodiens se (and keeping himself): our Holy Father now considers the consequences of the fear of God in respect of practical fidelity. Assiduous meditation on the will of God, His rewards and His punishments, will encourage the monk to watchfulness. Every moment, and especially at times of temptation, which perhaps occur periodically, he will be on his guard. Sad experience of his falls, and his daily examination of conscience, will reveal to him his weak points. He must abstain from sin and vice—that is, from every fault, whether habitual or not; and he must eliminate along with the fault the evil tendency which is its germ. St. Benedict enumerates the principal instruments of sin: thought, speech, eyes, hands, feet. And these various faculties, which serve as the material means of sin, are summed up in the will: *vel voluntatis propriæ*. But not only completed and external faults demand vigilance and resolution; we must be quick to cut off the desires of the flesh themselves, as soon as they begin to appear. The expression *desideria carnis*, with St. Benedict as with St. Paul, designates all the desires of the selfish life, of the life before baptism and profession, the sum of all tendencies which do not come from God or lead to Him. The flesh here signifies man in continual conflict with that Spirit, which realizes our divine sonship by its influence and its presence.

Æstimet se homo de cælis a Deo semper respici omni hora, et facta sua in omni loco ab aspectu Divinitatis videri, et ab Angelis omni hora Deo nuntiari.

Let him consider that he is always beheld from heaven by God, and that his actions are everywhere seen by the eye of the Divine Majesty, and are every hour reported to Him by His angels.

Therefore true fear of God is made up of knowledge and practical fidelity. This lesson seemed so important to our Holy Father that he takes it up again point by point, thereby giving a disproportionate space to the study of the first degree of humility. So we have again this general principle that we must be conscious of God's abiding presence. Up to this point, it would seem, St. Benedict has only spoken of the look we cast on Him, a look which suffers interruption, for it is characteristic of created beings not to exercise their powers at every instant. But God is pure act. His name is "the living and seeing God." The glance of His eye reaches even to the abyss; at all times and everywhere things are naked to His sight. When St. Benedict, with Holy Scripture, declares that God looks upon us from on high, as from an observatory, this means, not only that God is well placed so as to lose nothing of our doings, but also that He views us from the depths of the sanctuary of our souls. For God has in fact no other habitation than Himself and us, though He be present everywhere because of His universal activity.

So "from heaven" does not imply remoteness, but on the contrary the most complete intimacy; not separation but real union; it is not from outside but from within that God informs Himself continually of our life: and it is there, within our souls, that our look should seek to encounter His.[1]

We are never alone, God sees us always; and His angels, adds St. Benedict, apprise Him ceaselessly of our deeds. It would seem then that our Holy Father has not completely discarded the literal meaning of Jacob's ladder. No one will imagine that the angels convey information necessary to adequate knowledge. God employs these messengers out of His abundance, not out of His need. He associates them with the working of His providence, so that all may be accomplished in a regular hierarchical fashion; so that subjects too may become chiefs and kings; so that they may have the joy of co-operating in the building of the Church, the object of their eternal admiration (Eph. iii. 10; Heb. i. 14); so that from now onwards those who already possess eternity and those who still journey towards it may be united in a vast association of charity, zeal, and affection: "With whom we shall share the holy and most sweet city of God itself."[2]

Demonstrat nobis hoc Propheta, cum in cogitationibus nostris ita Deum semper præsentem ostendit, dicens: *Scrutans corda et renes Deus.* Et item: *Dominus novit cogitationes hominum, quoniam vanæ sunt.* Et item dicit: *Intellexisti cogitationes meas a longe;* et: *Quia cogitatio hominis confitebitur tibi.* Nam ut sollicitus sit circa cogitationes perversas, dicat semper humilis frater in corde suo: *Tunc ero immaculatus coram eo, si observavero me ab iniquitate mea.*

This the prophet tells us, when he shows how God is ever present to our thoughts, saying: "God searcheth the heart and the reins." And again: "The Lord knoweth the thoughts of men, that they are vain." And he also says: "Thou hast understood my thoughts afar off"; and "The thought of man shall confess to thee." In order, therefore, that he may be on his guard against evil thoughts, let the humble brother say ever in his heart; "Then shall I be unspotted before him, if I shall have kept me from mine iniquity."

After having recalled the directive principle of our moral life, St. Benedict shows what practical influence the fear of God ought to have on our actions, developing the paragraph *Et custodiens se*. . . . Leaving on one side the purely external act, which of itself has no moral character, our Holy Father deals successively with thought, manifestations of self-will, and desires. And it is not a mere care for method, the desire to adjust his didactic exposition to the laws of psychology, which led our Holy Father to speak first of intellect, and then of will, and finally of desire: we see that his aim is to form his monks from within. We may notice, too, that all the observations of St. Benedict are deduced from the words of Holy Scripture, acquiring thus a divine authority.

[1] *Cf.* S. Aug., *In Joannis Evang.*, tract. CXI., 3. P.L., XXXV., 1928.
[2] S. Aug., *De Civitate Dei*, l. XXII., c. xxix. P.L., XLI., 797.

Of Humility

God is the witness of all our thoughts. His glance, according to the seventh psalm (verse 10), "probes the reins and the heart." And again: "The Lord knoweth the thoughts of men, that they are vain" (Ps. xciii. 11). Likewise: "Thou hast understood my thoughts afar off" (Ps. cxxxviii. 3), and "The thought of man shall surely confess to thee" (Ps. lxxv. 11); thoughts which are mysterious to all lose their mystery at once to God. So the first degree of humility will consist in the monk[1] guarding himself from evil thoughts. And, to keep up his vigilance, he should voluntarily murmur in his heart the twenty-fourth verse of the seventeenth psalm, which speaks of the glance of God, of the purity that it demands, and of the method which assures this perfect cleanliness. "Then shall I be without spot in thy eyes, if I guard against my evil thoughts, against that which is the root of evil in me." For sin begins in thought and not in sense, in a deliberate look at the forbidden object, and not in a mere sight which is suddenly presented to us, or in a caprice of memory. There is no formal sin but in the will, and evil thoughts only exist because of perversities of will. St. Benedict devotes a moment to these last.

Voluntatem vero propriam ita facere prohibemur, cum dicit nobis Scriptura: *Et a voluntatibus tuis avertere.* Et item rogamus Deum in oratione, ut fiat illius voluntas in nobis. Docemur ergo merito nostram non facere voluntatem, cum cavemus illud quod dicit sancta Scriptura: *Sunt viæ quæ videntur hominibus rectæ, quarum finis usque ad profundum inferni demergit.* Et cum item cavemus illud quod de negligentibus dictum est: *Corrupti sunt, et abominabiles facti sunt in voluptatibus suis.*

We are, indeed, forbidden to do our own will by Scripture, which says to us: "Turn away from thine own will." And so too we beg of God in prayer that His will may be done in us. Rightly therefore are we taught not to do our own will, if we take heed to the warning of Scripture: "There are ways which to men seem right, but the ends thereof lead to the depths of hell"; or, again, when we tremble at what is said of the careless: "They are corrupt and have become abominable in their pleasures."

Of the two antagonistic wills, man's will and God's will, which is to prevail? Certainly God's, if we think of His omnipresence, His rights, His threats, and His promises. We are not bidden: "Act always against your own will," for such a behest would savour of Jansenism; but rather, "Beware of your personal and isolated will, separate yourself from all forms of your own will: for such is the formal command of the Scripture" (Ecclus. xviii. 30). And every time that we recite the Lord's Prayer, we beg God that His will may be fulfilled in us and fulfilled by us. Hence our life will show men the sincerity of our prayer.

If we wish to learn not to pursue the exercise of our own will, we must listen with holy fear to what Scripture says further: there are ways, practical habits, which seem to men right and fair, but the end of them

---

[1] We should, however, with all the manuscripts and the most ancient commentators, read *utilis* instead of *humilis*: a faithful brother, useful to his master; St. Benedict says similarly a little farther on, with Ps. lii. 4: . . . *et inutiles factos.*

engulfs us in the depths of hell (Prov. xvi. 25, xiv. 12). Our Holy Father once more warns us of the great danger of delusion, child of evil passion. Every passion is an adjustment of the being on a certain axis. When this adjustment is violent and resolute, it becomes the normal state and takes the place of conscience. Then that is good which is suitable, adapted, and favourable to it. We call this the good; and God Himself must speak according to it, for man is not ashamed to vex and bend and torture the words of Scripture, and he dares to seek in an alleged providential course of events the justification of his system and his pretended mission. But responsibility remains, even in delusion, when one was conscious of evil at the start and thereafter at certain lucid intervals; though it is not impossible that the sum of evil and suffering that is in the world does not come from malice alone, and that responsibility is diminished by delusion. For were this not so, would not the thing terrify us? If the good undergo trial, and if the part played by goodness in the kingdom of God is thereby diminished, this is not always the effect of pure wickedness, for blindness has its share in it. But it is possible that souls, which benefit by this sorry privilege of unconsciousness, expiate their misdeeds in proportion to the permanence of the consequences, and that the chastisement perseveres until the complete elimination from historical reality and the complex of things of all the disorder caused by delusion.

Besides the self-will of the proud man, which is shut up as it were in a strong castle and canonizes all his decisions, one meets the self-will of the man who is sluggish and cowardly, who refuses to react against himself, *negligentibus*. Often the two tendencies unite and support each other. Anything may happen then and very quickly. Thus is reached the wretched state described by the Rule and by the thirteenth psalm (verse 1). But perhaps our Holy Father here wished to indicate with a rapid stroke, by the side of culpable delusion, that other perverse state which is known as formal negligence and contempt for all that is most sacred. "The wicked man, when he is come into the depth of sins, contemneth: but ignominy and reproach follow him" (Prov. xviii. 3). Such dispositions may now and then appear in monasteries and reach their hateful climax.[2]

In desideriis vero carnis nobis Deum credamus esse præsentem semper, cum dicit Propheta Domino: *Domine, ante te est omne desiderium meum.* Caven-	And in regard to the desires of the flesh, we must believe that God is always present to us, as the prophet says to the Lord: "O Lord, all my desire

[1] As D. BUTLER remarks, St. Benedict cites a version other than the Vulgate; the expression *demergit* is a reminiscence of ST. MATTH. xviii. 6.

[2] ST. AUGUSTINE came to recognize this fact, and bade his people not to be scandalized. *Simpliciter fateor caritati vestræ coram Domino Deo nostro, qui testis est super animam meam, ex quo Deo servire cœpi: quomodo difficile sum expertus meliores quam qui in monasteriis profecerunt; ita non sum expertus pejores quam qui in monasteriis ceciderunt. . . . Quapropter etsi contristamur de aliquibus purgamentis, consolamur tamen etiam de pluribus ornamentis. Nolite ergo propter amurcam qua oculi vestri offenduntur, torcularia detestari, unde apothecæ dominicæ fructu olei luminosioris implentur* (*Epist.* LXXVIII., 9. *P.L.*, XXXIII., 272).

Of Humility

dum ergo ideo malum desiderium, quia mors secus introitum delectationis posita est. Unde Scriptura præcepit, dicens: *Post concupiscentias tuas non eas.*	is before thee." Let us be on our guard then against evil desires, since death has its seat close to the entrance of delight; wherefore the Scripture commands us, saying: "Go not after thy concupiscences."

Internal activity consists of thought and will; but St. Benedict is aware that, besides and beyond these two elements, there is a third which darkens the intellect and entraps, debases, and imprisons the will. Fleshly desire is that secret and base concupiscence, that instinct of sense which drives us towards persons or things, not because they are good but because they please us. Again, the conviction of the presence of God will introduce order among these stormy and subversive desires. As the prophet David said: "O Lord, all my desire is before thee" (Ps. xxxvii. 10).

To this lofty motive, proceeding from charity, our Holy Father adds another, less disinterested, but effective and within the reach of every soul. We should dread evil desires, because, in spite of their seeming sweetness and the pleasure we find in them, they are poison and sometimes deadly poison. Death is installed, so to speak, close to the entrance of evil delight: and death too often enters on the heels of delight. Therefore does Scripture bid us not to let ourselves be dragged along by our concupiscences and drawn in their train (Ecclus. xviii. 30): for they may lead us to perdition. After opening out this vista, our Holy Father now proceeds to summarize and conclude the whole teaching of the first degree of humility.

Ergo si oculi Domini speculantur bonos et malos, et *Dominus de cælo semper respicit super filios hominum, ut videat si est intelligens, aut requirens Deum;* et ab Angelis nobis deputatis quotidie die noctuque Domino factori nostro et Creatori omnium Deo opera nostra nuntiantur; cavendum est ergo omni hora, fratres, sicut in Psalmo dicit Propheta; ne nos declinantes in malum, et inutiles factos, aliqua hora aspiciat Deus, et parcendo nobis in hoc tempore (quia pius est, et expectat nos converti in melius), ne dicat nobis in futuro: *Hæc fecisti, et tacui.*	Since, therefore, the eyes of the Lord behold good and evil; and the Lord is ever looking down from heaven upon the children of men, to see who has understanding or is seeking God; and since the works of our hands are reported to Him, our Maker and Creator, day and night by the angels appointed to watch over us; we must be always on the watch, brethren, lest, as the prophet says in the psalm, God should see us at any time declining to evil and become unprofitable; and lest, though He spare us now, because He is merciful and expects our conversion, He should say to us hereafter: "These things thou didst and I held my peace."

St. Benedict is content to reiterate, under the form of an exhortation addressed to all and in the same key as the Prologue, the points which have been developed in this exposition. The eyes of the Lord are upon the good and the wicked; unceasingly from the height of heaven He looks upon the children of men, to discover whether there be among them an intelligent servant and one who seeks Him (Ps. xiii. 2); our guardian angels give an account to the Lord that made us of all our deeds every day, by night as well as by day.[1] So there is reason every moment to fear, my brethren, according to the warning of the prophet in the fifty-second psalm, that if we fall into evil and become unprofitable God is at that same moment watching us. He might punish us on the spot. Perhaps He will spare us in this life, for He is good and awaits our return to better dispositions; so at least we must fear lest He say to us in the next life: "These things thou didst and I held my peace; but now I am going to speak" (Ps. xlix. 21). This sentence nullifies the tacit objection which the sinner raises against the justice of God: "I have sinned, and what harm hath befallen me?" (Ecclus. v. 4). If God does not punish at once, it is because He would give the soul time to return to Him. There is no doubt, also, that it is in order to save the free and filial character of virtue; for virtue would easily become a bargain, and fidelity a vulgar piece of smart calculation, if the punishment followed immediately on the fault or if the good deed were at once crowned with its reward.

Secundus humilitatis gradus est, si propriam quis non amans voluntatem desideria sua non delectetur implere; sed vocem illam Domini factis imitetur dicentis: *Non veni facere voluntatem meam, sed ejus qui misit me.* Item dicit Scriptura: *Voluntas habet pœnam, et necessitas parit coronam.*

The second degree of humility is that a man love not his own will, nor delight in gratifying his own desires; but carry out in his deeds that saying of the Lord: "I came not to do mine own will, but the will of him who sent me." And again Scripture says: "Self-will hath punishment, but necessity wins a crown."

We remember, perhaps, that in Cassian the fear of God does not constitute a special degree, but is presented as in a sense the common basis of all the degrees of humility. At bottom St. Benedict's doctrine is the same. We should notice that henceforth he assigns no new motive for humility, but confines himself to indicating the methods and authentic forms through which humility should manifest itself. He too has spoken, primarily and at considerable length, of the fear of God; but, without setting this on one side, as did Cassian, he describes at the same time the negative consequences which it will have in our life as a whole. So that, in reality, abstention from the selfish actions which spring from our own will is the first degree of humility, with St. Benedict as with Cassian. The subsequent degrees describe the *positive* results of spiritual fear—viz., to do the will of God instead of one's own will (the second degree: Cassian did not distinguish it from the first); to do the will even of men when they hold God's place (the third degree); to do the will of God and superiors in heroic circumstances (the fourth degree), etc.

Therefore the second degree of humility is the realization in our

[1] The manuscripts have not got the words: *et creatori omnium Deo*, and the chief witnesses to the Carlovingian and Cassinese traditions read: *Domino factorum nostrorum opera nuntiantur.*

conduct of that which Our Lord said of Himself: "I have come not to do mine own will, but the will of him who sent me" (John vi. 38).[1] Instead of loving our own will, of taking joy in doing what we like and what our desires suggest, we shall imitate Our Lord Jesus Christ. The divine will of Our Saviour was wholly united with the will of His Father, and the same was true of His human will. But He had, as we have, an instinctive and indeliberate will, a natural will, a principle of interior reaction which impelled Him to choose certain things and avoid others. Now this will also bowed down before the will of His Father: "The chalice which my Father hath given me, shall I not drink it?" (John xviii. 11). Yet this was the chalice of which He had said shortly before: "Father, if it be possible, let this chalice pass from me." Truly he was a man and no beautiful statue; He felt human repugnance with a unique depth and an exquisite sensibility, and therefore He can be put before us as a model.

St. Benedict adds that our own spiritual interest urges us to submission. This little phrase is the crux of commentators. In the first place, should we read *voluptas* or *voluntas*? Since the context deals with self-will, it would seem that *voluntas* is the true reading; this conclusion is confirmed if we appreciate the antithesis to *necessitas*; and some manuscripts have this reading. Still the reading of the best manuscripts, and the one reproduced in the oldest commentators, is *voluptas*. This expression is in no way unexpected, for it is supported very naturally by the words *desideria sua non delectetur implere* (nor delight in gratifying his own desires); and the antithesis remains in some manner, for, according to St. Benedict's thought, will is here equivalent to pleasure, and at least the words sound much the same. But to what passage of Scripture does St. Benedict refer? The sentence is not to be found in the Bible. St. Benedict, so most commentators say, quotes from memory and gives the sense and not the words, as the writers of the New Testament and the Fathers have sometimes done. But then we should be able to produce a text with some likeness to our Holy Father's quotation, which is clean-cut and precise. Must we refer it to some lost text? That is a sort of hypothesis to which we should rarely have recourse. Can our Holy Father's memory have been a little at fault? Commentators have shrunk from this solution. Again, it is hard to suppose that he is quoting a proverb, since he refers expressly to Scripture. Some explain by saying that Scripture does not designate the sacred books exclusively; for does not the exposition of the eleventh degree of humility close with a non-scriptural quotation introduced by the formula *scriptum est* (it is written)? We might answer that this formula is much less precise than the word "Scripture."

Yet it may be a fragment of ecclesiastical literature. The Bollandists

---

[1] *Quod utique qui implere vult, sine dubio proprias sibi amputat voluntates, secundum imitationem ipsius Domini dicentis: Descendi de cælo non ut faciam voluntatem meam, sed voluntatem ejus qui misit me Patris* (S. BASIL., *Reg. contr.*, xii.). See also CASS., *Conlat.*, XXIV., xxvi.

have reproduced, from manuscripts and Mombricius, the Acts of SS. Agape, Chionia, and Irene, which are inserted in those of SS. Chrysogonus and Anastasia. This text, which they give as of great antiquity, is (happily for our hypothesis) different from that of Simeon Metaphrastes (tenth century). In it we read: " Sisinnius said: ' Are they not then polluted who have tasted of the blood of sacrifices ?' Irene replied: 'Not only are they not polluted, but they are even crowned: for pleasure hath punishment, but necessity wins (*parat*) a crown'" (Mombricius has *parit*).[1] The authenticity of these Acts is contested by Ruinart; but they may nevertheless be anterior to our Holy Father. Have we perhaps a more certain source in St. Optatus of Milevis, who writes: " Self-will hath punishment, necessity pardon " ?[2] It is possible; but the two formulas are not identical and still less the ideas. St. Optatus's meaning is that those deserve full chastisement who are in full possession of their freedom, while responsibility and therefore chastisement are less where there has been constraint. St. Benedict's meaning is that self-will incurs punishment, while necessity—that is, not an external and perverse constraint which leads us to evil, but a wise constraint which we put upon ourselves for the doing of good—merits a crown. If the borrowing from St. Optatus were established, we should have to go back to the hypothesis of a proverbial formula adapting itself to circumstances.

Tertius humilitatis gradus est, ut quis pro Dei amore omni obedientia se subdat majori, imitans Dominum de quo dicit Apostolus: *Factus obediens usque ad mortem.*	The third degree of humility is that a man for the love of God submit himself to his superior in all obedience; imitating the Lord, of whom the apostle saith: "He was made obedient even unto death."

Obedience again and always obedience; but these various degrees represent an advance, though they imply one another and are in germ contained in one another. To fulfil the will of God is comparatively easy; for He is Himself, His laws have a universal character and contain their own justification, and then He is invisible: *major ex longinquo reverentia* (distance increases reverence). But God requires us to submit our wills to the wills of other men, and that continuously and till death, without protest or any reservation: " in all obedience "; " to his superior "—*i.e.*, in general; and St. Benedict even adds later: " That the brethren be obedient to one another."

A little phrase, inserted in the precept, gives us its deep meaning and reassures us: it is " for the love of God " that we thus submit ourselves; our activity is always directed to God. When we obey for love, when our souls are raised aloft, then all becomes easy for us; our love invites sacrifice and every day it grows by reason of sacrifice

[1] *Acta SS.*, April., t. I., p. 250.
[2] *De Schism. Donat.*, l. VII., *post caput* vii. *P.L.*, XI., 1098. This passage has been restored to its place in chap. i. of the same book VII., in the edition of the Vienna *Corpus*, t. XXVI., p. 160.

accepted. This third degree of humility is especially Christian in that it requires us to imitate Our Lord, of whom St. Paul says that "He was made obedient even unto death" (Phil. ii. 8).[1] From Bethlehem to Calvary, and after, in the Holy Eucharist, the life of Our Lord has been nothing but obedience to creatures for love of His heavenly Father. He has not set any limits to this entire and glad giving of Himself, and He died to consummate it. If we are of the kin of Our Lord, if we are anxious to realize the meaning of Redemption, we shall desire no other method than His.

Quartus humilitatis gradus est, si in ipsa obedientia duris et contrariis rebus, vel etiam quibuslibet irrogatis injuriis, tacita conscientia patientiam amplectatur, et sustinens non lassescat, vel discedat, dicente Scriptura: *Qui perseveraverit usque in finem, hic salvus erit.* Item: *Confortetur cor tuum, et sustine Dominum.*

The fourth degree of humility is that if in this very obedience hard and contrary things, nay even injuries, are done to him, he should embrace them patiently with silent consciousness, and not grow weary or give in, as the Scripture says: "He that shall persevere to the end shall be saved." And again: "Let thy heart take courage and wait thou for the Lord."

The fourth degree of humility is heroic obedience, and by heroic we do not mean optional. The subject here is true monastic obedience, and every soul that is anxious to be faithful will often have occasion to use this blessed page, rich in experience and in saintliness, wherein our Holy Father develops a part of the monastic programme which was sketched at the very end of the Prologue: "we may by patience share in the sufferings of Christ."

Obedience may meet with objective difficulties: what is commanded may be hard, repugnant, even impossible, as St. Benedict says later. Or difficulties may come from the temper, or erratic ways, or want of tact, of those who command; they may treat us in an insulting way, or reproach us slightingly. Authority is a big subject: we may consider it as an element of unity, conservation, and happiness, and as a necessary element; but we cannot close our eyes to the fact that it is a dangerous instrument in the hands of a man. Those on whom the yoke presses heavily sometimes find it more intolerable than that anarchy which they dread. Lastly, such suffering always contains an imaginary element which aggravates the real grievance. Combine these three: the difficulty of the object, the difficulty that comes from the authority, the difficulties which we make for ourselves, and the result may be too much for our nature, which at length is stifled and exasperated. There are some who cultivate this frenzy, who lose their heads in it, and from it draw the germ of resolutions which upset and dishonour their whole life. Let four words of the Holy Rule, words of an incomparable precision, define the attitude of the truly humble monk.

[1] *Usque ad quem modum obaudire oportet eum, qui placendi Deo implere regulam cupit? Apostolus ostendit, proponens nobis obedientiam Domini : Qui factus est, inquit, obediens usque ad mortem, mortem autem crucis* (S. BASIL., *Reg contr.*, lxv.).

Tacita (silent). We must, at such times, know how to be silent, and that completely. To check the tongue or the pen is to keep one's strength whole, while if a man abandon himself to his words or anger, he is lost. It will be objected that one must complain, that suffering must be let breathe. No, says St. Benedict, be silent. And so as to have naught to say externally, make your interior thought be silent also: *tacita conscientia* (with silent consciousness). It is not enough for humility and obedience to be dumb, yet to indulge in concentrated, and sometimes apparent, anger. We must avoid secret plainings, inner protestations, endless recalling of the past, angry reminiscence. There are passages in our life which it is bad enough to have known once; why should we wish, by incessantly returning to them in thought, to make them eternal? This is to act like the child who has a small cut and inflames it by constantly touching it. Would that such reminiscences tended to stimulate our courage, penitence, or charity! Then all would be well. But the suffering which we cause ourselves, which comes from our persistent reawakening of some secret sorrow, is not wholesome. So we should let fall into darkness, oblivion, and nothingness all that which tends only to trouble our peace. We have an opportunity of exercising patience, which, as St. James says, is the work of perfection: "Patience hath a perfect work," and its work is to maintain in us, despite all, the order of reason and faith. Let us take our courage in both hands; let us grasp this blessed patience so tightly and so strongly that nothing in the world shall be able to separate us from it: *patientiam amplectatur*.

This is not the time for groaning, for self-justification, for dispute. We should not have been saved if Our Lord had declined to suffer. It is the time for bending our shoulders and carrying the cross, for carrying all that God wills and so long as He wishes, without growing weary or lagging on the road. "Son, when thou comest to the service of God, stand in justice and in fear: and prepare thy soul for temptation. . . . Wait on God with patience: join thyself to God and endure, that thy life may be increased in the latter end" (Ecclus. ii. 1 and 3). As we said in expounding the Prologue, there is no spiritual future for any but those who can thus hold their ground. When we promise ourselves to stand firm and to wait till the storm is past, then we develop great powers of resistance. Besides, all suffering has an end. It will blossom in glory and salvation, says Scripture; but only on condition that we persevere to this end (Matt. xxiv. 13). Be brave, it says again, and endure the Lord (Ps. xxvi. 14). Endure the Lord: true words, because your trial comes from His Providence, He helps you to endure, and the trial has no other end than to lead you to Him: our Holy Father at once proceeds to remind us of this.

Et ostendens fidelem pro Domino universa etiam contraria sustinere debere, dicit ex persona sufferentium: *Propter te morte afficimur tota die;*	And showing how the faithful man ought to bear all things, however contrary, for the Lord, it says in the person of the afflicted: "For thee we

Of Humility

æstimati sumus sicut oves occisionis. Et securi de spe retributionis divinæ, subsequuntur gaudentes, et dicentes: Sed in his omnibus superamus propter eum qui dilexit nos. Et item alio loco Scriptura: *Probasti nos,* inquit, *Deus, igne nos examinasti, sicut igne examinatur argentum; induxisti nos in laqueum; posuisti tribulationes in dorso nostro.*

suffer death all the day long; we are esteemed as sheep for the slaughter." And secure in their hope of the divine reward, they go on with joy, saying: "But in all these things we overcome, through him who hath loved us." And so in another place Scripture says: "Thou hast proved us, O God; thou hast tried us as silver is tried by fire; thou hast led us into the snare, and hast laid tribulation on our backs."

St. Benedict returns to the two classes of difficulties which he had mentioned earlier in a more rapid fashion; first objective difficulties, and then, in the succeeding paragraph, those which come from persons. *Sustine et abstine* said the Stoics (Endure and abstain). Here we are only required to endure; but this patience is no longer acquiescence in an impersonal law, which we accept because it is universal and inevitable; it is acquiescence in a personal will, a service rendered to God, and, through our courage, a measure of collaboration in His work of redemption: *pro Domino, propter te.* With such a conviction we could go even to martyrdom. *Et ostendens fidelem. . . .* To show how he who has faith, who is loyal to the Lord, should endure all things, including those most repugnant to nature, Scripture tells us that whose who suffer say: "For thy sake death threatens us all the day long, and we are treated as sheep destined for slaughter" (Ps. xliii. 22).

In truth we achieve by these sufferings nothing less than the conquest of God. As our courage increases, so does our hope grow. We are sure of our God, sure of eternal compensation. Joy is ours, and love draws us onward, ourselves and our cross. How well now we understand the programme of our life and our death! There is One who has loved me with an everlasting love, who has reached down to my wretchedness, who leads me with Him, gloriously, along His own blood-stained track, to the Father. Whatever is required of us, we shall succeed; nay, it would seem that we have already won, "through him that hath loved us" (Rom. viii. 37). We recognize everywhere the hand of God, and we kiss it affectionately, saying again with Holy Scripture: "Thou dost prove us, O God; thou dost put us to the trial of fire, even as men try silver; thou hast permitted us to fall unto the snare; thou hast laid tribulation on our shoulders" (Ps. lxv. 10–11).

Et ut ostendat sub priore debere nos esse, subsequitur dicens: *Imposuisti homines super capita nostra.* Sed et præceptum Domini in adversis et injuriis per patientiam adimplentes, percussi in maxillam, præbent et alteram, auferenti tunicam dimittunt et pallium, angariati milliario vadunt et duo, cum Paulo Apostolo falsos fratres

And in order to show that we ought to be under a superior, it goes on to say: "Thou hast placed men over our heads." Moreover, fulfilling the precept of the Lord by patience in adversities and injuries, they who are struck on one cheek offer the other: to him who takes away their coat they leave also their cloak; and being forced to

sustinent et persecutionem, et maledicentes se benedicunt.

walk one mile, they go two. With Paul the Apostle, they bear with false brethren, and bless those that curse them.

When the difficulty comes from those who command, we shall remember that we are cenobites and that we must go to God under the guidance of a superior. We should submit to this willingly and say with Holy Scripture: "Thou hast placed men over our heads" (Ps. lxv. 12). What does it matter if men trouble us, if they wound us with words ? God permits it. Obedient men, who have reached this degree of valour, march under the will of God as soldiers under their flag, through all obstacles, not suffering themselves to be turned aside or disturbed by anything. And such is their perfection, that not only do they preserve docility towards their superior and joyous affection, but in their earnestness they go beyond what is ordered; they ask in all sincerity and candour not to be spared; they never assume the air of victims. And so they fulfil the counsel of perfection given by Our Lord in St. Matthew (v. 39 *sq.*): Are you struck on the cheek ? Offer the other. Is your coat taken from you ? Let your cloak go too. The state officials requisition you for a mile ? Don't refuse to go two.[1] Plainly, and this the gospel text shows well, these metaphors need not be taken literally: Our Lord only wished to describe the spontaneity and generosity of Christian justice, as contrasted with the justice of the Pharisees. Our Holy Father follows this up by adding that if real persecutions come to us, not now from superiors, but from false brethren, again we have nothing to do but endure, and, in company with the Apostle St. Paul, answer curses with a blessing (2 Cor. xi. 26; 1 Cor. iv. 12). We have a living commentary on this teaching in the history of our Holy Father himself, when his own monks and Florentius tried to poison him.

With this fourth degree of humility is connected the celebrated question of "fictitious humiliations," which raised a lively controversy in the seventeenth century. Abbot de Rancé, adopting the extraordinary practices of some Eastern monks, introduced among his monks the custom of imputing imaginary faults to exercise their virtue. The method appealed to the spirituality of the time. In 1616, Dom Philip François, " Prior of Saint-Airy, sometime Master of Novices of the Order of St. Benedict of the Congregation of Verdun," along with some good teaching which he gave in his *Guide spirituelle tirée de la Règle de sainct Benoist pour conduire les novices selon l'esprit de la mesme Règle*," recommended that one should "impute to them some grave fault which they have not committed and punish them well for it."[2] In 1671 William Le Roy, commendatory Abbot of Haute-Fontaine in Champagne, having gone to pass some time at La Trappe to prepare himself there for the reform of his monastery, was shocked by these methods of humiliation, which in his view injured truth, justice, and charity, and, after discussing the matter with de Rancé, formulated his objections in a

---

[1] *Cf.* Cass., *Conlat.*, XVI., xxi.-xxiv.   [2] P. 473.

manuscript *Dissertation*. De Rancé replied vigorously: a long letter addressed to the Bishop of Chalons accused Le Roy of having interpreted these fictions in a bad sense and of maintaining a view which would "destroy all the sanctity of the Thebaid." The controversy went on for some years without creating much stir; but in 1677 the *Reply* of de Rancé, of which he had given some copies to his friends, was printed without his knowledge. Naturally Le Roy talked of publishing his *Dissertation*; meanwhile he put in circulation an *Elucidation* of the *Reply* and asked the advice of Bossuet. The latter, in a letter of August 16, 1677, urged his correspondent to let the matter rest and so secured the last word to his friend de Rancé.[1]

The Abbot of La Trappe expounded his theory of humiliations in his work *De la sainteté et des devoirs de la vie monastique*.[2] It was then that Mabillon entered the lists and respectfully submitted to de Rancé some *Reflections* (unpublished) on various points; he made his own the objections of M. Le Roy and for the same reasons.[3] But no one spoke so plainly as Dom Mège in his *Commentaire sur la Règle* (1687), wherein he criticized very fully these fictitious and outlandish humiliations, without however naming de Rancé.[4] The friends of the latter, and Bossuet among the first,[5] exerted themselves to such good purpose, that, after various vicissitudes, the *Commentary* of Dom Mège was forbidden for all the members of the Congregation of St. Maur in the Chapter of 1689. That same year de Rancé published *La Règle de saint Benoît nouvellement traduite et expliquée selon son véritable esprit*; and on the last day of the year appeared the *Commentary* of Dom Martène, announced two years before to Bossuet by Père Boistard, the General of the Congregation of St. Maur, as "more correct" than that of Dom Mège. And it is true that, except in a few points, the polemical tone is absent;[6] Martène even endeavours to justify historically a discreet use of humiliations. But for us the criticism of Dom Mège has lost none of its value. Not only is it no part of our custom to lie in order to prove the virtue of another, but we hold that superiors have no need of these factitious or violent methods to make sure of this virtue and cause its increase. In reality our Holy Father suggests absolutely nothing of the sort. And how easy it would become for monks, under this system of false imputations, to ignore all disagreeable observations, even when very well justified, on the ground that the Abbot is only seeking to try their virtue.

[1] URBAIN et LEVESQUE, *Correspondance de Bossuet*, t. II., pp. 35-46.
[2] Chap. xii.
[3] *Cf.* DUBOIS, *Histoire de l'Abbé de Rancé*, l. VII., chap. v. T. II., pp. 36 *ff.*
[4] Pp. 241-242, 290-334.
[5] See the letters to de Rancé of October 4 and November 11, 1687, and the notes of the editors URBAIN and LEVESQUE, *op. cit.*, t. III., pp. 426-429, 444-447. Bossuet at once had D. Mège's book suppressed by the authorities. " . . . May it remain banished from all places where true regularity and piety are known," he wrote to Mme. de Beringhen, March 28, 1689 (t. IV., pp. 15-16).
[6] See BOSSUET's letter to de Rancé of January 2, 1690 (URBAIN et LEVESQUE, *op. cit.*, t. IV., pp. 50-52).

Quintus humilitatis gradus est, si omnes cogitationes malas cordi suo advenientes, vel mala a se absconse commissa, per humilem confessionem Abbati non celaverit suo. Hortatur nos de hac re Scriptura, dicens: *Revela Domino viam tuam, et spera in eo.* Et item dicit: *Confitemini Domino, quoniam bonus, quoniam in sæculum misericordia ejus.* Et item Propheta: *Delictum meum cognitum tibi feci, et injustitias meas non operui. Dixi, pronuntiabo adversum me injustitias meas Domino, et tu remisisti impietatem cordis mei.*

The fifth degree of humility is to hide from one's Abbot none of the evil thoughts that beset one's heart, nor the sins committed in secret, but humbly to confess them. Concerning which the Scripture exhorts us, saying: "Make known thy way unto the Lord, and hope in him." And again: "Confess to the Lord, for he is good, for his mercy endureth for ever." So also the prophet says: " I have made known to thee my offence, and mine iniquities I have not hidden. I said, I will confess against myself my iniquities to the Lord: and thou hast forgiven the wickedness of my heart."

With the first four degrees the theory of humility is complete; we now know in what essentially consists the humility of the creature, the Christian, and the monk. What follows is only the application to certain circumstances in the monastic life of the principles already laid down. And—a point worth noting—we shall still for some time be occupied with internal elements; it would seem that the Rule makes a sort of proud claim to deal almost exclusively with such elements. To repeat, it is to the very sources of the moral life and to the depths where only God's eye can penetrate that we must carry our active efforts at correction; there is it that all should be regulated in the light of faith and in charity.

This degree is not concerned with sacramental confession. St. Benedict rarely speaks to us of divine or ecclesiastical law, since he supposes it known already. Besides Abbots were not always priests, and so could not receive confession *in ordine ad sacramentum*. What he speaks of here is a quite private affair, unofficial, a voluntary confiding of our wretchedness, what we know nowadays as "manifestation." Monastic tradition is unanimous in recommending this practice, for monks as well as for nuns. We have already quoted the wise words of the *Institutions* of Cassian, in speaking of the fifty-first instrument of good works; the tenth chapter of his second *Conference* might also be studied. St. Basil recurs frequently to that humble avowal of his secret faults which a monk should make, not, says he, to anyone at all, nor to one who pleases him, but to those who have the grace of state and proper capacity.[1] St. Benedict would like it to be to the Abbot himself; for it is only then that the procedure obtains its full effect. The Church, however, to prevent certain abuses, has reminded superiors that they have no right to exact manifestation of conscience.

These manifestations, says our Holy Father, deal with two matters. First with " all the evil thoughts that beset one's heart." Let us understand this well. According to St. Gregory, the history of temptation comprises three moments: suggestion, pleasure, consent. There

[1] *Reg. contr.*, xxi., cxcix., cc.

is no need to preserve and reveal to the Abbot what has been not even a suggestion, but only a lightning-like flash of thought; nor what has not caused real pleasure, because our soul at any rate, if not our sensibility, has remained unmoved. In the vague disturbances and confused movements of thoughts, inclinations, and impressions which make up our secret life, there are elements which we must know how to neglect; to attend to all is a weakness: *Nescire quædam magna pars sapientiæ* (Not to know some things is a great part of wisdom). But evil thoughts which are really ours, thoughts which abide with us, tendencies to which we surrender ourselves, inveterate companions of our thinking, these are the things which deserve to be brought out into the light. If they remain hidden they gradually overrun the soul. Likewise we must disclose the " sins we may have committed in secret."

The wholesomeness of this procedure is easily seen. All our external and public actions are controlled by regular authority, and we have a restraint also in human respect, propriety, and fear of ridicule; but our interior or hidden life is a thing apart. So St. Benedict provides this help to conscience and sends the monk to his Abbot. It is a practical application of the sentiment of the fear of God. Toothache is said to depart when one approaches the dentist's chair; it may be, too, that the mere thought: " I shall have to tell this," will often be enough to guard us against ourselves. In this then we may find an abundant source of security. A tempter does not care to have witnesses of his procedure. So it is notorious, as Cassian had remarked, that the devil dreads nothing more than the filial freedom with which we open our whole soul to our Abbot, knowing that such frankness shelters us from his arts and defends us against his shafts. God Himself guards us in the person of our superior. And all the texts here adduced (Ps. xxxvi. 5, cv. 1, xxxi. 5) regard the confidence given to the Abbot as given to Our Lord. They represent the avowal of our faults as a giving glory to God in its hopefulness and its praise of His mercy, as an infallible guarantee of His support and an assurance of pardon.

The most real benefit of the procedure is contained in the procedure itself. Without doubt it will obtain forgiveness for us, without doubt some guidance and practical advice will be provided us, and we shall accept it with eyes closed, without discussion or reservation; but its true and essential efficaciousness lies elsewhere. It establishes us in simplicity and absolute loyalty, it creates a profound unity in our life, a conformity between the inward and the outward. Certain little secret deceptions cannot withstand the determination to keep our souls always as an open book, to have nothing therein but what God and our neighbour may read, and to speak as we shall speak at the judgement seat of God. The peace and joy of our lives as monks depend largely on our freedom with the Abbot and his freedom with us.

Sextus humilitatis gradus est, si omni vilitate vel extremitate contentus sit monachus, et ad omnia quæ sibi	The sixth degree of humility is, for a monk to be contented with the meanest and worst of everything, and

injunguntur, velut operarium malum et indignum se judicet, dicens cum Propheta: *Ad nihilum redactus sum, et nescivi: ut jumentum factus sum apud te, et ego semper tecum.*

in all that is enjoined him to esteem himself a bad and worthless labourer, saying with the prophet: "I have been brought to nothing, and I knew it not: I am become as a beast before thee, yet I am always with thee."

The sixth degree of humility consists in accepting interiorly all the conditions of the monastic life and never being particular.[1] The monk will take all with a good grace, whether it be poverty of dwelling or clothes or food: *omni vilitate*. He will not allow himself to be surprised or discouraged by the base and menial character of tasks that may be entrusted to him; he will not be ashamed of the position that may be assigned to him and will not die of chagrin because he is forgotten in the distribution of dignities or favours: *vel extremitate*. Duties of considerable moment may sometimes come his way; he will not be conceited. Instead of being puffed up with his importance and regarding the trust committed to him as a tardy recognition of his capabilities, he will hold himself sincerely as an incapable workman, badly trained and predisposed of himself to all sorts of mistakes. Instead of promising himself to work wonders, he will put all his hope and strength in God alone; he will devote himself to every work that he is given, whatever it may be, with the same tranquil consciousness of his personal powerlessness, saying with the prophet: "Behold me brought to what I am, to nothing; I know naught. I am as a beast of burden before thee, and I am always with thee," that I may rest on thee (Ps. lxxii. 22-23).

To be content with anything does not mean that we must not bother much about slovenliness, neglect, boorishness of manners, and a whole assemblage of habits which may easily be a source of annoyance to others. There are no fictitious humiliations; but difficulties should not be added to those which are of rule. Nor yet does our Holy Father intend to prescribe conventual squalor and rudeness, nor even to condemn in advance what has lately been called "holy luxury"; though Martène, influenced by the principles of the early Cistercians and the Trappists, feels bound to deplore the sumptuous character of monastic dwellings.

Septimus humilitatis gradus est, si omnibus se inferiorem et viliorem, non solum sua lingua pronuntiet, sed etiam intimo cordis credat affectu, humilians se, et dicens cum Propheta: *Ego autem sum vermis, et non homo, opprobrium hominum, et abjectio plebis. Exaltatus sum, et humiliatus, et confusus.* Et item: *Bonum mihi quod humiliasti me, ut discam mandata tua.*

The seventh degree of humility is that he should not only call himself with his tongue lower and viler than all, but also believe himself with inmost affection of heart to be so, humbling himself, and saying with the prophet: "I am a worm and no man, the shame of men and the outcast of the people: I have been exalted, and cast down and confounded." And again: "It is good for me that thou hast humbled me, that I may learn thy commandments."

---

[1] *Cf.* S. BASIL., *Reg. contr.*, xxii.

A monk's humble appreciation of himself is not confined to the circumstances mentioned in the preceding degree, for it is universal and of universal application. The seventh degree embodies an element of comparison, in which certain authors would like to see, not a simple application of humility, but its very essence. Humility, to St. Bernard, is the virtue " by which a man, through truest self-knowledge, grows vile in his own eyes " (*qua homo, verissima sui agnitione, sibi ipsi vilescit*).[1] Wherein lies the comparison ? Must one believe himself inferior " to all things " ? It would surely be rather extreme to declare oneself inferior to beings who have not reason, to the devil, to the dust of the highway; moreover, it is hard to believe this, unless when we realize vividly, at certain times, how we abuse our power of turning from God, while irrational creatures obey Him without fail. One of the most characteristic marks of the saints is this eagerness to put themselves in the lowest place, to hold themselves cheap, to prefer themselves to none. In the most perfect characters, every grace of God but deepens in their eyes the abyss of their nothingness, and all the loving favours of Our Lord increase the conviction of their fundamental unworthiness. Can this be, as is sometimes said, " pious exaggeration," a fictitious and affected attitude ? It is undeniable that from one point of view we are all worth the same, since of ourselves we are worth nothing, and can do nothing but sin: " There is no sin that a man has committed, which another may not commit, except he be helped by God who made man." To this extent there is no difference between ourselves and others. To attain sincere and tried humility I shall not compare myself with my brethren, but I shall be attentive to my relation with God and to my worth in His sight. I know very little about my neighbour: if I see him do good, I should take edification therefrom; if, on the other hand, he do evil, my ignorance of his real dispositions should plead in his favour: " No one is bad, until he is proved so." We never know to what degree he is culpable, nor what influence heredity, previous training, and environment have had on him; we know not what he has been and what he is in God's sight, nor for what God destines him. How easy it would have been at Calvary to regard the good thief as a lost soul, or St. Paul himself as a wild fanatic at the martyrdom of St. Stephen![2] But at least we know ourselves well. " I know not," said the Count de Maistre, " what passes in the heart of a rogue; but there is enough in the heart of an honest man to make him blush." If anyone had treated us as we have treated Our Lord, we should have had no difficulty in regarding him as the basest of men. Have we not lied enough to God ? Have we not betrayed Him enough ? And how many days of fidelity have succeeded our repentances? An instant's reflection is enough to make us realize what we are and in what place we should put ourselves: inferior to all, more wretched than

---

[1] *De Gradibus humilitatis*, c. i. *P.L.*, CLXXXII., 942.
[2] *Cf.* S. Aug., *Liber de diversis* lxxxiii *quæst.*, *quæst.* lxxi., 5. *P.L.*, XL., 82. *De sancta virginit.*, lii. *P.L., ibid.*, 427.

all,[1] under the feet of all: "I am a worm and no man, the shame of men and the outcast of the people" (Ps. xxi. 7).

When he does not confine himself to mere verbal protestations, which are always easy,[2] but obeys a spontaneous and profound conviction,[3] then the monk shares in the humility of Him who, expiating all our misery in His own person, uttered on the cross the words of the prophet which we have just quoted. Then the soul recognizes, in the degradation to which it has fallen, the just punishment of its pride: "I raised myself up, and lo! I am cast down and confounded" (Ps. lxxxvii. 16). It understands all the spiritual profit of this humiliation thus accepted: "It is good for me that thou hast humbled me, for thus I shall learn to obey thee" (Ps. cxviii. 71).

| Octavus humilitatis gradus est, si nihil agat monachus, nisi quod communis monasterii regula, vel majorum cohortantur exempla. | The eighth degree of humility is, for a monk to do nothing except what is authorized by the common Rule of the monastery, or the example of his seniors. |

A monk who practises the seventh degree of humility finds the observance of the eighth a matter of course. He remains quietly in his place, as an anonymous unit, one of many; he seeks no exceptions or privileges; he does nothing that is out of the way or attracts notice, but only what is authorized by the common rule of the monastery and by the conduct—according to rule—of the seniors, by lawful custom.[4] This is not an invitation to sloth or apathy, nor to a sort of stoicism, a lack of filial simplicity, which would leave the Abbot the task of finding out for himself our weakness and our needs; our Holy Father only wishes to destroy every expression of self-will. We have by instinct a love of petty distinctions; it is only with some chagrin that we make up our minds to be ignored and lost in the crowd, especially if we were once honoured and exalted. We strive after originality, singularity, pose, effect. We would be personages and have our style, our own point of view, and our own manner of thought. All of which is a wretched revocation of that sacrifice of ourselves which we accepted on the day of our profession. Moreover, this need of self-assertion manifests itself most often in trivial, almost insignificant, matters, wherein all a man's selfishness seems to take refuge. It may be a small point of pronunciation, a personal peculiarity in the common ceremonial, exceptions in the refectory. And this degenerates into a passion, whether open or concealed, and sometimes into revolt. It is great virtue and real spiritual eminence to conform oneself always to the customs of the monastery and that even in external practices of devotion: *Ama nesciri*

---

[1] *Verba Seniorum: Vitæ Patrum*, III., 206. ROSWEYD, p. 531. — S. MACAR., *Reg.*, iii.—S. BASIL., *Reg. contr.*, lxii.

[2] *Cf.* CASS., *Conlat.*, XVIII., xi.

[3] The phrase is CASSIAN'S, in the parallel passage; it is found also in *Conlat.*, XXIV., xvi.; XII., xiii.

[4] CASS., *Instit.*, V., xxiii.; *Conlat.*, XVIII., iii.; II., x.: *Nullatenus decipi poterit quisque, si non suo judicio, sed majorum vivit exemplo.*

et pro nihilo reputari (Love to be unknown and to be counted for nothing).

Nonus humilitatis gradus est, si linguam ad loquendum prohibeat monachus et taciturnitatem habens, usque ad interrogationem non loquatur, monstrante Scriptura quia *in multiloquio non effugietur peccatum;* et quia *vir linguosus non dirigetur super terram.*

The ninth degree of humility is that a monk refrain his tongue from speaking, keeping silence until a question be asked him, as the Scripture shows: " In much talking thou shalt not avoid sin ": and, " The talkative man shall not be directed upon the earth."

In the eighth degree St. Benedict consented at last to speak of external works, and in that degree he has comprised our whole monastic activity. The three succeeding degrees, which might easily be united into one, deal with some more important details, with speech and certain concomitants of speech. A humble monk knows how to restrain his tongue, which is ever liable to misuse. He has the spirit of silence and a reverence for silence. In the presence of his superiors or his brethren he is wont, as it were, to await a summons[1] and a motive, before he speaks. Even in time of recreation one should observe moderation; yet conversation has its rights, and that is its hour. But would that we could speak only in time of recreation! There are those who are constantly at high pressure and cannot contain themselves. It has become necessity and second nature. They always suppose the matter is urgent, be it an excellent joke, or some confidence that will not wait, or a genial notion which must immediately be shared with friends. And it is futile to talk of silence before such as these, for they always think the criticism is meant for others. Let us beware of condoning our talkativeness, on the ground that after all it is only an external matter; for, alas! this external disposition is joined interiorly with a fund of pride, immortification, and spiritual dissipation. And we shall only succeed in correcting the secret enemy if we try to grapple with him in his visible manifestations. The result of this thoughtless stream of talk, as Scripture tells us, is unfailingly sin (Prov. x. 19); it means also loss of time—and that irremediably—scandal, and the slow destruction of our fraternal charity and spirit of obedience. The wordy man, the great talker, will never succeed, never find his way upon the earth: he will weary and offend both God and men (Ps. cxxxix. 12).

Decimus humilitatis gradus est, si non sit facilis ac promptus in risu, quia scriptum est: *Stultus in risu exaltat vocem suam.*

The tenth degree of humility is that he be not easily moved and prompt to laughter; because it is written: " The fool lifteth up his voice in laughter."

St. Benedict has already warned us several times against buffoonery, gainst the " loud, resounding laugh." We are well aware that a pleasant wit is a virtue; children would certainly not have surrounded Our

---

[1] *Usquequo servandum est silentium? usquequo interrogeris* (*Verba Seniorum: Vitæ Patrum*, VII., c. xxxii. ROSWEYD, p. 679).

Lord and sought His blessing, if He had not consented to smile and be agreeable. But the Holy Rule will not tolerate a habit of treating nothing seriously, of turning everything into jest. This infirmity of the mind is one of the most unpleasant traces of the spirit of the world. Even in the world it is irritating and in bad taste; it is considered the mark of a superficial mind and empty soul: " A fool lifteth up his voice in laughter " (Ecclus. xxi. 23). But for a monk it is incompatible with recollection and the sense of the presence of God. Moreover, it contains a rich store of self-love, the desire for display, of passing as a man of parts, a " devil of a fellow." There is this danger too: all this foolish gaiety stirs up an impure sediment, a sort of dangerous bottom of coarseness; reason and will fall partly into abeyance and we are thrown off our guard. And there is perhaps no loophole in a man's character through which temptation and evil suggestion get in more surely. Père Surin, who knew the ways of the devil, speaks in his book on the nuns of Loudun of a possessed nun who owed the fits of possession to a sort of rude high spirits, to which she used to surrender herself: she did not get rid of the devil until she had corrected this excessive gaiety.

Undecimus humilitatis gradus est, si, cum loquitur monachus, leniter et sine risu, humiliter et cum gravitate, vel pauca verba et rationabilia loquatur, et non sit clamosus in voce; sicut scriptum est: Sapiens verbis innotescit paucis.	The eleventh degree of humility is that when a monk speaks he do so gently and without laughter, humbly, gravely, with few and reasonable words, and that he be not noisy in his speech, as it is written: "A wise man is known in a few words."

St. Benedict has not prescribed absolute silence, but no one can fail to admire the number of precautions with which he has surrounded silence. In the ninth degree he asked us not to be too ready to speak; in the tenth, not to be too ready to laugh; he now describes the manner of the humble and well-instructed monk when he must make use of speech. He must do it gently, without laughter or jest, humbly, gravely, with few words and such as are reasonable, without shouting or noise,[1] following the example of Our Lord, of whom St. Matthew (xii. 19) says (after Isaiah), " He shall not contend nor cry out: neither shall any man hear his voice in the streets."

Instead of this text St. Benedict quotes another in which it is said that " the wise man is known in a few words." Though he says *scriptum est* (it is written), and we find an equivalent thought in several passages of the sacred books, notably in the tenth chapter of Ecclesiastes (verse 14), it is not from Holy Scripture that he has taken the verbal form of this maxim. As D. Hugh Ménard observed in his time, this is the hundred and thirty-fourth of the sentences of Sextus. Rufinus translated this collection from Greek into Latin[2] and offered it to the sister of his friend

---

[1] *Cf.* S. BASIL., *Reg. contr.*, cxxx.
[2] See this translation in the *Maxima Bibliotheca veterum Patrum* of MARGARIN DE LA BIGNE, t. III., p. 335; and in MULLACH, *Fragmenta Philosophorum græcorum*, t. I., p. 523.

Apronianus as a precious "ring," worthy of being worn on the finger. Men say, said he, that its author was Sixtus, Bishop of Rome and martyr. St. Augustine at first accepted this attribution, but later, being better informed, changed his mind. As for St. Jerome, he several times denounced with indignation the audacity of Rufinus for daring to ascribe to St. Sixtus an entirely pagan work containing doctrinal errors. The Decree of Gelasius condemned it. In fact, there has, it would seem, been a confusion between St. Sixtus II. and a Pythagorean or Stoic philosopher of the same name.[1] However, an English critic, Conybeare, has quite recently endeavoured to prove that the *Ring of Pope Xystus* is the work of a philosopher, retouched by a Christian living before A.D. 150, who may have been Pope Sixtus I.[2]

Duodecimus humilitatis gradus est, si non solum corde monachus, sed etiam ipso corpore humilitatem videntibus se semper indicet, id est, in opere,[3] in oratorio, in monasterio, in horto, in via, in agro vel ubicumque, sedens, ambulans, vel stans, inclinato sit semper capite, defixis in terram aspectibus, reum se omni hora de peccatis suis existimans, jam se tremendo Dei judicio præsentari existimet: dicens sibi in corde semper illud quod publicanus ille evangelicus, fixis in terram oculis, dixit: *Domine, non sum dignus ego peccator levare oculos meos ad cælum.* Et item cum Propheta: *Incurvatus et humiliatus sum usquequaque.*

The twelfth degree of humility is that the monk, not only in his heart, but also in his very exterior, always show his humility to all who see him: that is, in work, in the oratory, in the monastery, in the garden, on the road, in the field, or wherever he may be, whether sitting, walking, or standing, with head always bent down, and eyes fixed on the earth; that he ever think of the guilt of his sins, and imagine himself already present before the terrible judgement seat of God, always saying in his heart what the publican in the Gospel said with his eyes fixed on the earth: "Lord, I a sinner am not worthy to raise mine eyes to heaven." And again, with the prophet: "I am bowed down and humbled on every side."

For the last time let us remark the character of this antique spirituality which takes a man interiorly and makes of spiritual renewal a spontaneous and living work, the normal development of divine forces produced in us by baptism and the other sacraments. If humility be really in the heart it will appear in the body also, and will regulate all its movements; it will be like a new temperament, a nature made in humility replacing the old. This external manifestation is a thing natural and necessary: it is the very consequence of our oneness of being. So we should be on our watch against regarding this twelfth degree as the least of all, on the pretext that it concerns only the body. Deep sentiments, whether great love, great sorrow, or lofty thought, have always a dominant and despotic character. They work a change first

---

[1] *Cf. P.L.*, XXI., 40-42, 191-200.—HARNACK, *Die Ueberlieferung und der Bestand der altchristlichen Litteratur bis Eusebius*, p. 765.

[2] *The Ring of Pope Xystus, together with the Prologue of Rufinus, now first rendered into English with an historical and critical commentary* (London, 1910).

[3] The best supported reading is: *in Opere Dei*.

in the centre of our soul: the soul becomes as it were collected to a point; it makes a clean sweep; all that is not in accordance with this deep sentiment is treated as non-existent, or as accidental and negligible. Then there is a change at the circumference: the passion resounds to the very confines of our nature, and concentrates all our activity in its minutest forms; it wrecks our life or remakes it on its own plan. Man must perforce bear on him the trace of his vices; virtue, too, imprints its glorious stigmata on him, but less rapidly; for the more animal our impulses are, the more physical in their basis, the more readily do they stamp themselves on the sensibility and mould the body itself. Interior and exterior are conjoined, and we may sometimes prove it from the opposite direction; for deliberate external attitudes do partially modify the interior.[1]

When humility has laid hold of a soul, it embraces the whole man insensibly; it is like that Scripture unguent which begins with the head and then, little by little, makes its way to the fringe of the garment: "Like the precious ointment on the head, that ran down upon the beard, the beard of Aaron, that ran down to the skirt of his garment" (Ps. cxxxii. 2). The humble monk, says St. Benedict, enumerating the chief circumstances of the day and the diverse positions of the body, is recognizable everywhere and always. He neither walks, nor sits, nor stands, in the manner of the world, least of all like the vain or frivolous. His manner is not smug and conceited, he does not bully or rail, nor does he carry himself proudly and arrogantly. Habitually his head is gently bent, his gaze fixed on the ground. It has been remarked that the eyes of the saints, even when they are looking at some object, seem turned inwards, towards the hidden Beauty, so far and yet so near. Herein is a living lesson in humility: "that he always show his humility to all who see him." But there must be no stiffness or affectation. We need not think about the external effect of our humility, and still less must we aim at such effect, for to be anxious to edify by the display of virtue is always to run extreme risk of pride.

The exposition of the twelfth degree of humility is rounded off with a doctrinal reassertion of the principle of humility—that is, the fear of God, implying our looking to Him and His looking on us, eternal life being the issue. For Our Lord's look is not a Platonic gaze, a sort of infinite mirror in which created things are merely reflected; it is already a judgement. Undoubtedly this judgement will not be fully known to us until death has fixed its irrevocable seal upon our deeds; but we must never forget that God is our judge even here and now. He is our judge not only because He sees us and weighs us and registers our deserts, but also because He commences even now to execute sentence. When prayer is tasteless, reading ineffective, feast-days without savour, the truths of faith powerless to rouse, life without joy, grace attenuated, what is all this but the present operation of the justice of God? But even when things are not pushed to this extremity, even when we know we are in the

---

[1] *Cf.* S. AUG., *De cura pro mortuis gerenda*, c. v. P.L., XL., 597.

grace of God and feel His love, even then, says St. Benedict, we should ever be conscious of the load of our sins, and can ever without falsity regard ourselves as already standing before the dread judgement seat of God. And while, in the bottom of our hearts, we correspond with the exercise of divine justice by a continual act of humble repentance, of charity, and of adoration, we must keep exteriorly the only attitude that befits us, the attitude of the publican in the Gospel (Luke xviii. 13; Matt. viii. 8). Like him we must confess to God that we are unworthy to raise our eyes towards heaven and His purity.[1] Or we must repeat with the prophet: " Lo, I am bowed down always in humility" (Ps. cxviii. 107).

Ergo his omnibus humilitatis gradibus ascensis, monachus mox ad caritatem Dei perveniet illam, quæ perfecta foras mittit timorem; per quam universa quæ prius non sine formidine observabat, absque ullo labore, velut naturaliter ex consuetudine incipit custodire, non jam timore gehennæ, sed amore Christi et consuetudine ipsa bona et delectatione virtutum. Quod Dominus in operario suo mundo a vitiis et peccatis, Spiritu Sancto dignabitur demonstrare.

Having, therefore, ascended all these degrees of humility, the monk will presently arrive at that love of God which, being perfect, casts out fear: whereby he shall begin to keep, without labour, and as it were naturally and by custom, all those precepts which he had hitherto observed not without fear, no longer through dread of hell, but for the love of Christ, and of a good habit and a delight in virtue. Which God will vouchsafe to manifest by the Holy Spirit in His labourer, now cleansed from vice and sin.

This is the end. Save for the last sentence, it is taken almost verbally from Cassian.[2] So here we have the symbolical steps fixed into body and soul. When we have scaled them resolutely, without neglecting any—and for this a few days' retreat will probably not suffice—God will hasten to give us the promised recompense. This recompense is the same as that mentioned at the end of the Prologue: union with God in perfect charity. In both passages we read also of a fear which is driven out by love, and of an unspeakable sweetness which permeates the powers of the soul. It would seem that St. Benedict was anxious to fix clearly the nature of this fear which is driven out by perfect charity (1 John iv. 18): it is not chaste fear, which " abideth for ever and ever," but a cowardly fear, which keeps us to the performance of duty and magnifies its difficulties; and it is also servile fear, the dread of eternal punishment. For St. Benedict would have us substitute for this last motive, somewhat inferior and Jewish as it is, the influence of nobler motives—viz., love of Our Lord, a leaning towards the good, a delight in pleasing God.

Thanks to charity, all that the monk did not aforetime fulfil without

---

[1] The quotation is far from literal; it recalls a passage of the Prayer of Manasses printed at the end of our Latin Bibles: *Domine*, . . . *non sum dignus intueri et aspicere altitudinem cæli præ multitudine iniquitatum mearum.*

[2] *Inst.*, IV., xxxix.—*Cf. Conlat.*, XI., viii.—Compare with this ending to the chapter St. Augustine, *In Epistolam Joann.*, tract. IX., 2-9. *P.L.*, XXXV., 2045-2052.

dread, he now, when deeply attached to Our Lord, fulfils without effort, as it were spontaneously and naturally, by the influence of good habit, and with the secret charm that the practice of virtue brings to souls which are delivered from themselves. Love carries us, love has transfigured all; its unction has penetrated all the faculties of our being. There is no more inertia in us, no more difficulties in things; or, if there be still difficulty, it is the condiment of action, a stimulus to good, a motive the more for charity to display and prove itself. We are on the road to God, with souls all bathed in His love, with natures wholly inspired by His gospel and thoroughly Christianized. And assuredly joy is not lacking. The exclusion of all sensible and material pleasure has prepared us to enjoy the true pleasure and the true good. *Quæ major voluptas quam fastidium omnis voluptatis?* (What greater pleasure than aversion from all pleasure?) said Tertullian. Undoubtedly St. Benedict recommended the fear of God's presence as a medicine; but that which was the remedy of our convalescence becomes the generous nourishment and the delight of our health. Profound happiness, assured and invincible, is to live thus in God's sight, near Him and in Him.

And our Holy Father adds some words to which we may give the meaning either of a promise, or of a modest prayer or loving wish. The words take the form of a compact which our Holy Father makes with us, in the name of Our Lord. Such, says he, is the programme which Our Lord will deign to fulfil and show forth. He will not manifest it to the world, for where would be the good? But He will make it known to him in whom it shall be accomplished. After having, by means of humility, purified His servant and workman from vice and sin, He will pour forth in him without stint the substantial unction of His Spirit. This is the eternal rôle of the Spirit of God. Since, in the bosom of the Holy Trinity, He is the indissoluble bond, the living tie, and eternal embrace of Father and Son, so are attributed to Him *ad extra* (in external operation) all supernatural unions. He it is who unites us to Our Lord Jesus Christ and by Our Lord to the Father; He it is who gives us the temper for this region and this sanctuary where our life is established for ever. And we reach it by the one way which Our Lord traced and Himself followed: the humility of little children.

CHAPTER VIII

OF THE DIVINE OFFICE AT NIGHT

HAVING traced the main lines of the spiritual training of his disciples, St. Benedict now sets himself to organize liturgical and conventual prayer. He begins without any doctrinal introduction; but we may pause to ask ourselves what the Church and the old monastic legislators mean when, whether explicitly or not, they make the Divine Office the central and essential work of the religious and contemplative life.

Whatever may be the etymology of the word " religion,"[1] it implies, in its broadest acceptation, the idea of a relation towards God. In this sense the whole creation has a religious character. All things, in the very measure in which they possess being, are bound to God their Creator, Providence, and Last End. Ontologically all are true, beautiful, and good; all are in conformity with the ideal of the divine Artificer; all are a created expression of uncreated Beauty; all are in accord with His will and are good of Him and for Him, lending themselves with facility to His designs. The whole of this vast creation speaks of God and obeys Him; it is a sweet song in His ears, a surpassing act of praise. " The Lord hath made all things for himself " (Prov. xvi. 4). Not even moral evil can disturb the harmony of God's plan. Unwillingly and with disgust does creation endure the profanation of the wicked, who would turn it from its end; it groans in this servitude; and while waiting for its day of resurrection and recompense (Rom. viii. 19 *sq.*) it co-operates in the work of redemption and serves as the instrument of God's vengeance. Nor is all this a mere dream or an exaggerated fancy. Creation as a whole possesses in a true and special way a liturgical character. It resembles the divine life itself: for the Holy Trinity is a temple wherein, by His eternal generation, the Word is the perfect praise of the Father, " the brightness of his glory and the figure of his substance "; where the communion of Father and Son is sealed in the kiss of peace and in the personal joy which is their common Spirit. Glory has been defined as *clara notitia cum laude* (clear knowledge conjoined with praise); by the twofold procession of which we have just spoken God finds in Himself His essential glory. It is enough for Him; and the glory which He must receive from His works is only necessary on the creature's side; for God it remains accidental and exterior. Yet He may not renounce it: " I will not give my glory to another."

Furthermore, we should notice that this accidental glory of God is only complete on condition that it is at once objective, formal, and expressed. Objective glory is the real manifestation of the perfections

---

[1] *Summa*, II.-II., *q*. lxxxi., a. 1.

of God: all being, all life, all created beauty, whether natural or supernatural, is ontologically the praise of God. Formal glory is paid only by rational creatures, who alone are capable of appreciating objective glory and of tracing it to its source; and only in this act do we get religion and liturgy. Without saying anything in this place about the religion of the angels, we may at least remark the truly sacerdotal position of man in the midst of the lower creation. The Apostle says in his Epistle to the Hebrews : " Every high-priest taken from among men is ordained for men in the things that appertain to God, that he may offer up gifts and sacrifices " (v.1). Man himself is taken out of creation, raised above it, and made its priest, so that he may offer to God, in his own name and in the name of the whole world, an intelligent homage. By his very nature an abridgement of the universe—a " microcosm," as the ancients put it—his function is to collect the manifold voices of creation, as if all found their echo in his heart, as if he were the world's consciousness; and his mission is to give life to all with his thought and love, and to make offering of all, whether in his use of the world or in explicit praise. The religious system of the world is completed and made perfect only in him; he is the link between the world and God; and when this link is broken, then the whole creation is affected and falls: " cursed is the earth in thy work " (Gen. iii. 17).

Man's religion is not æstheticism, nor emotion, nor a blind deference to prejudices of upbringing, nor a cosmological theory, nor self-love and the love of humanity; it is not even " an affirmation concerning matters which lie beyond experience," nor the idea of the infinite; yet all these definitions have been advanced. Religion is a moral virtue, the most noble of all the moral virtues, and is akin to justice. It disposes us to pay God the worship that is His due. And the formal object of this worship, the fundamental motive of all religious acts, is the sovereign eminence of God, His infinite excellence as it is in itself : " We give Thee thanks for Thy great glory," and as it manifests itself for our sake in creation, conservation, providence, and all benefits.[1] If we had leisure to write the history of any religious act whatever, we should note with theologians that it always implies an intellectual appreciation of divine excellence, a humble self-abasement, the will to confess submission, and finally an actual recognition of the divine sovereignty, whether by way of an expressive act and confirmation of some sort, merely internal in character, or by an act which is at once internal and openly manifested. It is this last act which properly speaking makes the act of religion and worship, in which the glorification of God is consummated. However, a liturgy is something more than this; it is the sum of acts, words, chants, and ceremonies, by means of which we manifest our interior religion; it is a collective and social prayer, the forms of which have a character that is regular, definite, and determined.

The raising of man to the supernatural order made his relation to God more intimate and his religion more exalted. Nor has God been

[1] *Summa*, II.-II., *q.* lxxxi.—SUAREZ, *De virtute et statu religionis*, l. I., c. vi.

content with the priesthood of man for the uniting of Himself to creation. This link was fragile, and it broke; and perhaps God's very motive in allowing it to break was that He might replace it by another priesthood and make another humanity, no longer resting on Adam and on man, but on Jesus Christ and the Man-God. When He consented to run the risks of creation, it was because He was thinking of the incomparable glory that would be paid Him by His Word Incarnate, the Redeemer. It would be easy to show how the Incarnate Word completes the hierarchical series of the three sorts of glory of which we have spoken, how the whole creation, both natural and supernatural, is united to Him and incorporated with Him, the unique and eternal High-Priest, so as to offer to the Holy Trinity a single sacrifice of expiation, adoration, and thanksgiving, filling both time and eternity. To participate in His death and in His life by baptism is, in reality, according to St. Peter (1 Peter ii. 4 ff.), to share in His royal priesthood, so as to co-operate in the great liturgical act of which He is at one and the same time, and eminently, altar, priest, and victim. Nor has the Apostle Paul laid down any other programme for the Christian: "By him therefore let us offer the sacrifice of praise always to God, that is to say, the fruit of lips confessing to his name" (Heb. xiii. 15).

But all particular liturgies centre round, are merged in, and draw their strength from, the collective liturgy of that great living organism the Church, which is the perfect man and the fulness of Christ. The whole life of the Church expresses and unfolds itself in its liturgy; all the relations of creatures with God here find their principle and their consummation; by the very acts that in the individual as in the whole mass realize union with God, the liturgy pays God "all honour and glory." In it the Holy Spirit has achieved the concentration, eternalization, and diffusion throughout the whole Body of Christ of the unchangeable fulness of the act of redemption, all the spiritual riches of the Church in the past, in the present, and in eternity. And as the bloody sacrifice, and the entry of our High Priest into the sanctuary of heaven, mark the culmination of His work, so the liturgy has its centre in the Mass, the "Eucharist." The Divine Office and the Hours are but the splendid accompaniment, the preparation for or radiance from the Eucharist. It may be said that the two economies, the natural and the supernatural, meet in this synthetic act, this "Action" *par excellence.* So our Holy Father and other ancient writers[1] are well inspired when they call the liturgy in its totality the *Opus Dei* (Work of God): the work which has God and God alone for its direct object, the work which magnifies God, the work which works divine things, the work in which God is solely interested, of which He is the principal agent, but which He has willed should be accomplished by human hands and human lips.

---

[1] *Cf.* Hæft., l. VII., tract. ii., disq. iii.—Butler (*op. cit.*, p. 203) notes that the expression *Opus Dei* has the same sense in the *Rules* of St. Cæsarius as in St. Benedict, and he adds: *Apud alios scriptores antiquiores . . . significabat opera vitæ spiritualis vel asceticæ, ex. gr.* Basilii *Reg.*, 85, 86, 95, etc.

There are differences and special privileges among those who are consecrated priests and religious by the same baptism. God, by the sacrament of Holy Orders, associates some more intimately with the priesthood of His Son. Others are religious, not merely in the adjectival sense, like ordinary Christians, but substantially and essentially. Every authentic form of the religious life has for its first object the unifying of the powers of the soul, so as to make them combine for the contemplation and service of God. To be a religious is to belong to God alone, by a consecration and holocaust of one's whole self. "Religion, since it is a state in which a man consecrates his whole self and all his belongings to the worship of God, and so to speak immolates all, is without doubt a state of perfection."[1] We can well understand why the Church has entrusted the celebration of her liturgy especially to religious. In fact, apart from rare exceptions or dispensations, the Divine Office remains the first duty of every religious family. Religious, therefore, remain such in substance, even though the Church, desiring to secure full success for apostolic or charitable work, puts it into their consecrated hands. Yet, they are then religious "with addition," in view of work which is superadded and which, though religious because of its motive and relation to God, is not so directly and in its object.

But we monks are religious "without addition," we are religious only; we are given up to God to belong to Him solely. In our life no distraction and division is possible; our work is of the same nature as our life. We are not religious for the Work of God *and* for study, any more than for manual labour: for then our condition would be far inferior to that of the secular clergy who are directly concerned with souls. We do not deny that a contemplative can and should study; we do not dispute that erudite labours or apostolic works may be lawfully undertaken and successfully accomplished by monks. We content ourselves with the affirmation that the proper and distinctive work of the Benedictine, his lot and his mission, is the liturgy. He makes his profession so as to be in the Church—which is an association for the praise of God— one who glorifies God according to forms instituted by her who knows how God should be honoured and possesses the words of eternal life. He is wholly a man of prayer, and the diverse forms of his activity take spontaneously a religious colour, a quality of adoration and praise. Theologians enquire whether every good act which is performed with the formal design of honouring God becomes an act of religion and worship. St. Thomas, while recognizing a special value in acts which are produced directly by the virtue of religion and are its proper fruit, replies that all acts which are prescribed or determined by it take from this source a religious character.[2] Actions of this last sort are innumerable in a religious life; and especially because of the profound and total consecration of our very being to God's service there can scarcely be an act which escapes this transformation, provided the soul is careful often

---

[1] *Summa*, II.-II., *q.* clxxxvi., *a.* 1.
[2] *Summa*, II.-II., *q.* lxxxi., *aa.* 1 et 4.

to renew and ratify its profession. "If a man devote his whole life to the service of God, his whole life will belong to religion."[1]

But, beyond this personal and inclusive consecration which we share with all religious, we have, let it be repeated, a special vocation to prayer; the whole practical organization of our life is connected with and converges towards worship. The holy liturgy is for us, at one and the same time, a means of sanctification and an end. But it is especially an end. Our contemplation nourishes itself therein without cessation, and so to speak finds in the liturgy its adequate object and proper term.[2] This should be well understood. It is not a small matter, even from a practical point of view, to know our end with all exactitude, to find a definition so successful as to include both God and ourselves, His interests and ours, His glory and our happiness, the work of time and the work of eternity. There is no lack of definitions: we are told that our business is to "secure our salvation," "to procure the glory of God," "to realize our sanctification," "to attain union with God and His eternal life." These definitions are precise but of unequal value; though it is true that with a little explanation we may find the fulness of doctrine implied in all, and, for enlightened and generous souls, the first loses its tendency to lead in practice to lukewarmness and a commercial spirituality. The last is the best, and it is the one which our Holy Father adopts, in company with all the ancient writers. But none, save the second, suggests the idea of liturgy. And it is a pity; for after all our union with God is itself ordained for praise.

The supernatural beauty of Our Lord in us, that perfect resemblance to Him which the whole supernatural economy is engaged in forming, that divine imprint which the liturgy like some press is ever stamping on our souls, is not given to us that we should take our joy in it by ourselves, in selfish complacency. If we share more than others in the life and the experience of Him who has for His personal mission to reveal and glorify the Father, it is that we may share in His destiny, may with Him exercise that priesthood of which we have just spoken, may, like the ancients of the Apocalypse casting their crowns, or, like Our Lord on the Last Day, throw down before the throne of God our participated splendour. The value of the act depends upon the value of the agent; the adoration depends upon the adorer. And it is only because God "seeks those who will adore in spirit and in truth" that He has made us one with His Son by means of His Holy Spirit. In the wonderful passage with which the Epistle to the Ephesians begins, St. Paul makes it plain that the supreme end of creation and redemption, of that "recapitulation" of all things in Christ, is the liturgical witness to infinite Excellence and infinite Beauty: "He chose us in him before the foundation of the world, that we should be holy and unspotted in

[1] *Summa*, II.-II., *q.* clxxxvi., *a.* 1, ad. 2.
[2] See *The Spiritual Life and Prayer according to Holy Scripture and Monastic Tradition*, chaps. x., xx., xxii., xxiii. (By Madame Cécile Bruyère, Abbess of Ste Cécile de Solesmes.)

his sight in charity, who hath predestinated us unto the adoption of children through Jesus Christ unto himself: according to the purpose of his will: unto the praise of the glory of his grace, in which he hath graced us in his beloved son." Therefore there is a close connection between the three elements: union with God, the praise of God, the glory of God. Our individual and conventual sanctity expresses itself in that same liturgical prayer which realizes it most effectually; it is our blessedness to enter even here below into the life and joy of our God; it is to make all that created and uncreated being, which comes to us from the Father by way of the Word and Holy Spirit, flow back eternally by this same road of the Word and the Spirit towards its beginning that has no beginning, the Father.

Does our Holy Father speak of the liturgy immediately after describing the individual training of the monk because all our training and all our virtue are connected with our prayer? Is there purpose in this order? We may be allowed to think so, though it would be hard to prove it. What is certain is that St. Benedict has himself defined the monastic life as the " school of the Lord's service "; that he places the regulation of the liturgy in the forefront of his legislation; that he regulates this public prayer with more precision and care than anything else, leaving to individual initiative the measure and manner of private prayer; that he urges us finally " to set nothing before the Work of God." In fact all other monastic occupations depend upon this; the liturgy fixes our whole horarium; it claims almost all the hours of our day, and those the best hours. While a life devoted to study profits by the silence of the morning hours and the mental clarity that sleep has restored to push forward its learned researches at its ease, we for our part set ourselves to repeat the same psalms in the presence of the same God. Would a monk be faithful to the Rule and his conscience who should not give himself readily to this seeming waste, who should as far as possible husband the hours of the day so as to measure out parsimoniously what shall be given to God? Though our Holy Father calls the Office our *servitutis pensum* (meed of service), we never consider it as a task or forced labour; and if, at times, in an active and very busy ministry, some clerics are tempted to fulfil the duty of their Office with haste, or even to groan under the weight of this additional burden, there can never be any excuse for the monk to regard the Divine Office so.

What if the world does not understand this work of prayer and does not appreciate its purpose, except it be from an æsthetic standpoint? And yet how few are affected by the real and supernatural beauty of the rites of the Church or the sacred chant! We shall never be tempted so to reduce our life that the world may comprehend it; for our life is what God and St. Benedict and our own free act have made it. Discord with the world is a principle of ours, as old as the Gospel and as old as our Rule: *A sæculi actibus se facere alienum* (To keep aloof from worldly ways). The world is irreligious of its nature, professedly atheistic, sometimes with an atheism which is measured and knows its limitations, but at others with an aggressive atheism which stops at no lengths and at no measures. If the world does not understand the life of contemplatives, then why does it single them out for its persecution? Because the hatred of him who inspires the world is more clearsighted. Besides irreligion there is the vague religious sentiment of so many Christians, and, in a period of feverish activity and utilitarianism, an almost universal misunderstanding of the function of prayer. *Fas est et ab hoste doceri*: in the face of this naturalistic and impious conspiracy we are more than ever bound to be religious, completely and solely, and to assert what men deny or forget. And this not in a reactionary spirit, or from rivalry and contrast with other Orders, but from a fine and delicate sense of fidelity. Since we are, by special title, God's religious, we must, so to speak, offer Him compensation, and make our fidelity all the more loyal the more God is deserted: " You are they who have continued with me in my temptations. And I dispose to you, as my Father hath disposed to me, a kingdom; that you may eat and drink at my table, in my kingdom " (Luke xxii. 28-30).

Our ambition goes no farther than that. Yet we believe in the apostolic and social value of our prayer, and we believe that by it we reach directly not only God and ourselves, but our neighbours also. Even without speaking of its secret influence on the providential course of events, is not the spectacle of the Office worthily celebrated a very effective sort of preaching? Since the days of the primitive Church (Acts ii. 42-47) the Catholic liturgy has been a principle of unity for the people of God, and social charity has been created by it.[1] Can we hope to see the true and deep solidarity of Christendom restored, apart from that reunion of all around God, sharing in the same prayer and the same living Bread? However this may be, yet we are content to be makers of nothing that is visible or tangible, and to have no other usefulness than that of adoring God. We are glad and content to attain by the Work of God nothing but the essential end of all things, the end of the whole rational creation, the very end of the Church. So to act is to take here and now the attitude of eternity, and to rehearse for heaven; for, according to St. John, the work of those who are admitted into the heavenly Jerusalem is contemplation and a royal service: " The throne of God and of the Lamb shall be in it. And his servants shall serve him. And they shall see his face: and his name shall be on their foreheads. . . . And they shall reign for ever and ever" (Apoc. xxii. 3-5).

The methodical order in which St. Benedict sets out the parts of his liturgical legislation is obvious. He speaks to us first of the Night Office, then of the Day Office, and finally of the general discipline of the Divine Office, and of the dispositions which a monk should take with him to prayer. We may enumerate the subjects treated in these thirteen chapters, while noting that the titles given to them in the Rule do not always correspond exactly with their real contents.

[1] Read the general Introduction to the *Liturgical Year*.

VIII. The hour for the Night Office according to the season.
IX. The composition of the Night Office in winter.
X. The composition of the Night Office in summer.
XI. The composition of the Night Office on Sundays.
XII. The composition of the Morning Office on Sundays.
XIII. The composition of the Morning Office on ferias.
XIV. The composition of the Office on Saints'-days.
XV. The use of *Alleluia*.
XVI. The number of the Hours of the Day Office.
XVII. The composition of the six last Hours of the day.
XVIII. The distribution of the Psalter among the different Hours.
XIX.-XX. Attitude of mind and body during prayer.

In the liturgy, as in other observances of his Rule, St. Benedict shows an intelligent eclecticism. His *cursus* is composed of borrowings from the Roman and Ambrosian liturgies, and from the monastic liturgies of East and West, with some novelties and personal preferences. The whole forms a solid and stable framework, where all important details are foreseen; and doubtless St. Benedict wished, on this point as on others, to remedy the fluctuations of current monastic discipline. Yet the framework was not, as we shall see, absolutely rigid, although the time of improvisation and complete liturgical liberty was long past. Our Holy Father evidently only intended to regulate divine service in his own monasteries; but, since his work was the most complete, wisest, and most discreet which had appeared up to that time, it became little by little the sole monastic liturgy, and to some degree inspired the Roman liturgy itself. To avoid turning this commentary into a long and erudite work, we must leave to the general history of liturgical forms and to monastic history the study of the developments of the Divine Office, among the secular clergy as well as among monks, from the beginning to St. Benedict and from St. Benedict to our own day; for it would be to undertake a complete history of the Breviary. The work of Dom Suitbert Bäumer (translated from the German into French by Dom Biron) may be consulted with profit, and many references will be found there. The text of St. Benedict will furnish us only with the occasion for a few historical remarks.

The Work of God begins in the very heart of the night. This Night Office, the longest of all, is also the most ancient. It is not at all necessary to seek its origin in the expectation of the immediate return of the Saviour, of the παρουσία, but rather in the great Easter Vigil and in the other Vigils which the first Christians celebrated, after the pattern of this, on Sundays and certain fixed days. The programme of a Vigil recalls that of the morning and Sabbath prayer of the synagogues. It was often followed, whether at once or after an interval, by the Agape and the service of the Eucharist; yet not always, and it is distinct from the celebration of the mysteries. "They declared," wrote Pliny to Trajan, "that this was the sum of their fault or error;

Of the Divine Office at Night

that they were wont to meet together on a fixed day before morning, to make a song to Christ as to God by themselves and in turn . . .; which being done, they would separate and again meet to take food." Becoming attached very early to the Mass, the Vigil, or non-liturgical service, formed the Ante-Mass or Mass of the Catechumens. Dom Cabrol, after pointing out the analogies that exist between the arrangement of the Night Office and that of the Ante-Mass, adds that "the other Offices were formed on the model of the Night Office, which alone existed at first as a public Office"; there is the same liturgical design, though curtailed, in Lauds, Vespers, and the Little Hours.[1] While the faithful and even the clergy could not celebrate the Night Office daily, the monks were from the beginning assiduous in it, and we find the Night Office present among them all.

DE OFFICIIS DIVINIS IN NOCTIBUS.—Hiemis tempore, id est, a Kalendis Novembris usque ad Pascha, juxta considerationem rationis, octava hora noctis surgendum est, ut modice amplius de media nocte pausetur, et jam digesti surgant.

In winter-time, that is, from the Calends of November until Easter, the brethren shall rise at what may be reasonably calculated to be the eighth hour of the night; so that, having rested till some time past midnight, they may rise having had their full sleep.

For an accurate conception of the primitive Benedictine Office we must obviously set our minds free from modern conditions and the customs which time has introduced. In the first place, instead of fixing the hour of the Night Office according to the four seasons, our Holy Father, for simplicity, divides the year into two great divisions: winter and summer. The first extends from the Calends of November to Easter, the second from Easter to the aforesaid Calends. The question may be raised whether Calends means the first of November, the day on which they fall, or the 16th of October, the day on which one begins to count to them. In Chapter XLVIII., the expression *a Kalendis Octobris* (from the Calends of October) certainly means the 14th of September, the beginning of the Monastic Lent. Hildemar, interpreting the Rule according to the customs of the Roman Church, understands by the Calends of November either Sunday the 1st of November, or the Sunday which precedes the 1st of November, when this date falls within the first three days of the week, or the Sunday which follows the 1st of November when this date falls within the other three days. Calmet admits this explanation all the more readily because it appeared to him (wrongly, it would seem) indispensable "for the reconciling St. Benedict with himself . . . since he wishes the Office and psalter to be begun every Sunday and continued during the week." So we have two liturgical seasons instead of four. Our Holy Father's purpose is to proportion the Office to the length or brevity of the nights.

The ancients had also this special way of regarding days and hours. Without doubt the civil day among the Romans ran from midnight to

[1] D. CABROL, *Les Origines liturgiques*, Appendix I., pp. 317 *ff*.

midnight and was divided into twenty-four hours, which astronomers considered as equal or equinoctial; but in current usage the day was regarded as composed of two elements—viz., day and night. The length of day and night naturally varied with the season of the year; nevertheless the number of their divisions or hours remained the same: there were twelve hours of the day from sunrise to sunset, and twelve hours of night from sunset to sunrise. With midday and midnight as fixed points, there were six hours before midday and six hours after, six hours before midnight and six hours after.[1] So the length of each of these hours was constantly changing. In winter the night hours were longer than those of the day, and this was reversed in summer; only at the equinoxes of spring and autumn were day and night of equal length. The first hour of the day at the equinox commenced at what we call 6 a.m.; the first hour of the night at 6 p.m.; and the eighth hour of the night, beginning at 1 a.m., was "full" at 2 a.m.: *hora octava plena*.

Our Holy Father counted his hours in the Roman fashion.[2] The eighth hour of the night, of which he speaks, changed its position and moved about during the year, according as one went away from or approached the equinox. The rational determination of this eighth hour was to fix the hour of rising for his monks: *juxta considerationem rationis* (commentators usually understand these words of the discretion of St. Benedict's ordinance). Further, we may note that St. Benedict does not say at what point in the eighth hour his monks should rise: that too might vary with the season; probably it was nearer the beginning of the eighth hour in proportion as the nights were longer, and proportionally nearer the end when they were shorter. Perhaps the Abbot fixed in advance the exact moment of rising for each night, or rather for a week or more, striking a mean. There was need of considerable calculation in order to secure the monk a sufficient amount of sleep.[3] If sleep lasted a little more than half the night,[4] digestion would have had time to be completed and all would be ready for the Divine Office.

[1] *Vigiliæ* were military divisions of the night. While the Greeks divided the night into three watches of four hours each, the Romans divided it into four watches of three hours.

[2] However, D. Mège and other commentators think that St. Benedict divided day and night together into twenty-four hours of equal length.

[3] ST. COLUMBANUS treated his monks more roughly: *Lassus ad stratum veniat, ambulansque dormitet, necdum expleto somno surgere compellatur (Regula,* ix. P.L., LXXX., 216).

[4] Here again commentators have different interpretations. A monk, perhaps, had not to rise shortly after the middle of that period of time which constitutes the night, but to obtain an amount of sleep equal to somewhat more than half the night. To achieve this it would be necessary to correlate, according to the season, the expiration of the eighth hour (in the Roman sense) and bedtime. Let us suppose the date is the Calends of November: the night beginning at five o'clock in the evening and ending at seven o'clock in the morning has a length of fourteen equinoctial hours; if the monks, rising at the Roman eighth hour—that is, about 2.20 a.m.—went to bed at 7 p.m., they slept a little more than half the night—*i.e.,* seven hours and twenty minutes (*Cf.* HÆFT., l. VII., tract. ix., disq. iv., p. 777).

The monks going to bed after Compline, which was said at nightfall, could sleep in winter from six or seven o'clock in the evening until about two or even three o'clock in the morning. All through the year the time of rising oscillated, it would seem, between the hours of one and three o'clock; the custom of rising at midnight, as Martène remarks, arose from an inaccurate interpretation of the Rule and is not in conformity with tradition.

The difficulty of calculating the hour of rising was increased for the early monks by the fact that they had no striking-clocks or alarums. They had often to be content with an approximate time. The ancients determined the hour of the day from the height of the sun, from the length and direction of its shadow; they had invented, for the measurement of time, the gnomon, the sundial, the sun-clock. To measure duration they used the sand-glass, clepsydra, water-clock.[1] But monks did not always possess these instruments,[2] and had to listen for cockcrow or follow carefully the movements of the stars. Cassian observes that the monk whose duty it is to wake the brethren should not relax his vigilance on the plea that he has formed the habit of waking them at the same hour: "Although daily custom compel him to wake at the same hour, yet he should carefully and frequently calculate the time appointed for the community by the courses of the stars and so summon them to the duty of prayer."[3] An interesting little treatise of St. Gregory of Tours has come down to us with the title: *De cursu stellarum ratio, qualiter ad officium implendum debeat observari*[4] (The courses of the stars and how to observe them for the purpose of fulfilling the Office). The recital of a fixed quantity of prayers,[5] the calculation of the quantity of wax consumed in a candle, or of the difference of level in the oil of a lamp, were other elementary methods. The *Rule of the Master* requires two brethren to keep watch and consult the *horologium* frequently.[6] St. Benedict entrusts the duty of summoning the brethren to the Work of God to the Abbot in person, or to a zealous monk acting under the supervision of the Abbot; but he was obliged to foresee the possibility of forgetfulness and mistakes, and we shall find him consenting to an abridgement of the Office, if the monks' sleep has unluckily been prolonged.

Quod vero restat post Vigilias, a fratribus qui Psalterii vel lectionum aliquid indigent, meditationi inserviatur.	And let the time that remains after the Night Office be spent in study by those brethren who have still some part of the psalter and lessons to learn.

The monks did not go back to bed after the Night Office. The ancient monks feared that this supplementary rest made the soul lose the spiritual vigour that the sacred vigils had inspired and furnished an

---

[1] *Cf.* DAREMBERG et SAGLIO, *Dictionnaire des Antiquités grecques et romaines*, art. Horologium.
[2] *Cf.* HÆFT., l. VII., tract. ix.—CALMET, *in h. l.*   [3] *Inst.*, II., xvii.
[4] *Monumenta Germaniæ Historica : Scriptores rerum Merovingiarum*, t. I., pp. 854 *sq.*
[5] See the history of Adolius in *Hist. Laus.*, c. civ. (*Vitæ Patrum*, VIII. ROSWEYD, p. 769).   [6] Cap. xxxi.-xxxii.

occasion for illusions of the devil.[1] However, some legislators, especially the *Master*, and also some Benedictine abbots, were less strict. Even to strict regulations there were exceptions, the details of which may be found in Martène and Calmet: as, for example, when the monks had been awakened too soon or when they were suffering from sickness.

It would have been indiscreet, in the winter Vigils, to continue psalmody and lessons from half-past two until six o'clock. The lessons, as we shall see, were very long at that season. Yet there remained before Matins (*i.e.*, Lauds) an interval of varying duration: this period was to be devoted to study by those who needed to study some matter (literally: by those who are lacking at all in the psalter or lessons). In Low Latin, says Calmet, the word *meditari* has often the meaning of 'to study,' learn by heart or rote. We should remember that in St. Benedict's time illiterate or poorly instructed brethren and children were received into the monastery. A monk had to learn to follow the Office intelligently, and even to take his turn as reader or cantor. From the beginning of his monastic life he strove to commit the whole psalter to memory; the short lessons and most common liturgical formulas were also learnt by heart. Those who had every night to read the Scripture or the Fathers from manuscripts which were full of abbreviations, perhaps defaced by use and faded, by the dim light of a smoky lamp, and without the help of spectacles (adds Calmet): these generally required special preparation. If the reader failed to make himself understood his hearers could not turn to their books, as we can; for breviaries were not invented and manuscripts were rare. Finally, all had to penetrate deeply into the meaning of the sacred words. And for this preparation, indispensable to the worthy celebration of the Divine Office, St. Benedict chose the hours of silence and recollection; they supplemented the two hours of sacred reading (*lectio divina*) which were appointed daily for the monks. This ordinance of the Rule is not obsolete, and the reader must prepare even in our days. It is a sad spectacle to see a man who has learnt Latin floundering through ten lines of Scripture or the Fathers, with many wrong pauses, false accents, and mistakes of grammar. We should never treat Our Lord as a barbarian.

But what of the monks who know their lessons and psalter? how will they spend the time till Lauds? There is every reason to believe that they did not go back to bed. The time was left to the devotion of the monks or to the disposition of the Abbot, as Dom Hugh Ménard notes; St. Benedict has not elaborately determined the employment of every moment. The monks devoted these times to prayer and spiritual reading; but we may look in vain in our Holy Father or the ancients for a prescribed half-hour or hour of prayer, still less for a fixed method.[2]

[1] Cass., *Inst.*, II., xii.-xiii.; III., v.—However, Cassian mentions exceptions: *Inst.*, III., iv., viii.
[2] The Carthusians have no rule as to mental prayer. Nor had the disciples of St. Dominic and St. Francis until the sixteenth century, nor even the Society of Jesus at its origin. *Cf.* P. Bouvier, *L'Evolution de la piété* (*Etudes*, t. CXX. [1909], pp. 187-211).

We are sometimes asked, quite seriously, what could have been their " subjects for meditation." The holy liturgy furnished innumerable subjects and those always new. Private prayer drew its sap from the prayer of the Church and remained Catholic, simple, and living, like her. It had not yet entered anyone's head to imprison the movements of the soul in rigid moulds and to substitute for their joyous spontaneity of expression the dull commonplaces of the stereotyped formula. Who could exhaust the study of the psalms, the study of other portions of Scripture, the study of the holy Fathers, the study of the history of the Church and the saints ? And who can flatter himself that he has no further need for this study ? And again, even though long practice has familiarized us with the prayers of the liturgy, and precisely because of this familiarity, we must revivify all by constant study, if we do not want to become parrots, voice and members doing their duty mechanically without the intervention of the intelligence. The recitation of the psalms may become merely an exercise of voice and memory, so easily does everything human pass into the category of the unconscious and reflex.

A Pascha autem usque ad supradictas Kalendas Novembris, sic temperetur hora Vigiliarum agenda, ut parvissimo intervallo, quo fratres ad necessaria naturæ exeant, custodito, mox Matutini, qui incipiente luce agendi sunt, subsequantur.[1]

But from Easter to the aforesaid Calends of November, let the hour for the Night Office be so arranged that after a very short interval, during which the brethren may go out for the necessities of nature, Lauds, which are to be said at daybreak, may begin without delay.

In summer the determination of the eighth hour does not fix the commencement of the Night Office, which is determined by the relation between the hour of sunrise and the first Office of the day. Though this hour varies according to the season, yet it forms the fixed point from which to calculate the hour of rising. There must be time before dawn for the saying of the short Vigils; between this and Lauds the brethren must be given some moments for the necessities of nature; the study of the psalms and lessons is in this season removed to another time.[2]

Despite the shortness of the Night Office, the monks—going to bed later than in winter and rising at practically the same hour—had less sleep; so our Holy Father grants them a siesta after the meal which generally took place at the sixth hour (Chapter XLVIII.). We shall meet in Chapters XI. and XIV. the exceptions which modify the arrangements of the present chapter.

[1] The " received text " has modified the original with a view to greater clearness; here is the reading adopted by D. BUTLER: *Sic temperetur hora ut Vigiliarum Agenda parvissimo intervallo, quo fratres ad necessaria naturæ exeant, mox Matutini, qui incipiente luce agendi sunt, subsequantur.* = *Matutini, parvissimo intervallo . . ., mox subsequantur Vigiliarum Agenda.* And he rightly points out that the word *Agenda* is used as a noun, as it is farther on, in Chap. XIII.: it means the *Opus Dei.*

[2] CASSIAN mentions the morning service (Lauds) *quæ expletis nocturnis psalmis et orationibus post modicum temporis intervallum solet in Galliæ monasteriis celebrari* (*Inst.,* III., iv.).

CHAPTER IX

HOW MANY PSALMS ARE TO BE SAID AT THE NIGHT HOURS

QUOT PSALMI DICENDI SUNT IN NOCTURNIS HORIS.—Hiemis tempore, præmisso in primis Versu: *Deus in adjutorium meum intende, Domine ad adjuvandum me festina,* in secundo ter dicendum est: *Domine labia mea aperies, et os meum annuntiabit laudem tuam;* cui subjungendus est tertius Psalmus, et "*Gloria.*" Post hunc, Psalmus nonagesimus quartus cum Antiphona, aut certe decantandus. Inde sequatur Ambrosianum.

In winter time, after beginning with the verse, *Deus in adjutorium meum intende, Domine ad adjuvandum me festina,* let the words, *Domine labia mea aperies, et os meum annuntiabit laudem tuam,* be next repeated thrice; then the third Psalm, with a *Gloria,* after which the ninety-fourth Psalm is to be chanted with an antiphon, or at least chanted. Next let a hymn follow.

THE preceding chapter fixed the hour for the commencement of the Night Office and divided the liturgical year into two parts, winter and summer; the present chapter explains the composition of the Night Office in winter, while the next does the same for summer. Only the Office of the time and the ferial Office are here dealt with.

We have, to start with, a double series of preparatory prayers. The first series commences with the second verse of the sixty-ninth psalm: *Deus in adjutorium meum intende.* The Egyptian monks, according to Cassian,[1] had a great devotion to this sacred formula, which seemed to them to suit all times and circumstances. Yet there is nothing to prove that it formed part of the liturgy before St. Benedict. Nor is it clear that our Holy Father, who mentions it plainly for the Little Hours, prescribed it also for the Night Office. The doubt arises not only from the fact that the verses *Deus in adjutorium* and *Domine* have nearly the same sense and so make a tautology; but also and especially because the most authoritative reading of the manuscripts omits the verse *Deus,* etc. So it is probable that the monastic Night Office, like the Roman, commenced with the invocation taken from the fiftieth psalm (verse 17). St. Benedict would have it repeated three times, in honour of the Holy Trinity and to emphasize the insistence of the demand. It is very appropriate, since God alone can teach us to pray, and the work of praise thus begun is especially His work, the "Work of God."

Next comes the third psalm, chosen without doubt for the verse: *Ego dormivi et soporatus sum, et exsurrexi quia Dominus suscepit me.* Thanks to this psalm those who are late may arrive before the Invitatory. The psalm is followed by the short doxology, *Gloria Patri,* composed, or at least greatly popularized, at the time of the Arian controversies. The formula used at Monte Cassino was most probably the same as now;

[1] *Conlat.,* X., x.

for to its clause *nunc et semper*, etc., the Council of Vaison in A.D. 529, presided over by St. Cæsarius, had ordered the addition of the words *sicut erat in principio*, in imitation of what was said in so many places: " not only at Rome but also throughout the whole East,[1] and the whole of Africa and Italy."[2] Our Holy Father would have the *Gloria* said after each psalm (we may infer this from many passages of the Rule): this is the Western use, different, according to Cassian, from that of the whole East: " In this province, at the end of a psalm, one intones and all join loudly in *Gloria Patri et Filio et Spiritui Sancto*, a thing we have not heard throughout the whole East; there the psalm is usually finished by the cantor, all the rest being silent, and, when the psalm is ended, a prayer follows; only the antiphon is terminated by this praise of the Trinity."[3] St. Benedict has the *Gloria* also at the end of the canticles, at the end of certain responses, and after the *Deus in adjutorium* of the Day Hours.

Up to this point the preparatory formulas of the Office have had a very general character: with the ninety-fourth psalm a second preparation begins, including the Invitatory and the Hymn and having a more immediate relation, at least in actual usage, to the liturgy of each day. The Invitatory[4] is intended to dispel all torpor, whether of body or soul, to awaken fervour, and tune the instrument of praise. So it is given a special solemnity: it is chanted with an antiphon according to the manner which we shall describe; at least it should be chanted, *aut certe decantandus*, probably in the mode and with the melody of a psalm accompanied by an antiphon.[5] Nor is it only for the sake of solemnity that St. Benedict would have the Invitatory performed thus, for in Chapter XLIII. he recommends that it should be said " very slowly and protractedly " (*omnino protrahendo et morose*) so as to give the brethren plenty of time to arrive before the *Gloria* at its close and so avoid a humiliating penance.

We promised to leave to the liturgy course all questions which belong to it; yet we must say a word concerning the ancient psalmody,[6] or else leave unexplained or misunderstood several regulations of the Holy Rule. Our Holy Father makes a distinction between psalms said " without an antiphon, straight on " (*sine antiphona, in directum*) and

---

[1] D. HUGH MÉNARD (*Concord. Regul.*, c. xxiii., append. I, p. 343) conjectures that these words are an interpolation, *cum nusquam repereris sicut erat in principio tunc apud Græcos in usu fuisse ;* nor do the Greeks say them now.

[2] Can. v. MANSI, t. VIII., col. 727.   [3] *Inst.*, II., viii.

[4] *Cf.* D. BÄUMER: art. *Invitatorium* in the *Kirchenlexicon* of WETZER and WELTER.

[5] We leave to the specialists the task of telling us what was the sacred chant before our Holy Father and in his time. The Rule ordinarily employs vague phrases; to " say " the psalms, to " psalmodize " the psalms and canticles; sometimes, however, it is a little more explicit: *sex psalmi cum alleluia cantandi* (c. ix.); *modulatis, ut supra disposuimus, sex psalmis et versu* (c. xi.); *vespera quotidie quatuor psalmorum modulatione canatur* (c. xviii.) As to the lessons we know nothing: the Rule speaks of " reading," of " saying," and of " reciting " them. We know that responsories were " chanted." And that is all. See what CASSIODORUS says of the chanting of the psalms and *Alleluia*, and of *jubili*. *Cf.* BÄUMER, *Histoire du Bréviaire*, t. I., pp. 257-260.

[6] While we use much recent work we may not neglect the Preface of B. TOMMASI to *Responsorialia et Antiphonaria Romanæ Ecclesiæ*.

psalms said " with an antiphon " (*cum antiphona*). Let us deal with the second first. It is a species of what is called alternative psalmody, in which the voices answer or echo one another. When a single singer alternates with the choir we have what is called responsorial psalmody, a kind that was in current use during the early centuries and is frequently alluded to by the Fathers of the Church, as for example by St. Augustine. Our Invitatory is a *psalmus responsorius*, and everything would lead us to believe that with St. Benedict also, to say the ninety-fourth psalm *cum antiphona* meant, not merely to put an antiphon before and after it, but to interpolate a refrain after each verse or group of verses. This " response" of the choir was generally taken from the psalm itself, and was short and simple in melody.

Here, for St. Benedict, the antiphon performs the function of a response. Yet liturgists distinguish responsorial psalmody from antiphonal psalmody. Even if the latter is only a modification of the former, it certainly implies new and different elements; but the most characteristic difference is perhaps not that which is generally given, the alternation of choir with choir.[1] In the antiphonal psalmody of the fourth century—whatever may be its origin and the primitive meaning of the word ἀντίφωνος, which lends itself so readily to ambiguity—the novelty would rather lie, according to Bishop Petit,[2] in the fact that the interpolated refrains " are not taken from the psalm itself, but composed in their entirety; and finally that these refrains are no longer rendered in unison, as in responsorial psalmody, but in harmony and with modulations hitherto unknown." Dom Cagin had before this described, in his preface to the sixth volume of *Paléographie Musicale*,[3] the liturgical revolution which was effected " almost simultaneously at Constantinople, in Cappadocia, at Jerusalem, Antioch, and Edessa," and finally at Milan under St. Ambrose, " as a result of the same circumstances and on the same ground. It was everywhere a question of combating Arianism." And he concluded: " What is new is not perhaps the psalmody of two choirs in itself, but the psalmody of two choirs of the people . . . what is especially new is the hymn *literature* with its anthems or alternate strophes, with the anti-Arian doxology performing the function of ὑπακοή (response). . . . What is new, finally, is the Vigil Office, which was performed at Milan ' according to the custom of the East,'[4] like the psalms and hymns. . . ." " At this time," writes Paulinus, the biographer of St. Ambrose, " antiphons, hymns, and vigils first began to be in vogue in the church of Milan. And the devotion to these services remains to the present day, not only in the same church, but throughout almost all the provinces of the West."[5]

[1] The Jews were already familiar with methods analogous to the responsorial and antiphonal.
[2] In the article *Antiphone dans la liturgie grecque* of the *Dictionnaire d'Archéologie chrétienne et de Liturgie*.
[3] See also, in t. V., the *Avant-Propos à l'Antiphonaire ambrosien*, pp. 29-38.
[4] S. Aug., *Confess.*, l. IX., c. vi.-vii. *P.L.*, XXXII., 769-770.
[5] *P.L.*, XIV., 31.

How many Psalms are to be said at the Night Hours 147

The liturgy of Monte Cassino, for its part, is probably indebted to that of Milan. Though it be less animated and less rich than the Ambrosian service, the Benedictine Night Office is more so than that of which St. Benedict read a short description in the second and third books of the *Institutes* of Cassian. The psalmody of the Egyptian monks was of the simplest possible kind: one monk chanted the psalms, or a whole series of psalms (never more than six each), while the rest listened, seated and in silence; from time to time all rose and prostrated themselves for a secret prayer, then an old monk improvised or recited a prayer: "One comes forward to sing psalms to the Lord. And when, while all sit . . . and attend to the words of the cantor with all attention of heart, he has chanted eleven psalms separated by the interposition of prayers, with verses connected and uttered alike, finishing the twelfth with the response of Alleluia . . .," etc.[1] This is not even responsorial psalmody; yet there is, at the last psalm, a "response" of the hearers; and Cassian records the care of the Egyptian monks "that for the Alleluia response no psalm is used but such as in its title has the word Alleluia."[2] In Palestine and other parts of the East the psalmody was less monotonous and less fatiguing, although all took more share in it; the Vigils comprised three stages: "For after standing and singing three anthems, they sit on the ground, or on very low seats, and answer three psalms which one sings, each of which psalms is given them by a different monk, the brethren taking the duty in turn, and to these they add three lessons sitting again in silence."[3] But Cassian regards the custom of chanting twenty or thirty psalms in one night as an indiscreet novelty: "and these, too, protracted by the singing of antiphons and the addition of some modulations."[4] The Eastern monks, at any rate those of the desert, were long hostile to the introduction into their liturgy of canons and *troparia*.[5]

St. Benedict, like St. Cæsarius,[6] adopts antiphons, responses, and hymns. To chant the psalms with an antiphon probably means to insert a refrain between the verses. In that way the Office was made more solemn, longer, and more laborious. That is why our Holy Father

---

[1] *Inst.*, II., v.

[2] *Inst.*, II., xi.—In the *Rule* of St. Pachomius allusion is made several times to responsorial psalmody: xiv.-xviii., cxxvii.-cxxviii.

[3] *Inst.*, III., viii.—See the letter of St. Basil to the clergy of Neo-Cæsarea. P.G., XXXII., 760-765.

[4] *Inst.*, II., ii. What is the exact meaning for Cassian of the word "antiphon"? (Cf. also *Inst.*, II., viii.) In the ancient writers it means sometimes a chant in octaves, sometimes alternate recitation, sometimes the psalm itself or the composition executed in this manner, with or without the insertion of a refrain, sometimes the refrain, etc. See the *Peregrinatio ad loca sancta*, the author of which we may call Eucheria until better evidence is available.

[5] Cf. E. Bouvy, *Poètes et mélodes*, pp. 234 ff.

[6] *Reg. ad mon.*, xxi. Cf. especially: *Reg. monasterii sanctæ Cæsariæ*, xi. Acta SS., xii. Januarii (Holstenius does not give so complete a text). The *cursus* indicated is that of Lérins; the *Rule* of St. Aurelian gives nearly the same one. Père Blume (*Der Cursus S. Benedicti Nursini und die liturgischen Hymnen des 6-9 Jahrhunderts* . . ., pp. 35-39) cites this *cursus* of Lérins according to the Munich manuscript 28118.

suppresses antiphons for the Little Hours, if the community is not large, and at Compline (Chapter XVII.). The sixty-sixth psalm, which begins Lauds, the psalms of the Little Hours when the community is small, and those of Compline were said *directanee, in directum* (straight through, without interruption). This sort of psalmody appears also in the liturgy of St. Cæsarius and of St. Aurelian; it exists too, with the same rubric, in the Ambrosian liturgy, and consists in the whole choir executing the chant with one voice and continuously.[1] But, if we keep closely to the text of the Rule, all we have is a psalmody deprived of antiphons, without any indication of the manner of its execution.[2] It is not even certain, as Calmet judiciously remarks, that the psalms *cum antiphonis* (with antiphons) were chanted by two choirs. Perhaps the responsorial method, which was used by the Fathers of the East, and which we find shortly after St. Benedict's time in St. Aurelian, was preserved by him. Perhaps all the monks, who were capable of fulfilling this office worthily and were authorized by the Abbot, chanted the psalms in turn, whether alone or grouped in a *schola*, the choir repeating the antiphon which the soloist or *schola* had given out at the beginning.[3] "Let the Psalms and Antiphons be intoned by those whose duty it is, each in his order, after the Abbot. Let no one presume to sing or to read except such as can so perform the office that the hearers may be edified" (Chapter XLVII.; see also Chapter LXIII.). It is said also of one forbidden the common meal: "He shall intone neither psalm nor antiphon in the oratory, nor shall he read a lesson, until he have made satisfaction" (Chapter XXIV.).[4] We cannot argue that the expression *imponere* has, like "intone" with us, the sense of giving out the first words or first notes: for St. Benedict himself, in Chapter XLIV., gives it a wider meaning: "So that he presume not to intone psalm, or lesson, or anything else, in the oratory."

As regards responses, our Holy Father distinguishes the "short responsory" from the long one which followed the long lessons and was long enough in itself to be capable of abridgement if the brethren had risen too late (Chapter XI.). The long responsory was either a real "responsorial psalm" with a more elaborate melody, or perhaps a *historia* in scriptural or ecclesiastical style; its execution probably demanded special ability: but all that the Rule tells us is that a "cantor" here intervened.

Inde sequatur Ambrosianum: that is the hymn, borrowed from St. Ambrose and the liturgy of Milan.[5] Without raising any question

---

[1] *Cf.* Tommasi, *op. cit.*
[2] In any case psalmody *in directum* is not mere recitation *recto tono*, as D. Calmet remained "persuaded," in spite of Tommasi (Comment. on chap. xii.).
[3] Analogous usages still exist to-day in the liturgy of the Greeks. *Cf.* D. Placid de Meester, *Voyage de deux Bénédictins aux monastères du Mont Athos*, pp. 256-257.
[4] We cannot draw precise information as to St. Benedict's psalmody from those words of Chapter XLIII.: *Non præsumat sociari* choro psallentium *usque ad satisfactionem*.
[5] Consult: C. Blume, *Der Cursus S. Benedicti Nursini und die liturgischen Hymnen des 6-9 Jahrhunderts*, noticed in the *Revue B. néd.*, 1908, pp. 367-374; 1911, pp. 362-364.

as to the correctness of this attribution our Holy Father speaks according to current usage. The great bishop had, so to speak, won citizen rights for the hymn in the Western Church. At the very dawn of Christianity, in the Epistles of St. Paul for example (Rom. xiii. 11-12; Eph. v. 14; 1 Tim. iii. 16; 2 Tim. ii. 11-13), there are plain traces of these spiritual hymns in which the outpouring of the gifts of the Holy Spirit found free expression. But heretics abused this very popular instrument in order to sow their errors broadcast; the need arose of administering an antidote, and Catholic literature was enriched with valuable compositions. However, the Roman Church, doubtless ever watchful of danger, showed herself at first very reserved with regard to hymns and did not officially admit them into her liturgy until long after St. Benedict.

Deinde sex Psalmi cum Antiphonis. Quibus dictis, dicto Versu, benedicat Abbas, et sedentibus omnibus in scamnis, legantur vicissim a fratribus in codice super analogium tres Lectiones, inter quas tria Responsoria canantur. Duo Responsoria sine "*Gloria*" dicantur. Post tertiam vero Lectionem, qui cantat, dicat "*Gloria*"; quam dum incipit cantor dicere, mox omnes de sedilibus surgant ob honorem et reverentiam sanctissimæ Trinitatis. Codices autem legantur in Vigiliis, tam veteris Testamenti, quam novi, divinæ auctoritatis; sed et expositiones earum, quæ a nominatissimis, et orthodoxis, et catholicis Patribus factæ sunt.

Then six psalms with antiphons. These being said, and also a versicle, let the Abbot give the blessing: and, all being seated in their places, let three lessons be read by the brethren in turn, from the book on the lectern. Between the lessons let three responsories be sung—two of them without a *Gloria*, but after the third let the cantor say the *Gloria*: and as soon as he begins it, let all rise from their seats out of honour and reverence to the Holy Trinity. Let the divinely inspired books, both of the Old and New Testaments, be read at the Night Office, and also the commentaries upon them written by the most renowned, orthodox, and Catholic Fathers.

Psalmody is the essential part of the Office. As the ferial Office is divided into two nocturns, each of these has attributed to it six of the twelve psalms, which, traditionally, according to Eastern custom and angelical monition,[1] had to be recited every night. The versicle and its response, short utterances of the soloist and choir, revive the spirit of prayer and make the transition from the psalms to the lessons.

The synagogue also used to combine lessons with psalmody; the Law was read first and then the Prophets; finally, the person best qualified gave a homily: Our Lord did so on occasion (Luke iv. 16 *sq.*). The Christian Church adopted an analogous arrangement: Old Testament, the Acts or Epistles, the Gospel, and a sermon, read or spoken. We find the three lessons of the Ante-Mass of certain days in our Roman missal; and we know that the Ante-Mass is perhaps a relic of the ancient Vigil. At the Ante-Mass as in the Vigil there were sometimes read also the letters of holy bishops, such as St. Clement of Rome, the letters of the Churches, the Passions of Martyrs on their days. Without seeking to discover what was original in St. Benedict's choice and arrangement

---

[1] Cass., *Inst.*, II., v.

of lessons,[1] we may simply set down the fact that he prescribed readings from the Old Testament, from the New Testament, and from authorized commentaries of the Fathers. He does not tell us whether the three lessons of ferial Vigils were taken from these three sources and in this order; the eleventh chapter merely tells us that the lessons of the third nocturn on Sundays are from the New Testament and that the solemn reading of the Gospel comes last.

Nor do we know how far the duty of determining the lessons was left to the Abbot. It would seem that tradition and use had long before assigned appropriate portions of Scripture to the principal liturgical seasons, and these are sometimes the same lessons as now.[2] Moreover, the Acts of the Martyrs had to be read on their feast days; while in the fourteenth chapter our Holy Father requires the recital on the feasts of saints and on all solemn days of the psalms, antiphons, and lessons "belonging to the day itself." Doubtless more liberty was left to the Abbot with regard to the writings of the Fathers. St. Benedict recommends him to have read as Holy Scripture none but authentic and canonical books, and to choose, among the best known Fathers, those who were orthodox and Catholic. The true faith is the first consideration. At a time when manuscripts were scarce and critical capacity was rare, wrong or dubious doctrine might easily steal into souls by way of the church lessons; the more that at the beginning, in default of any formal decision of the Church, it was the fact of being read constantly in assemblies for worship that settled the authenticity and orthodoxy of the books themselves. The famous decree concerning public lessons, ascribed to Pope Gelasius,[3] is perhaps contemporaneous with our Holy Father. In his time were read especially St. Jerome, St. Ambrose, St. Augustine, and even Origen.

"When the versicle has been said, let the Abbot give the blessing." The reader asked from the president of the choir permission to be heard, and solicited by his agency the blessing of God;[4] our formula for this is very ancient. Smaragdus quotes a formula of blessing: "*Precibus omnium sanctorum suorum salvet et benedicat nos Dominus*, or another blessing of this sort." No distinction was yet made between Blessing and Absolution. It would seem that the Abbot did not give three

---

[1] CASSIAN says that the monks of Egypt, after chanting twelve psalms at the Office of the evening and of the night, have two lessons, one from the Old and one from the New Testament (*Inst.*, II., iv.). *In die vero sabbati vel dominico utrasque de novo recitant Testamento, id est unam de Apostolo vel Actibus Apostolorum et aliam de Evangeliis; quod etiam totis Quinquagesimæ diebus faciunt hi, quibus lectio curæ est seu memoria Scripturarum* (*ibid.*, vi.). In Palestine three lessons are recited (III., viii.—See the notes of the editor, D. GAZET).

[2] *Cf. Paléographie musicale*, t. V., p. 111, note.—D. BÄUMER, *Hist. du Bréviaire*, l. II., c. iv.,§ v.: "Lessons," t. I., pp. 380 ff.—D. BAUDOT, *Les Evangéliaires; les Lectionnaires*.

[3] THIEL, *Epistolæ Romanorum Pontificum genuinæ*, t. I., pp. 454 sq.—*Cf.* E. VON DOBSCHÜTZ, *Das Decretum Gelasianum* (Leipzig, 1912).—D. J. CHAPMAN, *On the Decretum Gelasianum de libris recipiendis et non recipiendis* (*Revue Bénédictine*, 1913).

[4] *Cf.* GRANCOLAS, *Commentaire historique sur le Bréviaire Romain*, t. I., p. 207.

blessings but only one,[1] in which the three readers who succeeded one another at the pulpit or lectern (*analogium* does not signify only the *ambo*) were considered to share. St. Benedict says expressly that the brethren read in turn, doubtless so that they might not be fatigued. As a fact the lessons were much longer then than now: St. Cæsarius speaks of " three leaves."[2] And this custom lasted for many centuries. " In the Cluniac order," says Calmet,[3] " the whole of Genesis was read in Septuagesima week, and the whole of Isaias in six week-days. St. Udalric relates that a monk, who marked the end of the lessons, was accused in Chapter of having cut them too short, since he had had only the Epistle to the Romans read in two week-days. Blessed John of Gorze[4] once read the whole of the prophet Daniel for a single lesson." The length of the lessons varied according to the length of the nights, and depended on the will of the presider and on custom.[5] They could not be recited by memory, as could the psalms: and our Holy Father mentions the codex placed on the lectern.

In the monasteries of St. Cæsarius and St. Aurelian the reader sat. St. Benedict only says that all the brethren are seated on benches, *in scamnis*, during the lessons (except during the reading of the Gospel: Chapter XI.), and during the responses, except at the *Gloria*. That would lead us to infer that the psalms were recited standing. The early Christians prayed thus; and commentators point out that St. Benedict regularly uses the word *stare* (to stand) when speaking of the ordinary posture of the monks in choir: *sic stemus ad psallendum . . .; post Abbatem stare . . .; in choro standum . . .; ultimus omnium stet.* And if our Holy Father does not order the monks to rise at the *Gloria* of the psalms, the reason is that they are already standing. As a matter of fact, too, the Greek monks sit only during the lessons; and we ourselves, even when we take advantage of the " misericords " of our stalls, are considered to be standing. We do not know how the lessons terminated. Some centuries after St. Benedict we learn that in certain churches the chief of the choir caused the reader to stop by the words: *Tu autem* (*siste* understood); the latter replied: *Domine miserere nobis*, and the choir: *Deo gratias*.

We have already spoken of the responsories which followed naturally on the lessons, *lectiones cum responsoriis suis*, and of which the last ended with the *Gloria*. We may mark what St. Benedict says about the devotion of the monks to the Holy Trinity, and be careful that our profound bows are something more than mere mechanical motions. St. Benedict only prescribes rising; but bows, genuflexions, and prostrations have always existed in the Church; and our Holy Father did not intend to write a complete ceremonial (genuflexion is mentioned in Chapter I.).

[1] In Chapter XI. St. Benedict mentions a blessing before the lessons of the third nocturn only, but it is permissible to think that one was given before those of the first two also.
[2] *Reg. ad mon.*, xx.
[3] Commentary on Chapter VIII.
[4] *Acta SS.*, Febr., t. III., p. 705.
[5] *Cf.* UDALR., *Consuet. Clun.*, l. I., c. i.

Post has vero tres Lectiones cum Responsoriis suis, sequantur reliqui sex Psalmi cum "*Alleluia*" cantandi. Post hos Lectio Apostoli sequatur, ex corde recitanda, et Versus, et supplicatio Litaniæ, id est, "*Kyrie eleison.*" Et sic finiantur Vigiliæ nocturnæ.

After these three lessons with their responsories let six more psalms follow, to be sung with an *Alleluia*. Then let a lesson from the Apostle be said by heart, with a verse and the petition of the Litany—that is, *Kyrie eleison*. And so let the Night Office come to an end.

There was no interval between the nocturns; but, as soon as the first ended, six more psalms were chanted, not now with an antiphon, but with *Alleluia*. We have met this use of *Alleluia* in Cassian. It is probable that with St. Benedict it was repeated, after the manner of an antiphon, in the course of the psalm. Then came a lesson taken from the Apostle St. Paul, short enough to be said by heart; and, after the versicle, the petition of the Litany—that is to say, as St. Benedict explains, *Kyrie Eleison*.[1] But the *Kyrie*, many times repeated, was only the beginning of a series of earnest supplications which in the early centuries used to end the principal liturgical functions: these are the *capitella* which are mentioned, for example, by the Council of Agde of A.D. 506, as well as by the Rules of St. Cæsarius and St. Aurelian, and they are the *preces feriales* preserved in the Roman breviary. Though St. Benedict does not speak here of the *Pater noster*, it is quite probable that it was recited and that secretly (see Chapter XIII.); it formed part of the Litany. According to many commentators and liturgists our Holy Father also implied the saying of the traditional collect, and only with this would the Night Office be finished, as in the case of all the other Hours. To this we shall have occasion to return.

[1] The Council of Vaison in 529 (can. iii. MANSI, t. VIII., col. 727) decrees: *Ut Kyrie eleison frequentius cum grandi affectu et compunctione dicatur*, . . . *ad Matutinos et ad Missas et ad Vesperam.*

CHAPTER X

HOW THE NIGHT OFFICE IS TO BE SAID IN SUMMER

QUALITER ÆSTATIS TEMPORE AGATUR NOCTURNA LAUS.—A Pascha autem usque ad Kalendas Novembris, ut supra dictum est, omnis psalmodiæ quantitas teneatur: excepto quod Lectiones in codice, propter brevitatem noctium, minime legantur, sed pro ipsis tribus Lectionibus una de veteri Testamento memoriter dicatur, quam breve Responsorium subsequatur, et reliqua omnia ut dictum est impleantur, id est, ut nunquam minus a duodecim Psalmorum quantitate ad Vigilias nocturnas dicatur, exceptis tertio et nonagesimo quarto Psalmo.

From Easter to the Calends of November let the same number of psalms be recited as prescribed above; only that no lessons are to be read from the book, on account of the shortness of the nights: but instead of those three lessons let one from the Old Testament be said by heart, followed by a short responsory, and the rest as before laid down; so that never less than twelve psalms, not counting the third and ninety-fourth, be said at the Night Office.

THE subject of this chapter throughout is ferial Vigils. The time is now summer, from Easter to November, when the nights are shorter. They still suffice for the psalmody, even with antiphons interspersed; but dawn comes too soon to give time for the long lessons of the Old and New Testaments and commentaries of the Fathers; and there must be no delaying of the hour of Lauds, which remains fixed to daybreak, nor any indiscreet shortening of the time of sleep. The necessary reduction must not effect the psalmody, for that is more directly addressed to God and is the part of the Office formally devoted to prayer. The three lessons of the first nocturn shall be replaced by a single lesson from the Old Testament, said by heart and therefore very short. Instead of the three long responsories, one only, and that a very brief one, shall be chanted. All is done to-day as St. Benedict prescribed.

The second portion of the Office is exactly the same as in winter: six psalms with *Alleluia* for the antiphon. There is no other difference between the Office of summer and of winter than the matter of the lessons and responsories. Our Holy Father insists that never less than the twelve psalms sanctioned by holy tradition shall be recited; and, to prevent all misunderstanding, he reminds us that the third and ninety-fourth psalms are not counted in this series of the twelve psalms of the Night Office.

CHAPTER XI

HOW THE NIGHT OFFICE IS TO BE SAID ON SUNDAYS

QUALITER DOMINICIS DIEBUS VIGILIÆ AGANTUR.—Dominico die temperius surgatur ad Vigilias, in quibus Vigiliis teneatur mensura, id est, modulatis, ut supra disposuimus, sex Psalmis, et Versu, residentibus cunctis disposite et per ordinem in subselliis, legantur in codice, ut supra diximus, quatuor Lectiones cum Responsoriis suis, ubi tantum in Responsorio quarto dicatur a cantante "Gloria"; quam dum incipit, mox omnes cum reverentia surgant.

On Sundays let the brethren rise earlier for the Night Office, in which the measure shall be observed. When six psalms and a versicle have been sung (as already prescribed), and all are seated on benches in their proper order, let four lessons with their responsories be read from the book, as before: and to the last responsory only let the reader add a *Gloria*, all reverently rising as soon as he begins it.

THE liturgy of Sunday Vigils deserved a special chapter; for this Office is, as was fitting, the most solemn and most complete. Its composition is to remain the same, says St. Benedict, throughout the year, without distinction of summer and winter. On Sundays the monks must rise earlier than during the week, because of the length of the Office, and in summer especially will the time of rising have to be put forward, if Lauds are to commence at dawn, *incipiente luce*. Since on this day there is no manual labour the monks are able to devote more time to prayer and to endure the fatigue of longer vigils.

Our Holy Father does not repeat what he has said already about the preparatory prayers. At the Sunday Night Office, he says, "the measure shall be observed." This does not mean discretion, nor the measure that will presently be given, but rather that which has been already fixed for the first nocturn of ferial Vigils. That is to say, explains St. Benedict, that six psalms (with their antiphons, of course) and the versicle shall be "modulated," as has been said previously. Then all shall take their seats, according to rank, in good order, and the lessons shall commence. These shall be read at the lectern from the book and by the brethren in turn, *ut supra diximus* (as said above). But this time there are four lessons with their respective responsories. Only at the fourth responsory, and not as before at the third, does the cantor add the *Gloria* and all rise in reverence. St. Benedict does not say from what source the lessons were taken, but we may conjecture that they were from Scripture, perhaps from the Old Testament.

Post quas Lectiones sequantur ex ordine alii sex Psalmi cum Antiphonis, sicut anteriores, et Versus. Post quos iterum legantur aliæ quatuor Lectiones cum Responsoriis suis, ordine quo supra.

After the lessons let six more psalms follow in order, with their antiphons and versicle as before; and then let four more lessons with their responsories be read in the same way as the former.

How the Night Office is to be said on Sundays

The second nocturn follows the first without an interval and starts with six psalms, taken according to their order in the psalter. They also have their antiphons, differing in this from the psalms of the ferial second nocturn which are chanted with *Alleluia*. After the versicle come four more lessons with their responsories, *ordine quo supra* (in the manner previously indicated)—that is, with the *Gloria* at the end of the fourth, all standing the while. These lessons were probably taken from the Fathers of the Church.

Post quas iterum dicantur tria Cantica de Prophetis,[1] quæ instituerit Abbas; quæ Cantica cum "Alleluia" psallantur. Dicto etiam Versu, et benedicente Abbate, legantur aliæ quatuor Lectiones de novo Testamento, ordine quo supra.

Next let three canticles from the prophets be said, as the Abbot shall appoint, which canticles are to be sung with an *Alleluia*. After the versicle, and the blessing given by the Abbot, let four more lessons from the New Testament be read as before.

There is a third nocturn; but in order not to exceed the sacred number of twelve psalms our Holy Father seeks material for the psalmody in the prophetical canticles of the Old Testament. The Abbot shall choose them at his pleasure, whether among all those in the Bible, or among those used by the liturgies. For the use of these canticles is considerably earlier than St. Benedict's time, if not among monks, at any rate in many churches of the East, in the churches of Milan and Rome, etc. The antiphon *Alleluia* accompanies the canticles, and so is always kept for the last portion of the psalmody. The versicle is said, the Abbot blesses the reader, as he has perhaps already twice blessed him, at the beginning of the lessons of each nocturn; then four lessons of the New Testament (Acts of the Apostles or Epistles) are read with their responsories and the *Gloria* after the fourth: *ordine quo supra* (as above).

Post quartum autem Responsorium incipiat Abbas Hymnum: "Te Deum laudamus." Quo dicto, legat Abbas Lectionem de Evangelio, cum honore et tremore stantibus omnibus. Qua perlecta, respondeant omnes: "Amen." Et subsequatur mox Abbas Hymnum: "Te decet laus." Et data benedictione incipiant Matutinos.

And at the end of the fourth responsory, let the Abbot begin the hymn *Te Deum laudamus*. After the hymn let the Abbot read the lesson from the Gospel, while all stand in awe and reverence. The Gospel being ended, let all answer *Amen*. Then let the Abbot go on with the hymn, *Te decet laus;* and after the blessing has been given, let them begin Lauds.

This is the solemn conclusion of the Night Office. The Abbot intones the *Te Deum*.[2] The order of lessons adopted by St. Benedict was admirable; after the Old Testament, the Fathers, and the apostolical writings, last of all came the Gospel, the very voice of Our Lord Jesus Christ, at the culminating point of the Office. All stood and a religious fear brooded over all: *cum honore et tremore stantibus omnibus*. The

---

[1] St. Benedict probably wrote *de Prophetarum, de Evangelia* (similarly in Chapters XII., XIII., XVII.). *Sic omnes fere codices antiqui; hi erant tituli voluminum S. Scripturarum* (D. BUTLER, *op. cit.*, p. 133).

[2] On the history of the *Te Deum*, see the work of D. CAGIN, *Te Deum ou Illatio?*

Abbot, because he held in the monastery the place of Christ, himself read the words of Christ. But, though he alone was reader, the community joined him in the unanimous profession of faith with which the reading ended. Some liturgists think the passage chosen from the Gospel was the one which was proper to the Sunday or feast and sung at the Mass of the day.

As soon as the Gospel is ended the Abbot intones the hymn *Te decet laus*, which is found in the seventh book of the *Apostolic Constitutions*. But what is the " blessing " of which our Holy Father next speaks ? We know, from the evidence of documents such as the *Apostolic Constitutions* and the *Peregrinatio Eucheriæ*, that the principal liturgical offices ended with litanies and prayers for all the needs of the faithful, with a prayer by the bishop, accompanied or followed by his blessing, and finally with the formula of dismissal. The words of St. Benedict recall all these usages. In speaking of the end of Offices he sometimes mentions the *supplicatio litaniæ, id est Kyrie Eleison* (IX., XIII.), *litaniæ* (XII.); sometimes simply the *benedictio* (XI.); sometimes *Kyrie eleison et missæ sint* (XVII.); sometimes *litaniæ et Oratio dominica et fiant missæ* (*ibid.*); for Compline finally: *Kyrie eleison et benedictio et missæ fiant* (*ibid.*); in Chapter LXVII. he writes: " At the last prayer of the Work of God let a commemoration be always made of the absent." In these various passages our Holy Father is alluding to well-known rites and does not think it necessary to be more precise. Perhaps he intends to designate the whole conclusion of an Office by citing only one of the elements which composed it, the Litany for example, or the blessing; or perhaps for St. Benedict the blessing which ends Vigils is merely a Collect or a developed *Benedicamus Domino*.[1] As to the term *missa*, it has in old writers many meanings, though these are very closely related: it signifies the dismissal of the faithful, the formula by which this was effected, the whole body of prayers which completed a liturgical function, the canonical Office itself, and finally the Mass. Our Holy Father, like Cassian, uses the word *missæ* in various senses:[2] sometimes it is synonymous with *completum est* (it is finished), sometimes perhaps it means the prayers which conclude the Office, and finally it signifies the Holy Sacrifice of the Mass (Chapters XXXV., XXXVIII., and LX.).[3]

" And after the blessing has been given let them begin Lauds," yet with that *parvissimum intervallum* (very small interval) between the Night Office and the first Office of the day spoken of in the eighth

[1] D. PLACID DE MEESTER puts forward the hypothesis that this blessing, as also the one before the lessons, was a formula of praise, a blessing of God, an acclamation analogous to those with which, in the Greek rite, certain Offices begin, or which make the transition between two parts of the same Office (*L'Office décrit dans la Règle bénédictine et l'office grec : Echos d'Orient*, 10th year, No. 67, November, 1907, pp. 342-344).

[2] See CALMET, Commentary on Chapter XVII.

[3] *Cf.* D. BÄUMER, *Ein Beitrag zur Erklärung von Litaniæ und Missæ in capp. 9-17 der heiligen Regel* (in *Studien und Mittheilungen aus dem Benediktiner- und dem Cistercienser-Orden*, 1886, t. II., pp. 285 *ff.*).—In ST. CÆSARIUS and ST. AURELIAN *missa* still has the sense of a reading or lesson.

chapter. Even on Sunday, at every season, the monks could go out then for a moment, as the beginning of Chapter XIII. makes abundantly plain: " On week-days . . . let the sixty-sixth psalm be said without an antiphon, straight on, and somewhat slowly, as on Sundays, in order that all may be in time for the fiftieth."

Qui ordo Vigiliarum omni tempore, tam æstatis quam hiemis, æqualiter in die Dominico teneatur: nisi forte (quod absit) tardius surgatur, quia tunc aliquid de Lectionibus breviandum est, aut Responsoriis. Quod tamen omnino caveatur, ne proveniat. Quod si contigerit, digne inde satisfaciat Deo in oratorio, per cujus evenerit neglectum.

This order for the Night Office is always to be observed on Sunday, alike in summer and in winter, unless perchance (which God forbid) they rise too late, in which case the lessons or responsories must be somewhat shortened. Let all care, however, be taken that this do not happen; but, if it should, let him, through whose neglect it has come to pass, make fitting satisfaction for it to God in the oratory.

This is quite plain, thanks to the explanations already given. The arrangement of Sunday Vigils does not vary in winter and summer. The hour of rising is early enough for the worthy and full performance of the Office before daybreak; for it must be finished by dawn. The quantity of the lessons themselves is fixed in advance, at least in a general way, by custom and the will of the Abbot. After St. Benedict's time we find the cantor, or some other competent person, preparing these lessons; sometimes the beginning and end of the lessons are marked on the manuscript by a drop of wax or a finger-nail scratch; or the superior himself might determine the appropriate amount on the actual occasion; then he would impose silence on the reader by some means or other, by the *Tu autem* of which we have spoken, or *sono gutturis* (by a cough) as Charlemagne used to do.[1]

Our Holy Father foresees only one occasion when it will be necessary to abridge the normal amount of lessons and responses, but not the psalmody or the rest—viz., when the signal for rising was given too late.[2] And since Sunday required an earlier hour for rising, it was on this day that the mistake could be most easily made. But St. Benedict would have the greatest care and watchfulness used to prevent such an occurrence; and he binds the monk, by whose negligence Our Lord has been cheated of a part of the common prayer, to public penance in the oratory.

[1] *De gestis Caroli Magni*, l. I., c. vii. *P.L.*, XCVIII., 1376.
[2] A regulation analogous to St. Benedict's is indicated by St. Cæsarius: *Si vero evenerit ut tardius ad vigilias consurgant, singulas paginas, aut quantum Abbatissæ visum fuerit, legant ; in cujus potestate erit, ut quando signum fecerit, quæ legit, sine mora consurgat* (*Reg. monasterii sanctæ Cæsariæ*, Acta SS., Jan., t. I., p. 736).—According to the *Customs* of Cîteaux, if the monks rose too soon the cantor should see that the twelfth lesson was lengthened.

CHAPTER XII

HOW THE OFFICE OF LAUDS IS TO BE SAID

QUALITER MATUTINORUM SOLEMNITAS[1] AGATUR.—In Matutinis Dominico die, in primis dicatur sexagesimus sextus Psalmus sine Antiphona in directum; post quem dicatur quinquagesimus cum "Alleluia." Post quem dicatur centesimus decimus septimus, et sexagesimus secundus; deinde Benedictiones et Laudes; Lectio de Apocalypsi una ex corde, et Responsorium, et Ambrosianum, et Versus, et Canticum de Evangelio, et Litaniæ, et completum est.

At Lauds on Sunday let the sixty-sixth psalm first be said straight on without antiphon. After this let the fiftieth psalm be said, with an *Alleluia*, and then the hundred and seventeenth and the sixty-second. Then the *Benedicite* and psalms of praise, a lesson from the Apocalypse, said by heart, a responsory, a hymn, a versicle, a canticle out of the Gospel, and the litany, and so let it come to an end.

THE subject of this chapter is Sunday Lauds, and of the next ferial Lauds; so the title is only correct if we join the two chapters together, a procedure which is suggested by the opening words of Chapter XIII.: *Diebus autem*. We are already aware that what was known to the ancients as Matins now goes by the name of Lauds. This Office was instituted some centuries before St. Benedict; it represents the hour of the victory of light over darkness, the hour of Our Lord's resurrection. Lauds is the natural complement of the Night Office, perhaps a double of it; at any rate they do not seem to have been separated at first. With St. Benedict too, save for winter ferias and the "short interval" of other days, the link between the two is a real one: "after the blessing has been given let them begin Lauds."[2] And at all times the preparation for Lauds is very short: perhaps it does not even include the *Deus in adjutorium*[3] and consists merely in the rather slow chanting of the sixty-sixth psalm, "without antiphon, straight on,"[4] "so that all may be in time for the fiftieth" as St. Benedict says in the next chapter.

The *Miserere*, the psalm of sorrow for sin, plays here to some extent the part of *Invitatory*; before singing of the appearance of the pure light and offering the Lord a detailed praise for all His benefits, the soul needs to purify itself and to recognize that God alone can make

---

[1] *Solemnitas* here, as in CASSIAN (*Inst.*, II., x.; III., iv., v., vi., etc.), is merely a synonym for Synaxis or Office.

[2] *Cf.* CASS., *Inst.*, III., iv. This joining of the Night Office and *Matutinum* is found also in the old Ambrosian Rite: D. CAGIN, *Te Deum ou Illatio ?* p. 417.

[3] We should not forget, however, that our Holy Father does not always give every detail of the rubrics and that he sometimes abridges. See the commentary on Chapter XLIII.

[4] For ST. CÆSARIUS also the Morning Office commences with a *directaneum* (*Reg. ad mon.*, xxi.). Notice in this liturgy and elsewhere the presence of the *Te Deum* and *Gloria in excelsis* at the end of Lauds.

it come forth from its darkness.[1] We learn from St. Basil that this psalm was already recited at the same hour in his time: "When day is breaking, let all with one voice and one heart sing the psalm of penitence, each making the words of sorrow his own."[2] St. Benedict would have it said with *Alleluia* as antiphon, and perhaps, too, *Alleluia* was said with the psalms that follow. Next comes the great psalm of the resurrection, the hundred and seventeenth: *Confitemini Domino quoniam bonu.*, set down for Lauds also in the Rule of St. Cæsarius *Ad monachos*.[3] Next comes the sixty-second psalm; *Deus, Deus meus, ad te de luce vigilo*, very appropriate to the Morning Office, the use of which St. Benedict had only to borrow from monastic and other liturgies. The same is true of the canticle *Benedicite*, the "blessings" as it is called by St. Benedict and St. Cæsarius, and of the psalms of praise (cxlviii., cxlix., cl.).[4]

A single lesson taken from the Apocalypse is recited by heart. There follows the responsory, doubtless a short one, the Ambrosian hymn, the versicle, and the canticle of the Gospel—*i.e.*, the *Benedictus*, chosen especially for the last verses: *Visitavit nos Oriens ex alto, illuminare his qui in tenebris et in umbra mortis sedent.*[5] Last come the "litanies"—*i.e.*, the *Kyrie eleison* and all the concluding formulas, and we are at the end, the dismissal.

---

[1] According to D. CALMET the *Miserere* may have been chosen because of the words: *Domine, labia mea aperies*, or because of these: *exultabunt ossa humiliata*, which recall the resurrection.

[2] *Epist. ad clericos Neocæsarienses*, 3. P.G., XXXII., 763-764.—*Cf.* CASS., *Inst.*, III., vi.

[3] Cap. xxi.   [4] *Cf.* CASS., *Inst.*, III., vi.

[5] "It is now generally believed, and that on good grounds, that the *Magnificat* was introduced into Vespers, as the *Benedictus* into Lauds, by St. Benedict" (BÄUMER, *Hist. du Bréviaire*, t. I., p. 253). *Cf.*, however, D. CABROL, *Dictionnaire d'Archéologie chrétienne et de Liturgie*, art. *Cantiques évangéliques*.

CHAPTER XIII

HOW LAUDS ARE TO BE SAID ON WEEKDAYS

Privatis diebus qualiter Matutini agantur.—Diebus autem privatis Matutinorum solemnitas ita agatur, id est, sexagesimus sextus Psalmus dicatur sine Antiphona in directum, subtrahendo modice, sicut in Dominica, ut omnes occurrant ad quinquagesimum, qui cum Antiphona dicatur.

On week-days let Lauds be celebrated in the following manner. Let the sixty-sixth psalm be said without an antiphon and somewhat slowly, as on Sundays, in order that all may be in time for the fiftieth, which is to be said with an antiphon.

ON weekdays which are not saints'-days[1]—*i.e.*, on ordinary ferial days—the Morning Office is celebrated as follows. The sixty-sixth psalm is said without an antiphon, straight on, and somewhat slowly, as on Sundays. So will all the brethren be in choir for the fiftieth psalm, which is part of the solemn psalmody and is not now said with *Alleluia* but with a special antiphon. These two psalms, with the psalms of praise of which St. Benedict speaks farther on, constitute the unchanging portion of the psalmody. In the next words we have the variable part.

Post quem alii duo Psalmi dicantur, secundum consuetudinem, id est, secunda feria, quintus, et trigesimus quintus. Tertia feria, quadragesimus secundus, et quinquagesimus sextus. Quarta feria, sexagesimus tertius, et sexagesimus quartus. Quinta feria, octogesimus septimus, et octogesimus nonus. Sexta feria, septuagesimus quintus, et nonagesimus primus. Sabbato autem, centesimus quadragesimus secundus, et Canticum Deuteronomii, quod dividatur in duas "Glorias."

After this let two other psalms be said according to custom; that is, on Monday, the fifth and thirty-fifth: on Tuesday, the forty-second and fifty-sixth: on Wednesday, the sixty-third and sixty-fourth: on Thursday, the eighty-seventh and eighty-ninth: on Friday, the seventy-fifth and ninety-first; and on Saturday, the hundred and forty-second, and the canticle from Deuteronomy, which must be divided into two *Glorias*.

Every day, after the *Miserere*, two psalms are to be said "according to custom." What is this custom? Is it a monastic custom current at Monte Cassino, or the custom of local churches, or Ambrosian custom, or Roman, such as is mentioned in reference to the canticles? We have no means of knowing. Nor do we know whether our Holy Father has taken the particular two psalms, as well as the practice of using two psalms, from the custom. However, he probably took over bodily this group of eleven psalms, chosen here and there in the psalter. But what was the original reason for their choice?[2] On Monday we have the fifth:

[1] The expression *diebus privatis* occurs also in the *Ordo psalmodiæ Lirinensis*.
[2] "A judicious person, who has given serious reflection to the matter," says D. Calmet, "thinks that St. Benedict wished to put at the first Day Hour psalms which speak of light and morning, and which are connected with the resurrection."

Verba mea, and the thirty-fifth: *Dixit injustus ;* on Tuesday the forty-second: *Judica me Deus,* and the fifty-sixth: *Miserere mei, Deus, miserere mei ;* on Wednesday the sixty-third: *Exaudi Deus, orationem meam,* and the sixty-fourth: *Te decet hymnus ;* on Thursday the eighty-seventh: *Domine, Deus salutis meæ,* and the eighty-ninth: *Domine, refugium factus es nobis ;* on Friday, the seventy-fifth: *Notus in Judæa Deus,* and the ninety-first: *Bonum est confiteri Domino ;* on Saturday, the hundred and forty-second: *Domine, exaudi orationem meam, auribus percipe.* In the Roman breviary, before the reform of Pius X., there were at Lauds each day, after the *Miserere,* a single special psalm and a canticle; the canticles were the same in the two liturgies; one of the psalms indicated by St. Benedict for each feria was present—and still remains—on the same days in the Roman breviary, with this difference that in the Roman breviary psalms cxlii. and xci. belong respectively to Friday and Saturday.

A single psalm is assigned to Saturday, because of the unusual length of the canticle from Deuteronomy appointed for this day. The canticle was divided into two *Glorias,* which means that it was divided into two portions each followed by the doxology *Gloria ;* the first part of the canticle took the place of one of the customary two psalms and the second part was the canticle itself. This leads St. Benedict to speak about the canticle.

Nam ceteris diebus, Canticum unumquodque die suo ex Prophetis, sicut psallit Ecclesia Romana, dicatur. Post hæc sequantur Laudes; deinde Lectio una Apostoli memoriter recitanda, Responsorium, Ambrosianum, Versus, Canticum de Evangelio, Litania, et completum est.	But on the other days let canticles from the prophets be said, each on its proper day, according to the practice of the Roman Church. Then let the psalms of praise follow, and after them a lesson from the Apostle, to be said by heart, the responsory, the hymn, the versicle, the canticle out of the Gospel, the litany, and so conclude.

Canticles are to be recited every day, not on Saturday only, and they are not to be the same each day, but each of the ferias is to have its own canticle, taken, like Saturday's canticle, from the repertory of the Roman Church. The Abbot had to determine the canticles of the third nocturn of Sundays, since the Roman Church used only psalms at the Night Office: and he could not take from it what it did not possess. But every day at Lauds it had a canticle taken from the prophets (*ex prophetis* in a broad sense); and St. Benedict in this matter adopts the custom and probably too the designation of the Roman Church. As D. Bäumer remarks, only a few churches of the West had adopted the Eastern custom of numerous canticles, and the introduction of this practice by St. Benedict " was, at least for the monks, something of a novelty."[1] While Sunday has the " blessings " of the Three Children,

---

[1] *Op. cit.,* t. I., p. 249. *Cf.* pp. 179 *ff.*—D. CABROL, *Dictionnaire d'Archéologie chrétienne et de Liturgie,* art. *Cantiques.*

Monday has the canticle of the twelfth chapter of Isaias; Tuesday the canticle of Ezechias; Wednesday the canticle of Anna; Thursday the canticle of Moses after the passage of the Red Sea; Friday the canticle of Habacuc; and Saturday that of Deuteronomy, in which Moses traces, before dying, the past and future history of Israel. After these canticles come the psalms of praise; then the short lesson taken from the Apostle St. Paul and recited by memory, the short responsory, the Ambrosian hymn, the versicle, the canticle from the Gospel, otherwise the *Benedictus*, the litany, and so the Office ends.

Plane agenda Matutina vel Vespertina non transeat aliquando, nisi ultimo per ordinem Oratio Dominica, omnibus audientibus, dicatur a priore, propter scandalorum spinas, quæ oriri solent, ut conventi per ipsius Orationis sponsionem, qua dicunt: *Dimitte nobis debita nostra, sicut et nos dimittimus debitoribus nostris*, purgent se ab hujusmodi vitio. Ceteris vero agendis, ultima pars ejus Orationis dicatur, ut ab omnibus respondeatur: *Sed libera nos a malo.*

The Office of Lauds and Vespers, however, must never conclude without the Lord's Prayer being said aloud by the superior, so that all may hear it, on account of the thorns of scandal which are wont to arise; so that the brethren, by the covenant which they make in that prayer when they say, " Forgive us our trespasses, as we forgive them that trespass against us," may cleanse themselves of such faults. But at the other Offices let the last part only of the prayer be said aloud, so that all may answer: " But deliver us from evil."

In prescribing the litany as the conclusion of the Office, our Holy Father most probably intends by that a whole complex of prayers of which the *Paternoster* was part; but he is anxious to make a formal and precise rule, peculiar to the monastic Office, for the liturgical use of the *Paternoster*. The rule which he lays down is to be invariable, and we see at once what store he set by it: *Plane* (i.e., *certe, omnino*) *agenda Matutina vel Vespertina non transeat aliquando* . . . (The Office of Lauds and Vespers must never conclude without the Lord's Prayer). There is no need to speak here of the beauty of this prayer, the most venerable and complete of all prayers, preserving ever in each of its petitions the divine unction that came to it from the lips of Our Lord.[1] From the earliest days of the Church it had its privileged place in private Christian prayer; the *Didache* bids everyone recite it three times a day, morning, noon, and night, at the traditional hours of Jewish prayer. It also had its place early in public prayer;[2] and numerous texts mention its solemn recitation at the Offices, both before our Holy Father and in his time.[3] The Council of Girone in A.D. 517 decreed: " That every day, after morning and evening Office, the Lord's Prayer be said by the priest."[4] St. Benedict also requires that no

---

[1] Cass., *Conlat.*, IX., xviii. *sq.*

[2] *Cf.* F. H. Chase, *The Lord's Prayer in the Early Church*, in the series *Texts and Studies*, ed. J. Armitage Robinson.

[3] See, for instance, the description of a service at Mt. Sinai in a document of the sixth century printed by D. Pitra, *Juris eccles. Græcorum hist. et monum.*, t. I., p. 220.

[4] Can. x. Mansi, t. VIII., col. 550.

celebration[1] of Lauds or Vespers should take place without the Lord's Prayer being recited at the end in its entirety by the president of the assembly, in the hearing of all the monks.

From the words of the *Paternoster* which are cited in the Rule, and from the explanation furnished by our Holy Father himself, we see clearly the special motive of this public recitation in choir. Undoubtedly it gave souls a special opportunity, at a time when some traces of Pelagianism still survived almost everywhere, for examination of conscience, for disavowal and sorrow, and made them put their trust in God alone for the escaping evil and temptation;[2] but St. Benedict has a different end in view. Even in communities which are united in all fraternal charity, little wounds may be caused, often without evil intent and from mere diversity of temperament. And these wounds, for all their triviality, yet when touched by thought or word may grow sore and fester. But they vanish when we find in God's goodness towards us a supernatural motive for charity towards our brethren. To use St. Benedict's simile, the thorns of scandal, which occasionally spring up in monasteries, then disappear. The petition of the *Paternoster*: "Forgive us our trespasses as we forgive" is a reciprocal contract, an engagement we enter into with Our Lord (*sponsio*).[3] Instead of imitating those Christians of whom Cassian writes: "When this prayer is sung in church by the whole people, they pass over this part in silence, doubtless that they may not seem to bind themselves . . .,"[4] the children of St. Benedict must take these words to themselves, let themselves be arraigned (*convenire*) and tried by them: they pronounce their own condemnation if they do not pardon one another and make reconciliation (*convenire* in another sense).

This solemn recitation of the Lord's Prayer shall take place only at the beginning and end of the day. At other Offices, *ceteris vero agendis*, only the last words are to be said aloud: *Et ne nos inducas in tentationem*, so that all may answer: *sed libera nos a malo*. Even in this less solemn form one might have opportunity to put one's soul into harmony with the thought of God, and to group in one prayer the intentions of all.

[1] *Agenda* means an Office, a portion of the *Work* of God.
[2] *Cf.* S. Aug., *Epist.* CLVII., CLXXVI., CLXXVIII. *P.L.*, XXXIII., 674, 762, 772.
[3] *Adjunxit plane et addidit (Dominus) legem, certa nos conditione et sponsione constringens, ut sic nobis dimitti debita postulemus secundum quod et ipsi debitoribus nostris dimittimus, scientes impetrari non posse quod pro peccatis petimus, nisi et ipsi circa debitores nostros paria fecerimus* (S. Cypriani *De Orat. Domin.*, xxiii. *P.L.*, IV., 535).
[4] *Conlat.*, IX., xxii.

CHAPTER XIV

HOW THE NIGHT OFFICE IS TO BE SAID ON SAINTS'-DAYS

IN NATALITIIS SANCTORUM QUALITER VIGILIÆ AGANTUR.—In Sanctorum vero festivitatibus, vel omnibus solemnitatibus, sicut diximus Dominico die agendum, ita agatur, excepto quod Psalmi, aut Antiphonæ vel Lectiones ad ipsum diem pertinentes dicantur. Modus autem supradictus teneatur.

On the Festivals of Saints, and all other solemnities, let the Office be ordered as we have prescribed for Sundays: except that the psalms, antiphons, and lessons suitable to the day are to be said. Their quantity, however, shall remain as we have appointed above.

OF the three kinds of Offices: ferial, Sunday, and festive, our Holy Father has now determined the first two, in what concerns Vigils and Lauds; a few lines are enough in which to regulate the festive Office, since it is like the Office of Sunday. The title of the chapter would restrict the similarity to Vigils only, but this is perhaps wrong, since St. Benedict expresses himself in general terms, without distinguishing between Vigils and Lauds; nor does he say any more on peculiarities of the festive Office in the Day Hours; and the Night Office needed especially this determination of the *modus*—that is, the quantity of psalmody and lesson. We may regret St. Benedict's extreme brevity, all the more because we have insufficient information from other sources concerning the festive Office among monks of that time.

For the feasts *de tempore*, the solemnities which commemorated the mysteries of Our Lord's life: such as Easter, Christmas, the Epiphany, etc. (St. Benedict probably means these by the words: *vel omnibus solemnitatibus*), the monastic calendar was from the first adapted to the calendar used by secular churches. The same was not the case with the feasts of the saints. It is true that some, such as the feasts of SS. Peter and Paul, St. Stephen, SS. James and John, St. Andrew, St. John the Baptist, etc., were at an early date common to all Christians; but in primitive times the feasts of martyrs and those of confessors (of somewhat later origin) were not celebrated except in the churches with which they were locally connected, or where there was at least some special local reason for their observance.[1] Monastic churches, being generally without such traditions, had few *natales* (Saints'-days) to commemorate; and this is undoubtedly the explanation of the silence of the ancient Eastern Rules in this matter. Sometimes the monks would leave their solitudes in order to keep the feast of a martyr with the clergy and the faithful; and it was in this way that the pilgrim Eucheria had (at Charra in Mesopotamia) the unexpected joy of meeting and conversing with all the monks of that district, who had to meet

---

[1] *Cf.* H. DELEHAYE, S.J., *Les Origines du culte des martyrs*, chap. iii., pp. 109 *ff.*

there in order to keep the anniversary of the martyr-monk Helpidius: "They told me," she writes, "that except at Easter and on this day they did not leave their retreats."[1] In the Rule of St. Cæsarius edited by the Bollandists there are special liturgical provisions, not only for Sundays and ordinary days (*privatis diebus*), but also for Easter, Christmas, the Epiphany, solemnities, "all feast-days," and especially for feasts of martyrs: "When feasts of martyrs are being celebrated, let the first lesson be read from the Gospels, the rest from the Acts of the Martyrs."[2]

So the monastic calendar was enriched little by little and copied the calendar of secular churches, which, moreover, were sometimes served by monks or had a monastery close to them. If our Holy Father was no conspicuous innovator in what concerns the *cultus* of the saints, he has at least secured it an honoured and regular place in the monastic liturgy. We know from St. Gregory that, when he took possession of Monte Cassino, St. Benedict dedicated an oratory to St. John the Baptist and another to St. Martin of Tours; and he makes us pronounce our vows before the relics of the saints, who are invoked as solemn witnesses.

On the feasts of saints and on all solemnities, the Work of God, (*agendum, ita agatur*) is to be performed in the same manner as has been laid down previously for Sunday—*i.e.*, at every season three nocturns, twelve lessons, twelve responsories. But St. Benedict adds a clause which limits and lessens the likeness of the festive Office to that of Sunday: it is to have its own psalms, antiphons, and lessons (we may note that there is no question of responsories or hymns). Long discussions have arisen among commentators as to the interpretation of the words: *ad ipsum diem pertinentes* (belonging to the day itself). Does this mean the psalms, antiphons, and lessons of the feria, or rather psalms, antiphons, and lessons specially assigned to the feast? Calmet holds the first opinion; D. Mège is decidedly in favour of the second; Martène, while recognizing the strength of the arguments adduced by the supporters of the latter view, leaves everyone free to estimate their value and comes to no decision.

Grammatically the text will bear either interpretation, so we must seek a solution elsewhere. St. Benedict, in the eighteenth chapter, requires of all his disciples the integral recitation of the whole psalter in a week; and he does not mean any hundred and fifty psalms, but the hundred and fifty psalms of the psalter. Now, this could only be achieved if at the Vigils of saints the psalms of the corresponding feria were recited. To those who answer that "St. Benedict was speaking conditionally, on the hypothesis that no feast-day would occur during the week," Calmet replies that "with such suppositions an author may be made to say anything." For St. Benedict the psalmody is the immovable framework of the Divine Office, and, though he leaves the Abbot free to arrange the psalter in some better way, yet, as we may repeat, he wishes the whole psalter to be recited each week. The festive character

[1] *Peregrinatio ad loca sancta*, ed. GAMURRINI, 1888, pp. 38-39.
[2] *Acta SS.*, Jan., t. I., pp. 735-736.

was sufficiently asserted by the special plan of the Office, copied from the Sunday, and by certain proper prayers. Again, do not the Little Hours now keep their psalmody unchanged even on feast-days, and has not the recent reform of the Roman Breviary combined the ferial and festal Office? However, as Calmet remarks, we cannot seek arguments in favour of one or the other interpretation of the text in customs subsequent to St. Benedict, albeit very ancient, nor in more recent ecclesiastical or monastic legislation.

Against those who understand the words *ad ipsum diem* of the current feria, the following objection is urged: St. Benedict speaks in the same way of the psalms as of the antiphons and lessons, enumerating these elements without distinction: we may infer, therefore, that their condition is the same. Now it seems clear that on feast-days neither the antiphons of the psalter nor the lessons of the feria could be said: for on ferias in winter there are only three lessons, and only one in summer, while the festive Office demands twelve; moreover, there are antiphons properly so called only in the first nocturn, while the festive Office requires them for both nocturns; therefore the ferial psalms were no more said than were the antiphons and lessons of the same feria. Calmet in reply contests the minor; " the lessons will be taken," he says, " from the same books as the ferial lessons came from, only instead of three there will be twelve; for antiphons either the antiphons of the same feria will be taken, or they will be drawn from a general antiphonary; and the same with the responsories. There would be a book containing a store of all these things, for it is impossible to doubt that, in St. Benedict's time and after, there were psalters, lectionaries, antiphonaries, and collections of responsories. . . ." One might allow that the lessons, like the canticles, perhaps also like the antiphons, were in fact proper to the feast and assigned by usage and the will of the Abbot, and maintain that the psalms did not necessarily go with the other elements among which they are enumerated. Then by this clause St. Benedict would have wished simply to distinguish the festal from the Sunday liturgy, each of these elements being arranged as best suited it. Unfortunately, in this explanation, the phrase *ad ipsum diem* has an indeterminate or rather a double sense, since at one time it means the feria, at another the feast.

Perhaps it would be better to admit that psalms, antiphons, and lessons were proper to the feast. That was the case in the liturgies of Milan and Rome which were known to St. Benedict; our Common Offices of saints, at least the Office for martyrs, were originally proper Offices. Eucheria remarks with interest that the church of Jerusalem adapted the liturgical texts to the mystery of the day: " Among all else this that they do is especially noteworthy: the psalms and antiphons are always appropriate, both those said at Vigils and those of the Morning Office; likewise those said during the day or at Sext and None and eventide; all are so apt and significant that they suit the occasion."[1] According to the Rule for the monastery of St. Cæsaria, as we have seen,

---

[1] *Peregrinatio*, p. 50.

certain lessons were taken from the Acts of the Martyrs whose feast was being celebrated; in the same document is contained the following ordinance: "On all feast-days at the twelfth hour the psalms of the third hour are to be said and three antiphons added, but the lessons are to be said of the matter in hand, that is of the feast-day itself." Is it not reasonable enough to think that our Holy Father adopted a similar practice? And he could prescribe a festal psalmody without sacrificing the great principle of the eighteenth chapter concerning the weekly recitation of the psalter, since feast-days were then exceptional and quite rare. He concludes by laying it down that the form of the festal Office, its general plan, the number and arrangement of its parts, should be the same as in the Sunday Office, whatever might be the feast or day on which it fell and its proper parts. So at the beginning a festal Office of three lessons was unknown.

CHAPTER XV

AT WHAT TIMES OF THE YEAR "ALLELUIA" IS TO BE SAID

ALLELUIA QUIBUS TEMPORIBUS DICATUR.—A sancto Pascha usque ad Pentecosten, sine intermissione dicatur "Alleluia," tam in Psalmis quam in Responsoriis. A Pentecoste usque ad caput Quadragesimæ, omnibus noctibus, cum sex posterioribus Psalmis tantum ad Nocturnos dicatur. Omni vero Dominica extra Quadragesimam, Cantica, Matutini, Prima, Tertia, Sexta Nonaque cum "Alleluia" dicantur. Vespera vero cum Antiphonis. Responsoria vero nunquam dicantur cum "Alleluia," nisi a Pascha usque ad Pentecosten.

From the holy feast of Easter until Pentecost, without interruption, let *Alleluia* be said both with the psalms and the responsories. From Pentecost until the beginning of Lent, it is to be said every night at the Night Office with the second six psalms only. But on every Sunday out of Lent let the canticles, Lauds, Prime, Terce, Sext, and None be said with *Alleluia*. Vespers, however, with antiphons. The responsories are never to be said with *Alleluia*, except from Easter to Pentecost.

CHAPTERS XIV. and XV. complete the arrangement of the Night Office, and with them we pass to the Day Offices; they treat of matters which concern both Vigils and the liturgy of the day. Our Holy Father devoted a special article to *Alleluia*, not merely *dignitatis causa* and out of respect for this glad cry so dear to souls in every age[1] and found, along with *Amen*, even in the liturgy of eternity; but rather and chiefly in order to regulate and extend its use. St. Benedict has it sung every day in the year except in Lent; in this we are far from the rigorism of the heresiarch Vigilantius, so vigorously trounced by St. Jerome, who would have kept *Alleluia* for the feast of Easter alone.

From Easter to Pentecost *Alleluia* must be said in the psalms and responsories, *sine intermissione* (without interruption). To understand the precise meaning of this phrase we must attend very carefully to the arrangements which follow and remember how St. Benedict in other chapters regulates the use of antiphons and *Alleluia*. During the whole of paschal time *Alleluia* is said at all responsories, both on Sundays and during the week. And in the psalmody there is no other antiphon but *Alleluia*, at the Night Office as well as at the Day Office, on Sundays as well as on ferias.

During the whole period from Pentecost to the beginning of Lent (there is no question yet of Septuagesima), *on ferial days*, *Alleluia* shall be said only at the six psalms of the second nocturn, as an antiphon. On these same days, at Lauds, Little Hours, and Vespers, the psalmody is interspersed with antiphons and not with *Alleluia*.

---

[1] See the account of the *Alleluia* in the *Dictionnaires de la Bible, de Théologie*, and *d'Archéologie chrétienne et de Liturgie*.

Sunday is in some sort a repetition of Easter-day: so *Alleluia* shall be used each Sunday, except in Lent, at nearly all the Hours: it shall be used for the canticles of the third nocturn, for the fiftieth psalm (and perhaps for those that follow) of Lauds, for the psalms of Prime, Terce, Sext, and None. But Vespers shall have antiphons and not use *Alleluia*.

As regards responsories, they shall be said with *Alleluia* only during paschal time. Our Holy Father makes no mention of adding *Alleluia* to certain versicles and antiphons, as is now done, but only to psalms and responsories: *tam in psalmis quam in responsoriis*.

CHAPTER XVI

HOW THE WORK OF GOD IS TO BE DONE IN THE DAY-TIME

QUALITER DIVINA OPERA PER DIEM AGANTUR.—Ut ait Propheta: *Septies in die laudem dixi tibi.* Qui septenarius sacratus numerus a nobis sic implebitur, si Matutini, Primæ, Tertiæ, Sextæ, Nonæ, Vesperi, Completoriique tempore, nostræ servitutis officia persolvamus. Quia de his Horis dixit Propheta: *Septies in die laudem dixi tibi.* Nam de Nocturnis Vigiliis idem ipse Propheta ait: *Media nocte surgebam ad confitendum tibi.* Ergo his temporibus referamus laudes Creatori nostro super judicia justitiæ suæ, id est, Matutinis, Prima, Tertia, Sexta, Nona, Vespera, Completorio, et nocte surgamus ad confitendum ei.

As the prophet saith: "Seven times in the day I have given praise to thee." And we shall observe this sacred number of seven if, at the times of Lauds, Prime, Terce, Sext, None, Vespers, and Compline, we fulfil the duties of our service. For it was of these Hours that he said: "Seven times in the day have I given praise to thee"; just as the same prophet said of the Night Office: "At midnight I arose to give thee praise." At these times, therefore, let us sing the praises of our Creator for the judgements of His justice: that is, at Lauds, Prime, Terce, Sext, None, Vespers, and Compline: and at night let us arise to praise Him.

WE now pass to the hours of the day in the strict sense, Lauds being only the conclusion of the Night Office, or the Office of dawn and morning. But, before fixing their content, St. Benedict desired to enumerate them clearly and to sum up the moments of the day and night when the monks devote themselves to the Work of God. However, he has already mentioned all the Hours except Compline, though only cursorily. So a more accurate title for the chapter might be: How many Offices there are in a day (of twenty-four hours).

We are not called upon to write the history of the Day Hours any more than was St. Benedict. Lauds and Vespers are the most ancient and the most solemn: "In the first half of the fourth century they were celebrated daily in public."[1] They were represented among the Jews by the morning and evening sacrifice; for the Jews had three traditional times for prayer: morning, noon (Sext and None), and evening. Several passages of the Acts show us the Apostles and their disciples praying at the hours that the Jews prayed in the Temple and the synagogues. We have already had occasion to observe that the *Didache* bade the faithful recite the Lord's Prayer three times a day. Whether our Hours of Terce, Sext, and None are connected or not[2] with this Christian practice, itself imitated from Jewish custom, it is certain that as early as the second century the three Hours of prayer are urged by Clement of Alexandria on all "those who appreciate the trinity of the holy

[1] D. BÄUMER, *op. cit.*, t. I., p. 82.   [2] *Ibid.*, p. 56, note 1.

mansions."[1] Tertullian is more explicit and gives mystical reasons for the choice.[2] But originally, it would seem, the chief idea was to address God at the three principal divisions of the civil day. The day was divided into twelve hours, calculated from sunrise to sunset, the sixth hour always corresponding to what we call midday; but only at the equinoxes did the third and ninth hours correspond to our 9 a.m. and 3 p.m. The end of the twelfth hour marked sunset; the "evening star," *Vesper*, appeared: and this was the hour of Vespers, *Lucernarium*, or lamp-lighting time; then began the first watch of the night.[3] To get Terce, Sext, and None into his scheme, our Holy Father had only to conform to a usage that had become practically universal and in particular to remember what St. Basil[4] and Cassian[5] had written about these Hours.

The Office of Prime dates from the time of Cassian, who relates its origin.[6] The researches of Père Pargoire have established the fact that Prime became a canonical Hour about the year 382 or 390 at the latest, and that it was instituted in a monastery at Bethlehem, not St. Jerome's. At Bethlehem, as in other monasteries, Lauds were said almost immediately after Matins, even in winter, without waiting for dawn; and, as a consequence, the brethren were allowed to lie down again until daybreak. But "the lazy abused this permission: since there was no community exercise to force them to leave their cells, instead of rising to work with hand or brain until the Hour of Terce, they formed the habit of waiting quietly in their beds for the signal to this Office. So there was a reform, and the elders decided that the custom of going to bed after the Night Office should continue, but that at sunrise, when work became possible, the community should assemble for the recitation of Prime."[7] This Hour is a double of the Morning Office, *altera matutina*, and psalms taken from Lauds were recited at it;[8] it is a morning prayer which perhaps all those might dispense with who chanted Lauds at daybreak, *incipiente luce*. However, as Cassian tells us, it was adopted almost everywhere: "It is now celebrated in the West

---

[1] *Stromat.*, l. VII., c. vii. *P.G.*, IX., 456-457.
[2] *De Oratione*, c. xxiii.-xxv. *P.L.*, I., 1191-1193.
[3] When Vigils were to last the whole night (παννυχίς) it was very natural to regard the *Lucernarium* as their prelude; and that is why some ancient sources look on Vespers as belonging to the Night Office.—St. Basil (*Reg. fus.*, xxxvii. *De Spiritu Sancto*, lxxiii. *P.G.*, XXXII., 205) speaks of the εὐχαριστία of the Evening Office; also St. Gregory of Nyssa, *De Vita sanctæ Macrinæ*. *P.G.*, XLVI., 985. *Cf. Apostolical Constitutions*, l. VIII., c. xxxiv.-xxxvii. *P.G.*, I., 1135-1140.—This name "Evening Eucharist" is very suggestive. It is clear, in fact, that the *Lucernarium* of the early centuries often had its Agape or non-sacramental Eucharist, accompanied by alleluia psalms and followed, on certain days, by the sacramental Eucharist. Things were so done, in the same order and at the same hour, at the Last Supper.
[4] *Reg. fus.*, xxxvii.   [5] *Inst.*, III., iii.   [6] *Ibid.*, iv.
[7] Pargoire, *Prime et Complies*, in the *Revue d'hist. et de littér. religieuses*, 1898, pp. 281-288.
[8] Cass., *Inst.*, III., vi. The *Matutina nostra solemnitas*, of which Cassian speaks at the end of chap. iii., is Prime and not Lauds. He never calls this new Office Prime. Prime is mentioned under this name in the *Rule* of St. Cæsarius given by the Bollandists.

especially," by which we must understand the Western monasteries, for secular churches were slower to adopt it.

The institution of the Hour of Compline (*Completorium*), which completes the Work of God, has often been attributed to St. Benedict; but our Holy Father has no need of other credit than that to which he is historically entitled. Perhaps the name is his; undoubtedly the spread of this Hour was due to its inclusion in the Benedictine scheme; undoubtedly also it is due to our Holy Father's initiative that Vespers became a day Hour and Compline took the place of the *Lucernarium* (Chapters XLI., XLII.): but there are at least two pieces of evidence in favour of the existence of Compline before St. Benedict; and Père Pargoire is of opinion that these texts certainly imply a special canonical Hour and not a simple evening prayer, or private devotional exercise.[1] St. Basil, enumerating the official hours of prayer, says that when the day is finished and complete (συμπληρωθείσης δὲ τῆς ἡμέρας) a εὐχαριστία (thanksgiving) was celebrated for all benefits received and pardon asked for all faults or errors committed: by this he means Vespers. Then he goes on: "Καὶ πάλιν τῆς νυκτὸς ἀρχομένης. . . . And again, when the night begins, we ask for sleep free from faults and evil dreams, by the recitation without fail of the ninetieth psalm [already used at Sext]."[2] The second piece of evidence is this: Callinicus, the disciple and biographer of St. Hypatius († June 30, 446), hegumenos (superior) of the monastery of Rufinianes, at "The Oak" near Chalcedon where St. John Chrysostom was condemned, narrates that his hero lived in seclusion during Lent, but did not fail to recite the Morning Office, Terce, Sext, None, *Lucernarium*, then the πρωθύπνια (the Office which precedes the first sleep), and finally the Midnight Office; in this way, adds the biographer, he fulfilled in the course of each day the words: "Seven times in the day have I given praise to thee for the judgements of thy justice."[3]

St. Benedict also is anxious to achieve, in the number of the Hours, the sacred total of seven. He does so, thanks to Prime, in the day itself, while St. Hypatius had to include the Night Office; so with St. Benedict *dies* (day) means the space between sunrise and sunset, while for St. Hypatius it is the whole liturgical day (νυχθήμερον). Cassian, who did not know Compline but counted Prime among the Hours, arrives at the number seven by including the Night Office; and he remarks that one of the advantages of the institution of the "second morning office" was just this realization to the letter of the words of David: "That number, which blessed David gives, though it have also a spiritual sense, is thus manifestly fulfilled according to the letter: 'Seven times in the day have I given praise to thee for the judgements of thy justice.' For by adding this Hour and so having these spiritual assemblies seven times in the day, we plainly praise God seven times a day."[4] Our Holy Father probably remembered this passage; but

---

[1] *Op. cit.*, pp. 456-467.
[2] *Reg. fus.*, xxxvii.
[3] *Acta SS.*, Junii, t. III., p. 325.
[4] *Inst.*, III., iv.

How the Work of God is to be done in the Day-time 173

since in his arrangement the number of Hours exceeded seven, he adds at once that the Prophet was there speaking only of the Day Hours, and alluded to the Night Office in another passage of the same hundred and eighteenth psalm. Therefore Holy Scripture itself summons us to praise our Creator seven times a day and once in the night.[1] To this are we bound as monks and as workmen of prayer: *nostræ servitutis officia persolvamus*.

More than this was achieved formerly: in very populous monasteries it was natural to organize the Work of God in such a way that choirs of monks relieved one another from hour to hour and the work of praise ceased neither day nor night. At St. Maurice of Agaune, for instance, at the beginning of the sixth century, we find the *Laus perennis* (perpetual praise).[2] And when monastic devotion could not adopt continuous psalmody, it often added various Offices to the *pensum servitutis* (meed of service) prescribed by St. Benedict, and the rubrics of our Breviary still mention on certain days the recitation of the Gradual Psalms, of the Penitential Psalms, and of the Office of the Dead. Without misconceiving the intention which dictated these practices, we may be allowed to remark that our Holy Father purposely abridged the liturgy of his predecessors and that he arranged the content of the Hours in a more discreet and wiser fashion. Does Our Lord gain much by an ever-increasing accumulation of prayers and new Offices? We must leave ourselves breathing-space. The generous must have the opportunity of doing something spontaneously and quite willingly. However, there is a form of *Laus perennis* which does not require an army of monks, which is open to each individual to realize: it is secret prayer, attention to God and the things of God, the attitude of submission and love, a certain constant contact with Beauty ever present. Thus, not only the monastery, but the soul of each monk, and the united chorus of all, may sing to God an uneasing song.

[1] In the first *Sermo asceticus*, which, if not St. Basil's, at least belongs probably to the fourth or fifth century, the author, like St. Benedict, cites these two texts: *Media nocte* . . . and *Septies* . . ., but he only counts seven Hours in all: the Night Office, the Morning Office, Terce, None, Vespers, and, in order to get seven, divides the midday prayer into two: the prayer before the meal and the prayer after. *P.G.*, XXXI., 877-878.

[2] *Cf. Dictionnaire d'Archéologie chrétienne et de Liturgie*, art. *Agaune*.

CHAPTER XVII

HOW MANY PSALMS ARE TO BE SAID AT THESE HOURS (OF THE DAY)

QUOT PSALMI PER EASDEM HORAS DICENDI SUNT.—Jam de Nocturnis, vel Matutinis digessimus ordinem psalmodiæ; nunc de sequentibus Horis videamus. Prima Hora dicantur Psalmi tres sigillatim, et non sub una " Gloria." Hymnus ejusdem Horæ post Versum *Deus in adjutorium meum intende* antequam Psalmi incipiantur. Post expletionem vero trium Psalmorum, recitetur Lectio una, Versus, et " Kyrie eleison," et missæ sint.

We have already disposed the order of the psalmody for the Night Office and for Lauds: let us proceed to arrange for the remaining Hours. At Prime, let three Psalms be said, separately, and not under one *Gloria*. The hymn at this Hour is to follow the verse *Deus in adjutorium* before the psalms are begun. Then, at the end of the three psalms, let one lesson be said, with a versicle, the *Kyrie eleison* and the concluding prayer.

WE have already, says St. Benedict, arranged the order of the psalmody for Vigils and Lauds; let us look now to the succeeding Hours. His object is to indicate the scheme or form of the Offices of the day, taking them in the order in which they occur; the substance of both night and day psalmody will be dealt with in the next chapter.

First we have the composition of Prime: the versicle *Deus in adjutorium*, then the *Gloria*, as laid down at the beginning of the eighteenth chapter, next the hymn proper to the Hour. In the same way do the three succeeding Hours begin. Moreover, the psalmody of Prime and of these three Hours consists of three psalms. In the monasteries of Palestine, Mesopotamia, and all that part of the East—Cassian tells us—Terce, Sext, and None consisted every day of three psalms;[1] those who adopted Prime used for that Hour psalms l., lxii., and lxxxix.[2] On Sunday, St. Benedict adds in the next chapter, Prime shall have by exception, not three psalms, but the first four sections of the hundred and eighteenth psalm. These psalms were to be said separately, each with its own *Gloria*, and not united above one *Gloria*, as are the last three psalms of Lauds. After the psalms comes a lesson, then the versicle, the *Kyrie eleison* and the *missæ*. We have briefly indicated in an earlier chapter what these concluding prayers might be and the various meanings of the word *missa*.[3] All that part of Prime which we say in chapter (the martyrology, prayers for manual labour, reading of the Rule) dates from the eighth and ninth centuries and originated in monastic customs.[4]

Tertia vero, Sexta, et Nona, eodem ordine celebretur Oratio: Versus, Hymni earundem Horarum, terni

Terce, Sext, and None are to be recited in the same way—that is, the verse, the hymn proper to each Hour,

[1] *Inst.*, III., iii. [2] *Ibid.*, vi.
[3] See the commentaries of MARTÈNE and CALMET on this chapter.
[4] *Cf.* D. BÄUMER, *op. cit.*, t. I., pp. 361-362, 374-375.

How many Psalms are to be said at these Hours

Psalmi, Lectio, Versus, "Kyrie eleison," et missæ sint. Si major congregatio fuerit, cum Antiphonis dicantur; si vero minor, in directum psallantur.

three psalms, the lesson and versicle, *Kyrie eleison* and the concluding prayer. If the community be large, let the psalms be sung with antiphons; but if small, let them be sung straight forward.

The best reading of the text for the beginning of this section is probably that which we have adopted, with the addition of *id est* (that is) before *Versus*. The prayer or portion of the Work of God which is celebrated at Terce, Sext, and None, is to have the same plan as Prime, comprising, that is to say, the verse *Deus in adjutorium*, a proper hymn, three psalms, etc. If the community is large the psalms of the four Little Hours shall be said with intercalated antiphons; otherwise they shall be said straight forward.[1] These Day Hours are brief, as was fitting for men who had work to do; they are simple, so that they can be recited by memory, even at the scene of one's toil (Chapter L.).

Vespertina autem synaxis quatuor Psalmis cum Antiphonis terminetur, post quos Psalmos lectio recitanda est, inde Responsorium, Ambrosianum, Versus, Canticum de Evangelio, Litaniæ et Oratio Dominica, et fiant missæ.

Let the Vesper Office consist of four psalms with antiphons: after the psalms a lesson is to be recited; then the responsory, the hymn and versicle, the canticle from the Gospel, the Litany and Lord's Prayer and the concluding prayer.

The Vesper psalmody is shorter than was that of the ancient *Lucernarium*, as for instance with the monks of Egypt[2] and St. Cæsarius; for it comprises only four psalms. Likewise, instead of several long lessons, St. Benedict requires only one, and that probably quite short and capable of recitation by heart, as in the case of the Little Hours; however, the reading which precedes Compline will go far to compensate. The psalms are to be said with antiphons. Next we have a responsory, the Ambrosianum (*i.e.*, the hymn), the versicle, the canticle from the Gospel (*i.e.*, the *Magnificat*), the litany, the Lord's Prayer, *et fiant missæ*.

Completorium autem trium Psalmorum dictione terminetur, qui Psalmi directanee et sine Antiphona dicendi sunt. Post quos Hymnus ejusdem Horæ, Lectio una, Versus, "Kyrie eleison" et benedictio, et missæ fiant.

Let Compline consist of the recitation of three psalms, to be said straight on without antiphons; then the hymn for that hour, one lesson, the versicle, *Kyrie eleison*, the blessing, and the concluding prayer.

St. Benedict keeps for another place what he has to say about the reading which preceded Compline (Chapter XLII.); the short lesson: *Fratres sobrii estote* . . . is a relic and a repetition of it in our actual liturgy. Compline is to consist first of three psalms without antiphons in the direct manner. Then comes the hymn proper to this last Hour of the day; so that Lauds, Vespers and Compline have their hymn *after* the psalmody. Finally there is a short lesson, a versicle, the *Kyrie*

---

[1] See the commentary on Chapter IX.   Cass., *Inst.*, II., vi.

eleison, the blessing and the concluding prayers or dismissal. We should recall what little was said concerning the blessing in Chapter XI., where St. Benedict spoke of the blessing at the end of Vigils: " And after the blessing has been given, let them begin Lauds." So the Night Office and the Day Hours end in the same manner. Let us remember also that in the ancient service the dismissal of the catechumens or of the faithful was only pronounced after a series of prayers in which the deacon and the bishop enumerated the intentions of all, and formulated the desires and sentiments of the assembly; after which the bishop gave his blessing. It is probable that at the end of Vigils and of Compline the Abbot too blessed all his children and accompanied the action with a formula of his own choice or one predetermined.[1] Monastic custom has preserved the blessing of Compline and given it a real importance. No one should be absent at that moment; it is an act of communion with brethren and Abbot; and the blessing should be carried to those in the monastery who cannot be present to receive it.

Commentators enquire why our Holy Father says nothing about Mass, though it is the culminating point of the liturgy. We may repeat that it was not St. Benedict's purpose to say everything: he passes over in silence points of ordinary ecclesiastical discipline; and, among properly monastic observances, he only mentions the chief, those which he adopts for his children and those which used to be defined by precise rules. He speaks elsewhere *en passant* of the Mass and Communion on Sunday and " solemn days " (Chapters XXXV., XXXVIII., LXIII.);[2] he allows the Abbot to have priests and deacons ordained for the religious service of the monastery and the *officium altaris* (Chapter LXII.); the Abbot may invite priests who embrace the monastic life to bless or to celebrate Mass: *aut Missam tenere* (Chapter LX.). Two centuries before St. Benedict's time, monks, like fervent Christians in the world, used to communicate very often and even daily; and it was not indispensable to do this at Mass since each individual could take the Holy Eucharist home with him.[3] Rufinus has preserved us this counsel of Abbot Apollonius: " He also advised that, if possible, monks should every day partake of the mysteries of Christ, lest perchance he, who should keep far from these, should find himself far from God."[4] The custom of daily Conventual Mass is very ancient, and Martène finds an example of it at the beginning of the fifth century in the life of St. Euthymius;[5] it was the custom too at Cluny.

[1] The Council of Agde in 506 decreed: *In conclusione matutinarum vel vespertinarum missarum, post hymnos, capitella de psalmis dicantur, et plebs collecta oratione ad vesperam ab episcopo cum benedictione dimittatur* (Can. xxx. MANSI, t. VIII., col. 330).
[2] CASSIAN wrote of the monks of Egypt: *Die sabbato vel dominica . . . hora tertia sacræ communionis obtentu conveniunt* (*Inst.*, III. ii.).
[3] S. BASIL., *Epist.* XCIII. *ad Cæsariam patriciam.* P.G., XXXII., 484-485.—Cf. D. CHAPMAN, *La Communion fréquente dans les premiers âges* (Paper read at the nineteenth International Eucharistic Congress held at Westminster, 1908, pp. 161-168 of the Report).—D. BESSE, *Les Moines d'Orient*, pp. 351-354; *Les Moines del'Ancienne France*, pp. 445-448. [4] *Hist. monach.*, c. vii. ROSWEYD, p. 464.
[5] *Acta SS.*, Jan., t. II., p. 309.—*Cf.* MARTÈNE, *De ant. monach. rit.*, l. II., c. iv.-viii.—CALMET, Commentary on Chapter XXXV.

CHAPTER XVIII

IN WHAT ORDER THE PSALMS ARE TO BE SAID

WE now know the number of the Hours and the plan of each of them; this long chapter is devoted by St. Benedict to the distribution of the psalms among the Hours of the day and the night. Leaving Lauds on one side, for he has fixed its psalmody in the thirteenth chapter, he determines successively the psalmody of Prime, of the three succeeding Hours, of Vespers, and of Compline. Since these Offices for the most part called for a special selection of their psalms, it was best to begin with them, while Vigils would share the psalms that remained. To fix the psalmody of each of the Hours, St. Benedict naturally follows their course throughout the week, and, as is natural too, begins with Sunday. The principle that guides this distribution of the psalter is that the whole should be said in the week; the same rule prevails in the Roman liturgy, while the Ambrosian fixes the period at two weeks. To realize this plan, our Holy Father had to adopt various arrangements which give his system of psalmody a rather complicated and perplexed character. He had, in fact, to take account of the traditional attribution of certain psalms to certain Hours, while at the same time making arrangements of his own, as for instance in the case of the Little Hours.

To begin with, we may note that the Rule divides the whole hundred and fifty psalms into three parts. The first portion, from the first to the nineteenth inclusively, is devoted, with three exceptions, to Prime on weekdays. The second, extending from the twentieth to the hundred and eighth, furnishes, again with three exceptions, the psalmody of Vigils and Lauds. The last, extending from the hundred and ninth to the hundred and forty-seventh, supplies our Holy Father with the psalms of Vespers, of the Little Hours of Sunday, and of Terce, Sext, and None on the other days of the week.

QUO ORDINE PSALMI DICENDI SUNT.—In primis, semper diurnis Horis dicatur Versus: *Deus in adjutorium meum intende, Domine ad adjuvandum me festina*, et " Gloria." Inde Hymnus uniuscujusque Horæ.

First of all, at the Day Hours, let this verse always be said: *Deus in adjutorium meum intende, Domine ad adjuvandum me festina*, and the *Gloria;* followed by the hymn proper to each Hour.

These few lines return briefly to the ordinary introduction to the psalmody of the Day Hours—*i.e.*, Prime and the three that succeed. The best manuscripts have not got the words: *semper diurnis Horis;* nevertheless this passage could not refer to all the Hours both of day and night indiscriminately, since the presence of the verse *Deus in adjutorium* at the Night Office and at Lauds is not proved; but chiefly because the " hymn proper to each Hour " precedes the psalmody only at Vigils and the Little Hours.

Deinde Prima hora, Dominica, dicenda sunt quatuor capitula Psalmi centesimi octavi decimi. Reliquis vero Horis, id est, Tertia, Sexta, et Nona, terna capitula supradicti Psalmi centesimi octavi decimi dicantur.

At Prime on Sunday four parts of the hundred and eighteenth psalm are to be said. At the other Hours—that is, Terce, Sext, and None—let three parts of the same psalm be said.

St. Benedict at once gives a privileged position to the hundred and eighteenth psalm. It is quite evident from the commentaries of the Fathers—Origen, St. Hilary, St. Ambrose, St. Augustine—that the longest of the psalms was also regarded as the richest in doctrine and the most profound: they saw in it an incomparable programme of the Christian life. We know that it is alphabetical: each verse of every eight consecutive verses commences with the same letter of the Hebrew alphabet; and, since there are twenty-two letters in this alphabet, the psalm consists of twenty-two strophes, or octonaries, which our Holy Father calls *capitula*. His intention is to apportion it among all the Little Hours of Sunday and the three last of Monday—that is, between seven canonical Hours; to this purpose twenty-one of the octonaries are devoted, since the psalmody of these Hours normally contains three psalms or portions of psalms. But rather than leave the single remaining octonary out in the cold on Monday, St. Benedict chose to give four *capitula* to Sunday's Prime.

Ad Primam autem secundæ feriæ dicantur tres Psalmi, id est, primus, secundus, et sextus. Et ita per singulos dies ad Primam, usque ad Dominicam dicantur per ordinem terni Psalmi, usque ad nonum decimum Psalmum; ita sane, ut nonus Psalmus et septimus decimus partiantur in binas " Glorias." Et sic fiat, ut ad Vigilias Dominica semper a vigesimo incipiatur.

At Prime on Monday let three Psalms be said—namely, the first, second, and sixth; and so in the same way every day until Sunday let three psalms be said at Prime in order, up to the nineteenth; the ninth and the seventeenth, however, being divided into two *Glorias*. Let it thus come about that at the Night Office on Sunday we shall always begin with the twentieth psalm.

We are still at Prime, but Prime of Monday. Rather than use them at Prime, Terce, and Sext, St. Benedict divides the last nine octonaries of the hundred and eighteenth psalm between Terce, Sext, and None of this day; for if the determination of the psalmody of the last three Little Hours throughout the week had to begin with None on Monday, some complication would ensue, at least in the exposition and in the text of the law. The question now, therefore, is to provide for the Psalmody of Prime for the week, and St. Benedict takes it quite simply from the beginning of the psalter. Prime of Monday shall have the first, second, and sixth psalms, the third psalm being reserved for the beginning of the Night Office, the fourth being the first psalm of Compline, and the fifth being consecrated by usage to Lauds of Monday.

For each of the remaining days till Sunday three psalms are taken in their sequence. But since the ninth and seventeenth are more lengthy and there is no time at this morning Hour for long psalmody, they are to be divided into two, each portion being followed by a *Gloria*. In this way the monks will be in a position to begin the Night Office of Sunday regularly with the twentieth psalm. The practice of dividing psalms was an old one and existed, for example, among the monks of Egypt, as Cassian tells us.[1]

Ad Tertiam vero, et Sextam, et Nonam secundæ feriæ novem capitula, quæ residua sunt de centesimo decimo octavo Psalmo, ipsa terna capitula per easdem Horas dicantur. Expenso igitur Psalmo centesimo octavo decimo duobus diebus, id est, Dominica et secunda feria, tertia feria jam ad Tertiam, Sextam, vel Nonam psallantur terni Psalmi, a centesimo nono decimo usque ad centesimum vigesimum septimum, id est, Psalmi novem. Quique Psalmi semper usque ad Dominicam per easdem Horas itidem repetantur (Hymnorum nihilominus, Lectionum vel Versuum dispositione uniformi cunctis diebus servata), et ita scilicet, ut semper Dominica a centesimo octavo decimo incipiatur.	At Terce, Sext, and None on Monday are to be said the nine remaining parts of the hundred and eighteenth psalm, three parts at each hour. This psalm having thus been said through in two days—that is, Sunday and Monday—let the nine psalms from the hundred and nineteenth to the hundred and twenty-seventh be said on Tuesday at Terce, Sext, and None—three at each Hour. And these psalms are to be repeated at the same Hours every day until Sunday: (the arrangement, nevertheless, of hymns, lessons, and versicles remaining the same every day), so as always to begin on Sunday from the hundred and eighteenth psalm.

For Terce, Sext, and None of Monday the last nine octonaries of the hundred and eighteenth psalm have been held in reserve. At the same Hours, from Tuesday to the following Sunday, the nine psalms which immediately succeed the hundred and eighteenth shall be said each day, three of them at each Hour. These are the first of the fifteen Gradual Psalms. Their brevity chiefly commended them to St. Benedict; for, as we said a short time ago, they are very suitable to Hours which monks may have to say by memory, at the scene of their labours. So these nine psalms are repeated regularly every day at the Hours to which they have been finally fixed; and this is done up to Sunday; but at that point the psalmody of the Little Hours shall start again at the hundred and eighteenth psalm.

The words *Hymnorum nihilominus . . . servata* form a parenthesis which commentators generally pass by without comment, and those who have deigned to speak of it do so inadequately. *Nihilominus* is an adversative conjunction implying an exception or contrast, and we may ask what are the contrasted elements. St. Benedict has just said that each day at the same Hours the same psalms are said; and it would seem at first sight, despite the " nevertheless," that the arrangement for the hymns, lessons, and versicles is to be the same: " the arrangement . . . remaining the same every day." Where, then, is the contrast ? We ought perhaps to attend more carefully to the thought and intention of St. Benedict than to its verbal expression. When he

[1] *Inst.*, II., xi.

wrote this sentence he was alluding to well-known liturgical practice and did not dream that his explanation, for all that it was intended to be clear, might be very puzzling to future commentators. Perhaps we should have understood the "nevertheless" better if it had been thrown to the end of the clause; for this seems to have been St. Benedict's meaning. He was bound to note that the nine Gradual Psalms were said at the same Hours of Terce, Sext, and None every day, but only from Tuesday up to Sunday, since Sunday had for all its Little Hours a special psalmody, taken from the hundred and eighteenth psalm, and Monday, being provided from another source than this psalm at Prime, had recourse to it for the three succeeding Hours. Here is a sufficiency of change and variety; and it is with the complexity of this scheme that St. Benedict contrasts the arrangement of the hymns, lessons, and versicles, which remains uniform every day, *cunctis diebus*.[1] At Tuesday's Terce, for example, the hymn, lesson, and versicle are the same as on Monday and Wednesday. So is it in our present liturgy except on Sundays and feast-days, when lessons and versicles are different.

Vespera autem quotidie quatuor Psalmorum modulatione canatur. Qui Psalmi incipiantur a centesimo nono usque ad centesimum quadragesimum septimum: exceptis iis qui in diversis Horis ex eis sequestrantur, id est, a centesimo decimo septimo, usque ad centesimum vigesimum septimum, et centesimo trigesimo tertio, et centesimo quadragesimo secundo. Reliqui omnes in Vespera dicendi sunt. Et quia minus veniunt tres Psalmi, ideo dividendi sunt qui in numero suprascripto fortiores inveniuntur: id est, centesimus trigesimus octavus, et centesimus quadragesimus tertius, et centesimus quadragesimus quartus. Centesimus vero sextus decimus, quia parvus est, cum centesimo quinto decimo conjun-

Vespers are to be sung every day with four psalms. And let these begin from the hundred and ninth, and go on to the hundred and forty-seventh, omitting those of their number which are set apart for other Hours—that is, from the hundred and seventeenth to the hundred and twenty-seventh, the hundred and thirty-third, and the hundred and forty-second. All the rest are to be said at Vespers. And as there are three psalms wanting, let those of the aforesaid number which are somewhat long be divided—namely, the hundred and thirty-eighth, the hundred and forty-third, and the hundred and forty-fourth. But let the hundred and sixteenth, as it is short, be joined to the

---

[1] See MARTÈNE, who quotes these explanations of HILDEMAR and BOHERIUS: according to them it is the quantity or number of hymns, lessons, and versicles of the Hours of each day that remain the same. In our view uniformity is observed rather in the quality.—Others think that the parenthesis does not necessarily contrast the régime for hymns, lessons, and versicles, with that of the psalmody; that *nihilominus* means either " besides, moreover," or " no less, likewise." St. Benedict would then simply say, and this with the object of rendering his arrangement of the Little Hours more precise if needed, that not only are the psalms he has just mentioned the same until Sunday, but that there is uniformity every day in the arrangement or disposition of hymns, lessons, and versicles; the law laid down elsewhere for the secondary parts of the Hours is to be observed every day: these parts shall have the same number and the same arrangement, leaving on one side their quality, of which St. Benedict says nothing. This remark would be of the same character as that with which the chapter begins and would complete it.

gatur. Digesto ergo ordine Psalmorum vespertinorum, reliqua, id est, Lectiones, Responsoria, Hymni, Versus, vel Cantica, sicut supra taxavimus, impleantur.

hundred and fifteenth. The order of the psalms at Vespers being thus disposed, let the rest—that is, the lessons, responses, hymns, verses, and canticles—be said as already laid down.

We pass to Vespers. For seven days, at the rate of four psalms a day, Vespers require twenty-eight psalms. The Benedictine liturgy, like the Roman and Ambrosian, makes the series of Vesper psalms begin with the hundred and ninth. The traditional psalm of the *Lucernarium*, psalm cxl., chosen for the sake of its verse: *Dirigatur oratio mea* . . ., occurs in this last portion of the psalter. Beginning with Sunday, says St. Benedict, the psalms are to be taken from the hundred and ninth to the hundred and forty-seventh inclusively, the three last psalms of the psalter forming the *laudes* of each day. This would give thirty-eight psalms, or more than are required, if some were not reserved for other Hours: the hundred and seventeenth belonging to Lauds of Sunday, the hundred and eighteenth and the first nine Gradual Psalms being applied as we have just seen, the hundred and thirty-third being the last psalm of Compline, and the hundred and forty-second being the second psalm of Saturday's Lauds. The hundred and sixteenth psalm, being short, is joined to the hundred and fifteenth. But after these arrangements we are left with three psalms too few; so the longest psalms of the Vesper series have to be divided into two—*i.e.*, the hundred and thirty-eighth, the hundred and forty-third, and the hundred and forty-fourth.

Digesto ergo. . . . Here again is a small clause which should not have escaped the attention of commentators. This remark seems parallel to that which terminates the preceding section; yet we may hesitate to give it the same interpretation. If the parallelism is complete and in the sense that we have indicated, we should translate thus: "The order of the psalms for Vespers is thus fixed; they are new every day, yet all else—*i.e.*, lesson, responsory, hymn, versicle, and canticle,[1] is performed as we have determined above in the preceding section, and remains unchanged throughout the week." But, to say nothing of the other liturgical items, was the hymn at Vespers always the same? There is no historical impossibility in the matter.[2] St. Benedict speaks of hymns proper to each of the Little Hours, but he nowhere says that the hymn for Vespers changes each day, any more than the hymns of Vigils, Lauds, and Compline. Furthermore, in his Rule he only regulates the Sunday and ferial office, and the little he says about feast-days does not allow us to conjecture that they enjoyed proper hymns. But perhaps, after all is said, our Holy Father's remark may only have the purpose of reminding us, in passing and with reference to the arrangements of the Vesper psalmody, of the composition of the

---

[1] We should, as a matter of fact, read the singular.
[2] Study on this point the *cursus* of St. Cæsarius and of St. Aurelian.

rest of the Office, that lesson, responsory, hymn, versicle, and canticle are as previously ordered—*i.e.*, in Chapter XVII.[1]

Ad Completorium vero quotidie iidem Psalmi repetantur; id est quartus, nonagesimus, et centesimus trigesimus tertius.

At Compline the same psalms are to be repeated every day—namely, the fourth, nineteenth, and hundred and thirty-third.

Compline has the same psalms every day: the fourth, *Cum invocarem*, the ninetieth, *Qui habitat*, and the hundred and thirty-third, *Ecce nunc benedicite Dominum*. We may note that St. Benedict in this place says nothing of the prayers which follow the psalmody; yet from this silence we can draw no conclusions towards a solution of our difficulties.

Disposito ordine Psalmodiæ diurnæ, reliqui omnes Psalmi, qui supersunt, æqualiter dividantur in septem noctium Vigilias, partiendo scilicet qui inter eos prolixiores sunt Psalmi, et duodecim per unamquamque constituantur noctem.

The order of psalmody for the Day Hours being now arranged, let all the remaining psalms be equally distributed among the seven Night Offices, by dividing the longer psalms into two, and assigning twelve to each night.

The psalmody for the Day Hours has been explained. The seven Night Offices shall share all the remaining psalms—all that have not yet been appropriated. This distribution is to be made equally, at the rate of twelve psalms for each night. There is left that part of the psalter which extends from the twentieth to the hundred and eighth psalm—*i.e.*, eighty-nine psalms; and, since we require eighty-four, we should have too many if the ninety-fourth psalm were not retained for the Invitatory, the nineteenth as the second psalm of Compline, and twelve others for Lauds. When these have been subtracted, there are nine psalms too few; we get out of this difficulty by dividing the nine longest psalms "into two *Glorias*," as St. Benedict said farther back. The Rule does not designate these psalms; but, according to Benedictine custom, they are the thirty-sixth, sixty-seventh, sixty-eighth, seventy-seventh, eighty-eighth, hundred and third, hundred and fourth, hundred and fifth, hundred and sixth. In the Ambrosian and Roman liturgies also, the psalmody of the Night Offices concludes with the hundred and eighth psalm.

Hoc præcipue commonentes, ut si cui forte hæc distributio Psalmorum displicuerit, ordinet, si melius aliter judicaverit, dum omnimodis id attendatur, ut omni hebdomada Psalterium ex integro numero centum quinquaginta Psalmorum psallatur, et Do-

Above all, we recommend that if this arrangement of the psalms be displeasing to anyone, he should, if he think fit, order it otherwise; taking care especially that the whole Psalter of a hundred and fifty psalms be recited every week, and always begun

---

[1] This explanation is doubtless similar to that referred to in the end of the note on page 180. But the explanation here does not do violence to the text, while in the parenthesis *Hymnorum* . . . there are expressions such as *nihilominus, dispositione uniformi*, which fit in with it badly. The two passages seem in reality rather different.

minico die semper a capite repetatur ad Vigilias: quia nimis iners devotionis suæ servitium ostendunt Monachi, qui minus Psalterio, cum Canticis consuetudinariis, per septimanæ circulum psallunt; cum legamus sanctos Patres nostros uno die hoc strenue implevisse, quod nos tepidi utinam septimana integra persolvamus.	afresh at the Night Office on Sunday. For those monks show themselves too slothful in the divine service who say in the course of a week less than the entire Psalter, with the usual canticles; since we read that our holy fathers resolutely performed in a single day what I pray we tepid monks may achieve in a whole week.

St. Benedict does not flatter himself that he has distributed the psalter in the best manner possible. With perfect humility and deference to the views of others, he emphatically (*præcipue*) admonishes any of his successors (he cannot here mean simple monks), who may discover an arrangement which seems preferable, to adopt it without scruple. So long as liturgical arrangements were not definitely consecrated by the Church, some Abbots took advantage of the permission accorded by our Holy Father. Councils such as those of Aix-la-Chapelle in A.D. 802 and 817 had to recall monastic communities to the pure and simple observance of the Rule. Even as concerns the distribution of the psalter St. Benedict's work is very wise; if there be some complexity in the arrangement of the psalms, we must recognize, at least from the point of view of the length of the Offices, that all the parts are successfully balanced and counterpoised.[1]

The only point which seemed essential to St. Benedict, and which every arrangement, whatever it might be, should safeguard before all else, was that the psalter should be said each week in its entirety—that is, with all its hundred and fifty psalms, so that the series might begin anew every Sunday at the Night Office. The principle that guided our Holy Father and the Roman Church is obvious: the Sovereign Pontiff emphasized it recently in the constitution *Divino afflatu*. The psalter was created by God Himself to be for ever the authentic formulary of prayer. With its thoughts and in its language God has willed to be praised and honoured. The psalms express the deepest, most varied, and most delicate sentiments of the human heart, and answer all its needs. They served the saints of the Old Testament; they have served the Apostles and the saints of all ages. And their words have been uttered by other and more august lips: for they were said and said again by Our Lady and Our Lord. In the pilgrimages to Jerusalem Our Lord and His Mother and St. Joseph chanted the Gradual Psalms. Some authors have thought that Our Lord used to recite the psalter every day, and that He was only continuing His prayer when in His Passion, raised aloft on the cross, He said: " My God, my God, why hast thou forsaken me ? " and again: " Into thy hands I commend my spirit."

Perhaps, in St. Benedict's time, some monks had begun to reduce

---

[1] *Cf.* Hæft., l. VII., tract. v., disq. iv. et v.—*Cf.* D. Cabrol, *La Réforme du Bréviaire et du Calendrier*,

the amount of their psalmody. To say in the course of a week the Psalter and the customary canticles is, adds St. Benedict, a minimum effort for those who are workmen of prayer. They would indeed show too great indolence and sloth, in the service of God that they have vowed, who should fail of this. While we read that our holy fathers[1] valiantly performed in one day this task of the psalter, God grant that we tepid monks may fulfil it at least in the course of a week. The purpose of this humble remark of our Holy Father's is to persuade his children not to reduce an Office adapted so considerately to the capacity of all and thereby constituting a wise mean; but he cannot have wished to suggest any depreciation of the *cursus* which he has just established, nor to invite experiment and indiscreet change. However, the phrase " we tepid monks " has more than once aroused the spirit of emulation in certain religious or in whole congregations, so that Offices were added to Offices. It goes without saying that private devotion may give itself full rein, under the direction of obedience; and a disciple of St. Peter Damian, St. Dominic Loricatus, succeeded in reciting twelve psalters and a half in twenty-four hours, while at the same time giving himself the discipline with both hands. " But these examples," concludes Calmet, " are more worthy of admiration than of imitation, and the excessive prolixity of Offices has met with the disapproval of several very judicious persons."

[1] . . . *Dixerunt inter se, ut prius ex more complerent orationes et psalmodiam, et postea cibum caperent. Cum autem ingressi fuissent, psallebant, totumque psalterium compleverunt* (*Verba Seniorum : Vitæ Patrum*, III., 6. ROSWEYD, p. 493).

CHAPTER XIX

HOW TO SAY THE DIVINE OFFICE

DE DISCIPLINA PSALLENDI.—Ubique credimus divinam esse præsentiam, et oculos Domini in omni loco speculari bonos et malos: maxime tamen hoc sine aliqua dubitatione credimus, cum ad opus divinum assistimus.

We believe that the divine presence is everywhere, and that the eyes of the Lord behold the good and the evil in every place. Especially do we believe this, without any doubt, when we are assisting at the Work of God.

THE last two chapters of the section on the Office are not concerned with technicalities, but specify the dispositions, especially the interior dispositions, which we should bring with us to the psalmody (that is to say, to the Work of God in general) and to private prayer.

"We believe that God is present everywhere, and that in every place the eyes of the Lord look attentively on the good and the evil. . . ." The words are a sort of brief allusion to the doctrine of the first degree of humility, that the fear of God must determine our attitude in all our prayers. They indicate the surroundings in which our life is passed: that we live in a sanctuary, very near to God, very close to His Heart. We should think often of this. An intelligent action, says Aristotle, is one *quæ de intrinseco procedit cum cognitione eorum in quibus est actio.* That is to say, it is an action which comes from within, not as a purely mechanical reaction, nor by constraint, but spontaneously, and is combined with knowledge of all that concerns the action, or at least of all important circumstances. Now our life is really intelligent, has a chance of interesting us, of developing and of succeeding, only if we become conscious of its character, of the serious and even solemn circumstances in which it is enacted. In simpler phrase than the philosopher, St. Benedict says: "We believe . . . we believe without any doubt." We must do honour to our faith, and we only do so when we submit ourselves practically to it. Apart from such practical submission, faith is nothing but a philosophic system or a Platonic ideal without practical issue. The monk is a believer and must take his faith seriously.

Now, faith tells us that God is everywhere present and that His gaze, though He be not seen, illumines all human activity; it tells us too that in every place and at every moment we are able, and sweet duty binds us, to live before Him and do Him homage. This homage, however, is private, not official, and has its source in personal love; it is quite free in its expression, and though it ever remains profoundly respectful, yet is it without forms and ceremonial. But the sacred liturgy pays God an official worship; and if God is not more present at the Divine Office than at private prayer, we are nevertheless especially bound to awaken and exercise our faith when we take part in this official audience, wherein all details are foreseen and all gestures regulated by the etiquette of God. God's audience-chamber is always open, but the Divine Office is a solemn levée. There God is enwrapped in more compelling majesty; we appear before Him in the name of the whole Church; we identify ourselves with the one, eternal High-Priest, Our Lord Jesus Christ; we perform the work of works.

Ideo semper memores simus quod ait Propheta: *Servite Domino in timore.* Et iterum: *Psallite sapienter.* Et: *In conspectu Angelorum psallam tibi.* Ergo consideremus qualiter oporteat nos in conspectu divinitatis et Angelorum esse, et sic stemus ad psallendum, ut mens nostra concordet voci nostræ.

Let us, then, ever remember what the prophet says: " Serve the Lord in fear ": and again, " Sing ye wisely "; and, " In the sight of the angels I will sing praises unto thee." Therefore let us consider how we ought to behave ourselves in the presence of God and of His angels, and so assist at the Divine Office, that mind and voice be in harmony.

Let us but think of it, and go through an act of supernatural understanding: *memores simus, consideremus.* Let us make our "composition of place," as modern methods of prayer have it. We are face to face with God. All creation is reunited. The Angels are around the altar. We are going to sing with them (Ps. cxxxvii. 1) and chant the triple *Sanctus* which they have taught us. Surely, then, we should vie with them in reverence and love. They veil their faces with their wings: we too are bidden by the prophet David, " Serve the Lord in fear " (Ps. ii. 11). And again, he says: " Sing ye wisely " (Ps. xlvi. 8)—that is, be aware not only of the words you pronounce, and the instruction they contain, but also and especially of Him to whom you speak. And, finally, let us remember that—in this more fortunate than were perhaps St. Benedict's monks—we have the Blessed Sacrament in our oratory.

How well we recognize our Holy Father's generous method, at once profound and spiritual! The way of constraint, though rules be absolute and rubrics perfect, is unable to produce more than an external perfection at the best. If the soul is distracted or the heart cold, if the Divine Office is nothing but a drill of body and voice, it will soon become tedious, with a deadly tedium. And this will be apparent, betraying itself in yawns and impatient movements, in wandering glances, in all sorts of irreverences. "What do you do during Mass?" a distracted soul was once asked. " I wait for it to end," was the answer. What, then, will you do in eternity, which will not end?

Many other conditions are necessary for the realization of our Holy Father's ideal. The community must have a high esteem for the Divine Office; and it is for superiors to maintain or restore this in every way and before all else. The individual, too, must have this esteem; it is heightened by study and by constant affectionate intercourse with Our Lord. How can one, who out of choir is occupied with everything but God, flatter himself that he will avoid distraction or lethargy at the Divine Office? Remote preparation for prayer is recommended by all the masters of asceticism.¹ They speak to us also of a proximate and immediate preparation; and our Constitutions have provided for it by securing us before each choir duty the few minutes, "*statio*" in the cloister. These are precious minutes, and it would be hard to exaggerate their importance, for then do we tune the soul, our spiritual instrument. We should therefore have the good sense not to pursue in the "*statio*" questions or lines of thought which we have begun; nor should it be a place for conversation or any sort of intercourse. "Before prayer prepare thy soul and be not as a man that tempteth God" (Ecclus. xviii. 23).

The entrance into the church, the attitude and various motions to be observed in choir, are regulated by the ceremonial and watched over by the master of ceremonies. But neither the one nor the other will be able to secure the execution, at once accurate and graceful, dignified and simple, of the liturgical motions, unless each individual contributes his whole presence of mind, his full measure of good behaviour, of spiritual courtesy, and finally of self-denial: for we must then especially take account of the whole body and co-ordinate our movements with those of others. All the ceremonies, even the smallest, will be exactly observed, in good order, yet without the obtrusive stiffness of soldiers on parade, if we are attentive to the meaning and purpose of the action that is being performed. Self-denial is perhaps more than ever indispensable in the case of the chanting; for it is better to suffer a little error than to sacrifice the combined movement, and the vocal unison, and to transform the choir into a prize-ring or a battlefield. The Constitutions bid us "not to spare the voice": which is not an invitation to drown all others; and when they describe the qualities of the true sacred chant, with its virile and quiet style, they do not intend to leave to the judgement of the individual a matter which is of right reserved to the choirmaster. In this field also we must use all diligence, and we need preparation; for the execution of certain parts of the Gregorian chant cannot be improvised; we must not, once we have made our profession, bid good-bye for ever to the study of the Gradual and Antiphonary. This will never be good enough for Our Lord; and, while we ought not to devote ourselves to such study merely to satisfy

¹ We should ponder these words of St. Basil, which our Holy Father had in mind in writing this chapter and the succeeding one: *Quomodo obtinebit quis ut in oratione sensus ejus non vagetur? Si certus sit assistere se ante oculos Dei. Si enim quis judicem suum videns vel principem, et loquens cum eo, non sibi credit licitum esse vagari oculis, et aliorsum aspicere, dum ipse loquitur; quanto magis qui accedit ad Dominum, nusquam debet movere oculum cordis, sed intentus esse in eum, qui scrutatur renes et corda? . . . Si possibile est obtinere hominem, ut in omni tempore et loco non vagetur mens sua; vel quomodo id fieri potest? Quia possibile est, ostendit ille qui dixit: Oculi mei semper ad Dominum. Et iterum: Providebam Dominum in conspectu meo semper; quia a dextris est mihi ut non commovear. Quomodo autem possibile sit, prædiximus; id est, si non demus animæ nostræ otium, sed in omni tempore de Deo, et de operibus ac de beneficiis ejus, et de donis cogitemus et hæc cum confessione, et gratiarum actione semper volvamus in mente, sicut scriptum est: Psallite sapienter* (Reg. contr., cviii., cix. Cf. ibid., xxxiv.--Cass., Conlat., V., xvii., xviii.).—*The Spiritual Life and Prayer*, chap. vii.

the æsthetic requirements of some hearers, and to keep up the reputation of a "*schola,*" yet we must remember that the chant and the psalmody are our form of apostolate and that we owe to souls this most effective preaching.

But it is not sufficient to assure the dignity and the good material execution of the Divine Office. Our minds must realize to whom word and song are addressed, and must be attentive to the thought of the Psalmist and of the Church. As the voice rings out the heart must grow fervent. And, to complete the harmony, our lives themselves must be brought into accord with thought and love and voice. Then, and then only, will the liturgy attain its twofold end, of honouring God and sanctifying our souls. Once again let us note well the method St. Benedict uses to inspire reverence in the oratory and attention at prayer. He does not think, as did other monastic legislators,[1] of combating distraction and sleepiness by making his monks weave baskets or mats during the long psalmody and lessons. The Work of God, with him, is all in its entirety to be performed in the House of God: "Let the oratory be what it is called; and let nothing else be done or kept there" (Chapter LII.). He takes for granted that we are Christians and that we use reflection; so he gives us no other rule than what is provided by our spiritual insight. "Let us consider," he says; by which words he invites us to eliminate all unreason, all discord between theory and deliberate practice, and to make of our whole life a constant exercise of harmony, loyalty, and delicate feeling. And our Holy Father sums up all his teaching in that phrase of antique ring: *Ut mens nostra concordet voci nostræ* (That mind and voice be in harmony). It recalls the words of St. Augustine[2] inserted by St. Cæsarius into his Rule for virgins:[3] "When you pray to God in psalms and hymns, let the heart feel what the voice utters."

[1] *Cf.* CALMET, Commentary on Chapter XI.
[2] *Epist.* CCXI., 7. *P.L.*, XXXIII., 960. In the *Enarratio in Psalmum* cxlvi. (2) we read: *Qui ergo psallit, non sola voce psallit; sed assumpto etiam quodam organo quod vocatur psalterium, accedentibus manibus voci concordat. Vis ergo psallere? Non solum vox tua sonet laudes Dei, sed opera tua concordent cum voce tua.* (*P.L.*, XXXVII., 1899.) In letter XLVIII. (3) to Abbot Eudoxius and his monks ST. AUGUSTINE writes: . . . *Sive cantantes et psallentes in cordibus vestris Domino, vel vocibus a corde non dissonis* . . . (*P.L.*, XXXIII., 188-189).
[3] C. xx.—Read a beautiful sermon on this theme by ST. CÆSARIUS, in the appendix to the sermons of St. Augustine, CCLXXXIV. *P.L.*, XXXIX., 2282-2283.

CHAPTER XX

OF REVERENCE AT PRAYER

De reverentia orationis.—Si cum hominibus potentibus volumus aliqua suggerere, non præsumimus, nisi cum humilitate, et reverentia: quanto magis Domino Deo universorum cum omni humilitate et puritatis devotione supplicandum est?

If, when we wish to make any request to men in power, we presume not to do so except with humility and reverence; how much more ought we with all lowliness and purity of devotion to offer our supplications to the Lord God of all things?

THIS chapter is not a repetition of the preceding one. The nineteenth chapter deals with conventual and official prayer, with the solemn audience accorded by Our Lord, and its title speaks of *disciplina*—that is, ceremonial; the twentieth deals with private prayers, and, to remove any danger arising from the greater freedom of such prayers, speaks to us of the respect (*reverentia*) with which we should always approach God.

The comparison and the *a fortiori* with which St. Benedict begins were suggested to him by his good sense and his reading;[1] but it is not impossible that he also had in mind in this simile a characteristic point of Roman life. Society was not yet levelled and made democratic. There was a powerful aristocracy, around which was grouped not only an army of slaves, but also a vast clientèle (*clientela*), composed of free men or enfranchised slaves, who lived attached to their master, under the name of friends, companions, or simply of clients; every day they would come to pay their duty to their master or to ask a favour, repaying in respect what they received in money or patronage.

> Si non ingentem foribus domus alta superbis
> Mane salutantum totis vomit ædibus undam.[2]

The clients were partly of the household of their master; they were associated with him in his rule and his interests, and so their requests were a sort of discreet indication of that which seemed to them fitting: they "suggest," as St. Benedict says, and the term becomes admirably theological when applied to our prayers. If we dare to approach the powerful of this world only with humility and reverence, if our sense of propriety and our own interest make us adopt before each of them the appropriate attitude, with how much greater reason ought our

---

[1] S. Basil., *Reg. contr.*, cviii. (*cf. Reg. brev.*, cci.).—Cass., *Conlat.*, XXIII., vi.—*Cf.* also Tertullian, *De Oratione*, xvi. (P.L., I., 1173-1174): *Siquidem irreverens est assidere sub conspectu, contraque conspectum ejus, quem quam maxime reverearis, ac venereris; quanto magis sub conspectu Dei vivi, angelo adhuc orationis astante, etc.*—S. Ephrem., *Parænesis* XIX. (*Opp. græc. lat.*, t. II., p. 95).

[2] Virgil, Georgics, l. II., 461-462,
> No portals proud of lofty palaces
> Pour from each room long waves of morning guests.
>   (trans., Royds.)

supplications to the Lord and Master of all things to be made in all humility, devotion and purity?

Humility, as we know, springs from the consciousness of what God is and of what we are in His sight. The habit of dealing with God, the facility with which He allows Himself to be approached, and the very humble forms which He takes when He comes down to us—none of these things should lessen our respect. One of the most certain marks of delusion is to treat God as an equal, as one who has made a bargain with us and with whom we are doing business. When Our Lord in the Gospel urged us to use trustful, earnest, even importunate prayer, He did not mean to encourage that strangely peremptory and exacting tone which is sometimes taken by the petitions—and such strange petitions too!—of the unenlightened faithful. Whatever the supernatural dignity to which God has raised us, there is never reason for our raising ourselves, for developing an audacious manner, or for forgetting we are speaking to God.

Purity is mentioned as many as three times in these few lines. We should understand it not only in the special sense of freedom from gross passions, but also of detachment from all created love and of the absence of all base alloy. Our prayers will be effective when we are able to say to God: " I undoubtedly have, unknown to myself, inclinations which You see and which displease You: I love them as little as You, and I disavow them." When our will, which is the source of every relation, is free from all irregular attachment, then God has established us in true purity. But St. Benedict does not say simply " purity ": his phrase is " devotion of purity." In the language of to-day devotion signifies the flame of charity, and is that disposition of habitual fervour in the service of God which makes us fulfil with promptitude, perseverance, and joy all our duties towards Him. But the Latin word *devotio* has a meaning which, while not very different, is more profound. *Devotio* is belonging, consecration, subjection, as a state, as a fixed, continuous, and even legal condition; and in the present case it is servitude accepted and loved, voluntary subjection to God and to all God's dispensations. In the eighteenth chapter we have the same sense of *devotio: Nimis iners devotionis suæ servitium ostendunt monachi* (Those monks show themselves too slothful in the divine service); and the liturgy invokes Our Lady *pro devoto femineo sexu* (for the consecrate feminine sex). *Puritas* then is enfranchisement from any alien servitude which should steal a part of our love or activity; and *devotio* means belonging wholly to Our Lord.

| Et non in multiloquio, sed in puritate cordis, et compunctione lacrimarum nos exaudiri sciamus. | And let us remember that not for our much speaking, but for our purity of heart and tears of compunction, shall we be heard. |

After having described in three words the interior dispositions with which we should approach God, St. Benedict now passes to the external and more material side of prayer. With Our Lord Himself,[1] with St. Augustine,[2] Cassian,[3] and all the Fathers, he urges us to avoid wordiness. The Jewish worship was not the only worship which, thanks to the priests, became a difficult and complicated ritualism, a religion of words and gestures; for ritualism and verbiage invaded the pagan cults and especially the Roman worship: " They think they are heard for their much speaking," as Our Lord said. However, many words do not make real prayer. We pray in words only that we may one day be free of words, and adore, praise, and love in silence that "Beauty which closeth the lips."[4] "They that adore him must adore in spirit and in truth" (John iv. 24). Prayer has its source in the heart; there is a prayer of the heart which is not tied to words. And this prayer is always heard, for the Spirit of God inspires it and gives it its form: " For, we know not what we should pray for as we ought: but the Spirit himself asketh for us with unspeakable groanings" (Rom. viii. 26). To pray in purity of heart is, as we have said, to display to the gaze and the heart of God the desire and affection of a soul which is free, which is disengaged from all base attachments and united to Him in conformity of will.

Et compunctione lacrimarum (and tears of compunction). The expression is borrowed from Cassian,[5] whose conferences on prayer should be read; and he also speaks often of true purity of heart and of pure prayer.[6] Compunction—though the *Imitation* tells us that it is better to have it than to define it—is that softening of heart caused in us, under the guidance of faith, by the remembrance of our faults and the consideration of the benefits of God. Our Holy Father several times in his Rule conjoins prayer and tears, as though the two things went naturally together; in the fifty-second chapter he says: "If anyone desire to pray in private, let him go in simply and pray, not with a loud voice, but with tears and fervour of heart." St. Gregory tells us that St. Benedict had the gift of tears; and what one day troubled the good Theoprobus was less the abundance and duration of his tears, than their deep sadness: " When he waited a long while yet did not see his weeping ended, and the man of God was not, as was his wont, weeping in prayer but in sorrowful lamentation, he inquired what might be the cause of so great a grief."[7] The gift of tears is regarded as the least of all the *charismata;* but it has the merit of not leading to pride and also of leaving no room for distractions at prayer; it drowns them all.

Et ideo brevis debet esse et pura oratio; nisi forte ex affectu inspirationis divinæ gratiæ protendatur. In

Therefore prayer ought to be short and pure, except it be perchance prolonged by the inspiration of divine

---

[1] MATT. vi. 7 ff. [2] *Epist.* CXXX., ad Probam, 20. P.L., XXXIII., 501-502.
[3] *Inst.*, II., x.; *Conlat.*, IX., xxxvi.
[4] B. ANGELA OF FOLIGNO: *The Book of Visions and Instructions*, c. xxi. English trans., CRUIKSHANK. New ed., N.Y. 1903.   [5] *Conlat.*, IX., xxviii.
[6] *Monachi autem illud opus est præcipuum, ut orationem puram offerat Deo, nihil habens in conscientia reprehensibile* (RUFIN., *Hist. monach.*, c. i. ROSWEYD, p. 453).
[7] S. GREG. M., *Dial.*, l. II., c. xvii.

conventu tamen omnino brevietur oratio, et facto signo a priore, omnes pariter surgant.

grace. But let prayer made in common always be short: and at the signal given by the superior, let all rise together.

St. Benedict enunciates the practical conclusion: our prayer should be short and pure, short so that it may be pure.[1] Such was the custom of the Egyptian monks, as is remarked by St. Augustine and Cassian; they preferred to keep in touch with Our Lord by many rapid ejaculations, rather than by long prayers, in which many superfluous petitions[2] are often made, which too are especially concerned with self, and which may degenerate into fatigue, torpor, and decay. We should, moreover, reflect on the inevitable danger, which would have been incurred in St. Benedict's day, and which is still incurred in our own time by minds of small culture and imperfectly formed souls, in being held officially to prolonged prayer. Previous training is indispensable for mental prayer, if it is to have any considerable duration. For a moment may find all said, and then the mind is off elsewhere. Sometimes we may recall it, but it is off again, no matter in what direction. Sometimes we do not even think of recalling it, and the time is spent in mental wanderings, so that we reach the end of our half-hour and wonder what part God has taken in the prayer that has just abruptly ended. And yet, at the very same time, we know our faith and our needs, and perhaps even our theology.

It goes without saying that our Holy Father has no thought of reducing the time which our fervour would give to God, for he formally provides for the case when divine grace stirs in us an interior movement of devotion and leads us to prolong our prayers. Provided that the work that is given us by obedience does not suffer and that we neglect none of our duties, this taste for prayer is wholly legitimate. But in order to avoid delusion and to consecrate all by obedience, we should not undertake prolonged prayers without previously obtaining the consent of the Abbot. The Constitutions fix the minimum time which should be devoted to prayer. And God grant that monks may ever have sufficient sense of their vocation for superiors to be dispensed from all inquiry and compulsion in this matter. However, no attempt is made to saddle us with a " method "; we are not forbidden to converse with God in peaceful meditation on Holy Scripture or the liturgy; for the *lectio divina* (sacred reading), which the Rule prescribes, is something more than a simple preparation for prayer; these two hours of reading enable our Holy Father to recommend that the prayers of his monks should be short, so as to be pure.

The last provision of this chapter is inspired again by discretion. If the individual be allowed, when divine grace moves him, to increase his private prayers, it is clear that it would scarcely be reasonable to require long additions to the daily liturgical duty from the whole com-

---
[1] *Cf.* St. Thomas, *Summa*, II.-II., q. lxxxiii., a. 14. *Utrum oratio debet esse diuturna.*
[2] *Hoc præcipue est in oratione petendum, ut Deo uniamur* (*Summa*, II.-II., q. lxxxiii., a. 1, ad 2).

Of Reverence at Prayer

munity. Therefore St. Benedict ordains that prayer in common should always be very short: *omnino brevietur*, and that all should rise at the same time, on the signal of the superior. Of what prayers is he treating? Cassian relates how the monks of Egypt after each psalm prayed for some moments erect and in silence, then prostrated on the ground, and almost immediately rose again, to unite their intention finally with the one who was reciting the collect: " But when he who is to make the collect has risen from the ground, all likewise rise, so that no one presumes either to kneel before he bends down or to delay when he rises, lest he should seem rather to have made a prayer of his own than to have followed the prayer of him who makes the collect."[1] But St. Benedict nowhere prescribes private prayer or a collect after each psalm: their place is taken by the antiphons. He would seem here to be alluding to the prayers with which the Offices ended (see Chapter LXVII.):[2] of which some were said in silence and mentally, while the monks either bowed or prostrated, and which the Abbot might abridge. For all its brevity, this conventual prayer was too much for that monk, mentioned in ᵗhe life of St. Benedict, whom a little black devil used to lure outside. "He could not stay at prayer, but as soon as the brethren bowed down in prayer, he would go out. . . . And when the man of God had come to the same monastery and at the appointed time, the psalmody being finished, the brethren were giving themselves to prayer,"[3] etc. St. Benedict never speaks of conventual prayers distinct from the Work of God: "When the Work of God is ended, let all go out with the utmost silence. . . . But if anyone desire to pray in private, let him go in with simplicity and pray" (Chapter LII.).

[1] *Inst.*, II., vii.; *cf. ibid.*, x.—The *Rule* of St. Pachomius said: *Cumque manum percusserit stans prior in gradu, et de scripturis quidpiam volvens memoriter, ut, oratione finiente, nullus consurget tardius, sed omnes pariter levabunt* (vi.).

[2] Cassian mentions the concluding prayer of the Offices: *Satis vero constat illum trinæ curvationis numerum, qui solet in congregationibus fratrum ad concludendam synaxin celebrari, eum qui intento animo supplicat observare non posse* (*Conlat.*, IX., xxxiv.). D. Baümer would read *orationis* instead of *curvationis*, and *non supplicat* (*Hist. du Brév.*, t. I., p. 149, note 1).

[3] S. Greg. M., *Dial.*, l. II., c. iv.

CHAPTER XXI

OF THE DEANS OF THE MONASTERY

WE enter now upon a portion of the Holy Rule which deals with the internal government and discipline of the monastery (XXI.-XXX.). St. Benedict begins by determining the principle of order and that hierarchical arrangement of parts which shall secure the right functioning of all. The authority of the Abbot initiates all regular activities, presiding over all and issuing sovereign decrees, and to it St. Benedict devoted the long chapter at the beginning of his Rule. But the Abbot must be seconded by officials acting under his orders and on his responsibility. Ordinarily this function appertains chiefly to the *præpositus* (the Prior), to whom St. Benedict makes a brief allusion at the end of this chapter. When he comes to deal with him professedly, in the sixty-fifth chapter, our Holy Father makes no secret of his repugnance for a dignity and an office which to his mind was dangerous on more than one count. After the Prior come the deans: but if the deans are able, in their respective departments, to secure work and discipline, then the general and comprehensive rule of the Prior may be easily dispensed with: " If possible, let all the affairs of the monastery be attended to (as we have already arranged) by deans, as the Abbot shall appoint; so that, the same office being shared by many, no one may become proud " (Chapter LXV.). So we may speak first of the deans.

DE DECANIS MONASTERII.—Si major fuerit congregatio, eligantur de ipsis fratres boni testimonii et sanctæ conversationis et constituantur decani: qui sollicitudinem gerant super decanias suas in omnibus, secundum mandata Dei et præcepta Abbatis sui. Qui decani tales eligantur, in quibus securus Abbas partiatur onera sua, et non eligantur per ordinem, sed secundum vitæ meritum, et sapientiæ doctrinam.

Should the community be large, let there be chosen from it certain brethren of good repute and holy life, and appointed deans. Let them carefully direct their deaneries in all things according to the commandments of God and the orders of their Abbot. And let such men be chosen deans as the Abbot may safely trust to share his burdens: let them not be chosen according to order, but for the merit of their lives and for their learning of wisdom.

The name and functions of the dean came from the camp to the monastery. In military language a *decanus* or *decurio* was one who had ten men under his command.[1] The cenobites of Egypt, with something of a military organization, were arranged in groups of ten. St. Jerome says: "They are divided by tens and hundreds, the tenth man presiding over nine; while the hundredth has ten provosts under him."[2]

[1] In the same way COLUMELLA says that workers in the fields should be grouped in tens (*De re rustica*, l. I., c. ix.).
[2] *Epist.*, XXII., 35. *P.L.*, XXII., 419.

And St. Augustine: "They give their work to those whom they call deans (*decani*) because they are set over ten. . . . These deans, while arranging all things with great solicitude and providing whatever their life needs for the weakness of the body, yet themselves give an account to one whom they call father." In this we recognize the idea and almost the phraseology of St. Benedict. He found in Cassian also many passages relating to deans.[2] Mentioning that the young monks are entrusted "to a senior who is in charge of ten juniors,"[3] Cassian notes that the office of dean dates from Moses, whose father-in-law Jethro gave him this good advice: "Provide out of all the people able men, such as fear God, in whom there is truth, and that hate avarice: and appoint of them rulers of thousands, and of hundreds, and of fifties, and of tens, who may judge the people at all times. And when any great matter soever shall fall out, let them refer it to thee, and let them judge the lesser matters only: that so it may be lighter for thee, the burden being shared out unto others" (Ex. xviii. 21–22). St. Benedict also would seem to have remembered this passage.

Deans only existed where the community was rather large, and it is possible to determine exactly what St. Benedict meant by "large." So long as a community consisted of twelve monks, as at Subiaco, or as at the commencement of the monastery of Terracina,[4] the Abbot could manage with one assistant. But since St. Benedict speaks of deans in the plural, and the plural implies at least two, and since each dean had ten monks under him (St. Jerome says nine), it would appear that a community became really "large" when it reached the number of eighteen or twenty religious.

Eligantur (let there be chosen). There is every reason to believe that in St. Benedict's time deans were chosen directly by the Abbot. The Abbot chose his deans just as he chose his Prior. If the community interfered, it was never to exercise a right or vindicate a privilege, but humbly to put its desires before the Abbot and to submit its preferences to him; it was no more than a presentation, and the Abbot and his monks acted in harmony and for the best interests of all. "But if the needs of the place require it, and the community ask for it reasonably and with humility, and the Abbot judge it expedient, let him himself appoint a Prior, whomsoever he shall choose with the counsel of brethren who fear God" (Chapter LXV.). And in Chapter LXII. our Holy Father, after having reminded any priest of the monastery that he must take his rank according to the date of his profession, provides for this exception: "Unless the choice of the community and the will of the Abbot should raise him to a higher place for the merit of his life." Nowadays deans do not rule over a fixed deanery, but have duties of kindly supervision over the whole community; in particular they have to set a good example, and to act as advisers to the Abbot, like the seniors.

[1] *De moribus Eccles. cathol.*, l. I., c. xxxi. P.L., XXXII., 1338.
[2] *Inst.*, IV., x, xvii.   [3] *Inst.*, IV., vii.
[4] S. Greg. M., *Dial.*, l. II., c. iii., xxii.

Modern Constitutions and Declarations have fixed, for each Benedictine Congregation, all that concerns the choice, number, and functions of the seniors and deans; most of them recognize the right of a community to be represented in the Abbot's Council by brethren elected by secret scrutiny. And it generally happens that the counsellors chosen by the community are more numerous than those chosen by the Abbot. But God grant that we may never have to invoke legislative contrivances to prevent the Abbot being in a minority in his Council. Such a course would introduce disunion into a monastery, would erect in permanency and consecrate a dualism and rivalry between Abbot and community. Practically, in a peaceful community, there is no difference between the case where the counsellors are chosen by the Abbot, according to the text of the Rule, and that where the majority are elected by the monks: for all are, by the same title, counsellors of the Abbot and of the community. The Abbot chooses counsellors, and counsellors are chosen for him; they are not to be either opponents or partisans.

Eligantur de ipsis (let there be chosen from it): deans shall not be chosen from seculars or even from other monks. It is hardly necessary to-day to observe that authority should only be entrusted to those who belong to the family. Yet it is sometimes good to remember that, save for the cases provided in Canon Law, externs, no matter who they be, have no right to interfere in our internal affairs; we are exempt, and have no need for legal guardianship or counsel. Perhaps, however, St. Benedict's remark is especially intended to remind the community that it should show deference and do honour to deans chosen from its bosom. *Et constituantur decani* (and let them be appointed deans): in which words is implied an official recognition of their title and perhaps also a ceremony of investiture. According to the *Rule of the Master* the rod of office was solemnly put into their hands.[1]

St. Benedict indicates by what signs the Abbot and his community may recognize those who are worthy to be elected. Age is not necessarily the determining factor, for deans must not be appointed by seniority: "let them not be chosen according to their order"; and it would be strange, in promoting a monk, to have regard to nothing but the date of his clothing, our Holy Father having several times repeated that age should neither raise prejudice against a man nor create a presumption in his favour. The old monks and counsellors of the Abbot, of whom St. Benedict spoke in the third chapter, are not necessarily candidates for the office of dean; the charge then implied, as we have said, an active rule and constant supervision, for which aged monks might often not have strength; for a man might be a senior and a wise counsellor and yet, for one reason or another, be incapable of managing a deanery. We may go farther still: aptitude, even marked aptitude, sound learning, and real virtue, are not always determining factors; there is needed a sum of qualities which our Holy Father reduces to two: *vitæ meritum, sapientiæ doctrinam* (merit of life, learning of wisdom). The deans are to be

[1] Cap. xi.—*Cf.* MÉNARD, *Concord. Reg.*, c. xxviii., p. 445.

chosen as were the first deacons, whom they resemble in their office. They are to have a good name among the brethren, so that men may bow willingly to their authority; their life must be edifying, since they have to help the Abbot in maintaining good observance. Besides meritorious life they need the "learning of wisdom"—that is to say, prudence, tact, and a feeling for what is spiritual and monastic; and it is here that training, experience, and age may be a great help. In brief, they must be such that the Abbot may have full confidence in them, and may with entire security leave many details to them and divide his cares among them.

This, in fact, is the purpose of the deans: to help the Abbot. When a house is starting and during all the period of "becoming," the superior may have to encroach on the spheres of particular officials; but in a fully organized monastery the Abbot should take care to provide himself with assistants and deputies, reserving for himself general direction only and the work inherent in his charge. He cannot successfully busy himself about everything, and our Holy Father wishes him to have quiet and leisure: "Let him not be violent or over anxious, not exacting or obstinate, not jealous or prone to suspicion, or else he will never be at rest" (Chapter LXIV.). Moreover, since he must grow old and die, he is well advised to think of the morrow and to initiate others into the government of the community, which does not die. Finally, this division of labour within the monastery does not merely relieve the Abbot and secure the future: it gives others the benefit of co-operation in the common work and a measure of responsibility. Whence it comes that no one is tempted to be wholly indifferent, to live in isolation, occupied solely with his own studies; and each only learns to love the better his home and his brethren.

Deans, says St. Benedict, must be solicitous for their deaneries. Solicitude does not mean arrogance or tyranny, but care and loving devotion. No one is put in authority that he may satisfy his vanity, and make himself friends either within or without the monastery, or take reprisals, or act with violence; but rather so that he may be more devoted to his monastic family and may serve it more intimately. Deans are bound to fulfil their office in its entirety: *in omnibus*. Formerly it was a charge of considerable complexity, requiring continuous care combined with decision and strength of character. The duties of deans at Monte Cassino were doubtless the same as among the Eastern monks spoken of in the passages of St. Jerome, St. Augustine, and Cassian previously quoted; they watched over their deaneries in the dormitory, in the refectory, and at manual labour; they saw to the observance of silence, gave permissions, and inflicted penances. A list of the chief functions of deans may be found in Martène. Sometimes, in places where deans did not exist, these functions were performed by the Claustral Prior. At Cluny, after the Abbot and the Grand Prior, came the Claustral Prior, assisted at need by another and aided in his supervision by masters of the children and young monks and by the *circatores*;

the name of "deans" was given to the brethren who controlled the working of the "villas" or farms situated in the neighbourhood of the monastery: *villarum provisores*.[1]

When St. Benedict wrote of deans that they should "govern their deaneries in all things," he had no intention of conferring on them an unlimited and uncontrolled power. In the first place there is a divine limit: "according to the commandments of God"; and then a limit on the side of the Abbot, "and the orders of their Abbot." For this authority must be exercised in unity of purpose with the Abbot, neither apart from him nor against him. The Abbot shares his government but does not abdicate it, and he may not become a stranger in his own house. Undoubtedly the monk who is in charge has no need, in the transaction of ordinary affairs, to interview the Abbot on details; but so soon as there are changes of some moment to be effected, or extraordinary matters to be dealt with, he should consult the Abbot and obtain his authorization. And supposing that the Abbot, on a particular day and as an exceptional case, should interfere in order to inspect or reform some point or other, the official who should be astonished as though he were distrusted, who should be irritated as though it implied want of consideration, and should protest against the supposed intrusion, or give it out that his Abbot is of one way of thinking but he of another, such a one would forget the rule: *according to the orders of his Abbot*. A man entrusted with a charge sees clearly only the requirements of his charge, is shortsighted and deficient in the sense of proportion; and he should be convinced that considerations of a wider scope must sometimes modify his programme or his habits. The power of a dean, again, is limited on the side of the brethren, since he rules only his deanery. He will avoid that ambitious and jealous spirit which makes a man extend the field of his jurisdiction as widely as possible: "This is my business, that concerns me; custom says that such and such a right or advantage belongs to my office." Wherever charity, self-effacement, and good sense are lacking, offices will supply matter for petty rivalry, and that the more easily since they overlap one another and no customary can achieve an exact delimitation of their frontiers.

We may make one last observation. St. Benedict uses the possessive pronoun "their" in alluding to the deaneries; but his intention thereby is not to suggest real possession and inalienable right, but simply appointment. There is no such thing here as possession by prescription, whether by a period of seven years or even of thirty. All the offices of the monastery are held *ad nutum*, on precarious tenure, even the office of dean or Prior. Every official should realize that his charge may pass into another's hands, that he may be deprived of it without the least shadow of injustice; for an opposite conviction would be a very subtle danger and a recrudescence of the spirit of ownership. If we are relieved of an office, we should rather quietly rejoice that we no longer have to

---

[1] BERNARD., *Ordo Clun.*, P. I., c. ii.—UDALR., *Consuet. Clun.*, L. III., c. v.

bear that responsibility, and be glad, according to the old saying, that Thebes has produced a worthier man.

Quod si quis ex eis aliqua forte inflatus superbia repertus fuerit reprehensibilis: correptus semel, et iterum, et tertio, si emendare noluerit, dejiciatur, et alter in loco ejus, qui dignus est, subrogetur. Et de præposito eadem constituimus.	And should any one of them, being puffed up with pride, be found worthy of blame, and after being thrice corrected, refuse to amend, let him be deposed and one put in his place who is worthy. And we order the same to be done in the case of the Prior.

If it happened that any dean, abusing his privileged position and swollen with self-importance, should be found blameworthy, this is how the Abbot should proceed. With the natural exception of notorious fault or scandalous resistance, and when it is only a question of bad tendencies or secret faults, a dean shall receive secret admonition up to three times.[1] Monks have two such secret admonitions, deans three, and the Prior four. If a dean refuse to amend, the Abbot has only one resource left—viz., to withdraw the offender from an office which has become a danger for himself and his brethren, and to entrust it to another who is worthy of it. An analogous line of conduct, says St. Benedict, shall be followed with regard to a proud or unruly Prior. Nevertheless, there shall be some differences of treatment; but of these our Holy Father says nothing here, since he proposed to speak of the Prior at greater length in the sixty-fifth chapter.

[1] *Quod si secundo aut tertio admonita emendare noluerit* . . . (S. CÆSAR., *Reg. ad virg.*, x.).

CHAPTER XXII

HOW THE MONKS ARE TO SLEEP

QUOMODO DORMIANT MONACHI.—Singuli per singulos lectos dormiant. Lectisternia pro modo conversationis, secundum dispensationem Abbatis sui, singuli accipiant.

Let them sleep each one in a separate bed, receiving bedding suitable to their manner of life, as the Abbot shall appoint.

ST. BENEDICT did not throw out the details of his Rule at random, without any order; yet it is hard to see, at first sight, what is the connection of this chapter with those which surround it. Probably our Holy Father, having spoken of the deans, wished to speak of the chief circumstances in which they had to exercise their duties, and of the methods put into their hands to secure obedience. Moreover, this question of the monks' sleep, being involved in that of the Night Office, is not out of place amid liturgical legislation, and Rules anterior to St. Benedict frequently treated the two together.

The regulation with which the chapter opens, that each brother should have a separate bed, seems to us nowadays quite superfluous. It is mere elementary decency and indispensable comfort. However, the old monastic Rules[1] thought it their duty to make the same provision, and Councils have legislated on the matter,[2] doubtless because the contrary practice existed in some houses. For manners were simple and the mode of life was voluntarily assimilated to that of the poor man and the peasant. Monks lay down to rest fully clad, on mats, mattresses, or planks.

So each brother is to receive a bed and bedding (*lectisternia*), the whole being suitable to the poverty and austerity of his way of life—that is the best explanation of the words *pro modo conversationis*—and according to the regulations of the Abbot. Our Holy Father keeps the list of bedding till Chapter LV.: " For their bedding let a straw mattress, blanket, coverlet, and pillow suffice." Monks are not to be surprised if their couch is somewhat hard: for it is merely a camp-bed whereon they stretch themselves for a few hours, and they themselves are soldiers, who, as St. Benedict says presently, should be ready to rise at the first signal. Nevertheless, the Abbot may give a more comfortable bed to the sick or aged, and adjust the amount and quality of the bedclothes to the climate or season.

Si potest fieri, omnes in uno loco dormiant; si autem multitudo non sinit, deni, aut viceni cum senioribus

If it be possible, let all sleep in one place; but if the number do not permit of this, let them repose by

---

[1] Except the *Regula cujusdam ad virgines*, xiv.
[2] *Cf. Conc. Turonense* II. (567), can. xiv. MANSI, t. IX., col. 795.

suis, qui super eos solliciti sint, pausent. Candela jugiter in eadem cella ardeat usque mane.	tens or twenties with the seniors who have charge of them. Let a candle burn constantly in the cell until morning.

Each is to have his own bed; but, so far as possible, there is to be one dormitory for all—that is to say, for all the professed monks; for, according to the fifty-eighth chapter, novices have separate accommodation: " Let him go into the cell of the novices where he is to meditate, to take his meals, and to sleep." St. Benedict wishes to have the perfect cenobitical life; so his sons must pray and work and eat together and have a common dormitory.[1] This is not, however, an innovation; for in the commentary of Martène may be found divers ancient testimonies in favour of the dormitory, in particular the witness of St. Cæsarius;[2] and there too may be read the history of the changes in custom with regard to this point. For long centuries Benedictine monks slept in a dormitory, in beds without screens, generally with the Abbot in the midst of them. Provided certain precautions were taken in the interest of hygiene and decency, no fault was to be found with this arrangement.[3] In the fifteenth century the fathers of Cluny and Bursfeld again condemn separate cells; but the dormitory is divided into cubicles, which really form so many little rooms where each may read and pray in peace. In the days when the monk's life was practically all absorbed by the Divine Office and manual labour, a brother would not go to the dormitory except to sleep or to read by his bed. However, the *lectio divina* (sacred reading) was generally taken in the cloister or the chapter-room, while copyists and illuminators worked in a common room known as the *scriptorium*. But the conditions of monastic life became rather different with the predominance of intellectual labours, the institution of lay brothers, new habits of piety, the intrusion of lay folk into the cloister, and the system of beneficed monks with each his separate apartment. It was easy to justify the use of cells by precedents taken from the history of the Eastern monks, or the monks of St. Martin, or Lerins, etc., and from the customs of the Carthusians and Camaldolese. Not to break completely with monastic antiquity, the cells were closed by a simple screen, or else the door had a small aperture with a movable shutter; while the name of " dormitory " was preserved for the corridor on to which the cells opened; and, finally, the light which St. Benedict says should burn until morning was faithfully kept in this same corridor all through the night.

The Rule does not consider any other arrangement than that of the dormitory; yet it leaves it to the Abbot to decide whether to assemble all in the same place, or, because of their numbers, to scatter them in different rooms, in their groups of ten (deaneries), or with many such groups together. In this last case, and in the absence of Abbot and Prior,

---

[1] *Cf.* S. Greg. M., *Dial.*, l. II., c. xxxv.
[2] *Reg. ad monach.*, iii.; *Reg. ad virg.*, vii.
[3] *Cf.* Udalr., *Consuet. Clun.*, l. II., c. v., ix., x.—*Constit. Hirsaug.*, l. I., c. lxix., lxx,

the monks were placed under the more immediate responsibility and supervision of their respective deans (that is the meaning here of the words *senioribus suis*). It was partly in order to enable the deans to exercise vigilance that the old customaries regulate so minutely the lighting of the dormitory. This was done, says Calmet, " by lights of wax, tallow, oil, wood, rush, or reed, but principally by torches of pine or fir." If we are to believe certain commentators, the deans must have had no right to close their eyes at all during the whole night; but St. Benedict makes no such demand of them; they could assure themselves that all was going well with less trouble, and go their rounds from time to time, as the customaries provide.

Vestiti dormiant, et cincti cingulis aut funibus, et cultellos ad latus non habeant dum dormiunt, ne forte per somnium vulnerentur dormientes; et ut parati sint monachi semper; et facto signo absque mora surgentes, festinent invicem se praevenire ad opus Dei, cum omni tamen gravitate et modestia.	Let them sleep clothed, and girded with belts or cords—but not with knives at their sides, lest perchance they wound themselves in their sleep— and thus be always ready, so that when the signal is given they rise without delay, and hasten each to forestall the other in going to the Work of God, yet with all gravity and modesty.

Monks must sleep clothed, and not, under the pretext of simplicity, in the manner of many of the ancients or of the peasants of Campania. Their clothing for the night, if not the same as that for the day, shall at any rate consist of the same elements—viz., the tunic, worn near the skin like a shirt and with its folds gathered in by a belt; probably also stockings or light shoes (*pedules*), which will be spoken of in Chapter LV.; finally the cowl, for our Holy Father writes in the same chapter: " It is sufficient for a monk to have two tunics and two cowls, on account of the nights and the need of washing." Drawers were given only to those on a journey. The scapular, being a working garment (*propter opera*) was out of place. It would seem that the belt used at night was different from that used during the day; the latter was the *bracile*, a large cincture acting as a pouch, while at night any sort of girdle would serve, of leather or cord: " girded with belts or cords, but not with knives at their sides."[1] Our Holy Father orders that their large knives, which were used for the most diverse purposes, should not, as in the daytime, be fastened to the belt: for it would be easy, even though the knife were in a case, to wound oneself in the unconscious movements of sleep, or to strike one's neighbours with it in the course of a nightmare.

When our Holy Father and other legislators bade monks keep their religious habit when sleeping, or at least some part of this habit, it was in the first place from motives of decency and poverty: for that was all the clothes they had. It was also from devotion to the vesture which symbolized their profession, and because it was a safeguard against the attacks of the devil. St. Benedict adds: " Let them sleep clothed and girded . . . and thus be always ready." The monk, as the soldier of

---

[1] According to D. BUTLER: *ut cultellos* . . .

Christ, should be always ready to run to the Work of God. Perhaps we have in this passage an allusion to the Gospel words: " Let your loins be girt and lamps burning in your hands. And you yourselves like to men who wait for their lord " (Luke xii. 35–6). As soon as the appointed signal sounded (Chapter XLVII.) all rose, without discussing the point with their pillows, and, probably leaving for the daytime the business of a quick toilet and change of habit, went down immediately to the oratory.[1] If there is one reason for regretting the ancient arrangement of the monastic dormitory, it is that it made it difficult for the lazy to indulge their laziness. A man might close his eyes and hide as well as possible under the coverlet, but it would be vain;[2] for he would not escape the feeling that he was a blot on the general promptness. The brethren have to be prompt and to strive who should be the first at the Work of God, yet with all gravity and modesty, adds our Holy Father prudently. It is the last time of all in which to indulge in small jests, or to rush madly down stairs and corridors, and in Chapter XLIII. St. Benedict repeats both counsels.

We should remember and practise the instruction: " When the signal is given . . . rise without delay." We must not rise piecemeal, bit by bit, but immediately and as it were mechanically: it is easiest in the end. The Divine Office, both the work and our disposition towards it, will suffer from the unhappy self-indulgence and petty calculation which give us an additional twenty minutes of sleep every morning. Eight hours of sleep is more than was granted by old rules of health:

> Sex horas dormisse sat est, pueroque senique;
> Da septem pigro: nulli concesseris octo.[3]

And even though punctual rising imply some weariness and mortification, let us face it resolutely. It is by such courage in details that we come to be morally stronger, more fully masters of our body, and lords over our passions. Moreover, the most wholesome mortifications are those which enter into the tissue of everyday life and are with difficulty perceived.

| Adolescentiores fratres juxta se non habeant lectos, sed permixti cum senioribus. Surgentes vero ad opus Dei, invicem se moderate cohortentur, propter somnolentorum excusationes. | Let not the younger brethren have their beds by themselves, but among those of the seniors. And when they rise for the Work of God, let them gently encourage one another, because of the excuses of the drowsy. |

These few lines are intended to secure the discipline of the dormitory and that moderate haste which has just been mentioned. In Chapter XLIII. St. Benedict fixes the order which the monks are to take in all assemblies of the brethren: precedence being determined by

---

[1] Cf. MARTÈNE, De antiq. monach. rit., l. I., c. i.
[2] The dark lantern of the Claustral Prior or the *circatores* easily found out those who lingered in bed or continued their sleep in the church. Cf. UDALR., Consuet. Clun., l. II., c. viii.—BERNARD., Ordo Clun., P. I., c. iii.—Constit. Hirsaug., l. I., c. xxviii.
[3] Six hours' sleep for old man and boy, seven for the sluggard, eight for none.

the date and hour of "conversion." In this place our Holy Father makes an exception of the case when the accident of their entry into religion has grouped many young religious together. Children and young people are great sleepers. These "younger brethren," if together in the dormitory, might either not wake, or be only too happy to enter into a conspiracy for mutual indulgence. They might often, too, be tempted to frolics. To obviate these various dangers St. Benedict would have their beds put among those of the older monks. The term *senioribus* (seniors), since it is contrasted with *adolescentiores* (younger monks), and is not as before accompanied by the possessive pronoun *suis* (their) should here be understood to mean religious of riper years and not the deans; the latter, besides, would have been too few for the plan proposed. If we understand the words *pro modo conversationis* at the beginning of the chapter to mean that the beds were arranged according to age, temperament, and gravity, we must admit, with some commentators, that St. Benedict gives the same counsel twice.

"When they rise." Not the young only must be encouraged: all the monks are to do this service for one another. The sleepy have always plenty of bad excuses for not rising, as nightmare, indigestion, cramp, headache, or the signal was not quite heard. These are the *somnolentorum excusationes*. St. Benedict, in the interests of the Office and of the common observance, empowers us to destroy all these illusions by discreet exhortation, *moderate;* a little noise is enough, or at need a shake of the bed. Would a few words be permitted? And does our Holy Father intend to make an exception to the rigid law of the night silence? It is not unlikely. Besides, we do not know when this time of silence ended, and it may have been precisely at the hour of rising and at the beginning of the monastic day. St. Basil recommends us to give the knocker-up a good reception, to welcome gratefully him who comes to draw us out of the humiliating state of sleep, wherein the soul loses self-consciousness, and to invite us to the work of glorifying God.[1]

We may add a final observation connected with the general subject of the chapter. Some people, before they go to sleep, review the intellectual work of the day so as to fix and assimilate the results; which is a good practice, if it be brief. St. Teresa tells us that she never went to sleep without thinking of the Garden of Olives, of that dreadful night and of the agony of Our Lord: which is a far better practice. The last thought of our day is of very great importance, for it influences our sleep and influences the morrow. It is quite possible for us to consecrate to God even the unconscious moments of slumber. Our last thought is like a seed entrusted silently to the earth: *Terra ultro fructificat* (The earth giveth fruit of itself); while it fades away, its blessed influence sinks slowly into our souls, impregnates them and permeates the whole.

[1] *Reg. contr.*, lxxv., lxxvi.

CHAPTER XXIII
OF EXCOMMUNICATION FOR FAULTS

THE duty of supervision and correction having been entrusted to the deans, they could not be left without the means to deal with non-observance of rule; therefore this chapter and the seven succeeding ones treat of punishment and the methods of its application.[1] All the old Rules abound in disciplinary provisions, and we shall have occasion to notice some of the items which St. Benedict has borrowed from them.[2] But nowhere before had a legislator formulated a code of such perfect sobriety, so prudent, discreet, and gentle in its holy rigour.[3] The evolution of manners has profoundly modified since his day both the nature of offences and the character of punishment; yet it is still useful to study the ideas of our Holy Father concerning the difficult duty of correction, even though the letter of his provisions has been in great measure abrogated by custom.

We may fix at once the plan of these eight chapters. The twenty-third enumerates first the principal faults to be punished, and then commences to describe the progressive series or hierarchy of corrections according to the Rule—viz., two secret admonitions, a public rebuke, excommunication, or corporal punishment. This is not an exhaustive list; but with the twenty-fourth chapter begins a long digression on excommunication, which is of two kinds, excommunication from meals (XXIV.), excommunication from meals and choir (XXV.). The two chapters that follow treat, the one of unlawful intercourse with the excommunicate (XXVI.), the other of lawful intercourse with them and the solicitude of the Abbot in their regard (XXVII.). Then St. Benedict resumes and completes, in the twenty-eighth chapter, the enumeration of the various methods of repression and cure—viz., the rod, earnest prayer, and, if all else is unavailing, expulsion. The twenty-ninth chapter fixes the number of times and the conditions under which expelled or renegade monks may be reinstated. Finally, the thirtieth chapter forms a little codicil on the punishments suitable for the young. Farther on, in Chapters XLIII.-XLVI., our Holy Father takes occasion to complete his code of punishments, treating of penances for faults of a less serious kind than those he deals with here. And in many parts of the Rule he uses the threat, in passing, of one or other of the monastic punishments.

[1] According to Abbot HERWEGEN, the eight chapters of this penal code would originally have formed a special fascicle, more for the use of the superior than of the monks; in the final redaction of the Rule they got the place they now have by pure chance (*Geschichte der benediktinischen Professformel*, p. 23, note 1).
[2] Consult the commentaries of MÈGE, MARTÈNE, CALMET.—MÉNARD, *op. cit.*, c. xxx.-xxxix.—HÆFTEN, l. VIII.—D. BESSE, *Les Moines d'Orient*, chap. ix.
[3] Compare the *Rule* of ST. PACHOMIUS, especially Nos. clx. onwards.

DE EXCOMMUNICATIONE CULPARUM.—Si quis frater contumax, aut inobediens, aut superbus, aut murmurans, vel in aliquo contrarius existens sanctæ regulæ, et præceptis seniorum suorum, contemptor repertus fuerit:

If any brother shall be found contumacious, or disobedient, or proud, or a murmurer, or in any way opposed to the Holy Rule, and the orders of his seniors, and a contemner:

We may note, first of all, that the faults contemplated by St. Benedict in this paragraph have their common basis in a rebellious will; or rather that he is concerned with this only, having no intention of cataloguing the infinite variety of offences, of which only a few are mentioned in the course of the Rule. Penances may be imposed for purely formal faults, so as to prevent negligence and make conscience more delicate; but severe treatment, with the rigour implied in these penal arrangements, is not meted out to imperfections; for there is not sufficient matter. Nor again is severity used against faults of thoughtlessness, ignorance, or impulse. Following the example of God, who considers only what comes from our deliberate will (Matt. xv. 17–20), St. Benedict is severe only with perversity of will, in its most formidable external manifestations.[1] There is, in the first place, formal rebellion. *Contumacia* (contumacy) is refusal to obey, directed against a present authority, open and obstinate resistance. It is audacious and insolent disobedience. Next comes grave disobedience, with no admixture of bravado; it is refusal to submit to the Rule or to some order that has been given. Then comes pride, habitual self-exaltation, self-inflation, and the worship of one's own worth, which is at bottom the secret principle of every failing in monastic life and the poisoned root of all the faults spoken of here.

Nothing of all this is very attractive; it reveals the beast, headstrong and restive: " Become not like the horse and the mule who have no understanding " (Ps. xxxi. 9). And yet we can see clearly that what our Holy Father detests most vigorously and most constantly denounces is a disposition to murmur: " or a murmurer." The murmurer is a sorry being, and it is just because he is such that he is a grumbler, discontented with everything and always in opposition. Yet he falls into line, he is in a material sense almost correct, and at need he may even be obsequious. He has not the unhappy courage of downright disobedience, for he does what he is told, though with a groan. But he carries here and there, to souls which he feels are prepared by their weakness and their sufferings, the accursed gospel of his murmuring. He is mean and cowardly, and at the same time dangerous. One might almost prefer the contumacious man, and the violence of his resistance, to the base and underhand scheming of the murmurer.

Vel in aliquo . . . Calmet enumerates the various meanings which

---

[1] *Si quis autem murmuraverit, vel contentiosus extiterit, aut referens in aliquo contrariam voluntatem præceptis* . . . (S. MACAR., *Reg.*, xii.). *Si inobediens quis fuerit, aut contentiosus, aut contradictor, aut mendax, et est perfrictæ frontis* . . . (S. PACHOM., *Reg.*, clxv. *Cf. ibid.*, cl.).

may be given to this section. The most natural is the following: " or else if he be found contemptuous, transgressing in some way or other the Holy Rule and the orders of his seniors, the deans." It forms a fifth kind of offence, being added to open resistance, serious disobedience, pride, and murmuring, and consists in the breaking of the Rule, accompanied with contempt. We may repeat that there could be no question of visiting every failing, no matter what, with the severity of the established penal code. But a want of harmony which may be slight and momentary may also become serious, constant, and unmanageable, and constitute what is called contempt; or if it be not formal contempt, which happily is very rare, at least it will be equivalent and practical contempt. Probably the evil dispositions here enumerated imply theological culpability, but St. Benedict does not consider them from that point of view; he punishes them only as contrary to monastic observance and the public promises of our profession.

... hic secundum Domini nostri præceptum admoneatur semel et secundo secrete a senioribus suis. Si non emendaverit, objurgetur publice coram omnibus. Si vero neque sic correxerit, si intelligit qualis pœna sit, excommunicationi subjaceat. Sin autem improbus est, vindictæ corporali subdatur.[1]

... let him, according to Our Lord's commandment, be once or twice privately admonished by his seniors. If he do not amend, let him be rebuked in public before all. But if even then he do not correct himself, let him be subjected to excommunication, provided that he understand the nature of the punishment. Should he, however, prove froward, let him undergo corporal chastisement.

This is, for ordinary cases, the procedure to be followed in the correction of the brethren; St. Benedict gives elsewhere the special points to be observed in the correction of deans, the Prior, and priests. He lays it down too, in Chapter LXX., that if a fault be public and such as to give scandal, it should receive an appropriate chastisement: " Let such as offend herein be rebuked in the presence of all, that the rest may be struck with fear." But so long as faults are not plainly scandalous, whatever be their gravity in other respects, the Holy Rule employs indulgence and pity. It is clearly inspired by the counsel of Our Lord in the Gospel: " But if thy brother shall offend against thee, go and rebuke him between thee and him alone. If he shall hear thee, thou shalt gain thy brother. And if he will not hear thee: take with thee one or two more, that in the mouth of two or three witnesses every word may stand. And if he will not hear them: tell the church. And if he will not hear the church: let him be to thee as the heathen and publican "

---

[1] *Cum vero inventa fuerit culpa, ille qui culpabilis invenitur, corripiatur ab Abbate secretius. Quod si non sufficit ad emendationem, corripiatur a paucis senioribus. Quod si nec sic emendaverit, excommunicetur* (Reg. Orient., xxxii.). Next come some particulars concerning excommunication from meals and prayer, and on satisfaction, almost in the same terms as those of our Rule; then a threat addressed to anyone who should talk with a rebellious monk: *simili modo culpabilem judicandum* (xxxiii.); finally sentence of exclusion is pronounced against the incorrigible monk *ne vitio ipsius alii periclitentur* (xxxv.).

(Matt. xviii. 15-17). So a private warning is first given and, if need be, repeated; and this is to be done by those only who hold a position of authority (see Chapter LXX.)—*i.e.*, the Abbot and the deans or seniors.

If secret admonition has no effect, then the delinquent is rebuked in public, and this is the second stage. The third consists in excommunication or corporal chastisement, for there are two methods of procedure according to the character and temperament of the delinquent. In the second chapter our Holy Father distinguished two classes of characters to which the Abbot should apply different treatment: " Those of good disposition and understanding let him, for the first or second time, correct only with words; but such as are froward and hard of heart, and proud, or disobedient, let him chastise with bodily stripes at the very first offence." It is hardly probable that in this passage St. Benedict would absolutely deprive of the double admonition these rough or rebellious natures, for it would seem from Chapter XXIII. to be part of the procedure to be applied to all. In the second chapter he is speaking in rather a general fashion about diversity of treatment and observes that one or two reprimands are enough for some, while others only yield to the argument of force. It would be waste of time, in the case of the latter, to indulge in many verbal rebukes and to delay punishment; the evil must be at once eradicated from the sensitive nature by methods which appeal to sense. And since the ineffectiveness in many cases of the most severe rebukes has been established, we then pass at once to the third stage in the procedure of correction. But this will not here be excommunication, for the *improbus* (froward) will either be glad of it as a new way of escaping observance, or else will not understand its nature or feel its sting.[1]

We shall explain excommunication in the succeeding chapters and describe its *nature;* in this place a word may be said about corporal punishment. Our forefathers did not hesitate to have recourse to it; and our Holy Father, who threatens offenders with it more than once in his Rule, only needed to remember the Rules of St. Pachomius and St. Cæsarius, the Lives of the Fathers, and, in a word, all tradition. The most common penances were reduction of food and drink, confinement,[2] and compulsory tasks; but above all there were the rod, the whip, and the ferula, the punishments of bad servants and children. Long before the rise of that voluntary practice of penance which St. Peter Damian propagated, the " discipline " was a penance in monastic[3] and indeed in ecclesiastical use, for certain Councils prescribe it for refractory clerics. In St. Benedict's language the word *disciplina* has various meanings, which can be determined only by the context. Thus in Chapter II. it means a line of practical conduct; in Chapter VII. the spiritual life and moral perfection; in Chapters LVI., LXII., LXIII.,

---

[1] *Cf.* S. Basil., *Reg. brev.*, xliv.
[2] *Cf.* Calmet, Commentary on Chapter XXV.
[3] Read Hæften, l. VIII., tract. v.—Martène, *De antiq. monach. rit.*, l. II., c. xi., col. 229 *sq.*—Calmet, Commentary on Chapter III.

and LXXI. regularity, good order and its safeguards; in Chapters XXXIV. and LV. a punishment or correction of some sort; in Chapter XXIV. corporal punishment, whether fasting or the rod. *Disciplina regularis, disciplina regulæ,* mean the sum of all monastic observances or submission to these observances (LX., LXII.); finally, *disciplina regularis* is either the graduated body of corrective methods provided by the Rule, or some of the degrees, and perhaps the punishment of the rod alone (III., XXXII., LIV., LXV., LXX.).

Nowadays, when a monk is to be punished with the discipline—a thing of extremely rare occurrence—he is himself charged with the execution of the sentence, out of the reach of curious eyes, and with no very formidable instrument. But things were not done quite in that way in the times of our ancestors. To begin with, this punishment—while not everywhere so common as in the régime of St. Columbanus, where strokes of the whip were current coin—was by no means unusual. It took place most frequently in public and in full chapter. The rod or whip was manipulated by the Abbot in person, or by a brother expressly deputed for this charitable duty. At Cluny,[1] as at Cîteaux, and to some degree everywhere, the blows fell on the bare shoulders, at least when it was a question of serious faults. The number of blows did not generally exceed thirty-nine, which was the Jewish measure, five times applied to the Apostle by his fellow-countrymen: "Of the Jews five times did I receive forty stripes save one" (2 Cor. xi. 24). In order not to violate the Law, which prescribed forty as the maximum (Deut. xxv. 3), they chose to keep below that number. The old monks, less scrupulous than the Pharisees, sometimes gave as many as a hundred stripes to great offenders. "Let him be extended and receive a hundred lashes," says the Rule of St. Fructuosus.[2] The Penitential of St. Columbanus speaks of a hundred and even of two hundred stripes; but the same code of punishment has this provision: "Let no more than twenty-five stripes be given at a time." The Rule of the Master is more formidable still: "Let them be beaten with rods to death"[3]—that is to say, observes Calmet,[4] "to the limit of endurance, with extreme rigour: for it was never really done to the death, and even in profane authors the phrase *cædere ad necem* (beat to death) is not to be taken literally, but as a figure of speech." A capitulary of Charlemagne,[5] reproduced by the Council of Frankfort in A.D. 794, thinks it necessary to urge Abbots not to put out the eyes or cut off the limbs of their monks "whatever be the fault committed": that kind of punishment should be left to seculars.

We need not either deplore or regret the severities of former days. When characters were ruder and less refined by a long process of education, when they sometimes stipulated for the benefits of confinement

---

[1] *Cf.* Pignot, *Hist. de l'Ordre de Cluny*, t. II., pp. 400-406. See statute lxiii. of Peter the Venerable. *P.L.*, CLXXXIX., 1043.
[2] C. xv. [3] C. xiii.
[4] Commentary on Chapter XXVIII.
[5] M. G. H., *Legum*, Sectio II., *Capitul. Regum Franc.*, t. I., p. 63.

or severe flogging as a precaution against their falls, this severity of regular discipline was often the only means of overcoming the rebellion of sense or the nerves. We should remember also that offences and misdemeanours of monks or clerics did not generally come before civil tribunals, so that it was necessary that ecclesiastical or monastic superiors should enforce the law themselves. All this is now changed; and if there occur disorders in face of which monastic authority is powerless, yet we must recognize that the dignity of monastic life has gained by the change. Therefore should monasticism, with all the more care, recruit itself from among those whose obedience is voluntary, eager, and joyous.

CHAPTER XXIV
WHAT THE MEASURE OF EXCOMMUNICATION SHOULD BE

QUALIS DEBEAT ESSE MODUS EXCOMMUNICATIONIS.—Secundum modum culpæ, excommunicationis vel disciplinæ debet extendi mensura: qui culparum modus in Abbatis pendeat judicio. Si quis tamen frater in levioribus culpis invenitur, tantum a mensæ participatione privetur.

The measure of excommunication or chastisement should be meted out according to the gravity of the offence, the estimation of which shall be left to the judgement of the Abbot. If any brother be found guilty of lighter faults, let him be excluded only from the common table.

HORACE pokes fun cleverly at the Stoics who asserted that there was no difference between offences, all being equally grave:

> Nec vincet ratio hoc, tantumdem ut peccet idemque,
> Qui teneros caules alieni fregerit horti,
> Et qui nocturnus divum sacra legerit. Adsit
> Regula, peccatis quæ pœnas irroget æquas,
> Ne scutica dignum horribili sectere flagello.[1]

Our Holy Father satisfies these requirements of Roman good sense and universal prudence in laying it down that the mode and measure of chastisement shall be proportionate to the nature and malice of the offence;[2] so there are to be different degrees, not only in corporal correction (*disciplina*), but in excommunication itself. Yet in order to avoid disputes, it is to be the Abbot's duty to estimate the gravity of offences and to fix the punishment incurred. Not that the Abbot may at his pleasure modify the objective gravity of faults, or put anything he likes under grave obligation (*sub gravi*); but he has the full right, in the interests of good observance, to decree severe penalties against faults otherwise light, which threaten to become chronic and to harm the community. This determination of offence and penalty is left, not to his caprice, but to his judgement and his conscience: "shall be left to the judgement of the Abbot."

St. Benedict has not thought it necessary to enlarge on the character and measure of corporal punishment, but he is anxious to be precise with regard to excommunication. Although a great deal of power is

---

[1] *Satires*, l. I., iii.,
> Nor can right reason prove the crime the same,
> To rob a garden, or, by fear unawed,
> To steal by night the sacred things of God.
> Then let the punishment be fairly weighed
> Against the crime; nor let the wretch be flayed,
> Who scarce deserved the lash. (Trans., FRANCIS.)

[2] *Digne correptus secundum arbitrium senioris vel modum culpæ* (S. MACAR., *Reg.*, xii.). *Pro qualitate culpæ erit excommunicatio* (*Reg.* I., SS. PATRUM, xv.). *Cf. Reg. Orient.*, xxxii.—S. CÆSAR., *Reg. ad virg.*, xi.

left with the superior, yet he cannot punish lighter offences (*lighter* is used by St. Benedict in a relative sense only) save by excommunication from the common table. The other form of excommunication excluded a man at one and the same time from table, oratory, and intercourse with his brethren. Many Rules before the time of our Holy Father, that of St. Cæsarius for example, mention this twofold excommunication. It is not impossible that the Church herself was inspired by monastic legislation, in making a clear distinction[1] between the greater excommunication, which cuts a man off from the society of the faithful, and the lesser excommunication which deprives him only of certain spiritual advantages, of the sacraments, and of the exercise of jurisdiction. The Apostles themselves seem to have made distinctions and shades of difference in the severity of excommunication; we might study and compare the character and effects of excommunication as pronounced by St. Peter, St. Paul, and St. John.

Commentators compare monastic excommunication with that pronounced by the Church and enquire what is its value and scope. I think we may support the opinion of Calmet. Whatever were the limits in St. Benedict's time to the privilege of exemption, it is not open to doubt —and the very text of the Rule proves it emphatically—that an Abbot possessed sufficient authority to pronounce a sentence of excommunication; it was the exercise of a power of jurisdiction, not of orders. And the effects of this sentence were identical with those of the Church's excommunication; the only difference lay in the immediate source of the excommunication and the special state of the monk so punished. The better to understand the scope of monastic excommunication we should remember the hierarchical constitution of the ancient Church and the bond of solidarity which held all its parts together. First one was in communion with a bishop and the faithful of a diocese, and then by means of this incorporation in a particular church one was a member of the Church universal, becoming part of the larger society by means of the lesser. To be admitted into special communion with another diocese it was necessary to produce *litteræ formatæ*. Many Councils speak of these testimonials and our Holy Father himself emphasizes the need of them. They showed that a man was at peace with his church of origin, whether monastic or secular. Sentence of excommunication pronounced by one bishop was notified to others from place to place, and the person affected, by the sole fact that he was excluded from the communion of his bishop, was excluded from the communion of the whole Church. Now a monastic family formed a small autonomous church in the bosom of the larger diocesan family. From the day of his profession a monk was a member of the Universal Church by means of his union with his monastic order, and only so. If he were

---

[1] In the early centuries there were different degrees of penance and excommunication: see J. MORINUS, *Commentarius historicus de disciplina in administratione sacramenti pænitentiæ*.—GABRIEL ALBASPINÆUS, *Observationes ecclesiasticæ*, l. II.—JACQUES ÉVEILLON, *Traicté des excommunications et monitoires*.

regularly excommunicated by his Abbot, and that for faults against ordinary morality or the special obligations of his state, he found himself *ipso facto* outside the Church, and was so regarded by all Christians. St. Gregory in the Life of our Holy Father relates how the man of God threatened two incorrigible nuns with excommunication, and the claim does not seem to him extraordinary; he merely expresses admiration for the fact that St. Benedict's threat was sufficient for God, that He treated these religious who had died in their sin as excommunicated, and then ratified, beyond the grave, the removal of the excommunication pronounced by His servant. The whole chapter is of very great interest.[1]

Privati autem a mensæ consortio, ista erit ratio: ut in oratorio Psalmum aut Antiphonam non imponat, neque Lectionem recitet, usque ad satisfactionem. Refectionem autem cibi post fratrum refectionem accipiat, mensura vel hora qua præviderit Abbas ei competere: ut si verbi gratia fratres reficiunt sexta hora, ille frater nona; si fratres nona, ille vespertina; usque dum satisfactione congrua veniam consequatur.

And this shall be the rule for one deprived of the fellowship of the table: he shall intone neither psalm nor antiphon in the oratory, nor shall he read a lesson, until he have made satisfaction. Let him take his meals alone, after those of the brethren, in the measure and at the time that the Abbot shall think best for him; so that if, for example, the brethren eat at the sixth hour, let him eat at the ninth: if they eat at the ninth, let him eat in the evening, until by proper satisfaction he obtain pardon.

Therefore the first and more gentle form of excommunication—after admonitions—was decreed against him who suffered himself to fall into offences, serious undoubtedly, but less grave than those presently to be mentioned. It meant first of all a penalty in the oratory. The guilty monk was not excluded from conventual prayer, but he no longer had the right to be heard in any special way, and was forbidden any individual part. He did not give out or intone any psalm or antiphon,[2] and recited no lesson; but he could, perhaps—for the Rule does not give us certain information on this point—mingle his voice with the voices of the choir. Certain later monastic customs forbade him to take his part in the conventual offering, or the kiss of peace, or the communion, or to celebrate Mass in public, etc. This isolation was to last until he had made fitting satisfaction and received absolution from the Abbot (see the last words of Chapter XLIV.). We must not confuse this excommunication with the penance imposed on monks who neglected to take their part in the prayers before a meal (Chapter XLIII).

The refectory was the chief scene of the lesser monastic excommunication: whence its name of excommunication *a mensa*. The monk still appeared in the oratory, for a part of conventual life might there be left him; but he was banished from the common table. He took his food

[1] *Dial.*, l. II., c. xxiii.
[2] The reader should remember what was said in chapter ix. concerning St. Benedict's psalmody.

alone, and that after the meals of the brethren. The words " in the measure and at the time that the Abbot shall think best for him " are not in the manuscripts and have been borrowed from the next chapter; nor is there any parallel between the conditions of the two sorts of excommunicated; and, as is remarked by commentators, the meals of one excommunicated *a mensa* were diminished only if he was unrepentant. His meals were merely put later: when his brethren, for instance, took their meal at the sixth hour—that is to say, during the whole summer save on fast days—the excommunicated monk took his at the ninth; when the community had theirs at the ninth hour—that is to say, from the beginning of the monastic Lent to the beginning of Lent proper—the excommunicated monk took his at the hour of Vespers (Chapter XLI.). In this matter, however, St. Benedict does not intend to lay down a complete and rigorous rule; it was the Abbot's business to decide according to the individual case. The penalty was to last until the monk, having made suitable satisfaction, received his pardon.

CHAPTER XXV

OF GRAVER FAULTS

De gravioribus culpis.—Is frater qui gravioris culpæ noxa tenetur, suspendatur a mensa simul et ab oratorio.

Let that brother who is found guilty of a more grievous offence be excluded both from the table and from the oratory.

GRAVER faults entail a more severe form of excommunication, excluding both from table and from oratory. We find a list of the chief faults of this kind in various Rules or Constitutions; but St. Benedict himself refrained from giving such a list. Yet he describes in emphatic words the isolation of the excommunicated monk. Save for some exceptions which are provided for later, all personal intercourse with him is broken off. We should note, however, the singular discretion with which all is done. Monastic excommunication is not exclusion, an absolute cutting off and final rupture of relations, such as is implied in the greater excommunication of the Church of to-day. Monastic excommunication resembles that pronounced by St. Paul, to which this chapter makes clear allusion; it has a remedial character and does not abandon the soul to perdition. There is always hope. Before proceeding to expulsion, which is the final act, trial must be made to see whether the monk is not terrified by the solitude created around him, and whether love of his religious family, more potent than punishments and reprimands, will not bring him to repentance. He is now scarcely *of* the monastery, but he is still *in* the monastery.

Nullis ei fratrum in ullo jungatur consortio, neque in colloquio. Solus sit ad opus sibi injunctum, persistens in pænitentiæ luctu, sciens illam terribilem Apostoli sententiam dicentis: traditum hujusmodi hominem Satanæ in interitum carnis, ut spiritus salvus sit in die Domini.

Let none of the brethren consort with him or speak to him. Let him be alone at the work enjoined him, and continue in sorrow of penance, remembering that dreadful sentence of the Apostle: "That such a one is delivered over to Satan for the destruction of the flesh, that his spirit may be saved in the day of the Lord."

He is as one plague-stricken, of his own act. Having become the enemy of God, he no longer has friends; he has no part any more in the community life, from which he has been the first to exclude himself by his fault. All avoid him. None may approach him, hold relations with him, or converse with him. There is now no place for him in the oratory.[1] Nor is he worthy to share even in the common toil. Not that he may wander idle, for he shall have his own fixed task, perhaps even a heavier task; but he shall perform it alone. And, according to the custom of certain monasteries, he shall be kept in confinement. He shall abide in penance and sorrow, and he shall have leisure, during the long

[1] *Cf. Reg. Orient.*, xxxii.

hours of his solitude, to meditate on and apply to himself the dreadful sentence of the Apostle: " such a one is delivered over to Satan for the destruction of the flesh, that his spirit may be saved in the day of the Lord" (1 Cor. v. 5).[1] All this should be well understood.

All creation obeys the law of community life; living beings do not develop and attain their end save by means of belonging to a society, or family, or hierarchical organization, of which the ideal pattern and term must be sought in the Blessed Trinity itself. This is true of men in general, it is still more true of the Church, and it is true also of a monastic body. We win salvation only by help of our family life; God's grace comes to us only in this living framework; we need the help of our Abbot and the prayers of our brethren. When sentence of excommunication interrupts this blessed current of divine influence and this pulsating life, we are no longer secure, or certain of anything. Ceasing to belong to the Church, to our spiritual family, to Our Lord and His jurisdiction, we pass into another hierarchical system and we are then exposed to the terrible familiarities and assaults of Satan. Even so God allowed the excommunication, pronounced by St. Peter against Ananias and Saphira, to entail their bodily death. The excommunication of Simon Magus caused him to be possessed by the devil. That of the incestuous Corinthian was intended to preserve the Church from all contagion and also to " deliver over to the tortures of the devil the body of the guilty man in order that his soul should be saved in the judgement of God." As in the story of the unstable monk whom St. Benedict let go,[2] there is always a dragon beyond the gates of the monastery, watching for the excommunicated and the renegade.

Doubtless our Holy Father by no means says that the tortures of Satan infallibly visit the excommunicated monk; but it is a threat, a warning not to remain impenitent, not to relapse ever into such an evil state. For in the ages of faith excommunication was regarded as a supreme peril, and the mere threat of it would fill souls with religious terror. But the sense of the supernatural has diminished; and it is this fact, coupled with an indubitable improvement in men's characters, which nowadays leads the Church and the monastic order to be very sparing of excommunication. Moreover, it happens only too frequently that those who deserve excommunication begin by excommunicating themselves.

Cibi autem refectionem solus percipiat, mensura vel hora qua præviderit ei Abbas competere; nec a quoquam benedicatur transeunte, nec cibus qui ei datur.	Let him take his portion of food alone, in the measure and at the time that the Abbot shall think best for him. Let none of those who pass by bless him, nor let the food that is given him be blessed.

[1] Cassian also cites this text in a passage which inspired St. Benedict in his writing of Chapters XXV. and XXVI. *Inst.*, II., xvi.
[2] S. Greg. M., *Dial.*, l. II., c. xxv.

Being banished from the oratory, the excommunicate monk is *a fortiori* banished from the common refectory. And the penance is more severe than in the preceding case; for not only is the hour of his meal delayed, its substance also is reduced, so that the rebel is attacked both in soul and in body. Our Holy Father leaves it to the Abbot to determine the hour and character of his repast. The brethren who meet the excommunicated monk do not reply to his salutation, do not say *Benedicite* to him (see Chapter LXIII.). Moreover, the food that is given to him does not receive the usual blessing.

We shall meet in Chapter XLIV. the series of expiations through which the excommunicate monk must pass before being reconciled with God and his brethren.

CHAPTER XXVI
OF THOSE WHO, WITHOUT LEAVE OF THE ABBOT, CONSORT WITH THE EXCOMMUNICATE

DE IIS QUI SINE JUSSIONE ABBATIS JUNGUNTUR EXCOMMUNICATIS.—Si quis frater præsumpserit, sine jussione Abbatis, fratri excommunicato quolibet modo se jungere, aut loqui cum eo, vel mandatum ei dirigere, similem sortiatur excommunicationis vindictam.

If any brother presume without the Abbot's leave to hold any intercourse whatever with an excommunicated brother, or to speak with him, or to send him a message, let him incur the same punishment of excommunication.

THE efficacy of excommunication would obviously be compromised and the remedy lose all its power, if it were not real; isolation is essential. But matters sometimes followed such a course as this. One of the brethren being excommunicated, certain wrongheaded people were tempted to take his part, to support him in his rebellion and so stir up something of a revolution. Other religious, united by some bond of blood or friendship with the guilty one, endeavoured to persuade themselves that nothing should stand in the way of the impulses and ties of nature and so broke the law of quarantine. Others finally allowed themselves to feel pity at the sight of this poor Holophernes,[1] so wickedly banished by the Abbot, and their thoughtless and harmful tenderness wrecked a course of treatment which they did not understand. Cassian writes as follows on this point: " If a monk be suspended from prayers for committing some fault, no one whatever has permission to pray with him . . .; and whoever, moved by inconsiderate piety, shall presume to hold communion with him in prayer before he be received back by a senior, makes himself partaker of his condemnation, for he hands himself voluntarily over to Satan, to whom the other had been committed for the amendment of his guilt: and he incurs a heavier responsibility inasmuch as by holding intercourse with him, whether for talk or for prayer, he adds fuel to his insolence and increases for the worse the contumacy of the offender."[2]

Apart from a special order of the Abbot, as explained at greater length in the next chapter, every brother who dares to associate with the excommunicated monk or to enter into relations with him of whatever sort, by conversation, or message, or by acting as his go-between, shares in his excommunication and will find himself involved in the same condemnation. This provision has seemed harsh to some commentators; and the more so because, in Canon Law, to have intercourse with one who is under the greater excommunication involves only lesser excom-

---

[1] An allusion to Racine's epigram on the *Judith* of Boyer:
> . . . Je pleure, hélas ! pour ce pauvre Holopherne,
> Si méchamment mis à mort par Judith.

[2] *Inst.*, II., xvi.

munication. But it would seem that in early times, among clergy as among monks, a notable infringement of the law of excommunication implied a full participation in the penalty of the excommunicate; there was no distinction made.[1]

[1] For instance, the Council of Orleans in 511 decrees in its xi. canon: *De his qui suscepta pœnitentia religionem suæ professionis obliti ad sæcularia relabuntur, placuit eos et a communione suspendi, et ab omnium catholicorum convivio separari. Quod si post interdictum cum eis quisquam præsumpserit manducare, et ipse communione privetur* (MANSI, t. VIII., col. 353). In the collections the authentic canons of the council are followed by others, of which the value is unknown; here is one that much resembles the text of our Rule: . . . *Nullus christianus ei ave dicat, aut eum osculare præsumat; . . . nemo ei jungatur in consortio, neque in aliquo negotio ; et si quis ei se sociaverit, . . . noverit se simili percussum anathemate. His exceptis, qui ob hanc causam ei junguntur, ut eum revocant ab errore, et provocent ad satisfactionem* . . . (MANSI, *ibid.*, col. 367).

CHAPTER XXVII

HOW CAREFUL THE ABBOT SHOULD BE OF THE EXCOMMUNICATE

QUALITER DEBEAT ESSE SOLLICITUS ABBAS CIRCA EXCOMMUNICATOS.—Omni sollicitudine curam gerat Abbas circa delinquentes fratres: quia *non est opus sanis medicus, sed male habentibus.*

Let the Abbot take care with all solicitude of offending brethren, for "they that are whole need not a physician, but they that are sick."

THIS is the final chapter of the digression on excommunication. It throws light on the whole subject of monastic penal legislation and makes St. Benedict's intention plain; and at the same time it reveals to us his fatherly solicitude. We know how variously human justice defends its exercise of the right of punishment, even to the extent of the death penalty. Some support the claims of absolute order, and maintain that those who will not accommodate themselves to it by obedience must do so by chastisement. This view is a true one, but it is cold and contemptuous; there is nothing for the guilty man but resignation. Others prefer to make the safety of society their basis, and punishment is then a security. The penalty, in protecting society against a recurrence of the faults punished, has a twofold action, both making it impossible for the criminal to do harm, and inspiring others with a wholesome fear: *Culpam pœna premit comes:* again a true view, but harsh and frequently ineffective. The Christian and monastic rule puts itself in the position of the delinquent, and, without at all disregarding the aims just considered, concerns itself before all with his correction, regarding him more as a sick brother than as a condemned criminal[1]. The ancient Rules and the Lives of the Fathers abound in edifying instruction on the mercy due to sinners, but none in our opinion contains anything comparable to this chapter, so characteristic of St. Benedict, and so full of his fatherly love, grave, strong, and considerate.

Omni sollicitudine . . . Though there be punishment, yet the monastery, the "house of God," is not a penitentiary, where the rebellious are cured only by violent repression and harsh treatment. The Abbot shall employ all possible solicitude and devotedness in favour of erring brethren. And as sole reason for this the Holy Rule invokes the words once used by Our Lord in justification of His infinite forgivingness: "They that are whole need not a physician, but they that are sick" (Matt. ix. 12). He came to redeem, to console, to heal; and woe to those self-sufficient souls who think they have no need of His compassion and His healing. Mercy is Our Lord's predominant virtue; it earned for Him the astonishment, the scandal, the very hatred of the evil casuists of His time, the Pharisees and doctors of the law. We have only to recall the episode of the woman taken in adultery, who was excommunicated by the doctors and condemned to stoning (John vii. 3–11). If God's heart is all goodness, the Abbot, who holds His place in the monastery, should always lean towards the side of mercy and love.

Et ideo uti debet omni modo ut sapiens medicus: immittere quasi occultos consolatores sympæctas, id est, seniores sapientes fratres, qui quasi secrete consolentur fratrem fluctuantem, et provocent eum ad humilitatis satisfactionem, et consolentur eum, ne abundantiori tristitia absorbeatur; sed sicut ait Apostolus: *Confirmetur in eo charitas*, et oretur pro eo ab omnibus.	To which end he ought to behave in every way as a wise physician, sending as it were secret consolers to sympathize with him—that is to say, some brethren of mature years and wisdom, who may, as it were secretly, console the wavering brother, induce him to make humble satisfaction, and comfort him, that he be not overwhelmed by excess of sorrow; but, as the Apostle saith, "Let charity be strengthened towards him," and let all pray for him.

Since the Abbot is appointed a physician of souls,[1] he shall act in every way[2] like a wise physician: he shall endeavour to find the effective remedy, or, rather, endeavour that the remedy of excommunication may have its full effect; he shall make use of the various means which his charity or experience may suggest to him. He shall, for example, send *sympæctæ* to the excommunicate monk. The words *quasi occultos consolatores* are a later gloss. The meaning of the word *sympæcta* has been much discussed, and very various not to say fantastic etymologies have been proposed; scribes too have often ill-treated it. Though the best reading is *senpectas*, it is very probable that the correct spelling of the word is *sympæcta* and that it is a transliteration of the Greek word συμπαίκτης (from σύν and παίζω) and means literally, one who plays with the child, or plays with another, a playfellow (*collusor*).[3] In Christian literature before St. Benedict, we find συμπαίκτης employed, and that in the figurative sense, only in the *Lausiac History* of Palladius. The *History* relates how Serapion Sindonita took the notion of selling himself to a company of actors, so as to convert them the more easily, and made an ascetic a party to his game or pious fraud: λαβών τίνα συμπαίκτην ἀσκητήν . . . .[4] Our Holy Father uses the word in an analogous sense. Because he adds immediately: "that is to say, some brethren of mature years and wisdom," it was thought that he was explaining the unusual word, and so some read not even *senpectas* but *senipetas*—*i.e.*, men approaching old age. And from this source come some unlikely interpretations. St. Benedict does in fact explain himself, but does it much more in the words "who may as it were secretly console . . ." than in those which follow directly after the phrase "that is to say." And his thought is as follows: the Abbot cannot intervene directly and himself approach the excommunicate, but he may have recourse to a

---

[1] S. BASIL., *Reg. contr.*, xxiv.
[2] *Omnimodo*, in one word, according to the best manuscripts.
[3] *Cf.* CALMET, *in h. l.*
[4] *Hist. Laus.*, c. lxxxiii. *P.G.*, XXXIV., 1180; ed. BUTLER, p. 109.

stratagem. There are in the community amiable and earnest brethren, in whom the excommunicated brother has confidence. They are monks of mature years and solid virtue, upon whom the complaints, or even the violent recriminations of the condemned man, will have no harmful effect; they are also skilful and diplomatic. So the Abbot makes them parties to his game of mercy and accomplices of his charity They shall go secretly to find the excommunicated brother, as though of their own accord and not as formal ambassadors; and their action will appear to him as though merely sanctioned by the Abbot.

Their function is first to console the brother and then to dispose him to amendment. His soul is still in a disturbed state, divided between anger and dread, between irritation and anxiety, *fluctuantem*. The loving intervention of the *sympæctæ* has as its object the calming of passion and helping of conscience; it will gently lead the excommunicated brother to make humble satisfaction, not from constraint, but from the desire to make amends. Yet before all else, as St. Benedict insists, he needs to be consoled. The *sympæctæ* will see to it that chagrin and shame do not crush him, that he be not " overwhelmed by excess of sorrow." St. Paul gave this counsel in the case of the incestuous Corinthian; and he proceeded to say that at such a critical time charity should be great, should show itself, and prevail in the treatment of him (2 Cor: ii. 7-8). While the discreet agents of the Abbot show their interest in the excommunicated monk directly, all the brethren must pray for him.[1]

We are very far in all this from those revengeful forms which human justice so readily affects, very far from the pharisaical spirit which requires implacable severity, very far from the tendencies, sometimes expressed in literature, which acknowledge only the virtue that has never fallen, and for which a momentary lapse has no cure but despair and suicide. That is the world all through: the most corrupt are the most implacable. We may also observe how the provisions of the monastic rule realize the ideal form under which penal justice should and can be exercised. The right to punish is normally exercised with success only by those who have endeavoured to exorcise the fault, who have proclaimed the moral law, who have not only refrained from cultivating violent and impious passions, the agents of crime, but have striven to diminish and, if possible, to suppress all revolutionary instincts. When a society incites to evil and corrupts both thought and morals, what right has it to set itself up as the judge of its own victims ?

Magnopere enim debet sollicitudinem gerere Abbas circa delinquentes fratres, et omni sagacitate et industria curare, ne aliquam de ovibus sibi creditis perdat. Noverit enim se infirmarum curam suscepisse animarum, non super sanas tyrannidem: et metuat	For the Abbot is bound to use the greatest care with erring brethren, and to strive with all possible prudence and zeal not to lose any one of the sheep committed to him. He must know that he has undertaken the charge of weakly souls, and not

[1] Nor does the *Rule* of St. Cæsarius *ad virgines* leave the excommunicate in absolute solitude: *Cum una de spiritualibus sororibus resideat* (xxxi.).

Prophetæ comminationem, per quem dicit Deus: *Quod crassum videbatis, assumebatis: et quod debile erat, projiciebatis.*

a tyranny over the strong; and let him fear the threat of the prophet, wherein God says: "What ye saw to be fat that ye took to yourselves, and what was diseased ye cast away."

St. Benedict repeats with great emphasis the first words of the chapter. The Abbot, he says, should exhibit the greatest solicitude with regard to erring brethren,[1] and should run, hasten, and expend all possible prudence and zeal, so as not to lose one of the sheep entrusted to him. God grant that an Abbot may never hold aloof from an erring brother with the scandalized horror of the Pharisee in the presence of St. Mary Magdalene! Nor should he ignore him and abandon the excommunicate to his passions and wounded pride, saying: "I cannot help it. If he wants to persevere in his rebellion, why, let him do it! I cannot give him my will instead of his own." Obviously you have not died for him, or you would throw him over less readily. "Yes, but he irritates me. He is so bitter and disloyal. . . ." He is all the more your concern. You are not a prince, or a pitiless justiciary, or an executioner. The Abbot's function, speaking generally, is not to exercise a haughty tyranny over strong souls, for God has entrusted to him the care and tendance and cure of souls weakly and infirm; and to this shall he give his special attention. St. Augustine wrote in the same sense of ministers of God living in the world: "Their care should be the cure of men rather than men who have been cured. They must endure the faults of men so as to cure them, for a plague must be endured before it can be cured."[2] So the Abbot must be on his guard against an attitude which is very natural, yet very selfish; let him, at need, remember the indignation of God, denouncing by the mouth of His prophet the harshness and rapacity of the evil pastors of Israel: You took to yourselves that which seemed to you fat and well-conditioned; but you spurned the lean. The whole passage of Ezechiel is an awe-inspiring threat (xxxiv. 3–4). But we do not ask the Abbot to be complaisant or weak, no more than to open the doors of his monastery to mediocrity or wretchedness of every sort.

Et Pastoris boni pium imitetur exemplum, qui, relictis nonaginta novem ovibus in montibus, abiit unam ovem, quæ erraverat, quærere; cujus infirmitati in tantum compassus est, ut eam in sacris humeris suis dignaretur imponere, et sic reportare ad gregem.

Let him imitate the loving example of the Good Shepherd, who, leaving the ninety and nine sheep on the mountains, went to seek one which had gone astray, on whose weakness He had such compassion that He vouchsafed to lay it on His own sacred shoulders, and thus bring it back to the flock.

St. Benedict contrasts the conduct of unworthy and mercenary shepherds with the example, the "loving example," of the tenderness

[1] The true reading, says D. BUTLER, is certainly *currere;* St. Benedict develops later on this idea of the Good Shepherd running in search of the lost sheep.
[2] *De moribus ecclesiæ cathol.*, l. I., c. xxxii. P.L., XXXII., 1339.

and condescendence of the Good Shepherd, as portrayed by Our Lord Himself in St. Matthew (xviii. 12–14) and in St. Luke (xv. 3–7, *cf.* John x.). The Good Shepherd had a hundred sheep, one of which strayed one day far from the flock. Then the Shepherd, leaving the ninety-nine in their folds on the hillsides which they pastured, went off to find the one deserter. He found it, hurt, perhaps, or refractory. And such was His pity for its weakness that He deigned to put it on His sacred shoulders and so bring it back to the flock.[1] The Gospel goes on to emphasize the joy of the Good Shepherd. And indeed to restore an erring soul to Our Lord is the highest joy that can be tasted here below. " My brethren, if any of you err from the truth and one convert him: he must know that he who causeth a sinner to be converted from the error of his way shall save his soul from death and shall cover a multitude of sins " (James v. 19–20). It need not be said that this ready and untiring condescendence of the Abbot expresses also what all the brethren should feel towards one another. There should be a general conspiracy of charity " lest he lose any of the sheep committed to him."

[1] St. Basil quotes the same gospel parable and the text: *non est opus valentibus*, etc., in a passage which resembles our Rule (*Reg. brev.*, cii.; see also *Reg. contr.*, xxvii.).

CHAPTER XXVIII

OF THOSE WHO, BEING OFTEN CORRECTED, DO NOT AMEND

DE IIS QUI SÆPIUS CORRECTI NON EMENDANTUR.—Si quis frater frequenter correptus pro qualibet culpa, si etiam excommunicatus non emendaverit, acrior ei accedat correctio, id est, ut verberum vindicta in eum procedat.

If any brother who has been frequently corrected for some fault, or even excommunicated, do not amend, let a more severe chastisement be applied—that is, let the punishment of stripes be administered to him.

OUR Holy Father here returns to the degrees of regular discipline which he began to enumerate in the twenty-third chapter. First of all he reviews briefly the particular chastisements already described: a brother, guilty of one of the faults which deserve chastisement, has been frequently corrected—*i.e.*, at least three times, twice secretly and once in public; he has been excommunicated or has suffered corporal punishment. But, for all this, he has not amended. Even excommunication has had no result, though it was thought that that would cure him. At this stage excommunication is supplemented by a more severe chastisement: the guilty man is beaten with rods. Corporal punishment is called more severe and more harsh, not because excommunication is a less serious penalty, but because bodily chastisement may perhaps more effectively subdue the animal man which has remained insensible to spiritual penalties; and also because there is in corporal punishment a note of servitude and as it were a stigma of disgrace. In the case of one with whom excommunication has not been tried, but who has had to submit to fasting or the rod immediately following on the admonitions, doubtless the same régime will be continued, only the strokes will be laid on somewhat more heavily.

Quod si nec ita se correxerit, aut forte (quod absit) in superbiam elatus etiam defendere voluerit opera sua, tunc Abbas faciat quod sapiens medicus: si exhibuit fomenta, si unguenta adhortationum, si medicamina Scripturarum divinarum, si ad ultimum ustionem excommunicationis vel plagas virgarum, et jam si viderit nihil suam prævalere industriam: adhibeat etiam, quod majus est, suam et omnium fratrum pro eo orationem, ut Dominus, qui omnia potest, operetur salutem circa infirmum fratrem

But if even then he do not correct himself, or perchance (which God forbid!), puffed up with pride, even wish to defend his deeds: then let the Abbot act like a wise physician. If he has applied fomentations and the unction of his admonitions, the medicine of the Holy Scriptures, and the last cautery of excommunication or corporal chastisement, and if he see that his labours are of no avail, let him add what is still more powerful—his own prayers and those of all the brethren for him, that God, who is all-powerful, may work the cure of the sick brother.

Plainly, in St. Benedict's eyes, a soul has an absolute value and must be treated with boundless patience. He puts the case of the guilty man not yet submitting and even daring, in a violent fit of pride, to justify himself and invoke right for his side. "Which God forbid!" says St. Benedict. Yet he knows too well that it is not unlikely. He has elsewhere condemned the unhappy facility which men have of calling that good which they desire, of worshipping their own ideas, of justifying thus the most shameful excesses. For conscience becomes seared. What had hitherto been merely weakness, becomes now a principle and a system. Still, there is no question yet of pronouncing irrevocable sentence.

The Abbot must continue to act like a wise physician.[1] He must review all the means which he might legitimately use to obtain a cure, and must make certain that he has neglected none. He has had, according to the methods of ancient medicine, to use every means to make the sickness emerge, to draw out to the surface the deep-rooted evil which was upsetting the vital functions. First he used fomentations, warm applications, fit to persuade the evil to depart; then ointments, the balm of his admonitions, as though to soften skin and flesh; and next the internal remedy of the Holy Scriptures. The word of God has a sacramental value, and acts on souls like a charm. Its lucid and sweet sentences can free the soul from its fever. Obviously admonition, whether private or public, and the good advice of the *sympæctæ* should be inspired pre-eminently by supernatural doctrine, and remind the guilty one of the familiar passages of Holy Scripture, containing the rule of morality and monastic perfection. If these preliminary measures failed, the Abbot decided to cauterize with the hot iron of excommunication, or to lance with the sharp points of the scourge. But he may be forced to conclude that his skill makes no way against the evil.

What human effort cannot achieve, prayer may obtain from God. For Him no situation is desperate. The treasuries of His mercy hold graces capable of converting the most hardened heart. Is He not the God who brings the dead to life (Rom. iv. 17)? "To the Almighty Physician nothing is incurable; He gives up none."[2] So let the Abbot still act like a wise physician, says St. Benedict; let him use a remedy more potent than the others, his own prayers and those of the brethren, in order that God, with whom all things are possible, may restore health to the sick brother. By this is meant a supplication more insistent and more general than that mentioned in Chapter XXVII.; it is a sort of formal suit to God, at once respectful and filial, by the whole community.

Quod si nec isto modo sanatus fuerit, tunc jam utatur Abbas ferro abscissionis, ut ait Apostolus: *Auferte malum ex vobis.* Et iterum: *Infidelis si dis-*	But if he be not healed even by this means, then at length let the Abbot use the sword of separation, as the Apostle says: "Put away the evil one

---

[1] The metaphors which follow are inspired by CASSIAN, *Inst.*, X., vii.
[2] S. AUG., *Enarr.* II. *in Ps.* lviii. 11. *P.L.*, XXXVI., 712.

cedit, discedat: ne una ovis morbida omnem gregem contaminet.	from you." And again: "If the faithless one depart, let him depart," lest one diseased sheep should taint the whole flock.

Finally, if the unfortunate man is not cured by the last remedy, there is nothing for it but amputation. The excommunicated man becomes a danger. He may infect the whole community with his malady, for one diseased sheep can taint a whole flock. The duty of charity to the community—always more important than the individual—demands the removal of any element that is incorrigible, forming as it does a scandal and a permanent danger. This is the advice of St. Paul: " Put away the evil [or the evil one] from your midst " (1 Cor. v. 13). " Nor is this done from cruelty, but from mercy, lest he destroy many by the infection of his disease," says St. Augustine in a passage which may be compared with our description of the degrees of regular discipline.[1] St. Cyprian, too, writes as follows: " I should not think them worthy to mix with virgins, but like infected sheep or sick cattle they should be kept away from the virgin flock, holy and pure, lest by contagion they should pollute the rest."[2] And the more so as the man is no longer merely sick; he is dead. All that the Abbot does is to recognize a severance which has already been effected by the expelled man himself. He has decided. There is nothing for it but to accept his incorrigible blindness: " If the faithless one wishes to go, let him go," says St. Benedict, taking another sentence of St. Paul in an accommodated sense (1 Cor. vii. 15).

Expulsion is provided for also in more ancient Rules, for example in those of St. Macarius[3] and St. Basil;[4] and St. Benedict clearly has some such legislation in his mind. Some Rules did not venture to decree expulsion: " Though a man be immersed in an abyss of frequent and most serious faults," says St. Isidore,[5] " still he should not be expelled from the monastery . . . lest perchance he, who could have been cured by a long course of penance, may, when cast forth, be devoured by the devil." Seclusion and confinement, perpetual if necessary, were preferred. But the common law of the Church has recognized the lawfulness and expediency of expulsion and has determined the juridical forms by which competent authority may proceed to effect it.

[1] *Epist.* CCXI., 11. *P.L.,* XXXIII., 962.
[2] *De habitu virginum,* xvii. *P.L.,* IV., 456. The expression *ovis morbida* occurs several times in St. Jerome: *Epist.* II. *P.L.,* XXII., 331; *Epist.* XVI., 1. *P.L., ibid.,* 358; *Epist.* CXXX. *ad Demetriadem,* 19. *P.L., ibid.,* 1122.
[3] C. xvii., xxvii.–xxviii.
[4] *Reg. contr.,* xxx. *Cf. Reg. brev.,* xxxviii., xliv., lvii., lxxxiv., cii.
[5] C. xv.

CHAPTER XXIX
WHETHER THE BRETHREN WHO LEAVE THE MONASTERY ARE TO BE RECEIVED AGAIN

Si debeant iterum recipi fratres exeuntes de monasterio.—Frater qui proprio vitio egreditur, aut projicitur de monasterio, si reverti voluerit, spondeat prius omnem emendationem vitii pro quo egressus est, et sic in ultimo gradu recipiatur, ut ex hoc ejus humilitas comprobetur.

If any brother, who through his own fault departs or is cast out of the monastery, be willing to return, let him first promise entire amendment of the fault for which he left; and then let him be received back into the lowest place, that thus his humility may be tried.

THIS chapter rounds off the last and at the same time softens its severity. The incorrigible brother having been expelled may presently be moved by grace, so that, like the Prodigal Son, returning to himself he desires to go back to God. And while speaking of expulsion, our Holy Father allows of another case, where the leaving of the monastery is the work of the religious himself, impelled by the evil spirit of instability or by some vicious motive or other.[1] St. Benedict is careful to add "through his own fault": for it may occasionally happen that such departure is regular, sanctioned by the Abbot or legalized by the Church. Of such cases we shall say nothing, as, for instance, of the case where a man thinks it his duty to escape from surroundings which appear to him inobservant and disedifying, or passes to a stricter form of religious life. Nor again shall we seek to determine whether secularization, sought and obtained, is not sometimes, to the eye of conscience, a euphemism for religious apostasy.

Regulus is said to have pleaded earnestly before the Roman Senate against an exchange of prisoners between Carthage and the Roman State; his view was that a Roman who had suffered himself to be taken captive without a struggle, could not afterwards fulfil his duty valiantly.

> Auro repensus scilicet acrior
> Miles redibit ? Flagitio additis
> Damnum ![2]

A bad soldier restored to the war would prove himself a bad soldier again. So to ransom a prisoner was to throw your money away and not to gain a soldier. All of which is distinctly Roman in sentiment; but

---

[1] D. Butler adopts this text: *Frater qui proprio vitio egreditur de monasterio, si reverti voluerit, spondeat prius omnem emendationem pro quo egressus est.* And D. Chapman, reviewing Traube, strove to show that the reading of the "received text" and of the most ancient manuscripts was a clear case of misguided interpolation (*Revue Bénéd.*, 1898, p. 506). Without disputing the authority of the Carlovingian and Cassinese tradition, it is, however, possible to give a probable sense to our text. Why should an expelled monk not come to a better mind ? Do not the arrangements of this chapter appear to be a natural consequence of what precedes ?

[2] Horace, *Odes*, Bk. III., v.

St. Benedict's attitude, in opening his arms to the renegade and the expelled monk, and giving them the chance of repairing the past by a better life, is truly human and is in conformity with the ways of God.[1]

There are two conditions set to this act of mercy, and both have the same purpose: to show that the returned brother has nothing in common with him who fled or was expelled. St. Benedict lays it down that the brother who so presents himself should first of all promise fundamental amendment of the fault which occasioned his departure: to this extent he is no longer, interiorly in his will, the same man as the former. And this change of identity expresses itself externally under a form which has no doubt the character of a punishment and a trial, but which may also be a delicate and skilful act of considerateness. When he enters he takes rank as though he then first came. There has been a misdeal and all must begin again. He takes his order anew from entrance and conversion, and inherits naught from the evil monk who went forth. Besides, says our Holy Father, his humility will thus be tested and assurance obtained that he has amended and intends to become a new man.[2] St. Benedict does not mention other requirements, but it is probable that there was a public confession and apology followed by absolution, as in the case of the excommunicate (Chapter XLIV.). Martène cites in full various ritual forms for the reception of renegades.

| Quod si denuo exierit, usque tertio recipiatur. Jam vero postea sciat, omnem sibi reversionis aditum denegari. | Should he again depart, let him be taken back until the third time. But let him know that after this all way of return is denied him. |

We have seen how our Holy Father strives to avert and delay expulsion; it remains now to observe how this penalty, though the end of so long a process, seems to him by no means final. We must admire such abounding charity. All other considerations yield to that of saving a soul from destruction. A brother leaves for the first time and he is received when he returns. A second time he leaves and a second time is received on the same terms as before. And the same happens after a third departure: "let him be taken back until the third time."[3] But he must know that henceforth all way of return is barred to him. There must be a limit; mercy has not been stinted, but these goings and comings must not become a mere game for the runaway and vexation for the community; we cannot favour instability, a thing specifically combated by our Holy Father.

Nevertheless, in certain monasteries, for example at Cluny, the repentant monk was received back after a greater number of fruitless

---

[1] St. Basil is more strict: *Reg. fus.*, xiv.

[2] *Qui absque commonitione fratrum recesserit et postea acta pænitentia venerit, non erit in ordine suo absque majoris imperio* (S. Pach., *Reg.*, cxxxvi.).

[3] This explanation of *usque tertio* is proposed by the author of *Explication ascétique et historique de la Règle de saint Benoît*, t. I., p. 429. In this way the reception of the monk on his first leaving the world and coming to the monastery is not counted among the three receptions.—The critical editions read: *usque tertio ita recipiatur.*

attempts. They believed that they were thus following St. Benedict's true intention. It was observed, with more subtlety than exactitude, that the text said that the monk who leaves more than three times must know that all return to the monastery is forbidden. Yes, said commentators, he must know that, he must know that he has no right to a fourth pardon. The threat will do him good. But the Abbot is free to decide differently; and though the door is closed to the monk, the Abbot may open it. Peter the Venerable himself had recourse to this kindly trick of interpretation in defending to St. Bernard the leniency of Cluny. However, he rested his case principally on more solid proofs. Would you then, he asked, introduce a new Gospel and put limits to mercy? What was to become of declarations such as that of Our Lord to St. Peter: "Lord, how often shall my brother offend against me, and I forgive him? Till seven times? Jesus saith to him: I say not to thee, till seven times, but till seventy times seven times" (Matt. xviii. 21–22).[1]

[1] PETRI VENER., *Epist.*, l. I., *Ep.* XXVIII. *P.L.*, CLXXXIX., 127.

CHAPTER XXX

HOW YOUNG BOYS ARE TO BE CORRECTED

De pueris minori ætate, qualiter corripiantur.—Omnis ætas vel intellectus proprias debet habere mensuras. Ideoque quoties pueri, vel adolescentiores ætate, aut qui minus intelligere possunt quanta pœna sit excommunicationis, hi tales dum delinquunt, aut jejuniis nimiis affligantur, aut acribus verberibus coerceantur, ut sanentur.

Every age and understanding should have its due measure. As often, therefore, as boys, or those under age, or such as cannot fully understand the greatness of the penalty of excommunication, commit faults, let them be punished by severe fasting or sharp stripes, in order that they may be cured.

JUST as punishments should be graduated to suit the fault, so should they be proportioned to the years, understanding, and education of the individual. St. Benedict has already noted this, in the chapter on the Abbot and in the twenty-third chapter, so far as concerns understanding, but without explicit mention of differences of age. A reminder, therefore, at the close of his code of punishments, that many of its provisions by no means suited the young, was not out of place. " Every age and every degree of intelligence should have its proper measure," its own methods of correction: this is the general principle. And our Holy Father proceeds at once to apply it to three classes of persons: children, adolescents, and those of limited understanding or small culture.

The Rule does not determine the limits of childhood and adolescence, and this doubtless of set purpose; for full responsibility and exact discretion do not come to all at the same age. Farther on (in the seventieth chapter) St. Benedict lays it down that in what concerns external supervision the conditions of infancy (*pueritia*) should cease at the completion of the age of fourteen—that is to say, at the age when Roman children generally discarded the *toga prætexta*.[1] Adolescence, according to St. Isidore (who seems in this matter to have inspired the commentators), lasted to the age of twenty-eight. But it is clear that most monks could be brought under the full discipline of the Rule long before the expiration of this period. St. Benedict does not distinguish between boys and the younger religious; what he requires is that there should be a special and identical régime for all in whom animal impulses predominate.

A first principle in education is to take men on the side by which they may be reached: by their intelligence if they have such; by their senses if intelligence is not yet sufficiently developed. Now, what is a child ? A being, doubtless, rich with future promise, but for the present scarce revealing any phenomena but those of the animal life.

[1] *Sancta constitutione promulgata, pubertatem in masculis post quartum decimum annum completum illico initium accipere disposuimus* . . . (Justinian, *Instit.*, I., tit. 22; published A.D. 533).

As we observed in the second chapter, it is by means of sweetmeats, or dry bread and the lash, that we teach him the ABC of conscience, the distinction between good and evil. To excommunicate such a one would be cruelty and folly; nor should we propose seriously to imprison children. In the case of the adolescent, we have got intelligence, but also the pride of intelligence as it awakens; there is conscience, but with it are crude or violent passions; we have to deal, not with dormant powers as in the case of the child, but with rebellion. Finally, by the side of these two classes must be ranged those persons who remain children all their lives, with nothing in their souls to check the impulses of instinct. Such persons, as St. Benedict insists, are little suited to comprehend the scope of a moral penalty like excommunication.

So, when characters such as these commit faults, appeal must be made to their bodies, whether for repression or weakening. They may be weakened by severe fasting (by *nimiis* St. Benedict cannot mean excessive and indiscreet); their extravagances may be repressed by well-directed stripes. "In order that they may be cured": for thus shall be established true moral health—that is to say, the ordered and tranquil play of every energy, the balance and harmony of body and soul: *Mens sana in corpore sano.*

CHAPTER XXXI

OF THE CELLARER OF THE MONASTERY

WE enter, with Chapter XXXI., upon that section of the Rule which is concerned with the working and material conditions of the monastery. The community has property, does work, and possesses tools for work; it must live and support itself. All this goes to make a considerable department, which is entrusted to the immediate or mediate care of him whom St. Benedict calls the "cellarer of the monastery," and whom other Rules call the provider, or the procurator, or, as Cassian does, the economus, who "presides over the deaconry."[1] In ancient writers the *cellarius* was a trusted servant who had charge of the cellar and the office, and distributed their victuals to the slaves. But, in St. Benedict's use, as for St. Pachomius and to some extent for all monks, the whole temporal administration devolved on the cellarer. We may easily measure the importance which St. Benedict attached to his office by the length of the chapter devoted to him, by the qualities which are required of him, and by the variety of the counsels that are given him. Among the sources of this chapter we may single out for special mention the twenty-fifth chapter of the *Regula Orientalis*.[2]

DE CELLERARIO MONASTERII.—Cellerarius monasterii eligatur de congregatione sapiens, maturus moribus, sobrius, non multum edax, non elatus, non turbulentus, non injuriosus, non tardus, non prodigus, sed timens Deum, qui omni congregationi sit sicut pater.	Let there be chosen out of the community as Cellarer of the monastery, a man wise and of mature character, temperate, not a great eater, not haughty, nor headstrong, nor offensive, not dilatory, nor wasteful, but a God-fearing man, who may be like a father to the whole community.

The cellarer shall be elected or chosen by the Abbot; of that there can be no doubt, since St. Benedict entrusts to the Abbot the care of providing for the hierarchical organization of the monastery; but, in so important a matter, one which concerns the whole community, the Abbot shall take advice, if not of all the brethren, at least of the more prudent (Chapter LXV.). The cellarer shall be chosen from the bosom of the community: for it is obvious that to entrust the management of the possessions of the monastery to an outsider would be unkind to the community by ignoring them and would also be dangerous for the individual appointed. And should not a monastery be administered monastically? A layman might be cleverer or more acquainted with business: but he might see just the business side and no other and fail to give things the importance which they have in reference to God. There is profitable business which we should despise, and unprofitable

---

[1] *Conlat.*, XXI., i.; *Inst.*, V., xl.
[2] *Cf.* S. BASIL., *Reg. contr.*, cxi., cxii., cxiii.

business which charity bids us undertake. Only sons of the house know what suits the dignity of the house; and only a brother can set the souls of his brethren before temporal advantage. Finally, manual labour, and the different offices connected with it, are too much part of the web of our lives to be dependent on a stranger. All this is plain; but perhaps our Holy Father merely means that *he* should be chosen from among all the brethren who possesses the requisite assemblage of qualities.

St. Benedict enumerates the cellarer's virtues with extreme care. Nor is it difficult to explain such requirements. Monastic life depends on peacefulness and security, the individual living without care for material things and having no relations with the outside world. There are, however, three or four monks whose life is sacrificed to the well-being of all, who are denied this prayerful serenity and this recollection, and who by their very office are endangered, so that the rest may be saved. Such are the infirmarian, the guestmaster, the cellarer, and the Abbot. The cellarer, says St. Benedict, should be a "wise" man—that is, circumspect and prudent, able to consider many points at the same time, and in his decisions to give due weight to each: wisdom is eminent knowledge, able to judge and ordain by reason of its eminence. He must be "of mature character." His years, or in default of years his innate seriousness ("a spotless life is old age," Wisd. iv. 9), will guard him from interior and exterior dangers. He must be "temperate,[1] not a great eater";[2] for, being in charge of the department of supplies and provisions, he must not be tempted to secure himself worldly comforts and privileges in food and drink that would soon degenerate into gluttony. Perhaps this counsel was especially opportune at a time when manners were barbarous and tended to excess; for nowadays we should be more inclined to advise the Abbot to choose a cellarer who both ate and drank. In fact it would be dangerous to entrust the victualling of the community either to an ascetic, a monk who lived very meagrely and always well within the average, or to a monk whose life was nothing but exceptions and who did not follow the general régime. The first cannot estimate correctly; his measure is too small: for we naturally take ourselves as the standard and are easily unmerciful with grievances which we ourselves do not feel. This state of things leads inevitably to murmuring, and would make many unable to face the essential work of their lives. On the other hand, we have a régime of exceptions, spreading from one to another through the whole monastery.

Non elatus: he must not be proud. His office undoubtedly gives him an occasion for pride. The uniting of many functions in his hands, the dependence of all on him, the very custom which the Abbot wisely follows of keeping nothing in his own possession, but himself receiving what he needs from the cellarer: this subordination of all to him may insensibly become a temptation. *Non turbulentus:* he must not be

---

[1] *Cf.* CALMET., *in h. l.*
[2] *Reg.* I., SS. PATRUM, xii.: . . . *Qui cellarium fratrum contineat. Debet talis tantummodo eligi, qui possit in omnibus gulæ suæ suggestionibus dominari.*

turbulent and a source of confusion; he should be of an equable and peaceful temper. Turbulence and caprice are everywhere and always objectionable: but they would be especially so in the case of one who has such serious responsibilities. *Non injuriosus:* he must not insult people, a thing to which impatience leads so quickly. The more various the interests he has to consider, the more resolute should be his calm serenity. We may add that this serenity implies constant union with God and cannot come merely from temperament. He especially should often repeat those words of the seventy-fifth psalm: "And his place is in peace and his abode in Sion." He must not be slow (*non tardus*) through avarice or meanness or natural carelessness; for the business entrusted to him generally demands promptitude. *Non prodigus:* he should not be wasteful, with a taste for extravagant expenditure. Nay, he shall be forgiven for being somewhat careful, a little close-fisted, so as to be a check on a hundred factitious requirements. In any case he must be exact, and get a clear idea of things, nor give the misguided man all he asks for a journey or purchase of any sort. The "fear of God" shall guide all his actions and inspire his decisions. And in temporal matters the cellarer must be "like a father to the whole community," not a mere business man, or harsh and heedless bailiff.

Curam gerat de omnibus: sine jussione Abbatis nihil faciat. Quæ jubentur, custodiat: fratres non contristet. Si quis autem frater ab eo forte aliquid irrationabiliter postulat, non spernendo eum contristet, sed rationabiliter cum humilitate male petenti deneget. Animam suam custodiat, memor semper illius apostolici præcepti, quia *qui bene ministraverit, gradum bonum sibi acquirit.*

Let him have the care of everything, but do nothing without leave of the Abbot. Let him take heed to what is commanded him: let him not sadden his brethren. If a brother ask him for anything unreasonably, let him not treat him with contempt and so grieve him, but reasonably and with all humility refuse what he asks for amiss. Let him be watchful over his own soul, remembering always that saying of the Apostle, that "he that hath ministered well purchaseth to himself a good degree."

Up to this point our Holy Father has been giving a rapid summary of the qualities which should determine the choice of a cellarer. He now speaks of his duties in general, describing his relations with the Abbot, and with his brethren, and finally what he should be himself. "Let him have the care of everything." To separate the offices which supply the material wants of the community and set them in a mere relation of juxtaposition to one another would be to open the door to disorder, waste, jealousy, and negligence. Not that one man is to do everything; but things will not be done and done well except there be a single directive authority. This authority the cellarer should have. Nothing should be withdrawn from his vigilant care. He shall be responsible for all; yet, as St. Benedict adds, he shall do nothing without leave of the Abbot, and his activities are to be controlled by his instructions:

" let him take heed to what is commanded him." Of course in practical concerns and matters of finance the Abbot will always be very ready to adopt the opinion of his cellarer, since more than any other he is conversant with such and is competent to deal with them. But, when all is said, the Abbot remains responsible and from him must come the decision. So after putting these various offices into the hands of the cellarer, St. Benedict would have these offices and their controller, the cellarer, remain unquestionably in the hands of the Abbot.

He is not to sadden the brethren.[1] Here we have the most thorny problem of his administration. If every request were reasonable and discreet, and the function of the cellarer a mere giving of consent, there would be no need to bother about finding a prudent and judicious man for the post. But the cellarer must be able to say no, when a request is unjustified or unreasonable. Undoubtedly the cellarer's duty is simplified by the fact that he gives nothing save by express or tacit permission of the Abbot; but there still remains scope, in the ordinary duties of his office, for the exercise of this wise counsel of our Holy Father. He may be asked for what is unreasonable. Let him learn to refuse it reasonably—that is, explaining the refusal, simply, humbly, sweetly, without insult or taunt; so that the brother who prefers the unreasonable request may not be able to charge him with impatience or prejudice, whether in the substance or the manner of his refusal. There is a manner of giving which enhances the gift; so, too, there is a manner of refusing which softens the refusal: spiritual tact will find this manner.[2] St. Benedict's aim is to banish murmuring, to secure gentleness with souls, and to spare the Abbot those troublesome appeals which the aggrieved monk naturally brings to his tribunal. The cellarer must be amiable. He has not to be a sort of hedgehog in the community, getting into an attitude of defence whenever anyone approaches him, because he guesses what the matter is. If people are compelled to take their courage in both hands when they have any request to make of him, and if they only make up their minds to face him in the last extremity, then monastic poverty is in great danger; for, to avoid these painful interviews, the brethren will be strongly tempted to provide themselves with what is necessary, and presently with what is superfluous.

Animam suam custodiat. In these words we have the duty of the cellarer as regards himself. He must guard his soul against the dissipation inevitably induced by the care of material things and somewhat frequent relations with the world. He should be a more interior man and a better monk than his brethren. The more he is drawn out to the external by the nature of his occupations, the more should he turn in

---

[1] *Ne contristes fratrem tuum, quia monachus es* (*Verba Seniorum: Vitæ Patrum*, III., 170. ROSWEYD, p. 526).

[2] *Supplicem nullum spernas, et cui dare non potes quod petierit, non eum spernas; si potes dare, da; si non potes, affabilem te præsta* (S. AUG., *Enarr.* I. *in Psal.* ciii. 19. P.L., XXXVII., 1351).

Of the Cellarer of the Monastery

to his centre and to God, and so escape dissipation and aridity. Such is the meaning generally given to St. Benedict's words, and the interpretation is accurate. Yet we may bring out the meaning more fully, if we consider the motive which goes with the counsel—viz., that the cellarer should remember the reward that is promised him. The words "let him be watchful over his own soul!" recall the Gospel sentence: "In your patience you shall possess your souls" (Luke xxi. 19); for to watch over and to possess the soul mean the same. Perhaps dissipation is not the only danger to which a cellarer is exposed; he may let his soul escape his grasp by impatience or ennui. Great is his temptation, every day and every moment and lasting for years; for the capable cellarer is a precious pearl and is jealously kept. His life does not belong to himself; unwittingly a conspiracy of all is formed against his peace; he is most exposed to the petty importunities and annoyances of the brethren. And if he has a taste for the things of the mind and for piety, how heroic is that abnegation which purchases the peace and security of all! Yet the cellarer should not dwell upon his toil and sacrifice and servitude, but remember only what the Apostle said of deacons who fulfilled their duties diligently: "They that have ministered well shall purchase to themselves a good degree and much confidence in the faith which is in Christ Jesus" (1 Tim. iii. 13.)[1] For God is just and without doubt will give a large share of the merits of the community to those whose devotedness permits the community to serve Him in peace. The "good degree" here promised is not promotion in the worldly sense: it is a better position henceforth and for ever in nearness to God.

Infirmorum, infantium, hospitum, pauperumque cum omni sollicitudine curam gerat, sciens sine dubio, quia pro his omnibus in die judicii rationem redditurus est. Omnia vasa monasterii cunctamque substantiam, ac si altaris vasa sacrata conspiciat. Nihil ducat negligendum: neque avaritiæ studeat, neque prodigus sit, aut extirpator substantiæ monasterii; sed omnia mensurate faciat, et secundum jussionem Abbatis sui.

Let him have especial care of the sick, of the children, of guests, and of the poor, knowing without doubt that he will have to render an account of all these on the Day of Judgement. Let him look upon all the vessels and goods of the Monastery as though they were the consecrated vessels of the altar. Let him not think that he may neglect anything: let him not be given to covetousness, nor wasteful, nor a squanderer of the goods of the monastery; but do all things in proper measure, and according to the bidding of his Abbot.

The Rule, considering more in detail the duties of the cellarer, specifies the privileged objects of his care and determines the true character of his administration. The sick and children of the monastery, guests, and the poor that present themselves: all these have an especial title to the good offices and the generosity of the cellarer. The Abbot

---

[1] The *First Rule of the* HOLY FATHERS also said: *Studere debet qui huic officio deputatur, ut audiat: Quia qui bene ministraverit, bonum gradum acquirit; et animæ suæ lucrum facit* (xii.).

and community count upon him to exercise those works of mercy which are expected from a monastery. And, in order to awaken his zeal, St. Benedict treats him as he did the Abbot, appealing to his conscience and reminding him that without doubt he will have to render an account of all his deeds on the Day of Judgement.

All the tools and vessels of the monastery, all its goods, whether real or personal, must be regarded by him and treated as though they were the consecrated vessels of the altar. This is a strong statement and would even seem exaggerated; yet it is common to the ancient monastic Rules. To the question: "How should workers care for the tools or implements of their work?" St. Basil answers: "First they should treat them as though they were the vessels of God, even as those already consecrated to His service. Then as not being able without them to profit by their devotedness and zeal. . . . If a man misuse them, he is to be adjudged guilty of sacrilege; if a man destroy them by his negligence, he incurs the same charge; for all things which are appointed for the use of the servants of God are without doubt consecrated to God." The same teaching is to be found in the first *Rule of the Holy Fathers* and in Cassian.[1] Despite the legal arrangements which communities are forced to adopt in order to resist the encroachments of an infidel State, the only true proprietor of monastic property is God, neither one nor many religious nor the corporate community itself. Both persons and property belong to God. What consecration does for the vessels of the altar is done for monks by their profession, for their property by its devotion to God's service. Perhaps it is this quality of monastic property, more than its actual value, which commends it to the rapacity of God's enemies. But our use of God's resources, which as our Father He gives for our enjoyment and entrusts to our administration, must be guided by the inspiration of faith. Neither Abbot nor cellarer may make away with or squander these resources without dishonouring God and frustrating His designs; their consciences will even forbid them to surrender part to iniquitous exaction, with the purpose—in itself very human—of possessing the rest in peace. The property may be taken from them; but they may not give it away or divert it from its true end.

Nihil ducat negligendum. . . . Since all the possessions of the monastery, movable or not, are the property of God, the cellarer may treat none with negligence. No sort of economy, as we are told, should be despised; but here it is a question not of economy, but rather of respect and supernatural fidelity. Negligence in such circumstances may easily acquire the malice of sacrilege. *Neque avaritiæ studeat:* by which remark St. Benedict would anticipate and prevent the mistake of a cellarer who should interpret the previous counsel to suit his own wishes. For the desire to amass and to keep, which is impossible of realization by the other religious, may be realized by him. The habit of handling money, the need of skilful management and carefulness, combined, it may be, with a natural leaning towards excessive economy:

---

[1] S. BASIL., *Reg. contr.*, ciii., civ.—*Reg.* I. SS. PATRUM, xii.—CASS., *Inst.*, IV., xix., xx.

all these, assisted by age, may make a man who has renounced personal ownership, the very type of a proprietor, in the pretended interest of the community. What ingenious reasons self-interest can find to satisfy its desires and bring about ownership under the very shelter of the vow of poverty! So he accumulates, and defends against all approach and against all use with which he does not agree, possessions of which he is only the temporary administrator; he creates an unlimited reserve, though the property, like the persons of a monastery, once they pass a certain point, should fructify for God—that is, serve for the foundation of new centres of teaching and prayer.

There is another danger: prodigality, the squandering of the resources of the monastery. To see a religious house go bankrupt is not an edifying spectacle; nor should it groan under a burden of debt. As we have already remarked, religious poverty requires a margin of subsistence. A monk should never be forced by the notorious distress of his house to provide for himself, to go begging from all sides, to importune parents and benefactors. The worst may be feared if the cellarer is a "hustler," enamoured of imposing purchases, which are no sooner made than they are found useless and sold at a loss; if he is partial to mining shares and remote speculations; if he has an incorrigible love for bricks and mortar. Rather than abandon himself to covetousness or prodigality, let him listen to our Holy Father's appeal and do all things in proper measure, keeping the mean between both extremes. If he would not give way to inclination or temperament, let him keep the Abbot informed of his administration, and follow in all things the orders and views of his superior, who must not stand aside.

Humilitatem ante omnia habeat, et cui substantia non est quæ tribuatur, sermo responsionis porrigatur bonus, quia scriptum est: *Sermo bonus super datum optimum.*

Let him above all things have humility; and to him on whom he has nothing else to bestow, let him give at least a kind answer, as it is written: "A good word is above the best gift."

St. Benedict has treated of the qualities and duties of the cellarer in a general and theoretical fashion; he now considers him in the actual and concrete exercise of his office, so as to emphasize anew the attitude which is expected from him towards the Abbot and towards his brethren. "Let him above all things have humility." To meet the special difficulties of his charge the cellarer should, as we have said, be a better monk than all; therefore should he possess, more deeply and strongly entrenched in his soul, that virtue which makes the monk, humility. Humility has been defined as "submission to God and to every creature for love of God"; to which we would fain add "peaceful and constant union with God." By the assiduous practice of this union the cellarer will spare himself a thousand blunders and his neighbour many a petty annoyance. Let us admire once more St. Benedict's spiritual skill. Instead of describing minutely the methods and particular means which the cellarer must use, instead of furnishing him with a ready-made mind, he educates him from within and gives him a soul.

The humility of the cellarer will show itself especially, says the Rule, in his manner of refusing monks what he cannot or ought not to give them. He should remember that he is their brother and their equal, their servant rather than their master, and that the favours which he grants or withholds are not his nor personal to him. A rough or contemptuous refusal is cruel. And, if you must disappoint, you need not do it tauntingly. How excellent is kindness, and how little it costs! Just a word of regret, some small compensation, a promise, an affable air, a friendly smile. If the money or object which is asked for cannot be given, then "let him give at least a kind answer": which words are almost those of Ecclesiasticus (xviii. 16–17): "A good word is above the best gift."

Omnia quæ ei injunxerit Abbas, ipse habeat sub cura sua; a quibus eum prohibuerit, non præsumat.	Let him have under his care all that the Abbot may enjoin him, and presume not to meddle with what is forbidden him.

A third time St. Benedict reminds the cellarer that he should conform in all things to the orders and directions of his Abbot; a thing required by humility and obedience. Office is made easy when one is determined to be absolutely docile. Perhaps this third instruction has a new meaning. As we said a moment ago, it is very important that the whole material administration of the monastery should be unified. But one man cannot manage the manifold interests of a great monastery, nor need he necessarily possess all-round aptitude. So the Abbot may relieve a cellarer of the immediate care of several matters. Some cellarers will want to keep everything in their own hands, while others will disburden themselves according to their own good pleasure; either attitude is harmful and dangerous. The difficulty is met and solved by the Abbot's authority: he must himself choose the different officials and define exactly the scope and limits of their offices. So let the cellarer look to all that the Abbot may enjoin him, but let him not meddle with matters in which he has been requested not to interfere. To appeal to monastic custom, to vindicate haughtily the supposed rights of his office, and to search the chronicles of the Order for proof of his case—such procedure would be childish.

Fratribus constitutam annonam sine aliquo typo vel mora offerat, ut non scandalizentur, memor divini eloquii, quid mereatur *qui scandalizaverit unum de pusillis.*	Let him distribute to the brethren their appointed allowance of food, without arrogance or delay, that they be not scandalized: mindful of what the Word of God declares him to deserve, who "shall scandalize one of these little ones."

It is to the cellarer, as we shall see in the succeeding chapters, that St. Benedict entrusts the care and distribution of food. The Rule determines what should be given to the monks at each meal; it provides for certain cases when the Abbot may somewhat increase and alter the allowance of food and drink. By *cònstitutam annonam* St. Benedict means this fixed portion, the regular allowance given to those serving under the standard of God. Perhaps, by an extreme care for the finances of the monastery or from fear of scarcity to come, the cellarer might sometimes be tempted to reduce the portion fixed by the Abbot, or at least to grant it with regret, with a sort of jealousy and a disagreeable reluctance. The Life of St. Benedict gives a sketch of one of these too conscientious cellarers.[1] A cellarer might even go so far as to season with ungracious comment the portion that he has been compelled to give. Our Holy Father warns him against a temper which would wound charity and obedience and true monastic poverty: *sine aliquo typo vel mora offerat*.[2] Refusals, grumbling, and niggardliness would cause trouble in the community. For men are not angels, and they must eat; neither are all men perfect, and, when they have just cause to complain, they do complain. Our Holy Father sets such value on peace and charity in the community that his language becomes severe and he recalls the Gospel menaces against those who sow discord and give scandal, be it only to one of the little children of God (Matt. xviii. 6).

Si congregatio major fuerit, solatia ei dentur, a quibus adjutus, et ipse æquo animo impleat officium sibi commissum. Horis competentibus dentur quæ danda sunt, et petantur quæ petenda sunt: ut nemo perturbetur, neque contristetur in domo Dei.	If the community be large, let helpers be given to him, by whose aid he may with peace of mind discharge the office committed to him. Let such things as are necessary be given and asked for at befitting times, that no one may be troubled or grieved in the house of God.

The intention of these last words is to secure the cellarer himself some peace and leisure. In the first place, if the community is large, the Abbot shall give him assistants, so that he may be able to discharge the office committed to him with an equable and tranquil soul. But it will relieve him more than all else if the brethren are considerate and take care to make their requests to him only at the proper times; while on his part he should give what he has to give in due time and at fixed hours. The brethren should know how to wait for a suitable opportunity, and should ask themselves, when they go to the cellarer, whether he is not occupied by business of greater moment. That man has neither good manners nor charity who jumps up as soon as he feels a need and runs off to the cellarer, at any hour of the day and of silence time, immediately the notion enters his head. We may remark that the

---

[1] S. Greg. M., *Dial.*, l. II., c. xxviii., xxix.

[2] The scribes sometimes wrote *typo*, sometimes *typho*: the latter reading is the better. The word is Latinized Greek: τύφος, smoke, smoke of pride or arrogance; in Hippocrates it means torpor, stupor, lethargy. If St. Benedict had this latter sense in mind, *typus* and *mora* would be very nearly synonymous; what he wanted to say was: without arrogance, *cum humilitate*, as before and for a third time. St. Benedict's words recall St. Augustine: *oblationes pro spiritibus dormientium . . . super ipsas memorias non sint sumptuosæ, atque omnibus petentibus sine typho et cum alacritate præbeantur* (*Epist.* XXII., 6. *P.L.*, XXXIII., 92).

recollected and studious wait most willingly and are most economical of the time of others.

We might give to St. Benedict's words a general application. There is practically but one man in the monastery to whom this rule does not apply—that is, the Abbot. He is yours wholly. You may be passing his room and you go in, with nothing to say or ask for, but simply because your heart is so inclined. You receive his blessing and you are dismissed, if he is very busy, or else you chat for a moment. It is the Abbot's privilege to be accessible at every hour, and that is the advantage of his office; good monks will take care that they do not deprive him of it. Having made this observation let us hold fast to St. Benedict's principle: that no one should be troubled or grieved in the house of God. We were created and put in the world to be happy. Superiors have no mission to try the patience of their monks by deliberate rebuffs, nor have monks to burden beyond measure the shoulders of those who carry them. The monastery is the "house of God," and therefore the house of peace and the threshold of eternity: *Urbs Jerusalem beata, dicta pacis visio.*

CHAPTER XXXII

OF THE TOOLS AND PROPERTY OF THE MONASTERY

De ferramentis vel rebus monasterii.—Substantiæ monasterii in ferramentis, vel vestibus, seu quibuslibet rebus, provideat Abbas fratres, de quorum vita et moribus securus sit: et iis singula, ut utile judicaverit, consignet custodienda atque recolligenda. Ex quibus Abbas breve teneat: ut dum sibi in ipsa assignata fratres vicissim succedunt, sciat quid dat aut quid recipit. Si quis autem sordide aut negligenter res monasterii tractaverit, corripiatur; si non emendaverit, disciplinæ regulari subjaceat.

Let the Abbot appoint brethren, on whose manner of life and character he can rely, to the charge of the tools, clothes, and other property of the monastery; and let him consign the various things to their charge, as he shall think fit, to be kept and to be collected after use. Of these let the Abbot keep a list, so that as the brethren succeed to different employments, he may know what he gives and what he receives back. If anyone treat the property of the monastery in a slovenly or negligent manner, let him be corrected; and if he do not amend, let him be subjected to the discipline of the Rule.

THE connection of this chapter with the preceding one is obvious. Both treat of the property of the monastery, and the thirty-second mentions some of those assistants that the cellarer was promised in the thirty-first.

The Abbot has to entrust to brethren whose good life and steady character he knows, and in whom he can repose all confidence, whatever tools, clothes, or other movable property the monastery may possess. He must assign to each, according as he thinks fit, a special department, with the duty of guarding and preserving the implements pertaining to his department. To prevent their being lost, they will see to their return, after use, to the regular place; *consignet custodienda atque recolligenda.* So the cellarer does not himself choose his assistants, but is given them by the Abbot. One will have charge of tools, another of clothes, another of the library, and so on. The immediate control of the commissariat and the kitchen remains in the hands of the cellarer.

There is nothing to prove that in St. Benedict's time tools were given out for a week only, and that all the offices here mentioned changed their holders periodically, as in the service of the kitchen, and in conformity with the ordinance of St. Pachomius: "When the week is finished all tools shall be brought back to one house; and let those who follow every week know what to give out to the various houses."[1] St. Benedict foresees, however, that the brethren will follow one another in the custody of the things entrusted to them; and, since they might be tempted to accuse one another of negligence, he

---

[1] St. Pach., *Rule.* lxvi.; *cf.* xxv., xxvi., xxvii.

makes a point of fixing responsibility. So the Abbot, never abdicating his position, must keep by him an account and inventory (*breve*) of all things given out; in order that he may know exactly what he gives and what is given back to him. This is that excellent precaution of accurate book-keeping. Calmet appositely notices the analogies between our Holy Father's arrangements and those of the Latin agricultural writers, Columella and Varro.

In the third and final sentence of this chapter our Holy Father declares that punishment will be inflicted on those who treat the property of the monastery in a slovenly or careless manner—viz., a reprimand, and if that be unsuccessful, the application of the various penalties comprised in the discipline of the Rule. " If any of the brethren shall treat anything negligently," says the first *Rule of the Holy Fathers*, " let him know that his part is with that king who drank in the sacred vessels of God's House with his concubines, and let him remember the punishment he earned."[1] In the world a man is impelled to care for himself and his possessions, to be thrifty and businesslike, by different motives: by consideration for his well-being and the well-being and social standing of his family, and by the sentiment of personal ownership. Children are rarely careful, because they have little foresight; communists and socialists, who give all ownership to collective bodies or to the State, will with difficulty solve the problem of work and economy. The monastic life alone has found the means, while suppressing personal ownership, of furnishing work, economy, and carefulness, not with any ordinary motive or stimulus, but with the most powerful of all: the conviction, that is, that we work for God and that our respect is paid to His property. Yet it is imperative that these considerations should not remain in the region of abstract theory, but be practically realized by the individual in his conduct. This done, it is not external order only and health that benefit by scrupulous care of clothes, person, cell, books, tools, and all else, but our souls also, our delicacy of conscience, our spiritual family, and even God Himself.

[1] C. xxii. And St. Cæsarius: *Quæ cellario sive canavæ, sive vestibus, vel codicibus, aut posticio, vel lanipendio præponuntur, super Evangelium claves accipiant, et sine murmuratione serviant reliquis. Si quæ vero vestimenta, calceamenta, utensilia negligenter expendenda vel custodienda putarint, tanquam interversores rerum monasterialium severius corrigantur* (Reg. ad virg., xxx.).

CHAPTER XXXIII
WHETHER MONKS OUGHT TO HAVE ANYTHING OF THEIR OWN[1]

SI QUID DEBEANT MONACHI PROPRIUM HABERE.—Præcipue hoc vitium radicitus amputetur de monasterio, ne quis præsumat aliquid dare aut accipere sine jussione Abbatis, neque aliquid habere proprium, nullam omnino rem, neque codicem, neque tabulas, neque graphium, sed nihil omnino: quippe quibus nec corpora sua, nec voluntates licet habere in propria potestate.

Above all let the vice of private ownership be cut off from the monastery by the roots. Let none presume to give or receive anything without leave of the Abbot, or to keep anything as their own, either book or writing-tablet or pen, or anything whatsoever; since they are permitted to have neither body nor will in their own power.

AGAIN it is in reference to the cellarer and his office that our Holy Father describes for us the position of monks with regard to temporal goods, and tells us under what conditions and in what measure they may use them. Before St. Benedict's time, as after it, poverty was always one of the three essential obligations of the religious life; and if our Holy Father does not require his disciples to take an explicit vow of chastity or poverty, the reason is that they are included in the promise to observe monastic customs and the monastic mode of life: that is in the vow of *conversio morum*. That the monk is poor by the very fact of his state of life was a principle universally accepted; and so St. Benedict is able to embark without any preface, and so to say *ex abrupto*, on his provisions for the exclusion of all personal ownership.

"Above all let this vice of private ownership be cut off from the monastery by the roots ";[2] farther on he calls it "this most baneful vice." Such words as these, for all their appearance of extreme and rather excessive vigour, are yet not more than prudent. For in this matter nothing is trivial. Doubtless poverty belongs to the more external side of our religious promises; for while I give God my will by obedience and my body by chastity, it would seem that by poverty I only give external goods and the rights attaching to them. But for the very reason that poverty is more external it is more open to menace, just as the most advanced works of a fortress are those first attacked by the enemy. So long as these works remain intact and stoutly defended, the fortress has nothing to fear; but if they be taken the most central parts are no longer secure, and it often happens that those works are turned against a position, which were laboriously constructed for its defence. Experience teaches that religious apostasy nearly always begins with some breach of poverty. Infidelities multiply and con-

---
[1] This is ST. BASIL's title, or rather his question: *Si debet habere aliquid proprium, qui inter fratres est?* (*Reg. contr.*, xxix.).
[2] Both thought and phrase come from CASSIAN, *Conlat.*, XVI., vi.

science slumbers. A man speaks thus to himself: "The thing is so trivial; I should certainly get permission if I asked. And I cannot be bothering the Abbot with these petty details. Perhaps he would not understand how useful these things are to me, how necessary for my health and my studies. This has been of great service to me before now; it is so convenient and I am used to it. I have a prescriptive right to it." When personal ownership is re-established, under whatever form, we are no longer in God's house, but in our own, among our goods and chattels or in "furnished apartments"; for our relation to God is instantly changed. Again there is *meum* and *tuum*; self-interest reappears and with it jealousy and conflict; for our relations to our neighbours are also instantly changed. We return to the conditions of ordinary worldly life, but with a mean and base addition, the disgrace of a broken vow.

After having proscribed the vice of ownership in general, St. Benedict enumerates the different acts of ownership which are forbidden to monks —viz., giving, receiving, and keeping.[1] The qualification: "without leave of the Abbot" will be explained later. So as to preclude all the petty devices of self-interest and to keep off all too liberal interpretations of the law, our Holy Father declares in forcible terms that a monk may own nothing whatsoever (*nullam omnino rem*)—not even trivial things, not even articles of prime necessity to students, such as books, writing-tablets, pens. All these things are given us only *ad usum*, not for a use which is of right and perpetual, but for a use of fact, revocable at pleasure by the superior. And St. Benedict repeats the point in the words: *sed nihil omnino*. We shall find the same rigorous ordinance in the fifty-eighth chapter, and the sentence which follows occurs there too, though in a less complete form. From the moment of their profession monks may possess nothing, "since they are no longer permitted to have either body or will in their own power."[2] What is our Holy Father's exact meaning ? Would he suggest that, since the monk has given his person to religion, it should be much easier for him to consent to the abandonment of his property, which is external to himself and of less value ? Or would he merely mark the fact that the monk's dispoliation must be quite radical, "since neither body nor will is any longer in his own power." It seems to us that the words of St. Benedict have here

---

[1] As sources of this chapter we may indicate once for all the following: S. PACH., *Reg.*, lxxxi., cvi.—S. ORSIESII *Doctrina*, xxi.–xxiii.—*Reg.* II. SS. PATRUM., i.—*Reg. Orient.*, xxx.–xxxi.—S. BASIL., *Reg. contr.*, xxix.–xxxi., xcviii.-xcix.—S. AUG., *Epist.* CCXI., 5 (*P.L.*, XXXIII., 960).—SULP. SEV., *Vita B. Martini*, x. (*P.L.*, XX., 166).— S. CÆSAR., *Reg. ad mon.*, i.–iii., xv., xvi.; *Reg. ad virg.*, *passim.*—CASS., *Inst.*, IV., xiii.

[2] *Qui seipsum et membra sua tradidit in alterius potestatem propter mandatum Domini* (S. BASIL., *Reg. contr.*, cvi.).—*Ne sui quidem ipsius esse se dominum vel potestatem habere cognoscat* (CASS., *Inst.*, II., iii.).—See also S. MACAR., *Reg.*, xxiv.—We read in the *Constitutiones monast.*, c. xx. (inter opp. S. BASILII. *P.G.*, XXXI., 1393): *Tu autem mortuus es, et toti mundo crucifixus. Rejectis enim terrenis divitiis amplexus es paupertatem; et cum te ipse dicasti Deo, Dei factus es thesaurus . . . Nihil omnino possidens, nihil habes quod largiaris. Imo etiam cum ipsum corpus obtuleris et de cætero ne illius quidem potestatem habeas, tanquam quod res sit Deo consecrata, tibi eo uti non licet ad humanum usum.*

a juridical force, a formal practical reference. Goods, which of themselves belong to no one, do not become ours save by means of two acts: the first an act of our positive will, for no one can be an owner in his own despite, and even for an inheritance acceptance is necessary; the other an act of our body, which occupies the object and awards it, whether by its labour or by some external form, to the person. If one or other of these elements be wanting, and *a fortiori* if there be neither internal act of will nor external occupation, ownership does not exist. Now this, to St. Benedict's mind, is precisely the case of the monk: he is incapable of possessing, since his body and will, the necessary instruments of personal appropriation, belong to him no more.

Does this mean that profession makes the religious radically incapable of the act of acquisition or of exercising any sort of ownership? To appreciate the point perfectly we should remember that according to the actual legislation of the Church vows are of two kinds, simple and solemn. The simple vow of poverty leaves the religious the bare ownership of his property, but does not permit him its administration or use save under the control of his superior; for the monk's will must be made competent by the will of his Abbot. The case is different with the solemn vow. To be quite precise the solemnity of the vow consists in the intervention of the Sovereign Pontiff; for the vow is regarded as uttered in his presence and accepted by him. Henceforth he alone may dispense, since it is the common character of every case that is taken to Rome and in which Rome intervenes, though it be incidentally only, to be withdrawn *ipso facto* from any inferior jurisdiction. The solemnly professed monk loses both the bare ownership and the administration of his property; yet he may be empowered by the Holy See to perform certain acts of ownership, notwithstanding his vow and without breaking it, as is proved by certain papal decisions of the eighteenth and nineteenth centuries. In certain cases the Church has authorized religious to attest the reality of their ownership under oath before the civil courts. But, for all that, they do not cease to be poor, since even then they are owners only within the limits set by obedience and by the will of the Holy See. So we cannot say unreservedly that solemn profession entails an absolute and final incapacity to possess.

Moreover, even without taking into consideration extraordinary cases and dispensations, it is correct and wise to hold that, in a general way, the monk in solemn vows always remains capable of real acquisition, that the *animus domini* can really exist in him. The terse axiom of canon law which decides the point says so twice in the words: *Quod monachus acquirit monasterio acquirit*. A monk acquires property, and acquires it for his monastery; whether it be by labour, gift, bequest, or inheritance. He is incapable of acquiring for himself *in proprietate*, with rights of ownership; but acquires for the monastery to which he belongs. His union with the monastery and incorporation in it are so complete that, except he has settled in due time (before his vows) what shall become of anything that comes to him later, the monastery inherits at once all the property that falls to a monk. We should not regard the system of "la mort civile" (civil death) which was introduced in France during the fifteenth century as an ideal state of things for monasticism. By this system religious were, so to say, struck out of the list of the living, both in their active and passive relations, so that any legacy, instead of going to them and their monastery, passed by law to their heirs. This was an injustice, a perverse precaution against the excessive extension of mortmain, a socialistic ordinance suppressing ownership by State authority, a prelude to the spoliations of the eighteenth century. Some have found the theory of "civil death" in the laws of Justinian; but a close perusal shows, on the contrary, that these laws sanctioned the bestowal of a monk's property on the monastery and even authorized a bequest to be made in favour of the monastery in certain cases. St. Gregory the Great[1] cites these laws and bases his action on their decision, so far as they were Christian and equitable; but there is nothing to prove that he wished to give them ecclesiastical authority.

Omnia vero necessaria a patre monasterii sperare; nec quicquam liceat habere, quod Abbas non dederit aut permiserit. Omniaque omnibus sint communia, ut scriptum est, nec quisquam suum esse aliquid dicat aut præsumat.	But let them hope to receive all that is necessary from the father of the monastery; nor let them be allowed to keep anything which the Abbot has not given or permitted. Let all things be common to all, as it is written, nor let anyone say or assume that aught is his own.

So far St. Benedict has given only negative precepts; now he tells us how the monks are provided with the things indispensable for their life and state. They must expect to receive them from the father of the monastery, and they must not keep anything whatever that the Abbot has not given or permitted. We should take careful note that herein consists the true essence of our poverty. For there are different types of poverty. There is the poverty of St. Cajetan and apostolic men; there is poverty relieved by manual labour; there is poverty relieved by begging; there is poverty with community of goods; there is the poverty of the Capuchins and Friars Minor of the observance, who may possess neither real nor personal property. And all are good; all have their origin in facts of history which gave each its special character. St. Benedict's conception is as follows. We are children of a family, forming the family of God and remaining minors till eternity. We live in our Father's house, the house of God. All the possessions of the monastery are His and He dispenses to us what we need by the hands of the Abbot, His representative. We are poor, not when we are in want of all things and suffer from scarcity,[2] but when we have nothing

---

[1] *Epist.*, l. IV., *Ep.* VI.; l. IX., *Ep.* VII., *Ep.* CXIV. *P.L.*, LXXVII., 672–673, 945–947, 1044–1045. See the edition of Ewold and Hartman, M.G.H.: *Epist.*, t. I., pp. 237–238; t. II., pp. 185–186, 215–216.

[2] Nor was this the ideal of St. Gregory the Great, who wrote: *Religiosam vitam eligentibus congrua nos oportet consideratione prospicere, ne cujusdam necessitatis occasio aut*

in our possession save what the Abbot has given us or permitted us to keep. The Abbot is responsible to God both for what he refuses and for what he gives; yet each individual should help him to fulfil his rôle of guardian of poverty by reducing his requirements.[1] It appears to us that a man has the Benedictine spirit when he takes naturally to these elementary principles.

Not even when certain possessions are left to the disposal of a monk is there ownership; no one should make anything his own, whatever it be, either in thought or word. This is the monastic tradition.[2] All is common, and the same property is for the use of all. This is a holy, well-regulated communism, and not anarchy. It is a return, prudently and with limitations, to the conditions of the Church of Jerusalem (Acts iv. 32). God alone possesses, and we rely upon Him, thus realizing the ideal traced in the Sermon on the Mount. We retain no single care, our liberty is complete. Nothing embarrasses or occupies our activity, in the way that possession of any sort generally does; for every proprietor is the slave of his property, often belonging only half or even less to the things of God. That is why the religious soul should be free of it all, free from all material possessions, from all immoderate desires, from all deliberate attachment to any good which is not God. Riches, in themselves, are neither good nor bad; nor is poverty itself good, save when it permits us to enjoy the Sovereign Good in all completeness. Is not, therefore, that form of poverty the best which most effectively conduces to this leisure of soul and union with God?[3] Poverty, as St. Benedict understands it, secures us our subsistence and banishes all care, secures us a position of legitimate and necessary independence, secures us liberty to go to God, secures our obedience and submission to the Abbot, secures our fraternal charity, since there is no longer " mine and thine," secures our charity towards God, and our perfection.

Quod si quisquam hoc nequissimo vitio deprehensus fuerit delectari, admoneatur semel et iterum: si non emendaverit, correctioni subjaceat.	But if anyone shall be found to indulge in this most baneful vice, and after one or two admonitions do not amend, let him be subjected to correction.

---

desides faciat aut robur, quod absit, conversationis infringat (Epist., l. III., Ep. XVII., P.L., LXXVII., 617; M.G.H.: Epist., t. I., p. 175). And again: *Officio pietatis impellimur monasteriis provida consideratione ferre consultum, ne hi qui Dei servitio deputati esse noscuntur necessitatem aliquam possint, quod avertat Dominus, sustinere (Epist., l. II., Ep. IV. P.L., LXXVII., 541; M.G.H.: Epist., t. I., p. 109).*

[1] We should congratulate ourselves on the fact that our Constitutions absolutely forbid *peculium*—*i.e.*, any money deposit, testamentary reservation, or income left to the free disposal of the monk. Even when authorized by Rule, this custom is hardly in accordance with the spirit of true monastic poverty. The Abbot himself, by our Constitutions, is subject to the requirements of the perfect common life.

[2] *Hanc regulam videamus districtissime nunc usque servari, ut ne verbo quidem audeat quis dicere aliquid suum magnumque sit crimen ex ore monachi processisse codicem meum, tabulas meas, grafium meum, tunicam meam, gallicas meas, proque hoc digna pænitentia satisfacturus sit, si casu aliquo per subreptionem vel ignorantiam hujusmodi verbum de ore ejus effugerit* (Cass., *Inst.*, IV., xiii.).

[3] Read St. Thomas, *Summa contra Gent.*, l. III., c. cxxx.–cxxxv.

Our Holy Father threatens with chastisement all who should be convicted of any yielding to this detestable vice of ownership. Such a monk is to be warned a first and second time; if he does not mend his ways he is to be subjected to the grades of regular correction. Monastic antiquity ever showed itself very severe on this point. We may recall the story of the napkins told in the Life of St. Benedict.[1] St. Gregory the Great also tells of one of his monks who had secreted three gold coins. He did not allow the brethren to assist him on his deathbed and gave orders for him to be buried in a dunghill, with a little ritual which vividly impressed the monks and provoked a general restitution of all articles which had passed into private use, whether secretly or through the proper channels.[2] This custom of burying monks guilty of the vice of ownership in a dunghill, or in unconsecrated ground, is found elsewhere.[3] The ordinary punishment was excommunication. At Cîteaux and among the Carthusians it was the custom to proclaim it solemnly on Palm Sunday against all *proprietarii*.[4]

[1] S. Greg. M., *Dial.*, l. II., c. xix.
[2] *Dial.*, l. IV., c. lv. *P.L.*, LXXVII., 420.
[3] *Cf.* S. Hieron., *Epist.* XXII., 33. *P.L.*, XXII., 418.
[4] *Cf.* Martène, *in h. l.*

CHAPTER XXXIV

WHETHER ALL OUGHT TO RECEIVE NECESSARY THINGS ALIKE

Si omnes debeant æqualiter necessaria accipere.—Sicut scriptum est: *Dividebatur singulis, prout cuique opus erat.* Ubi non dicimus, quod personarum (quod absit) acceptio sit, sed infirmitatum consideratio. Ubi qui minus indiget, agat Deo gratias, et non contristetur: qui vero plus indiget, humilietur pro infirmitate, et non extollatur pro misericordia; et ita omnia membra erunt in pace.

It is written: "Distribution was made to everyone, according as he had need." By this we do not mean that there should be respecting of persons (God forbid!) but consideration for infirmities. Let him, therefore, who needs less thank God and be not distressed; and let him who requires more be humbled because of his infirmity and not puffed up by the mercy that is shown to him: so all the members shall be in peace.

THIS chapter is the complement of the preceding one, for it develops and expounds the words: "But let them hope to receive all that is necessary from the father of the monastery." We shall find the ordinances of these two chapters summarized at the end of the fifty-fifth.[1] They are very characteristic of the spirit of our Holy Father and mark an epoch in the history of monasticism. The religious life began with great austerity which was exacted from all. The time was the morrow of the persecutions, and souls were raised to the pitch of heroism, ready and even trained for martyrdom. God wished strongly to emphasize the idea of renunciation and to give a vigorous impulse to the development of monastic institutions. A picked body of men and characters of exceptional strength were needed; those who could not satisfy these high requirements returned to or remained in secular life; as we may see illustrated in St. Antony's method of testing the vocation of St. Paul the Simple. But St. Benedict's idea is different. Without ceasing to be a picked body—and therefore, like all such, not very numerous—the religious community is to be accessible to men of very various temper and very unequal vigour. Perfection is to be its normal end, but not its condition. There shall be discretion, moderation, and restraint in observances. More than this, the monastic life shall model itself on the life of the family and not on a military organization. In an army a man is to some degree an anonymous unit, bound to furnish the standard amount of work and service; when his

---

[1] St. Benedict had in mind the words of St. Augustine: *Non dicatis aliquid proprium, sed sint vobis omnia communia: et distribuatur unicuique vestrum a præposita vestra victus et tegumentum; non æqualiter omnibus, quia non æqualiter valetis omnes, sed unicuique sicut opus fuerit. Sic enim legitis in Actibus Apostolorum: Quia erant eis omnia communia et distribuebatur singulis prout cuique opus erat. . . . Quæ infirmæ sunt ex pristina consuetudine, si aliter tractantur in victu, non debet aliis molestum esse, nec injustum videri, quas fecit alia consuetudo fortiores. Nec illas feliciores putent, quia sumunt quod non sumunt ipsæ: sed sibi potius gratulentur, quia valent quod non valent illæ* (Epist. CCXI., 5, 9. P.L., XXXIII., 960, 961).—*Cf.* S. Basil, *Reg. contr.*, xciv.

capacity for endurance is lowered and he becomes a defective unit, he is removed and his place and number taken by another. In a family, on the contrary, the weaker member gets additional attention; and while a military chief must ignore all aspects of the individual which do not concern his duty, and consider almost exclusively the total effect, the father of a family is concerned with each of his children in particular, —" he calleth his own sheep by name "—and nothing which affects them leaves him unaffected.

Nor does St. Benedict attempt to reduce all his monks to one uniform level. " As it is written ": once more he borrows the exact design of the religious life from the conditions of the primitive Church (Acts iv. 35). In practice, taking man individually, inequality and not equality is the rule; and consequently their treatment should be proportionate and not identical. All efforts that are made to escape this law of nature involve mistakes and cruelties. And, to return to the Abbot, he should give to the brethren according to their real needs; by which we do not mean caprices or claims. The business of settling what is necessary does not appertain to the individual; for some temperaments would set everything down as necessary; but all have the right to ask, and humility and simplicity will know how to do it. The Abbot does not ordinarily delegate his powers in this matter of poverty to any official of the monastery, precisely because of the special gravity which we have seen belongs to the subject, and also because of the disastrous results which would follow if a monk were free to get permissions from several sources and then combine the various permissions thus obtained.

Nothing is simpler than a system of absolute equality, in which government becomes a matter of bureaucracy and mere administration, without soul or pity. But, when we have a system of proportional equality, and when account has to be taken of individuals, then the ruler's task is a very delicate one indeed. There is danger for the Abbot, danger for the monk who obtains permission, danger for his brethren. Against this threefold peril St. Benedict warns us in the rest of the chapter. First he reminds the Abbot of the principle already expounded in the second chapter, that he is bound to be attentive to the infirmities of each, without acceptance of persons or the pursuit of his own inclination. But our Holy Father proceeds to add that the Abbot has a right to count on the discretion and good spirit of the brethren. The government of a house would quickly become impossible, if all set themselves, in the spirit of a narrow and slavish self-interest, to watch jealously the permissions and relaxations granted to one of their number by the father's authority. St. Benedict delineates with delicate skill the attitude to be taken by monks with regard to exceptions from the common régime. He who needs less, he tells us, should thank God and not be distressed that he does not receive special attention; he who needs more should be humbled on account of his weakness and not puffed up by the mercy which is shown him. In this way there will be

Whether all ought to receive Necessary Things alike 253

neither quarrels nor rivalry in the monastery, and all the members of this mystical body of the Lord will abide in peace.

Ante omnia, ne murmurationis malum pro qualicumque causa, in aliquo qualicumque verbo vel significatione appareat. Quod si deprehensus fuerit quis, districtiori disciplinæ subdatur.	Above all things let not the pest of murmuring, for whatever cause, by any word or sign, be manifested. If anyone be found guilty in this let him be subjected to the most severe punishment.

In St. Benedict's eyes, monastic peace is a benefit which surpasses all others, as murmuring seems to him the worst of all evils. Above all things, he says, let not the pest of murmuring show itself, for any cause or in any form whatever, whether in word, or in act, or in some attitude that implies discontent. A man may say: " I will make no approaches; I will keep out of his way; I will assume a mask of reserve or offended dignity, and so let authority perceive that it has failed in its duty." Now, that is sheer anarchy; for authority is destroyed if it become subordinated to its subjects. Even should the Abbot take certain measures, in this matter of exceptions to the common régime, which seem to us unjustifiable, murmuring is a greater evil still. St. Benedict says, "for whatever cause." And he stipulates that any monk who is found guilty of murmuring should be subjected to very severe chastisement.

CHAPTER XXXV

OF THE WEEKLY SERVERS IN THE KITCHEN

DE SEPTIMANARIIS COQUINÆ.—Fratres sic sibi invicem serviant, ut nullus excusetur a coquinæ officio, nisi aut ægritudine, aut in causa gravis utilitatis quis occupatus fuerit; quia exinde major merces acquiritur. Imbecillibus autem procurentur solatia, ut non cum tristitia hoc faciant, sed habeant omnes solatia, secundum modum congregationis aut positionem loci. Si major congregatio fuerit, cellerarius excusetur a coquina; vel si qui, ut diximus, majoribus utilitatibus occupantur. Cæteri vero sibi sub charitate invicem serviant.

Let the brethren so serve each other in turn that no one be excused from the work of the kitchen unless on the score of health, or because he is engaged in some matter of great utility; for thence greater reward is obtained. Let the weaker brethren, however, be helped that they may not do their work with sadness: and let all generally have assistance according to the number of the community and the situation of the place. If the community be larger, the cellarer shall be excused from the service of the kitchen; and any others who are engaged (as we have said) in matters of greater utility. But let the rest serve one another in turn with all charity.

MAN needs a local habitation; he needs a roof over his head and the means to exercise his activities, since he is born to labour; and he needs food that he may live. This last need is imperious and recurrent, even for monks; wherefore St. Benedict has to devote several chapters to the regulation of meals. All that concerns kitchen, refectory, and cellar was put, as we have said, under the immediate jurisdiction of the cellarer. Our Holy Father deals first with the servers of the kitchen, that is, with the brethren who prepare the food and serve at table; for this twofold duty was fulfilled by the same persons.[1] There was not yet any distinction between choir-monks and lay brothers.[2]

All the brethren are to serve one another in turn with all charity. In this they will imitate the Lord, who declared that He had come into the world only to serve: " not to be ministered unto, but to minister." Cassian tells us that in the East, save in Egypt,[3] all the monks in their turn spent a week thus in the kitchen. We may easily imagine that these untrained cooks would not always produce an appetising and dainty repast; but tastes were simple, especially in the East. Salted herbs, says Cassian, seemed to them a delicious feast;[4] the monks of Egypt

---

[1] Does St. Benedict really intend to distinguish between the kitcheners and table sewers, when he writes, in Chapter XXXVIII., that the reader will take his meal *cum coquinæ hebdomadariis et servitoribus*? It is more likely that the servers are brethren given as assistants to the officials of the week.

[2] The principal source of this chapter is chapter xix. of the fourth book of the *Institutes* of CASSIAN.

[3] *Inst.*, IV., xxii.   [4] *Ibid.*, xi.

Of the Weekly Servers in the Kitchen

were content with fresh or dried vegetables; and it was a royal banquet (*summa voluptas*) when they were served monthly with hashed leeks, salted herbs, ground salt,[1] olives, and tiny salted fish.[2]

No one shall be dispensed from the service of the kitchen, says St. Benedict. The more humiliating it is and irksome, the greater will be the recompense, and charity too will grow (we should in fact read *major merces et caritas acquiritur*). At the French Court of former days even the commonest services conferred a title of nobility or presupposed it: the butler, chamberlain, and constable were great personages. The spiritual nobility who form Our Lord's royal court rank above all others, and all monastic offices are honourable. Our Holy Father, however, recognizes the Abbot's right to exempt certain of the brethren from the service of the kitchen: those in ill-health, those who are engaged in more important and exacting duties, such as the cellarer of a large community, and undoubtedly the Abbot as well. Some ancient Rules[3] except the Abbot expressly, while others would have him serve on certain days, if he be free. At Cluny, at least in its early days, the Abbot performed the service of the kitchen and waited at table on Christmas-day, in company with the cellarer and the deans; the Customs also order that the Abbot should be put in the list of servers when his turn comes, but as a supernumerary.[4] From motives of discretion our Holy Father would have help given to the weak, and ordains that the holders of this office should have the assistance of as many brethren as are required by the condition and number of the community, or the arrangement of the monastery; for the kitchen may be in the basement, the well very far away,[5] etc. It is important that the work should be well performed, but also that the brethren should perform it without sadness.

Egressurus de septimana, sabbato munditias faciat. Linteamina, cum quibus sibi fratres manus aut pedes tergunt, lavet: pedes vero tam ipse, qui egreditur, quam ille qui intraturus est, omnibus lavent. Vasa ministerii sui munda et sana cellerario reconsignet; qui cellerarius item intranti consignet, ut sciat quid dat aut quid recipit.

Let him who is ending his week's service clean up everything on Saturday. He must wash the towels with which the brethren wipe their hands and feet; and both he who is finishing his service, and he who is entering on it, are to wash the feet of all. Let him hand over to the cellarer the vessels used in his work clean and in sound condition; and let the cellarer hand them to the one entering on his office, that he may know what he gives and what he receives.

After enunciating and explaining the common duty of mutual service our Holy Father enters upon certain technical details, in the interest of cleanliness and good order. Every Saturday the outgoing

---

[1] *Cf.* CALMET, *in* c. xxxv.   [2] *Inst.*, IV., xi.
[3] For instance, the *Rule* of ST. CÆSARIUS *ad virgines*, xii.
[4] UDALR., *Consuet. Clun.*, l. I., c. xlvi.—BERNARD., *Ordo Clun.*, P. I., c. i.—*Constit. Hirsaug.*, l. II., c. xiv.
[5] As in one of the Subiaco monasteries: S. GREG. M., *Dial.*, l. II., c. v.

official [1] of the week is to clean up (*munditias faciat*) in the kitchen and in the refectory. On him falls the duty of washing the towels with which the brethren dry their hands and feet. Every Saturday too, assisted by his successor, he washes the feet of the brethren, in memory of the *mandatum* of Our Lord and as wages for the work of the whole week, as Cassian says. Finally, St. Benedict bids him return the vessels used in his work to the cellarer, clean and in good condition (*munda et sana*) such as they stood in the inventory made or checked the previous week. Constant supervision was necessary in this service, which changed hands each week and gave scope for negligence; and this supervision was reserved to the cellarer, who kept by him an inventory of the articles entrusted to the week's official, just as the Abbot kept the list of all tools and instruments distributed to the holders of the various offices (Chapter XXXII.).

Septimanarii autem, ante unam horam refectionis, accipiant super statutam annonam singulos biberes, et panem: ut hora refectionis, sine murmuratione et gravi labore, serviant fratribus suis. In diebus tamen solemnibus usque ad Missas sustineant.

An hour before the meal these weekly servers shall receive, over and above the appointed allowance, a draught of wine and a piece of bread, so that they may serve the brethren at meal time without murmuring or excessive fatigue. On solemn days, however, let them wait until after Mass.

Here we have another act of condescension on the part of the Rule. Breakfast did not exist in those days, and St. Benedict speaks only of two meals, never of three. Now the weekly servers of the kitchen, besides the fatigue of their duties, would also have their dinner hour delayed. They did not take their places with their brethren when these had been served, as the *Rule of the Master* prescribes;[2] an observation in the thirty-eighth chapter shows that they ate after all the others, along with the reader—*i.e.*, "at second table," as we say nowadays. In order that they may be able to serve without excessive fatigue and without murmuring,[3] our Holy Father grants each of them a drink and a piece of bread, one hour before the common meal. Calmet says: "The word *biber*, from which comes *biberes*, is low Latin and signifies, in the monastic rules, a small vessel containing enough wine for a draught, to refresh oneself." We should translate the words *super statutam annonam* as meaning that it is over and above the ordinary fixed allowance, and not, with some commentators, that it is to be taken from the ordinary allowance; for—we may quote Calmet again—"the preposition *super* in Latin, like *hyper* in Greek, naturally signifies superabundance and not subtraction." We may add that our Holy Father's intention is not to deduct from the ordinary allowance, but to balance by means of a little addition the labours attached to the duty of kitchener. He

---

[1] St. Benedict speaks of the weekly servers sometimes in the singular, sometimes in the plural.
[2] *Reg. Magistri*, xxiii.
[3] *Sine murmure serviant sororibus suis* (S. Aug., *Ep.* CCXI., 13. *P.L.*, XXXIII., 964).

proceeds to observe that this small anticipation of their meal is on solemn days—that is to say feast-days and Sundays—incompatible with the requirements of Communion and the Eucharistic fast. On such days all communicate, and this at the Conventual Mass. The kitchen officials were not to take advantage of the merciful provision of the Rule to omit Holy Communion or break the fast; in spite of the added fatigue of the long liturgy they were to wait until after Mass—that is, to something less than an hour before the common meal—to take their food.[1]

Intrantes et exeuntes hebdomadarii, in oratorio mox Matutinis finitis, Dominica, omnium genibus provolvantur, postulantes pro se orari. Egrediens autem de septimana dicat hunc versum: *Benedictus es Domine Deus, qui adjuvisti me, et consolatus es me*. Quo dicto tertio, accipiat benedictionem egrediens. Subsequatur ingrediens et dicat: *Deus in adjutorium meum intende, Domine ad adjuvandum me festina*. Et hoc idem tertio repetatur ab omnibus. Et accepta benedictione, ingrediatur.

On Sunday, as soon as Lauds are ended, both the incoming and outgoing servers for the week shall cast themselves on their knees in the presence of all and ask their prayers. Let him who is ending his week say this verse: *Benedictus es, Domine Deus, qui adjuvisti me et consolatus es me;* and when this has been said thrice, let him receive the blessing. He who is entering on his office shall then follow, and say: *Deus in adjutorium meum intende, Domine ad adjuvandum me festina*. Let this also be thrice repeated by all; and having received the blessing let him enter on his office.

The chapter ends with the description of a liturgical rite in two parts —viz., absolution for the outgoing servers of the week and installation of the incoming. On Sunday, immediately after Matins (*i.e.*, Lauds) the first prostrate at the feet of all the brethren in the Oratory, begging their prayers.[2] They recite thrice (all together, or the senior monk only) the verse *Benedictus es* (Ps. lxxxv. 17); then the superior gives the blessing, doubtless by saying a collect. Those entering on their week follow, saying thrice the verse *Deus in adjutorium*, which the choir repeats after them (St. Benedict does not say whether the choir repeated also the *Benedictus es*); when the blessing has been received[3] they have entered on their week. Thus they were invested with their charge in the name of Our Lord, and a duty of a very material kind and one often grievous to nature was consecrated by prayer. It became from that moment a religious and meritorious work, accomplished for the glory of God.

[1] *Cf.* PAUL THE DEACON, Commentary *in c.* xxxv.
[2] *Ab omnibus fratribus oratio prosequatur, quæ vel pro ignorationibus intercedat vel pro admissis humana fragilitate peccatis, et commendet Deo velut sacrificium pingue consummata eorum devotionis obsequia* (CASS., *Inst.*, IV., xix.). Among the Eastern monks this was done after the evening meal on Sundays.
[3] The two prayers which we use come from Monte Cassino and Cluny (UDALR., *Consuet. Clun.*, l. II., c. xxxv.).

CHAPTER XXXVI

OF THE SICK BRETHREN

WE may remember that in Chapter XXXI. St. Benedict confided the sick and children to the care of the cellarer; we may remember also that in Chapter XXXIV. the Holy Rule would have more attention given to those who require more. To make his meaning plain and to clear up some points, our Holy Father, after settling the conditions of service in the kitchen, treats separately of the care due to the sick and infirm (Chapter XXXVI.), the aged and children (Chapter XXXVII.). The chapters form a kind of parenthesis, and after them St. Benedict returns to the subject of the refectory and meals.

DE INFIRMIS FRATRIBUS.—Infirmorum cura ante omnia et super omnia adhibenda est, ut sicut revera Christo, ita eis serviatur, quia ipse dixit: *Infirmus fui, et visitastis me.* Et: *Quod fecistis uni de his minimis meis, mihi fecistis.* Sed et ipsi infirmi considerent in honorem Dei sibi serviri, et non superfluitate sua contristent fratres suos servientes sibi. Qui tamen patienter portandi sunt: quia de talibus copiosior merces acquiritur. Ergo cura maxima sit Abbati, ne aliquam negligentiam patiantur.

Before all things and above all things care must be taken of the sick, so that they may be served in very deed as Christ Himself; for He has said: "I was sick and ye visited me" and, "As long as ye did it to one of these, my least brethren, ye did it to me." But let the sick themselves consider that they are served for the honour of God, and not grieve their brethren who serve them by their importunity. Yet must they be patiently borne with, because from such as these is gained more abundant reward. Therefore the Abbot shall take the greatest care that they suffer no neglect.

In this matter, again, the inspiration of faith must guide our conduct. In a general way, Our Lord is near us, taking the form of our neighbour whoever he may be. Nay, our neighbour is Christ. We live with His Real Presence; for we meet with naught else but God, both in us and around us. We are ever serving God, and our acts of love ascend to Him. "All that ye shall do to one of these my little ones, ye shall do to me" (Matt. xxv. 40). This is more especially true of our religious brethren and of their consecrated persons; and when they suffer, they resemble our Lord Jesus Christ all the more. Therefore they shall be served just as though they were Christ Himself, for He says: " I was sick and you visited me " (Matt. xxv. 36). A gain indeed for the sick, but our gain also. Is not this ideal of faith enough to give abundant peace and joy to those visited by sickness and debility, and to inspire also in those who tend them true tenderness of heart ? It is this very thought, more than a sentiment of natural compassion, that caused our Holy Father's emphasis of language: " Before all things and above all things care must be taken of the sick, and they shall be served in very deed as Christ Himself."[1] No other Rule displayed so much solicitude with regard to the weak and suffering.

In return for this supernatural tendance with its character of reverence, the sick shall endeavour really to resemble the Lord by their gentle humility, self-denial. and moderation. They shall remember that these attentions are paid, not to their poor persons, but to God hidden in them. They shall be careful not to sadden by unreasonable demands and unrestrained importunity (*superfluitate sua*) the brethren who are employed in their service, as their brethren and not as their servants. According to the author of the *Imitation of Christ* it is hard to grow holy in illness: *Pauci ex infirmitate meliorantur* (I. xxiii.). We become impatient, effeminate, almost luxurious. Temperament reasserts itself, and with the help of the devil nature becomes insolent again. The habit of living on exceptions and a special régime stealthily saps the spirit of monastic observance, and we practically become persuaded that sickness dispenses us from being monks Active suffering is perhaps less dangerous from this point of view than a perpetual state of indisposition and what is now called neurasthenia. To souls who are tempted to occupy themselves excessively with the care of their health, who are always complaining and always in search of new remedies, we might recommend the careful reading of a chapter in the *Way of Perfection*. St. Teresa writes: " Believe it, daughters, when once we begin to subdue these bodies of ours they do not so much molest us. There will be enough to observe what ye have need of. Take no care for yourselves except there be a manifest necessity. Unless we resolve once for all to accept death, and the loss of our health, we shall never do anything."[2] The letters of the Saint show us, however, how far she busied herself with the health of others and how she exercised her ingenuity in procuring small luxuries for the sick. A monk, even if seriously ill, ought to be able to do without extraordinary and expensive remedies, such as a periodical " cure " at some watering-place; and he will never ask the help of his family.

Even if the sick show themselves exacting, says St. Benedict, they must be patiently borne with, since from them is gained a more abundant reward. Moreover, so that no excuse for complaint may be given, and to realize fully what Our Lord expects from our charity, the Abbot must watch with the greatest care that the sick are not treated with neglect nor suffer from the unskilfulness or ignorance of anyone.

Quibus fratribus infirmis sit cella super se deputata, et servitor timens Deum, et diligens ac sollicitus. Bal-	And let a cell be set apart by itself for the sick brethren and an attendant be appointed who is God-fearing,

---

[1] *Quali affectu debemus infirmis fratribus ministrare ? Sicut ipsi Domino offerentes obsequium, qui dixit: Quia cum fecistis uni ex minimis istis fratribus meis, mihi fecistis* (S. BASIL., *Reg. contr.*, xxxvi.). And St. Basil also adds in the second part of this rule and in the next that the sick should show themselves worthy of such honour.

[2] Chapter XI.

neorum usus infirmis, quoties expedit, offeratur. Sanis autem, et maxime juvenibus, tardius concedatur. Sed et carnium esus infirmis, omninoque debilibus pro reparatione concedatur. At ubi meliorati fuerint, a carnibus more solito omnes abstineant.

prompt, and painstaking. Let the use of baths be granted to the sick as often as it shall be expedient; but to those who are well, and especially to the young, baths shall be seldom permitted. The use of meat, too, shall be permitted to the sick and to the very weak, that they may recover their strength; but, when they are restored to health, let all abstain from meat in the accustomed manner.

There shall be special accommodation in the monastery for the sick, for all who cannot follow the common observance, and who need special care, a purer air, and more quiet. In the great abbeys of former days the infirmary was almost a second monastery, with its own church,[1] cloister, kitchen, refectory, and dormitory. Our Holy Father evidently means each monastic family to care for its sick in the monastery itself. And we might well be astonished should a religious express the desire to go seek his cure with his parents, or friends in the world. Likewise, it would be far from consistent with the spirit and traditions of the Benedictine Order to collect in a single *sanatorium*, or in a retreat, all the sick of a Congregation or a province. We should deprive them thus of that share in the religious life which is compatible with their state and leave them to finish their days in very prosaic fashion. Above all, we should deprive communities of the advantage of their charity and of the edification generally given by the sick and the old. Those who are on the threshold of eternity have a special title to the delicate attentions which they can only receive from their Abbot and their brethren. To prepare them to appear in the presence of Infinite Purity, to complete the work of forming them to the image of God, surely this is to serve Christ in their persons and to win for ourselves the blessing and gratitude of God. The arrangements for the sick in the Congregation of St. Maur are noteworthy. In order that they might never have to suffer by the pecuniary distress of a particular monastery, all the expenses—viz., medicines (except white sugar), doctors' fees, and the fees of chemists and surgeons, food purchased for them, journeys, etc. —were charged to the Congregation and had to be regulated by the Diet.[2]

The *cella* for the sick is to be entrusted to the infirmarian, whom

[1] The old Customaries dispense the sick from the Divine Office only in very serious cases. This is what we read in the *Disciplina Farfensis: Illi fratres qui non valent surgere, eant famuli servientes eis et educant illos sustentantes ulnis suis in ecclesia, atque collocent ut melius potuerint. Ingratum nulli apparere debet hoc factum; quia sæpe vidimus in eodem die fratrem finire ex hac luce et ad Christum transire, etiam in ipsa ecclesia exhalare spiritum. Quis de talibus dubitet quod non statim ad regnum polorum penetrent ?* . . . *Ita debent opus Dei per omnia agere sicut sani in monasterio, præter quod leniter atque cursim dicant.* . . . *Illi vero qui ita nimietate infirmitatis detinentur quod nullo modo consurgere valeant, mox ut monasterio fuerint celebrata nocturnalia obsequia, annuat ille qui ordinem tenet duobus fratribus qui illis divinum opus decantent,* etc. (l. II., c. lii.).

[2] *Regula S. P. Benedicti cum declarationibus Congregationis S. Mauri* (1663), pp. 144-145.

St. Benedict calls the "attendant" (*servitor*), but who was certainly a monk and not a secular. The infirmarian is to have assistants, if necessary; St. Benedict implies as much by using the plural *servitoribus* at the end of this chapter. Our Holy Father finds three words adequate to sum up the personal qualities of a good infirmarian. He must be God-fearing—that is, habitually guided by the spirit of faith in all his dealings with the sick; he must be prompt, for those who suffer are tried by long delays; and he must be attentive and kind.[1] We might add that he has a right to absolute obedience from his patients. To doctor yourself in your own fashion, or according to the prescriptions of brethren who have no authority to interfere, is a very dangerous form of self-will: "since they are permitted to have neither body nor will in their own power." Moreover, it is by no means profitable for monks to take pleasure in discussing their health with one another.

Without here entering into detail with regard to the treatment required by various diseases,[2] St. Benedict only considers two sorts of relief—viz., baths and the use of flesh meat. We know how plentiful at Rome were the *thermæ* or public baths. Every great house had its baths, and they formed part of the daily programme of every gentleman. Monasticism complied with this custom in a measure; and Cassiodorus, St. Benedict's contemporary, installed baths in his monastery of Vivarium. They were indispensable in a hot country for monks who devoted themselves to manual labour and did not wear underclothing. And obviously monks did not go to the public baths, first because they rarely dwelt in a town, and then because such public bathing would have had its dangers. St. Benedict requires that baths be offered to the sick, not sparingly, but as often as health may be benefited by them. "But to those who are well, and especially to the young, baths shall seldom be permitted." Our Holy Father does not dispense the healthy and the young from a measure of precaution which is doubly necessary in community life. Certainly he makes a limitation; but this limitation is not inspired by a sort of foolish panic, otherwise he would simply have forbidden the use of baths. The word *tardius* (lit., more slowly) should be considered in the light of Roman custom and of the generous treatment which St. Benedict employs towards the sick. It is notorious that baths, especially hot baths, when very frequent, have the result of enervating the body, and of inducing sloth and a sort of decay of the will. St. Benedict did not want worldly manners in his monasteries; yet he stipulates that baths be offered to the sick, while being permitted, at rarer intervals, to those in health.[3] The ancient monks often took our Holy Father's

---

[1] *Cf.* S. CÆSAR., *Reg. ad virgines*, xxx.

[2] On the subject of bloodletting (*minutio*) and the employment of doctors by the ancient monks, see CALMET, *in h. l.*—On the treatment of sick, dying, and dead monks, see HÆFTEN, l. XI., tract. v.—MARTÈNE, *De ant. monach. rit.*, l. V., c. viii.–xiii.—PIGNOT gives a summary of the customs of Cluny: *Hist. de l' Ordre de Cluny*, t. II., pp. 434–435, 463–473.

[3] *Lavacra etiam, cujus infirmitas exposcit, minime denegentur: sed fiat sine murmuratione de consilio medicinæ. . . . Si autem nulla infirmitate compellitur, cupiditati suæ non præbeatur assensus* (S. CÆSAR., *Reg. ad virg.*, xxix.).

restriction too literally. Paul the Deacon observes that they bathed once, twice, or three times a year. Calmet writes: "At present, especially in temperate regions, the use of them is almost abolished. Likewise there is now no question in monasteries of regular household baths. In case of sickness permission is given to go to the public baths, with the reservations and precautions of which we have spoken." But hygiene and charity may take this matter differently without injuring monastic austerity or the spirit of mortification.[1]

St. Benedict adds that the sick and those who are very weak[2] may eat meat "that they may recover their strength" (*pro reparatione*). And, to mark plainly the character of this concession, our Holy Father would have it end so soon as their health no longer requires it. Then, all will abstain from meat in the accustomed manner (*more solito*).[3] The same recommendation is repeated in Chapter XXXIX., and we may reserve our commentary till then.

Curam autem maximam habeat Abbas, ne a cellerariis aut servitoribus negligantur infirmi: quia ad ipsum respicit, quicquid a discipulis delinquitur.	Let the Abbot take all possible care that the sick be not neglected by the cellarers or their attendants; because he is responsible for whatever is done amiss by his disciples.

For the second time the Abbot is required to take very great care of the sick. He must watch that they be not neglected by the cellarers or the infirmarians; for he is responsible for all the shortcomings of his disciples. Let us add that no one in the monastery may be indifferent to the sick; all should remember them in their prayers and visit them with the permission of the Abbot. But the ordinances of the Rule do not lapse in the case of the sick, and their cells should never be turned into parlours.

---

[1] On the care of tonsure and beard among the ancient monks, see Hæften, l. V., tract. ix.—Martène, *De ant. monach. rit.*, l. V., c. vii.—Calmet, Commentary on Chapter I.

[2] We should read *infirm* ‹ *omnino debilibus*.

[3] *Pullos et carnes nunquam sani accipiant; infirmis quicquid necesse fuerit ministretur* (S. Cæsar., *Reg. ad mon.*, xxiv.). *Quia solet fieri, ut cella monasterii non semper bonum vinum habeat, ad sanctæ Abbatissæ curam pertinebit ut tale vinum provideat, unde aut infirmæ, aut illæ quæ sunt delicatius nutritæ, palpentur* (S. Cæsar., *Reg. ad virg.*, xxviii.). *Ægrotantes sic tractandæ sunt, ut citius convalescant; sed cum vires pristinas reparaverint, redeant ad feliciorem abstinentiæ consuetudinem* (*ibid.*, xx.).

CHAPTER XXXVII

OF OLD MEN AND CHILDREN

DE SENIBUS VEL INFANTIBUS.—Licet ipsa natura humana trahatur ad misericordiam in his ætatibus, senum videlicet et infantum: tamen et regulæ auctoritas eis prospiciat. Consideretur semper in eis imbecillitas, et nullatenus eis districtio regulæ teneatur in alimentis; sed sit in eis pia consideratio, et præveniant horas canonicas.

Although human nature of itself is drawn to feel pity and consideration for these two times of life—viz. for old men and children—yet the authority of the Rule should also provide for them. Let their weakness be always taken into account, and let the full rigour of the Rule as regards food be in no wise maintained in their regard; but let a kind consideration be shown for them, and let them anticipate the regular hours.

MERE humanity, says St. Benedict, will give us sympathy and indulgence towards these two periods of life, old age and childhood; yet the authority of the Rule should also intervene in their favour. Charity is something better than mere philanthropy, and the fundamental motive of our actions should be supernatural. Moreover, we must note carefully that dispensations, permissions, and kindly interpretations of the Rule, appertain still to the Rule and emanate from authority; they have not their source in caprice, arbitrary action, or relaxation.

Therefore regard shall always be shown towards the weakness of children and the aged, and the austerity of the Rule as to food shall by no means be applied to them.[1] Instead they shall be treated with a tender considerateness and permitted to eat before the regular hours (*præveniant horas canonicas*). In one word, everything shall be done so that the monastic life, which does not consist in levelling and uniformity, may remain possible for them. St. Benedict did not think it proper to enter into precise details, but has left all to the discretion of the Abbot. It is his duty to determine, in each case, when childhood ends and when old age begins; to decide whether one or several supplementary meals should be granted, or only some small instalments, analogous to the solace supplied to the kitchen servers, readers, and monks who have been employed in some fatiguing occupation. We know from a sentence in Chapter LXIII. that the children had their meals with the community. Discussing the words *in alimentis*, D. Ménard observes that the exceptions spoken of by St. Benedict concerned the quality rather than the quantity of food, for we find in Chapter XXXIX. the

---

[1] *Vinum tantum senes accipiunt, quibus cum parvulis sæpe fit prandium, ut aliorum fessa sustentetur ætas, aliorum non frangatur incipiens* (S. HIERON., *Ép.* XXII., 35. P.L., XXII., 420). *In cena mensa ponitur propter laborantes, senes et pueros, æstusque gravissimos* (S. HIERON., *Præfatio in Reg. S. Pachom.*, 5).

words " the same quantity shall not be given to young children, but a lesser amount than to their elders." The child's stomach, says D. Ménard, is too small to digest an abundance of viands; an old man's stomach is too cold, and indulgence in an ill-regulated diet might destroy the little heat that is left; as Hippocrates teaches.

CHAPTER XXXVIII

THE WEEKLY READER

De hebdomadario lectore. — Mensis fratrum edentium lectio deesse non debet; nec fortuito casu, qui arripuerit codicem legere audeat ibi, sed lecturus tota hebdomada, Dominica ingrediatur.

When the brethren are taking their meals there should always be reading. Yet no one shall presume at haphazard to take the book and read; but let him who is to read throughout the week enter on his office on Sunday.

READING must never be lacking at the public meals. Cassian[1] tells us that this custom comes from the Cappadocian[2] monks and not from those of Egypt; St. Benedict found it in St. Cæsarius as well.[3] The purpose is clear, and was as follows. Though their meals were frugal in the extreme, it aimed at distracting attention from that poor pittance and at moderating the animal satisfaction in eating and drinking by an appeal to the things of piety and the mind; that is the motive invoked by St. Basil. However, Cassian notes another: "It cannot be doubted," he says, "that the Cappadocians adopted this practice, not so much for the spiritual nurture of their minds, as for the purpose of cutting short superfluous and idle talk and especially those disputes which arise at most meals; they saw no other way of suppressing them." Monastic tradition adopted this reading at table unanimously. Often it even took the plural *mensis* of the text quite literally, so that there was reading at first table—*i.e.*, at the community meal; reading at second table—*i.e.*, the servers' meal; reading at the table of the Abbot and guests; reading for the sick; and even at the meals of monks on a journey.

What was read? Calmet says: "In the Order of St. Benedict, Sacred Scripture was more commonly read; and since each part of the year has its special books of the Scriptures to be read in choir, what was not read in the choir was read in the refectory, in such a way that, in the course of the year, the whole of the Scriptures was read both in the choir and in the refectory. Often the homily begun at Matins was continued in the refectory. The Acts and Passions of the saints and martyrs were also read there. . . ." The Rule too was read, perhaps from the time of St. Benedict himself; for he says: "We wish this Rule to be read frequently in the community so that no brother may plead ignorance as an excuse" (Chapter LXVI.) Custom now adds to this list certain historical works which are concerned in some way with Church matters or the monastic life. We may profit much by the reading in the refectory. If the refectory be a place where we recruit our bodily

---

[1] *Inst.*, IV., xvii. [2] *Cf.* S. Basil., *Reg. brev.*, clxxx.
[3] *Sedentes ad mensam taceant, et animum lectioni intendant. Cum autem lectio cessaverit, meditatio sancta de corde non cesset. Si vero aliquid opus fuerit, quæ mensæ præest sollicitudinem gerat, et quod est necessarium nutu magis quam voce petat. Nec solæ vobis fauces sumant cibum, sed et aures audiant Dei verbum* (Reg. ad virg., xvi.). *Cf. Reg. ad mon.*, ix.

strength, it is also a place where prayer is easy and intellectual labour very sweet and almost unconscious.

Let us speak now of the reader. His office is grave, and it should be fulfilled with gravity. The first-comer, chosen haphazard, or even appointed by his own choice and impelled by the desire of self-display, shall not seize the book and make himself, impromptu, the reader for a meal; reading in the refectory is to be a regular office, commencing on the Sunday and continuing throughout the whole week. At the end of the chapter, in a final sentence which seems to have been added at the dictate of experience, St. Benedict comes back to this regulation. Neither individual will, nor chance and circumstances, nor the order of the community, should designate those who are to read or chant, whether in refectory or choir; the Abbot must choose those who can make themselves heard and understood, and be really useful to their brethren: who can " edify " them. In the time of St. Benedict not everyone could read; and even nowadays to be able to read well in public in a large refectory is not a common gift. Aptitudes differ, but in any case it is difficult to read without preparation. If we respect ourselves and our audience we shall prepare carefully. A man must be able to divide clauses intelligently, and to break up a period in such a way as to give each portion of it its proper value. And this may be realized even in the style of reading called *recto tono* (monotone); for properly speaking there is no such reading, since intelligence and accentuation are every instant modulating quite perceptibly the note on which the reading is read. It is not necessary to have a powerful voice, nor even a clear one; but it is important to know the voice which you have and the place in which you are reading, and to adjust yourself to these conditions. The settled purpose of making yourself heard at both ends of the room involves an unconscious adaptation of means to end. We should read slowly, articulate mute syllables, without swelling the voice on the open ones, and remember that we are not reading privately nor holding a conversation. In the midst of noise and when minds are inevitably distracted, it is indispensable that the meaning should reach each one where he sits and that no effort should be needed to catch it.

Qui ingrediens, post Missas et communionem petat ab omnibus pro se orari, ut avertat ab eo Deus spiritum elationis. Et dicatur hic versus in oratorio tertio ab omnibus, ipso tamen incipiente: *Domine labia mea aperies, et os meum annuntiabit laudem tuam;* et sic accepta benedictione, ingrediatur ad legendum.

Let this brother, when beginning his service, ask all after Mass and Communion to pray for him, that God may keep from him the spirit of pride. And let this verse be said thrice in the oratory by all, he, the reader, first beginning: *Domine labia mea aperies, et os meum annuntiabit laudem tuam.* And so, having received the blessing, let him enter on his reading.

Investiture in this office, as was the case with the kitchen servers, is accomplished by a blessing. The blessing of the reader took place after Mass and Communion on Sundays. The brother begged the prayers of all, either in words, or by prostrating or bowing in the middle of the choir. He said thrice the verse *Domine* (Ps. l. 17) and the whole community repeated it after him. Then the Abbot gave the blessing, probably chanting a collect; " and so, having received the blessing, let him enter on his reading." We have preserved the whole of this rite,[1] and in the collect we ask God to avert from the reader " the spirit of pride and ignorance."[2] Our Holy Father mentions only pride explicitly. In his time, as we may repeat, only a picked few could read Latin well, without clumsiness or barbarism. Moreover, this spiritual precaution against vanity is always seasonable; for the reader occupies a conspicuous position; he alone is speaking amidst universal silence; he is tempted to think that he is producing a great effect; and he is liable to look round him to make sure of the general admiration.

Summumque fiat silentium ad mensam, ut nullius mussitatio vel vox, nisi solius legentis, ibi audiatur. Quæ vero necessaria sunt comedentibus et bibentibus, sibi sic invicem ministrent fratres, ut nullus indigeat petere aliquid. Si quid tamen opus fuerit, sonitu cujuscumque signi potius petatur quam voce. Nec præsumat ibi aliquis de ipsa lectione, aut aliunde quicquam requirere, ne detur occasio maligno, nisi forte prior voluerit pro ædificatione aliquid breviter dicere.

Let the greatest silence be kept at table, so that no whispering nor voice, save the voice of the reader alone, be heard there. Whatever is required for eating and drinking the brethren shall minister to each other so that no one need ask for anything. But should anything be wanted, let it be asked for by the noise of some sign rather than by the voice. Let no one ask any question there about what is being read or about anything else, lest occasion be given to the Evil One; unless, perhaps, the superior should wish to say something briefly for the edification of the brethren.

Complete and profound silence should reign at table, a strict law which has prevailed always and everywhere among monks.[3] No whispering should be heard in the refectory, nor any other voice but that of the reader. Interchange of ideas is forbidden, even though performed in a low voice, and into your neighbour's ear. It would be very bad taste to read your letters during the reading, or some book of your own which interests you more. Likewise we should give up mocking and sly applications or allusions, made by means of gestures or smiles or fixed looks; doubtless we have not got to be impassive as statues in the refectory, no more than in the oratory; but these petty manifestations, even though they hurt no one, are seldom becoming.

[1] And we have also adopted the very ancient custom of asking a blessing before the reading which accompanies each meal. *Cf.* UDALR., *Consuet. Clun.*, l. II., c. xxxiv.

[2] The form we employ is very like the one already indicated by SMARAGDUS: *Averte, quæsumus, Domine, ab hoc famulo tuo spiritum elationis, ut humiliter legens, sensum et intellectum capiat lectionis.*

[3] See the enactments collected by MARTÈNE in his Commentary.—*Est autem eis et in capiendo cibo summum silentium* (RUFIN., *Hist. monach.*, c. iii. ROSWEYD, p. 458). *Tantum silentium ab omnibus exhibetur, ut, cum in tanta numerositas fratrum refectionis obtentu consederit, nullus ne muttire quidem audeat præter eum, qui suæ decaniæ præest, qui tamen si quid mensæ superinferri vel auferri necessarium esse perviderit, sonitu potius quam voce significat* (CASS., *Inst.*, IV., xvii.).—*Cf.* S. PACH., *Reg.*, xxxiii.—S. CÆSAR., *Reg. ad virg.*, xvi.

Not even fraternal charity excuses a breakage of silence. Cassian tells us that in the monastery of St. Pachomius " each monk had his hood lowered over his eyes, so that he could see only the table and the food placed before him, and so that none could note the manner in which his neighbour ate nor the quantity of his portion." St. Benedict is more amiable and courteous, prescribing that the brethren shall serve each other with all that is necessary for the meal, so that no one may have need to ask for anything, and the law of silence be kept, and of charity also. No one should be so absorbed in his own business as to be unable to perceive what his brethren lack. Moreover, there are the *hebdomadarii* and the kitchen servers, moving to and fro and attentive all through the meal. If there be need to ask anything from your neighbour or the servers, it should be done by means of a sign, by some recognized sound, rather than by words: *Sonitu cujuscumque signi potius petatur quam voce.* Several ancient Rules express themselves in the same terms. Evidently some moderate sign was intended, for a great clatter would have been as prejudicial to recollection and the reading as talking. Modern monastic customs have suppressed all signs of a noisy character; only in cafés is the waiter summoned by striking a glass or the table.

The refectory silence may be broken not only by noise and by exchange of words relative to the serving, but also, St. Benedict says, by questions about the reading or some other subject. No one would venture in practice to address a question to the superior at this time; but we may be tempted to engage in a little dialogue with a neighbour. The Rule does not allow it, *ne detur occasio*, so that every occasion of levity, disputation, and pride may be suppressed. The word *maligno* (to the Evil One) does not belong to the original text, but is a gloss added by analogy with two other passages of the Rule (in Chapters XLIII. and LIV.).

The hours when we give our bodies what they require in order to live are dangerous hours, as are those immediately after the meal; it is wise to protect oneself then against the attacks of the devil; which is one of the reasons why we sanctify our meals with prayer, reading, and silence. Our Holy Father allows only the superior (*prior*) to say a few words " for edification," but briefly, and he need not consider himself obliged to do so.[1]

Frater autem hebdomadarius accipiat mixtum prius quam incipiat legere, propter communionem sanctam, et ne forte grave sit ei jejunium sustinere: postea autem cum coquinæ hebdomadariis et servitoribus reficiat.	The brother who is reader for the week shall receive a sop before he begins to read, on account of the Holy Communion, and lest it be too hard for him to fast so long. He shall take his meal afterwards with the weekly cooks and servers.

These final directions concern the meal of the weekly reader. In the first place, before commencing to read,[2] he is to receive a *mixtum*.

---

[1] *Nec alicujus audiatur sermo, nisi divinus, qui ex pagina proferatur, et ejus qui præest Patris* (Reg. I. SS. Patrum, viii.). *Ad mensam specialiter nullus loquatur, nisi qui præest, vel qui interrogatus fuerit* (S. Macar., Reg. xviii.).

[2] Perhaps immediately before and not *ante unam horam* as the kitchen servers: these latter needed to be fortified for the immediate preparations of the meal, the most trying part of their work.

The word *mixtum* meant for the ancients wine mixed with substances which tempered its taste and strength, or wine diluted with water, and so contrasted with *merum* (unmixed wine); sometimes it merely means wine or any beverage, just as the word *miscere* (to mix) signifies to pour out for drinking. It is possible that by the "mixture" granted to the reader St. Benedict means only a cup of wine diluted with water;[1] but it is certain that, shortly after his time, many assimilated it in practice to the little extra allowance granted to the kitchen servers, the *singulos biberes et panem*, and the *mixtum* became a draught of wine with some pieces of bread steeped in it.

Our Holy Father gives two reasons for this custom. Both are valid only for the first meal, which was often the sole meal of the day. And the first reason given, "on account of the Holy Communion," holds only for Sundays and solemn feasts, the days on which all the monks received Holy Communion. In this case the *mixtum* certainly plays the part of an ablution. In the first centuries of the Church (as still done now at certain liturgical functions, such as ordination, profession, etc.) communicants were given a draught of unconsecrated wine (sometimes with a morsel of bread), in order to help the swallowing of the sacred species and to prevent any accident. In St. Benedict's practice the meal probably followed Mass very closely.[2] And it is possible that the custom of Monte Cassino was the same as that which we find in the Rule of the Master, where dinner commenced with the distribution of blessed wine with some morsels of bread steeped in it; the Master orders that the reader also should take this beverage and he gives as reason: "As soon as the Abbot first of all at the table has taken his wine, let the reader also take his lest he spit out the Sacrament, and so let him begin to read."[3] On Sundays and feast-days, according to St. Benedict's provision, the kitchen servers also took their little refection after Mass, and, on those days, in company with the reader. When there was not Holy Communion, the *mixtum* at least took the edge off hunger, and allowed the monk to wait without excessive fatigue for the meal which reader, weekly servers, and cooks took together. Our Holy Father does not tell us whether the reader received this *mixtum* before supper also.

Fratres autem non per ordinem legant aut cantent, sed qui ædificent audientes.	The brethren, however, are not to read or chant according to their order, but such only as may edify the hearers.

The explanation of this short sentence is given at the beginning of the chapter.

---

[1] Cf. *Explication ascétique et historique de la Règle de saint Benoît*, chapter xxxviii.
[2] Cf. PAUL THE DEACON, Commentary *in* c. xxxv., pp. 333–334.
[3] *Reg. Magistri*, xxiv.; cf. *ibid.*, xxvii. Read the commentary of CALMET on our text, and especially, in the *Ouvrages posthumes* of MABILLON (t. II., pp. 272–320), the *Traité où l'on réfute la nouvelle explication que quelques auteurs donnent aux mots de Messe et de Communion qui se trouvent dans la Règle de saint Benoît*, and the *Addition au précédent traité*.

CHAPTER XXXIX

OF THE MEASURE OF FOOD

DE MENSURA CIBORUM.—Sufficere credimus ad refectionem quotidianam tam sextæ, quam nonæ, omnibus mensis cocta duo pulmentaria, propter diversorum infirmitates: ut forte qui ex uno non poterit edere, ex alio reficiatur. Ergo duo pulmentaria cocta fratribus sufficiant; et si fuerint inde poma, aut nascentia leguminum, addatur et tertium.

We think it sufficient for the daily meal, whether at the sixth or the ninth hour, that there be at all the tables two dishes of cooked food, because of the variety of men's weaknesses: so that he who may not be able to eat of the one may make his meal of the other. Therefore let two cooked dishes suffice for the brethren; and if there be any fruit or young vegetables, let a third dish be added.

IF the Fathers of the desert could have read this chapter of the Rule they would perhaps have regarded its provisions as lax. Some of their masters[1] certainly recommended discretion in abstinence and fasting, quite in St. Benedict's fashion; but the most generous measure of an Eastern monk is less than the fare which our Holy Father allows daily to his disciples, comprising as this does three courses. And yet St. Benedict only puts this régime forward with reserve, as a reasonable mean allowance (*sufficere credimus*), leaving the Abbot power to add to it. Such considerateness is easily justified if we recognize the entirely relative value of mortification[2] and remember the end at which our Holy Father was aiming. He wished to make the monastic life accessible to souls that might be deterred by extreme austerity. He wished to adapt his Rule to Western constitutions, and to a more rigorous climate, which compels men to compensate for the lack of external warmth by the use of more potent bodily fuel. We must add that he wrote for men who not only performed long liturgical duties, but also laboured in the open air for part of the day. The fare which he gives his monks is practically peasants' fare, simple and plentiful.

At all the tables[3] (that is to say, at those occupied by the monks in small groups, under the presidency of the deans; or else at the community table, the servers' table, and the Abbot's)—at all the tables two cooked dishes (*cocta duo pulmentaria*)[4] shall be served; St. Benedict does not think it suitable or even possible to be precise as to their nature. Usage

---

[1] S. BASIL., *Reg. fus.*, xix.—CASS., *Conlat.*, II., xvi.–xxvi.

[2] CASS., *Conlat.*, XXI., xi.–xvii.

[3] In spite of what CALMET says, the best reading of the manuscripts is certainly this, and not *omnibus mensibus*, at every season; the fact is that a difference was sometimes made between the régime of summer and that of winter: *Cf.* CATO, *De re rustica*, c. lvi.–lviii. Cato would have workers receive a *hemina* of wine in the fourth month, three *heminæ* in the ninth, tenth, and eleventh. He speaks in the same place about the *pulmentarium* of olives.

[4] *Pulmentarium* means a dish of any sort, but especially stew, mash, or pudding: *cf.* CALMET, *in h. l.*

has varied enormously in this matter, nor need we attempt to summarize it. Vegetables have always formed the basis of monastic fare; eggs, fish, and milk products appeared more rarely at their table in former days. At Cluny they served cooked beans every day, and this was the staple dish *par excellence*.[1] St. Benedict naturally does not order the eating of the two dishes; he allows them so that all appetites may be satisfied and that all may recruit their strength: *propter diversorum infirmitates*. He adds that, thanks to the two courses, a brother who cannot eat of one will be able to make his meal on the other. But have we the right, according to the Rule, to patronize both ? Commentators are agreed among themselves, and with custom, in answering in the affirmative. So let two cooked dishes suffice for the brethren, continues St. Benedict; and let a third be added of fruit or fresh vegetables, if they can be procured easily—that is to say, if they are in the monastery garden (*si fuerint inde* [or *unde*]).

The menu our Holy Father has just given is that of the whole day— the quantity of food supplied each day or the daily fare—whether there were two meals or only one, both in Lent and during the rest of the year. At least that is the best-founded interpretation[2] of the very concise phrase of the Rule: " for the daily meal whether at the sixth or the ninth hour." St. Benedict only speaks of the meal at the sixth or ninth hour; when dinner was at the sixth hour there was supper in the evening, but the meal at the sixth hour was the chief one and probably furnished supper not only with that third part of bread of which St. Benedict speaks presently, but also with such articles of food as were better suited to a frugal supper. On the fast-days appointed by the Rule, dinner was at the ninth hour; during the ecclesiastical Lent, the sole meal was taken in the evening; but the quantity of food was always the same, St. Benedict leaving it to the discretion of each individual to make such retrenchment as was compatible with health and obedience (Chapter XLIX.). Most ancient monastic customaries confirm these comments.

Panis libra una propensa sufficiat in die, sive una sit refectio, sive prandii et cenæ. Quod si cenaturi sunt, de eadem libra tertia pars a cellerario servetur, reddenda cenaturis.

Let a pound weight of bread suffice for each day, whether there be but one meal, or both dinner and supper. If they are to sup let a third part of the pound be kept back by the cellarer and given to them for supper.

Every day, whether there be but one meal or both dinner and supper, a pound of bread shall suffice, a generous pound of full weight, turning the scale definitely (*propensa*). If there be supper, the cellarer shall reserve the third part of this pound. Markings made in the baking probably facilitated this partition.[3] Endless discussions have arisen as to the exact quantity of the " pound weight," just as with the *hemina*

---

[1] BERNARD., *Ordo Clun.*, P. I., c. vi., xlvii.—UDALR., *Consuet. Clun.*, l. II., c. xxv.
[2] See especially the Commentary of CALMET.
[3] *Cf.* S. GREG. M., *Dial.*, l. I., c. xi. *P.L.*, LXXVII., 212.

of wine spoken of in the next chapter.¹ All these researches have their interest for curiosity and erudition, but they have none whatever as true commentary and elucidation of the Rule. Even if we suppose that measures, while keeping the same names, have not varied with time and country, it is clear in the case before us that our Holy Father employs the customary measures in an approximate and not in an exact way. His pound of bread is something over a pound, the capacity of his *hemina* is perhaps calculated in a way that would satisfy the requirements of weaker brethren. But what is still more decisive is the care which the monks of Monte Cassino took to preserve the weight of bread and measure of wine fixed by our Holy Father. They carried them to Rome in A.D. 581, when they were driven out by the Lombards;² perhaps Petronax and the restorers of Monte Cassino recovered them, thanks to Pope Zachary (A.D. 741-752);³ finally, Theodemar, Abbot of Monte Cassino, sent to Charlemagne the measures of bread and wine as determined by St. Benedict.⁴ All these precautions were superfluous, if the pound and the *hemina* were invariable measures, known to all and in current use. And it is quite clear that they were not preserved as memorials of our Holy Father, but as special standards appointed by him.⁵ The Roman pound was equivalent, according to recent calculations, to 327·45 grammes (11¼ ounces avoirdupois approx.).⁶ This would be a small amount as the daily ration of men working in the fields. Calmet says there is reason to believe that St. Benedict did not take the Roman pound, containing 12 ounces (Roman), but the pound of commerce, containing 16.⁷ Many commentators find even this too small. Our Constitutions wisely declare that, since the value of St. Benedict's pound is unknown, bread shall be given without restriction.

Quod si labor forte factus fuerit major, in arbitrio et potestate Abbatis erit, si expediat, aliquid augere, remota præ omnibus crapula, ut nunquam surripiat monacho indigeries: quia nihil sic contrarium est omni christiano quomodo crapula, sicut ait Dominus noster: *Videte ne graventur*

If, however, their work have been greater, it shall be at the will and in the power of the Abbot, if it be expedient, to make some addition, provided that excess be before all things avoided, that no monk suffer from surfeiting. For nothing is more contrary to any Christian life than excess, as Our Lord

---

¹ *Cf.* Hæften, l. X., tract. iii.-iv.—Lancelot, *Dissertation sur l'hémine de vin et sur la livre de pain de saint Benoist et des autres anciens religieux* (Paris, 1667; second and more complete edition, 1668).—Mabillon, *Acta SS. O.S.B.*, Sæc. IV., P. I., Præf., 152-165.

² *Cf.* Pauli Diac., *De gestis Langobardorum*, l. IV., c. xviii. *P.L.*, XCV., 548.

³ *Ibid.*, l. VI., c. xl. *P.L.*, XCV., 650-651.

⁴ Pauli Diac., *Epist*. I. *P.L.*, XCV., 1585.

⁵ There is preserved at Monte Cassino a bronze weight of 1550 grammes (nearly 3¾ lb.), which Dom Tosti thinks is the *libra propensa* of St. Benedict: *Della vita di San Benedetto*, capo v. (edizione illustrata, p. 194). But is not this the weight of a loaf which was divided among several monks? (*Cf.* Calmet, Commentary on Chapter XXXIX., pp. 39-40).

⁶ Daremberg and Saglio, *Dictionnaire des Antiquités grecques et romaines:* Libra, iv.

⁷ In France the Paris pound, which was most widely spread, contained 16 ounces, each equivalent to 30·59 grammes (1·08 oz. avoir.).

corda vestra in crapula et ebrietate. Pueris vero minori ætate non eadem servetur quantitas, sed minor quam majoribus, servata in omnibus parcitate.	says: "Take heed to yourselves lest perhaps your hearts be overcharged with surfeiting and drunkenness." And let not the same quantity be allotted to children of tender years, but less than to their elders, frugality being observed in all things.

However large already the ordinary daily allowance of food and drink, St. Benedict still leaves the Abbot the power to add to it, if he think fit, as for example in the case of extraordinary toil. So he does not purpose to drive all his monks by rule to heroic mortification and extreme severity towards the flesh. The Abbot's function is not to crush his monks, but to establish a just ratio between their work and the physical recruitment which it requires. Only he must beware of excess. Above all things, his adjustments must never favour gluttony, and a monk must never be surprised by the shameful consequences of excess: (*indigeries*). For nothing is so degrading, not alone for a monk, but for any Christian, as such excess. Our Lord was addressing all His followers when He said: "Take heed to yourselves lest perhaps your hearts be overcharged with surfeiting and drunkenness" (Luke xxi. 34). St. Benedict adds that the children in the monastery shall have a quantity suitable to their age; and, along with the considerate treatment that they merit, there will also be in all things such austerity as is agreeable to the life which they have already professed.

In our days, perhaps, the tendency to excess will display itself rather in fastidiousness and singularity than in gluttony properly so called. And, strangely enough, it is actually necessary sometimes to persuade people to eat, just as though they were Manicheans and eating was sinful. We sometimes meet with wrongheaded folk who regard eating and drinking as a humiliating function, and do themselves great injury by their monomania. Such as these need watching and even constraint. But, apart from these pathological cases, the Abbot leaves each individual free to decide in God's sight what he should take and what deny himself. We eat to live; we take what is needful to sustain us in our work, and fit us to face our duty; and always must we observe that rule of good breeding, health, and mortification which bids us stop before satiety.[1] Nor should the refectory and its business become the preoccupation of our lives, a constant and harassing anxiety.

The idea of compensations and additions to the ordinary fare has generally been well understood and realized under various forms. The customaries and cartularies of the Middle Ages often mention extra courses and the distribution of "pittances." At Cluny, in the end, they regularly added to the beans and other vegetables a "general" or "pittance" of eggs, fish, and cheese. By "general" was meant a portion served to each monk on a special plate; the "pittance" was a dish for two.[2] Modern stomachs cannot manage the solid meals of our ancestors.

[1] *Cf.* Cass., *Inst.*, V., viii.—S. Aug., *Confess.*, l. X., c. xxxi. *P.L.*, XXXII., 797 *sq.*
[2] Udalric gives this definition, *Consuet. Clun.*, l. II., c. xxxv.; *cf.* l. III., c. xviii.

It is true that they submitted to blood-letting, often a monthly occurrence; but to compensate at once for this lowering treatment, the patient was given a substantial " general " and submitted to a thorough régime of feeding up.

Carnium vero quadrupedum ab omnibus abstineatur comestio, præter omnino debiles et ægrotos.	But let all abstain from eating the flesh of four-footed animals, except the very weak and the sick.

We may remind ourselves of what St. Benedict said in reference to the sick in the thirty-sixth chapter: "The use of meat too shall be permitted to the sick," etc. In this place also we have the same prohibition for the healthy and the same exception for the seriously ill or weak. But St. Benedict here makes the scope of his prohibition more precise by the words *carnium vero quadrupedum*, thus forbidding the flesh of four-footed animals. Does the phrase exclude other sorts of flesh, so that fowls would be permitted? However strange it may appear to us, it would seem to be incontestable that, in St. Benedict's time and for centuries afterwards, birds were considered by many— we do not say by all[1]—as fare compatible with abstinence. You could deny yourself such flesh meat for mortification, but it was recognized to be flesh of an inferior quality; though it might be more delicate and more agreeable to the taste than the flesh of quadrupeds, it was less nourishing and less apt to stimulate the passions. And did not Genesis say that the birds and fishes were created on the same day and both alike taken from the waters? Why not treat waterfowl as fish, for they live on them and taste like them? Whatever be the value of the reasons formerly alleged in justification of the practice of treating bipeds as abstinence-fare, it was a custom, and everyone knows that moral theologians still in our own days allow certain waterfowl on abstinence days. They would, however, surprise us on a monastic table; and for us the question has been practically decided.[2]

[1] S. Cæsarius expressly forbids birds, except for the sick: *Reg. ad mon.*, xxiv.; *Reg. ad virg.*, *Recapitulatio*, xvii.

[2] The history of this matter is well summarized in the Commentary of Calmet. Read also: Herrgott, *Vetus disciplina monastica*, Præf., pp. xii-xxxii.—D. Grégoire Berthelet, *Traité historique et moral de l'abstinence de la viande et des révolutions qu'elle a eues depuis le commencement du monde jusqu'à présent*, etc. (Rouen, 1731), P. III., chapters i.-ii.—D. Mège maintained that St. Benedict forbade the flesh of birds.

CHAPTER XL

OF THE MEASURE OF DRINK

De mensura potus.—*Unusquisque proprium habet donum ex Deo: alius sic, alius vero sic. Et ideo cum aliqua scrupulositate a nobis mensura victus aliorum constituitur. Tamen infirmorum contuentes imbecillitatem, credimus heminam vini per singulos sufficere per diem.*

"Everyone hath his proper gift from God, one thus, another thus." And therefore it is with some scruple that we determine the measure of other men's living. Yet, making due allowance for the weakness of some, we think that a *hemina* of wine a day is sufficient for each.

THE whole of this chapter is a striking illustration of that fatherly discretion which we have so often remarked; the care with which the most ordinary details of our life are regulated is obvious and touching. First we have a formal recognition of the differences between us in body, in soul, and in grace: " Everyone hath his proper gift from God, one thus, another thus " (1 Cor. vii. 7). And because of this individual variety our Holy Father confesses that it is only with some misgiving and timidity that he ventures to determine matters which concern the lives of others. An absolutely invariable and rigid measure —a bed of Procrustes to which both great and small must needs adapt themselves—is out of the question. Nor should a man take himself as the standard to which all must conform. What, then, shall be our fixed point ? We shall consider the weakness of the small and feeble: of those who are little ones as regards physical strength, as well as of those who are not rich in moral vigour. Considering all these cases, we think, says St. Benedict, that a *hemina* of wine a day is sufficient for each monk. The Roman *hemina* was almost a quarter of a litre (nearly a half-pint).[1] But we should remember what was said in the last chapter.

Quibus autem donat Deus tolerantiam abstinentiæ, propriam se habituros mercedem sciant. Quod si aut loci necessitas, vel labor, aut ardor æstatis amplius poposcerit, in arbitrio prioris consistat, considerans in omnibus ne subrepat satietas aut ebrietas.

But let those to whom God gives the gift of abstinence know that they shall receive their proper reward. If either the situation of the place, the work, or the heat of summer require more, let it be in the power of the superior to grant it, care being taken in all things that surfeit or drunkenness creep not in.

After laying down the reasonable mean allowance, the Rule, in its care for the spirit of mortification, for obedience, and for considerateness, provides for the principal cases that may occur. A monk may think himself able to do without wine, whether entirely or in part; God has given him vigorous health and inspired a secret desire for this abstinence.

---

[1] Daremberg et Saglio, *Dictionn. des antiquités grecques et romaines*, art. Hemina. [The Roman *sextarius* is generally equated with the English pint (more accurately = ·96 of a pint). The *hemina* was half of the *sextarius*.]

Let him ask permission, as required in Chapter XLIX., and, if he obtain it, give up wine. He will gain merit both for his generosity and for his docility.

But the allowance of wine may be too small. The climate may be rigorous, there may be extraordinary work, or else it is the height of summer and the heat is extreme. Such circumstances seem to call for a little more. The superior may grant it, but he should take great care that none insensibly reach drunkenness or even a state of surfeit which approximates thereto. Commentators give details of the wine allowed at the end of meals or outside mealtimes. At Cluny, besides the regular amount of wine served at the meal (the " justice," as it was called), there was sometimes given also a " charity " of wine, or the *pigmentum*, a compound of wine, honey, cinnamon, and cloves.

Licet legamus vinum omnino monachorum non esse; sed quia nostris temporibus id monachis persuaderi non potest, saltem vel hoc consentiamus, ut non usque ad satietatem bibamus, sed parcius: quia *vinum apostatare facit etiam sapientes.*	Although we read that wine is by no means a drink for monks, yet, since in our days they cannot be persuaded of this, let us at least agree not to drink to satiety, but sparingly: because " wine maketh even the wise to fall away."

St. Benedict seems to be a little ashamed of his leniency and to remember regretfully the heroism of the Fathers of the East. "We read," he says, "that wine is by no means the drink of monks." The passage occurs, word for word, in the collected *Verba Seniorum*.[1] It is said also in the Life of St. Antony that neither he nor other fervent ascetics used flesh meat or wine.[2] This usage was, however, not general: the *Lausiac History*, for example, shows that the monks of Nitria drank wine;[3] so too did the monks of St. Cæsarius. In our days, St. Benedict continues, it is impossible to convince monks that the axiom of the ancients is true. Therefore they shall drink wine, since they must, but they shall at least agree not to drink to satiety,[4] for "wine maketh even the wise to fall away" (Ecclus. xix. 2). At Monte Cassino, as at Vicovaro,[5] St. Benedict drank wine. He might easily have astonished all by his mortifications—he was an expert and might have lived as he did at Subiaco. But, when he became father of a religious family, he put himself into harmony with the dispositions and lawful usages of his monks.

Ubi autem loci necessitas exposcit, ut nec suprascripta mensura inveniri possit, sed multo minus, aut ex	But where the place is such that not even the aforesaid measure can be supplied, but much less, or none at

---

[1] *Narraverunt quidam abbati Pastori de quodam monacho qui non bibebat vinum, et dixit eis: Quia vinum monachorum omnino non est (Verba Seniorum: Vitæ Patrum*, V., iv., 31. Rosweyd, p. 570).
[2] S. Athanasii, *Vita S. Antonii*, c. vii. P.G., XXVI., 853.—*Cf.* S. Aug., *De moribus eccles. cathol.*, l. I., c. xxxi. P.L., XXXII., 1339.—S. Hieron., *Ep.* LII., 11; *Ep.* XXII., 35. P.L., XXII., 536-537; *ibid.*, 420.
[3] C. vii. (Rosweyd, p. 713).
[4] *Ut non usque ad satietatem persistamus in edendo* (S. Basil., *Reg. contr.*, ix.).
[5] S. Greg. M., *Dial.*, l. II., c. iii.

toto nihil, benedicant Deum qui ibi habitant, et non murmurent. Hoc autem omnino admonentes, ut absque murmurationibus sint.	all, let those who dwell there bless God and not murmur. This above all do we admonish, that they be without murmuring.

Therefore the *hemina* shall be the standard, a mean between total abstinence and excess. But we must provide for the case when even this limited measure cannot be got. The monastery may be poor, the country may produce no wine, with the result that much less may be procurable or even none at all. In that case the monks must bless God, from whom are both wine and lack of wine, and face this small hardship bravely. It will not kill them. We are like soldiers: "Everyone that striveth for the mastery refraineth himself from all things. And they indeed that they may receive a corruptible crown: but we an incorruptible crown" (1 Cor. ix. 25). We should never murmur or grow sad on account of such matters. Our Holy Father reiterates the advice, warning monks who are deprived of their portion of wine to abstain also from murmuring.

CHAPTER XLI

AT WHAT HOURS THE BRETHREN ARE TO TAKE THEIR MEALS

QUIBUS HORIS OPORTEAT REFICERE FRATRES.—A sancto Pascha usque ad Pentecosten ad sextam reficiant fratres, et ad seram cenent.

From the holy feast of Easter until Whitsuntide let the brethren dine at the sixth hour and sup in the evening.

ST. BENEDICT divides the year into four parts as regards the times of meals. From Easter till Whitsuntide there is no fast, in accordance with the ancient discipline of the Church. It is certain also, though St. Benedict says nothing on the point, that Sundays were not fast-days. There were two meals, one in the middle of the day, at the sixth hour, and the other in the evening before sunset, at an hour which would naturally vary according to the season. In Greek and Roman customs the midday meal was a summary affair; for the monks it was the chief meal of the day.

A Pentecoste autem, tota æstate, si labores agrorum non habent monachi, aut nimietas æstatis non perturbat, quarta et sexta feria jejunent usque ad nonam; reliquis vero diebus ad sextam prandeant. Quæ prandii sexta, si opera in agris habuerint, aut æstatis fervor nimius fuerit, continuanda erit, et in Abbatis sit providentia. Et sic omnia temperet atque disponat, qualiter et animæ salventur, et quod faciunt fratres, absque ulla murmuratione faciant.

But from Whitsuntide, throughout the summer, if the monks have not to work in the fields, nor are harassed by excessive heat, let them fast on Wednesdays and Fridays until the ninth hour, but on other days dine at the sixth. Should they have field labour, or should the heat of the summer be very great, let dinner at the sixth hour be the rule, at the discretion of the Abbot. Let him likewise so temper and arrange all things that souls may be saved and that the brethren may fulfil their tasks without any murmuring.

From Whitsuntide throughout the summer, the Easter régime holds good, except that Wednesdays and Fridays are to be fast-days. These same days were days of penance for all Christians in the early centuries.[1] But St. Benedict differentiates these fast-days from the fast of Lent, putting the single meal at the ninth hour—that is, towards three o'clock in the afternoon. In some places the ninth hour was the time for breaking fast, not only at this season but also in Lent.[2] On other days, says St. Benedict, dinner shall be at the sixth hour. Because he does not speak of supper, and because some ancient documents such as the Rule of St. Fructuosus and the Rule of the Master exclude it expressly, some

---

[1] *Cf.* S. EPIPH., *Adv. Hæreses*, l. III., t. ii.: *Expositio fidei*, xxii. P.G., XLII., 825–828.
[2] *Cf.* SOCRAT., *Hist. eccles.*, l. V., c. xxii. P.G., LXVII., 625–646.—CASS., *Conlat.*, II., xxvi.; XXI., xxiii.

commentators doubt whether they had both *prandium* and *cena* at Monte Casino in summer.[1] But it is the custom of the whole Order to grant two meals on days which are not fast-days.

Our Holy Father allows an alleviation of the summer régime in the case of heavier toil or excessive heat. Hours were longer in this season, and it might often be a severe trial to wait till the ninth hour for a meal. "Let dinner at the sixth hour be the rule "; so that throughout the week, even on Wednesdays and Fridays, dinner shall be at that time. Probably there was also supper in the evening, so that the fast was completely dropped. It is left to the fatherly wisdom and foresight of the Abbot to determine when this was suitable. St. Benedict adds that he must also so contrive and arrange all things that souls may be saved, and the work of the brethren be fulfilled without murmuring. Here, as always, we find care for measure and moderation, fear of murmuring and complaint, though this be entirely secret. Better to dispense with the fast than to expose the brethren to discouragement or distress.

Ab Idibus autem Septembris, usque ad caput Quadragesimæ, ad nonam semper reficiant fratres.	From the Ides of September until the beginning of Lent let the brethren always dine at the ninth hour.

The third period, which we know as the monastic Lent, extends from after the Ides of September, when the Calends of October begin—that is, from September 14—until the ecclesiastical Lent. In this period dinner was at the ninth hour. There is nothing to show that there was a collation on fast-days. But we should remember that the quantity of food was the same at all times. On fast-days that was served at one meal which was else served at two, the difference being that the hour of this single repast was more or less retarded.

In Quadragesima vero usque ad Pascha, ad Vesperam reficiant. Ipsa tamen Vespera sic agatur, ut lumine lucernæ non indigeant reficientes, sed luce adhuc diei omnia consummentur. Sed et omni tempore, sive cenæ, sive refectionis hora sic temperetur, ut cum luce fiant omnia.	During Lent, however, until Easter let them dine in the evening. But let this evening meal be so arranged that they shall not need lamps while eating, and that all things may be finished while there is yet daylight. Indeed, at all times of the year, let the hour, whether for dinner or supper, be so arranged that everything be done by daylight.

From the beginning of Lent (Ash Wednesday or Quadragesima Sunday)[2] until Easter there shall be one meal and that at the hour of Vespers, after the Office. This was for many centuries the most common practice of the clergy and the faithful.

---

[1] St. Jerome, in his preface to the *Rule of St. Pachomius* writes: (5) *Bis in hebdomada, quarta et sexta Sabbati ab omnibus jejunatur, excepto tempore Paschæ et Pentecostes. Aliis diebus comedunt qui volunt post meridiem; et in cena similiter mensa ponitur, propter laborantes, senes, et pueros, æstusque gravissimos. Sunt qui secundo parum comedunt; alii qui prandii, sive cenæ uno tantum cibo contenti sunt.* Cf. Ladeuze, *Étude sur le cénobitisme pakhomien*, pp. 298-299.

[2] Cf. *Dictionn. d'archéol. chrét. et de Liturg.*, art. *Caput Jejunii*.

Our Holy Father wished the Lenten meal to be taken before sunset, a forestalling of the time which would be some relief to the brethren. The hour of Vespers shall be fixed so as to allow the meal to be finished in daylight without any need of a lamp. The reader will not require a light, and the brethren, moreover, will be less tempted to distractions during the meal. Conversation would have been easy in a badly lighted refectory. St. Benedict makes a general rule of this. Throughout the year the hour of supper, or the hour of the single meal, shall be so arranged that all is fulfilled by daylight. It may be objected that this would in winter put dinner very near supper. Calmet replies to this: " (1) that St. Benedict was speaking of Italy where he wrote and where the days of winter are longer than in France, Germany, or the North. (2) That it is by no means certain that he granted supper to his monks from the feast of the Exaltation of the Cross till Easter, on days when dinner was at the sixth hour any more than on days when it was at the ninth. (3) But supposing that he did grant it, it was more in the nature of a light lunch than of a supper."

CHAPTER XLII
THAT NO ONE MAY SPEAK AFTER COMPLINE

LET us recall the division of the Rule suggested in the first chapter. The central portion, from the twenty-first to the fifty-seventh chapters inclusively, concerns legislation and the internal order of the monastery. It is subdivided into three parts—viz., XXI.-XXX., dealing with the deans and their duties and the code of punishments; XXXI.-XLI., dealing with the cellarer and so with all that is connected with his office in a more or less immediate way. We now come to the subject of regularity and observance. It is not hard to see how this chapter is connected with the previous one and based on it.

UT POST COMPLETORIUM NEMO LOQUATUR.—Omni tempore silentio debent studere monachi, maxime tamen nocturnis horis, et ideo omni tempore, sive jejunii, sive prandii.

Monks should study silence always, but especially during the hours of the night; and this shall hold of all times, whether fast-days or not.

St. Benedict takes silence first, as though to remind us that it is the most important item in monastic observance. Superiors speak repeatedly of the observance of silence, and we are inclined to regard it as a vague commonplace, a subject taken up when there is nothing else to say. Yet they only imitate our Holy Father. Without repeating the doctrinal and practical reflections made in the sixth chapter, we may well observe again that silence, like poverty and mortification, has only a relative value. Silence is not perfection, absolute silence is not sanctity. There are natures which from timidity, or a deep-seated tranquillity, dislike self-expression. Silence is, then, a matter of temperament and no virtue. For its value consists in a voluntary and deliberate relation to perfection and God. Silence is an aid to prayer, the condition and effect of interior recollection, the guardian and sign of charity.

Recollection is so bound up with the goal of the monastic life that St. Benedict writes with insistence and some imperiousness. He does not merely invite. Monks ought, he says, at all times without exception, and even when they are speaking, to study and love silence. *Omni tempore silentio debent studere monachi.* Those words give us the general rule, to be modified in its application according to times, places, and subjects of conversation. St. Benedict, as we have remarked elsewhere, nowhere prescribes the absolute suppression of speech. He recognizes degrees of silence; the very diversity of these degrees and the special condemnation sometimes pronounced on certain sorts of conversation—all these detailed measures of prevention would be out of place in a house where there was never any talking. Our Holy Father here gives the night silence a privileged place.[1] Religious orders

---

[1] Some testimonies in favour of the night silence occur previously to St. Benedict: *Nemo alteri loquatur in tenebris*, says the *Rule* of ST. PACHOMIUS (xciv.). *Finitis igitur psalmis et cotidiana congregatione, sicut superius memoravimus, absoluta, nullus eorum vel ad modicum subsistere aut sermocinari audet cum altero* (CASS., *Inst.*, II., xv.).

have all adopted from him a measure which is justified on many grounds. In the first place it was in the interest of good order, when all the monks slept in the same dormitory, and the vigilance of the Abbot and deans was as a matter of fact somewhat relaxed. It is further a matter of mortification. For while all is silence and recollection, our will readily submits itself to what external things require, and we put ourselves simply in unison with nature. When all noise is stilled, imagination becomes less active, thoughtfulness and prayer more easy. In the secret places of our souls there is produced an effect like that which resulted from the coming of the Angel of deliverance, described in the Book of Wisdom and applied by the Church to the coming of our Lord: "While all things were in quiet silence and the night was in the midst of her course, thy almighty word leapt down from heaven from thy royal throne . . ." (Wisdom xviii. 14-15).

Besides the general counsel of silence, three things are dealt with in this chapter—viz., reading or spiritual conferences, Compline, and the night silence. The end of the first sentence presents a difficulty. The punctuation we have adopted[1] differs from that of the editions of Schmidt and Wölfflin, which put a full stop after the word *horis* and a colon after the words *sive prandii*. With either punctuation the clause *et ideo* etc., is both the conclusion of the general precept which precedes and an introduction to the details that follow. The sense would seem to be: Monks should practise silence at all times, but especially at night. So at all times, whether fast-days or not, things should be done as follows. Then in a long digression St. Benedict indicates how the monks are to prepare for the night silence and when it is to begin, whether the day be one on which there are two meals or only one. He is thinking in the latter case of the fast-days of the Rule and does not explicitly consider the fast-days of the Church, a thing which we shall explain. After this digression, with the words *Et exeuntes a Completorio*, we come back to the topic of the night silence.

A third system of punctuation, of fairly wide acceptance, makes the words *Et ideo* begin a new sentence and puts a simple comma before *si tempus fuerit prandii;* but this reading raises the following difficulty. If we understand by fast-days the fasts of the Rule, as well as those of the Church, it is not accurate to say in general that as soon as supper is ended there follows spiritual reading; for on the fast-days of the Rule there was most probably no supper, but only the one repast at the ninth hour. If we take the words to refer to the fast of Lent, the statement is accurate; but then the two alternatives "fast-days or not" do not exhaust the meaning of the words "at all times," since the fast-days of the Rule are excluded. With our punctuation we may very well take the words "fast-days" to mean all such days of whatever sort.

[1] Followed by D. Guéranger in his French translation of the Rule.
[2] *Omni tempore* seems here to mean: all the year, every day, although at the beginning of the chapter we gave it a wider meaning: at every time, in all circumstances, always.

Si tempus fuerit prandii, mox ut surrexerint a cena, sedeant omnes in unum, et legat unus Collationes, vel Vitas Patrum, aut certe aliquid quod ædificet audientes; non autem Heptateucum, aut Regum: quia infirmis intellectibus non erit utile illa hora hanc Scripturam audire; aliis vero horis legantur.	If it be not a fast-day, as soon as they shall have risen from supper let all sit down together, and let one read the *Conferences* or *Lives of the Fathers*, or at least something else which may edify the hearers; but not the Heptateuch, nor the Books of Kings: for it will not profit those of weak understanding to hear those parts of Scripture at that hour; let them be read at other times.

On days when there are two meals, as soon as supper is ended, the brethren shall rise, assemble, and sit together in one place, and one of them begin the reading. St. Benedict does not say where this took place, and the custom of the Order has been very various. Most often reading and Compline took place in the chapter-house or in the cloister, sometimes in the oratory, or even in the refectory.[1] Nowadays all is done in the oratory. Besides the chief purpose of edifying the monks, preparing them for the night, and leaving their minds full of spiritual thoughts, our Holy Father had another intention in instituting this reading. It was a practical one, and is revealed in the last words of the succeeding sentence. For the length of the reading is calculated so that all the monks may be able to assemble for a last conventual prayer. The kitchen servers and the reader, who have their meal at second table, the infirmarians, guestmasters, and all occupied in any special duty, will thus have the means of rejoining their brethren. If need be they must hurry somewhat: "so that during the reading all may come together (*concurrentibus*, running together), even such as may be occupied in some work enjoined them."

St. Benedict indicates the substance of this reading—viz., the *Collationes* or Conferences (of Cassian), the *Lives of the Fathers*, or at least some book capable of edifying the hearers. Some parts of Scripture with approved patristic commentaries might be read. But the Rule excludes the Heptateuch (*i.e.*, the Pentateuch plus the Books of Joshua and Judges) and the Books of Kings (probably including the Book of Ruth).[2] These being historical narratives might disturb some imaginations, and in any case were not quite adapted to the restful purpose of this evening reading. Or else St. Benedict wished to spare his monks, among whom were children and boys, some narratives quite Oriental in their freedom. "It will not profit those of weak understanding to hear those parts of Scripture at that hour, but they shall be read at other times." The whole Bible is from God. It was not written for unbelievers. St. Benedict's intention, therefore, is not to make an expurgated edition of the Sacred Books, for the use of those who might be tempted to explain them in the light of their evil experiences, but merely to take precautions to ensure us a quiet night and quiet awakening.

[1] *Cf.* MARTÈNE, *De ant. monach. rit.*, l. I., c. xi.
[2] *Cf.* S. AUG., *De doctrina christiana*, l. II., c. viii. *P.L.*, XXXIV., 40–41.

Si autem jejunii dies fuerit, dicta Vespera, parvo intervallo, mox accedant ad lectionem, ut diximus, et lectis quatuor aut quinque foliis, vel quantum hora permittit, omnibus in unum concurrentibus[1] per hanc moram lectionis; si quis forte in assignato sibi commisso fuerit occupatus, occurrat.[2]

If it be a fast-day, then a short time after Vespers let them assemble for the reading, as we have said; four or five pages being read, or as much as time allows, so that during the delay provided by this reading all may come together, even such as may be occupied in some work enjoined them.

This probably refers to the monastic fasts, two days a week from Pentecost to September 14, and every day from then to Lent. On these days dinner was at the ninth hour. Vespers followed at its proper time, and then, after a brief interval, all assembled for the reading as previously explained. The kitchen servers would be free long before, but other brethren might be occupied in various tasks, whether in the monastery or its surroundings. They must hasten to join the community and arrive, at latest, towards the end of the reading. It would appear that it hardly lasted more than a half-hour, sufficient for the reading of four or five pages of manuscript. But St. Benedict does not wish to fix it too precisely, adding that it should last as long as time allows. On days when there had been supper, or when that meal was taken late, in summer for instance, or when work was heavier, the Abbot might shorten the reading. Nowadays we do not exceed ten minutes; but we have reading or a spiritual conference before the evening meal.

St. Benedict has nothing special to say about Lent or other ecclesiastical fasts, since, in what regards reading and Compline, all would be the same as on days when there were two meals. The reading would follow immediately after the single evening meal.

Omnes ergo in unum positi compleant; et exeuntes a Completorio nulla sit licentia denuo cuiquam loqui aliquid. Quod si inventus fuerit quisquam prævaricari hanc taciturnitatis regulam, graviori vindictæ subjaceat; excepto si necessitas hospitum supervenerit, aut forte Abbas alicui aliquid jusserit. Quod tamen et ipsum cum summa gravitate et moderatione honestissime fiat.

When all, therefore, are gathered together let them say Compline; and when they come out from Compline no one shall be allowed to speak further to anyone. If anyone be found to evade this rule of silence, let him be punished severely; unless the presence of guests should make it necessary, or the Abbot should chance to give some order. But even this must be done becomingly, with the greatest gravity and moderation.

Note again the importance which St. Benedict attaches to the presence of all at Compline. All tasks shall cease and all the brethren unite at this last hour of the day: *omnes in unum positi compleant.* Then shall Compline be said; its structure our Holy Father has given elsewhere (Chapters XVII.–XVIII.).

[1] *Convenientibus in unum fratribus ad concinendos psalmos, quos quieturi ex more decantant* (Cass., *Inst.*, IV., xix.).
[2] *Occurrat* belongs only to the "received text"; and this whole passage is variously punctuated by editors.

On coming out from this hour, no one shall be free to say anything whatever to any of his brethren: *nulla sit licentia denuo cuiquam loqui aliquid.* Whosoever is convicted of a violation of this rule shall be subjected to very severe punishment. St. Benedict does not say what this was; but, in ancient times, it sometimes took the form of excommunication. Custom is still exacting in this matter and good monks will endeavour to keep the night silence in all its integrity.

Nevertheless, all rules remain subordinate to discretion and even the gravest precepts have no other aim except charity. Our Holy Father enumerates briefly the chief circumstances when one must overlook the rule—viz., if guests have to be attended to, if the Abbot has orders to give. One may imagine other cases, such as fire, the sickness of a brother, robbery;[1] any of which reasons would be more than enough to justify the breaking of the night silence. But, as St. Benedict remarks, though silence gives way before the higher law of charity, it never loses all its rights. We should only say what is necessary, with great gravity, in few words, and with all possible moderation and restraint.

As we said in commenting on the twenty-second chapter, the Rule does not tell us when the night silence ended, and it may have ended at rising. From the time of St. Benedict of Aniane it lasted in certain monasteries until Prime and the meeting of the brethren in the chapter-house. With us it ceases with the versicle *Pretiosa* at Prime.

[1] D. MÉNARD notes that the ancient monks often observed the night silence when away from the monastery and on a journey; he tells how St. Stephen of Obazine, and, on another occasion, two monks of Cluny, when attacked by robbers or barbarians, kept an imperturbable silence.

CHAPTER XLIII

OF THOSE WHO COME LATE TO THE WORK OF GOD, OR TO TABLE

WE now start a series of four chapters which may be regarded as the complement of the monastic penal legislation (in XXIII.-XXX.). They are more in place here than earlier. For our Holy Father treats in fact of observance, regularity, and punctuality; these are the chief subjects of these chapters. They contain punishments for small breaches of observance and for purely material faults. We are told how to expiate all the little injuries we may do to the peace and good order of the community, slight and even involuntary irreverences towards God and sacred things. And since public penances most often have the oratory or refectory for their scene and occasion, it was natural not to speak of them until meals had been dealt with. Finally, apropos of satisfactions, St. Benedict describes the manner of them for brethren excommunicated both from oratory and table or from table alone (Chapter XLIV.).

DE IIS QUI AD OPUS DEI VEL AD MENSAM TARDE OCCURRUNT.—Ad horam divini Officii, mox ut auditum fuerit signum, relictis omnibus quælibet fuerint in manibus, summa cum festinatione curratur: cum gravitate tamen, ut non scurrilitas inveniat fomitem. Ergo nihil operi Dei præponatur.

At the hour of Divine Office, as soon as the signal is heard, let each one lay aside whatever he may be engaged on and hasten to it with all speed, and yet with seriousness, so that no occasion be given for levity. Let nothing be put before the Work of God.

In oratory and refectory the whole community is united and there the external bond of conventual life is realized. Therefore should punctuality be especially in evidence at these duties. St. Benedict deals first with the Divine Office, giving the precept, the mode of its fulfilment, and finally the motive. As soon as the signal for Office is heard, each one should go with all speed, leaving unfinished any other work, whatever hand or brain has been occupied with.[1] It is obvious, and St. Benedict thought it unnecessary to remark, that one would not abandon thus abruptly whatever charity or good sense would bid him

[1] *Itaque considentes intra cubilia sua et operi ac meditationi studium pariter inpendentes, cum sonitum pulsantis ostium ac diversorum cellulas percutientis audierint ad orationem scilicet eos seu ad opus aliquod invitantis, certatim e suis cubilibus unusquisque prorumpit, ita ut is, qui opus scriptoris exercet, quam repertus fuerit inchoasse litteram finire non audeat, sed in eodem puncto, quo ad aures ejus sonitus pulsantis advenerit, summa velocitate prosiliens ne tantum quidem moræ interponat, quantum cœpti apicis consummet effigiem, sed inperfectas litteræ lineas derelinquens non tam operis conpendia lucrare sectetur quam obedientiæ virtutem exsequi toto studio atque æmulatione festinet. Quam non solum operi manuum seu lectioni vel silentio et quieti cellæ, verum etiam cunctis virtutibus ita præferunt, ut huic judicent omnia postponenda et universa dispendia subire contenti sint, dummodo hoc bonum in nullo violasse videantur* (CASS., *Inst.*, IV., xii.).

keep or continue for a moment. Extreme haste should also be tempered with gravity, for we are not bidden to run in the literal sense of the word. Dissipation should not be caused and justified by a gross interpretation of the Rule, and that in duties which we should approach with great recollection.

The supernatural zeal with which St. Benedict would have us fulfil all the behests of obedience is ever justified, for it is God who gives the orders; but this is especially true when the work is the Work of God *par excellence*, that essential and unique work towards which are ordained all God's operations *ad extra*. Nothing, says St. Benedict, should be put before the Work of God. Which principle, borrowed by him from monastic tradition,[1] has remained the proud motto of all his children. Let us never be slow to appear in the audience chamber of God; there is the one interest of life. Moreover, regularity is the school of abnegation. Let us be forgiven for repeating that it is the truest mortification, sounding the very depths of our wills, though it remain unnoticed by men. Monastic punctuality is not mechanical or constrained. It has its source in deep conviction, in a glad spontaneity of faith and love. Our souls are identified with the law, and thus arises an orthodox form of that immanence of which men now speak so much.

Quod si quis ad nocturnas Vigilias post " Gloriam " Psalmi nonagesimi quarti (quem propter hoc omnino protrahendo et morose volumus dici) occurrerit, non stet in ordine suo in choro, sed ultimus omnium stet, aut in loco quem talibus negligentibus seorsum constituerit Abbas, ut videatur ab ipso vel ab omnibus, usque dum completo opere Dei, publica satisfactione pæniteat. Ideo autem eos in ultimo aut seorsum judicavimus debere stare, ut visi ab omnibus, vel pro ipsa verecundia sua emendentur. Nam si foras oratorium remaneant, erit forte talis qui se aut recollocet et dormiat, aut certe sedeat foris, vel fabulis vacet, et detur occasio maligno; sed ingrediatur intro, ut nec totum perdat, et de reliquo emendetur.

Should anyone come to the Night Office after the *Gloria* of the ninety-fourth psalm (which for this reason we wish to be said very slowly and protractedly), let him not stand in his order in the choir, but last of all, or in the place set apart by the Abbot for such negligent ones, so that he may be seen by him and by all, until, the Work of God being ended, he do penance by public satisfaction. The reason why we have judged it fitting for them to stand in the last place or apart, is that, being seen by all, they may amend for very shame. For if they were to remain outside the oratory, there might be one who would return to his bed and sleep, or else sit outside and give himself to idle tales, and so give occasion to the Evil One. Let him, therefore, enter, that he may not lose the whole, and may amend for the future.

The common purpose of the penances which our Holy Father now begins to appoint is undoubtedly to repair the offence against God and

---

[1] *Cursum monasterii super omnia diligas.—Ad horam vero orationis dato signo qui non statim prætermisso omni opere quod agit paratus fuerit, foras excludatur, ut erubescat; quia nihil orationi præponendum est* (S. MACAR., *Reg.*, ix., xiv.). *Orationi nihil præponas tota die* (S. PORCARII *Monita: Revue Bénédictine*, October, 1909, p. 478).

the slight scandal given to the brethren; but they have as well a remedial character, tending to wean us from all inclination to self-will or carelessness. Whoever arrives after the *Gloria* of the ninety-fourth psalm, in the Night Office, must not take his order in the choir. He has displayed too little zeal to deserve, though he be now ready, to join the common psalmody. The *Invitatory* had been chanted slowly and much drawn out with set purpose of considerateness. He shall take his place last of all, or else apart, in a special place appointed by the Abbot for such delinquents (*talibus negligentibus*). He will be seen there by the Abbot and his brethren and will feel a salutary shame. But this is not the whole of his penance; for when the Office is over, he shall make public satisfaction, probably in the choir or at the doors of the church.

So St. Benedict allows the late-comer into the oratory, but appoints him the last place or puts him in the pillory of the lazy. In this he departs from the custom of the monks of Palestine as he found it described in Cassian. With them a monk, who did not arrive at the Night Office before the prayer which followed the second psalm, had to remain outside the oratory, taking part in the Office from a distance only, and when the brethren came out had to prostrate at the feet of all, asking their pardon. At Terce, Sext, and None he had to arrive before the end of the first psalm if he would escape the above penalty.[1] It may be that for the fervent Eastern of refined nature such temporary excommunication was a severe lesson. But St. Benedict knew that in the West of his day such a proceeding would have been dangerous for certain ruder natures. We have judged it fitting, he says, to relegate such careless ones to the last place, or to a place apart and conspicuous, so that, in default of high motives, their shame may produce amendment. But to allow a monk, even as a punishment, to remain outside the oratory would be to expose him to a thousand temptations. The lazy man would regard it as a positive encouragement, return to bed, and continue his slumbers, judging that excommunication certainly had its good points. Another might sit solitary outside;[2] or else indulge in gossip with other late-comers or with strangers. Now a monk without protection of prayer, or rule, or work, or the society of his brethren, would be a sure prize for the enemy. Our Holy Father puts it quite directly: "and so give occasion to the Evil One." The devil is always looking for opportunities; but as long as we are safeguarded by the helps of our conventual life we may laugh at him. For we ourselves hold the key that opens and shuts our souls, and none enters but he to whom we grant

---

[1] CASS., *Inst.*, III., vii.—The *Rule* of ST. MACARIUS (xiv.) also excludes the late-comer.—This is the regulation of ST. PACHOMIUS: *Quando ad collectam tubæ clangor increpuerit per diem, qui ad unam orationem tardius venerit, superioris increpationis ordine corripietur, et stabit in loco convivii* (penance in the refectory). *Nocte vero, quoniam corporis infirmitati plus aliquid conceditur, qui post tres orationes venerit, eodem et in collecta et in vescendo ordine corripietur* (ix-x).—ST EPHREM, *Paraenesis xviii*, wherein monks are exhorted to rise in haste for the "Work of the Lord," and to enter the oratory, even if Office has begun (inter S. EPHREM. *opp. græc. lat.*, t. II., pp. 93-94).

[2] We should read *sedeat sibi foris*.

admittance. If the late-comer be admitted into the oratory, St. Benedict adds, anxious to justify his innovation to the full, he does not lose the whole advantage of the Divine Office; and he is constrained to amend for the future; or: makes satisfaction for what he has omitted and for the negligence that he has shown.

Diurnis autem Horis, qui ad opus Dei post Versum et " Gloriam " primi Psalmi qui post Versum dicitur, occurrerit, lege qua supra diximus, in ultimo stet loco: nec præsumat sociari choro psallentium usque ad satisfactionem, nisi forte Abbas licentiam dederit permissione sua; ita tamen, ut satisfaciat reus ex hoc.

At the Day Hours let him who comes to the Work of God after the Verse and the *Gloria* of the first psalm which is said after the Verse stand in the last place, as ordered above; nor let him presume to join the choir in their chanting until he have made satisfaction, unless the Abbot allow him: yet even so let him make satisfaction for his guilt.

One who comes late for the Day Hours, arriving after the *Gloria* of the first psalm which follows the versicle *Deus in adjutorium*, must be punished as before. He must take the last place, or else (St. Benedict does not mention this explicitly) go to the place appointed for the negligent. Until he has made satisfaction he is not to be permitted to join his voice with the voices of the choir in their chanting. It may be asked whether late-comers were denied all share in the Office, or merely forbidden to chant, whether alone or in the " schola " (*choro psallentium* are St. Benedict's words), psalms, antiphons, or lessons, in the same way as this was forbidden to those excommunicated from the table (Chapter XXIV.) and those excommunicated from oratory and table before their complete reconciliation (Chapter XLIV.).[1] Did they do nothing but listen ? Did they recite what they could in a very low voice ? Did they take part in certain " responses," or in chanting which was performed by the whole choir? We cannot say. The words " that he may not lose the whole " would seem to indicate more than a purely passive rôle. Nor can we say, from the mere text of the Rule, whether this exclusion could be continued for many Offices, when the negligence was more grave, or was habitual, or when complete satisfaction was long coming. But St. Benedict tells us that the negligent monk could take his usual place and duty in choir by express invitation of the Abbot; as, for example, when he was in charge of a duty which without him would be unfulfilled or fulfilled imperfectly. It would not do to disorganize the common prayer for the sake of punishing one man's tardiness. However, even then, the guilty man must make public satisfaction after the Office.

It has been remarked that St. Benedict is more lenient with those who come late for Matins than with laggards at the Day Offices; and the reason is not obscure. At the Night Office they have until after the Verse, psalm iii., and the Invitatory; at the Day Hours they are punished if they come after the first psalm. But what does St. Benedict mean by

[1] See p. 148.

the Day Hours? Cassian,[1] in a passage which our Holy Father uses with modifications, describes the penances done by the Palestinian monks when they arrived late for the Night Offices (*in nocturnis conventiculis*), or else for Terce, Sext, and None (*in Tertia, Sexta vel Nona*). Cassian says nothing of other Hours. Lauds could be included under the Night Office, Compline probably did not yet exist in those parts, and Prime was of quite recent institution. But what of Vespers? Was the rule of penance the same for this as for the Night Offices?[2] Yet, whatever may have been Palestinian custom, we have no right to infer an exact agreement between the arrangements mentioned by Cassian and those of St. Benedict. If our Holy Father really intends to speak of Lauds and the succeeding Hours, we must recognize that all the Hours have the verse *Deus in adjutorium*, a fact not mentioned explicitly in his set treatment of the Office save for Prime, Terce, Sext, and None.[3] And we should allow that at Lauds laggards have till after the *Gloria* of the sixty-sixth psalm, which is purposely said slowly like the Invitatory, "that all may be in time for the fiftieth" (Chapter XIII.).[4] Perhaps, finally, the fact that St. Benedict does not here mention the hymn, between the *Deus in adjutorium* and the first psalm, is a proof that he wishes to include in one precise formula the Day Offices which have the hymn before the psalmody (Prime, Terce, Sext, and None) and those other Offices where the hymn comes after (Lauds, Vespers, and Compline).

Ad mensam autem qui ante Versum non occurrerit, ut simul omnes dicant Versum et orent, et sub uno simul omnes accedant ad mensam: qui per negligentiam suam aut vitium non occurrerit, usque ad secundam vicem pro hoc corripiatur: si denuo non emendaverit, non permittatur ad mensæ communis participationem, sed sequestratus a consortio omnium reficiat solus, sublata ei portione sua vini, usque ad satisfactionem et emendationem. Similiter autem patiatur, qui ad illum Versum non fuerit præsens, qui post cibum dicitur.

He who does not come to table before the Verse, so that all may say it praying together and sit down to table at the same time, must be corrected once or twice if this be through negligence or fault. If after this he do not amend, let him not be suffered to share in the common table, but be separated from the company of all and eat alone, his portion of wine being taken from him until he makes satisfaction and amends. He is to undergo the same punishment who is not present at the Verse which is said after meals.

St. Benedict now ensures the conventual character of meals. In the main it is not hard of realization, for there are decisive reasons urging all the monks to be present and that without great delay; whereby we achieve a complete reunion. But if all are present for the meal they should likewise be present for the prayers before and after. There

---

[1] *Inst.*, III., vii.   [2] See p. 171, note 3.   [3] See pp. 158 and 177.
[4] Is it not precisely in allusion to Lauds and in order to prevent any confusion between psalm lxvi. and psalm l. that St. Benedict speaks specifically of the first psalm *qui post versum dicitur*?

was, therefore, at that epoch—and the custom is as old as Christianity[1]—a form of Blessing before meals and Grace after meals. St. Benedict alludes to both as the "Verse."[2] And he requires three things at the beginning of meals: that all should assemble before the Verse, that they should say it and pray together, and finally that all should sit down together (*ut sub uno simul omnes accedant ad mensam*). By this regulation and the one concerning the end of the meal our Holy Father perhaps intends to exclude the custom followed by the monks of St. Pachomius, who went to the refectory as they wished and left when it suited them.[3] At any rate, it is plain that in St. Benedict's conception a monastery is a fraternal fellowship, closely knit together, wherein all follow the same horarium, wherein all are blessed and consecrated, and all works, even the most ordinary ones, are sanctified, by prayer.

He who from carelessness or caprice does not arrive before the prayer shall first be corrected once or twice. So St. Benedict prudently makes a distinction between negligence in coming to the Divine Office and a late arrival at meals. The latter fault is less serious. However, if two corrections do not cause amendment, the guilty one must thenceforth be forbidden to share in the common table.[4] This is not the excommunication from meals provided in the twenty-fourth chapter, but a penalty analogous to that just decreed against the laggard at the Office. The refectory, like the choir, had a place allotted to the careless where they were to eat by themselves separated from the society of their brethren and deprived of their portion of wine. They had not to take their meals at second table or outside the refectory.[5] This is proved by St. Benedict's requirements before the laggards may recover their wine and their right place: they had to make satisfaction and amend; but it would be impossible to manifest their improvement in punctuality unless they were kept in the common refectory. Our Holy Father decides finally that the same punishment should be inflicted on the monk who goes out before Grace.

---

[1] To give a blessing before breaking bread is the familiar action of Our Lord (Luke xxiv. 30–35) and of the Apostles (Acts xxvii. 33–35). This blessing occurs in the Agape of the early Christians. Read on this subject chapters ix. and x. of the *Didache*, the interpretation of which has been fixed in a quite final manner by D. CAGIN (*L'Eucharistia*, part II., viii.).

[2] On the prayers at monastic meals *cf.* MÉNARD, *Concordia Regularum*, pp. 765–766.—HÆFTEN, l. X., tract. i., disq. vi.—MARTÈNE, *De antiq. monach. rit*, l. I., c. ix.

[3] *Sunt qui secundo parum comedunt; alii qui prandii, sive cenæ uno tantum cibo contenti sunt. Nonnulli gustato paullulum pane egrediuntur. Omnes pariter comedunt. Qui ad mensam ire noluerit, in cellula sua panem tantum et aquam, ac salem accipit* (S. HIERON., *Præf. in Reg. S. Pach.*, 5). But when the monks of ST. PACHOMIUS came to the refectory they had to come at a fixed hour, for we read in the same Rule: *Si quis ad comedendum tardius venerit, excepto majoris imperio . . ., aget pænitentiam, aut ad domum jejunus revertetur* (xxxii.).

[4] *Quæ signo tacto tardius ad opus Dei, vel ad opera venerit, increpationi, ut dignum est, subjacebit. Quod si secundo aut tertio admonita emendare noluerit, a communione, vel a convivio separetur* (S. CÆSAR., *Reg. ad virg.*, x.).

[5] ST. BASIL condemns late-comers to wait for the next day's meal (*Reg. contr.*, xcvii.); he distinguishes, however, between guilty and excusable late-coming.

Nec quisquam præsumat ante statutam horam, vel postea, quicquam cibi vel potus percipere. Sed et si cui offertur aliquid a priore, et accipere renuerit, hora qua desideraverit, hoc quod prius recusavit aut aliud omnino non percipiat, usque ad emendationem congruam.

And let no one presume to take any food or drink before or after the appointed time; but if something is offered to anyone by the superior and he refuse it, and afterwards wishes to have what he had rejected or some other thing, let him get neither this nor anything else till he makes proper satisfaction.

If negligent monks were free to eat and drink before or after the appointed hour, they would certainly have recompensed themselves for the loss of their wine and their penance at the common meal; and they would have had little zeal for amendment. But St. Benedict forbids eating or drinking, no matter how small a quantity, apart from the refectory and the conventual meals.[1] Moreover, it would have been unseemly for a monk to eat at any time or to drink when he had opportunity, seeking a little dessert in the vineyard or the orchard. Nor is it in the power of the cellarer, or of him whom we call the "depositary," to consider the needs of each individual, to distribute kindly largesse, or to show a tender thoughtfulness for one or other of the brethren. Furthermore, in the refectory, you must get permission if you would exchange one dish for another which you think more suited to your stomach. And since the spirit of singularity and self-indulgence is very subtle and very hard to conquer, we should ever be on our guard, more especially as we advance in years, against seeking our ease and likes and preferences.[2] Finally, it may not be quite unnecessary to remark that, if the laws of our common life and of mortification forbid us giving ourselves anything whatever outside of mealtime, poverty also forbids us to offer a brother what we think we should deny ourselves. We are poorer than the poor themselves and cannot even dispose freely of our superfluity. To mix up some dish or other, without partaking of it, so as to show that we have touched it, and to transform it thus into something which we may give to others, would be to some degree a mistaking of true monastic poverty.

St. Benedict forbids a monk to give or receive irregularly, but he recognizes the superior's right to grant a solace or some small addition, whether in the course of the common meal or outside it. And our Holy Father would have the monk accept with humility and courtesy what the Abbot's considerateness offers him. Not that he means to oblige the brethren to take indiscriminately and wholly any addition which they think excessive or harmful. He must accept graciously, but he may graciously excuse himself. For what St. Benedict wishes to banish is false austerity, ill-temper, and intractableness. A man may refuse haughtily and repenting soon come to ask for what he

---

[1] *Ante quam vel post quam legitimam communemque refectionem summa cautione servatur, ne extra mensam quicquam cibi penitus ori suo quisquam indulgere præsumat*, etc. (Cass., *Inst.*, IV., xviii.).

[2] *Cf.* S. Basil., *Reg. contr.*, xc.

had refused. The superior, says St. Benedict, should then remember his incivility, and not only refuse what is asked, but also every sort of favour, perhaps even necessary things, until the brother begs parden and repairs his fault suitably.[1]

[1] The meaning we give to the words of St. Benedict is, it seems, almost the same as that of the passage in ST. BASIL which inspired them: *Si quis iratus fuerit, nolens accipere aliquid eorum quæ ad usum præbentur? Iste talis dignus est etiam ut si quærat non accipiat, usquequo probet is qui præest; et cum viderit vitium animi curatum, tunc etiam quod corporis usibus necessarium fuerit præbebit* (Reg. contr. xcvi.). See also the question which precedes this.

CHAPTER XLIV

OF THOSE WHO ARE EXCOMMUNICATED, HOW THEY ARE TO MAKE SATISFACTION

ST. BENEDICT continues his enumeration of the means by which faults against observance are expiated, of the penances by which we regain favour. If small mistakes call for punishment and penance, more serious and very grave faults require such *a fortiori*. In outlining the ascending series of punishments deserved by these two last classes of faults our Holy Father (in Chapters XXIV. and XXV.) described the condition of those excommunicated " from oratory and table " and " from table." He now tells us how both may obtain pardon. To emerge from the full regular excommunication, a whole series of graduated and wise expiations had to be traversed, in which four stages may be distinguished.[1]

DE IIS QUI EXCOMMUNICANTUR, QUOMODO SATISFACIANT.—Qui pro graviori culpa ab oratorio et a mensa excommunicatur, hora qua opus Dei in oratorio celebratur, ante fores oratorii prostratus jaceat, nihil dicens; nisi tantum posito in terram capite et prostratus, pronus omnium de oratorio exeuntium pedibus se projiciat. Et hoc tamdiu faciat usque dum Abbas judicaverit satisfactum esse.

He who for graver offences is excommunicated from the oratory and the table must, at the hour when the Work of God is being performed in the oratory, lie prostrate before the doors of the oratory, saying naught; only let him, with his face on the ground and body prone, cast himself at the feet of all as they go forth from the oratory. And let him continue to do this until the Abbot judge that satisfaction has been made.

The excommunicated monk, who has submitted and consented to be reconciled with God and his brethren, is treated as were public penitents in the early centuries. At the hour when the Work of God is celebrated, at all Offices, he prostrates before the doors of the oratory, saying nothing. Possibly our Holy Father's intention was to keep him there during the whole of the Office, and the words *nihil dicens* are meant to forbid him taking any part in the liturgy. Many historical texts support this interpretation.[2] However, to stay thus at the door during the whole Office of the long winter nights would be a painful process,[3] especially if we take the words *prostratus jaceat* literally. Does it not seem that St. Benedict himself explains his meaning when he adds, immediately after *nihil dicens*, the clause beginning *nisi tantum?* The excommunicated monk must be at the doors of the oratory while

---

[1] There is some verbal reminiscence of CASSIAN (*Inst.*, II., xvi.; IV., xvi.) in this chapter.
[2] See the *Rule* of ST. FRUCTUOSUS (xiv.), and the *Rule of the Master* (xiv.).—MÉNARD, *Concordia Regularum*, pp. 532–533.
[3] It is true that there was usually, before the church, a covered *atrium*; penitents and catechumens stayed there.

the brethren are going out; he must say nothing, but lying prostrate, with his face in the dust, cast himself at the feet of all, whether before each in turn or while the whole community defiles past him. The first remedy for every evil is humility, and humiliation is the means to obtain humility. Moral virtues are acquired by exercise, by the accumulation, and repetition of acts. The excommunicate must continue to act thus, says the Rule, until the Abbot judges that this first satisfaction is complete and sufficient.

Qui dum jussus ab Abbate venerit, provolvat se ipsius Abbatis pedibus, deinde omnium vestigiis fratrum, ut orent pro eo.	Then, when the Abbot bids him, let him come and cast himself at the feet of the Abbot, and next at those of all the brethren, that they may pray for him.

This is the second stage. At the invitation of the Abbot the penitent comes and casts himself at his feet, and then at the feet of all the brethren begging their prayers, whether by word or merely by his suppliant attitude. The excommunication evidently will soon be removed and the guilty one restored to his place in the family. St. Benedict does not tell us in what place this second stage was enacted.

Et tunc, si jusserit Abbas, recipiatur in choro, vel in ordine, quo Abbas decreverit: ita sane, ut Psalmum aut Lectionem vel aliud quid non præsumat in oratorio imponere, nisi iterum Abbas jubeat.	And then, if the Abbot so order, let him be received back into the choir, in such a place as he shall appoint: yet so that he presume not to intone psalm or lesson or anything else in the oratory, unless the Abbot again command him.

When the Abbot ordains it, the penitent is received back into the choir, but takes his rank as the Abbot judges fit, not necessarily that which he held before his fall. And in order to make him realize that his state is still only one of convalescence, he is forbidden to chant or to recite (probably by himself or in the "schola") psalms, lessons, or other liturgical pieces of the same character. He will not have the right to raise his voice in the presence of God and his brethren until formal authorization by the Abbot. If St. Benedict is prudent in his use of punishments, he does not care for quick and wholesale amnesty, that facility of pardon which encourages a recrudescence of the same faults.

Et omnibus Horis, dum completur opus Dei, projiciat se in terram, in loco in quo stat, et sic satisfaciat, usque dum ei jubeat Abbas, ut quiescat ab hac satisfactione.	Moreover, at every Hour, when the Work of God is ended, let him cast himself on the ground, in the place where he stands, and so make satisfaction, until the Abbot bids him cease from this satisfaction.

Although he has regained his place in the common prayer, the penitent monk still owes a last satisfaction. At the end of each Hour he must prostrate on the ground, in the same place as he holds in choir; and he must repeat this satisfaction until the Abbot bids him cease and be at rest (*quiescat*). We may note carefully that it is not said that the monk then recovers the place he held before his fault. Our Holy Father recognizes elsewhere that the Abbot has the right to degrade a man for well-founded reasons, *certis ex causis* (Chapter LXIII.).

| Qui vero pro levibus culpis excommunicatur tantum a mensa, in oratorio satisfaciat usque ad jussionem Abbatis; et tamdiu hoc faciat, usque dum benedicat, et dicat: Sufficit. | But those who for small faults are excommunicated only from the table must make satisfaction in the oratory so long as the Abbot shall command; let them do so till he bless them and say: It is enough. |

The procedure was naturally less complex and more gentle when it was a matter only of the minor excommunication, called excommunication from the table because it operated chiefly in the refectory. In the choir, the excommunicated man was only deprived of the right to intone psalms and antiphons and recite lessons—until he had made satisfaction, adds St. Benedict (Chapter XXIV.). Our Holy Father confines himself here to directing that this satisfaction should be made in the oratory and last as long as the Abbot thinks suitable, being repeated until he gives his blessing and says: It is enough. But in what did this satisfaction consist? It would seem that it was nothing else but the prostration of which our Holy Father spoke in the preceding sentence. Since the Rule gives no precise directions we may interpret it by itself, from the passage which is nearest and most connected in sense.

We cannot embark on the history of monastic custom with regard to the satisfaction performed by the excommunicated. Let us observe only that the text of the Rule has never been abrogated. It remains still and it may be put into force. And though occasions for the incurring or infliction of excommunication be much rarer than once they were, yet they are still possible. Given the occasion, it would be the strict duty of the Abbot to apply the penalties of the Rule, if he were forced thereto by obstinacy or by prolonged and formal contempt.

CHAPTER XLV

OF THOSE WHO MAKE MISTAKES IN THE ORATORY

DE IIS QUI FALLUNTUR IN ORATORIO.—Si quis, dum pronuntiat Psalmum, Responsorium, aut Antiphonam, vel Lectionem, fallitur: nisi cum satisfactione ibi coram omnibus humiliatus fuerit, majori vindictæ subjaceat; quippe qui noluit humilitate corrigere, quod negligentia deliquit. Infantes vero pro tali culpa vapulent.

If anyone while reciting a psalm, responsory, antiphon, or lesson, make a mistake, and do not make satisfaction, humbling himself there before all, let him be subjected to greater punishment, as one who would not correct by humility what he did wrong through negligence. But children for such faults are to be whipped.

FROM this point we are no longer concerned with grave irregularities but with purely formal mistakes, at the most with offences due to some negligence or inadvertence. The ancients teach us not to be too easygoing even in such small matters.[1] In the oratory, in particular, where all is sacred and where the work performed is of supreme importance, where routine, laziness, and sleepiness are ever to be feared, any mistake calls for immediate expiation and such as is suited to its gravity. If anyone, says the Rule, makes a mistake in reciting a psalm, responsory, antiphon, or lesson, he owes satisfaction. The error may be a fault in pronunciation, by which we substitute one word for another or curtail a word, or else a fault in chanting, or the intoning of a wrong versicle; St. Benedict does not go into detail, but employs the general phrase: "while reciting." Nor does he say what the satisfaction was. But we may suppose with some probability that he meant a humiliation imposed on himself by the delinquent, by kneeling or prostrating in his place before the eyes of all. Such, with minor differences, are now and have always been, in the diverse branches of the Order, the ordinary choir penances.

It is not necessary that our fault should have caused appreciable disturbance or discord, nor even that our neighbours should have noticed it. It is not a question of æsthetics, but of religious justice. Imperfection has appeared where there should be full and continuous perfection, so that we have a real debt to pay to the Majesty of God. Our religion takes its whole character from the idea we have of God, and the attitude which this idea makes us adopt before Him. Under the New Covenant, God has not loaded us with a weight of manifold ritual ordinances, because He thought that charity would suffice to regulate our attitude in the presence of His Beauty. There are attentions which we should not expect of slaves, but should be astonished not to find in sons. Our penances should be done spontaneously, generously, with zealous faith and love. They should be done at once, without

---

[1] In writing this chapter and the one following St. Benedict had in mind the *Institutes* of CASSIAN, IV., xvi.

debate or secret self-justification. There is nothing better for making conscience delicate than this generous reparation for trivial faults and errors of frailty. Our Holy Father decrees that he who will not punish himself and correct his negligence by an act of humility must incur a more severe penalty.[1] Since he voluntarily abandons his character of a son in order to adopt again the internal attitude of the slave, he shall be treated for the slave that he would be, and will not be the gainer thereby.

" But children for such faults are to be whipped." We know that there were children in the monastery, that they were real religious, and that they were present at all the Offices. The Rule comes to the assistance of consciences not yet fully developed and stipulates that their mistakes in chanting or psalmody should be punished with the rod.[2] The old customaries, particularly that of Udalric,[3] describe in detail the procedure for the correction of children.

[1] *Nisi pro neglegentia præsenti confestim vera humilitate subnixius satisfacere festinarit* (Cass., *Inst.*, III., vii.).

[2] It is better to interpret the words *pro tali culpa* of any fault committed by the boy in the chant or psalmody, than of the fault of not humbling himself.

[3] *Consuet. Clun.*, l. III., c. viii. et x.

CHAPTER XLVI
OF THOSE WHO OFFEND IN ANY OTHER MATTERS

DE IIS QUI IN ALIIS QUIBUSLIBET REBUS DELINQUUNT.—Si quis dum in labore quovis, in coquina, in cellario, in ministerio, in pistrino, in horto, in arte aliqua dum laborat, vel in quocumque loco, aliquid deliquerit, aut fregerit quippiam, aut perdiderit, vel aliud quid excesserit,[1] et non veniens continuo ante Abbatem vel congregationem, ipse ultro satisfecerit et prodiderit delictum suum; dum per alium cognitum fuerit, majori subjaceat emendationi.

If anyone while engaged in any sort of work, whether in the kitchen, the cellar, the office, the bakehouse, or the garden, in any craft, and in any place, shall do anything amiss, break or lose anything, or offend in any way whatsoever, and shall not come at once before the Abbot, or the community, and of his own accord do penance and confess his fault, but it be known by means of another, let him be subjected to greater punishment.

ST. BENEDICT here deals with the penance due for faults committed outside the oratory. He first enumerates the principal offices of the monastery in which faults might occur: the kitchen, cellar, office,[2] bakehouse, and garden. Then he uses general phrases to cover all: in practising any craft or fulfilling any work in any place, if anything be broken, lost, or spoilt, and damage, or trouble be caused to the community—in a word, if any fault of inattention, negligence or awkwardness be committed. In all these cases the offender must come at once, confess his fault, and do penance, before the Abbot if the Abbot be alone, before the Abbot and community if all the brethren are assembled together, which would ordinarily be the case.[3] This penance probably consisted of kneeling or prostration. St. Benedict would have it be voluntary: *ultro satisfecerit* (of his own accord do penance), and fulfilled with zeal: *veniens continuo* (come at once). The worthy Goth at Subiaco, who let the blade of his tool fall into the lake, acted in this manner.[4]

In a numerous community, often scattered and toiling in various places, much going and coming and loss of time would obviously be caused, for the Abbot and for each member, if the smallest offence or damage had to be brought at once to the knowledge of all. So monastic custom established the " chapter of faults," which is held in chapter several times a week, and in which each accuses himself of faults against observance, or some small damage for which he is responsible. The

---

[1] D. BUTLER reads: . . . *excesserit ubi ubi, et non veniens* . . .

[2] It is difficult to determine the exact meaning of this word. Some ancient manuscripts read *in monasterio*.

[3] *Qui vas fictile fregerit* . . . *aget pænitentiam vespere in sex orationibus. Si quis aliquid perdiderit, ante altare publice corripietur* (S. PACH., *Reg.*, cxxv., cxxxi.).—*Si quis gillonem fictilem* . . . *casu aliquo fregerit, non aliter neglegentiam suam quam publica diluet pænitentia, cunctisque in synaxi fratribus congregatis tamdiu prostratus in terram veniam postulabit*, etc. (CASS., *Inst.*, IV., xvi.).

[4] S. GREG. M., *Dial.*, l. II., c. vi.

penances, which cannot prudently be performed in church or even in the chapter room, are generally fulfilled in the refectory.

St. Benedict foresees the case of a monk who from false shame or a refractory spirit conceals one of these external faults or formal errors. In such a case, when what has occurred is learnt by means of another, the penance must be more severe.[1] The Abbot might be informed by the deans or the brethren, and the words of our Holy Father: *dum per alium cognitum fuerit* (but it be known by means of another), are not sufficient to prove that the practice of denunciation existed in those days. According to that monastic custom each monk had to make known in chapter the faults he had noticed in others. There is no doubt that it existed almost universally in the ninth century; Cluny and Cîteaux adopted it. It was suppressed by the Congregation of Monte Cassino, the Congregation of SS. Vitonus and Hydulphus, and the Congregations connected with them; but it is still in force among the Cistercians.[2] We must walk warily in examining the merits of a practice which has such abundant and venerable authority; yet it is easy to discover the reasons which have led us to abandon it. The duty of fraternal correction, fulfilled in that public fashion by all for the benefit of all, is yet the most delicate of duties. Charity is much endangered. A sort of narrow and jealous surveillance easily spreads and entangles all in its meshes. How easily will all sorts of petty rivalries, revenges, and reprisals vent themselves under cover of this regularized denunciation! Doubtless these dangers would vanish if the monks, denouncers as well as denounced, were all perfect. But then, to what purpose the denunciation? Abbot de Rancé replied that ill-consequences, however real, should not make us forget the benefit which may be got from this practice both by the good and by the lukewarm. Of course a religious who sees acts or tendencies which are a serious danger for the monastery or for one of the brethren should never shelter himself behind the condemnation which the world reserves for the informer and dispense himself from telling the Abbot. That would be to undervalue the honour of his brethren and the charity which he owes to all. After all, the hive is of more value than one bee, and certainly of more value than a hornet. Nor are the complaints of him whose fault is thus revealed really admissible.

Si animæ vero peccati causa latens fuerit, tantum Abbati, aut spiritualibus senioribus patefaciat, qui sciant curare sua, et aliena vulnera non detegere aut publicare.	If, however, the guilt of his offence be hidden in his own soul, let him manifest it to the Abbot only or to the spiritual seniors, who know how to heal their own wounds, and not to disclose or publish those of others.

Is our Holy Father here contrasting public confession of faults against the Rule, and penance for such, with secret confession of theological faults? More probably he refers to an extra-sacramental manifestation,

---

[1] *Si hoc ultro confitetur, parcatur illi et oretur pro ea. Si autem deprehenditur atque convincitur . . . gravius emendetur* (S. AUG., *Epist.* CCXI., 11. *P.L.*, XXXIII., 962).

[2] MARTÈNE, *De ant. monach. rit.*, l. I., c. v.

this regulation having then the same purpose as the fifty-first instrument of good works and the fifth degree of humility. Whether there be theological guilt or not, though the interior fault remain quite a formal one, the result of inadvertence, surprise, or impulse, though it be only a temptation, a disturbing mood, or an obstinate obsession—the brother, with filial purpose and loyal desire to amend, should manifest his state candidly—not to the whole community, since there has been no scandal or notoriety—but to the Abbot or to the spiritual seniors. As we have said elsewhere, the ancients regarded this practice as an indispensable means of spiritual progress, and as a source of peace and security. So we shall tell the Abbot, even though he look austere and we fear his judgement and the results of our confidence. Whatever may be the Abbot's character and worth in other respects, has he not, for his children, a sort of sacramental character? Has he not a right to know what is going on in his house and in his monks? By "spiritual seniors" St. Benedict probably means all those who have an important part in the government of souls. Failing the Abbot, manifestation should be made to them. They are "spiritual" men, instructed in the ways of God; having triumphed over the devil in their own case, or at least reduced his power, by the experience thus acquired they may be useful to others. They know how to heal their own wounds and the wounds of others. And, adds St. Benedict, we may count on their discretion; they will not reveal or publish the fault confessed.[1]

These two chapters just ending, besides their formal instruction, are useful also as showing us the system of our monastic life with respect to the interior culture of the soul. We do not belong to the active life, and we cannot have a twofold existence. The fact that we have definitely broken with the world removes from us a number of dangers. We are in habitual contact with God and holy things, as though wrapped ever in a cloud of fragrant incense. Even our hours of toil should bring us close to God; for they do not dissipate our attention. And, besides, we should be watchful the whole day long; we should at once repair and expiate before our brethren absolutely all the small infidelities to which nature has succumbed. What does all this mean but examination of conscience, not examination at a fixed hour and for a stated time, but continuous and assiduous examination, which nothing may escape? Let men who are plunged in the cares and perils of the apostolic ministry, ever liable in the very course of their activities to outstep the bounds and to yield overmuch to inclination—let such as these fortify themselves with manifold and minute examinations of conscience; for such they are both right and prudent. But the needs of our souls are different, and for them our Holy Father has otherwise provided. Were we to inflict on ourselves these endless investigations, the result would only be to increase our sense of self-importance, to exhaust and trouble us, perhaps even to poison our lives. Let us, then, replace this superfluous inquiry by regularity, absolute fidelity, perfect charity, and tranquil union with God.

[1] The best reading would appear to be as follows: *Qui sciant curare et sua et aliena vulnera, non detegere et publicare.*

CHAPTER XLVII

OF SIGNIFYING THE HOUR FOR THE WORK OF GOD

De significanda hora operis Dei.—Nuntianda hora operis Dei, die noctuque sit cura Abbatis, aut ipse nuntiare, aut tali sollicito fratri injungat hanc curam, ut omnia horis competentibus compleantur.

Let the announcing of the hour for the Work of God, both by day and night, be the Abbot's care: either by giving the signal himself or assigning this task to such a careful brother that all things may be done at the fitting times.

AGAIN the subject is regularity and orderliness. Since the Work of God forms the pivot of the monastic day, it is supremely important that the times for the Office should be fixed with care and punctually notified. Now, in an epoch when the length of the hour varied from day to day and when the methods of determining time were often rudimentary (see the commentary on the eighth chapter) we can understand why the duty of signifying the hour for the Work of God was given to the Abbot in person. He carries all responsibility. And in spite of the multiplicity of his occupations, St. Benedict is not afraid to entrust to him the care of calling the monks to prayer, seven times during the day and once at night. A wise provision, precluding disorder and disputes among the brethren; thus murmuring is banished and all are inspired with a greater esteem for the Divine Office.

Nevertheless, the Abbot's labours, or absence, or ill-health, might obviously make him unable to fulfil this duty; so that our Holy Father allows him to entrust it to an attentive and diligent brother. The latter shall see that all the Office is fulfilled in its entirety and at the fitting times (see the end of Chapter XI.). Nowadays Abbots delegate their power to an official, yet remain concerned that the work should be done with exactitude.

Commentators take occasion of this chapter to describe the various methods formerly employed in monasteries for the awaking or warning of the brethren. They knocked at doors,[1] or used such various instruments as horns, wooden trumpets,[2] clappers, rattles, etc. The nuns of St. Paula were summoned to Office by the singing of *Alleluia*.[3] In the Benedictine Order, perhaps from the very time of St. Benedict,[4] the thing most often used was a bell or hand-bell. Remembering the beautiful prayers in the Pontifical for the blessing of bells and the solemn consecration given to them, we shall not doubt that their sweet and penetrating tones are the very voice of God and that we should answer their appeal with glad haste.

[1] Cass., *Inst.*, IV., xii.   [2] S. Pach., *Reg.*, iii.
[3] S. Hieron., *Epist.* CVIII., 19. P.L., XXII., 896.
[4] It is narrated in the Life of St. Benedict how St. Romanus used to let down bread to him in his hermitage by means of a rope and to warn him by means of a bell fixed to this rope (S. Greg. M., *Dial.*, l. II., c. i.). The *signum* alluded to in the Rule (Chapters XXII., XLIII., XLVIII.) is probably a bell.

Of Signifying the Hour for the Work of God 303

Psalmos autem, vel Antiphonas, post Abbatem, ordine suo, quibus jussum fuerit, imponant. Cantare autem aut legere non præsumat, nisi qui potest ipsum officium implere, ut ædificentur audientes. Quod cum humilitate, et gravitate, et tremore faciat, et cui jusserit Abbas.

Let those, who have been ordered, intone the psalms and antiphons, each in his order, after the Abbot. Let no one presume to sing or to read except he can fulfil the office so that the hearers may be edified. And let it be done with humility, gravity, and awe, and by him whom the Abbot has appointed.

After having secured its regular commencement, St. Benedict makes an ordinance designed to safeguard the dignity of the work of God itself. The brethren must not intone or chant[1] the psalms and antiphons by chance, under the impulse of caprice or on their personal initiative. Several conditions are to be fulfilled before a monk may perform these duties. He must have received an order and have been regularly designated. The brethren shall intone psalms and antiphons in their turn and in order of seniority, " after the Abbot," as is natural. No one shall undertake to sing or read, if he be not capable of performing the office to the edification of the hearers. The duty of selecting, and of deciding the question of capacity, devolves on the Abbot.[2] Finally, when fulfilling the charge appointed to them, the brethren must display humility, gravity, religious fear, and a great spirit of submission.

[1] See the discussion in Chapter IX of this commentary on the primitive monastic psalmody and the probable meaning of the word *imponere*.

[2] *Adstantibus ad orationem nullus præsumat sine præcepto qui præest Patris psalmi laudem emittere* (*Reg.* I. SS. Patrum, vi.).

CHAPTER XLVIII

OF THE DAILY MANUAL LABOUR

De opere manuum quotidiano.— Otiositas inimica est animæ. Et ideo certis temporibus occupari debent fratres in labore manuum, certis iterum horis in lectione divina.

Idleness is the enemy of the soul. Therefore should the brethren be occupied at stated times in manual labour, and at other fixed hours in sacred reading.

THIS chapter gives us much more than is promised in the title. It deals not merely with manual labour, but with all monastic labours, with all that occupies the hours left free by the Office. It legislates for the use of time, giving the horarium of a Benedictine day.

According to his custom our Holy Father begins with a general precept: "Idleness is the enemy of the soul.[1] Therefore should the brethren be occupied, at stated times in manual labour, and at other fixed hours in sacred reading." Though St. Benedict alludes explicitly only to the dangers of idleness, he was not blind to the positive benefit and intrinsic value of work. Its advantages are manifold. We may see in work a potent means of diversion and a remedy for many temptations, we may recognize the weakness and softness of all that has not constant exercise, and finally we may remember that all life and all happiness imply action, contemplation itself being only the supreme activity of mind and heart united, an act of clinging with all our being to Him who is. Work is not simply a penalty and a punishment; it is a divine law anterior to sin, of universal validity. How, then, should monks escape it? Nay, they are doubly bound to work, since their life always includes some austerity and penance, and since that indwelling of God in the soul to which they aspire is only promised to those who toil perseveringly. Sweet toil! said St. Augustine regretfully, as he thought of the ceaseless worry that beset his episcopate.[2] Our Holy Father groups the chief monastic occupations under three heads: the Work of God, sacred reading, and manual labour (*Opus Dei, lectio divina, opus manuum*).

There is nothing but good to be said of manual labour.[3] From the very beginning, in various degree, it figures in the programme of the

---

[1] A reminiscence of St. Basil: *Et Salomon: Otiositas inimica est animæ* (*Reg. contr.*, cxcii.). D. Butler notes that this sentence is not from Solomon and does not occur in the Greek text of St. Basil (*Reg. fus.*, xxxvii.). We read in Ecclesiasticus (xxxiii. 28–29) only: *Mitte* (*servum*) *in operationem, ne vacet; multam enim malitiam docuit otiositas.*

[2] St. Benedict quotes some expressions verbally from this passage of the treatise *De opere monachorum: Quantum attinet ad meum commodum, multo mallem per singulos dies certis horis, quam in bene moderatis monasteriis constitutum est, aliquid manibus operari, et cæteras* (vel *certas*) *horas habere ad legendum et orandum, aut aliquid de divinis litteris agendum liberas* (c. xxix. *P.L.*, XL, 576).

[3] There is a full dissertation on manual labour in the Commentary of Martène.

religious life. It would seem that its first purpose is to reduce the body to subjection, to shake off its inertia, to destroy those desires and instincts which find in it their source and their fuel. So manual labour is a process of mortification. It allows us at the same time to consecrate to God our physical strength itself. Is there need to allude to its eminently hygienic character, especially in the young, for monks who devote long hours to the Office and to study? Accidentally, too, it may be a means of humility, and its servile character may be repugnant to certain natures; though it is hard to see what humiliation there is in digging the ground or breaking stones on a road. Finally manual labour sometimes becomes for monks the regular means of earning their bread; and, in every monastery, it is required at least by the daily necessities of life. But after one has in a general way proclaimed the indispensable nature of manual labour, after one has emphasized its advantages and even affirmed that, in a concrete case, it is necessary for an individual to the exclusion almost of any other, it remains true that material toil has no efficacy of itself for the formation of an intelligent nature and less still for the development of the supernatural life. Of the two forms of toil, the one servile, and the other liberal, with the intellect for its basis, it seems to us easy to recognize the absolute superiority of the second over the first, and to fix the proportion in which the two should normally be represented among us.

The success of the Holy Rule and the cause of its diffusion is the common connection of all the ordinances contained in it with an ideal of life which it set out to realize, and a primary and essential work. Our understanding of the Rule and appreciation of our vocation depend upon an exact and practical grasp of this connection. St. Benedict's master thought is that we should *seek God*. There are only two legitimate attitudes towards God: to enjoy Him when we possess Him, to seek Him as long as we do not possess Him fully. God is by nature hidden and invisible, He dwells in light inaccessible. " Verily thou art a hidden God, God of Israel, the Saviour " (Isa. xlv. 15). Even when He reveals Himself, He is still hidden: in creation, in the incarnation, in redemption, in the Eucharist. He reveals Himself more and hides Himself more; He is at once God giving Himself, and God incommunicable. And our life, when it is truly the life of Christ, becomes hidden with Him: " Ye are dead and your life is hidden with Christ in God " (Col. iii. 3). We sometimes wonder why it is that the dead we have loved most dearly never reveal themselves to us and seem to cease all relation with us. " If souls still intervened in the affairs of the living," said St. Augustine, " my mother Monica would speak to me every night, she who followed me over land and sea and whose one love I was."[1] Our dead are silent, because they must not disturb the economy of our faith; but above all because they belong to God, and, being His, adopt His ways and enwrap themselves in His mysteriousness. So we must seek God. The renunciations involved in our vows and in our whole life

[1] *De cura pro mortuis gerenda*, c. xiii. P.L., XL., 604.

set our souls free for this blessed seeking. We lose ourselves to find God, as the Gospel says and as St. John of the Cross sings so admirably:

> For no beauty created
> Myself will I lose,
> But alone for that Beauty,
> Which words cannot name,
> Which may happily be found.

The sacraments, prayer, the constant exercise of faith, hope, and charity, these things bring us near to God and make us enter little by little into union with Him. The "sacred reading" (*lectio divina*) prescribed by our Holy Father has no other purpose than this.

We should mark the phrase *lectio divina* carefully.[1] It is not merely intellectual activity and culture of the mind; so it is beside the point to commend St. Benedict for an intention which can scarcely have been his. It is the work of the intelligence, if you will, but of the intelligence applying itself to divine mysteries and divine learning; it is the work of the supernatural intelligence—that is to say, of faith. It is the organized totality of those progressive intellectual methods by which we make the things of God familiar to us and accustom ourselves to the contemplation of the invisible. Not abstract, cold speculation, nor mere human curiosity, nor shallow study; but solid, profound, and persevering investigation of Truth itself. We may say that God alone is the object of this study, its inspiration and its chief cause; for it is not only pursued under His gaze, but in His light and in very intimate contact with Him. It is a study pursued in prayer and in love. The name *lectio* is only the first moment of an ascending series: *lectio, cogitatio, studium, meditatio, oratio, contemplatio* (reading, thinking, study, meditation, prayer, contemplation); but St. Benedict knew that the remaining degrees would soon come if the soul were loyal and courageous. So it is to contemplation and union with God that the monastic *lectio divina* tends. The hours which our Holy Father would have us devote to this reading every day are essentially hours of prayer.

We have already answered those who enquire whether the ancient monks practised prayer, whether they had a set method, and what was the subject of their prayer. Apart from the Divine Office (which after all *is* surely prayer), apart from some moments of private prayer, "short and pure," which St. Benedict permitted to those who felt attracted to it, all were bidden to devote prolonged study to Sacred Scripture—the book of books—to the Fathers and the words of the liturgy. So, by ordinance of the Rule, the whole day was to be passed in the presence of God. The method of prayer was simple and easy. It was to forget self and to live in habitual recollection, to steep the soul assiduously in the very beauty of the mysteries of faith, to ponder on all the aspects of the

---

[1] It occurs in ST. AUGUSTINE: *Illud sane admonuerim religiosissimam prudentiam tuam, ut timorem Dei non irrationabilem vel inseras infirmiori vasi tuo, vel nutrias divina lectione gravique colloquio* (*Epist.* XX., 3. *P.L.*, XXXIII., 87).—*Erigunt nos divinæ lectiones* (*Sermo* CXLII., c. i. *P.L.*, XXXVIII., 778).

supernatural dispensation, under the inspiration of that Spirit of God which alone can teach us how to pray (Rom. viii. 26). For sixteen centuries, clerics, religious, and simple lay folk knew no other method of communicating with God than this free outpouring of the soul before Him, and this "sacred reading" which nourishes prayer, implies it, and is almost one thing with it.

Let us reassure ourselves. The absence of systematic method, of books containing short ready-made meditations, does not mean disorder, nor lead inevitably to dissipation of energy and distraction of mind. The ancients were not without certain practices for fixing thought and concentrating the soul; they did not disdain all spiritual discipline. Especially did they think it needful, for souls immersed in the manifold cares of the world, to remind them of Our Lord's advice: "But thou, when thou shalt pray, enter into thy chamber and, having shut the door, pray to thy Father in secret" (Matt. vi. 6). But they thought that the words of God, of the saints, and of the liturgy, meditated and repeated without ceasing, had a sovereign power of withdrawing the soul from anxious self-consideration, in order to possess it wholly and introduce it into the mystery of God and His Christ. Once there, the need of beautiful considerations or of the well-constructed arguments of a keen intellect vanished; there is need for naught but contemplation and love, in all simplicity. So, from the beginning of our conversion, the work of purgation is achieved by acts of the illuminative and unitive ways, and thus our transformation in God begins to be realized: "But we all, beholding the glory of the Lord with open face, are transformed into the same image, from glory to glory, as by the Spirit of the Lord" (2. Cor. iii. 18). In order that prayer may become an easy matter it is enough that we realize the treasure which baptism has given us, and, with St. Paul's help, understand what it means to be redeemed in Christ and to live with His life. Whatever be the suitability of methods for this or that class of the faithful, we may be permitted to preserve what Father Faber calls "the badge of the old Benedictine ascetics."[1] We are in the happy condition of Benjamin, the best loved son: "The best beloved of the Lord shall dwell confidently in him. As in a bride chamber shall he abide all the day long: and between his shoulders shall he rest" (Deut. xxxiii. 12).

The majority of St. Benedict's predecessors, even anchorites hidden in desert solitudes, devoted several hours of the night and of the day to spiritual study, especially to the study of the Scriptures. St. Pachomius would have the illiterate who joined him learn to read. Our forefathers considered that sacred study was required of all those to whom God gave intelligence and leisure. Contemplation itself is endangered as soon as it claims to be self-sufficient. For God never comes to the succour of sloth with extraordinary illumination; His works are arranged in orderly fashion, and He does not grant such

---

[1] *All for Jesus*, c. viii., § 8.—See D. GUÉRANGER's Preface to his translation of the *Exercises* of St. Gertrude.

favours save at His own pleasure and to those who can learn in no other way. Although St. Benedict counted among his monks more than one slave and barbarian, and although they all remained, with few exceptions, in the lay state, yet he reserved a relatively large amount of time for the *lectio divina*. He had himself abruptly broken off his secular studies and retired from the world *scienter nescius et sapienter indoctus*[1] (knowingly ignorant and wisely unlearned); but he took up later the assiduous study of Scripture and the Fathers, and his Rule betrays quite considerable reading. He lays it down that the Abbot should be " learned in the law of God " (Chapter LXIV.). For many centuries now the Black Monks have given a large place to study. Manual labour, without having been deliberately or completely abandoned, has been gradually replaced by mental labour. And we believe that this change is abundantly justified by the alteration in the intellectual, social, and economic conditions of modern times, and by the present position of monasteries. All choir monks must now be fit for the priesthood; and the Church has lately insisted on the necessity of study even for religious vowed to the contemplative life. She expects from them an apostolate of the mind, an influence on the Christian thought of their contemporaries; she sometimes entrusts to them, by exception, the work of preaching and instruction—but without ever dispensing them from being monks. And perhaps we may be allowed to insist on a matter which we think is no personal fancy, but a fundamental part of the monastic spirit.

First, then, under pain of suffering the springs of our prayer to dry up, we must reserve the best moments of the day for " sacred reading " properly so called. To what studies shall we give ourselves beyond our spiritual reading ? All that is valuable and useful for the Church is valuable and useful for us; but it goes without saying that, except for special works of obedience, the sciences known as ecclesiastical have a right to our choice, especially such as best suit the ordinary conditions of our life and are more fitted to unite us with God. Nevertheless, we should note that a monk does not specialize at pleasure according to his own inclinations; our studies, as well as all else, and with even more reason than manual labour, should be directed, controlled, and consecrated continually by the will of the Abbot.

But although we apply ourselves regularly to the study of theology, ecclesiastical history, patrology, or liturgy, it is of importance to know how to work and in what spirit. There are so many ways of studying a book. Let it be, for example, the manuscript of one of St. Augustine's sermons. One might describe its state, count its parts, recognize the style of its writing, determine its date. Or one could go farther, and attempt some measure of historical reconstruction, comparing the text with that of other manuscript or printed copies, with other works of St. Augustine, and with other authors; asking oneself when the sermon was delivered and to what audience; collecting from its pages all that would help to a better knowledge of the period, etc. Of course, such re-

[1] S. GREG. M., *Dial.*, l. II., præf.

searches are profitable and even necessary, and thoughtful men may even glean from them things of much moment for their instruction. Yet it is undeniable that such textual study is inadequate. What would become of the man who refused to eat until he had made a chemical analysis of every dish, separating what was harmful from what was nutritious? He would die of inanition. There is a third method, more scientific and more philosophical, which passes from the text to the meaning. There are major and minor premises and many various conceptions to be arranged methodically in one coherent whole and made part of a scheme of thought. But we should recognize well that this work, being purely abstract and academic, does not exhaust the content of the book. Divine truth is of greater worth; and those who confine themselves to such study will ever remain in the antechamber, studying God and never learning to know Him. How is it that a man may sometimes succeed in making theology itself the most wearisome, sterile, and frigid of all sciences? Because he regards it in a merely human and bookish manner, and sees in it only material for examination.

The definite acts, which should be the outcome of all those hitherto mentioned, are a heartfelt and practical assent to truth, a real assimilation of it, and an entire sympathy of soul. Clearly to see the spiritual theses of our faith will do us no good, if our will shuts itself off from the truth known, and if thought, love, and act do not work together. True knowledge is that which develops our faith and increases our charity. Moreover, charity, after having received from faith, gives it something in its turn; for we know better that which we love more, and we see according as we are. This is really fruitful study, the science of monks and of saints. Here is the normal occupation of our minds and a preparation for the beatific vision.

Work, as we said a moment ago, is a powerful diversion and saves us from a thousand temptations, a thing which is especially true of intellectual work. Yet it is not, like a sacrament, infallible in its operation, since we may study divine things in such a way as to remain ever ignorant of them. After all, the efficaciousness of our study is not to be measured by its material object or by its duration; we shall appreciate its value by its coefficient of moral dispositions, by a certain quality of attentiveness, a certain spiritual well-being, a certain loyalty and liberty of soul, by an awareness and an ever-deepening appreciation of God. The story of Æsop's banquet comes to my mind. He wished to set before his friends the best thing in the world, and it was found to be tongue; and the worst thing in the world, and again it was tongue. Study seems to me to be in like case. Perhaps it is the best of all created things; but when it deviates from its true end, it is worse than aught else. One may take occasion from philosophy, theology, and Scripture to lose one's own faith and destroy the faith of others. Knowledge by itself is not dangerous; and if some wise men are proud, so are some fools. But knowledge which has no influence on our sanctification is very likely to make us proud. " Lay up to yourselves treasures in heaven: where neither rust nor the moth doth consume, and where thieves do not break through and steal" (Matt. vi. 20). Purely human knowledge is exposed to rust, and the moth, and thieves; and a day comes when nothing is left of your living encyclopædia. The other sort of knowledge is divine by title, eternal in its fruit, and incorruptible of its very nature; it cannot be taken from us nor can we ourselves abuse it or make it a cause of vanity. It is profitable only for eternity. That is the only sort of knowledge which the Church and the world expect from priests and monks. God grant that we have not left the world and taken our vows in order to belong body and soul to science and criticism, to be devoted collectors of bibliographical notes. It is desirable that monastic work should be conscientious and methodical, and never fritter itself away on mediocre subjects;[1] but we must not take God *and* study as our ideal, we must not look to intensive production and realize all too literally the traditional learned Benedictine, who rivals the pupils of the École des Chartes or the members of the Académie des Inscriptions. What a sorry apostolate! The day that we sacrifice on the altar of study our conventual life, the solemn performance of the Office, monastic regularity and stability, we lose our whole character, and almost our title to exist. Let us remember in what miserable fashion the Congregation of St. Maur ended. As soon as there is any human consideration, whether reputation, riches, or knowledge, which we put into the scale against God and which we use as a pretext for robbing Him, then our fall is near.

So we must be on our guard against a naturalistic spirit: we must not cut down our prayers, or even lessen our esteem for them, in the interests of a quite unreal advantage to be gained by sacred learning. We should also fear the critical spirit, that narrow, crabbed, pedantic disposition which dissects all things distrustfully. We should avoid the carping spirit, for which authority is always in the wrong, *a priori*, especially actual present authority, the spirit which welcomes all mistrust. Those who doubt and deny win immediate fame. And the deference refused to tradition, to antiquity, to authority, is given at once and wholly, with infinite thoughtlessness, to the notions of some writer or other, to one of those prophets of the hour who trumpet the vague phrases: progress, evolution, broad-mindedness, and dogmatic awakening. This is intellectual foolery. And it seems to me that good sense and dignity require from us not only an attitude of reserve, but above all a spirit of tranquil resistance and conservatism. Conservation is the very instinct of life, a disposition essential for existence. We shall be truly progressive if we hold fast to this spirit, for there is no progress for a living organism which does not preserve continuity with its past. We belong to a traditional society, the Church. In his Conference with the Protestant minister Claude " sur la matière de l'Église," Bossuet observes " that there was never a time when the world did not possess a visible and speaking authority, to which obedience had to be given. Before Jesus Christ there was the Synagogue; when the Syna-

---

[1] Read MABILLON, *Traité des études monastiques*.

gogue was doomed, Jesus Christ Himself came; when He departed He left His Church, to which He sent His Holy Spirit. If you could bring back Jesus Christ, teaching, preaching, and working miracles, I should have no further need of the Church; likewise, if you take the Church from me, I need Jesus Christ in person, speaking, preaching, and deciding with miracles and an infallible authority."[1] Christians, clerics, and monks, we receive our teaching from the Church alone. Neither science nor criticism is our mother; the Church alone, who gave us birth and nourished us, has the right to form our souls for eternity. In dogma, morals, liturgy, history, and in Sacred Scripture especially, it is ever the Church which speaks and expounds. Hence the character of monastic teaching and of monastic studies: we take from the lips and from the heart of the Church the thought of God.

Ideoque hac dispositione credimus utraque tempora ordinari: id est, ut a Pascha usque ad Kalendas Octobris mane exeuntes, a prima usque ad horam pene quartam laborent, quod necessarium fuerit. Ab hora autem quarta usque ad horam quasi sextam lectioni vacent. Post sextam autem surgentes a mensa, pausent in lectis suis cum omni silentio; aut forte qui voluerit sibi legere, sic legat, ut alium non inquietet. Agatur Nona temperius, mediante octava hora; et iterum, quod faciendum est, operentur usque ad vesperam.

We think, therefore, that the times for each may be disposed as follows: from Easter to the Calends of October, on coming out in the morning let them labour at whatever is necessary from the first until about the fourth hour. From the fourth hour until close upon the sixth let them apply themselves to reading. After the sixth hour, when they rise from table, let them rest on their beds in all silence; or if anyone chance to wish to read to himself, let him so read as not to disturb anyone else. Let None be said rather soon, at the middle of the eighth hour; and then let them again work at whatever has to be done until Vespers.

In order to banish idleness the monk's day is to be devoted, at fixed hours, to manual labour and the study of sacred things. And this, continues our Holy Father, is the way in which we think we should apportion the time. In the eighth chapter, when determining the time for the beginning of the Night Office, St. Benedict divided the year into two seasons; in the forty-first chapter, dealing with the hours of meals, he divided it into four periods; in the forty-second chapter, apropos of the reading at Compline, he is content with two; and in this place finally he divides it into three. The first period extends from Easter to the Calends of October—*i.e.*, to September 14, on which day began the counting from the Calends (*decimo octavo Kalendas Octobris*); it is the same date as that signified in the forty-first chapter by the phrase *ab Idibus Septembris:* from the close of the Ides of September.[2]

[1] Bar-le-Duc edition, 1863, t. V., p. 348.
[2] These words cannot in this chapter mean the day on which the Calends fall—*i.e.* October 1: in fact, St. Benedict would have the brethren take their meal at None after September 14 (Chapter XLI.), at Sext from Easter to what he here calls the "Calends of October"; now the two ordinances would be irreconcilable, the one fixing September 14, the other October 1, if we understood the words *usque ad Kalendas Octobris* to mean the day on which the Calends fall.

Let us repeat what was said in the eighth chapter about the division of the day among the ancients. It was divided into twenty-four hours of unequal length according to the season; the twelve day hours were counted from the rising to the setting of the sun; they were longer in summer and shorter in winter.

During summer the brethren shall go out in the morning, probably after Prime, and occupy themselves in necessary work until the fourth hour. From the fourth hour until about the sixth they shall devote themselves to reading. Terce might be said in the fields (Chapter L.); Sext is said in the monastery. When the sixth hour is ended and the meal finished, the brethren shall rise from table and may then rest on their beds. This was the siesta, always indispensable for Italians, and granted here to monks with good reason, because during all this period the heat was greater, work larger in amount, and nights shorter. Our Holy Father would have the night silence observed during this time. And charity demands it, for the conversation of some would disturb the sleep of the rest. Yet no one is forced to lie down; he may continue the reading he had been engaged on before dinner, but on the express condition that he reads in a very low voice and to himself alone, so as not to annoy anyone. Apparently the ancients were accustomed when reading, if not to read aloud, at least to pronounce the words; and St. Augustine remarks on St. Ambrose's contrary practice.[1] After the siesta the brethren recite None (*agatur Nona*), though the ninth hour has not yet begun, it being about the middle of the eighth: *temperius, mediante octava hora*. Then they return to manual labour until evening, until the hour of Vespers.

Si autem necessitas loci, aut paupertas exegerit, ut ad fruges colligendas per se occupentur, non contristentur; quia tunc vere monachi sunt, si de labore manuum suarum vivunt, sicut et Patres nostri et Apostoli. Omnia tamen mensurate fiant propter pusillanimes.	If, however, the needs of the place or poverty require them to labour themselves in gathering in the harvest, let them not grieve at that; for then are they truly monks when they live by the labour of their hands, as our Fathers and the Apostles did. But let all things be done in moderation for the sake of the faint-hearted.

This passage might be applied to any season, but it is particularly appropriate for summer and the beginning of autumn, for that is the time of harvest and fruit-gathering. It is difficult to see how, from such a passage as this just read, certain well-known exaggerations could arise. St. Benedict foresees—he does not exact it—that conditions of locality or poverty may oblige the monks themselves to gather the fruits of the earth. The monks might live in a solitary region; the monastery might possess vast landed property and have only a few servants. If the crops were not to perish on the ground the monks had to be employed. And

---

[1] *Cum legebat, oculi ducebantur per paginas, et cor intellectum rimabatur, vox autem et lingua quiescebant. . . . Sic eum legentem vidimus tacite, et aliter numquam* (Confess., l. VI., c. iii. *P.L.*, XXXII., 720–721).

St. Benedict takes occasion of this possibility to remind us that manual labour is not only good and useful, and sanctified by obedience, but also that the holy Apostles and the Fathers of the desert were not ashamed to devote themselves to it. The remark was not superfluous. In the East manual labour kept a less servile and coercive character than in the West. Even rich folk often learnt a craft, working for occupation or to give alms to the poor. St. Paul wove Cilician sail-cloth, proudly resolving not to burden the churches. But the West is more practical and more industrial; with a different climate and vigorous muscles there is more expenditure of physical strength, so that labour was naturally left to slaves And our Holy Father thinks it necessary to plead in its favour, as St. Augustine had done at some length in his treatise *De opere monachorum* (Concerning the work of monks). Monks should never find manual work beneath them, especially those who have been slaves, says the holy Doctor. And to live by the work of one's hands, as did our fathers and the Apostles, is to be truly a monk; it is to devote oneself to a very monastic occupation and to realize a primitive ideal.[1] But our Holy Father nowhere says that monks are not monks or are less monks when they do not live by the labour of their hands. It is impossible to misunderstand his thought if we note that he here speaks of harvest as of an exceptional thing and an extraordinary labour. Yet even then, he adds, the law of discretion holds good. All must be done with moderation, on account of the weak. The Abbot shall be careful never to crush the community under an excessive load of work.

A Kalendis autem Octobris usque ad caput Quadragesimæ, usque ad horam secundam plenam lectioni vacent; hora secunda agatur Tertia; et usque ad Nonam omnes in opus suum laborent, quod eis injungitur. Facto autem primo signo nonæ horæ, disjungant se ab opere suo singuli, et sint parati, dum secundum signum pulsaverit. Post refectionem autem vacent lectionibus suis, aut Psalmis.	From the Calends of October until the beginning of Lent let the brethren devote themselves to reading till the end of the second hour. At the second hour let Terce be said, after which they shall all labour at their appointed work until None. At the first signal for the hour of None all shall cease from their work, and be ready as soon as the second signal is sounded. After their meal let them occupy themselves in their reading or with the psalms.

From the Calends of October—that is to say, from the beginning of the monastic Lent (September 14)—till the beginning of Lent proper, there is a new rule for manual labour. The great labours are over; perhaps it is inside the monastery rather, and in the various workshops of the enclosure, that the monks are then employed. The day hours are growing shorter and shorter; the hours of the night being abundantly

---

[1] *Ne ipsi quidem (monachi Romani) cuiquam onerosi sunt, sed Orientis more, et Pauli apostoli auctoritate manibus suis se transigunt* (S. AUG., *De moribus eccles. cathol.*, l. I., c. xxxiii. P.L., XXXII., 1340).—*(Antonius) gaudebat quod sine cujusquam molestia ex propriis manibus viveret (Vita S. Antonii,* versio EVAGRII, 50. P.G., XXVI., 915).

sufficient, there is no question now of a siesta. From morning till the end of the second hour the brethren devote themselves to reading. When the second hour is ended they say Terce. Then, until the ninth hour, each is employed in his appointed task.[1] The Office of None (and probably the others too) is announced by two signals. At the first signal all leave their work at once and prepare for the Office, which begins after the sounding of the second signal. Then follows the meal. Then the brethren take up again their reading of the morning, or study the psalms. Perhaps the words *lectionibus suis* (their reading) designates especially the lessons of the Night Office, as in the eighth chapter: "And let the time that remains after the Night Office be spent in study by those brethren who have still some part of the psalter and lessons to learn." Our Holy Father intends, therefore, that the substance of the "sacred reading" and of study should be taken primarily from the liturgy. This reading continued until Vespers. If we add this reading to that of the morning and to that which could follow the Night Office in winter, we obtain a large amount of spiritual study. The Rule nowhere speaks expressly of conferences. It is probable, however, that the Abbot gave his monks the benefit of the doctrine which St. Benedict expects him to possess. Sometimes doubtless the reading was done by one only, by the Abbot or a dean, and anyone might ask questions. This was one of the recognized methods of teaching in ancient times and St. Benedict has some allusions to it (Chapter IV., fifty-sixth instrument, Chapter VI., Chapter XXXVIII.).

In Quadragesimæ vero diebus, a mane usque ad tertiam plenam, lectioni vacent, et usque ad decimam plenam operentur quod eis injungitur. In quibus diebus Quadragesimæ, accipiant omnes singulos codices de bibliotheca, quos per ordinem ex integro legant: qui codices in capite Quadragesimæ dandi sunt.

In Lent, however, from the morning till the end of the third hour, let them devote themselves to reading, and, after that, work at their appointed tasks till the end of the tenth hour. In this time of Lent let them receive a book each from the library, to be read consecutively and straight through. These books are to be given out at the beginning of Lent.

We have here the third and last period, the time of Lent. Reading is then to be taken in the morning to the end of the third hour. After that, till the end of the tenth hour, the monks have to busy themselves in the work that has been ordered them. In these arrangements we may note that there is no mention of Mass on weekdays.

In the next chapter our Holy Father recommends special application to reading during Lent; he here makes provision so that none may lack books and evade so necessary an obligation. The monastery shall possess a library and one large enough for each monk to receive a manu-

---

[1] *Omni tempore usque ad tertiam legant: post tertiam unusquisque sibi opera injuncta faciat* (S. Cæsar., *Reg. ad mon.*, xiv.). *Post horam secundam unusquisque ad opus suum paratus sit usque ad horam nonam, ut quidquid injunctum fuerit, sine murmuratione perficiat* (S. Macar., *Reg.*, xi.).

script.¹ These will be given out at the beginning of Lent, a practice which still obtains. We receive from the hands of the Abbot himself the book by means of which God is to instruct us. " To be read consecutively and straight through:" it is not enough to skip the pages, to read carelessly in a random and perfunctory manner such passages as seem less tedious; our Holy Father would have us read through in order. He requires serious study and not that rapid, superficial manner of reading which is only a graceful form of laziness. The Rule does not fix a date for the restoration of such books, nor does it say that they have to be read in their entirety during Lent.

Ante omnia sane deputentur unus aut duo seniores, qui circumeant monasterium horis quibus vacant fratres lectioni, et videant, ne forte inveniatur frater acediosus, qui vacet otio aut fabulis, et non sit intentus lectioni: et non solum sibi inutilis sit, sed etiam alios extollat. Hic talis, si (quod absit) repertus fuerit, corripiatur semel et secundo: si non emendaverit, correctioni regulari subjaceat, taliter ut ceteri metum habeant. Neque frater ad fratrem jungatur horis incompetentibus.

Above all, let one or two seniors be deputed to go round the monastery at the hours when the brethren are engaged in reading, and see that there be no slothful brother giving himself to idleness or to gossip, and not applying himself to his reading, so that he is not only useless to himself, but a distraction to others. If such a one be found (which God forbid) let him be corrected once and a second time; and, if he do not amend, let him be subjected to the chastisement of the Rule, in such a way that the rest may be afraid. Moreover one brother shall not associate with another at unsuitable hours.

After the enunciation of the precept of sacred reading there follow certain disciplinary measures to guarantee its observance. We suspect that in St. Benedict's time there were novices—perhaps even older monks—who felt little attraction for the deciphering of cumbrous manuscripts and would have preferred working in the fields to the Sermons of St. Augustine on the psalms, or to some other and more subtle commentator. It was for their benefit, to assist their consciences, that St. Benedict instituted the *circatores*. " Above all," he says, " let one or two seniors be deputed to go round the monastery at the hours when the brethren are engaged in reading." They will ascertain what is going on. Perhaps they will meet an easygoing brother, one with no taste for things of the mind and weary of seeking God, *acediosus*.² Instead of applying himself to his reading, he dreams and dozes, or else he gossips. A man afflicted with ennui propagates his own condition, and laziness is contagious. So this brother not only wastes his own time and harms himself, but also distracts the rest. When the *circator* meets with such a defective monk—which God forbid—he must himself reprimand him secretly or have him admonished by the Abbot once or twice. But if the guilty man does not amend, he is to be subjected to

---

[1] Some particulars on the ancient monastic libraries are given in HÆFTEN, l. IX., tract. iv., disq. v·, and CALMET, Commentary on Chapter XLVIII.

[2] *Cf.* St. Thomas, II.–II., *q.* xxxv., on *acedia*.

the chastisement of the Rule, in such sort that all the rest may be inspired with fear.

The observation that succeeds has a general reference and concerns all seasons of the year, and all times of silence. One monk must not associate with another, or converse, at unsuitable hours. Many dangers are thus removed. Once more, thanks to these few words, we see that St. Benedict's monks had regular hours when they could converse.

Dominico die lectioni vacent, exceptis iis qui variis officiis deputati sunt. Si quis vero ita negligens et desidiosus fuerit, ut non velit aut non possit meditari aut legere, injungatur ei opus quod faciat, ut non vacet. Fratribus infirmis vel delicatis talis opera aut ars injungatur, ut nec otiosi sint, nec violentia laboris opprimantur, ut effugentur. Quorum imbecillitas ab Abbate consideranda est.

On Sunday let them devote themselves to reading, save such as are assigned to the various offices. But if anyone be so negligent and slothful as to be unwilling or unable to read or meditate, he must have some work given him that he be not idle. For weak or delicate brethren let such work or craft be enjoined that they will not be idle and yet will not be oppressed by weight of labour so as to be driven away. The weakness of such brethren must be considered by the Abbot.

Here, finally, are some exceptions to the rules laid down in this chapter. Something needed to be said of Sunday. On this day, in every season, manual labour ceases and all the brethren are occupied in reading,[1] save such as are employed in duties which cannot cease—the work of the kitchen, for example.

St. Benedict then provides for the case of a monk who is so negligent and slothful that he will neither read nor meditate. *Aut non possit* (or unable): perhaps even he cannot, because of a habit of intellectual indifference, or else from defect of nature, without culpability on his part. That he may not remain unoccupied, some task shall be given him. Without doubt our Holy Father would have this done on the other days of the week as well and not on Sunday only. However, it might be more necessary on Sunday, for, during the long hours devoted by the community to reading, some occupation would have to be found for the negligent or illiterate consistent with Sunday restrictions.

Not only should the duration of manual labour be fixed prudently; its kind also should be adapted to the powers of the individual. St. Benedict wrote previously: "But let all things be done in moderation for the sake of the faint-hearted." He here pleads again in favour of the weak or delicate. They should not remain idle and yet they should not be oppressed by too heavy a weight of labour, so as to be discouraged and even tempted to flee from the monastery.[2] They shall be entrusted with some easy task, and appointed to work suitable to their state of health. This consideration for their weakness is left to the conscience and to the heart of the Abbot.

[1] *Dominicis diebus orationi tantum et lectionibus vacant* (S. HIERON., *Epist.* XXII., 35. *P.L.*, XXII., 420).

[2] *Ne plus operis fratres compellantur facere; sed moderatus labor omnes ad operandum provocet* (S. PACH., *Reg.*, clxxix.).

CHAPTER XLIX

OF THE OBSERVANCE OF LENT

De Quadragesimæ observatione.—Licet omni tempore vita monachi Quadragesimæ debeat observationem habere; tamen quia paucorum est ista virtus, ideo suademus istis diebus Quadragesimæ omni puritate vitam suam custodire, omnes pariter negligentias aliorum temporum his diebus sanctis diluere.

Although the life of a monk ought at all times to have about it a Lenten observance, yet since few have strength enough for this, we exhort all, at least during the days of Lent, to keep themselves in all purity of life, and to wash away during that holy season the negligences of other times.

ST. BENEDICT had occasion in the preceding chapter to describe certain of the ordinary observances of Lent; but so important is this season in a Christian and monastic life[1] that he devotes a special chapter to it, wherein are set before all certain optional practices, and especially the supernatural dispositions which will give value to what they do.

We should not misunderstand the nature of St. Benedict's declaration " that the life of a monk ought at all times to be marked by Lenten observance." Lent, according to the popular view, is a portion of the year given over to fasting, abstinence, and practices of mortification. The world, which is always impressed by what hits it hardest, regards Lent as so much stinting of food and drink; it is more alive to the culinary hardships of this season than to its real and fundamental purpose of penance. But in St. Benedict's conception, Lent has a wider meaning. When he expresses the desire that the life of a monk should be a continual Lent, he is not speaking of Lenten fare; for that would be to upset the regulations he has made elsewhere and to leave a monk the dangerous liberty of eating or not as he pleased, and of eating at his own hours, and it would imply want of discretion. Moreover it does not appear that our Holy Father intends to embark his monks on a régime of endless austerities and extraordinary mortification. He is speaking of the Lent of the spirit, a Lent which will fit in with any horarium and suit all states of bodily health, which, moreover, is far superior to the Lent of the body, this being but a means to help us to achieve the other.

This true Lent involves two elements, negative and positive, an element which disjoins and an element which unites. It consists in the first place of the elimination of sin, and even of imperfection, in the suppression of all that cannot be reconciled with God's Will for us, with the dignity of our vocation and the seriousness of our vows. And the Lent of the spirit is complete when good works are practised and the soul clings more closely to God. Now the monk's life should at every time be an endeavour to fulfil this programme of sanctity. The very

---

[1] *Cf.* Cass., *Conlat.*, XXI.

reality of our incorporation with Our Lord and daily liturgical co-operation with His mystery should be enough to stamp our lives with the mark of a continually increasing fidelity. But St. Benedict shows his knowledge of men, for he says: " few have strength enough for this." We always lag somewhat behind our ideal, and even in perfect loyalty there are defects of execution. So the purpose of Lent is to furnish us with an opportunity of repairing and expiating the negligences of other times. It is a time, moreover, of recollection, of more attentive docility, of spiritual activity: " keep themselves in all purity of life." St. Benedict here uses the word purity in its broad and comprehensive sense, understanding by it the life of unity and unmixed union with God, the absence of all base alloy in the inner principle which determines our activity: " Whoso are led by the Spirit of God, they are the sons of God "; wherein is virginity of heart. To keep our souls in all purity and to efface the negligences of the rest of the year, these are two counsels connected as cause and effect: for we do not strike at the faults of other times save by our fidelity in the present.[1]

| Quod tunc digne fit, si ab omnibus vitiis nos temperemus: orationi cum fletibus, lectioni, et compunctioni cordis, atque abstinentiæ operam demus. | This we shall worthily do if we refrain from all sin and give ourselves to prayer with tears, to holy reading, compunction of heart, and abstinence. |

St. Benedict now develops his meaning, giving in detail the points with which the individual's observance of Lent may be concerned. First comes the negative element, abstinence from all vices and evil habits. This is fundamental; for it is idle to add new practices, to conceive a fine plan of bodily austerities, when our hearts remain voluntarily full of pride, jealousy, sloth, and murmuring.

Then we have the positive element in which prayer comes first. The Pharisees put the external work and material performance before all else; but a Christian thinks first of prayer. St. Benedict requires prayer accompanied by tears—that is, prayer intimate and earnest, springing from love and " compunction of heart." We recognize here the teaching of Chapter XX. So, in Lent, private prayer shall be more frequent and more fervent, while official prayer, the divine service, shall be better prepared and performed with greater care. We shall also apply ourselves specially to the study of divine things, *lectioni*,

[1] St. Benedict is inspired by several passages of ST. LEO THE GREAT: *Hæc autem præparatio, licet omni tempore salubriter assumatur, ... nunc autem sollicitius expetenda est. ... Scientes enim [adversarii nostri] adesse sacratissimos Quadragesimæ dies, in quorum observantia omnes præteritæ desidiæ castigantur, omnes neglegentiæ diluuntur.—Debebatur quidem tantis mysteriis ita incessabilis devotio et continuata reverentia, ut tales permaneremus in conspectu Dei, quales nos in ipso paschali festo dignum est inveniri. Sed quia hæc fortitudo paucorum est . . . magna divinæ institutionis salubritate provisum est, ut ad reparandam mentium puritatem quadraginta nobis dierum exercitatio mederetur, in quibus aliorum temporum culpas et pia opera redimerent, et jejunia casta decoquerent.—Deo ita demum sacrificium veræ abstinentiæ et veræ pietatis offerimus, si nos ab omni malitia contineamus* (De Quadrag., Sermo I., 2. P.L., LIV., 264; Sermo IV., 1 et 6. P.L., ibid., 275, 280).

which explains the reference in the previous chapter to Lenten books. We should note that our Holy Father does not suggest extraordinary practices, but a full and more generous accomplishment of the ordinary duties of our state. To this he appends a counsel of self-restraint: *abstinentiæ*, perhaps giving to this word, as to the word Lent, a wider signification than that sanctioned by current usage. Nor could it have referred to abstinence from meat, for this was continual in monasteries.

Ergo his diebus augeamus nobis aliquid ad solitum pensum servitutis nostræ: orationes peculiares, ciborum et potus abstinentiam, unusquisque super mensuram sibi indictam aliquid propria voluntate cum gaudio Sancti Spiritus offerat Deo: id est, subtrahat corpori suo de cibo, de potu, de somno, de loquacitate, de scurrilitate, et cum spiritualis desiderii gaudio sanctum Pascha expectet.	In these days, then, let us add something to the usual meed of our service: as private prayers, and abstinence from food and drink, so that everyone of his own will may offer to God, with joy of the Holy Spirit, something beyond the measure appointed him: withholding from his body somewhat of his food, drink, and sleep, refraining from talk and mirth, and awaiting holy Easter with the joy of spiritual longing.

The monastic life was defined as a "school of the Lord's service." So we have a task, a service to fulfil, according to strict justice and the requirements of our vows. But the good and generous servant goes beyond what is prescribed: *augeamus aliquid* (let us add something).[1] And St. Benedict proceeds to enumerate some Lenten practices—viz., special prayers, which chiefly concern the soul, and privations in food and sleep, with a more scrupulous abstinence from talking and dissipation, for the conquest of the body. Abstinence, fasting, and vigils are the standard methods of bodily mortification. We may remind ourselves that in Lent our forefathers took only one meal and that in the evening; therefore it required some strength of soul to reduce further an already frugal régime. "So that everyone may offer something": would it not be a fair interpretation of St. Benedict's meaning if we recognized in this phraseology a brief allusion to the discretion and moderation which should characterize our observance, even in Lent? A multiplicity of external works is another mark of the piety of the Pharisee.

But what we should discover in these words, more than anything else, is an indication of the inner dispositions from which our Lenten practices should proceed: they should have the gracious quality of an "offering made to God." An offering is by definition something spontaneous, so the monk will take counsel with his generosity and himself choose his gift, *propria voluntate* (of his own will); and if obedience intervenes, it will not be to reduce initiative or manly resolution,

---

[1] Another reminiscence of St. Leo: *Omnem observantiam nostram ratio istorum dierum poscat augeri.... Ad mensuram consuetudinis nostræ necessariis aliquid addamus augmentis* (*De Quadrag., Sermo* II., I. *P.L.*, LIV., 268).—*Debet esse aliquid quod Quadragesimæ diebus addatur* (vel *augeatur*): *sed ita, ut nihil ostentationis causa fiat, sed religionis* (S. Ambros., *De virginibus*, l. III., c. iv. *P.L.*, XVI., 225).

but to guide them and make them fruitful. An offering should be joyous, " with joy of the Holy Spirit ": " for God loveth a cheerful giver " (2 Cor. ix. 7). We know that the Pharisee when he fasted had a long and disagreeable face: "they disfigure their faces" (Matt. vi. 16-18). Isaias saw them "bowing their heads low and lying on sackcloth and ashes" (lviii. 5).[1] But Our Lord requires a different attitude from souls which are at peace with Him, which are loved by Him, and which carry within them infinite Love, Beauty, and Joy; " but thou, when thou fastest, anoint thy head, and wash thy face." Our Holy Father knows his New Testament. He is not at all blind to the fact that in Lent there are special obstacles to joy: physical obstacles, such as a rebellious stomach or a heavy head; spiritual obstacles, such as petty temptations, and attacks of those nasty " black birds."[2] When there is physical suffering or moral depression, the enemy is never far distant; neither is God, fortunately, nor His angels; therefore the Church is careful to commit us to the good angels at the very beginning of the holy season of Quadragesima.[3]

Besides, as the Rule reminds us, Lent will end. We should anticipate the joy of paschal time and let it influence the weeks of expectation. The joy meant is " the joy of spiritual longing "; the joy of the stomach, which has a base longing of its own, is not here referred to. "And awaiting holy Easter with the joy of spiritual longing ": we can catch a glimpse in these few words of the great sweetness of Easter to our Holy Father. Thus is joy mentioned twice in a few lines, for in fact joy is always a duty. Even in its most austere moments and in its penitential exercises the monastic life should keep that tranquil character and that accessibility which St. Benedict wished it to have: " In the setting forth of which we hope to order nothing that is harsh or rigorous."

Hoc ipsum tamen, quod unusquisque offert, Abbati suo suggerat, et cum ejus fiat oratione et voluntate: quia quod sine permissione patris spiritualis fit, præsumptioni deputabitur et vanæ gloriæ, non mercedi. Ergo cum voluntate Abbatis omnia agenda sunt

Let each one, however, make known to his Abbot what he offers, and let it be done with his blessing and permission: because what is done without leave of the spiritual father shall be imputed to presumption and vainglory, and merit no reward. Everything, therefore, is to be done with the approval of the Abbot.

Additional mortifications, though undertaken spontaneously, must be submitted to the judgement of the Abbot, whom our Holy Father here calls the "spiritual father." There can be no excess in the theological virtues, but in the moral virtues excess is easy, for they consist in a wise mean between two extremes, and their immediate object is a thing which is not good of itself or for itself, but in virtue of its relation to an absolute good. Mortification is only a relative good: otherwise

---

[1] *Missale Romanum, Epistola feriæ* vi. *post Cineres.*
[2] S. Greg. M., *Dial.*, l. II., c. ii.   [3] *Missale Romanum, Dom.* i. *Quadrag.*

every Indian fakir would be perfect.[1] It is good because it establishes us in moral health and reduces the demands of our bodies or of self-will; because it helps us to expiate and make amends for sin; and above all because it associates us with the sufferings of Our Lord Jesus Christ; it is good as a method and as a means, not as an end. Now there is room here for errors, both doctrinal and practical. Not only is it possible to fail in moderation, but even, by a strange reversal of the very principles of Christianity, to make the whole supernatural life consist in the " mortification " of penance. It is possible to exceed in audacity, to slay the ram that Isaac may live. An attraction towards severe mortification may be a matter of temperament, of natural violence, or morbid excess of refinement, or nothing but a form of pride. Very frequently an ardent desire of bodily mortification is not united with interior obedience and with mortification of the understanding. There is no future for the soft soul, nor yet for those who are extremely mortified, if their penances be not accompanied with a very great docility and submission of spirit. St. Benedict indicates the sole method of avoiding illusion, that we should tell the Abbot our good desires and follow his guidance in everything.

Our Holy Father gives another motive for such recourse to our superior. A monk has ceased to belong to himself, his whole activity is determined by the Rule and by the will of the Abbot.[2] It would not do, under pretence of perfection, and by means of particular observances, which may be excellent in themselves but are not authorized, to escape for a whole Lent from that absolute subjection which is the very essence of our monastic life. Whatever we might do in these dispositions would have no supernatural character, nor bring us any merit. Whatever is done without the permission of the spiritual father, says St. Benedict, shall be imputed to presumption and vainglory, and merit no reward.[3] Once more are we put on our guard against pharisaical tendencies, against ostentation in good deeds: " Sound not a trumpet before thee, as the hypocrites do in the synagogues and in the streets, that they may be honoured by men. Amen I say to you, they have received their reward " (Matt. vi. 2). In our little mortifications we should forget everything save the regard and the joy of our heavenly Father. St. Benedict, besides speaking of the permission of the Abbot, mentions his prayers as well. We may always count on the prayers of our Abbot, and our prayers should habitually be united with his.

[1] As Father Faber remarks; *Growth in holiness*, chapter xi.
[2] *Sine (præpositi) voluntate nullus frater quidquam agat* (*Reg. II. SS. Patrum*, i.).
[3] *Cf.* S. Basil., *Reg. contr.*, lxxxix., clxxxi., clxxxiv.—Cass., *Inst.*, V., xxiii.—Hæften, l. X., tract. viii., disq. vi.—Udalr., *Consuet. Clun.*, l. II., c. lii.

CHAPTER L

OF BRETHREN WHO ARE WORKING AT A DISTANCE FROM THE ORATORY OR ARE ON A JOURNEY

THESE two short chapters (L. and LI.) take account of possible exceptions to the perfect punctuality and regularity treated of in the preceding chapters. They might be joined under one title. Their purpose is to settle cases of conscience, created by temporary withdrawal or prolonged absence, with regard to two duties: first, the Divine Office; secondly, conventual meals. The fiftieth chapter tells us how those brethren are to perform the Hours who cannot be in the oratory with the community, either because their work keeps them in the fields or because they are on a journey.

DE FRATRIBUS QUI LONGE AB ORATORIO LABORANT, AUT IN VIA SUNT.—Fratres qui omnino longe sunt in labore, et non possunt occurrere hora competenti ad oratorium, et Abbas hoc perpendit quia ita est, agant ibidem opus Dei, ubi operantur, cum tremore divino flectentes genua.

Those brethren who work at a great distance and cannot come to the oratory at the proper time (the Abbot judging such to be the case) should perform the Work of God there where they are working, bending their knees in godly fear.

We may note in the first place that St. Benedict regards all his monks as strictly bound to the Office; yet in those days monks were not generally clerics. Brethren who have gone to work in the fields must contrive to return, in time to celebrate each of the liturgical Hours in the oratory, if the distance is not too great, and also, doubtless, if they can leave their work without serious inconvenience; but this second proviso, though established in monastic tradition, is not mentioned by St. Benedict.

Those who are too far away (*qui omnino longe sunt*) must say the Office where they are. And, to cut short indecision, the Abbot is to decide whether they shall return or not. This obviously refers to exceptional cases. All manual work, in St. Benedict's plan, should ordinarily be performed within the enclosure (Chapter LXVI.), and in such sort that the brethren may easily assemble for the Work of God. But it may often happen that the monastery has more distant possessions. In such cases the crops shall be gathered by workmen. The Rule nowhere provides for large agricultural undertakings, which should habitually absorb the activities of the community and compel many monks to be absent all day or for whole weeks far from the centre of conventual life.

The custom of reciting certain parts of the Office in the fields existed before St. Benedict: it is mentioned by the Rules of St. Pachomius and St. Basil.[1] On which point Martène observes that "we should not wonder that monks performed the Divine Office in the fields, since they also took the midday sleep there, to refresh their bodies." Perhaps it is easier to sleep in the fields than to recite the Office there reverently. So our Holy Father recommends the observance of the same supreme reverence and the same vigilance as in choir. God is nowhere absent, and if the thought of His presence is familiar to monks, as St. Benedict would have it be, they will recollect themselves without trouble. The place of their work thus becomes as sacred as the oratory. The customary ceremonial is observed there: bows, genuflexions, prayers said kneeling or prostrate: *cum tremore divino flectentes genua;* which words do not mean that the whole Office is recited kneeling, but rather that the same rubrics are kept as in choir. There is question, probably, only of a Little Hour, and practically all could be recited from memory.[2]

Similiter qui in itinere directi sunt, non eos prætereant Horæ constitutæ: sed ut possunt, agant ibi, et servitutis pensum non negligant reddere.	In the same way let not the appointed hours pass them by who are sent on a journey: but, as far as they can, let them perform them there and not neglect to pay their due of service.

Here we have the case of monks on journey. The question has been asked: to what refer the words "in the same way"? The Cluniacs held with good reason that they applied to the phrase "let not . . . pass them by"; the Cistercians that they referred to the words "bending their knees." As a matter of fact universal monastic custom was practically this. When the time for reciting the Hour seemed to have come a monk got down from his horse (long journeys were rarely made on foot), took off his travelling gloves and headgear, and prayed in the same way and in the same posture as he would have done in choir; when the Hour was started thus, he remounted his horse and continued the psalmody. When the roads were too muddy, when there was rain or snow, the genuflexion before the Office was dispensed with and the *Miserere* recited instead: such at least was the Cluniac custom, as Peter the Venerable reminds St. Bernard.[3] Our Holy Father suggested such discreet action when he wrote: "as far as they can let them perform them there."[4] These words leave a margin for the interpretation of superiors and monks; they must celebrate the Work of God as well as possible. If they had been bound to recite the Office exactly as in choir and in its entirety, they would have had to carry with them large manuscript books. Breviaries were then, and for long after, unknown. Before their appearance, however, there is evidence of the use of manu-

---

[1] *Si in navi fuerit, et in monasterio, et in agro et in itinere, et in quolibet ministerio, orandi et psallendi tempora non prætermittat* (S. PACH., *Reg.*, cxlii.).—*Si corporaliter non occurrat adesse cum ceteris ad orationis locum, in quocunque loco inventus fuerit, quod devotionis est expleat* (S. BASIL., *Reg. contr.*, cvii.).—See also CASS., *Inst.*, II., xv.
[2] See the interesting particulars given by the *Rule of the Master*, lv.
[3] *Epist.*, l. I., *Ep.* XXVIII. *P.L.*, CLXXXIX., 132.
[4] We should read: *agant sibi*, they shall say the Office by themselves.

scripts containing certain portions of the Office and a selection of prayers and lessons for travellers.[1] So St. Benedict could not give more exact instructions. What he wishes is that monks should do what they can. " And not neglect to pay their due of service ": for it is a debt of justice and a sacred obligation.[2]

In the words " let not the appointed Hours pass them by " some commentators see a command to recite each Hour at its proper time. St. Benedict would have been surprised at a monk saying Lauds, for instance, at sunset or bedtime. We may also remember that there are places which are less favourable to a pious and becoming recitation of our Office; and finally, that apart from the cases provided for in moral theology, no one nowadays is free to shorten his Office and suit it to the exigencies of his journey.

[1] *Cf.* CALMET, Commentary on Chapter L.
[2] On the antiquity and universality of this obligatory recitation, for clerics as for monks, *cf.* MABILLON, *De Liturgia gallicana: Disquisitio de cursu gallicano*, vi., pp. 426–439.

CHAPTER LI

OF BRETHREN WHO DO NOT GO FAR AWAY

De fratribus qui non satis longe proficiscuntur. — Fratres qui pro quovis responso proficiscuntur, et ea die sperant reverti ad monasterium, non præsumant foris manducare, etiamsi a quovis rogentur: nisi forte eis ab Abbate suo præcipiatur. Quod si aliter fecerint, excommunicentur.

Brethren who go out on any business and expect to return to the monastery on the same day must not presume to eat abroad, even though they be asked by anyone at all; except permission be given by their Abbot. If they do otherwise let them be excommunicated.

THE title of this chapter is not a sufficient indication of its real purpose. The preceding chapter laid down rules of conduct for monks with regard to the Divine Office; the present chapter tells them what they must do with regard to meals.

The chapter deals with brethren who are sent out officially on some business (*pro quovis responso*).[1] St. Benedict says nothing about monks who travel far; these would obviously have to accept the hospitality they found on the road. Or else they would carry their provisions with them—a necessary course in the desert—and then the sun would sometimes dry up the wine-skins, as it did for those brethren who went to visit St. Antony; or sometimes the ass which carried their food expired on the road.[2]

Whenever monks see that they can return to the monastery the same day they must be careful not to sit at table with layfolk. St. Benedict foresaw the excuses of those who travel. "The journey is hard. It is so hot. I was importuned so. Were they not people of standing, or devout folk?" None of these excuses will do: "even though they be asked by anyone at all."[3] However, the Abbot may possibly grant permission; that is the meaning we should give here to the word *præcipiatur*. The *Rule of the Master* gives a short dialogue held between a monk and his Abbot and enumerates all the circumstances in which we should accept or refuse invitations.[4] For ourselves, if the superior's permission is only tacit and presumed, we should be very careful how we use it. Of course, if seriously fatigued, we should accept refreshment without scruple. Cassian relates that two young solitaries let themselves die of hunger rather than touch some figs they were carrying to a sick man.[5]

Our Holy Father pronounces the penalty of excommunication against transgressors (perhaps excommunication from the table), since

---

[1] See Chapter LXVI.
[2] S. Athanasii *Vita S. Antonii*, 54. P.G., XXVI., 919-922.—*Verba Seniorum: Vitæ Patrum*, V., x., 2. Rosweyd., p. 596.—S. Pach., *Reg.*, liv.
[3] An incident in St. Benedict's Life may serve for commentary on this chapter: S. Greg. M., *Dial.*, l. II., c. xii.
[4] Cap. lxi.   [5] *Inst.*, V., xl.

by this breach of rule they become layfolk again. The common life is expressed especially in the conventual character of the Divine Office and meals. Even though a monk cannot take his repast at the same hour as his brethren, it is desirable that he should take it at the monastery after his return. The tables of layfolk were not made for us; neither their wines nor their talk suit us. Men sometimes employ the pretext of edification; but is not the edification much more real when we are only rarely seen ? Would not people of the world be rather surprised that monks should accept invitations so readily ? If they eat and drink little, they will be suspected of hypocrisy; if they have good appetites and appreciate good wine, they will be charged with excess. Our Holy Father wishes that at every instant and in every place the monk should remain a monk and preserve all that he can of his profession. Let us beware of thinking that once we are outside the monastery it is good form to walk, gaze, and act as do men of the world and to be monks only in dress.

CHAPTER LII

OF THE ORATORY OF THE MONASTERY

De oratorio monasterii.—Oratorium hoc sit, quod dicitur; nec ibi quidquam aliud geratur, aut condatur.

Let the oratory be what it is called; and let nothing else be done or kept there.

ST. BENEDICT likes to have things exact, consistent and harmonious. When speaking of the Abbot he requires him to justify his name by his deeds: *Et studeat nomen majoris factis implere;* when treating of the Divine Office he counsels us to put our minds in harmony with our voices: *Mens nostra concordet voci nostræ;* so also here, in the matter of the oratory, which by definition and name is the place of prayer (*domus orationis*), he would have this title be fully justified: "let it be what it is called." We recognize in all this the same lofty interest in good order. Love of order is one of the most noble forms of conscience; by this it touches æsthetics and the cult of beauty. And, at the same time, it is the best proof of our submission to law, since the moral law was summed up by the ancients in this simple dictum: "Be what you are," *Vivere naturæ convenienter oportet,* manifest in your acts that which is in your being.

So the oratory shall be used only for the things of prayer. *Nec ibi quidquam aliud geratur aut condatur.*[1] Nothing foreign to it shall be done there. The oratory must not be like a workshop; St. Benedict has no weaving of mats during the psalmody.[2] Nor shall meals be taken there, as in certain churches mentioned by St. Augustine.[3] Nor again is it a dormitory. *Aut condatur:* nothing shall be deposited there save what belongs to the Divine Office; it must not become a sort of lumber room where all manner of things are heaped confusedly, books, tools, and garments.

Expleto opere Dei omnes cum summo silentio exeant, et agatur reverentia Deo; ut frater, qui forte sibi peculiariter vult orare, non impediatur alterius improbitate.

When the Work of God is finished let all go out with the utmost silence, and let reverence be paid to God; so that a brother who perchance wishes to pray by himself may not be hindered by another's importunity.

The oratory belongs exclusively to God and to those who pray to Him. When the Work of God is finished, all must withdraw in very

---

[1] This prescription of the Rule has been adopted by Canon Law (Can. *Oratorium,* 6. Dist. xlii.) and the canons of Councils have often quoted it. It is, besides, a reminiscence of St. Augustine in his letter CCXI. *ad monachas* (7); and the whole passage has certainly inspired St. Benedict: *Orationibus instate horis et temporibus constitutis. In oratorio nemo aliquid agat, nisi ad quod est factum, unde et nomen accepit; ut si aliquæ etiam præter horas constitutas, si eis vacat, orare voluerint, non eis sint impedimento, quæ ibi aliquid agere voluerint.*
[2] *Cf.* S. Pach., *Reg.,* v. et vii.
[3] *Confess.,* l. VI., c. ii. *P.L.,* XXXII., 719–720.

strict silence, thus showing their reverence towards God's Majesty (*et agatur reverentia Deo*). Commentators who understand these words of a salutation or genuflexion to the Cross or the Blessed Sacrament would seem to be wrong. St. Benedict means us to appreciate the sanctity of the place, not to leave it noisily, and never to stay there to talk. Honour due to God requires this, as does also our own spiritual interest, since the sweetness left in our hearts by the Office may evaporate in a moment. But the Rule adds yet another motive.

Profound silence shall be observed in the oratory from affectionate consideration for our brethren, and, "that a brother who perchance wishes to pray by himself may not be hindered by another's importunity." We must in passing take note of this private prayer, of which St. Benedict nowhere speaks formally, any more than of spiritual conferences. The little that is said of it here and in Chapter XX. is enough to establish the fact that the monks of former days did not ignore it, and that the Rule and the Abbot's authority allowed them to take from manual labour or study some moments for prayer. But St. Benedict leaves this practice in some sort optional and free: " a brother who perchance " ... " if another wish." Apparently our Holy Father wished to signalize the time immediately after Office as especially favourable for prayer; the soul is then quite full of God, and, as we know, there is an intimate connection between a monk's prayer and the Divine Office. The church is also implicitly indicated by the Rule as the place *par excellence* for prayer. Finally, the words which follow would appear to outline a method.

Sed si alter vult sibi forte secretius orare, simpliciter intret et oret; non in clamosa voce, sed in lacrimis et intentione cordis. Ergo qui simile opus non facit, non permittatur, expleto opere Dei, remorari in oratorio, sicut dictum est, ne alius impedimentum patiatur.	But if another wish perchance to pray by himself, let him go in with simplicity and pray, not with a loud voice, but with tears and fervour of heart. And let him who is not similarly occupied be not permitted to stay in the oratory after the Work of God, lest another should be hindered, as has been said.

St. Benedict's principal object[1] is to protect recollection, by saving his monks from the noise of much going and coming, and from the din of unnecessary talk. If there be one place in this world where we have a right not to be molested or given over to the mercy of the talkative it is surely the oratory. It is closed to all who do not intend to pray there, and it is also closed, for the same reasons, to those whose too demonstrative piety might annoy their brethren. Let us not forget that the Rule was first written for men of the South, and that external forms of devotion always follow temperament. Moreover, some of the monks of Monte Cassino had doubtless been barbarians and peasants.

---

[1] *Cf.* Cass., *Inst.*, II., x. Read the whole chapter and the ones following, which St. Benedict had in mind while writing Chapter LII.—S. Basil., *Reg. contr.*, cxxxvi.— S. Cypr., *De oratione dominica*, c. iv. et v. *P.L.*, IV., 521–522.

Of the Oratory of the Monastery

St. Benedict reminds us, for the benefit of those who would not be restrained by education from certain extravagances, that cries, loud supplications, and sighs must be absolutely banned from a monastic oratory. Intention, the secret fervour of the heart—this it is which makes prayer; and if tears come, let them be tears of silence and tenderness. Our Holy Father's rapid sketch of the man of prayer is truly admirable: " Let him go in with simplicity and pray. . . ."[1]

Therefore, concludes St. Benedict, all those who do not confine themselves, apart from the Divine Office, to this silent prayer, shall be excluded from the oratory in the name of fraternal charity.

[1] *Omni cordis intentione (orent)*, said Cassian, *Inst.*, II., xii. On *intentio cordis* see Cassian again, *Conlat.*, I., vii.; IV., iv.; IX., vi.–vii.; XXIII., xi.; and *Inst.*, V., xxxiv.— *Vera postulatio non in oris est vocibus, sed in cogitationibus cordis. Valentiores namque voces apud secretissimas aures Dei non faciunt verba nostra, sed desideria. Æternam etenim vitam si ore petimus, nec tamen corde desideramus, clamantes tacemus. Si vero desideramus ex corde, etiam cum ore conticescimus, tacentes clamamus. . . . Intus in desiderio est clamor secretus, qui ad humanas aures non pervenit, et tamen auditum Conditoris replet* (S. Greg. M., *Moral. in Job*, l. XXII., c. xvii. *P.L.*, LXXVI., 238).

CHAPTER LIII

OF THE RECEPTION OF GUESTS

THE regulations contained in this long chapter may be summarized under four heads. St. Benedict first speaks of those who enjoy monastic hospitality. Then he describes the usual ceremonial for the reception of a guest. Then he arranges certain details of claustral organization concerning hospitality. And, in conclusion, he guards against the recollection of the monastery being disturbed by the presence of guests.

DE HOSPITIBUS SUSCIPIENDIS.—Omnes supervenientes hospites tamquam Christus suscipiantur, quia ipse dicturus est: *Hospes fui, et suscepistis me.* Et omnibus congruus honor exhibeatur, maxime tamen domesticis fidei et peregrinis.

Let all guests that come be received like Christ Himself, for He will say: "I was a stranger and ye took me in." And let fitting honour be shown to all, especially, however, to such as are of the household of the faith and to pilgrims.

St. Benedict begins with words of generous welcome, laying down the primary motive of hospitality, based on faith and charity. Guests shall be received as Our Lord Himself, so that He may be able to say to us on the Day of Judgement: "I was a stranger and ye took me in" (Matt. xxv. 35).[1] Therefore hospitality is not merely an act of philanthropy or worldly courtesy, nor one inspired by the desire of popularity or influence, but rests on the conviction that we receive Christ Himself in the persons of guests, and the will to honour Him wheresoever He hides Himself, with the certainty that He will recompense us in eternity. And surely it is a remarkable thing that, in the passage of the Gospel from which our Holy Father took his text, the judgement passed by Our Lord concerns no other matter but charity, and this as expressed in attention paid to strangers and the sick.

Hospitality is a profoundly human activity, even considering it altogether apart from the supernatural.[2] The East especially has been faithful to it from the remotest antiquity; the Arab recovers delicacy of conscience when guests are brought into his tent. In the Old Testament the Patriarchs were great hosts. And the Church has preserved God's law of hospitality with infinite care. St. Paul the Apostle often recalls it: "Forget not hospitality; for thereby some have entertained angels unawares" (Heb. xiii. 2). A bishop should be "hospitable" (1. Tim. iii. 2), and likewise a Christian widow (*ibid.* v. 10). The most ancient monuments of Christian literature regulate hospitality, and determine the prudent measures with which it should protect itself in a

---

[1] *Adventantes fratres quasi Domini suscipiamus adventum . . . qui dicit: Hospes fui et suscepistis me* (RUFIN., *Hist. monach.*, c. vii. ROSWEYD, p. 464).

[2] *Cf.* S. AMBR., *De officiis*, ii., 103. *P.L.*, XVI., 131.

pagan world.[1] The Fathers praise it and practise it; who does not know the story, for example, of St. Gregory and his thirteenth beggar ?[2] As to monks it is their glory to guard, almost alone, the traditions of hospitality. Before, as well as after, our Holy Father, we undoubtedly find it practised in all religious families, but the holy Patriarch formulated its perfect code. The better to understand its seasonableness, we should remember that in the sixth century inns were rare, and that often there were even no roads; we may read in the Dialogues of St. Gregory of the misadventures to which a traveller overtaken by night was exposed.[3] Monasteries were located precisely in deserted places; in them was refuge to be sought.

All who come must be received, says the Rule. In principle no one should be refused, since the motive of hospitality, which St. Benedict immediately recalls, is valid for all, since there is something of God in all souls, for all are loved by Him. Nevertheless, although the Rule does not set this down explicitly, some reservations are necessary. In the first place all that our Holy Father says of the reception of guests into the monastery shows that he did not mean to extend hospitality to women. Yet there have been monasteries—Cluny, for instance—which established hospices outside the enclosure for the reception of women and young children.[4] Hospitality had to be refused also to professional malefactors and to notoriously dangerous folk. Nor could the Church's enemies and notorious heretics partake of the monks' bread.[5] Surely all the ceremonial of hospitality is applicable only to Catholics. However, despite all precautions, undesirable folk might find their way into a monastery. So the *Rule of the Master* prescribes that two brethren should sleep in the guest-house and close the door securely, so that none might escape by night and carry off the bedding or other objects. Nowadays we may be even a little more particular. In receiving unknown guests we should think not only of individual charity, but of the common security. And now that inns and hotels are plentiful, there is no cruelty in closing the door on doubtful characters.

Furthermore, we may observe that there are charitable institutions which have hospitality as their whole purpose or as part of their purpose; these bear names in accord with their function. There are others which are hospitable, but by extension of meaning and not by definition. The latter case is ours. Hospitality is not an essential part of Benedictine life, but only an integrating part; as such it is capable of expansion or contraction according to need and time, of being adapted to circum-

---

[1] *Cf.* S. Clement., *Epist. ad virgines;*—the *Doctrina Apostolorum.*
[2] Read also St. Nilus, *Tract. ad Eulogium,* 23-24. *P.G.,* LXXIX., 1123-1126;— and Peter of Blois, *Epist.* XXIX. *P.L.,* CCVII., 98-100.
[3] *Dial.,* l. III., c. vii. *P.L.,* LXXXVII., 229 sq.
[4] The same usage existed in the monasteries of St. Pachomius: *cf.* S. Pach., *Reg.,* li.
[5] *Nobis in monasterio hospitalitas cordi est; omnesque ad nos venientes, læta humanitatis fronte suscipimus. Veremur enim ne Maria cum Joseph locum non inveniat in diversorio, ne nobis dicat Jesus exclusus: Hospes eram, et non suscepistis me. Solos hæreticos non recipimus* (S. Hieron., *Apologia adv. libros Rufini,* l. III., 17. *P.L.,* XXIII., 469).—*Cf.* S. Basil., *Reg. brev.,* cxxiv.

stances, proportioned to resources, calculated according to rules of prudence, and, finally, subordinated to the highest laws of the monastic life.

Omnes supervenientes. Guests may arrive at any hour and even without warning, for in St. Benedict's time it was difficult to give notice: *incertis horis supervenientes hospites.* But with modern postal facilities a word of warning is more natural and safer, if we would cause neither surprise nor confusion. Monks, however, should not be too exacting on this point, for monastic hospitality should be ready for everything, even for surprises.

"And let fitting honour be shown to all." In the person of the stranger who presents himself, we receive, said St. Ephrem,[1] not a man, but God Himself; so there should be no accepting of persons. But though goodwill and interior dispositions be the same for all, yet the external expression of our respect should be regulated according to the status of the guest, and St. Benedict prescribes that fitting honour (*congruus honor*) should be shown to all. This is mere prudence and charity. If we paid a commoner the honours of a prince, would we be treating him suitably and putting him at his ease? Does a layman expect the same reception as a bishop? Bernard of Monte Cassino says: "Coarse bread, herbs, and beans are enough for a poor man; but a rich man is scarce content with pork, or beef, or tender fowls."

There are three classes of guests for whom St. Benedict requires special attention. First, *domestici fidei* (those of the household of the faith). This perhaps means our brethren in the Faith, those of the same supernatural household and family, agreeably to the words of the Apostle: "Now therefore you are no more strangers and foreigners: but you are fellow citizens with the saints and of the household of God" (Eph. ii. 19). "Let us work good to all men, but especially to those who are of the household of the faith" (Gal. vi. 10). A warmer welcome shall be given to a Christian than to a Jew or an infidel. But might not the words "those of the household of the faith" mean stranger monks or clerics? It is precisely to these that St. Pachomius orders greater consideration to be shown.[2]

Peregrini. Pilgrims belong to God in a special way. They are seeking God, and we should help them to find Him, giving them, wherever they halt, a substitute for their native land. A little farther on our Holy Father again prescribes this great solicitude towards pilgrims, and orders it to be extended also to the poor. "Because in them Christ is more received. For the very fear we have of the rich procures them honour." It is unnecessary, St. Benedict shrewdly remarks, to require that respect and those attentions for the rich and powerful which they will obtain without any trouble. The magnificence of their persons

---

[1] *Testamentum* (inter S. EPHREM. *opp. græc. lat.*, t. II., p. 244).
[2] *Quando ad ostium monasterii aliqui venerint, si clerici fuerint aut monachi, majori honore suscipiantur* (Reg., li.).

and of their train, the honour they confer on those whom they visit, the hope, it may be, of obtaining some favour from them: all these sentiments help us to receive them well. But with poor people there is little danger of obsequiousness. Yet they are more grateful, because they are less accustomed to attentions. And in them especially is Christ received; they are the privileged members of Our Lord Jesus Christ, of Him who lived on the earth as a pilgrim, as a poor man, as a stranger ever in quest of a lodging: " The foxes have holes and the birds of the air nests: but the Son of Man hath not where to lay his head " (Matt. viii. 20). We should observe that St. Benedict uses Christian phraseology: he speaks not of strangers but of guests.

Ut ergo nuntiatus fuerit hospes, occurratur ei a priore vel a fratribus, cum omni officio charitatis:	When, therefore, a guest is announced, let him be met by the superior or brethren with all marks of charity.

In order to describe the ceremony of his reception St. Benedict begins at the gate of the monastery and follows the guest through the whole course of his visit. The Eastern monks were sometimes accustomed to meet guests in a body.[1] But cenobites could be somewhat less demonstrative than the solitaries of Nitria and Scete. St. Pachomius and St. Basil[2] would not have the whole community turn out for all guests that came; and, if we read St. Benedict properly, his regulation is the same. The community might be engaged at the Divine Office, or scattered here and there, employed in various tasks, when a guest arrived. Moreover, we may imagine the embarrassment which some visitors would feel if met by a levy *en masse* of the whole community. Above all, what disorder would be occasioned in the monastery if all had to assemble at the gate for every arrival at any hour! So we should suppose that the ceremonial here indicated—and monastic customs have interpreted it thus—was applied with more or less solemnity according to circumstances of time, place, and person. Often, undoubtedly, porter and guest-master alone appeared. On other occasions the reception was conventual, and the brethren were probably warned by a predetermined signal. In spite of its brevity, the Rule distinguishes cases where the superior (*prior*) received a guest, and cases where this duty fell to " brethren," not necessarily meaning the whole community, but brethren who had charge of guests, or else the deans, or those who happened to be free.

[1] *Ubi peregrinos fratres advenire senserunt, continuo velut examen apum, singuli quique ex suis cellulis proruunt, atque in obviam nobis læto cursu et festina alacritate contendunt, portantes secum quamplurimi ipsorum urceos aquæ et panes, secundum quod Propheta corripiens quosdam dicit: Quia non existis filiis Israel in obviam cum pane et aqua* (2. Esdr. xiii. 2). *Tunc deinde susceptos nos adducunt primo cum psalmis ad ecclesiam, lavant pedes, ac singuli quique linteis quibus utebantur abstergunt, quasi viæ laborem levantes, re autem vera vitæ humanæ ærumnas mysticis traditionibus abluentes* (RUFIN., *Hist. monach.*, c. xxi. ROSWEYD, pp. 477-478).

[2] S. PACH., *Reg.*, l.-li.—S. BASIL., *Reg. fus.*, xxxii., xlv.; *Reg. brev.*, cccxiii.

Et primitus orent pariter, et sic sibi socientur in pace. Quod pacis osculum non prius offeratur, nisi oratione præmissa, propter illusiones diabolicas.	Let them first pray together, and thus associate with one another in peace; but the kiss of peace must not be offered until prayer has gone before, on account of the delusions of the devil.

Before all else they shall pray together, and that in the oratory, as St. Benedict specifies presently. The early Christians received no one without good credentials. The faithful of one diocese were not admitted to communion with another church without letters of recommendation (*litteræ commendatitiæ, litteræ formatæ*).[1] In early times the Creed served to distinguish Catholics from those who were not such; it was the password. In the Arian period Catholics marked themselves off from heretics by means of a paper bearing the Greek initials of Father, Son, and Holy Ghost: Π.Υ.Α–Π. The same idea may have disposed St. Benedict to make prayer the prelude to reception; when the guest consents to it, then he is at peace with the Church. Thus a visitor is admitted to communion with us only after we are sure that he is himself in communion with God.

But our Holy Father, in insisting that this prayer should come before all else, suggests another motive: " on account of the delusions of the devil." The Fathers of the East, by whose ordinances the Rule is directly inspired, are more explicit. It sometimes happened that the devil took human form in order to introduce himself into a monastery and molest the monks; a preliminary prayer was the most effective way of neutralizing any diabolical influence. Rufinus says it was a rule that prayer should always precede greeting.[2] Moreover, to fortify oneself against contact with heretics, or other perverse folk, would also be to frustrate " the delusions of the devil "; it is too true that corrupt and vicious people, besides their evil habits and uncleanness, carry with them an unhealthy atmosphere.

After prayer comes the kiss of peace. This was the ancient form of greeting between Christians: " Salute one another with a holy kiss," says St. Paul. Rufinus mentions also the fraternal kiss of monks and their guests.

In ipsa autem salutatione omnis exhibeatur humilitas. Omnibus venientibus sive discedentibus hospitibus, inclinato capite, vel prostrato omni corpore in terra, Christus in eis adoretur, qui et suscipitur.	And in the salutation itself let all humility be shown. At the arrival or departure of all guests, by bowing the head or even prostrating with the whole body on the ground, let Christ be adored in them, who indeed is received.

[1] On the ancient *tessera hospitalitatis cf.* DAREMBERG et SAGLIO, *Dictionnaire des antiquités grecques et romaines, art. Hospitium.*—According to TERTULLIAN, what unites all churches is *communicatio pacis, et appellatio fraternitatis, et contesseratio hospitalitatis* (*De præscript.*, c. xx. *P.L.*, II., 32).

[2] *Forma hujusmodi inter monachos observatur, ut si quis ad eos veniat . . . ante omnia ut oratio fiat, ut nomen Domini invocetur: quia si fuerit aliqua transformatio dæmonis, continuo oratione facta diffugiet* (*Hist. monach.*, c. i. ROSWEYD, pp. 456–457).—*Cf. Verba Seniorum: Vitæ Patrum*, V., xii., 15. ROSWEYD, p. 614.

This paragraph may be regarded as a parenthesis, determining the general character of the welcome given to guests, and, so to speak, the tone of the greetings addressed to them. Our Holy Father has already bidden us meet them with all cordiality: " with all marks of charity "; he now tells us to greet them with " all humility "; presently we shall be invited to treat them with " all kindness." It is not a question of worldly politeness, but of supernatural courtesy and humility. We know that monastic humility shows itself in submission to God and to every creature for love of God: and since it is Christ chiefly whom we recognize in guests, we shall not be ashamed to reverence Him profoundly in them. Before all who arrive or depart we shall bow or prostrate, probably according to the dignity of the guest.[1] The practice of prostration has perforce been abandoned.

Suscepti autem hospites ducantur ad orationem, et postea sedeat cum eis prior, aut cui jusserit ipse. Legatur coram hospite lex divina, ut ædificetur, et post hæc omnis ei exhibeatur humanitas.	When the guests have been received let them be led to prayer, and then let the superior, or anyone he may appoint, sit with them. Let the divine law be read before the guest for his edification; and afterwards let all kindness be shown him.

The parenthesis finished, St. Benedict takes up again his description of the ceremonial of hospitality. The guest having been received into the monastery shall be conducted first to the oratory, as has been said, and then saluted and embraced. The brethren, who have perhaps assembled to receive him, return to their work; and the Abbot, or a monk appointed by the Abbot, shall stay with him and keep him company.

Following the custom of the ancient Fathers St. Benedict desires that the " divine law " should be read to guests " at once," meaning by " divine law " a passage of Holy Scripture or of a Catholic author, some such matter as formed the spiritual reading (*lectio divina*) of the monk himself. The guest is certainly treated as one of the family. This reading edifies him and prepares him to benefit by his sojourn in God's house. There is preserved at Monte Cassino a collection of short exhortations, for the use of guests, extracted from St. Gregory. While the soul is receiving this spiritual nourishment, a material repast is being prepared in the kitchen. But customs have changed. Perhaps travellers complained of being kept too long waiting for supper and bed. The divine law is now read to them only in the refectory.

After the reading, continues our Holy Father, the guest must be treated with all possible " kindness," and given any comforts that he needs. St. Benedict here uses the word *humanitas* in the sense of loving

---

[1] *Sæpe dixit* (abbas Apollo) *de suscipiendis monachis, quod oportet adorare fratres advenientes: non enim ipsos, aiebat, sed Deum adorasti* (PALLAD., *Hist. Laus.*, c. lii. ROSWEYD, p. 751).—*Cf.* RUFIN., *Hist. monach.*, c. ii. ROSWEYD, p. 458.—*Verba Seniorum: Vitæ Patrum*, III., 195. ROSWEYD, pp. 528–529.—*Vita Porphyrii*, xxxv. P.G., LXV., 1227–1228.

care and assistance, as did Rufinus[1] and Cassian,[2] from whom this expression is borrowed. And the Rule indicates quite a series of delicate attentions, describing the quasi-festival that will be observed on account of the guest.[3]

Jejunium a priore frangatur propter hospitem; nisi forte præcipuus sit ille dies jejunii, qui non possit violari. Fratres autem consuetudines jejuniorum prosequantur.	Let the superior break his fast for the sake of the guest, unless it happens to be a principal fast-day, which may not be broken. The brethren, however, shall observe their accustomed fasting.

Most guests were Christians and knew what was meant by an ecclesiastical fast; neither they nor the Abbot could dispense themselves from it. But the superior might break the fast of the Rule, which was less strict. Charity is of more value than fasting. And perhaps the guest would be reluctant to partake of the monastic table, if his companion would only eat very little.[4] However, St. Benedict observes that the dispensation from the fasts of the Rule only concerns the guests and the superior, and also, according to Chapter LVI., those religious who assist him at this meal or take his place. The rest of the brethren shall remain faithful to the fast, so that the coming of guests may never introduce relaxation into the monastery. We shall see presently how the inner organization of hospitality allowed the claims of charity and observance to be reconciled.

In the words " all kindness " some commentators—Bernard of Monte Cassino and Turrecremata, for example—think they find permission for the serving of flesh meat to guests. But the opposite practice prevailed almost everywhere, and the Cistercians maintained it habitually. People do not come to monasteries for good cheer; a sumptuous meal would rather scandalize guests.[5] Nevertheless, while doing no injury to the law of monastic poverty and monastic frugality, we should not impose on them the severity of our own fare.

Aquam in manibus Abbas hospitibus det; pedes hospitibus omnibus tam Abbas, quam cuncta congregatio lavet; quibus lotis, hunc versum dicant: *Suscepimus, Deus, misericordiam tuam,*	Let the Abbot pour water on the hands of the guests; let both the Abbot and the whole community wash the feet of all guests. When they have been washed let them say this verse:

---

[1] *Habebat* (abbas Isidorus) *hospitalem cellulam, in qua adventantes hospitio recipiat et omni humanitate refoveat* (*Hist. monach.*, c. xvii. ROSWEYD, p. 476).

[2] *Inst.*, V., xxiv.; *Conlat.*, II., xxv.; XXI., xiv.

[3] *Cumques alutans nos orasset more sibi solito, pedes hospitum propriis manibus lavat, et docere nos ex Scripturis quæ ad ædificationem vitæ ac fidei pertinent, cœpit.*

Et ut vidit nos, statim prior adoravit usque ad terram, et surgens osculo nos suscepit. Ubi autem ingressi sumus monasterium, oratione prius (ut moris est) data, pedes nostros propriis manibus lavat, et cetera quæ ad requiem corporis pertinent adimplevit (RUFIN., *Hist. monach.*, c. ii. et vii. ROSWEYD, pp. 458, 464).

[4] Cf. CASS., *Inst.*, V., xxiv.-xxvi. And elsewhere also (*Conlat.*, II., xxvi.) CASSIAN notes: *Satis absurdum est, ut fratri, immo Christo mensam offerens non cum eo cibum pariter sumas aut ab ejus refectione te facias alienum.*

[5] To those astonished at being too well treated might be read the anecdote recounted in the *Verba Seniorum: Vitæ Patrum*, III., 5. ROSWEYD, p. 493.

in medio templi tui. Pauperum autem et peregrinorum maxime susceptio omni cura sollicite exhibeatur: quia in ipsis magis Christus suscipitur. Nam divitum terror ipse sibi exigit honorem.

"*Suscepimus, Deus, misericordiam tuam in medio templi tui.*" Let special care and solicitude be shown in the reception of the poor and of pilgrims, because in them Christ is more received[1]. For the very fear we have of the rich procures them honour.

The Abbot shall pour water on the hands of guests and wash their feet. Because the Abbot holds the place of Christ in the monastery, therefore is this function reserved to him, recalling the condescension of Our Lord to His Apostles at the Last Supper and expressing Christian humility and charity. In ancient times, to pour water on the hand of those who were going to table was the act of a servant or disciple;[2] with St. Martin[3] it became the act of a monk wishing to honour his guests; and St. Benedict makes it a rule. This practice is still observed, and takes place at the door of the refectory when the guest is first led in. As to the washing of the feet, a regular element in the ritual of ancient hospitality, it no longer agrees with our Western manners and has long been suppressed; we must honour guests, not embarrass them.

We should understand well in what sense the Rule would have the whole community proceed with the Abbot to the washing of the feet of all guests. As D. Mège remarks, guests would have good reason to complain "if they had to endure being washed and washed again as many times as there were monks." The text probably means that all the religious should fulfil this charitable office in turn; and it was thus that the business was performed formerly in many monasteries.[4] Not all guests had their feet washed, this privilege being by preference reserved for the poor, who are mentioned expressly in the succeeding words of the Rule. But perhaps our Holy Father intended the whole community to be present at what has since been called the *Mandatum* (Maundy) and to take part in it, as we do on Holy Thursday or on the eve of the clothing of a novice. This interpretation also can appeal to ancient customs. There was a fixed time each day for the *Mandatum*, for a guest's feet were not washed in this conventual manner at the moment of his arrival, which would have caused considerable disturbance and disorganization of the horarium. In monasteries of the Middle Ages the guests used to be assembled—generally in the chapter-room—before or after the meal, or else in the evening after Compline. St. Benedict orders that a short prayer from the forty-seventh psalm should be

---

[1] *Ne avertas oculum, aut inanem dimittas pauperem: ne forte Dominus in hospite aut in paupere ad te veniat* (S. MACAR., *Reg.*, xx.).

[2] *Est hic Eliseus, filius Saphat, qui fundebat aquam super manus Eliæ* (IV. *Reg.*, iii., 11).—*Cf.* S. ATHANASII, *Proœm. Vitæ S. Antonii. P.G.*, XXVI., 839.

[3] SULP. SEVER., *Vita B. Martini*, xxv. *P.L.*, XX., 171.

[4] Thus PETER THE VENERABLE writes to St. Bernard: *Facimus quod possumus, et per totius anni spatium, unaquaque die tribus peregrinis hospitibus manus et pedes abluimus, panem cum vino offerimus, Abbate in ordine suo id faciente, nullisque, nisi infirmis, qui hæc implere non valent, exceptis (Epist.*, l. I., *Ep.* XXVIII. *P.L.*, CLXXXIX., 131).

recited after the *Mandatum*, so as to give thanks to God for the visit He has paid to the monastery in the persons of the guests.

After having been received thus into the family, guests conformed as far as possible to its régime and took their part both in prayers and work; of all of which St. Benedict says nothing. The monks of Nitria let their guests rest for a week; then they employed some in kitchen, bakery, or garden, others in reading and study. Silence was observed in the guest-house till midday, but they could talk then.[1] Abbot Isaias invites guests to render all service of which they are capable.[2] The *Rule of the Master* would have a guest compelled to work if he stays more than forty-eight hours.

Coquina Abbatis et hospitum per se sit, ut incertis horis supervenientes hospites, qui nunquam desunt monasterio, non inquietent fratres.	Let the kitchen for the Abbot and guests be apart by itself; so that guests, who are never lacking in a monastery, may not disturb the brethren, coming at uncertain hours.

The claustral organization necessary to cope with the duties of hospitality embraces two elements: the kitchen and its servers, the guest-house and the guest-master.

In order to ensure order and peace in the monastery St. Benedict gives it three kitchens: one for the community (Chapter XXXI.), one for the sick (Chapter XXXVI.), and one for the Abbot and guests (Chapter LIII.). Thanks to this arrangement, guests may arrive at any hour without their arrival and the care of preparing a meal for them disturbing the community. The example of Cluny has often been cited, where the Pope, the Emperor, and several kings with numerous suites, might stay without impairing the tranquil regularity of monastic life. But the custom early prevailed, in certain places, of the Abbot eating with guests in the common refectory, one kitchen sufficing for the two tables. Or else, as Paul the Deacon notes, the two kitchens were placed near together and a " turn " allowed the passage of dishes from one to the other.

In quam coquinam ingrediantur duo fratres ad annum, qui ipsum officium bene impleant. Quibus, ut indigent, solatia administrentur, ut absque murmuratione serviant: et iterum quando occupationem minorem habent, exeant, ubi eis imperatur, in opera. Et non solum in ipsis, sed et in omnibus officiis monasterii ista sit consideratio; ut quando indigent, solatia accommodentur eis; et iterum quando vacant, obediant imperanti.	Let two brothers who are able to fulfil this duty well be placed in this kitchen for the year. If they need it let help be afforded them, that they may serve without murmuring. On the other hand, when they have not much to occupy them, let them go forth to other work, wherever they are bidden. And not only with regard to them, but also in all the offices of the monastery let this consideration be shown, so that when they need it, help may be given them, and again when they are idle they may do what they are bidden.

---

[1] PALLAD., *Hist. Laus.*, c. vii. ROSWEYD, p. 713.
[2] *Oratio* III., 3. P.G., XL., 1110.

Two of the brethren are appointed to the charge of this guest-kitchen. While all the monks have to work in turn in the community-kitchen, and serve for a week, the kitcheners for guests remain at their office for a whole year. Why this difference? The reason is that the dignity of guests called for a more careful cuisine, and only the more skilful brethren were appointed to it: " who are able to fulfil this duty well "; and they were kept at it for a whole year just because of their skill and practice.

And since the work could vary much in proportion to the number of guests, the Rule is discreetly and prudently anxious that no one should be overworked or left idle. When many guests come, help shall be given; when the guest-house is empty or nearly so, the monks habitually occupied there shall not regard themselves as dispensed from conventual work, but shall go where obedience sends them. St. Benedict takes occasion of this to tell us that none of the officials of the monastery should be overworked, or on the other hand withdraw themselves from obedience and daily toil: " *obediant imperanti.*"[1]

| Item et cellam hospitum habeat assignatam frater cujus animam timor Dei possideat; ubi sint lecti strati sufficienter; et domus Dei a sapientibus sapienter administretur. | Moreover, let a brother whose soul is possessed by the fear of the Lord have the guest-house assigned to his care. Let there be sufficient beds provided there; and let the house of God be wisely governed by wise men. |

No monastery is complete without a guest-house. A whole history of monastic guest-houses might be written. This *cella hospitum* is evidently not a cell, a single apartment where all the guests were huddled together; it is a house, a regular and complete habitation. In the Life of St. Benedict, where we have the account of the plans for the monastery of Terracina supplied by the Patriarch in a dream, mention is made of a place for the reception of guests.[2] Probably from the very time of St. Benedict the guest-house was separated from the rest of the monastery. The Rule does not fix its exact position; but monastic custom, in conformity with the spirit and intentions of St. Benedict, placed it apart from the cloister, dormitory, and refectory of the religious, generally quite near the entrance gate. This was already the practice in the time of St. Pachomius.

At Cluny, where hospitality was exercised on a large scale, the guest-house was in two parts: the guest-house proper, under the jurisdiction of the guest-master, and receiving rich or well-to-do travellers; and the almonry, administered by the almoner and receiving poor travellers, pilgrims, the sick, and the poor of the neighbourhood.[3] The daily *Mandatum* of which we spoke above took place in the almonry. The history of " hospices," built near monasteries and by their agency, connects itself with this chapter on hospitality. From the sixth and seventh centuries monastic hospices were numerous in Gaul.

---

[1] The authoritative reading is *imperatis*. [2] S. GREG. M., *Dial.*, l. II., c. xxii.
[3] *Cf.* PIGNOT, *Histoire de l'Ordre de Cluny*, t. II., pp. 456-463.

The guest-house cells should have suitable furniture, of better quality, doubtless, than that used by the monks. St. Benedict mentions the bed only, perhaps as being—after the refectory table—what the guest most needs. And care must be taken that there is a sufficient number of beds fully equipped: *ubi sint lecti strati sufficienter.*

Our Holy Father defines in a single phrase the virtues he requires of the guest-master: the " fear of God " should be to him as an enclosure in which his soul rests captive: *cujus animam timor Dei possideat.* The guest-master has special duties and special dangers. We expect him to be prudent and even shrewd; he needs charity, unfailing patience, much self-denial; he needs both zeal and caution. The honour of the community, its good name, the edification of strangers, all depend largely on him. He is the first to deal with postulants, and prepares the way discreetly for the novice-master. We may imagine the perils of this office: distraction of spirit, distaste for the things of God, for Office, and for study which has become so difficult, and an exaggerated interest in outside matters. His conversation should never be worldly, under pretext of adapting himself to the mentality of some visitors. There are matters of which he may confess his ignorance; who expects him to have the information of a Reuter's Agency ? Nor is he required to set himself up as permanent director and instructor. Finally, a delicate disinterestedness will prevent him from appropriating as personal to himself those friendly feelings which are directed to other brethren or to the whole community. Summing up, St. Benedict says that the guest-house, which in a monastery is especially the house of God, should be entrusted to wise men, who may administer it wisely.

Hospitibus autem, cui non præcipitur, nullatenus societur neque colloquatur: sed si obviaverit aut viderit, salutatis humiliter, ut dictum est, et petita benedictione, pertranseat, dicens sibi non licere colloqui cum hospite.	Let a monk who is not so bidden on no account associate or converse with guests. But if he chance to meet or to see them, after humbly saluting them, as we have said, and asking their blessing, let him pass on, saying that he is not permitted to talk with a guest.

This last remark gives us St. Benedict's whole mind on the character and measure of our relations with the outside world. Hospitality as described in this chapter is a duty of faith, since it is Our Lord whom we receive in the persons of guests; a duty of charity also and an apostolate, for it is not possible to come into contact with the recollected and attractive dignity of the monastic life without obtaining supernatural benefit. Sometimes we teach by our words and sometimes by our books, but most of all do we teach by our lives. Instruction in this form cannot be questioned. The Acts of the Apostles tell us how pagans were edified by the spectacle of the first Christian community. A real though insensible impression is produced on all those who attend our services, and on priests and cultivated folk who visit the monastery, and these spread the influence among their acquaintance.

But St. Benedict would have this inner apostolate harmonize with the essential conditions of our life, so that the practice of charity may never impair peace and observance. Our Holy Father prescribed some precautionary measures before; he now requires that guests be committed exclusively to the care of the guest-master, and the rest of the brethren excused from this duty. Analogous arrangements are found in most ancient Rules.[1] Careless, dissipated, and gossiping monks seek contact with the world most readily. Nor is that strange, for they already belong to it by their life; not knowing what to do with their time, they give it to any comer. There is hardly another matter in which nature deludes itself so easily. Those men most greedily desire converse with people of the world, for whom such people are most dangerous. And even though we should have all qualities necessary for edification, we cannot practise an apostolate piously and profitably which is not directed by obedience.

If it happens, says St. Benedict, that a monk meets a guest unexpectedly, he must conduct himself politely, salute him with humility as mentioned before, furnish any information that is sought, and then retire, excusing himself on the ground that he may not prolong the conversation. We have no reason to blush at such an avowal. As we may repeat, it is giving people of the world a false idea of the monastic life to persuade them by exaggerated cordiality, or by conversations entered upon at once without previous permission, that we have nothing to do, that we are glad of any excuse to escape from solitude and silence. Let us take care never to let them think that our life resembles their own. And if we walk through the monastery with guests we should respect the appointed places of silence; visitors will moderate their voices in proportion as we restrain ours. St. Benedict adds " and asking their blessing ": which is an allusion to the ancient custom according to which a monk meeting a superior or elder said: *Benedicite ;* by the same formula was the supernatural dignity of guests recognized. (See the commentary on Chapters LXIII. and LXVI.).

Throughout the last lines of this chapter we discover once more, as at a glance, what is the monastic ideal and what our Holy Father expects of us. We are not obliged to do good—is it often real good ?— to our own detriment, we are not bound to accomplish all the good that is possible in this world and at any price. It would be buying influence

---

[1] S. Pach., *Reg.*, l.-li.—S. Basil., *Reg. fus.*, xxxii.-xxxiii.—Cass., *Inst.*, IV., xvi.— St. Benedict quotes verbally the *First Rule* of the Holy Fathers: *Venientibus (hospitibus) nullus nisi unus cui cura circa hospitale fuerit injuncta occurrat et responsum det venientibus. Orare vel pacem offerre non liceat ulli nisi primo videatur ab eo qui præest Patre; et oratione simul peracta, sequatur ordine suo pacis officium reddere. Nec licebit alicui fratri cum superveniente sermocinari; non sit illi cura interrogandi unde venerit, ad quid venerit, vel quando ambulaturus sit, nisi soli qui præest Patri, aut quibus ipse jusserit. Venientibus vero fratribus ad horam refectionis non licebit peregrino fratri cum fratribus manducare, nisi cum eo qui præest Patre, ut possit ædificari. Nulli licebit cum eo loqui nec alicujus audiatur sermo, nisi divinus qui ex pagina proferatur, et ejus qui præest Patris, vel quibus ipse jusserit loqui, ut aliquid de Deo conveniat* (viii.).

and reputation too dearly, if we bought them at the expense of an essential part of our Rule. And this is the more undeniable in that other Orders have now undertaken the work of preaching and ministering to souls; we are no longer needed. It is not fitting that we should desert our life of prayer and silence to become regular clerics, supernumeraries or casuals, or that we should scatter our energies in a great variety of works for which we are in general poorly prepared. We have the right to hold fast to the essential conditions of the monastic institute, to that which has, moreover, always constituted the special, normal, and distinctive function of monks. Except for rare and sometimes splendid exceptions, this is all that the Church requires of us. And of what has a feverish age more need than of the spectacle of men living only by God and for God, assiduous in the praise of His beauty, and sharing in every manifestation of Catholic life by the sure and efficacious means of liturgical prayer?

CHAPTER LIV

WHETHER A MONK OUGHT TO RECEIVE LETTERS OR TOKENS

SI DEBET MONACHUS LITTERAS, VEL EULOGIAS SUSCIPERE.—Nullatenus liceat monacho nec a parentibus suis, nec a quoquam hominum, nec sibi invicem litteras, aut eulogias vel quælibet munuscula accipere aut dare, sine præcepto Abbatis sui.

On no account shall it be lawful for a monk to receive, either from his parents or anyone else, or from his brethren, letters, tokens, or any little gifts whatsoever, or to give them to others, without the permission of his Abbot.

IT is difficult to see the connection between the chapter on hospitality and this on presents. Like certain portions of Chapters LV. and LVII., this chapter completes rather the teaching of Chapters XXXIII. and XXXIV., on poverty; Chapter LVI. is a codicil to Chapter LIII.

A monk, as we know already, is incapable of receiving, giving, or alienating anything whatsoever without the permission of the Abbot.[1] That is the strict principle. St. Benedict ranges the persons from whom gifts may come in three classes; parents, external friends, brethren in religion. Then he enumerates things which may be given: letters, *eulogiæ* or pious presents, and any little gifts whatsoever.[2]

"Letters." Our separation from the world to be effective must be external: such as is produced by our leaving it, by enclosure, by our habit, by silence; but it should be internal also: and if intercourse is assiduously maintained by visits and letters, it is clear that our thoughts remain with the world: "No man, being a soldier to God, entangleth himself with secular business: that he may please him to whom he hath engaged himself" (2 Tim. ii. 4).[3] Perhaps we write too many letters. Why can we not confine ourselves to those demanded by politeness, charity, and real utility? Would it not be rather strange that more letters should go out of a monastery than come in? We should drop not only all frivolous, trivial correspondence, but also such as is of a purely worldly character. Let us also remember the dangers of letters of "direction." And when we write, let it be always with sobriety, and moderation, and in a supernatural spirit. There are anecdotes which may be told in recreation, but with which it would be foolish to entertain our correspondents. There are certain details or events of our family life which we have no right to communicate even to our parents or to religious. A monk is safeguarded by having to obtain permission to

---

[1] *Nemo ab altero accipiet quidpiam, nisi præpositus jusserit* (S. PACH., *Reg.*, cvi.).

[2] ST. AUGUSTINE (*Epist.* CCXI., 11. *P.L.*, XXXIII., 962) speaks of nuns surreptitiously receiving *litteras vel quælibet munuscula.—Cf.* S. CÆSAR., *Reg. ad virg.*, xxiii.—S. ORSIESII *Doctrina*, xxxix.

[3] *Cf.* CASS., *Inst.*, V., xxxii.

write; moreover, our Constitutions bind us to give our letters open to the superior and in the same way to receive those that come.[1]

"Tokens." The practice of sending a friend something from your table existed among the pagans of antiquity and survived in Christian times. The morsel of blessed bread which is distributed (in France) to the faithful in the course of High Mass, as a token of communion between them, is the *eulogia* par excellence. In the fourth century we find St. Paulinus of Nola sending little loaves of bread to his friends—to St. Augustine, for instance.[2] Presents were also made of fruit, images, medals, relics; and all these things received the generic name of *eulogiæ*.[3]

The Holy Rule supposes that presents come chiefly from outside; yet it foresees that there may occur between religious of the same or different monasteries some interchange of letters and *eulogiæ*. Doubtless "little presents strengthen friendship"; but, even apart from poverty, there are other motives which forbid monks these civilities as long as they remain clandestine. St. Benedict's prohibition is precise and complete; it embraces all cases, and demolishes in advance all vain excuses. We have broken with the world, and we are poor by profession.

| Quod si etiam a parentibus suis ei quicquam directum fuerit, non præsumat suscipere illud, nisi prius indicatum fuerit Abbati. | And if anything be sent to him, even by his parents, let him not presume to receive it, except it have first been made known to the Abbot. |

After laying down the principle St. Benedict speaks of presents given by parents: they may not be appropriated without the Abbot's permission. We cannot be made owners in spite of ourselves and in spite of the Rule. So it would be superfluous to protest that a present is a personal gift, or a souvenir, or has cost the monastery nothing. When any presents whatsoever come to a brother, they should first be handed to the Abbot. The Abbot often does not look at them and has them distributed whatever they may be; but he never means to put them *ipso facto* at the disposition of the brother to whom he sends them. Permission is still required before the brother may use either a part or the whole. Whatever is not granted must go without delay to the religious who has charge of such things. Let us recall what was said in Chapter XXXIII. on the extreme watchfulness which we should employ in all that concerns poverty; in this matter there are no trivial details.

| Quod si jusserit suscipi, in Abbatis sit potestate, cui illud jubeat dari; et non contristetur frater, cui forte directum fuerat, ut non detur occasio | If he order it to be received, let it be in the Abbot's power to appoint to whom it shall be given; nor let the brother to whom it chance to have |

[1] Cf. Cass., *Inst.*, IV., xvi.—S. Cæsar., *Reg. ad mon.*, xv.
[2] S. Paulini *Epist.*, III.-V. *P.L.*, LXI., 164 *sq.*
[3] Cf. Mabillon, *Acta SS. O.S.B.*, Sæc. i., p. 310.—Venantius Fortunatus, *Carmina, passim.*—See the Comments of Martène and Calmet on this passage of the Rule.—The poisoned bread which Florentius sent to St. Benedict was a *eulogia* (S. Greg. M, *Dial.*, l. II., c. viii.).

diabolo. Qui autem aliter præsumpserit, disciplinæ regulari subjaceat.[1]

been sent be grieved, lest occasion be given to the devil. Should anyone, however, presume to act otherwise, let him be subjected to the discipline of the Rule.

Some present or other arrives and is handed to the Abbot; the Abbot receives it and then transmits it to the monk to whom it was sent (*quod si jusserit suscipi*), but adds, at once or somewhat later, the unexpected clause: " You shall give it to such and such a brother." To be grieved in these circumstances would be the mark of a very small soul. It betrays attachment to things, and shows that our happiness consisted in possessing God *and* them. Such grief reveals the depths of the soul. And, at the same time, it is perilous; for it disarms us, and by means of it the devil sows all sorts of foolish feelings in us: regret that we left the world, distaste for our life, hostility towards the Abbot as not loving us, jealousy of the brother to whom our cherished present has gone.

" Should anyone presume to act otherwise." Most commentators say that St. Benedict would have the severity of regular discipline employed only against one who appropriated an article wrongfully, and not against one who evinces disappointment, unless perhaps this leads him to scandalous excesses.

We should remember that, in this matter of poverty, there are three things to be distinguished: the vow, the virtue, and the spirit of poverty.

We observe the vow if we abstain from acts which are forbidden us, or rather which we have forbidden ourselves in taking the vow: if we possess nothing, dispose of nothing, destroy nothing. But the vow is much endangered if we do not go on to the virtue, which leads us not only to fulfil our vow indifferently well, but to practise renunciation and privation with facility, promptitude, and joy. The virtue, in its turn, is complete only if it be connected with its most lofty motive. We must have the spirit of poverty, which is to regard ourselves as being united to God and obliged to be like Him. We did not leave the world to enter solitude, but rather to go into the society of God. We are not poor in order to be poor, but to be rich with God and rich like God. God Himself is poor, for He has but Himself; yet He is infinite wealth, since He possesses in Himself the fulness of all things. This is the last word about our poverty. And at this height the three vows of religion reunite, even as the three theological virtues meet in union with God.

[1] All these ordinances are as old as monachism, as is shown by a curious regulation of St. Pachomius (lii.), and especially by this passage of St. Augustine (Letter CCXI., 12): *Etiam illud quod suis vel filiabus vel aliqua necessitudine ad se pertinentibus in monasterio constitutis aliquis vel aliqua contulerit, sive vestem sive quodlibet aliud inter necessaria deputandum, non occulte accipiatur; sed sit in potestate præpositæ, ut in commune redactum, cui necessarium fuerit, præbeatur. Quod si aliqua rem sibi collatam celaverit, furti judicio condemnetur* (*P.L.*, XXXIII., 963). Reproduced in part by St. Cæsarius, *Reg. ad mon.*, i.; *Reg. ad virg.*, xl.

CHAPTER LV

OF THE CLOTHES AND SHOES OF THE BRETHREN

DE VESTIMENTIS, ET CALCEAMENTIS FRATRUM.—Vestimenta fratribus secundum locorum qualitatem ubi habitant, vel aerum temperiem dentur, quia in frigidis regionibus amplius indigetur, in calidis vero minus. Hæc ergo consideratio penes Abbatem sit.

Let clothing be given to the brethren suitable to the nature and climate of the place where they live: for in cold regions more is required, in warm regions less. It shall be the Abbot's duty, therefore, to consider this.

IT has sometimes been thought that St. Benedict had a presentiment, or a prophetic knowledge, that his Rule would spread and be received widely in Christian Europe, and that this led him to say here that clothing should be adapted to climatic conditions and their variety. That may be so; but it is certain that the differences of temperature which exist between Sicily and the Sabine country, between Monte Cassino and Terracina, were sufficient to justify this prudent ordinance. So monks shall be clothed variously according to differences of latitude and conditions of climate. St. Benedict differs in this point from some modern founders, who have determined the colour, cut, and stuff of clothing with the greatest nicety. He does not even begin with a principle of poverty, but with a precept of discretion, wherein is revealed once more the breadth of his spirit. And his ordinance has the further purpose of precluding excess, fancifulness, or confusion. The Abbot, and the Abbot alone, shall decide what may form part of a monk's wardrobe; it shall be his to say if some addition should be made to the common allowance, or to suppress and modify some of its constituents.

Nos tamen mediocribus locis sufficere credimus monachis per singulos cucullam et tunicam: cucullam in hieme villosam; in æstate puram et vetustam; et scapulare propter opera; indumenta pedum, pedules et caligas.

We think, however, that in temperate climates a cowl and a tunic should suffice for each monk: the cowl to be of thick stuff in winter, but in summer something worn and thin: likewise a scapular for work, and shoes and stockings to cover their feet.

Though he has left the care of clothing to the Abbot, St. Benedict consents to indicate—always with a certain discreet timidity—what should be allowed in temperate regions.

Let us note first that our Holy Father clearly means to give his monks a distinctive costume. Perhaps the warning which he addresses to monks and which we shall explain presently: *De quarum rerum omnium* . . . has misled people and made them think that St. Benedict was indifferent, not only to the quality and colour of the material, but also to the character and distinctive form of the habit. Erasmus, for example, alleges that St. Benedict and his monks were clothed like everyone else.

But Erasmus was deceived by prejudice and a too rapid and careless reading. Without any doubt St. Benedict asked and received from St. Romanus a special habit: " He asked for the habit of a holy life."[1] We shall be accurate if we say that St. Benedict was inspired by various contemporary customs, and that the exclusive employment of certain articles of clothing was sufficient to make them distinctive. Why should monks have rejected the custom of antiquity, which gave each social class its special costume ? Soldiers had theirs, and so had philosophers even, being distinguishable by their *pallium* (robe), staff, and long beard. Tertullian's obscure and difficult treatise *De pallio* might be consulted on this point. Moreover, the first monks had good reasons for the choice of a special costume.

The monastic habit distinguishes us from the rest of men, and that is its primary justification. It also reminds us, and that incessantly, of our supernatural state: by its austerity, by its form, by all its details, it warns us that we are no longer of the world and that there are a thousand worldly matters to which we have bidden farewell. The monks of antiquity delighted in investigating the symbolism of the religious habit,[2] which is suggested also by the sacred liturgy. We should read the forms for the blessing and imposition of the monastic habit in our ritual. Just because of this blessing, which makes it sacramental, our habit guards us, is a part of our enclosure and completes it: it holds us in the sweet captivity of God. And perhaps we should not seek elsewhere for the motive of that disfavour, or rather hatred, which the religious habit encounters from the devil and his agents. It is a bad sign when a priest or a monk is eager and glad to return to what the liturgy calls " the ignominy of worldly dress." The cowl does not make the monk, but what service it renders him ! There is a real relation between our dress and our state; there are things which we feel to be impossible, conduct which we shall never attempt, just because we wear the livery of God. Let us esteem and venerate it, but especially the cowl, whose generous folds will enwrap us even in death.

Our Holy Father did not create this monastic habit in all its entirety, but selected from the elements furnished by tradition with his usual discrimination. In such a matter usage varied greatly, according to times and places, and we cannot attempt to trace its evolution here. Nor is it wise, when illustrations are lacking, to construct an exact theory as to the costume described by customaries and commentaries; for it is not always possible to identify certain items. St. Benedict considers it sufficient in temperate regions if each monk has a cowl and a tunic. In winter the cowl shall be of rough or thick stuff; in summer, of stuff which is lighter or worn by use. (We are not told that the tunic changes with the seasons.) At work the cowl shall be replaced by a less ample garment, the scapular. To write the history of cowl and scapular would

---

[1] S. Greg. M., *Dial.*, l. II., c. i.
[2] Cass., *Inst.*, I.—Sozom., *Hist. eccles.*, l. III., c. xiii.-xiv. *P.G.*, LXVII., 1065-1081.—S. Dorothei *Doctrina*, i., 12-13. *P.G.*, LXXXVIII., 1632 *sq.*

necessitate a treatment beyond the scale of this commentary; we must confine ourselves to a few notes.

Originally the cowl was merely a cap or hood (*cucullus, cucullio*) covering the head and the nape of the neck, its conical form recalling the skin caps—once called *cuculli*—of grocers and druggists. It was the ordinary headgear of peasants[1] and children. Very popular in Italy and in Gaul, the hood was doubtless popular also throughout the whole Empire, for we meet a similar headdress with the same name (κουχούλιον) among the first monks of the East.[2] Besides the practical motives which made them adopt it, there were considerations also of a symbolical kind. The hood reminds monks, says Cassian,[3] that they should imitate the innocence and simplicity of children, since they have returned to spiritual childhood. This is to regard profession as a second baptism; just as the neophyte's head was covered in baptism, so was the monk's in profession. The hood was the most venerated part of the monastic habit and was worn day and night.

The cowl of which St. Benedict speaks is certainly something more than a hood. It is the *vestis cucullata*—i.e., a garment fitted with a hood (*cucullus*).[4] Columella advises that labourers in the fields should be protected against bad weather with skins having sleeves (*pellibus manicatis*) or hooded cloaks (*sagis cucullis* or *cucullatis*); and Palladius prescribes skin tunics with hoods (*tunicas pelliceas cum cucullis*).[5] For monks, as for layfolk, the cowl might be of rough material or of the skins of animals; it then resembled, apart from its hood, the *melota* of the Eastern monks (μηλωτή, a sheepskin, from μῆλον=sheep), which was a nightdress or travelling garment and could on occasion serve as a wallet.[6] Perhaps it was a sheepskin of this kind with a hood that our Holy Father wore at Subiaco.[7] We cannot describe with exactitude

---

[1] *Cf.* DAREMBERG et SAGLIO, *Dictionnaire des antiquités grecques et romaines*, t. I., fig. 2094.
[2] See, for instance, the *Rule* of ST. PACHOMIUS, *Lausiac History* (ed. BUTLER) pp. 89–90, 92, 98.   [3] *Inst.*, I., iii.
[4] Some traces remain of the use of the words *cuculla* and *cucullus* before St. Benedict's time to denote a hooded garment. SIDONIUS APOLLINARIS offers one such to Abbot Chariobaudus: *Nocturnalem cucullum, quo membra confecta jejuniis, inter orandum cubandumque dignanter tegare, transmisi; quanquam non opportune species villosa mittatur hieme finita, jamque temporibus æstatis appropinquantibus* (*Epist.*, l. VII., Ep. XVI. *P.L.*, LVIII., 586). And the clothing of St. Germanus of Auxerre, according to his biographer CONSTANTIUS, was *cuculla et tunica* (*Acta SS.*, Julii, t. VII., p. 204).—*Cf.* S. HIERON., *Vita S. Hilarionis*, c. xlvi. *P.L.*, XXIII., 52.—S. PAULINI *Poema* XXIV. ad *Cytherium*, vers. 389–390. *P.L.*, LXI., 622.—ENNODII, *Epist.*, l. IX., Ep. XVII. *P.L.*, LXIII., 156.
[5] COLUMELLA, *De re rustica*, l. I., c. viii.; l. XI., c. i.—PALLADIUS, *De re rustica*, l. I., c. xliii.   [6] S. PACH., *Reg.*, xxxviii.
[7] ST. GREGORY tells us that the shepherds *dum (illum) vestitum pellibus inter fruteta cernerent, aliquam bestiam esse crediderunt*; and the boy Placid when rescued from the water said he had seen above his head *Abbatis melotem* (*Dial.*, l. II., c. i. et vii.). THEODEMAR, in his letter to Charlemagne, explaining what the cowl was, what shapes it had taken and what names received in different places, observed that its first and original name was *melota: Cucullam nos esse dicimus, quam alio nomine casulam vocamus. . . . Illud autem vestimentum quod a gallicanis monachis cuculla dicitur et nos cappam vocamus, quod proprie monachorum designat habitum, melotem appellare debemus, sicut et hactenus in hac provincia a quibusdam vocatur* (*P.L.*, XCV., 1587).

the shape of a cowl in the time of St. Benedict, for the hood could be fixed to divers garments (*lacerna, casula, pænula, sagum:* overcoat, mantle, cloak, coat); moreover, St. Benedict may mean by *cuculla* any monastic habit with a hood, whatever its special shape, dimensions, and material. The most ancient monastic cowls that we know are shaped like a full chasuble, reaching to the feet and having no openings in the sides.[1] That explains why it was necessary to take off the cowl for manual labour. In later times, in order to free the arms, the *casula* was slit along the sides, and the two portions fastened together at intervals by straps or bands, which came to be called " St. Benedict's stitches " or " joints "; this shape of garment occurs in many documents from the ninth to the twelfth century.[2]

Cowls with sleeves were in use from the tenth century, these sleeves being at first rather narrow.[3] The hood underwent a series of transformations: under the influence of Cistercian and Franciscan custom it grew long and tapering; in some places it became very full, falling over the shoulders like a veil and forming two lappets in front: this shape survives in the English Congregation.

The origin of the scapular is somewhat obscure. We find no mention of a garment of this name before St. Benedict. Etymologically it would be a garment designed to protect the shoulders (*scapulæ*) or to fit the shoulders: but in what way ? Our Holy Father merely says: " likewise a scapular for work "; nor is the scapular mentioned at the end of the chapter in the small list of articles necessary for a monk. Learned authorities have identified it, but without much reason, with the sort of corset or belt which the Eastern monks used for tucking up their garments and preventing them blowing about during their work;[4] many Greek authors have described this shoulder garment shaped like a cross under various names. More probably the primitive scapular of the monks of Monte Cassino was a small cowl, a tunic or frock with a hood, like that used by the peasants of the district. Theodemar, speaking of the scapular, says that it is so called because it covers chiefly the shoulders and head: " Almost all the peasants in this country use this garment; in place of it we have a covering made of coarser stuff after the manner of a *melota*, except that it has sleeves reaching to the hands."[5] This tunic sometimes had short sleeves and sometimes was

---

[1] *Cf.* MARTÈNE et DURAND, *Voyage littéraire de deux religieux bénédictins de la Congrégation de Saint-Maur*, t. II., p. 154.—MABILLON, *Acta SS. O.S.B.*, Sæc. V., Præf., p. xxxi.

[2] *Cf.* MABILLON, *Annales O.S.B.*, t. II., p. 353.—BERNARD DE MONTFAUCON, *Les Monuments de la monarchie française*, t. I., pl. xxviii.—ROHAULT DE FLEURY, *La Messe*, t. VIII., pl. dcxliv.—SEROUX D'AGINCOURT, *Histoire de l'art par les monuments*, t. III., p. 80; t. V., pl. lxix.—We may often be at a loss to decide whether the thing spoken of is a cowl, or a scapular, or some liturgical garment.

[3] *Cf. Le Miniature nei codici Cassinesi*, Disp. V., Tav. i.; Disp. VI.—See the reproductions of miniatures of a Cluny manuscript of the twelfth century in D. L'HUILLIER, *Vie de saint Hugues*, pp. 298, 360, 512.

[4] *Cf.* CASSIAN, *Inst.*, I., v.

[5] *P.L.*, XCV, 1588.—See two reproductions of peasants clad in hooded tunic, in the *Revue archéologique*, May–June, 1892, pp. 331 and 333.

without them. It was often slit open at the sides and the two parts joined by one or several fastenings or joints; in the course of centuries these fastenings disappeared, the flaps grew longer, and the scapular became what we now wear.[1] At Cluny, in the eleventh century, only the cowl and the frock, which was worn over it, were known; there was no scapular.[2] The cowl was formed of two long strips of material which reached to the ground, after covering the shoulders and part of the arms;[3] the hood was fitted to it. The cowl was reserved for professed monks; while the frock, an ample robe with long sleeves, was permitted to the novices; except for these last the frock had no hood.

Cucullam et tunicam: the tunic is the undergarment; we should remember that the ancients did not use underclothing. The tunic (λεβιτών, κολοβή, *colobium*) was used by the monks of all countries; it had short sleeves or no sleeves at all, and was usually made of cloth. Anchorites often wore tunics made of goats' hair or camel hair, true hair shirts, the use of which Cassian would allow only to very fervent religious who have a special vocation; for the clothing of a monk he prefers less unusual material, yet such as is coarse and common.[4] This, as we shall see, is exactly our Holy Father's view. The tunic was not loose, but held in by a girdle of leather or linen. St. Benedict does not speak here of the girdle (*bracile*) but mentions it a little farther on; at night the monks were to sleep " girt with belts or cords " (*cincti cingulis aut funibus*), as said in Chapter XXII.

Pedules et caligas. It is difficult to identify these coverings of the feet (*indumenta pedum*); antiquaries dispute lengthily about them, at which D. Mège is much amused.[5] The monks of some countries[6] generally went barefoot, like the poor, which is a sort of footgear that does not wear out, being renewed by nature. The solitaries of St. Pachomius used sandals. The *pedules* prescribed by St. Benedict are perhaps stockings, or socks, or light indoor footgear. The *caligæ* are not necessarily what we call shoes, but may be military sandals bound by straps and clasping foot and ankle firmly, a very convenient and very healthy sort of footwear. Field work obviously required more solid

---

[1] The ancient forms of the scapular are to be found in: MABILLON, *Acta SS. O.S.B.*, Sæc. V., Præf., p. xxxi; *Annales O.S.B.*, t. I., p. 505.—*Antiphonaire du B.* HARTKER: *Paléographie musicale*, II. Series, t. I., p. 11 of the reproduction of the manuscript.— *Le Miniature nei codici Cassinesi*, Disp. II., Tav. i.; Disp. IV., Tav. i.; Disp. VI., Tav. iv.; MABILLON reproduces the first of these miniatures in his *Annales*, t. I., p. 109. —MARTÈNE et DURAND, *Voyage littéraire de deux religieux bénédictins de la Congrégation de Saint-Maur*, t. II., p. 64.

[2] SMARAGDUS had already written: *Cucullam dicit ille quod nos modo dicimus cappam. . . . Quod vero ille dicit scapulare propter opera, hoc nos modo dicimus cucullam.*

[3] *Cf.* MABILLON, *Acta SS. O.S.B.*, Sæc. V., Præf., pp. xxxii–xxxiv.—The Cluniac cowl is described in a curious dialogue between a monk of Cîteaux and one of Cluny (of the second half of the twelfth century): MARTÈNE et DURAND, *Thesaurus novus anecdotorum*, t. V., col. 1638–1639.—It would seem that this cowl-scapular is the relic of a cowl in the form of a *casula;* see the description of the cowl in the *Disciplina Farfensis*, l. II., c. iv.

[4] *Inst.*, I., ii.

[5] Commentary *in h. l.*—Read especially CALMET.   [6] CASS., *Inst.*, I., ix.

Of the Clothes and Shoes of the Brethren

"*caligæ*" than those worn in the house. St. Gregory the Great tells us of *caligæ clavatæ* (nailed boots) which were worn during work in the monasteries of St. Equitius.[1]

De quarum rerum omnium colore aut grossitudine non causentur monachi, sed quales inveniri possunt in provincia qua degunt, aut quod vilius comparari potest. Abbas autem de mensura provideat, ut non sint curta ipsa vestimenta utentibus eis, sed mensurata.	Of all these things and their colour or coarseness let not the monks complain, but let them be such as can be got in the region where they live, or can be bought most cheaply. Let the Abbot be careful about their size, that these garments be not short for those who wear them, but fit well.

Monks should not discuss the colour or quality of their clothing, even in the secrecy of their hearts. This advice is also given by Cassian and St. Basil.[2] There must be no affectation, vanity, or effeminacy. That material shall be chosen which is generally used in the district, and which can be bought most cheaply.[3] This passage would seem to prove decisively that St. Benedict determined nothing as to the colour of our habit. The natural impulse was to seek something of an austere and inconspicuous shade. White and black, grey and brown, were adopted by preference; but there was often a mixed and motley result: a white tunic, for instance, with black cowl and scapular. A great mass of historical evidence on this point may be found collected in the commentaries of Martène and Calmet. Black was the prevailing colour, at least for outer garments, and Cluny held jealously to it,[4] while Cîteaux declared for white, a choice attributed to St. Alberic. The colour of the habit was discussed between Cîteaux and Cluny, and Peter the Venerable took up the defence of black—and of charity and discretion at the same time—in several letters to St. Bernard.[5]

In the Rule of St. Basil it is a monk's business to say if his clothing is "too large or too small for his height."[6] But St. Benedict would have the Abbot see to all, no detail being too small for his affectionate solicitude. Therefore he shall take care that the garments suit the stature of each, not being excessively full or long, so as to cause pride or inconvenience; nor, on the other hand, excessively short, thereby easily becoming ridiculous. St. Benedict mentions the second defect only.

Accipientes nova, vetera semper reddant in præsenti, reponenda in vestiario propter pauperes. Sufficit	When they receive new clothes let them always give back the old ones at once, to be put by in the clothes-

---

[1] *Dial.*, l. I., c. iv. *P.L.*, LXXVII., 173. *Cf.*, *ibid.*, l. III., c. xx. *P.L.*, *ibid.*, 269 *sq.*

[2] Cass., *Inst.*, I., ii.—S. Basil., *Reg. fus.*, xxii.

[3] St. Benedict is quoting a passage of St. Basil, but one which concerns food: *Sed si quid est, quod in unaquaque provincia facilius et vilius comparatur* (*Reg. contr.*, ix.).

[4] D. Mayeul Lamey has recently essayed to prove that the Cluniac habit was russet, of the natural colour of brown wool (*Œuvres choisies*, pp. 240-261).

[5] Petri Venerab., *Epist.*, l. I., *Ep.* XXVIII. *P.L.*, CLXXXIX., 116-117; l. IV., *Ep.* XVII. *P.L.*, *ibid.*, 332 *sq.*

[6] *Reg. brev.*, clxviii.

enim monacho duas tunicas et duas cucullas habere, propter noctes, et propter lavare ipsas res. Jam quod supra fuerit, superfluum est, et amputari debet. Et pedules, et quodcumque est vetustum, reddant, dum accipiunt novum.

room for the poor. For it is sufficient for a monk to have two tunics and two cowls, as well for night wear as for convenience of washing. Anything beyond this is superfluous and ought to be cut off. In the same way let them give up their stockings, and whatever else is worn out, when they receive new ones.

When a monk receives new clothes, he is not free to keep his worn-out garments by him to be utilized still at his pleasure; which would be a sad return to the vice of ownership, since necessities only are allowed and all superfluity must be curtailed. Moreover, we are able to take even from our poverty what may be given to those poorer than ourselves, but on condition that the alms is given by the Abbot or the brethren charged with this duty; for by what title would a monk distribute objects, even of a most worthless kind, if they in no way belonged to him? So our Holy Father ordains that all shall be deposited in the clothes-room.[1]

Two tunics and two cowls shall be enough for each. St. Benedict says nothing of the other less important parts of the habit, which perhaps, especially in the case of the *pedules* (stockings), exceeded the number of two. Cassian before him spoke of the use of two tunics, " for day and night wear."[2] St. Basil would have only one, while St. Pachomius allowed two *cuculli*, two tunics, " and one already worn with wear for sleep or work."[3] We know from St. Benedict himself that monks slept clothed: they kept on their tunics—a matter of mere decency—and probably also their cowls. The ancient monks had, it would seem, a special tunic, girdle, and cowl for night; there is no mention of the scapular, which was not needed except for work. Perhaps they wore these clothes even during the Night Office. So the monks of Monte Cassino received two tunics, and two cowls, more or less thick according to the season. Our Holy Father gives another reason for having these two sets of garments: the necessity of parting with them for a time while they were being washed—that is, if they could be washed, for clothes made of the skins of animals do not take readily to washing.

Femoralia hi qui diriguntur in via, de vestiario accipiant; qui revertentes lota ibi restituant.

Let those who are sent on a journey receive drawers from the clothes-room, and on their return restore them washed.

Here we have an exceptional article of monastic clothing: *femoralia*, breeches, drawers, trunk-hose. The monks, like most of the ancients

---

[1] Borrowed from St. Cæsarius: *Indumenta ipsa cum nova accipiunt, si vetera necessaria non habuerint, Abbatissæ refundant, pauperibus aut incipientibus, vel junioribus dispensanda (Reg. ad virg.,* xl.).—Cato too recommended that, when slaves were given new clothing, their old clothes should be collected, but it was to use them in another way: *De re rustica,* c. lix.
[2] *Conlat.,* IX., v.   [3] S. Hieron., *Præf. in Reg. S. Pach.,* 4; *Reg.,* lxxxi.

who wore long garments, hardly used them save for reasons of health or travel. St. Martin's monks did not wear them; St. Fructuosus allows them to his; the Master does the same; but in general the early monks seem to have regarded the habitual use of drawers as a relaxation. Paul the Deacon holds to the words of the Rule; Theodemar says that at Monte Cassino most preferred to do without them; and Hildemar says: "Where the brethren generally receive and wear drawers, they should receive them in chapter, like the rest of their clothing. . . . But monasteries where all receive and wear them are not praiseworthy." Cluny adopted the use of drawers, and Peter the Venerable had to defend the practice against the Cistercians.[1] According to Ordericus Vitalis, St. Robert suppressed them for the monks of Molesmes.[2] In default of drawers, properly so called, loin-cloths or pants were sometimes used.

Qui revertentes lota ibi restituant. The brethren, when they return from their journey, must restore the drawers to the clothes-room, having first washed them. They did their washing themselves, on which topic the customaries furnish us with abundant detail. We need not dwell upon the care which the monks bestowed on their persons, but we should note our Holy Father's interest in cleanliness. If we were hermits we might dress as we pleased, with the least possible trouble; we might even say, with St. Hilarion, that it was superfluous to wash a hair shirt: *Superfluum est munditias in cilicio quærere.* "Monks," said a Father of the desert, with some exaggeration of language, "should wear a cloak such that, if they left it on the ground, it might remain there for three days without anyone being inclined to pick it up."[3] But we are cenobites and belong to a family; out of respect for our family and consideration for our brethren we should have constant care for cleanliness and tidiness: they generally indicate purity and refinement of soul.

Let us remember the spirit which guided our Holy Father in determining the monastic dress. He did not wish to mortify us by means of the habit, but to secure perfect detachment and poverty. He would give us what is necessary and even something more, so as to leave monastic life its holy joy, its sober liberty, and its peace. He wished to prevent all discontent and murmuring. He wished to secure a certain gentlemanliness inside the monastery, and especially, perhaps, outside, as is shown by the ordinance which follows.

Et cucullæ et tunicæ sint aliquanto his, quas habere soliti sunt, modice meliores; quas exeuntes in viam accipiant de vestiario, et revertentes restituant.

Let their cowls and tunics also be a little better than those they usually wear; they must receive these from the clothes-room when setting out on their journey, and restore them on their return.

Monks going on a journey receive from the clothes-room cowls and tunics somewhat better than those they wear usually. Some customaries add that, when a person of quality comes to the monastery, the brother

---
[1] *Epist.*, l. I., *Ep.* XXVIII. *P.L.*, CLXXXIX., 123.
[2] *Hist. Eccles.*, P. III., l. viii., 25. *P.L.*, CLXXXVIII., 637.
[3] *Apophthegmata Patrum.* P.G., LXV., 227.

who attends him should receive more fitting clothes.[1] This is an act of consideration towards visitors. Such was the conduct of Our Lord Himself, who in His intercourse with the Jews did not imitate the austerity of St. John the Baptist: " The Son of Man came eating and drinking." St. Benedict does not want to be ashamed of his sons when they appear in the world. But what of poverty and edification? Carelessness and dirt do not edify, nor are we bound to advertise our poverty. The Abbot is not told to have a patch sewn on to every new habit which he gives, so that it may appear old and worn. And St. Benedict held, with Cassian, that we " should avoid the opposite defect " to excessive care and nicety as to dress, " and not attract notice by affected negligence."[2]

If we dwell upon such small points, it is because they concern, not external appearances only, but the very form of monastic perfection itself. And St. Benedict, who began as an anchorite and was familiar with extreme poverty, knew what he was doing when he fixed the characteristic features of our life. There is a virtue and a sanctity which we may liken to light that has been resolved through a prism. There are souls who have the spirit of poverty, or of mortification, or zeal and a kind of supernatural impetuosity, in an extreme degree. The spectrum of such sanctity contains a bar of vivid red, and men see it better, perhaps imitate it with less difficulty, though their gestures be awkward. Of course all the virtues have a fragmentary and relative character: so fragmentary that our attention should never be devoted to one in such a way that the rest are eclipsed; relative, because all are preparatory and relative to contemplation, to the constant, deep exercise of faith, hope, and charity. Besides the prismatic sanctity, of which we have spoken, there is a white sanctity, where all tints are merged in a perfect simplicity and equality. Such sanctity makes less stir; it is less noticed, and the unobservant do not notice it at all. But it is enough that God recognizes it as a more perfect likeness to Our Lord and to His Mother.

| Stramenta autem lectorum sufficiant: matta, sagum, læna et capitale Quæ tamen lecta frequenter ab Abbate scrutanda sunt, propter opus peculiare, ne inveniatur. Et si cui inventum fuerit, quod ab Abbate non acceperit, gravissimæ disciplinæ subjaceat. | For their bedding let a mattress, blanket, coverlet, and pillow suffice. These beds must be frequently inspected by the Abbot because of private property, lest it be found therein. And if anyone be found to have what he has not received from the Abbot, let him be subjected to the most severe discipline. |

After clothes, furniture. We should not forget that the ancient monks did not have cells but slept in a dormitory, so that

[1] HILDEMAR, *in h. l.*
[2] *Inst.*, I., ii.—*Abbas Agathon* . . . *in omnibus cum discretione pollebat, tam in opere manuum suarum quam in vestimento. Talibus enim vestibus utebatur, ut nec satis bonæ, nec satis malæ cuiquam apparerent* (*Verba Seniorum: Vitæ Patrum*, III., 75. ROSWEYD, p. 512).

their whole furniture was a bed. The bedding comprised four items.

Matta. According to Calmet, this was very probably a rush-mat, or at best a quilted straw mattress, but certainly not a mattress stuffed with hair or wool.

Sagum. A covering, or heavy sheet. Some ancient commentators thought the *sagum* was a sack stuffed with straw or hay. " But I think," says Calmet, " that *sagum* in this passage properly signifies a bed covering, of a finer and lighter character then the *læna;* that the *sagum* served to cover the brethren in the summer and the *læna* in winter; or better that in summer they only used the *sagum*, while using both *sagum* and *læna* in winter.

Læna. A covering, more or less shaggy or furry.

Capitale. A bolster of straw, or hair, or perhaps of feathers.

At Cluny the bedding conformed to the regulations of the Rule, but they allowed as many coverlets as the season demanded. In winter these were made of the skins of sheep, goats, or cats. Peter the Venerable had to forbid luxurious furs. Our customs have added little, and have abolished coverlets of fur. We should obey them faithfully with the greatest strictness. Yet the monastic bed remains, in spite of them, none too easy to leave at four o'clock in the morning.

St. Benedict imposes on the Abbot the duty of looking to the poverty of bed and cell. The monk of Monte Cassino naturally had no cupboard or other furniture whatever; the bed was the only place where he could hide anything for his personal use unknown to the Abbot.[1] The ancient Rules also—as, for instance, those of St. Isidore, St. Fructuosus, and St. Donatus—order superiors to make these domiciliary visits.[2] Paul the Deacon and Hildemar describe in detail the usual ceremonial in their time. In the morning the Abbot announced to the monks assembled in chapter that he was going to make a visitation and he deputed for this purpose four or five brothers " of good life." After making their investigation the brethren returned, sometimes with considerable booty: they set down before each offender the matter of his offence, and the Abbot invited the culprits to explain the origin of the articles discovered. Perhaps Abbots nowadays keep this point of the Rule less faithfully. Of course, they may easily see in a glance, when they enter a cell, the various objects which it contains. Moreover, in a well-ordered and busy house, the Abbot trusts somewhat to the good sense and good taste of all, and relies on each making from time to time a careful inventory of his furniture. We should take particular care with regard to library books, and not let our cells become like the cave

---

[1] The expression *opus peculiare*, hard to translate exactly, is borrowed from CASSIAN, *Inst.*, IV., xiv. and xvi.; VII., vii.

[2] One might be tempted to suppose that what St. Benedict and the ancient monks had in mind was the discovery of some superfluity in bedding; but this was not so. The bed sometimes became a secret store: *Quidquid ad manducandum vel bibendum pertinet nulla de sororibus præsumat circa lectum suum reponere aut habere* (S. CÆSAR., *Reg. ad virg.*, xxviii.).

of Cacus, from which there was no return; charity and poverty are here concerned. And such habits are all the more dangerous as supplying a justification for others; for one will accumulate in order to forestall the operations of another. St. Benedict calls for the greatest severity against such offences, chiefly because of the tendency which they reveal.

Et ut hoc vitium peculiare radicitus amputetur, dentur ab Abbate omnia quæ sunt necessaria: id est, cuculla, tunica, pedules, caligæ, bracile, cultellus, graphium, acus, mappula, tabulæ, ut omnis auferatur necessitatis excusatio.	And in order that this vice of private ownership may be cut off by the roots let the Abbot supply all things that are necessary: that is, cowl, tunic, stockings, shoes, girdle, knife, style, needle, handkerchief, and tablets; so that all plea of necessity may be taken away.

The Abbot is bound both to repress petty greediness and to give necessaries generously; thus will excuses based on necessity be abolished and the vice of ownership be in a fair way of being suppressed and cut out by the roots. St. Benedict enumerates a certain number of objects which should be distributed to each monk. We know the first of these already: cowl, tunic, and footgear. We have here some others. *Bracile:* this was the belt used during the day, large enough to serve as a receptacle, instead of pockets. From it hung the knife (*cultellus*) which was used in the refectory and elsewhere; in it was kept the handkerchief (*mappula*). We may remember the story of that monk of St. Benedict's who concealed handkerchiefs " in his bosom."[1] Each person received also a needle (*acus*), and with it, doubtless, some thread, for repairing small defects in his clothing, and finally waxen tablets (*tabulæ*) and a style (*graphium*).

A modern monastic outfit is somewhat more elaborate, though it is perhaps less so than that of a Cluniac monk in the eleventh century.[2] We have to get permission if we would add an overcoat to our equipment, or a skull-cap, or a *clémentine;* and it is certainly more perfect to fall in with the common rule, leaving it to our superiors to see that we lack no necessary. A monk should be able to renounce many items of comfort.

A quo tamen Abbate semper consideretur illa sententia Actuum Apostolorum, quia *dabatur singulis, prout cuique opus erat.* Ita ergo et Abbas consideret infirmitatem indigentium, et non malam voluntatem invidentium. In omnibus tamen judiciis suis Dei retributionem cogitet.	Yet let the Abbot always be mindful of those words of the Acts of the Apostles: " Distribution was made to everyone, according as he had need." Let him, therefore, consider the infirmities of such as are in want, and not the ill-will of the envious. Nevertheless, in all his decisions, let him think of the judgement of God.

The teaching contained in these few lines is familiar and recalls especially Chapter XXXIV. The Abbot, says St. Benedict, shall never

---

[1] S. Greg. M., *Dial.*, l. II., c. xix.
[2] *Cf.* Bernard., *Ordo Clun.*, P. I., c. v. -Udalr., *Consuet. Clun.*, l. III., c. xi. —Pignot, *Histoire de l'Ordre de Cluny*, t. II., pp. 431-432.

Of the Clothes and Shoes of the Brethren

think of imposing a uniform rule: he should have the indulgent and dexterous spirit of a father. He shall give to each according to his real needs, as was done in the Church of Jerusalem (Acts iv. 35), even though he thus expose himself to the discontent of some.[1] He shall be attentive to the weakness of those who are in want, and never consider the evil dispositions of the envious. In a well-united monastic family the Abbot shall always have the right to be something of an accepter of persons, as we have said already. There shall be privileges and privileged persons: and the privileges shall go automatically to the small and the weak, to those who require more consideration and to those of whom one is not sure. Charitable impulse shall always make us regard every exception by which a brother may benefit as justifiable and as our own.

But, in order to banish delusion and unenlightened sympathy, St. Benedict reminds the Abbot once more of the account which he shall have to render of all his decisions at the judgement seat of God.

---

[1] ST. BASIL had already written: *Hi qui præsunt, observabunt regulam illam quæ dicit: Dividebatur unicuique prout opus erat. Debent enim unumquemque prævenire ut secundum laborem etiam solatia refectionis inveniat* (*Reg. contr.*, xciv.).—See also ST. AUGUSTINE, Letter CCXI., 5. *P.L.*, XXXIII., 960.

CHAPTER LVI

OF THE ABBOT'S TABLE

DE MENSA ABBATIS.—Mensa Abbatis cum hospitibus et peregrinis sit semper. Quoties tamen minus sunt hospites, quos vult de fratribus vocare, in ipsius sit potestate. Seniorum autem unum aut duo semper cum fratribus dimittendos procuret, propter disciplinam.

Let the table of the Abbot be always with guests and pilgrims. But as often as there are few guests, it shall be in his power to invite any of the brethren he wishes. Let him take care, however, always to leave one or two seniors with the brethren, for the sake of discipline.

THE Rule contains few chapters shorter, and, it would seem, clearer, than this; yet there are few which have given rise to so much controversy. How, it has been asked, could St. Benedict order the Abbot to have his meals regularly with guests and pilgrims: *cum hospitibus et peregrinis* ?[1] Our Holy Father having said elsewhere that guests are never lacking in a monastery, the Abbot will have to be a permanent absentee. But that, we are told, is *a priori* impossible: for, both from a disciplinary and a financial point of view, it would entail disorder and a serious danger of monastic decadence; moreover the Abbot himself would be in some danger if he had to take his meals and even spend his days with layfolk, separated from his community. Martène exclaims: "Who can say how many evils arise both in spirituals and in temporals, when the Abbot is feasting while the community fast?"

In actual fact, *a posteriori*, all the ancient Rules place the Abbot in the common refectory. Most commentaries, commencing with Hildemar's, and the customaries of observant monasteries of all periods, are against a literal interpretation of St. Benedict's words. Councils even, like that of Aix-la-Chapelle in A.D. 817, forbid the Abbot to have his meals apart. At Cluny, says Peter the Venerable, our Abbots always eat with us, save when they are sick, or in exceptional cases entertain certain guests.[2] Wherever an attempt has been made to hold to the literal sense of the Rule abuses have broken out. And the commentators of the seventeenth century, Martène, Mège, and Hugh Ménard, combating them with an indignation which is abundantly justified, protest against so disastrous an interpretation. For them the text can mean only this: guests are to be entertained at the Abbot's table, but it shall be in the common refectory, in a special place of honour. And they all spend much ingenuity in solving the difficulties which are put to them.

For the opposite interpretation has its supporters. Bernard of Monte Cassino, Haeften, Perez, and Calmet, refuse to distort the plain

---

[1] PAUL THE DEACON gives another explanation: *Hospites sunt qui de eadem regione sunt, id est de prope; peregrini sunt, qui de alia regione sunt.*
[2] *Cf. Epist.*, l. I., *Ep.* XXVIII. P.L., CLXXXIX., 133.

meaning of the Rule, confirmed as it is by other passages. For instance, Chapter LIII. says: " Let the kitchen for the Abbot and guests be apart by itself; so that guests, who are never lacking in a monastery, may not disturb the brethren, coming at irregular hours." Would it not seem, from these words, that the Abbot and his guests really have their kitchen apart and a special refectory?[1] The reason St. Benedict gives for this measure is that, the hours of arrival of guests being uncertain and variable, their meals would not be at the same time as the fixed meals of the community. Therefore special cooks and a separate table were needed. At this the Abbot would take his place, not surely at any moment of the day, but at the times when the chief meals for guests occurred, the community meanwhile keeping its own régime and timetable. Nor could guests be compelled to wait for their dinner till None, during the monastic Lent. And that is why St. Benedict prescribes, again in Chapter LIII., that the Abbot or one who presides at the table of the guests, the " superior," should break his fast, " unless it happens to be a principal fast-day, which may not be broken;" for, in this case, both guests and monks should wait for the canonical hour. Therefore we must admit that, on days when the Abbot broke the fast of the Rule " for the sake of the guest," he ate at a different hour from the brethren, and—except he took a second meal!—did not appear in the common refectory on that day. . . . But, if guests are never lacking in a monastery, has the Abbot a wholesale dispensation from fasting from September 14 to Lent? We should not take St. Benedict's dictum that guests are never lacking in a monastery in such a literal and absolute way; he must have foreseen that the Abbot would be free sometimes. But we must take literally the commands which follow: "Let the superior break his fast . . ." and: " Let the table of the Abbot be always with guests."

However, the supporters of the hypothesis of a common refectory are very subtle and have an answer to all difficulties even to that raised for them by the words: " But as often as there are few guests, it shall be in his power to invite any of the brethren he wishes." These words obviously imply a separate refectory, to which the Abbot might summon, when there was not a great concourse of guests, some brother known to the guests or more fitted to edify them. Now, what would be the object, in a common refectory, of summoning some of the brethren to sit near you and the guests? To secure them a good dinner? Or was it that the Abbot and his table companions might not be left in isolation, however relative? And of course there is silence in this common refectory and all attend to the reading: " Reading must not be wanting while the brethren eat at table" (Chapter XXXVIII.). Will the Abbot and these privileged brethren chat while the rest keep silence and follow the reading? Surely not; for that would mean sheer disorder. In the description of the reception of guests in Chapter LIII. there is no suggestion that guests took their meals in silence in the monks' refectory.

And if it were still possible to have doubts as to the reality of these

[1] *Cf. Reg.* I. SS. PATRUM, viii.: *Venientibus fratribus ad horam refectionis, non licebit peregrino fratri cum fratribus manducare, nisi cum eo qui præest Patre, ut possit ædificari.*

two refectories, it would be enough to read the third and last sentence of the present chapter, which seems to us decisive. There, says Martène after Hildemar, " carnal Abbots " triumph. True, and only prejudice or prepossession—however creditable—could dispute it. If the Abbot and seniors remained in the common refectory, why the recommendation that one or two seniors be left with the brethren in the interests of discipline? But here is a last argument urged against our view. In Chapter XXXVIII. our Holy Father supposes that the superior may wish to say a few words, for edification. St. Benedict's hypothesis would be vain, it is argued, if the Abbot were never with his monks, but with the guests " who are never lacking in a monastery." We have already replied that these last words should be taken in a broad sense, and that the Abbot might in fact sometimes find himself with the community: as, for instance, if the guests arrived after the meal of the Abbot and brethren. We should observe also that the word superior (*prior*) does not in the Rule designate the Abbot alone, but a superior of any sort; and it may apply here to him who presides at the community meal in the absence of the Abbot.

We ought to say a word on the motives which made St. Benedict ordain that the Abbot should take his meals with guests. He remembered that St. Paul urged the superiors of ecclesiastical communities to be hospitable. Hospitality was an exercise of charity and a proof of Christian brotherhood, things which were very necessary at that period; it was, above all, an excellent method of spreading the Gospel. The conversation of the Abbot, whom St. Benedict wished to be a man of learning and virtue, combined with the spectacle of the monastic life to form an attractive sort of preaching. The recruitment of the monastery was in part effected by this hospitable intercourse. And thus the Abbot, while occupied with guests, was by no means deserting his house, but was working for it. Moreover, the character of conventual life was somewhat different then from what it has become since. Nowadays, if an Abbot were not with his monks in the refectory and at recreation, he would never be with them, since, except for the Divine Office and the spiritual conference, the whole day is employed in labours at which we work alone. But in St. Benedict's time all worked together in the fields and together returned to the monastery, and the Abbot, who accompanied his monks everywhere, even to the dormitory, could the more easily abstract some of his time in favour of guests.

While we hold fast to the spirit which inspires this chapter, we have only to congratulate ourselves on the modifications introduced by usage and the authority of the Church. The Abbot should not now take his meals apart from the community. Certainly, though we should not take ridiculous precautions against guests, perpetual contact with them would be prejudicial to the recollectedness and work of the Abbot. Guests and he generally meet immediately after meals or at other fixed times. In exceptional cases—which, moreover, are justified by monastic tradition—the Abbot takes his meal with them apart; but most often they are introduced into the common refectory.

CHAPTER LVII

OF THE ARTIFICERS OF THE MONASTERY

DE ARTIFICIBUS MONASTERII.— Artifices, si sunt in monasterio, cum omni humilitate et reverentia faciant ipsas artes, si tamen jusserit Abbas. Quod si aliquis ex eis extollitur pro scientia artis suæ, eo quod videatur aliquid conferre monasterio, hic talis evellatur ab ipsa arte, et denuo per eam non transeat, nisi forte humiliato ei iterum Abbas jubeat.

Should there be artificers in the monastery, let them ply their crafts in all humility and submission, provided the Abbot give permission. But if one of them be puffed up by reason of his knowledge of his craft, in that he seems to confer some benefit on the monastery, let such a one be taken from it and not exercise it again, unless perchance, when he has humbled himself, the Abbot bid him resume.

THE first part of this chapter relates to the crafts and mechanical arts exercised within the monastery; the second to the fruit and produce of these labours.

All the brethren are available for rough work or for that which is easily executed. But there are tasks of a special character which require an apprenticeship and belong only to *artifices* (artificers or artisans). So St. Benedict supposes that there are craftsmen in the monastery, perhaps even real artists: painters, sculptors, or illuminators. They may have learnt their crafts in the world, or had their training in the monastery. For our Holy Father wishes that all arts necessary for the upkeep of the house should be cultivated therein. He does not merely tolerate them, but formally desires them; yet he is aware, here as in Chapter LXVI., that this will not always be possible.

St. Benedict is consistent when he decides that advantage may be taken of the skill of those brethren who know a craft; for he never thinks of deliberately thwarting aptitude and taste, under pretext of mortification. Only one condition is required: the order or permission of the Abbot. The monk is expected to exercise his craft " in all humility and submission." Special knowledge distinguishes a man among his fellows, and measures have to be taken to guard against self-sufficiency. Moreover, the community generally benefits by these special capacities; and the more real the benefit, the easier for him who procures it to find cause for pride or non-observance. Whenever any enterprise, manufactory, or money-making concern is annexed to a monastery the danger exists. " One year with another," a man may say, " I am worth so much to the community. The rest do nothing but eat and drink, while I supply the Abbey finances with a considerable annual sum." One can only avoid the danger of such a situation by having a solid religious spirit. St. Augustine foresaw this before St. Benedict: " Nor let them be puffed up if they benefit the common funds from their own resources." Cassian has the same thought. St. Ephrem also bids a monk not to take pride in what he may contribute; and St. Basil, like our Holy Father, urges the superior not to tolerate such an abuse.[1]

The monk's soul is worth more than all else. The moment the Abbot sees pride, or a mercantile spirit, or insubordination and particularism, creeping in by way of these small occupations he should ignore any pecuniary loss, which is never irreparable, and safeguard souls at all costs. The words of the Rule are emphatic: " Let such a one be taken from his craft and not exercise it again, unless perchance, when he has humbled himself, the Abbot bid him resume it."

Si quid vero ex operibus artificum venumdandum est, videant ipsi per quorum manus transigenda sunt, ne aliquam fraudem præsumant inferre. Memorentur Ananiæ et Saphiræ: ne forte mortem quam illi in corpore pertulerunt, hanc isti, vel omnes qui aliquam fraudem de rebus monasterii fecerint, in anima patiantur.

And if any of the work of the artificers is to be sold, let those, through whose hands the business has to pass, see that they presume not to commit any fraud. Let them remember Ananias and Saphira: lest perchance they, and all who deal fraudulently with the goods of the monastery, should suffer in their souls the death which these incurred in the body.

Perhaps this is a fitting place to review the list of manufactures or enterprises which are compatible with the external dignity of our life, with the nature of a monastery, and with our traditions.[2] The matter is at once important and delicate. Tradition has determined what is suitable and what is not so for the various branches of religious families. We should abstain from laying down universal laws on such matters. Every superior is to some degree a judge of what he owes to himself, of what he owes to his monastery, of what is required by the interconnection of different houses, and of what they are sometimes constrained to do in order to meet financial stress. The Carthusians make liqueur, or rather a father and some lay brothers are thus employed. The Trappists manufacture chocolate, cheese, and beer, and farm their land; that is their accepted practice. For ourselves we are not the " sole manufacturers and patentees " of any product. If for the publication of liturgical books and other monastic works, and to aid in the diffusion of truth, we control a printing-press, so be it. It is a kind of conventual preaching; we are only taking up again our old traditions and by means of a press multiplying the manuscripts which formerly we transcribed and illuminated. To go outside this is to expose ourselves sometimes to serious mistakes; it is to enter again, and that by the wrong door, upon all the responsibilities and preoccupations of the world, to escape from our religious life, *et propter vitam vivendi perdere causas*. It has yet to be proved that Our Lord cares much for our exercising any industry.

But supposing the farm annexed to a monastery produces more than

---

[1] S. AUG., *Epist.* CCXI., 6. *P.L.*, XXXIII., 960.—CASS., *Inst.*, IV., xiv.—S. EPHR., *Paræn.*, xxvi. (*opp. græc. lat.*, t. II., p. 114).—S. BASIL., *Reg. fus.*, xxix.
[2] *Cf.* S. BASIL., *Reg. fus.*, xxxviii.

is required for the monks themselves: wine, for instance, or honey, or vegetables; what is to be done with the surplus? Some of the Eastern Fathers used to unweave their mats and baskets and begin over again. Cassian tells us that Abbot Paul, who lived seven days' journey from any habitation, used at the end of the year to burn the baskets with which his cave was encumbered. But the majority sold their work in the towns.[1] Nor are we forbidden to imitate them. Having attended to the duty of almsgiving, we may then provide for our monastery. But St. Benedict would surely not have cared to see his monks going to fairs and public markets.[2] He desires that all crafts should be exercised in the monastery enclosure: " so that there may be no need for the monks to go abroad." How, then, could he wish his monks to go abroad, not merely to buy, but to engage in trade?

Selling shall be done by means of agents. And St. Benedict warns the Abbot and monks to see that these agents deal honestly. They might be tempted to make a commission on the sales. The work is conscientiously done, the wine is not adulterated, and there are plenty of buyers. The vendors may be induced, by the very excellence of the merchandise they are offering, to put the price high, and pocket the difference. Perhaps they are dependants of the monastery and think it only natural to enrich themselves at its expense. But St. Benedict recalls the case of Ananias and Saphira (Acts v.): the deed which drew down upon the pair the severity of God and St. Peter was rather like that forecasted in the Rule. They had sold their field; instead of handing over the whole price to the community, they took some pocket money for themselves out of it and gave St. Peter what remained, completing the transaction with a lie, and that a concerted one. It would seem that St. Benedict regarded the fault committed by Ananias and Saphira as venial and as punished with bodily death only;[3] in which he followed the interpretation of several Fathers, such as Origen, St. Augustine, and Cassian.[4] But the fault of the monastery agents is more serious; for the stuff they deal with is only a deposit, and a sacred deposit at that, since all monastic property belongs to God. Therefore they shall suffer in their souls.

In ipsis autem pretiis non surripiat avaritiæ malum, sed semper aliquantulum vilius detur, quam a secularibus datur: ut in omnibus glorificetur Deus.	In the prices themselves let not the vice of avarice creep in, but let goods always be sold a little cheaper than by men of the world, that God may be glorified in all things.

Monks must avoid all that resembles greed and the desire of unlimited accumulation: *avaritiae malum.* How unworthy of a religious is greed

[1] *Inst.*, X., xxiv.
[2] St. BASIL manifests the same repugnance: *Reg. fus.*, xxxix.
[3] However, PAUL THE DEACON and HILDEMAR think that St. Benedict does not claim to settle the question as to their spiritual death: he considers only the bodily punishment.
[4] ORIGEN., *Comm. in Matth.*, l. XV., 15. *P.G.*, XIII., 1297-1298.—S. AUG., *Contra Epist. Parmeniani*, l. III., c. i. *P.L.*, XLIII., 84.—CASS., *Conlat.*, VI., xi.

of gain! St. Jerome, from whom our Holy Father borrowed his portrait of the Sarabaite, tells us that they sold dear: " They put part of the produce of their work into the common stock, that they may have their food in common . . . and as though their craft were holy and not their lives, they ask a greater price for what they sell."[1] St. Benedict requires the exact contrary. The products of monastic toil shall always be sold at something less than the ordinary price; in order that religious may not cause protests and anger which would recoil on God; in order that people of the world may find edification in their accommodating and disinterested spirit, and that, even in money matters, they may find means for a sort of apostolate: " That God may be glorified in all things " (1 Pet. iv. 11).[2]

A little supernatural pride will easily secure us against all unseemly astuteness and permit us to be faithful to the spirit of the Rule, if not always to the letter. For there are economical conditions and exterior interests of which we must take account. In times when there was no commercial competition, nor, as nowadays, over-production, and especially when monks were employed in producing objects of the first necessity, no rivalry was possible, and the lower rate of monastic prices was sheer gain for the public. But, as things now are, monasteries which flooded the public markets with manufactured articles at prices below those current would cause a ruinous fall of values, bankruptcies, and enmities. If monks are obliged to make more profit than they would like, they can always restore it in alms. When the business is small and cannot constitute serious competition, it is permissible to sell cheap; likewise, when one is working a patent, there is more liberty of action. But whether we lower the price or raise it, the essential point is to realize always the Benedictine motto: " That God may be glorified in all things " (*Ut in omnibus glorificetur Deus*).

Lay brothers. We may take occasion of this chapter (LVII.) to say a word about lay brothers. Their history is yet to be written. It has, however, been sketched by M. Raymond Chasles in his thesis for the École des Chartes,[3] and by Father Eberhard Hoffmann, a Cistercian of Mehrerau.[4] The dissertation of Martène in the Preface to the sixth volume of the *Veterum scriptorum . . . amplissima collectio* may also be read; also Calmet in his commentary on the second chapter of the Rule; and Mabillon, in the Preface to the sixth Benedictine century (P. II.).

The commentators of the seventeenth century seem to have been mistaken in asserting that lay brothers existed before St. Benedict and

---

[1] *Epist.* XXII., 34. *P.L.*, XXII., 419.
[2] Some ancient writers had given the same counsel: EVAGRIUS, *Rerum monachalium rationes*, viii. *P.G.*, XL., 1259-1260.—ISAIAS, *Reg.*, lix., lxi.
[3] École nationale des Chartes, Positions des thèses, 1906, pp. 43-49: *Étude sur l'Institut monastique des frères convers et sur l'oblature au moyen âge; leur origine et leur rôle* (xi.-xiii. cent.).
[4] *Das Konverseninstitut des Cisterzienserordens in seinem Ursprung und seiner Organisation* (Fribourg, 1905). Reviewed in the *Revue Bénédictine*, April, 1906, p. 289.

even in his institute. In the earliest Western monasteries, as at Lérins under Faustus, in the fifth century, there were monks who were clerics, and monks who were laymen; there were lettered monks and illiterate; nor is it at all surprising that the heavier work was entrusted by preference to the latter. But they did not form a separate class. Moreover, many monasteries had servants and even slaves on their lands, but these were not monks.

Many passages of the Rule seem to forbid any distinction between monks (for instance the words of Chapter II.: " Let him make no distinction of persons in the monastery "); and there is no text to prove the existence of a distinct class, specially dedicated to the material services of the monastery. Allusions to lay brothers have been found in the ordinances concerning the sick, the guests, and the porter; but they are not convincing. Chapter XXXVIII. says that the reader at meals shall eat " with the weekly servers of the kitchen and the attendants ": but this is not enough to establish the existence even of purely lay servants; yet M. Chasles draws that inference. But it is undeniable that at Monte Cassino there were, besides the educated and cultured monks, peasants and quondam slaves, such as the worthy Goth mentioned in the Life of St. Benedict. There are those who " can neither meditate nor read " (Chapter XLVIII.); some are unable to write their profession paper (Chapter LVIII.). The Abbot obviously would not choose clerics and priests from among these " simple folk," as St. Benedict calls them; and they would have to be given work suited to their capacity. But apart from that they were distinguished in no respect from the rest of the monks. They went to the Divine Office and took part in it to the best of their ability; their memories gradually learnt the psalms and hymns.

From the eighth to the tenth century—and here we are summarizing the conclusions of M. Chasles—a change came over monastic practice. The Work of God took more considerable proportions than in St. Benedict's time. Monks were very numerous. The difference between educated and illiterate was accentuated; little by little lay *famuli* (servants) gave way to religious exclusively occupied in manual work, with a special liturgical Office of a very simple character.[1] Cluny had lay brothers. They were monks, but had no seat in chapter; in church they took their place in the lower choir; some, however, were employed in the ritual; and those who had good voices even acted as cantors and were vested in the cope. The lay brothers had a special habit and wore beards, whence their name of *barbati* (bearded); in the earliest times the name of *conversi* applied to all monks. There was also in monasteries a class called " oblates," whose history is intimately bound up with that of lay brothers. Children brought up in the cloister were often called *nutriti* (nurslings) to distinguish them from *conversi*, or those who came of their own accord.

[1] Our lay brothers also recite an Office, composed of the *Pater*, *Ave*, and some short prayers taken from our Hours.

The institution of lay brothers reached its full development in the eleventh century. It was established in Germany, thanks chiefly to Abbot William of Hirschau, who was much influenced, as is well known, by the Customs of Cluny. Haymo, his biographer, has left us a summary of the Rule for lay brothers at Hirschau. As at Cluny, the business of the kitchen was entrusted to them. Lay brothers played an important part at the end of the eleventh century. In the twelfth they appeared in all the abbeys of Western Europe. They are found among the Camaldolese, Vallombrosians, and Carthusians. But it was at Cîteaux above all that they held an important position. Customs and a Rule were drawn up for them. Some of them were to dwell in the abbey, others in the "granges," others with high secular personages; some were assigned to the service of the abbeys of Cistercian nuns. The more recent Congregations of Monte Cassino, Bursfeld, St. Vanne, and St. Maur also had their lay brothers. There was, moreover, among the Maurists, another class called "commis" (officials) who were charged especially with external works and the relations of the monastery with the outside world; after probation they took a vow of stability. Finally, there were "perpetual servants," bound to the monastery by civil contract.

It should be observed that our Constitutions, taken in this case from those of the Maurists, order that none should be admitted as lay brothers save those who possess aptitude for their work. Above all we should note that they are as truly religious and monks as are the choir monks. Therefore they should have such instruction and training as will enable them to live up to their vows. They are all, whether novices or professed, under the spiritual direction of the lay brother master. As regards their work they are under the cellarer; apart from him and the fathers assigned to the charge of them, no one has a right to put any duty on them or to require their services; if lay brothers are not the domestic servants of the community, they are still less the servants of any individual monk. Perfect courtesy and considerate charity should regulate all our relations with them; every species of petty familiarity should be severely repressed, as well as all unjustifiable conversation; both their interest and ours demand this. Let us also beware of scandalizing simple souls by certain ways which are scarcely monastic, and by notorious breaches of Rule.

Their life is humble, silent, hidden, and more severe in some respects than that of the choir monks; and, as the Maurist Declarations set it down, they should not be advanced to Orders nor undertake higher studies. Strict observance of these two last points is indispensable for the safeguarding of their monastic vocation; and those who seek to enter the clerical state nearly always meet with failure. Their laborious days may easily become one long colloquy with the Lord; and the spectacle of such glad and peaceful fidelity is the most valuable of all their services.

CHAPTER LVIII
OF THE DISCIPLINE OF RECEIVING BRETHREN INTO RELIGION

THE portion of the Rule which begins with this chapter and extends to the sixty-sixth inclusively is quite clearly defined, and deals first with the recruitment of the monastery, then with its hierarchical arrangement and regular order. To exhaust the topic of recruitment our Holy Father speaks successively of novices in general, of children, of priests, and of stranger monks. The present chapter, which gives us the general methods by which a community is recruited, comprises three main divisions: the reception of candidates, their probation or novitiate, and their final admission. This last part treats of the solemn forms of admission, and then of the monk's obligation to dispose of all his property. Here we have a number of questions, the importance and interest of which invite us to extend our commentary.

DE DISCIPLINA SUSCIPIENDORUM FRATRUM.—Noviter veniens quis ad conversionem, non ei facilis tribuatur ingressus: sed sicut ait Apostolus: *Probate spiritus, si ex Deo sunt.* Ergo si veniens perseveraverit pulsans, et illatas sibi injurias, et difficultatem ingressus, post quatuor aut quinque dies visus fuerit patienter portare, et persistere petitioni suæ, annuatur ei ingressus, et sit in cella hospitum paucis diebus.

To him that newly comes to conversion, let not an easy entrance be granted, but, as the Apostle says, "Try the spirits if they be of God." If, therefore, he that comes persevere in knocking, and after four or five days seem patiently to endure the wrongs done to him and the difficulty made about his entrance, and to persist in his petition, let entrance be granted him, and let him be in the guest-house for a few days.

"*One that newly comes to conversion.*"—The conversion here spoken of is simply the religious life, so called from its being a turning towards God. This phraseology accorded with the ecclesiastical language of the time,[1] and is very felicitous; man turns from sin, from the world and its frivolity, in order to direct his life towards the supreme reality and uncreated beauty. However, when he presents himself at the monastery, and so at the house of God, he does but respond to the call of God Himself—*i.e.*, to vocation.

[1] Illi quorum conversioni consulere voluimus . . . says ST. AUGUSTINE (*Epist.* LXXXIII., 2 et 3. *P.L.*, XXXIII., 292), and a little farther on: *Cum quisque ad monasterium convertitur, si veraci corde convertitur,* etc.—*Si quis ad conversionem venerit* (S. CÆSAR., *Reg. ad mon.*, i.; *Reg. ad virg.*, Recapitulatio, viii.).—D. BUTLER (*S. Benedicti Regula monachorum*, pp. 140–141) says that the best attested reading everywhere in the Rule is *conversatio: Conversatio morum: lectio omnino certa sed haud facilis intellectu.* Conferri potest CASSIANUS, *c. Nest.*, V., i.: *per bonorum actuum conversationem.* . . . *Conversio non usurpabatur a S. Benedicto; converti vero bis invenitur* (ii., lxiii.). *Conversatio* (= *vita monastica*) *et conversio erant ambo in usu communi.*—Cf. D. ROTHENHÄUSLER, *Zur Aufnahmeordnung der Regula S. Benedicti*, II., *Conversatio morum*, pp. 20 sq.—D. HERWEGEN, *Geschichte der benediktinischen Professformel*, II., i. *Conversatio und conversio im Regeltext*, pp. 47 sq.

Vocation.—We must limit the use of this term and not make it signify any expression of our activity. We speak of the soldier's vocation, the engineer's vocation, the vocation to the married state or common vocation. These are actual states, the result of strictly personal choice, the product of circumstances, aptitudes, and tastes. Doubtless these choices do not escape the laws of Providence, yet they do not imply a very special invitation of God, as does vocation properly so called. This comprises three elements: a special call of God—to a high supernatural state—to which call the intelligent creature should respond with free co-operation. And in this sense there are only three vocations: vocation to the Faith, for heretics and infidels, which is universal and obligatory under pain of damnation; religious vocation, which is, as we hope to show, universal and yet a matter of counsel; vocation to the ecclesiastical state, which is special and is addressed to a select few, chosen by name from among Christian folk and designated by the Church. Here we are concerned with religious vocation only.

A general vocation to the religious life may be distinguished from an individual vocation. The first is the universal invitation addressed by Our Lord to all the faithful: "If anyone wish to come after me" (Matt. xvi. 24); "If thou wouldst be perfect" (*ibid.* xix. 21). This vocation has been given once and for all, and Our Lord's words have never been retracted. Neither the State nor the Church has any power here. God has called souls and opened the gates of perfection to them. It is not merely permission or leave, but a positive invitation addressed to the whole Church. Everyone baptized is by that act sufficiently called by God to a life which is the fulfilment of baptism. But, in actual fact, Our Lord's offer does not reach all efficaciously; it may be that a soul is inattentive; it may be that it does not consent to follow the divine counsel; it may be that at the hour when God's call reaches its ear, it finds that it has taken on itself obligations which forbid it making any response; it may be that it is without certain dispositions of soul or body which are strictly requisite. God respects the play and course of secondary causes, and in practice only a picked few are capable of following His call: "Not all take this word, but those to whom it is given. . . . He that can take, let him take it" (Matt. xix. 11–12).

The doctrinal principle of a universal vocation having been carefully safeguarded, it remains true that there is an individual and, so to speak, a privileged vocation. But our ideas should be clear with regard to this "special" vocation also. Vocation to the religious life cannot necessarily mean a positive call, a revelation, a supernatural and imperative intimation: "Thou shalt be a religious." Nor is it any more true, necessarily, that vocation is the command of a confessor. The confessor may advise, he can and should enlighten; he can weigh the chances of success, because he knows the soul's dispositions: but he cannot command, in any sense whatever. God himself does not command. Souls are free. It is infinite imprudence, and want of reverence for souls, to claim to choose their state of life for them, when the consequences are felt in

Of the Discipline of receiving Brethren into Religion

time and in eternity. Do parents and meddling, merciless directors bear the consequences of the decision which they impose by main force on a too docile and trustful soul? Vocation is a personal matter.

But, we may ask further, what is the form under which God speaks to souls, when He would draw them to Him? To confine the infinite variety of His methods within the compass of a formula or a catalogue is impossible. For God all means are good. Vocation may be a matter of sensible attraction, an inclination of the heart towards the religious life, the love of the chant and of beautiful services: a form which it very naturally takes among the young. But this sensible attraction is not an indispensable element. Vocation is sometimes an impression that dates from infancy: we have never contemplated our life in any other than monastic surroundings; we are influenced, perhaps, by the example of a relative. Or it may be an ideal of perfection that suddenly forces itself upon us.

Vocation may consist in an intellectual appreciation of the moral superiority of the religious life and in the strong resolve: " It is the better way and I will follow it." Perhaps this is the purest type of vocation. Sometimes a man is guided by a sort of practical and utilitarian impulse: " I shall have no more visits to receive or make, no more confessions, no more sermons, no domestic worries. I shall have leisure for prayer and study and shall live in peace." This sort of vocation is the vocation of middle age, of one who has already been wounded by contact with life.

Or it may be suffering which turns souls towards God; or again discontent, moral unrest, inability to be happy elsewhere. Our Lord, when He would direct us towards His ends, sows secret bitterness over all the joys of our life, and we meet naught but sadness and bruises if we step aside from the way traced by Him, a way, as the prophet says, that is marked out with hewn stones: " He hath shut up my ways with square stones " (Lam. iii. 9). Finally, there are cases where the religious life, while remaining in the abstract a counsel of perfection, yet becomes in the concrete an obligation: as when experience forces us to recognize that we need the cloister, that there only is our eternal salvation perfectly secure. In brief, vocation is never lacking; God's call takes so many forms, that one of them is always at hand and he who enters always has good reasons for entering.[1]

Again, we must not fail to remark—and the very words of the Rule invite us to do so—that all these diverse ways in which the universal call manifests itself to the individual do but constitute the material and determinable element in vocation; the formal and determinant element is the firm resolve to seek God and perfection. " If thou wouldst be perfect?" Do you wish it? " Who is the man that would have life and desires to see good days?" said St. Benedict in the Prologue. When all is said, this is the essential element and often the only one

[1] Abbot Paphnutius explained to CASSIAN that there were three kinds of vocation: *Primus ex Deo est, secundus per hominem, tertius ex necessitate* (*Conlat.*, III., iii.-v.).

that matters. For, of the two other elements, the concrete manifestation of God's counsel and personal aptitude, we have said that the first is never lacking; and of the second we may say that it is sometimes created or at least developed, when the will is generously determined. This explains why our Holy Father's ordinances for the admission of a postulant and the training of a novice have as their sole purpose the testing of his will.

Should there be long deliberation and much consultation? St. Thomas says not.[1] What, he asks, shall we deliberate about? On the excellence of the proposed resolution? But it cannot be disputed that it is a good thing, nay, a very good thing; and to doubt this, though it were but for an instant, would be to give the lie to Our Lord. Must we deliberate about our powers, whether we have the necessary strength to carry out our resolve? Some of our friends will tell us that we are doing a foolish thing, a thing impossible for our nature. Others, better advised, will reply: " You have the resources of your will, which are boundless; prayer will procure you the infinite strength of God. Children and women have done it; you can surely do as much." St. Thomas admits that there may be deliberation on three points: Is our health sufficient? Have we debts? What form of religious life suits us best? Here we may consult and interrogate; but we should ask few people and such as are discreet, prudent, competent in supernatural matters, well-informed on the character of the monastic life, and even predisposed in its favour. One may deliberate, too, with oneself, but let it be done quickly. And above all we should reflect on the most expeditious means to rid ourselves of all obstacles.

After having seen what religious vocation is in general, it will not be superfluous to say a word as to the qualifications prudently required for the contemplative life, and in particular the monastic and Benedictine contemplative life. An immortal soul—the same baptized—the same from that moment endowed with the supernatural faculties of which contemplation is the proper exercise: this is enough, no more is needed. Does the condition seem simple and easy to be realized? Yet it is the principal one of all, and the fundamental one; it might almost be said that it is the sole condition, given a determined will.

Very ordinary health is adequate to our monastic duty. But the important thing required of a candidate for the contemplative life is a certain equipoise of temperament, a thing not always very common in our age of impulsive and neurotic natures. A man who vows himself to the monastic life with a rather weak head and defective intellect will there lose all that is left, or at least will become a burden to his brethren and a danger to the community. An exaggerated preoccupation with health, with oneself, with the honour and attention one deserves, is a very bad omen; hypertrophy of the ego may be the first sign of insanity. Yet we do not reject a candidate because we find in him certain slight faults or egoistic tendencies; otherwise no one would be chosen.

A man need not be a Plato or an Aristotle for the work of Christian contemplation. But it would certainly be presumptuous to-day to

[1] II.-II., *q.* clxxxix., *a.* 10.

enter the contemplative life and to become a choir monk, we do not say without some previous education—for that is forbidden by the Holy See—but without a real taste for the things of the mind. The contemplative life does not consist in dreaming and doing nothing. Beware of those who neglect study on the ground that we are vowed only to pure contemplation, or that, according to the Apostle, "knowledge puffeth up." Taking our life as a whole, a taste for true and wholesome doctrine is a guarantee of perseverance, of worthiness, and of progress, safer often than a certain kind of piety.

The postulant must intend to take his faith seriously and must be valiant. In a monastery our livelihood is assured; we have not the external prick of necessity, nor the stimulus that action brings with it. If a contemplative be not courageous, he will quickly become a loiterer, a deserter of perfection, a useless thing. There is required of him also a love of quiet and silence, a certain detachment from the world, from politics, from external activity, from a ministry which he has freely abandoned, even, we would fain add, from the affairs of his family. We have not to provide for our brothers and sisters, nephews and nieces; our prayers and our fidelity will be more efficacious with God than human activities for which we are no longer competent. The candidate should also have a good character and a certain youthfulness of soul; critical, peevish, and unsociable temperaments are poorly suited to a rule which requires continual contact with brethren and filial submission to the Abbot.

Finally, an excellent sign of a vocation to the contemplative life is described in the passage of Ecclesiasticus: *Pulchritudinis studium habentes, pacificantes in domibus suis:* the just men of old studied beauty, they caused peace and order in their houses. Study of beauty does not necessarily mean artistic taste or artistic talent; but it implies the habit of doing nothing by halves, of realizing perfect purity, and a delicacy of disposition that does not suffer the petty passions of the world we have renounced to enter our souls again under any disguise. Courtesy and refinement also, in our relations with God as with our brethren, flow from this love of beauty; as do likewise an intelligent love of the Divine Office, of its rites and of its chants.

The reception of candidates.—A man believes that God is calling him to the Benedictine life; he is "converted"; he comes and knocks at the door. Strange to say, it does not open at once, and his reception is very reserved, not to say disagreeable: *Non ei facilis tribuatur ingressus.* It was the same among the Fathers of the East.[1] St. Benedict's first

[1] *Si quis accesserit ad ostium monasterii volens sæculo renuntiare, et fratrum aggregari numero, non habebit intrandi libertatem, sed prius nuntiabitur Patri monasterii, et manebit paucis diebus foris ante januam* (S. PACH., *Reg.* xlix.).—*Hebdomada pro foribus jaceant; nulli cum eis de fratribus jungantur, et semper dura et laboriosa eis proponantur. Si vero perseveraverint pulsantes, eis non negetur ingressus* (*Reg.* I. SS. PATRUM, vii.).—*Ambiens quis intra cœnobii recipi disciplinam non ante prorsus admittitur, quam diebus decem vel eo amplius pro foribus excubans indicium perseverantiæ . . . demonstraverit* (CASS., *Inst.*, IV., iii.). There are also resemblances between this chapter of St. Benedict and several passages in ST. BASIL (*Cf. Reg. fus.*, x. sq.).

observation is a warning against receiving promiscuously all who present themselves. They are generally unknown; their past, the secret motives which impel them to the monastic life, their possession of the requisite qualities, are all unknown. In St. Benedict's time there were special reasons for a very careful scrutiny. Besides men who were known or were furnished with letters of recommendation, there came strangers, slaves, barbarians, ex-soldiers; perhaps also characters were in general less refined than in the East.

Moreover, St. Benedict knew that the monastic life was God's reserve. Now, it is not prudent to recruit a picked body of troops by chance. Such a corps does not want those defectives who encumber and retard the progress of the whole. It is unwise to seek numbers at any price; God has no need of big battalions: sufficient for Him the three hundred soldiers of a Gideon. We must not induce souls to impose on themselves obligations out of proportion to their strength; nor must we receive men indiscreetly and bequeath to those that come after us a heritage of difficulties. Moreover, to receive everyone or nearly everyone is not the way to get many subjects, since the very condition of a monastery's recruitment is that excellence and edifying influence which chance elements are incapable of securing. The history of monasticism proves that want of strictness in the reception of subjects contributed largely to the decline of certain houses.[1] To sum up, both the interests of God and the interests of the Church are at stake; so too are the interests of the monastery in the present and in the future, and the interests of the candidates themselves. Without doubt the special motives that formerly caused a certain severity in this matter no longer hold to-day; there are now no slaves, and those who present themselves are Christians, often even clerics and priests; we know what they are, thanks to the testimonial letters prescribed by Canon Law and to private information. Nevertheless the general motives still remain. Experience proves that precautions are not superfluous, since a good number of those received do not persevere. So wise are the regulations of our Rule, that the year's novitiate and the methods of trial there exacted have been adopted by the Church and extended to all sorts of religious orders.

When our Holy Father shows so much reserve in receiving those who knock at the door, he is obviously no friend to military methods of recruiting. There is a kind of pressing solicitation which, so to speak, forces the candidate to stand and deliver. We must always avoid the methods of the press gang in our pursuit of postulants, nor shall we use alluring advertisement. In spite of kindly invitations and although there be no absolute rule on this point, we shall not go to colleges and seminaries, there to seek the increase of our communities. Providence has its own ways of making souls know the monastery where it would have them be. Yet is it legitimate and praiseworthy, while avoiding any kind of compulsion, to exhort a soul that seems predisposed to the religious life; that is the teaching of St. Thomas.[2] Nor is it indiscreet

---

[1] *Cf.* Hæften, l. IV., tract. ii.   [2] II.-II., *q.* clxxxix., *a.* 9.

sweetly and moderately to press one who is visibly called, yet temporizes without any solid motive. We must know how to help, encourage, and, as our Holy Father presently says, " win souls."

From one point of view admission into the Benedictine Order is perhaps subject to less complicated conditions than is the case with some modern forms of the religious life: one cannot become a Jesuit, Dominican, or Franciscan, without very definite qualities. Suppose a man have none of the qualities necessary for a preacher, or a professor, or a missionary; he cannot, without rashness, enter an Order which is devoted expressly to the mission, to teaching, or to the work of preaching. Of course no one will think of becoming a monk merely because all other doors are closed to him. Yet it remains true that for the Benedictine life there is scarcely but one aptitude required of us—viz., the interior purpose of sanctifying our souls. And this aptitude exists when a man is determined to develop the powers of his baptism. As we have already observed, the formal constituent of religious vocation in general is a vigorous will; and it is with the candidate's will that the scrutiny of superiors should chiefly concern itself. The more uniform our existence is, the more withdrawn from the world and disengaged from the torrent of modern life, which flows towards noise, display, and action, the more openly contrary to the temper created in almost all our contemporaries by social influences, the less can we consent to lower its standard.

St. Benedict's idea is so exactly that which we have just expressed, that he seems to have had no other intention, when fixing the novitiate tests, than to discover the seriousness, determination, and generosity of the will.[1] For if the candidate be one of those who will and will not (" the sluggard willeth and willeth not "), if his will have only conceived one of those indecisive resolutions in which the lazy perish (" desires kill the slothful "): the necessity he is under of waiting at the door, the very rebuffs of his first reception, will make this appearance of a vocation vanish in smoke, and he will retrace his steps congratulating himself that he went no farther.

Therefore, the postulant shall be left knocking at the door, says St. Benedict. Yet it shall be partly opened, though it be to tell him unpleasant things. He may be told, for instance, that he is too old or too young, that he has not health or energy enough to become a monk, that there is no room for him. The Fathers of the East were very skilful in varying these tests. Read, for instance, the account of St. Antony's reception of Paul the Simple, or the reception given by St. Pachomius to Macarius of Alexandria in disguise.[2] We see why the monk who attended the door and was charged with the reception of postulants had to be chosen from among those of greatest experience.[3] At the end of four or five days of this treatment, if the candidate holds

---

[1] *Cf.* S. BASIL., *Sermo asceticus de renuntiatione sæculi.* P.G., XXXI., 626 sq.— S. GREG. M., *Expositio in I. Reg.*, l. IV., c. iv., 17. P.L., LXXIX., 245.
[2] PALLAD., *Hist. Laus.*, c. xxviii. et xix.–xx. ROSWEYD, pp. 730, 723.
[3] *Cf. Vita S. Pachomii*, c. xix. *Acta SS.*, Maii, t. III., p. 303.

firm and remains, entrance shall be granted him: but only entrance into the guest-house, which, as we have said, is a separate building. There he must remain some days, as the Rule prescribes with no more precise determination of time; during this period, again, exact knowledge may be gained of his character. According to some ancient monastic customs, he was employed to wait on the guests. Cassian says that after admission and clothing the candidate was entrusted to the guest-master for a year, and then to the novice-master.[1] It will be observed that the candidate makes his way into the Benedictine family only gradually and by stages, with a slow and prudent progress; first comes the door, then the guest-house, then the novitiate, and finally entrance into the community.

Clothing and postulantship.—In the actual Solesmes practice the candidate remains some days in the guest-house; that was the custom at Cluny and among the Maurists. Then he is given a cell in the novitiate and follows the novitiate exercises. At the end of a fortnight he may receive the habit. But he comes first before the Abbot and his Council, and a certain number of questions are put to him concerning his canonical fitness for the religious life.[2]

After clothing begins the period of postulantship. We may regard it as taking the place of the first tests to which our forefathers made newcomers submit, but only if we note that it was, as such, unknown to them. A distinction between the postulantship and novitiate will be searched for in vain not only in St. Benedict but everywhere else. The postulantship was an invention of the last Maurists. After the royal edict professing to reform religious orders, promulgated by Louis XV. in March, 1768, which forbade profession before the age of twenty-one,[3] the Congregation of St. Maur published in 1770 a new edition of its Constitutions. In this document the "first probation" becomes a regular organized stage, through which all candidates must pass, under the religious habit and in special houses; its normal duration is a year, but it might last as many as fourteen months or as few as six. The postulants were entrusted to a "Director of probationers" (*Director probandorum*) and a Zelator. Their horarium and exercises were almost the same as those of the novices, save that the latter devoted themselves exclusively to studies "calculated to develop piety and train the memory," while the postulants, under the guidance of the Zelator, added to the study of the rubrics, chant, New Testament, Rule, etc., the study of Latin, French, Greek, and Hebrew. "Let them be taught the rules for correct reading and speaking, and

---

[1] *Inst.*, IV., vii.
[2] This set of questions is ancient; it occurs in large part in the Ceremonial of St. Augustine of Canterbury (*Customary of the Benedictine Monasteries of St. Augustine, Canterbury, and St. Peter, Westminster*, edited by Sir Edward Maunde Thompson, London, 1902, vol. I., p. 6).—There already existed in the institute of St. Pachomius an examination previous to admission: *Reg.* xlix.
[3] *Cf.* Prat., S.J., *Essai historique sur la destruction des Ordres religieux en France au XVIIIe siecle*, pp. 182 ff.

the elements of Geography, Chronology, and History: so that they may be instructed in virtue and knowledge together." Our constitutions, which in the matter of the postulantship are indebted to the Maurists, follow them also in the determination of its length. But with us postulants are put with the novices and undergo an absolutely identical probation.

The postulantship has been introduced into many religious families, but Canon Law does not order it for choir monks. Clement VIII., in the decree *Cum ad regularem* (March 19, 1603), stipulated that all candidates should be instructed in the Rule, the vows, and the special nature of the institute, before receiving the habit—that is to say, before commencing the novitiate proper. The fact is that in the time of Clement VIII. only two clothings were known: the clothing of the novice and the clothing of the professed monk. To-day we have three: the clothing of the layman, of the novice, and of the professed. But the two first are only duplicates of the profession clothing. And from the very rite itself it is plain that this clothing is the most important and has a decisive effect. Then only is the candidate required to choose between his worldly garments and the garments of religion, then only is the monastic habit given in its entirety, then only does it receive a special blessing, then only is its meaning and virtue set forth in detail. And while the clothing of a postulant takes place in chapter, and the clothing of a novice in chapter and in church at the end of Mass, the clothing of a professed monk is performed in the very course of the Holy Sacrifice.

In St. Benedict's practice—he parted with Cassian on this point[1]—clothing coincided with profession, as we know from the very terms of this fifty-eighth chapter. The novitiate was made in lay clothes, which differed less than now from the garments of religion; when probation was finished, the novice renounced the livery of the world and received the monastic habit and the tonsure. Such was then the common practice in the West, as witnessed by the Rules of St. Cæsarius, St. Aurelian, St. Ferreolus, St. Fructuosus, the Master, the Fifth Council of Orleans of A.D. 549, the third novel of Justinian. The Council of Aix-la-Chapelle in A.D. 817 still insists: "Nor let the novice be tonsured, nor change his former vesture, until he promises obedience." However, since the ninth century, the practice has been introduced in the West—already known, as we have said, to some Easterns—of giving the habit and the tonsure at the commencement of the novitiate.[2] At Cluny in the eleventh century there was a clothing at the beginning of the year's novitiate. The Cistercians adopted this custom, and it spread also amongst nuns. Nowadays, unless an approved Rule formally authorizes the contrary, or there is a special dispensation, it is common law that the novitiate be made in the habit of religion. Finally, since the

[1] *Inst.*, IV., v.–vi.
[2] *Cf.* HILDEMAR, Comment. *in cap.* lviii.—*Vita S. Bened. Anian.*, c. vi. *P.L.*, CIII., 356.

creation of the postulantship, the clothing is in practice anticipated still earlier.[1]

| Postea sit in cella novitiorum, ubi meditetur, et manducet, et dormiat. | Afterwards let him be in the cell of the novices, where he shall meditate, eat, and sleep. |

The novitiate.—After the candidate has been clothed as a novice he is a true member of the monastic family and enjoys the privileges of novices as recognized in Canon Law.

The novitiate house (*cella novitiorum*), according to our Holy Father's notion, is distinct from the habitation of the monks, somewhat in the same way as the guest-house. The novices have their own refectory, their own dormitory, and a special place where they meditate—that is to say, where they pray and study divine things. It is highly probable that St. Benedict admitted novices to the Divine Office and to the manual labour in which the whole community took part: the very enumeration of what is done in the novitiate suggests this and seems to exclude other special exercises. Moreover, early monastic history gives us no positive evidence of an absolute separation. At Cluny, when the novices were not very numerous, they slept and ate with the professed monks. They were always present at the Offices in the lower choir of the church. In chapter they were present only for the explanation of the Rule.

The separation of novices and professed became canonical by the decree *Cum ad regularem* of Clement VIII. The new *Codex* ordains: "Let the novitiate be separated, as far as possible, from the part of the house occupied by the professed, so that novices, except for a special reason and with the permission of the superior or their Master, may have no communication with the professed, nor the professed with novices (Can. 564)." The unauthorized intercourse of a novice with a choir monk is regarded by our Constitutions as a fault *simpliciter gravis* (of itself serious). The object is to secure a single uniform training and to keep novices concentrated exclusively on the process of their monastic initiation. But doubtless this separation cannot among us have the absolute and uncompromising character which it takes in certain more modern religious bodies. A Benedictine monastery is a family of which the novices are the children. They are not merely in a relation of juxtaposition to the rest, but are thrown with them constantly all through the day. Before admitting them to profession, it is right that the community should observe them carefully and come to know them. Yet it remains true that the mere fact of being a

[1] All the Ceremonial which is actually used by the Congregation of France, and which other Benedictine families have adopted, was composed by D. GUÉRANGER. The Abbot of Solesmes utilized and combined materials taken from various ancient rituals for profession and the clothing of novices. A portion of these materials will be found in MARTÈNE, *De ant. monach. rit.*, l. V., c. ii.; *De ant. eccl. rit.*, l. II., c. ii.—See the Declarations, Constitutions, and Ritual of the Congregation of St. Maur.

Of the Discipline of receiving Brethren into Religion 377

professed monk, or even a senior, is not sufficient to legitimize direct interference with novices when they merit reprimand or admonition.

Again, a monastery, because it is a family, has the right to train its own novices. Among the Maurists only one or two houses in a province possessed a novitiate. The practice of having one novitiate for a whole Congregation has real advantages, which have decided many Orders or branches of an Order to adopt it. Perhaps a closer union between the members of diverse monasteries is thus secured; and small communities are dispensed from having a novitiate, where, with a very modest number of candidates, it would yet be necessary to employ several religious. Finally, it is easier thus to secure the candidate a complete and uniform training. However, the disadvantages are also real; and the actual practice of our Congregation is for each superior to educate his own children. This usage is in conformity with the traditions of the Order and with the mind of St. Benedict—who, by the way, never contemplated a Congregation. It is a recognition of the autonomy of each monastery. Nevertheless an Abbot may entrust his novices to another house; and a recent General Chapter expressed the desire that the same horarium and a common course of reading and study should be followed everywhere.

| Et senior ei talis deputetur, qui aptus sit ad lucrandas animas, et qui super eum omnino curiose intendat et sollicitus sit, si vere Deum quærit, et si sollicitus est ad opus Dei, ad obedientiam, ad opprobria. Prædicentur ei omnia dura et aspera, per quæ itur ad Deum. | Let there be assigned to him a senior, who is skilled in winning souls, who may watch him with the utmost care and consider anxiously whether he truly seeks God, and is zealous for the Work of God, for obedience, and for humiliations. Let there be set before him all the hard and rugged ways by which we walk towards God. |

The Novice Master.—Having entered the novitiate, the candidate is placed under the control of a master: such is the universal practice, as old as the monastic life itself. Does St. Benedict mean that each novice should have a master, as was the custom among many Eastern monks? That is the opinion of Haeften and of some other commentators. But it may be disputed. St. Basil and Cassian, who inspired our Holy Father, take for granted that the novices are numerous, and Cassian speaks of an " elderly monk guiding the ten religious whom the Abbot has entrusted to his charge."[1] The words of the Rule, like those of the *Institutes* (of Cassian) speak only of a novice and deal with the individual; but this is only a method of exposition; in actual fact the novice might belong to a group. Supposing, as is quite likely, that many candidates present themselves at a monastery, how will the *cella novitiorum* (novitiate house) work, if each has to have his own master? Moreover, as Martène observes, the separation of novices from the

[1] *Inst.*, IV., vii.

community, explicitly indicated by the Rule, would be nothing but an unrealizable ordinance, if each novice was entrusted to a senior.

So St. Benedict probably intended that there should be one Master of Novices, but he did not therefore intend him to be omnipotent. When a novitiate is the novitiate of a whole Congregation or of a province, there is reason for leaving him his independence, since it is justified by the Constitutions and by custom. To permit Abbots and local superiors to enter the single novitiate at their pleasure and to exercise their authority in it, would be to contravene the very law of a house which belongs to the Congregation, and depends on the Diet or General Chapter. But when each monastery has its own novitiate, when the Novice Master is nominated by the Abbot and when the latter may always, if he so will, keep this charge for himself, to refuse to let him interfere in the affairs of his novitiate would be at once an audacious, inconsistent, and futile act. Therefore the Novice Master should never regard his charge as a fief which he must defend jealously against the intrusions of the Abbot as understanding nothing about it. The novices do not belong to the Novice Master; he is merely the Abbot's representative among them. This incontestable principle once laid down, it is clear that the first care of a Novice Master should be to know the Abbot's mind and how he conceives the training of his subjects. He should study only to be obedient, docile, intelligently and lovingly pliant. Without doubt it is his mission to lead souls to Our Lord (*aptus ad lucrandas animas*), but there is no going to Our Lord save by way of the Abbot. He has to train disciples and sons for his Abbot; therefore he shall not seek to be anything but a disciple and a true son. This is good sense and order, and procures the security and peace of all. Thus only shall the novices make real progress, and the Novice Master be truly loyal; for he is trusted with full confidence.

And this same principle, that the Novice Master is the Abbot's representative, determines the general character of his activity. Sharing in the fatherhood of the Abbot, he shall have, along with reverence for souls, a deep and supernatural tenderness for all and for each. He shall not disdain their regard and their trust in him, because they need trustfulness and submission that they may grow; yet he shall never take advantage of it to the point of engrossing what after all does not belong even to the Abbot, but to God. He must readily believe that his work is not his own, but Our Lord's and the Abbot's, who work through him. He may take St. John the Baptist as his patron saint and with him say: " I am not the Christ, but am sent before him. He that hath the bride is the bridegroom: but the friend of the bridegroom, who standeth and heareth him, rejoiceth with joy because of the bridegroom's voice. This my joy therefore is fulfilled. He must increase: but I must decrease " (John iii. 28–30).

St. Benedict would have the Novice Master be a senior—if not old in years, at any rate mature in prudence and in the understanding of supernatural things. A Master's business is to teach: *Loqui et docere magistrum condecet* (Chapter VI.); and our Holy Father has himself indicated the substance of this teaching. First and foremost it consists of the Rule, customs, and traditions of the Order. The special counsel given by our Holy Father to the Abbot: " And especially let him observe this present Rule in all things," concerns the Novice Master also. He must expound it to the newcomers and maintain with discretion, yet firmly and uncompromisingly, the true spirit of the monastic institute. He will also, of course, instruct them in all that concerns the interior life. Holy Scripture, the Liturgy, and the Fathers being the very sources of Benedictine piety, a taste for them must be instilled in the novitiate.[1]

Our Holy Father requires the Master of Novices not only to teach and enlighten souls, but also, by means of various ascetical methods, to re-form them, to turn them towards God, to train them to virtue and perfection, to bear them along—in a word, to " win " them for God.[2] According to our Holy Father he must be careful, cautious, and observant: *Omnino curiose intendat et sollicitus sit.* And in order to facilitate this scrutiny, the novice should lay bare his whole soul. There are some who preserve an obstinate silence, others who talk endlessly, and always about themselves; but it is better to be something talkative than to " close up." The careful observation of the Novice Master is not that bitter zeal which St. Benedict condemns elsewhere, that extreme severity which exacts from all at every moment the maximum of perfection. Nor do we want a minute supervision; for what is the good of pressing heavily on souls so as to excite in them a precocious fervour, which too often is factitious and transient? What is the good of forcing them to endless self-analysis? Nay, they are called to leave the region of self and sweetly to turn towards eternal Beauty and Purity: " Hearken, O daughter, and see, and incline thy ear, and forget . . ." (Ps. xliv.). " But we all, beholding the glory of the Lord with open face, are transformed into the same image from glory to glory, as by the Spirit of the Lord " (2 Cor. iii. 18).

St. Benedict himself indicates the signs which shall guide the Master in his investigation, and so at the same time gives the disciple his programme: *Si vere Deum quærit.* Does he seek God? God seeks man: " And the Lord, seeking his own workman in the multitude of the people to whom he thus cries out "; and man on his part should seek God. " That they should seek God if haply they may feel after

---

[1] The Constitutions of Chezal-Benoît contained this ordinance: *Novitii per totum annum sui novitiatus nihil aliud discant præter Regulam B. Patris N. Benedicti, ceremonias nostræ societatis, officium divinum et quæ ad illud pertinent, vitas Patrum et collationes eorundem.* Our Constitutions, which here again borrow from St. Maur, forbid during the novitiate " profane and curious studies "—that is to say, critical or erudite labours—and generally all that is not concerned with spiritual and professional training; then they add: *Sedulam operam cantui gregoriano, ceremoniis, rubricisque dabunt; demum excolendæ memoriæ, ne pereat aut languescat, satagent.*

[2] *Constituit* (Pachomius) *præpositos qui sibi ad lucrandas animas, quæ ad eum quotidie confluebant, adjutores existerent* (*Vita S. Pachomii*, c. xxv., *Acta SS.*, Maii, t. III.).

him or find him, although he be not far from every one of us" (Acts xvii. 27). This and nothing else is what is done in the monastic life. Why should we be ashamed of this work before people of the world? God is the only interesting being, and the postulant should realize that from the first moment of his conversion. The Novice Master will soon discover whether a soul is turning itself wholly in this direction.

This seeking God will show itself especially in a great zeal for the Divine Office: *si sollicitus est ad opus Dei*. There is the novice secure of finding the Lord, of talking with Him, of putting himself in harmony with Him: " The sacrifice of praise shall glorify me: and there is the way by which I will show him the salvation of God " (Ps. xlix. 23). Since his whole life must be spent in the Work of God, the novice shall use all effort to gain a liturgical spirit, and superiors shall notice whether he is eager to take his place in the church, whether he is content there in the spirit of faith and abides without weariness, whether he provides and prepares for the ceremonies and lessons.

When the novice seeks God he remembers also that the only way that leads securely and quickly to Him is the way of obedience: *Scientes se per hanc obedientiæ viam ituros ad Deum* (Chapter LXXI.) For St. Benedict, as we know, all virtue is manifested and summed up in an interior attitude which may be called obedience or humility. The Novice Master should therefore principally—as urged by all monastic history—habituate the novices to profound docility, to a supreme reverence for authority, very far removed from every sort of questioning, though this be polite or even purely secret. In their desire to break down pride the ancients employed methods which sometimes rather astonish us.[1]

Our Holy Father is doubtless recalling Cassian and also St. Basil[2] when he requires his novices to be eager for humiliations (*ad opprobria*). However, save for the preliminary tests which St. Benedict himself imposes on candidates at the doors of the monastery (which, moreover, may have been very moderate in character), we nowhere in the Holy Rule find allusion to certain deliberate vexations, of a factitious and unjustifiable character, and calculated to exasperate human nature. We have spoken of them already in connection with the fourth degree of humility. We said that God's methods and the methods of the Rule are enough to try a soul. One would hardly feel at one's ease under an Abbot who believed himself bound in conscience to be a trial to his monks, and regarded them rather as patients or victims. The humiliations spoken of by St. Benedict are much rather the trials implied normally in the ordinary course of a religious life. The servile works in which monks were employed, the care of cattle, harvesting, the reclaiming of land, the kitchen service, all these formed so many humi-

[1] *Cf.* Cass., *Inst.*, IV., iii.
[2] *Prius autem quam corpori fraternitatis inseratur, oportet ei injungi quædam laboriosa opera et quæ videantur opprobrio haberi a sæcularibus*, etc. (*Reg. contr.*, vi.).

Of the Discipline of receiving Brethren into Religion

liations for the native pride and refinement of patricians.[1] Moreover, the monastery had no comforts; provision was made for living and for cleanliness, but not for comfort. Finally, a noble might have to rub elbows with one of his former slaves, sometimes even receive orders from him. We see at once in what the humiliations consisted and in what they still consist. Does some regular task mortify an evil tendency of yours? Well, do it bravely. God alone counts; things and events do not matter; to work miracles or to work in the kitchen is all one; it is enough that the task be ordered and willed by God. The soul thus faces all things with the same tranquil zeal. This, we admit, is a description of perfect virtue, but generous souls reach it quickly or tend vigorously towards it.

Prædicentur ei omnia dura et aspera per quæ itur ad Deum (Let there be set before him all the hard and rugged ways by which we walk towards God). We should recall what was said at the end of the Prologue. There are real difficulties in the monastic life; the road which leads to God is sown with roughness and pain.[2] The novice will not be slow to find this out for himself. Yet he must be told, in order that he may not have too great a surprise and may arm himself with courage. But this warning should be discreet, so as not to frighten, and so as to observe the truth. Moreover, the postulant, wholly plunged in the joy of his first meetings with the Lord, and proud of his first renunciation, would scarcely believe us or at least would misunderstand the character of these hardships. God of His mercy leaves many things hidden designedly. Enough that the novice is ready to accept all. The ritual of profession renews this warning and asks his formal acceptance.

The Novice Master, therefore, should speak somewhat in this way: In the first place there are the general conventual hardships of the monastic life, which has certainly not been organized with a view to gratify nature. Next, and especially, there are particular trials for each individual. And hardship always assails us at the point where we are most sensitive and least prepared. Such and such vexations, which would have been nothing in the world, become almost unbearable in the monastery; God generally permits an enormous disproportion between the cause of the hardship and the hardship felt. Some brother, or father, or the Abbot especially, becomes a burden to us: " He does not speak to me; he does not understand me; he keeps all his affection for others. The notions that prevail here are very strange and one has to adopt them. I had a very good way of thinking, and now it is found too broad or too narrow, and I have to revise my views. What a nuisance!——" So a man fosters his weariness, and talks about it; his little wound festers; he becomes despondent.

[1] *Cf.* S. BASIL., *loc. ult. cit.*
[2] VIRGIL had spoken of a race *dura et aspera* (*Aen.*, v., 730) ; but the true sources of St. Benedict are rather the following: *Via regia suavis ac levis est, licet dura et aspera sentiatur* (CASS., *Conlat.*, XXIV., xxv.).—*Satis duram atque asperam vitam . . . habuit* (PALLAD., *Histor. Laus.*, versio antiqua: apud *Parad. Heracl.*, 41. ROSWEYD, p. 970). —*Semper dura et laboriosa eis proponantur* (*Reg.* I. SS. PATRUM, vii.).

Sometimes it seems that perseverance is only secured by natural and petty motives. Sometimes, too, the temptation takes this form: " Why did I not choose another Order? After all, the monastic and contemplative life is not the only one. There are plenty of other ways of being a religious; I might be a Dominican, or a Capuchin, or a Jesuit: a Dominican especially. Then there are the Carthusians; they have almost continual silence, and one has not to associate with people——"

Let us add that, in a monastery, the absence of distractions and diversion gives us over entirely to our grievance. As we noted in commenting on the Prologue, the sufferings of contemplatives resemble the pains of purgatory: the fire penetrates to the marrow, to the most intimate fibres of our being; it is a slow burning, as in a closed vessel, stifling and choking. Every movement becomes painful, as with a man whose outer skin has been removed: " The soul tosses and turns upon back and side and face; but all is hard."[1] Verily it is painful, this contact with God, the contact of our ugliness with His beauty, of our darkness with His light. St. John of the Cross explains it admirably. Until the day when God shall be our supreme joy, He is the great trial. " For the word of God is living and effectual and more piercing than any two-edged sword and reaching unto the division of the soul and the spirit, of the joints also and the marrow: and is a discerner of the thoughts and intents of the heart " (Heb. iv. 12). Furthermore, there are certain privileged sufferings which would be intolerable and mortal, if God did not sustain us by His grace; but they are the prelude to union with Him. Let us not imagine that our little novitiate troubles have something to do with these sufferings.

One wretched way of escaping the *dura et aspera* (hard and rugged ways) is to make oneself a quiet bourgeois existence, to seek to be one of those whose lives are without glory and without disgrace, whom heaven likes not and hell will not receive in its depths,[2] of those who are saved, but barely and prosaically. " He who soweth sparingly shall also reap sparingly: and he who soweth in blessings shall also reap blessings " (2 Cor. ix. 6). If we read the fourteenth chapter of *The Spiritual Life and Prayer* on the First Purification, we find that " those who forget themselves sometimes pass these painful stages, however hard they may be, very cheerfully; but they appear very painful, and are in fact doubly so, to those who love their spiritual comfort too well. Therefore what is needed is to remain tranquilly on the cross, to adore, to let the physician cut the sore at his pleasure, to make an effort to keep very close to God, whose touch wounds only to heal. Let us take care also not to magnify our sufferings by imagination and by a turning in upon self which strains and irritates us. Certain unhealthy temperaments have a tendency to seek a sort of morbid pleasure, not free from pose, in suffering: but " no sorrow is desirable."[3] Sorrow is never anything but

---

[1] S. Aug., *Confess.*, l. VI., c. xvi. P.L., XXXII., 732.
[2] Dante, *Inferno*, III., 32–42.   [3] S. Aug., *ibid.*, l. III., c. ii. P.L., XXXII., 684.

Of the Discipline of receiving Brethren into Religion

a means; and often our sufferings, being due to unfaithfulness, are such that we might easily be rid of them. As to the others, it is far more important to accept them well when they come, than feverishly to solicit them from God. "Upon the bars I did not deny Thee, O God, and when put to the fire I confessed thee, O Christ; Thou hast proved my heart and hast visited me in the night, Thou hast tried me with fire: and iniquity was not found in me."[1]

Et si promiserit de stabilitatis suæ perseverantia, post duorum mensium circulum legatur ei hæc Regula per ordinem, et dicatur ei: Ecce lex, sub qua militare vis; si potes observare, ingredere: si vero non potes, liber discede. Si adhuc steterit, tunc ducatur in supradictam cellam novitiorum, et iterum probetur in omni patientia. Et post sex mensium circulum relegatur ei Regula, ut sciat ad quod ingreditur. Et si adhuc stat, post quatuor menses iterum relegatur ei eadem regula.

And if he promise steadfastly to persevere in stability, after the lapse of two months let this Rule be read in order to him and let him be told: "Behold the law under which you desire to fight; if you can keep it, enter; if you cannot, freely depart." If he still stand firm, let him be taken to the aforesaid cell of the Novices, and again tried in all patience. And after the lapse of six months, let the Rule be read to him again, that he may know to what he is entering. Should he still stand firm, after four months let the same Rule be read to him once more.

Choosing, petition, and scrutiny.—St. Benedict has no very pronounced interest in anything about the candidate save the temper of his will. The novitiate trial is to be continued only if the candidate "promise steadfastly to persevere," if his intention of giving himself to God in the monastery is thoroughly solid. But since the quality of our will is in proportion to our knowledge; since we remain attached to that only which we have freely chosen; since we are bound to fulfil only what we have promised: for all these motives of elementary prudence and wisdom, St. Benedict would have the candidate made to know the laws of his new life exactly. The year of novitiate is marked by this presentation of the Rule at intervals and by a threefold choosing.[2]

According to St. Benedict's words it would appear that this official reading of the Rule, consecutively and in its entirety, *per ordinem*, was done after the two, or six, or four months, if not at one sitting, at least during the days which preceded the ceremony of choosing. The ancient

---

[1] Office of St. Lawrence the Martyr.

[2] St. Benedict's predecessors had written: *Si quis de sæculo ad monasterium converti voluerit, Regula ei introeunti legatur, et omnes actus monasterii illi patefiant. Qui si omnia apte sustinuerit sic digne a fratribus suscipiatur in monasterio* (S. MACAR., *Reg.*, xxiii.).—And ST. CÆSARIUS: *Quæcumque ad conversionem venerit, in salutatorio ei frequentius Regula relegatur; et si prompta et libera voluntate professa fuerit se omnia Regulæ instituta completuram, tamdiu ibi sit quamdiu Abbatissæ justum ac rationabile visum fuerit* (*Reg. ad virg.*, Recap., viii.).—An analogous provision occurs among the statutes of a burial society, in a Latin inscription of the second century: *Tu qui novos (= novus) in hoc collegio intrare voles, prius legem perlege et sic intra, ne postmodum quæraris aut heredi tuo controversiam relinquas* (ORELLI-HENZEN, *Inscriptionum latinarum selectarum amplissima collectio*, no. 6086).

customaries mention these three readings and these three choosings.[1] In actual fact the Rule is read to novices in the course of the months of probation. It is not read to each individual by himself, but to the whole community, three times a year among us, in chapter and in the refectory. Moreover, it should be explained in its entirety during the novitiate. The Council of Aix-la-Chapelle, in A.D. 817, recommended: " That all monks, who are able, should learn the Rule by heart." We still have two solemn ceremonies of choosing: before the novice receives the habit and before profession.

If this reading and this formal arraignment have not driven the candidate away, if he " stands firm," he is taken back to the novitiate and tried " in all patience "—that is to say, trial is made to see whether he can suffer, without being disconcerted, all the little worries of community life. The patience of which our Holy Father here speaks is rather that of the novice than of his masters, which for its part should never fail: for we must imitate God, who knows how to wait. Our Constitutions, agreeing in this with more ancient Constitutions, such as those of Chezal-Benoît and of the Maurists, prescribe an examination of the novices by chapter, at certain fixed dates; this is the function that we call the " novices' chapter "; it is held at the Ember-days.

The duration of the novitiate proper is fixed by our Holy Father at a year, as is proved if we add together the three periods of two, six, and four months which precede the choosings. Whatever be the facts about the novitiate of St. Pachomius,[2] other legislators, such as St. Cæsarius, St. Fructuosus, and St. Ferreolus, require a year's trial. Sometimes the superior had power to reduce the period of probation, even to a notable extent. Such reductions were customary at Cluny, and Peter the Venerable justifies them to St. Bernard.[3] A year was a judicious mean; and therefore the Benedictine usage has passed into the *Corpus Juris*, in the Decretals, and has been consecrated by the Council of Trent.[4] The Council even decreed that profession made before the age of sixteen and without a year's novitiate is null. Its legislation is severe on this point. But the discussion of all these questions may be left to the Canonists. When the year's novitiate is complete the candidate is received or dismissed; yet it is not irregular for the superior to prolong the probation some months. These eleventh-hour attempts, or a second novitiate, generally have no great success.

The candidate's choice is not sufficient of itself to admit him to pro-

[1] Here is the reply of a candidate at St. Ouen in Rouen (fourteenth to fifteenth century): " My lord, for this I do not trust in myself, but in God and our Lady, St. Mary, and in all the saints, men and women, and in you, my lord, and the holy community of this house—that I shall be obedient even to death. And should the devil wish me to retract this, I beg you, my lord, to have me constrained by force " (MARTÈNE, *De ant. eccl. rit.*, l. II., c. ii. T. II., col. 465).
[2] MGR. LADEUZE considers " that the novitiate did not exist among the cenobites of St. Pachomius as a regular and general institution " (*Etude sur le cénobitisme pakhomien pendant le IVᵉ siècle et la première moitié du Vᵉ*, pp. 280–282).
[3] *Epist.*, l. I., *Ep.* XXVIII. *P.L.*, CLXXXIX., 117 *sq.*
[4] And by the new *Code.*

fession: there is needed as well the consent of the body, and this, according to our custom, the novice asks humbly on his knees in the middle of chapter. In ancient monastic practice the candidate also made a last petition and was questioned as to his dispositions. Our Constitutions, in prescribing a similar course, are indebted to the Maurists and other Benedictine Congregations,[1] but with this difference, that the ceremony comprises nothing else but the reading of a long and solemn formula. We should note besides that the phrase " make a petition " has not, in modern usage, quite the same meaning as in the Rule. The *Petitio*, according to St. Benedict's ideas and the custom of his time, was at once a request for admission, a promise, and the schedule, or written and signed instrument, testifying for ever to the obligations contracted.[2] This written petition was then preceded, it would seem, by a verbal promise: " Let him make a promise of stability. . . . Let him draw up a petition containing this promise." Subsequently—and this is manifest in the very tenor of the documents—the verbal promise was sometimes made only after the drawing up of the legal instrument.

In the verbal promise the text of the Rule was reproduced without addition: *Promitto de stabilitate mea*, etc. As to the written formula or petition, which was also without doubt originally short, this became fuller after the seventh century, developing into a little speech in which the novice described the reality of the trial he had undergone, asked admission to the household of God and His servants, proclaimed his good resolutions, mentioned the saints, the relics, and the Abbot, and ended as we do in our form. Later on the long formula was abridged. And in this way the schedule, or petition, was confused with the verbal promise uttered before or after it. A fusion of the two produced a summary, and that is the nature of the form in actual use. The verbal formula of the eighth and ninth centuries is cited sometimes in documents of that period alongside the long formula of petition in this shape, for instance: *Ego ille, Domne Abba N., obedientiam vobis secundum Regulam S. Benedicti, juxta quod in ista petitione continet, quam super istud altare posui, coram Deo et Sanctis ejus, in quantum mihi ipse Deus dederit adjutorium, Deo et vobis promitto custodire, et in quo possum, ipso auxiliante, conservo.*[3] Our petition formula is only an ancient profession schedule, somewhat abridged and adapted to its new purpose; or, more accurately, it is a compilation formed from many different documents of the same character.[4]

[1] See, for instance, the *Ceremoniale monastico-benedictinum* of the Bavarian Congregation of the Holy Angels (1737), p. 189.
[2] *Cf.* D. ROTHENHÄUSLER, *Zur Aufnahmeordnung der Regula S. Benedicti*, I., i. 2, pp. 9 *sq*.
[3] M. G. H.: *Legum*, Sectio V., *Formulæ*, p. 569.
[4] These documents are to be found in BALUZE, *Capitularia Regum Francorum: Nova collectio formularum*, nos. xxxiii. and xxxii., t. II., pp. 576 and 574; in MABILLON, *Acta SS. O.S.B.*, Sæc. IV., P. I., pp. 694–695; and in the recent and critical edition of the *Monumenta Germaniæ Historica: Legum*, Sectio V., *Formulæ Merowingici et Karolini Aevi*, p. 479, n. 42, and p. 570, n. 31.—A formula much resembling that given by BALUZE in no. xxxiii. is cited by HERRGOTT in his *Vetus disciplina monastica*, p. 591; it may be

We might seek in vain in the petitions of former days for that mention of the "suffrages" of the community which is introduced in ours. The reason is that the novice was admitted to profession in virtue of the Abbot's decision; it was the right of the father of the family to grant a place in his household to his newborn son. The Abbot stood guarantee to the community for the good dispositions of the candidate whom he received. He was the witness *par excellence*, in this world, of the profession promises, just as the saints, whose relics they had, were their witnesses in heaven. So we find St. Benedict prescribing that the petition be made " in the name of the saints . . . and of the Abbot there present "; the latter received the petition in the name of God, and the candidate became truly *his son*. However, the Abbot did not fail to take the advice of his community.[1] According to the Statutes of Lanfranc,[2] he asks the brethren if he may proceed to the profession; there is the same direction in the Bursfeld Ceremonial;[3] the " novices' chapters," of which we said a word, were designed for the enlightenment of the Abbot. But, after all, it is he who decides, and there is no voting; if there be sometimes mention of a " scrutiny," it is only in its etymological sense of an examination.[4] Present-day legislation is different; but to-day still, the decision of the Abbot carries most weight in the matter of admission, not so much on the score of the double vote that the Constitutions give him, as because it is he who presents, and because he presents only those of whom he is morally sure.

The vows of religion.—Before entering upon the third portion of the chapter, and in order not to have to interrupt the description of the ritual of profession, we may briefly review the theological basis of the vows of religion, and examine closely the form used by the Benedictines.

The supernatural perfection of man consists essentially in charity, not initial or incipient charity, but charity dominant and supreme; it consists in an eminent degree of charity, or in the complex of all those forces which unite us to God deeply, solidly, and in a stable and continuous fashion. And the " perfect life " is defined by its tendency towards perfection, by a manner of living (*modus vivendi*) designed to realize and increase perfection. Now, this is obtained by the full and generous accomplishment of the precepts, which are all nothing but particular manifestations of the law of charity. But, for all that, we do not arrive at this full observance of the precepts and at perfect charity save by the practice of certain counsels. A counsel, on its negative side,

---

found also in the M. G. H.: *l. c.*, p. 568, and in D. ALBERS: *Consuetudines monasticæ*, vol. III., p. 178. The formula which D. ALBERS cites immediately before this one is the same as that of no xxxii. in Baluze, as that printed by DU CANGE, *Glossarium* (*Profiteri*), and by LÉOPOLD DELISLE, *Littérature latine et histoire du moyen âge*, p. 16. —See also the formula given by SMARAGDUS and quoted in MARTÈNE, *Commentary*, p. 763.—*Cf.* D. HERWEGEN, *Geschichte der benediktinischen Professformel*.

[1] See Chapter III. of the Holy Rule and the Commentary of PAUL THE DEACON.
[2] MARTÈNE, *De ant. monach. rit.*, l. V., c. iv., col. 646.
[3] MARTÈNE, *op. cit.*, l. V., c. iv., col. 656.
[4] MARTÈNE, *De ant. eccl. rit.*, l. II., c. ii. T. II., col. 484.

guarantees a precept, and, at the same time, defends and protects charity; on its positive side it increases charity while being at the same time its fruit; it is at once the cause and index of perfection. The perfect life, or life of perfection, is therefore assured by the practice of the counsels; thus the exercise of the counsels is a mark of the perfect life.

But the perfect life may exist even in the world and is not necessarily the religious life. The latter is the "state of perfection"—that is to say, the perfect life organized and comprising certain special elements. It will not be out of place to say a word concerning each of these.

We should remember, in the first place, that the religious life is not distinct from the Christian life, it is not something new superadded to Christianity, but is one of its states, its achievement and full flower. This state is not purely interior, but has as well a visible and external character. It implies stability, a legal and *de jure* permanence. The religious life is instituted with a view to personal perfection, at least primarily. We enter upon it by personal resolve and personal action. And the obligation is contracted in precise terms under an exterior and visible form, in a way that the Church can ascertain.

It is contracted in view of a good which is over and above the precepts —that is to say, in view of the counsels, of works which prepare, exercise, and increase perfection. The counsels to which the religious life binds us are not merely interior; nor does the religious life bind monks to all counsels, but primarily to the three great evangelical counsels, and to the good determined for each form of the religious life[1] by its own end and its special laws. Poverty, chastity, and obedience are at one and the same time a means of enfranchisement by the sacrifice of three great concupiscences, a giving to God of the whole man with all his external goods, his body and his soul, and a means of union with God; for, according to the theologians, the vows of religion, besides being a guarantee and a security, have at the same time the character of an offering and a holocaust. Much might be said on the subject of the vows: the more so that the true conception of their scope and excellence is nowadays often misunderstood. A vow really adds something to a good work and is a very efficacious instrument of perfection; it creates a bond which of its nature decisively enfranchises him who takes the vow, a bond which purposely fixes the will in the good vowed. Thanks to the vow, a good work becomes an act of worship and adoration, and not only the fruit but the sap and the tree itself are consecrated to God.[2] Profession is nothing else but the taking of the vows of religion.

But, in order that the giving of ourselves by the three main vows of religion should make us religious, it must be accepted in the name of God by the Church; and the Church in this case is represented by the prelate or any other competent person. Profession being, as we shall explain, a contract, the intervention of two parties is indispensable.

[1] *Cf.* D. Guéranger, *Règlement du Noviciat* (current under the title: *Notions sur la vie religieuse et monastique*). See also: Mgr. Gay, *De la vie et des vertus chrétiennes considérées dans l'état religieux*, t. II., chap. ix.-xi.

[2] *Cf.* St. Thomas, *Summa* II.-II., q. lxxxviii., a. 6.

The profession should be made and the vows practised under a Rule approved by the Church: as the Rules of St. Basil, St. Benedict, St. Augustine, and St. Francis, on one or other of which "constitutions" now are based. The Popes have allowed some Orders to live under a Rule of their own, not derived from one of the four just mentioned. Finally, the religious life, in virtue of canonical regulations, now requires submission to a superior, and also a common life, which varies in degree according to the Order.

Without entering in detail into the distinction between simple and solemn vows, it will be well to say a word about it. Solemnity does not mean perpetuity, for there are simple vows with perfect perpetuity, as in the Congregations which take only simple vows. Still less does it consist in the liturgical ceremonies, or even in the publicity with which the vows are taken, though the law ordains that the monk's parish priest must be notified. Solemnity makes the monk incapable of performing acts contrary to the vows, in such a way that these acts become not merely illicit, but null and void, but this incapacity might be regarded rather as a consequence of solemnity than as its essential element, and it is sometimes attached to simple vows, as for instance to the vows taken by the Jesuit scholastics and coadjutors.

The Church has not made any pronouncement on this question of the essential character of solemnity, but there can be no doubt that it is an institution of ecclesiastical origin. The Church decides the special conditions which must be fulfilled in taking solemn vows, and the Church can dispense from the obligations which result from them, or from the solemnity, while at the same time leaving the vows intact.

Nevertheless it remains true that solemn vows, because of the incapacity which they imply, strip the monk completely and bind him more closely to his Order; they set him in a more perfect state, and the Church secures the full privileges of exemption to every religious body in which solemn vows are taken.

Perpetual vows, whether simple or solemn, cannot now be taken before the age of twenty-one, and until after three years at least of temporary vows.

"Let the vows be taken according to the Benedictine form—viz., of stability, conversion of manners, and obedience according to the Rule of our Holy Father St. Benedict, to be observed in the sense explained by the Constitutions." So speak our Constitutions.

Stability. We should remember that one of the principal objects of our Holy Father was to combat degraded forms of the monastic life, especially "gyrovagy." It was a great evil. The vows of religion, although perpetual, often became illusory when a man set himself to run about the world and change his monastery as caprice suggested. Monastic legislation admitted these changes of monastery too easily.[1]

[1] *Cf.* FAUSTI RHEGIENSIS, *Sermo* vii. *ad monachos. P.L.*, LVIII., 885.

St. Basil, without failing to recognize that there are sometimes good reasons for passing to another house, yet lays down the principle of stability in the monastery.[1] *Instabilitas* is condemned by Cassian.[2] St. Cæsarius of Arles makes stability a primary condition of admission: " In the first place, if any one come to conversion (*i.e.*, religious life), let him be received on this condition that he persevere there until death."[3] The Fourth Ecumenical Council forbade monks to quit their monasteries without the bishop's authorization,[4] and the Council of Agde (A.D. 506) laid it down that a monk belonged to his house and his Abbot.[5] But it really seems that St. Benedict was the first to bind a monk to his monastery by an express vow; and in the passage of the Rule which enumerates the elements of his promise the vow of stability holds the first place.

Stability therefore has the precise meaning of permanence in the supernatural family in which profession is made, of permanence in the monastery, and not merely the general meaning of perseverance in good or in the religious life. " From that day forward he cannot depart from the monastery," says St. Benedict. As early as the Prologue he alludes to "perseverance until death in the monastery"; it the end of the fourth chapter the monastic enclosure, with stability in the assembly of the brethren, was put before us as the sole workshop wherein the instruments of the spiritual craft might be used successfully. Finally, in the sixty-first chapter, St. Benedict indicates the method which must be followed in succouring victims of the vagrant habit (gyrovagy), if there be any hope of a cure.

Monastic stability is not the rigid enclosure of nuns; it is not opposed to such an egress as is authorized by the Abbot, nor even, nowadays at least, to a passing into another house of a Congregation, when permission is granted. We vow stability " according to our Constitutions ": now these provide for the case when a monk may, by means of an authentic instrument, set his stability in a monastery other than that of his profession: as when a man leaves his own house either for his personal good, or to help a community, or to assist in a new foundation. If stability is in conflict with obedience, the latter must prevail; for, to repeat, the stability we vow does not imply absolute immovability. It may be said that stability consists in a deep and lasting belonging to a family, normally to the very monastery of one's profession.

Conversion of manners. In general this means abandonment of a sinful or worldly life, and the direction of our activity towards the supernatural. But we should take these words in the exact sense attached to them in the time of our Holy Father. Conversion of manners meant the religious life itself, considered in the elements with-

---

[1] *Reg. fus.*, xxxvi. *Cf.* also the *Constitutiones monasticæ*, c. xxi. P.G., XXXI., 1393–1402.
[2] *Inst.*, VII., ix.
[3] *Reg. ad mon.*, i.; *Reg. ad virg.*, i.—*Cf.* also the *Rule* of ST. AURELIAN, i.
[4] Can. iv. MANSI., t. VII., col. 382.
[5] Can. xxxviii. MANSI, t. VIII., col. 331.

out which it cannot exist, especially in chastity and poverty (obedience is presently mentioned expressly). Let us not be astonished that our form of profession contains no explicit mention of poverty and chastity: this omission is traditional and is found in the diverse branches of the Order.[1] Nor have Carthusians, Canons Regular, Carmelites, and Dominicans an express mention of the three vows; some have only the vow of obedience.[2] The monks of St. Basil take only the vow of chastity.

Obedience well deserved to be the matter of a special promise: it is the most lofty form of conversion of manners; it is the sacrifice of soul and will; it embraces of itself the whole supernatural life and the whole religious life. Moreover, his definite purpose of distinguishing cenobites from anchorites on the one hand and from sarabaites on the other, induced St. Benedict to make obedience an explicit vow. Bernard of Monte Cassino remarks judiciously that in emphasizing thus the vows of stability, conversion of manners, and obedience, our Holy Father distinguishes his monks from the gyrovagues by stability, from the sarabaites by conversion of manners, and from the anchorites by obedience to a superior and a written rule.

We take our vows "according to the Rule of St. Benedict, as interpreted by our Constitutions." This calls for several observations.

We do not vow to practise all the counsels, which would be rather hard of fulfilment, since some are mutually exclusive and contradictory (poverty and almsgiving, for instance), and their number is infinite. As we have already remarked, every form of the religious life is based upon the observance of the three great substantive counsels, to which are added those counsels which are appropriate to the end of the institute. By making our profession as Benedictines, we engage to live according to the Rule of St. Benedict; therefore we shall not go about making ourselves a motley collection from other Rules as the accident of devotion leads us. Still less are we justified in adding to or subtracting anything whatever from our Rule and Constitutions, with a view to the greater perfection of the community. Neither the Abbot, nor the Superior General, nor General Chapter can of themselves modify them in a notable degree; they are competent only to interpret them, to propose changes and to test them. That Benedictine life, which is our duty, is also our right. Even as regards the essential vows—chastity being excepted—obedience and poverty are understood and practised in each Order in a way to some degree peculiar to the Order: and we have a right to the special character of the Benedictine Rule. The ideal of our observance is bound up with an accurate understanding of our Holy Father's spirit. Yet we should be on our guard; for it is fatally easy for egoism, folly, or delusion to persuade a monk that his superior has not got the true mind of St. Benedict, or that he oversteps his rights.

We make profession to live "according to the Rule": but to what extent does the Rule bind us? Is faithful observance merely a matter

---

[1] *Cf.* Hæften, l. IV., tract. vi., disq. vi.
[2] *Cf.* St. Thomas, *Summa* II.-II., *q.* clxxxvi., *a.* 8.

of the individual's consistency, or of propriety, or of honour—or is conscience concerned, and to what extent? The question is a delicate and complicated one, but very practical. Here we can give some conclusions only.

The religious Rule involves obligation. It involves obligation, and that under the ordinary theological conditions, for all the ordinances of natural law, of divine positive law, and of ecclesiastical law, which it embodies and promulgates to its subjects. It involves an obligation of conscience, more or less grave, in all that constitutes the matter of the vows: infringement in this case having the malice of sacrilege. We do not vow to keep the Rule absolutely: otherwise all that it contains would be matter of the vows; but only to live " according to the Rule." It involves an obligation of conscience in the special cases where the Rule, or the superior, prescribes something in formulas of command which appeal to the vow of obedience.

Some Rules take the trouble to specify the points which bind under pain of mortal or venial sin. Others announce that, save for the cases enumerated above, they do not bind under sin, but only to the enduring of the prescribed penalty (*sed solum ad pœnam taxatam sustinendam*). Others specify nothing, which is the case with the ancient Rules and ours in particular. Casuistry was not according to the spirit of those times, and it is probable that they never dreamt that disputes might arise on this point.

Yet there have been disputes among the theologians of the Order.[1] Without plunging into the heart of the discussion, it may be affirmed that our Holy Father intended to make of his Rule something other than a series of optional counsels of perfection, something other, too, than a sort of police code, than a system of personal penalties designed to inspire fear by their severity. His monks are not slaves, who obey the menace of the lash; the Abbot is not a "prefect of discipline." Practically, whatever be the obligation of the Rule in itself,[2] there are few infringements of it which do not become theological faults in virtue of malice which originates elsewhere. The secret motive which inspires transgression often has an immoral complexion, as of laziness, pride, or gluttony. There may also be formal contempt for some point or other of observance,[3] such contempt as might constitute a grave fault if it extended to the whole Rule. Moreover, there may be scandal of a more or less serious nature: we may contribute to the relaxation of general discipline. On all these points delusion is easy and habits of inobservance are easily formed, especially in the matter of silence, studies, and prayer: it is thus that a man finds himself on the downward slope that leads to contempt.

In these matters we need delicacy of conscience, not scrupulosity,

---

[1] *Cf.* D. Mège, *Comment. sur la Règle*, Avertissement, pp. 36 *ff.*—J. Rottner, *Margarita cælestis*, q. XI., a. ii., pp. 520 *sq.*
[2] Read D. Guéranger, *Règlement du Noviciat*, chap. ii.
[3] *Cf.* St. Thomas, *Summa* II.-II., q. clxxxvi., a. 9., ad. 3.

nor an awkward rigidity, which ignores shades of difference and that prudent " epikia " of which moralists speak. Above all let us not forget that we have a real obligation of conscience to tend towards perfection and have solemnly vowed it; that the Rule is the very form of this perfection which we have vowed, and that its liberality and discretion do not leave self-will free to recover itself in detail. Sons need only to know what their Father loves and what he expects of them.

Et si habita secum deliberatione, promiserit se omnia custodire, et cuncta sibi imperata servare, tunc suscipiatur in congregatione, sciens lege Regulæ constitutum, quod ei ex illa die non liceat egredi de monasterio, nec collum excutere de sub jugo Regulæ, quam sub tam morosa deliberatione licuit ei recusare aut suscipere.	And if, having deliberated with himself, he promise to keep all things, and to observe everything that is commanded him, then let him be received into the community, knowing that it is decreed by the law of the Rule that from that day forward he may not depart from the monastery nor shake from off his neck the yoke of the Rule, which after such prolonged deliberation he was free either to refuse or to accept.

The character and consequences of profession.—Before describing profession, St. Benedict briefly indicates what happens when the novitiate trial is complete and the candidate has made up his mind: he promises to observe the whole Rule; he is received into the community; and his engagement is irrevocable. Our Holy Father here emphasizes especially the character and the moral consequences of an act for which the novice has had opportunity to prepare himself with all completeness. The consequences, so far as material goods are concerned, shall be mentioned only at the end of the chapter.

Profession is a considered act. There has been leisure to think about it and to deliberate, leisure large and abundantly sufficient: *tam morosa deliberatio*. The novice has been required to weigh the reasons for and against, and to refuse or accept the burden: *licuit recusare aut accipere*. Before committing himself, he has examined the matter for a last time in the depths of his soul: *habita secum deliberatione*. For profession is not a jest or an elegant mockery entailing no consequences.

Its principal character is that of oblation, as we see clearly from the formula which accompanies it: *Suscipe me, Domine*, from the part of the Mass at which it is made, and from the very words of the Rule. Now, according to St. Benedict, this giving must be entire, comprising the whole man, both in his being and in his activity: so much so that St. Benedict bases the ensuing incapacity of the monk to possess anything whatever upon the absolute character of the gift: " Who may not have their bodies or their wills in their own power " (Chap. XXXIII.), and in the last paragraph of the present chapter " . . . no power even over his own body." It is a sacrifice in which the victim is consumed wholly. No one thinks, on the day of his profession, of making reserva-

Of the Discipline of receiving Brethren into Religion

tions, of bargaining shamefully with God, of arranging that such and such a point of the Rule shall not bind him. On that day we do not even take precautions against eventual requirements, and possible excesses of authority. On that day we say: " Lord, I write my vow small that You may be able, in the blank spaces and on the margin, to write all that You wish; You are not one to haggle with. Set down the unexpected, the painful, the impossible; it makes no matter, You shall be obeyed." Our bond remains as we made it. We shall have to render an account of it according to its true value, and not according to subsequent mitigation and abatement: " For by thy words thou shalt be justified: and by thy words thou shalt be condemned " (Matt. xii. 37).

Profession, therefore, is an engagement of honour, or rather of strict justice. Our word once given, we must keep it—even when it is given to the living God. As we shall see later, profession is also a contract, and a twofold contract: with God who gives us His life in exchange for ours, with our monastic family, which gives us a share in all its supernatural goods, in return for a promise of submission and fidelity. If we arrive ever at such a state as practically to say that our contracts do not bind us, we mock God, says St. Benedict, recalling the words of St. Paul (Gal. vi. 7): *Ut si aliquando aliter fecerit, ab eo se damnandum sciat quem irridet.*

Finally, profession is a definitive and irrevocable act.[1] Did we intend to make a terminable contract? Can the belonging of the soul to God, and of God to the soul, which profession implies, have a precarious and temporary character? It must last for eternity. He who loves does not look forward to the day when he shall cease to love. St. Benedict had besides a special motive in adding the remark: *Sciens . . . quod ei ex illa die,* etc. As we have said, he does not want any of those gyrovagues who come and go at their pleasure, nor does he want sarabaites. And in plain language he warns those who would join his family of the conditions of the life led therein: a man may not go forth any more; he is stable and abides under the yoke of a Rule.[2]

The ceremonial of profession.—After something of a campaign of private and conventual prayers,[3] the blessed day of profession comes at last, a day of unique importance to the soul, to be ranked only with the day of baptism and the day of its entry into eternity. The community assemble in the chapter room after Terce and the novice comes forward to make a last petition and a last choice.[4] " Son, you know the law under which you wish to fight, you know upon what you are entering.

---

[1] *Cf.* S. Basil., *Reg. fus.,* xiv. *Constitutiones monasticæ,* c. xxii. P.G., XXXI., 1401 sq.—S. Joann. Chrysos., *Adhort.* II. *ad Theodorum lapsum.* P.G., XLVII., 309.—S. Cæsar., *Reg. ad mon.,* i.

[2] *Jugo regulæ colla submittentes* (*Vita Macarii Romani,* 2. *Vitæ Patrum,* I. Rosweyd, p. 225).

[3] The Customs of Cluny said: *Commendat (Abbas) fratribus ut in orationibus suis recordentur eorum, et aliquando, si videtur, unum psalmum, post singulas Horas in illo die pro eis cantari* (Udalr., *Consuet. Clun.,* l. II., c. xxvi.).

[4] This choosing of dress was in vogue among the Maurists also.

Lo, now before you are the garments of your former worldly condition, and the clothing of holy religion: choose in the sight of God and His saints, choose which of these your soul seeks and desires." After the choosing of the monastic habit the procession[1] returns to the oratory.

The profession shall take place there, as St. Benedict prescribed, for it is eminently a religious and liturgical function. It takes place during Mass and at the time of the Offertory. Our Holy Father does not say so, but everything leads us to believe that such was really the custom in his time. Let us note that the vows were to be placed " on the altar ": doubtless along with the offerings of the faithful; for, in the next chapter, he prescribes that the written petition of a child offered by its parents should be wrapped, with its hand and with the offerings (of the faithful), in the altar-cloth: *Et cum oblatione ipsam petitionem et manum pueri involvant in palla altaris et sic eum offerant.* The Council of Aix-la-Chapelle, in A.D. 817, interprets the *cum oblatione* of Chapter LIX. in that way. The most ancient tradition puts the profession during the Holy Sacrifice. In the eighth century St. Theodore of Canterbury says in his Capitulary that the profession took place during Mass celebrated by the Abbot.[2] The same was the custom at Cluny[3] and in many other places. The statutes of Lanfranc leave it to the choice of the Abbot to bless the monk " before the Introit if he do not celebrate the Mass, or after the Gospel, whether he celebrate or no ";[4] but it is clear from what follows that the second method was more in favour. Almost everywhere, in fact, the profession was made after the Gospel, or the Credo, and before the Offertory. However, in his first commentary on the Rule, Peter Boherius says that it took place after the Offertory.[5] Among the Maurists also profession came after the Offertory.

The custom of some modern Congregations is to have the profession outside Mass; those which make it in the course of the Mass are authorized by a decree of 1894 to adopt the Jesuit ceremonial, which consists in pronouncing the vows before the priest who holds the Sacred Host, immediately before receiving Communion.[6] We are free to consider the ancient custom more profoundly symbolical.

[1] We then sing that same psalm cxxv.: *In convertendo*, which the five first monks of Solesmes sang when going from the parish church to the restored monastery, July 11, 1833.

[2] According to the ancient monastic canons, the Abbot should himself celebrate the Mass, if he can, and receive the profession, thus performing the " blessing " of the monk. In liturgical parlance it is not a " consecration," for monks do not form part of the ecclesiastical hierarchy; and, according to ST. DENIS, it is the business of priests to bless them (*De hierarch. eccl.*, c. vi.).

[3] BERNARD., *Ordo Clun.*, P. I., c. xx.

[4] Cap. iii., ap. MARTÈNE, *De antiq. monach. rit.*, l. V., c. iv., col. 646.—*Cf.* BERNARD, *Ordo Clun.*, P. I., c. xv., xx.   [5] *Cf.* MARTÈNE, Commentary, p. 769.

[6] Compare this custom with that which is found mentioned in the *Liber ordinum* of the Mozarabic liturgy, edited by D. FÉROTIN; the evidence is at least as old as the eleventh century, but is probably older. It is there said (cols. 85–86) that after the profession of a *conversus* who is not a cenobite, when the prayers are finished, *datur ei sancta communio;* for a cenobite, the ritual is the same, except that, after the Communion, *tota jam explicita missa*, he deposits his profession form on the altar and sings the *Suscipe*.

Before describing the ceremony of profession we should enquire what it was before our Holy Father's time. Canonists distinguish two sorts of profession, tacit and explicit, and observe that the former was the only one in use primitively: it consisted of acts equivalent to formal profession and having the validity of a contract. It may be said that the taking or reception of the monastic habit, and often also the tonsure, were enough, in the early centuries, for the making a monk or a nun; hermits made their profession in a more simple manner still; generally they contrived to receive the habit from the hands of an elderly monk. Sometimes even, a famous nun gave it to a man, as Evagrius of Pontus received it from Melania the Elder.[1]

The giving of the religious habit was among monks doubtless accompanied at an early date by prayers, and surrounded with some solemnity, but we are not so well informed on this point as on the giving the veil, and the consecration of virgins, the liturgy of which is very ancient. St. Pachomius says merely that after the preliminary trials the candidate shall be handed over to the brethren: " Then they shall strip him of his worldly garments and clothe him in the monk's habit, and pass him on to the door-keeper, that he may bring him before all the brethren at prayer time; and he shall sit in the place that shall be commanded him."[2] St. Nilus only gives us very summary information when he says: "When, then, did you put on the venerable monastic habit? What Abbot applied his hand, saying good words?"[3] It is hard to determine the character of the ceremonial used by St. Basil. There were witnesses. Questions were put to the novice and there was profession " clear and plain." Doubtless there was also a fixed form.[4] As to the written promise, the most ancient example of it which we have[5] would seem to be the engagement which Schenoudi of Atripé, of the Upper Thebaid (A.D. 452), made his monks sign.[6] St. Isidore also requires a written document, and Mabillon cites a form of this *pactum* (compact).[7] The same custom obtained among the monks of St. Fructuosus (seventh century).[8]

---

[1] PALLAD., *Hist. Laus.*, c. lxxxvi. ROSWEYD, p. 764. [2] *Reg.*, xlix.
[3] *Epist.*, l. II., *Ep.* XCVI. *P.G.*, LXXIX., 243.
[4] S. BASIL., *Reg. fus.*, xii, xiv., xv. *Epist.* CXCIX. (*P.G.*, XXXII., 719.) *Reg. brev.*, ii.
[5] In a sermon attributed to FAUSTUS OF RHEGIUM (fifth century) mention is made of the *chirographum de quo se monachus debitum ex tota fide promiserit implere* (*P.L.*, LVIII., 875).
[6] Here it is, according to the Coptic text and the German translation of LEIPOLDT (*Schenute von Atripe*, pp. 109, 195–196): " The contract. Each shall say thus: I bind myself before God, in His holy place, even as the words witness which my mouth pronounces: I will not defile my body in any way, I will not steal, I will not perjure myself, I will not lie, I will not do ill in secret. If I transgress that to which I have bound myself, then I will not to enter into the kingdom of heaven; for I well see that God, because of the contract I have made before Him, will destroy my soul and my body in the gehenna of fire, because I shall have transgressed the contract that I have made." *Cf.* LADEUZE, *Étude sur le cénobitisme pakhomien pendant le IVᵉ siècle et la première moitié du Vᵉ*, pp. 208, 314 *ff*. Also: the review of LEIPOLDT's work in the *Revue d'hist. eccl's.*, t. VII., pp. 76 *ff*.
[7] S. ISIDORI *Reg.*, IV.—MABILLON, *Annales O.S.B.*, l. XII., xlii. T. I., p. 332.
[8] *Reg.*, xxii.: see a formula for this pact in *P.L.*, LXXXVII., 1127 *sq.*

Whatever may be said as to the customs from which St. Benedict drew inspiration, and of the correspondences which exist, for instance, between the Benedictine ceremonial and that given by St. Denis in the sixth chapter of his *Ecclesiastical Hierarchy,* it is undeniable that our Holy Father has here again accomplished work of a profoundly original character. He organized and defined monastic profession, and made it a juridical act, complete in itself and of considerable solemnity. We recognize the hand of a Roman, and a Roman of a noble and vigorous line. It was the common practice of all peoples, and especially of the Hebrews, to surround contracts with guarantees, symbolical actions, witnesses, so as fully to determine their sense and to ensure their faithful fulfilment; but nowhere more than at Rome were public and private transactions accompanied with a profusion of forms which had to be scrupulously observed under pain of nullity. The necessity of combating the instability of the sarabaites and gyrovagues combined with these racial tendencies to suggest this ceremonial to our Holy Father.[1]

So the Benedictine profession is pre-eminently a contract, a bilateral contract, between the novice on the one side, and God and the brethren on the other: I give myself wholly and for ever to God and to the monastic Order, that God and the monastic Order may admit me to communion with them, may put me in possession of their life. It is adoption into God's family: the candidate is denominated " he who is to be received " (*suscipiendus*); he gives himself to be received and accepted: and the fact of reception makes him a son of the family.

Suscipiendus autem, in oratorio coram omnibus promittat de stabilitate sua, et conversione morum suorum, et obedientia, coram Deo et Sanctis ejus, ut si aliquando aliter fecerit, ab eo se damnandum sciat quem irridet. De qua promissione sua faciat petitionem ad nomen Sanctorum quorum reliquiæ ibi sunt, et Abbatis præsentis. Quam petitionem manu sua scribat: aut certe, si non scit litteras, alter ab eo rogatus scribat; et ille novitius signum faciat, et manu sua eam super altare ponat. Quam dum posuerit, incipiat ipse novitius mox hunc versum: *Suscipe me, Domine, secundum eloquium tuum, et vivam : et non confundas me ab exspectatione mea.* Quem versum omnis congregatio tertio respondeat, adjungentes: " Gloria Patri." Tunc ipse frater novitius prosternatur singulorum

Let him who is to be received make before all, in the oratory, a promise of stability, conversion of manners, and obedience, in the presence of God and His saints, so that, if he should ever act otherwise, he may know that he will be condemned by Him whom he mocks. Of this promise of his let him make a petition in the name of the saints whose relics are there, and of the Abbot there present. Let him write this petition with his own hand; or at least, if he knows not letters, let another write it at his request, and let the novice affix a sign to it, and place it with his own hand upon the altar. When he has placed it there, let the novice himself presently begin this verse: " *Suscipe me, Domine, secundum eloquium tuum, et vivam : et non confundas me ab exspectatione mea.*"

---

[1] D. ROTHENHÄUSLER, *Zur Aufnahmeordnung der Regula S. Benedicti,* compares ingeniously the ordinances of this passage of the Rule and the juridical customs of the time.

pedibus, ut orent pro eo, et jam ex illa hora in congregatione reputetur.	And this verse let the whole community thrice answer, adding thereto *Gloria Patri*. Then let the brother novice cast himself at the feet of all, that they may pray for him; and from that day let him be counted as one of the community.

A contract or public act such as profession requires witnesses. There are heavenly witnesses: " in the presence of God and His saints "; and there are earthly witnesses: the Abbot, the brethren, and all the faithful there present. Nothing shall be done in a corner.

But first of all, according to our practice, the candidate is interrogated solemnly as to his dispositions with regard to the obligations he is going to contract. The same is done before baptism and before the consecration of a bishop. " Let him make a promise of stability."[1] There have been examinations and preliminary scrutinies during the year of novitiate, but a final one is needed. The candidate replies to a series of precise and plain questions by the repetition of *Volo* (I will). This oral promise is nowadays completed by the reading of the document containing the vows.

For there is such a document, called by St. Benedict the " petition," a new juridical guarantee, supplementing the necessarily transient character of mere words. Our Holy Father sees to it that it be an instrument well and duly drawn. It is written by the candidate with his own hand. If he cannot write, he must ask one of his brethren to write it in his name. It is localized. The expression " let him make a petition in the name of the saints whose relics are there " undoubtedly means that he takes for witnesses and guarantors the saints of the abbey, those who more especially are a part of the monastic family, who are more immediately present, who are the recognized protectors. But as a consequence the profession is localized before the eyes of God and His saints and even before the eyes of men; for, according to the view of our forefathers, just as there was no monastery without a church, so there was no church without relics: and a monastery was known as the monastery enriched with such and such relics. It is dated, dated especially by the name of the Abbot there present, of the then Abbot, *et Abbatis præsentis;* indicating that this profession was made under such and such an Abbot. It is signed. The novice affixes to it a sign or *the* sign: words which do not necessarily mean his name or signature, but perhaps a conventional mark of any sort, adopted by the individual in order to attest his private transactions, and such that even the illiterate

[1] Perhaps it was even the case, in St. Benedict's practice, that the *promissio* was made under the form of question and answer (as among the Greeks: *cf.* ST. DENIS, *De hier. eccl.*, c. vi.—*Eucologium* of the Greeks, ed. GOAR (1647), pp. 469, 477 *ff.*). *Cf.* D. ROTHENHÄUSLER, *Zur Aufnahmeordnung der Regula S. Benedicti*, p. 3.—The admonition in our Ceremonial, *Dominus noster Jesus Christus*, and the interrogatory which follows are borrowed from the ancient ritual of Abbot Orderisius of Monte Cassino (MARTÈNE, *De ant. monach. rit.*, l. V., c. iv., col. 640). Next come four splendid prayers which are found in the Gregorian Sacramentary: *Ordo ad faciendum monachum*.

could make it. The " sign " *par excellence*, formerly much employed as a signature, is the cross. For long the profession document was signed by a simple cross, as is still the case in the majority of the Congregations of our Order. However, monastic antiquity shows some cases of signature by name.[1] Hildemar says that the novice should write his name, or, " if he does not know letters," trace the sign of the cross in the presence of the brethren.[2]

The novice, even though he is a layman, signs his vows on the altar itself, on the stone whereon Our Lord Jesus Christ offers and immolates Himself. And St. Benedict would have him deposit them there with his own hand. Thenceforth the promise and offering of the novice are consecrated things. Finally, that the petition may better resist the effects of time, we write it upon parchment, as is done in all very important ecclesiastical transactions. According to our Holy Father himself, it shall be kept in the archives of the monastery and never returned to the monk.[3]

" When he has placed it there, let the novice himself presently begin this verse: *Suscipe*." After all the juridical guarantees of which we have spoken comes a prayer, designed to assure their efficaciousness.

Our Holy Father, who knew the Psalter thoroughly, found no more appropriate formula than this simple verse of the hundred and eighteenth psalm. The novice is standing, in the presence of God. He addresses himself in turn to each of the three Divine Persons. And the general sense of his prayer, chanted and made still more expressive by liturgical actions, is undoubtedly that of a supreme affirmation of his sacrifice, but above all of a humble and trustful appeal for its acceptance. Having done all that is in his power, the novice begs God to fulfil on His side the engagements entailed in the contract. God has engaged to receive and accept; He has given His word; His fidelity is pledged. The novice is sure that God will not fail him, and he does not distrust Him or take precautions against Him. But, prostrating in the dust, he begs Him to let it be even so and to deign to accept him as His son. If we are unfaithful, the contract is violated and without fruit: God is mocked and we are disappointed and frustrated. Therefore, it is really against his own frailty that the novice wishes to fortify himself: *Suscipe me, Domine, secundum eloquium tuum, et vivam : et non confundas me ab exspectatione mea*. Grant that I may be really " given " and really " received," truly received because truly given, and that both of us may be able to keep our word. Both my gift and Yours rest wholly in Your blessed hands.

God's answer, it would seem, is not slow in coming. First of all, as its

---

[1] *Cf.* HÆFTEN, l. IV., tract. v., disq. vi.

[2] Our lay brothers sign with a cross. The choir-monks (since August 15, 1840) add their names beneath the cross. In order to prevent the possibility of fraud and to have the fact of profession certified beyond question, we have borrowed from the Congregation of St. Maur the custom of adding to the profession form an instrument in which the Abbot attests what has been done.

[3] Though an enfranchised slave was given the deed recording his purchase. *Cf.* D. ROTHENHÄUSLER, *op. cit.*, p. 16, note 2.

Of the Discipline of receiving Brethren into Religion

visible manifestation, comes the acceptance of the brethren, incorporation into the society of God's children. This incorporation is made manifest immediately after the chanting of the first *Suscipe*: for all the brethren take it up in chorus; and they do not say *Suscipe eum*, but *Suscipe me;* so that there is already vital union, and the entire community joins with the newly professed in presenting the oblation. The word *tertio* has always been taken to mean a threefold repetition. The combined *Suscipe* ends, as St. Benedict prescribes, with the praise of Father, Son, and Holy Ghost; nor is there any need to emphasize the appropriateness of this doxology.

After the public prayers in which the principal duties of the professed monk are enumerated, and all the graces which will help him to face them asked,[1] the blessing and imposition of the monastic habit take place. The clothing, of which our Holy Father speaks a few lines farther on, took place, then, in the oratory, doubtless at the end of the ceremony. Usage has varied on this last point, and the clothing has sometimes been put after the Communion. As we have said already, it has always been an essential part of the profession ceremony, and has often even sufficed alone.[2] Before the clothing we sing the *Veni Creator*, as was done by the Maurists and others; which indicates that the act is specially entrusted, by appropriation, to the Divine Person who unites and consummates. So does God take complete possession.[3] Therefore, after the clothing, is sung the antiphon *Confirma hoc Deus*.

The clothing is the external manifestation of the transformation which has been wrought within; the old man, the sinner, has been destroyed; he has given place to the new man, to him who lives of God and for God, a " new creature." It is a restoration, a new edition, a completing of what was done in baptism; and at baptism also the neophyte was given a special and symbolical garment. " It may reasonably be said," says St. Thomas, "that by entry into religion a man obtains the remission of all his sins. . . . Wherefore we read in the Lives of the Fathers that they who enter religion obtain the same grace that the baptized obtain."[4] Tradition is unanimous in regarding profession as a second " baptism "; and everyone may benefit by an examination

---

[1] Observe especially the prayer *Clementissime*, which D. GUÉRANGER found in MARTÈNE, *De ant. monach. rit.*, l. V., c. iv., cols. 648–649, and which the latter had taken from an old ritual of Aniane. It may go back to a very high antiquity; it forms part of an *Ordo conversorum*, in the *Liber ordinum* of the Mozarabic liturgy published by D. FÉROTIN (cols. 83–85).—The Preface which follows is found (in the form of a prayer) in the *Ordo romanus* of HITTORP (*De divinis Ecclesiæ catholicæ officiis*, col. 155).

[2] *Quid petis?* Benedictionem habitus mei (Ritual of the English Benedictine Congregation).

[3] We may note, all the same, that the insertion of the *Veni Creator* at this point is a little surprising; and historically it is a relatively recent practice (*cf.*, however, the Statutes of LANFRANC: MARTÈNE, *De ant. monach. rit.*, l. V., c. iv., col. 647).

[4] *Summa*, II.–II., q. clxxxix., a. 3.—We read in a sermon attributed to FAUSTUS OF RHEGIUM: *Abrenuntianti publica pœnitentia non est necessaria, quia conversus ingemuit et cum Deo æternum pactum inivit. Ex illo igitur die non memorantur ejus delicta quæ gessit in sæculo, in quo facturum se justitiam de reliquo promiserit Deo* (P.L., LVIII., 875–876).

of the analogies which exist, as regards ritual and doctrine, between profession and baptism.[1]

The monastic habit signifies the state of perfect innocence and spiritual childhood:[2] " May they be to him the covering of his sins," as one of the prayers at the clothing says; it signifies the life of Our Lord Jesus Christ penetrating us and enfolding us wholly: " For as many of you as have been baptized in Christ have put on Christ " (Gal. iii. 27): especially does the cowl signify this unique grace and our belonging to the society of the perfect, the livery of which we shall wear thenceforth. The habit is at once the mark of this belonging, and the means or instrument of our separation from the world: " strong armour and a safe defence," as the ritual says again. Finally—and this is plainer to see in the ceremonial for the consecration of Virgins—it symbolizes the adornment and embellishment of the espoused soul, for profession may be regarded also as a marriage feast. And just as the Church, in giving the white robe to the newly baptized, bids him guard it without spot until the day of the eternal marriage feast, so the Abbot asks on behalf of the newly professed " that he may be brought joyfully with his wedding garment into the heavenly banquet of our most sweet Spouse, the Lord Jesus Christ, there to reign for ever."

Monastic tradition would have the newly professed keep on his cowl (and formerly he kept his head covered with the hood) during the days which follow immediately on this second baptism: even as the newly baptized kept for some time their white garments and the cap or veil.[3] The Abbot uncovered the head at a time appointed; and—like baptism again—this was a little liturgical ceremony, taking place generally in church after the Conventual Mass, but sometimes in the chapter house.

The professed monk, therefore, has been "adopted" by God and belongs henceforth to the family of God. But to be one of the family of God is to dwell in the society of the three Divine Persons, and in the society of the members of Our Lord Jesus Christ, which is the Church. Baptism made us all " one " in Christ; profession, on its part, aggregates us to the society of those who are specially vowed to God, between whom there is a community of goods, prayers, and work, as in the primitive Church. The *Suscipe* taken up by the community already showed this union, as we have said; but St. Benedict would have a formal rite

---

[1] *Cf. Religiosæ Professionis valor satisfactorius constanti traditione necnon et intrinsecis præcipuis quibusdam argumentis defensus*, auct. ROBERTO COLLETTE, O.C.—On the " new name " given to the professed monk, see HÆFTEN, l. IV., tract. viii., disq. ii., iii., and iv.

[2] See CASSIAN, *Inst.*, I., iii.

[3] *Cf.* THEODORE OF CANTERBURY, *Pænitent.*, iii. *P.L.*, XCIX., 928.—PAUL THE DEACON (Commentary *in cap.* lviii.) is insistent on it and speaks of eight days. The Council of Aix-la-Chapelle in 817 prescribed three days only (cap. xxxv. MANSI, t. XIV., col. 396). [In the English Benedictine ritual the newly professed monk wears his hood over his head until the Conventual Mass of the " third day " after his profession, except when in his cell. The hood is fastened in that position by the Abbot at the end of the profession ceremony, and unfastened by him before the Communion at the Mass of the " third day."]

Of the Discipline of receiving Brethren into Religion

of adoption into the monastic family. And just as on the day of their baptism it is by becoming the children of the Church that men become the children of God, and partake in the supernatural life, even so, on the day of profession, it is by becoming children of the monastery that they partake in the perfect supernatural life. When the newly professed has asked the prayers of the Abbot and received from him his paternal kiss, then all the brethren embrace the chosen one, who asks them to pray for him, as the very words of the Rule prescribe; and they answer him with a cordial *Proficiat* (may it profit thee).[1] Among the Maurists and generally the newly professed passed into the stalls for this ceremony, but at Monte Cassino the brethren came to him, and the kiss of peace was given kneeling, as though to mark the supernatural respect and holy affection of all these consecrated souls. Such is also our practice.[2]

The profession is now accomplished. According to the rite attested by the most ancient documents, as for instance by the writings of Paul the Deacon and Hildemar, the neophyte prostrates before the altar, " enfolded wholly " in his cowl, as the rituals say, that of the Maurists for example. " You are dead, and your life is hid with Christ in God " (Col. iii. 3). " We are buried together with him by baptism into death " (Rom. vi. 4). In order to express this notion of death in a striking way, modern monastic custom[3] has devised the ceremonial of pall and lighted candles. Dom Guéranger, in his conferences, apologized for having preserved a usage " from which the faithful draw some edification," but which he considered to be rather too theatrical and likely to cause misunderstanding of the true effect of profession. In fact, there lies there not only the corpse of the old man, but also, and this more than anything, a living man, a man renewed; there is a living victim, " a pure, holy and unspotted victim," reunited to the victim on the altar, offered and accepted with that victim, and enwrapped by the deacon in the fragrance of the same incense.

Then the Mass continues. Motionless, and silent like the Lamb of

---

[1] The two formulas: *Ora pro me, pater*, and *Proficiat tibi, frater*, are found in a manuscript ritual of Corbie, cited by Martène (*De ant. monach. rit.*, l. V., c. iv., cols. 654 and 655).—As to the kiss of peace, of which St. Benedict does not speak, it is mentioned in the *Rule of the Master* (eighth century), in the Pontifical of Alet (ninth century: Martène, *De ant. eccl. rit.*, l. II., c. ii. T. II., col. 454), in Hildemar, etc.

[2] Psalm xlvii. is sung during this ceremony, the antiphon being its verse *Suscepimus, Deus*, dear to St. Benedict (Chapter LIII.); also psalm cxxxii., the psalm *par excellence* of monastic brotherhood (read the *Enarratio* of St. Augustine on this psalm).—Both are indicated in the Pontifical (with the *Miserere* between them) for the blessing of an Abbot who is not professed.

[3] For instance, the ritual of the Congregation of St. Maur of 1666. We should recognize that, according to Paul the Deacon, they sang over the professed monk the *Miserere*, the *De profundis*, and, adds this commentator, *cæteros psalmos qui ad hoc pertinent*. See also Hildemar, *in h. l.*—We sing the Litany of the Saints, and it is prescribed also by the rituals of other Congregations. It is an imitation of what is done at ordinations and at the consecration of virgins. St. Benedict limited himself to writing: *et orent pro eo*; and it would seem that, primitively, these prayers comprised some psalms, then the *litaniæ*, the *supplicatio litaniæ—i.e.*, the *Kyrie eleison* repeated— a series of verses and responses, and finally the prayer. (See Paul the Deacon and Hildemar.)

God, the newly professed suffers himself to be immolated and consumed mystically by the Eternal High-Priest. How sweet that Mass and that Communion! Our whole monastic life should resemble this Profession Mass. *Supplices te rogamus, omnipotens Deus, jube hæc perferri, per manus sancti Angeli tui in sublime altare tuum, in conspectu divinæ Majestatis tuæ*. . . . Then comes the *Paternoster*, which is an appeal to the Tenderness, Beauty, and Purity of God, with its tranquil and full petition. Holy Communion completes the baptismal illumination: even so the newly professed should, according to our most ancient customs, receive the Body and the Blood of the Lord, and, like the neophytes once more, they shall communicate each day of this period in white (*in albis*).

Finally, the newly professed monk is given official possession of his stall in choir. Thus the rights acquired by profession are sealed, and henceforth the monk shall keep the rank thus given to him. The choir is now his true place, for he has been chosen and blessed for the work of praise. In the case of nuns there is even a solemn giving of the book of the Divine Office. However, our ceremonial, in accord once more with tradition, would have the neophyte fulfil no choir duty alone for three days. Formerly, too, he kept complete silence, hidden night and day in his cowl and conversing with God.[1]

Res si quas habet, aut eroget prius pauperibus, aut facta solemniter donatione, conferat monasterio, nihil sibi reservans ex omnibus: quippe qui ex illo die nec proprii corporis potestatem se habiturum sciat. Mox ergo in oratorio exuatur rebus propriis quibus vestitus est, et induatur rebus monasterii. Illa autem vestimenta, quibus exutus est, reponantur in vestiario conservanda, ut si aliquando, suadente diabolo, consenserit ut egrediatur de monasterio (quod absit), tunc exutus rebus monasterii, projiciatur. Illam tamen petitionem, quam desuper altare Abbas tulit, non recipiat, sed in monasterio reservetur.

If he have any property let him either first bestow it on the poor, or by solemn deed of gift make it over to the monastery, keeping nothing of it all for himself, as knowing that from that day forward he will have no power even over his own body. Forthwith, therefore, in the oratory, let him be stripped of his own garments wherewith he is clad, and be clothed in those of the monastery. Those garments which are taken from him shall be placed in the clothes-room, there to be kept, so that if ever, by the persuasion of the devil, he consent (which God forbid) to leave the monastery, he may be stripped of the monastic property and cast forth. The petition, however, which the Abbot received on the altar shall not be given back to him, but shall be kept in the monastery.

[1] The Ceremonial in actual use in the English Congregation still lays it down that the newly professed are to converse during these three days with none but their confessor. [This is the full rubric: *Tunc denique Professus a Magistro deducitur ad locum suum inter Professos, et usque ad Missam conventualem tertii post diei, in qua ad sacram Synaxim accedit, nemini loquitur nisi Confessario suo; nec in choro actibusve conventualibus quidquam ita recitat ut a ceteris monachis audiatur. Item, extra cellam suam, caputium super caput semper gerit.*]

Of the Discipline of receiving Brethren into Religion

Arrangements with regard to property.—What shall the monk do with his property, supposing he has any? Our Holy Father concludes the chapter by dealing with this point, and his regulations echo the teaching of the ancient monks.[1]

" Let him first bestow it "—that is, before profession, or else before the putting on of the monastic garments as mentioned presently. The candidate can and ought to dispose freely of his property, both actual and possible. He is free to choose whom he shall give it to, for all that is required of him is to despoil himself, completely and finally, without keeping anything for himself, whether within the monastery or without, without securing for himself any benefit such as a small regular income. All monastic rules have insisted vigorously, as we know, on the incompatibility of possession of any sort with the true religious life.

St. Benedict does not say anything about parents. It would seem that the ancients were not very partial to donations made to one's family. St. Cæsarius, for instance, speaks plainly about them in his second letter to Abbess Cæsaria.[2] Monastic profession consecrates the whole man to God, and since his property is in some sort part of him, the best use the candidate can make of it is to offer all to God in the person of His poor. That is the express counsel of Our Lord: " Sell what thou hast and give to the poor "; and it is the first thought which occurs to St. Benedict: " either let him first bestow it on the poor." Obviously, however, if a man's parents are in need, his charity should begin with them. The monastery, too, may lawfully be considered, for the monastery is of our kin and the monastery is poor. Therefore, our Holy Father, without maintaining that anything must be asked from the candidate or his parents, without neglecting to suggest both here and in the next chapter that we must proceed in this matter with much moderation, is less severe than Cassian and St. Basil: the former would have nothing accepted from the novice, the latter speaks only of donation made to the poor and recommends that nothing be accepted from the parents.[3]

Monastic tradition is in agreement with St. Benedict's views, and his reserved attitude. Paul the Deacon and Hildemar report the curious little dialogue which took place between Abbot and novice on this

---

[1] *Qui si susceptus fuerit, non solum de substantia quam intulit, sed etiam nec de seipso ab illa judicabit hora. Nam si aliquid prius erogavit pauperibus, aut veniens in cellulam aliquid intulit fratribus, ipsi tamen non est licitum ut aliquid habeat in sua potestate* (S. Macar., *Reg.*, xxiv.). And St. Cæsarius: *Vestimenta laica non ei mutentur nisi antea de facultate sua chartas venditionis suæ faciat, sicut Dominus præcepit dicens: Si vis perfectus esse, vade, vende omnia quæ habes, da pauperibus, et veni, sequere me. Certe si non vult vendere, donationis chartas, aut parentibus, aut monasterio faciat, dummodo liber sit; et nihil habeat proprium. Si vero pater ejus aut mater vivat et non habet potestatem faciendi: quando illi migraverint, cogatur facere. Quæcumque secum exhibuit Abbati tradat; nihil sibi reservet; et si aliquis de propinquis aliquid transmiserit, offerat Abbati. Si ipsi est necessarium, ipso jubente habeat; si illi necesse non est, in commune redactum cui opus est tribuatur* (*Reg. ad mon.*, i.; cf. *Reg. ad. virg.*, iv.).—See also: S. Basil., *Reg. fus.*, viii.-ix.; *Reg. contr.*, iv.-v.—S. Aug., *Epist.* LXXXIII. P.L., XXXIII, 291 sq.—Cass., *Inst.*, IV., iii.-vi.

[2] *P.L.*, LXVII., 1133.   [3] *Reg. fus.*, ix.; *Reg. brev..* ccciv.—Cass., *Inst.*, IV., iv.

point.¹ According to actual usage a pension is allowed to be paid during the novitiate, but by no means exacted. A man may quite well bring with him nothing but his " good will," as says the founder of Cluny. The dowry of nuns is often the very condition *sine qua non* of the existence of the convent, and is a practice approved by the Holy See. But the Church, while recognizing that monasteries have the right to accept the donations of those who are going to be professed, has always taken care to preclude all practices and compacts of a simoniacal character. Canon Law fixes the time when the novice should dispose of his property, which is two months only before profession—nowadays, two months before solemn profession.

The donation ordered by St. Benedict would seem from the Rule to take place in the very course of the profession ceremony. But the text may be taken otherwise. Besides it is not impossible that, everything having been arranged previously, a solemn declaration was made at the profession that one wished to dispose of one's property in such and such a way. We should perhaps, understand a passage in the *Rule of the Master* in this way.²

St. Benedict prescribes that, if donation be made to the monastery, it should be done according to the accepted legal forms, so that the intention of the donor may be plain beyond dispute, so that the support of the law may be assured, and so that the monastery may be safe against dispossession or legal process. The Master would have the act of donation, which was drawn up on the entrance of the candidate, countersigned by monk witnesses, the bishop, the priest, the deacon, and the clergy of the place, and deposited on the altar.³ Martène has proved that this placing of donation documents on the altar is no isolated instance;⁴ and some of the forms employed have come down to us.⁵ " Keeping nothing for himself . . ." St. Benedict has already expressed himself in much the same terms in the thirty-third chapter, and we explained his meaning in that place.

Mox ergo. . . .   So as to realize completely and manifest exteriorly

---

¹ The Abbot having reminded the novice of the command *Vende omnia tua: Si ille dixerit: quia in hoc monasterio volo tribuere; tunc dicat illi Abba: Frater, Deo adjuvante, nobis non est necessaria tua res; eo quod nostra indigentia habemus unde suppleatur. Sunt enim alii pauperiores nobis, aut etiam monasteria, vel certe parentes tui forte plus sunt pauperes quam nos, et ideo melius est ut pro mercede illis tribuas qui plus indigent quam nobis. Si autem ille dixerit: quia volo pro mercede animæ meæ magis in hoc monasterio tribuere quam alteri dare; tunc donare debet rem suam aut pauperibus aut in monasterium* (PAULI DIAC., Commentary *in cap.* lviii.).

² Cap. lxxxix.

³ Cap. lxxxvii., lxxxix.   When the brother deposits his deed on the altar he should say: *Ecce, Domine, cum anima mea et paupertate mea, quidquid mihi donasti tibi reconsigno et offero, et ibi volo ut sint res meæ ubi fuerit cor meum et anima mea: sub potestate tamen monasterii et Abbatis, quem mihi, Domine, in vice tua timendum præponis . . ., unde quia per eum nobis tu omnia necessaria cogitas, ideo nihil nos oportet peculiare habere, quia tu nobis de omnibus es idoneus et in omnibus sufficis solus; ut jam nobis vivere et spes Christus sit et mori lucrum.*

⁴ Commentary *in h. l.*

⁵ For instance, that cited by DE ROZIÈRE in his *Recueil général des formules usitées dans l'Empire des Francs du Ve au Xe siècle* (Part I., no. cxciii.).

Of the Discipline of receiving Brethren into Religion

this basic incapability, the newly professed is stripped, in the very oratory, of his worldly garments and clothed in those of the monastery. Consequently, the novitiate in St. Benedict's time was certainly made in secular clothes, as we observed before. St. Benedict uses here again the words of St. Pachomius and Cassian;[1] like them, he would have the secular garments deposited in the clothes-room. Without doubt they were not kept there in reserve for an indefinite period, for in case a monk should leave it would be easy to find him substitutes.

Such abandonment of the monastery, in spite of the vow of stability, was frequent enough at that period for St. Benedict to consider the question as to how many times one should be received back who has left or been dismissed by his own fault (Chapter XXIX.). In the case of certain headstrong natures the temptation was so violent that practical precautions were taken against it. It is not uncommon to find in the ancient profession rituals a request addressed by the candidates to the Abbot that he would lock them up securely on the day when the devil should tempt them to quit the monastery, or that he would drag them back by force if they have deserted. The Abbot had a penal code and prison cells at his disposal. But our Holy Father did not prescribe either constraint or coercion for the fugitive; yet he will not let him carry the vesture of his holy profession into the unknown, for a deserter has no right to it, and to wear it in the world would cause scandal. And St. Benedict wishes also to prevent a man taking advantage of his habit to obtain admittance into another monastery, as did the gyrovagues. Canon Law has fixed the procedure to be observed with regard to those who are expelled or secularized, and preserves the monastic regulation which forbids them to wear the religious habit.

So the old discarded vesture of the world may be returned, as says St. Benedict; but one thing is never returned, a thing which the deserter might wish to bear off or to destroy. This is the document containing his vows, which has been received by the Abbot on the altar of the Lord, and which will bear witness eternally in favour of the rights of God against the violator of the contract.

[1] *Tunc nudabunt eum vestimentis sæcularibus et induent habitu monachorum. . . . Vestimenta autem quæ secum detulerat, accipient qui huic rei præpositi sunt, et inferent in repositorium et erunt in potestate principis monasterii* (S. Pach., *Reg.*, xlix.). —*In concilio fratrum productus in medium exuatur propriis, ac per manus Abbatis induatur monasterii vestimentis. . . . Illa vero quæ deposuit vestimenta œconomo consignata tamdiu reservantur donec profectus et conversationis ejus ac tolerantiæ virtutem . . . evidenter agnoscant. Et siquidem posse eum inibi durare tempore procedente perspexerint . . ., indigentibus eadem largiuntur. Sin vero . . ., exeuntes eum monasterii quibus indutus fuerat vestimentis et revestitum antiquis quæ fuerant sequestrata depellunt. . . . Deposita monasterii veste pellatur* (Cass., *Inst.*, IV., v.–vi.).

CHAPTER LIX
OF THE SONS OF NOBLES OR THE POOR THAT ARE OFFERED

THE preceding chapter described the reception of adults; the present one speaks of the reception of children. This does not mean children received into the monastery temporarily as *alumni*, to be educated there, but children given permanently and devoted to the religious life. These regulations of the Rule are now obsolete, the ancient discipline having been modified and the Council of Trent having refused to recognize the validity of profession made before the completion of the sixteenth year. But if we would appreciate correctly the question of fact and the question of right, the historical and the doctrinal aspect of the matter, it is important not to let our judgement be affected by present-day legislation, and particularly by the lessening of the religious sense.[1]

The practice of parents consecrating their children to God goes back very far in the history of the Old Testament. Without speaking of the extraordinary offering of Abraham, nor even of the vow of Jephte (Judg. xi.), we know that the young Samuel was presented in the Temple and consecrated to its service by his mother Anna (1 Kings i.). St. John the Baptist and Our Lady were offered in the same way. And it was even a general law with the Jews that the firstborn belonged to the Lord, unless they were "ransomed" by their parents. Moreover, the rights of the father of a family were in antiquity almost sovereign. St. Paul the Apostle takes it for granted that a father has the right either to give his daughter in marriage or to consecrate her to God: "For he that hath determined, being steadfast in his heart, having no necessity, but having power of his own will, and hath judged this in his heart, to keep his virgin, doth well" (1 Cor. vii. 37). To consecrate a daughter to virginity does not seem to the Apostle an infringement of the true liberty of the individual; it was a sort of slavery which he could not think much of who ventures to advise Christian slaves to abide in their state, and, instead of seeking enfranchisement, to serve conscientiously and heartily: "Wast thou called, being a bondman? Care not for it: but if thou mayest be made free, use it rather" (1 Cor. vii. 21). "Servants, be obedient to them that are your lords according to the flesh, with fear and trembling, in the simplicity of your heart, as to Christ . . . with a good will serving, as to the Lord, and not to men" (Eph. vi. 5, 7).

In early times, Christians thought it quite natural that they should

---

[1] Read, with the various Commentaries, MÉNARD, *Concord. Regul., in b. l.*—HÆFTEN, l. IV., tract. i.—MABILLON, *Acta SS. O.S.B.*, Sæc. IV., P. II., Præf., 199; Sæc. VI., P. I., Præf., 36. *Vetera Analecta*, pp. 155–158.—THOMASSIN, *Ancienne et nouvelle discipline de l'Eglise*, P. I., l. III., chaps. lvi.–lix.

Of the Sons of Nobles or the Poor that are Offered

offer their children to monasteries. It is a practice " found in many places in Egypt, in the Thebaid, Palestine, Syria, and in Asia Minor," says the author of the *Monks of the East* (*Moines d'Orient*), who cites much interesting evidence.[1] Undoubtedly there were sometimes abuses and disadvantages in these precocious professions, for St. Basil, while maintaining the principle of the admission of children, requires that they be not asked to make their profession until they have reached an age when they can act with full knowledge and liberty.[2] St. Benedict, who took more than one hint from those famous pages on the reception and education of children, has yet not accepted them in their entirety; and in particular he has not thought it his duty to adopt St. Basil's caution with regard to the age of profession, and to depart from the Western custom.

In the West, in fact, and that too before St. Benedict's time, parents were accustomed to bind their young children finally to the religious life. Thomassin[3] cites a passage from a letter of St. Augustine in favour of a discipline analogous to St. Basil's, but it does not appear to us very conclusive. Nor is there anything to prove that the young oblates, of whom St. Jerome speaks in the letters cited by the same author, were not vowed for life: of Asella it is said, " While still wrapped in the clothes of childhood and scarce beyond her tenth year, she was consecrated, receiving thus the glorious pledge of future blessedness." St. Cæsarius allows the nuns to receive girls at six or seven years of age; and he is not speaking only of children who were to be educated in the monastery.[4] St. Gregory of Tours speaks of such offerings, and of the offering of slaves by their masters, as of an old and common practice.[5] The Fifth Council of Orleans (A.D. 549)[6] recognizes that girls enter the religious life either of their own will (*propria voluntate*) or by their parents offering them; and the First Council of Mâcon (A.D. 583) excommunicates oblates who should abandon the monastery.[7] Children vowed to the clerical state were given the choice, at a fixed time, either of making a vow of chastity, which allowed them to proceed to sacred Orders, or of marrying and so remaining in the lower Orders.[8] Let us turn now to the text of the Rule.

DE FILIIS NOBILIUM VEL PAUPERUM, QUI OFFERUNTUR.—Si quis forte de nobilibus offert filium suum Deo in monasterio, si ipse puer minori ætate est, parentes ejus faciant petitionem quam supra diximus. Et cum obla-

If perchance any noble shall offer his son to God in the monastery, let the parents, should the boy himself be not old enough, make the petition of which we spoke before. And, together with the offerings, let them

---
[1] Chapter V., p. 121.
[2] *Reg. fus.*, xv. *Cf. Reg. contr.*, vii.
[3] *Ancienne et nouvelle discipline de l'Eglise*, P. I., l. III., chap. lvi., no. xii.
[4] *Reg. ad virg.*, v.
[5] *In gloria martyrum*, 75. M. G. H.: Script. rer. merov., t. I., p. 538. *In gloria confessorum*, 22. M. G. H.: *ibid.*, p. 762. *De virtutibus S. Martini*, ii., 4. M. G. H.: *ibid.*, pp. 610–611.
[6] Can. xix. MANSI, t. IX., col. 133. [7] Can. xii. MANSI, t. IX., col. 934.
[8] *Concil. III. Carthag.* (397), can. xix. MANSI, t. III., col. 883.—*Tolet. II.* (527) can. i. MANSI, t. VIII., col. 785.—*Vasense III.* (529), can. i. MANSI, t. VIII., col. 726

tione ipsam petitionem et manum pueri involvant in palla altaris, et sic eum offerant.

wrap that petition and the hand of the child in the altar-cloth, and so offer him.

By nobles, our Holy Father, using the language of his time, means the rich, though, as Hildemar observes, many noble by birth are poor, and many commoners wealthy. Perhaps St. Benedict was thinking, when he wrote these lines, of Eutychius, father of St. Maurus, and of Tertullus, father of St. Placid.[1]

St. Benedict supposes that the child is too young to write his petition —that is, his vows—himself. This age is fixed variously in the Customaries from ten to fourteen years. It is the business of the parents (that is to say, according to the commentators and custom, of the father and mother; of the mother if the father be dead, sometimes of other relatives, or of a guardian[2])—it is the business of the parents to promise stability, conversion of manners, and obedience in the name of their child; they have to draw up the "petition of which we spoke before": which words are of themselves enough to prove that we are dealing with a true profession, a profession as real as that of adults and formulated in practically the same terms.[3]

The vows are deposited on the altar along with the offerings—that is, with the bread and wine offered for the sacrifice, of which the child himself and his parents would give their share. Therefore we are here again in the oratory and at Mass. The offerings, the petition, and the hand of the child are wrapped in the "altar-cloth." Does this mean what we now call the corporal, which formerly was much more ample and was probably the only altar-cloth? Or does it mean, as Paul the Deacon explains it, the veil which covered the offerings?[4] There should be witnesses present, as our Holy Father remarks at the end of the chapter, and their numerous signatures are to be found at the foot of the profession documents which have been preserved. St. Basil made the same recommendation.[5]

De rebus autem suis, aut in præsenti petitione promittant sub jurejurando, quia nunquam per se, nunquam per suspectam personam, nec quolibet modo ei aliquando aliquid dent, aut tribuant occasionem habendi. Vel certe, si hoc facere noluerint, et aliquid offerre voluerint in eleemosynam monasterio pro mercede sua, faciant ex rebus, quas

With respect to their property they must in the same petition promise under oath that they will never either themselves or through an intermediary, or in any way whatever, give him anything, or the means of having anything. Or else, if they are unwilling to do this, and desire to offer something as an alms to the monastery for

---

[1] S. Greg. M., *Dial.*, l. II., c. iii.
[2] *Cf.* Martène, Commentary *in b. l.*, p. 784.
[3] Specimens of these petitions (later than the time of St. Benedict) are to be found in Mabillon, *Vetera Analecta*, pp. 155–158; Martène, Commentary *in b. l.*, p. 785; L. Delisle, *Littérature latine et histoire du moyen âge*, pp. 9–16; etc.
[4] Commentary *in b. l.*
[5] *Oportet infantes voluntate et consensu parentum, immo ab ipsis parentibus oblatos, sub testimonio plurimorum suscipi; ut omnis occasio maledicti gratia excludatur hominum pessimorum* (*Reg. contr.*, vii.).

Of the Sons of Nobles or the Poor that are Offered

dare volunt monasterio donationem, reservato sibi (si ita voluerint) usufructuario. Atque ita omnia obstruantur, ut nulla suspicio remaneat puerò, per quam deceptus perire possit (quod absit), quod experimento didicimus.

their advantage, let them make a donation to the monastery of the property which they wish to give, reserving to themselves, if they so wish, the usufruct. And so let every way be blocked that the child may have no sort of expectation, by which he may be misled and perish (which God forbid), as we have learnt by experience may happen.

As in the fifty-eighth chapter, after regulations which concern persons come regulations concerning property. The child has become a monk; his profession is final and not merely provisional; it is not fictitious, or existing only in the desire of his parents. The child is poor, and that absolutely and for ever. It is important, therefore, to settle the question not of his present possessions—he is too young to have any—but of the property which may come to him some day from his family. Matters must be so arranged, says St. Benedict with vigour of language, that all communication with the world, on account of this property, should be closed to him; that every way may be blocked to the thought that this property might come to him should he return to the world. If it were open to the oblate to think that he might one day have property on some title or other, he might be deceived by this mirage; he might easily become a renegade and lose his soul.[1] God forbid, exclaims St. Benedict; but we have learnt by experience that such evils do happen.[2]

Infringements of the law of poverty are a danger for all monks; but the very conditions in which the child is vowed to poverty make it necessary to regulate this matter with especial prudence. The parents bind themselves by an oath, in words which are embodied in the petition, never to give anything themselves, or by an intermediary, or in any way whatever, or to give the means of possessing anything. Our Holy Father has here adopted the legal style, exhausting all hypotheses.

Such a procedure, the first proposed to the parents by St. Benedict, is tantamount to disinheriting the child. He suggests another course, but very cautiously, as he did in the previous chapter with respect to adults. If they are unwilling to act thus—viz., to swear that their child shall never have part in their fortune, let them offer with him some property, which may stand for his share of the inheritance. Just as the adult, if he wishes, may offer himself with his property, so the child is offered with whatever the parents agree to relinquish. But the gift is nothing really but an alms to the monastery: *pro mercede sua* (for their advantage), as a return for what the monastery does for their child; or, according to the interpretation of Paul the Deacon and many

---

[1] CASSIAN says of the monk who should keep some resources in the world: *Sed ubi primum exorta fuerit qualibet occasione commotio, fiducia stipis illius animatum, continuo de monasterio velut funda rotante fugiturum* (*Inst.*, IV., iii.).

[2] *Quod omnimodis observari debere, multis sunt experimentis frequenter edocti*, wrote CASSIAN also, but with reference to troubles which may be caused in a monastery by the acceptance of the property of the candidate (*Inst.*, IV., iv.).

others, for the salvation and ransom of their souls. Care must be taken that the act of donation is drawn up in proper form; and the parents shall reserve to themselves the income of the property abandoned, if they wish to do so. We have already observed that St. Benedict, St. Basil, and Cassian feared these gifts made to the monastery.

Similiter autem et pauperiores faciant. Qui vero ex toto nihil habent, simpliciter petitionem faciant, et cum oblatione offerant filium suum coram testibus.	Let those who are poorer do in like manner. But those who have nothing whatever shall simply make the petition, and offer their son along with the offerings and before witnesses.

St. Benedict ranges the parents of oblates, from the point of view of their fortunes, in three classes: the nobles or rich, those who possess less, those who possess nothing at all. The "poorer" (*pauperiores*) are to observe the same regulations as the rich. As to poor folk, whose children are received with equal readiness and affection, they have merely to write the petition or get it written, and present their child with the offerings of bread and wine in the presence of witnesses.[1]

The same line of conduct with regard to oblates was pursued after our Holy Father's time. St. Isidore, the Master, and others sanction it in the West.[2] Councils legislated on the matter. For instance, the Fourth Council of Toledo (A.D. 633) decrees thus: "A monk is made by the consecration of his parents or by his own profession; by whichever of these he is bound, it shall hold him. Wherefore, we close against them the way of return to the world and forbid all such returning."[3] St. Gregory II. (A.D. 715-731), in a letter to St. Boniface, declares that the oblate is no longer free to marry.[4] The tendency to approximate to Eastern discipline, which showed itself at the beginning of the ninth century, was due to abuses. Some families found it a useful method of disposing decently of weakly, lame, or stunted children, or of providing for younger sons without worldly prospects. Laxity entered monasteries in consequence. Some Councils (as for instance that of Aix-la-Chapelle in A.D. 817),[5] without forbidding parents to offer healthy children, decreed that oblates should confirm their profession by a personal act, when they were of an age to make such. But these decisions were not by any means observed everywhere. The Council of Worms in A.D. 868[6] again binds oblates to remain always in the

---

[1] We know from Chapter II. that the religious life was by no means forbidden to slaves. The previous consent of their masters, or enfranchisement, was doubtless required, as the Council of Chalcedon (451) prescribes (can. iv. MANSI, t. VII., col. 374). See also the letter of GELASIUS to the bishops of Lucania (c. xiv. MANSI, t. VIII., col. 41). —ST. BASIL (*Reg. fus.*, xi.). Masters sometimes offered their slaves to God; sometimes, too, the master, entering religion, was followed by his slaves (S. GREG. TURON., *In gloria confessorum*, 22. M. G. H.: *Script. rer. merov.*, t. I., p. 762. *De virtutibus S. Martini*, ii., 4. M. G. H.: *ibid.*, pp. 610–611. *Histor. Franc.*, x. 29. M. G. H.: *ibid.*, pp. 440–442.—*Vita S. Romarici*, 4: MABILLON, *Acta SS. O.S.B.*, Sæc. II., p. 400).

[2] ST. AURELIAN (*Reg. ad mon.*, xlvii.) requires a formal instrument *quando ætate probati fuerint*.   [3] Cap. xlix. MANSI, t. X., col. 631.

[4] *Ep.* XIV. *ad Bonifacium episc.*, 7. P.L., LXXXIX., 525.

[5] Cap. xxxvi. MANSI, t. XIV., col. 396.   [6] Can. xxii. MANSI, t. XV., col. 873.

monastery; and in the second half of the ninth century the old practice had regained the upper hand.

At Cluny oblates were numerous and the customs furnish interesting details with regard to them. They were treated as true religious; and, if it was the rule that in their fifteenth year they should read their vows and be blessed with all the ceremonial of an adult's profession, this by no means proves that their engagement was not regarded as irrevocable from the very beginning. On the contrary, precisely because they were regarded as professed, they were not given the cowl anew at the age of fifteen. The same customs are found at Farfa, Bec, and elsewhere.[1] As a proof that Cluny certainly viewed the act of offering as creating a real and final bond between the child and the monastery, we find them refusing to let St. Bernard's relative, Robert, pass over to Clairvaux. The incident is well known. We know that it occasioned the vigorous letter that is placed at the head of St. Bernard's correspondence, and that the Pope, being consulted, decided in favour of the black monks. St. Bernard did not deny that the child belonged to God and to the monastic life; but in this affair, as in a parallel case treated of in the course of another letter,[2] he maintained that the oblate could, when grown up, pass freely to the religious family of his choice; especially, he added, when this was more fervent and of a stricter observance. Doubtless Cluny did not much relish the reasoning of the holy Doctor.[3]

The fundamental juridical effects of oblate profession having been disputed, it was but a step farther to allow them to return to the world if they wished. Undoubtedly, Clement III. ratified the decree of the Fourth Council of Toledo; but his successor, Celestine III., acknowledged that oblates possessed the sorry liberty of returning to the world, and this discipline prevailed little by little over the old; but this does not at all prove that the old discipline was an abuse, or exorbitant, or arising from a false interpretation of the Rule, but merely, as it has been expressed, "that the faith of the peoples had grown old."

To appreciate the customs of antiquity we need the antique soul; to appreciate Christian practice we need the Christian soul. Let us remember in the first place that the notion of paternal omnipotence, the *patria potestas* of the Romans, certainly had an influence on this institution. But is that notion pagan ? If so, how comes it that the Old and New Testaments recognize this discipline in part, and that the Church sanctioned and adopted it for so many centuries ? Indeed, the attacks which are made on the oblate system are based on a major premiss which is greatly in need of cogent proof and will not quickly

---

[1] *Cf.* MARTÈNE, *De ant. monach. rit.*, l. V., c. v., col. 659 *sq.*
[2] *Epist.* CCCLXXXII. *P.L.*, CLXXXII., 585 *sq.*
[3] *Epist.* I. *P.L.*, CLXXXII., 67 *sq.*; *Epist.* CCCLXXXII. *P.L.*, *ibid.*, 585–586: *Videat prudentia vestra quid habeat plus vigoris et rationis, utrum illud quod factum est de ipso per alium ipso nesciente, an illud quod sciens et prudens de se ipso fecit.* . . . *Ego autem dico, quod votum parentum integrum manet, et oblatio eorum non est exinanita sed cumulata. Nam et idem offertur quod prius oblatum est; et eidem offertur cui prius oblatum est; et quod prius a solis parentibus oblatum fuerat, nunc offertur a filio.*

get it, this namely, that a man is subject to those laws only the obligation and burden of which he has freely accepted. We are creatures, without having willed it, Frenchmen, without having willed it, men of the twentieth century, without having desired it in any way; we have become Christians and we have been committed to God's service, without our opinion being asked.[1] If a man reflects he quickly recognizes that he is a being of whom God disposes at His pleasure, of whom God Himself disposes, whether directly or by intermediaries, but always as his master.

May not retrospective concern about this institution come, in fact, from a too prevalent misconception of liberty? The power to choose evil or a lesser good, personal independence with respect to good or evil, a narrow and jealous individualism—what is all this but the diminution of liberty? True liberty consists in a profound belonging, in a conscious and loved adhesion, to the good and to God. If we do not take this point of view, it is hardly possible to understand education, which has for its end precisely this, to create in us a prejudice in favour of the good, even before we know what it is. And those who would have every Frenchman belong to the State more than to the family, and that he should be trained at the State University or forfeit all social standing, are only turning to their own use the procedure for which they reproach the Church.

When Tertullus, the senator, offered his young son Placid to St. Benedict, he did not think that he was acting tyrannically; he believed that he was thus assuring the safety and eternal life of his son; and he persuaded himself that neither the child nor God would ever blame him for his decision. As a matter of fact the majority of children offered in this way afterwards joyously clung to the profession that had been made for them. And if there were some who would gladly have returned to the world, are they much to be pitied for having been constrained to remain with God? And instead of letting our minds be possessed by the abuses and inevitable defections occasioned by the system, should we not rather bless it for having given us St. Maurus, St. Placid, the Venerable Bede, St. Gertrude, and so many others? So we have no reason to be ashamed of this fifty-ninth chapter. Had it been applied to ourselves, we should have known God only, we should have no memories but of Him, we should have nothing to unlearn: where would be the misfortune?[2]

[1] On this comparison between infant baptism and the "oblature," read THOMASSIN, *Ancienne et nouvelle discipline de l'Eglise*, P. I., l. III., chap. vi. T. I., cols. 1762-1763.

[2] With this chapter may be connected the question of "adult oblates": internal oblates, who give themselves to the monastery in order to live there the life of the monks and under a rule, with or without a religious habit; external oblates, who are, so to speak, the fringe of the monastic garment. Properly speaking, such oblates do not form a third order; they belong, as do the monks, to the monastery of their profession.

We said, in speaking of lay-brothers, that their history is closely connected in its origins with that of oblates; the same is true of the history of "recluses."

Here, too, something might be said about "monastic schools," which also were divided into internal and external schools. *Cf.* LÉON MAITRE, *Les Ecoles épiscopales et monastiques de l'Occident depuis Charlemagne jusqu'à Philippe-Auguste, 768-1180.*—CLERVAL, *Les Ecoles de Chartres au moyen âge.*—PORÉE, *Histoire de l'Abbaye du Bec*, t. I., chaps. iii. iv., vii., xv.

CHAPTER LX

OF PRIESTS WHO MAY WISH TO DWELL IN THE MONASTERY

DE SACERDOTIBUS, QUI VOLUERINT IN MONASTERIO HABITARE.—Si quis de ordine sacerdotum in monasterio se suscipi rogaverit, non quidem ei citius assentiatur: tamen si omnino perstiterit in hac petitione, sciat se omnem Regulæ disciplinam servaturum, nec aliquid ei relaxabitur, ut sit sicut scriptum est: *Amice, ad quid venisti?*

If anyone of the priestly order ask to be received into the monastery, let not assent be too quickly granted him; but if he persist strongly in this request, let him know that he must keep all the discipline of the Rule, and that nothing will be relaxed in his favour, to fulfil what is written: "Friend, whereto art thou come?"

IN early times, as we have already noted, monks belonged to the ranks of the laity. There were, however, in every monastery some priests and clerics; and to them our Holy Father devotes the whole of Chapter LXII., which completes the teaching of this chapter. So far from being mutually exclusive the two orders may be co-ordinated harmoniously and the two lives combined; monks become clerics and clerics embrace the monastic life, and this alliance of the two states honours the religious and sanctifies the priestly life; as St. Jerome says: "Monks and clerics, whose priesthood is adorned by their vows and vows by their priesthood."[1] For the moment St. Benedict is concerned only with the reception that shall be given to those of the priestly order who wish to be admitted, whether they be bishops, priests, deacons,[2] or lower clergy. (Our Holy Father distinguishes the two classes of clerics both in this chapter and at the end of the next.)

The monastic life is distinct from the priestly life in its end, its duties, and its graces. We shall not think of denying that the secular priest should work for his perfection: was it not said to him when the priestly dignity was conferred: "Realize what you do, imitate what you perform" (*Agnosce quod agis, imitare quod tractas*)? And to prove that the realization of perfection is no cloistral monopoly, we have only to recall here the example of the saintly Curé d'Ars. Nor shall we make the comparison, so famous and so often ill understood, between the state of acquired perfection, the episcopate, and the state of perfection yet to be acquired, the religious state. Nor do we dream of establishing any comparisons between persons. We deal with the theology of the matter. Now it is certain that the religious life is the perfect life organized, secured by the practice of counsels and vows, and that the priest himself enters it without losing status. It is incontestable also that the Church is solicitous to maintain and safeguard the sacred right of all clerics to enter, should they wish, an active or contemplative Order. Bishops,

---

[1] S. HIERON., *Epist.* LII. *ad Nepot.*, 5. *P.L.*, XXII., 532.
[2] We may regard deacons as forming part of this order (HILDEMAR, *in h. l.*).

because of the spiritual bond which binds them to their church, require the permission of the Sovereign Pontiff in order to become religious. As to clerics in sacred orders, Canon Law requires them only to give respectful notice to their ordinary, and to make arrangements with him so that souls may not suffer thereby and be left without a pastor.[1] Even when there is a shortage of priests, bishops have too much of the supernatural spirit and too deep a sense of the Communion of Saints not to favour religious vocations.

If it be always permissible for a cleric, one who is already " converted to the clerical state," as ancient Councils express it, to seek admittance into a monastery for a new and more complete " conversion ": it is also allowable for the monastery not to be too ready or in too great a hurry to receive him: " Let not assent be too quickly granted him." Care must be taken therefore not to forestall him, and not to yield save to long and urgent importunity: " If he persist strongly in this request." Without permitting ourselves to be dazzled by the honour or advantage that such vocations may bring to the monastery, it is prudent to test them exactly as any others—more than others, says Hildemar. And the same commentator adds, with Paul the Deacon, that a priest had to pass through the same stages as a layman, including even the humiliating wait at the door. But our Holy Father—so careful of the honour due to a priest—could not intend to submit him to the annoyances and insults which usually preceded admittance.[2]

The fears of the Holy Rule are still justifiable. In the seminary, when men are being prepared for the functions and duties of the priestly life, constant stress is laid on the incomparable dignity of the priesthood. The priest stands in a special relation to the virginal motherhood of Our Lady; the fact that he holds authority and jurisdiction over Our Lord's Person exalts him above kings and even above angels; and this teaching is accurate. But we also know well that when supernatural dignity is conferred on us, we are singularly ready to stress the grandeur and privilege, and not the responsibility and obligation. Nuns are never at a loss for words in which to proclaim themselves the spouses of Jesus Christ; yet it would be rash to say that they always do the will of their Spouse. A too exclusive sense of our personal dignity is a poor disposition for a life characterized by humility and obedience.

Moreover, a priest, especially if he be somewhat advanced in years, comes with a soul already formed, with a clear-cut character, with habits, or even a fixed system of thought. In such circumstances it is difficult for him to be freely and calmly accessible to ideas and practices which are far from familiar to him, and may seem unsuitable, if not incorrect.

---

[1] The reader is referred to the canonists: PIATUS MONTENSIS, O.M.C., *Prælectiones juris regularis;* VERMEERSCH, S.J., *De religiosis;* and especially the solid dissertation of Père NILLES, S.J., in his *Selectæ disputationes academicæ juris ecclesiastici.*

[2] *Cum autem clericus aliquis ad virum sanctum ut monachis adscriberetur accedebat, ordini quidem ejus deferebatur reverentia, quemadmodum divina nobis lex præscribit; quantum vero ad observantiam canonis fratres obligantis attinet, præstabat illam talis æque ac ceteri* (*Vita S. Pachomii,* c. iii. *Acta SS.,* Maii, t. III., p. 303).

Inclination of a very human sort will make him critical; and it will seem, granted his experience, that he has entered only to correct his brethren and reform the abbey. A secular priest is so placed that he must hold himself aloof from the world and preserve an attitude of defence; but in the monastic life no grosser fault can be committed than to be on one's guard. Whoever purposes to become a monk must consent to that complete reformation of the self which implies the effacement of our own will. Long exercise of authority, though quite lawful and supernatural authority, may have made a priest, despite himself, something of a " boss " and director; or the habit of an easy life, without constraint or intellectual occupation, may have softened his character. Yet, to succeed, one side of our heart must have remained naïve, simple, and affectionate; we must rediscover something of youthfulness and joyous courage.

But, after all, if the candidate is not of the stamp of those we have just described, or if his goodwill is such that he has a chance of success, it is not imprudent to receive him. Nevertheless St. Benedict says nothing of this reception, but observes immediately that the priest should know well that if he enters he will be bound to keep all the discipline of the Rule, without any relaxation being made in his favour He must meditate on the words of the Gospel: " Friend, whereto art thou come ?" Was it not to sanctify yourself and to obey ? The words occur in St. Matthew (xxvi. 50), and were addressed to Judas; but we are free to think that St. Benedict used the quotation apart from its context. The Fathers of the Desert used an equivalent formula when they wished to remind themselves of the realities of their vocation: St. Arsenius often asked himself: " Why did you leave the world ?" (*Propter quid existi ?*).[1] So St. Bernard, to whom this sentence is generally attributed, did no more than imitate the ancients.[2]

| Concedatur ei tamen post Abbatem stare, et benedicere, aut Missam tenere, si tamen jusserit ei Abbas. Sin alias, nullatenus aliqua præsumat, sciens se disciplinæ regulari subditum, et magis humilitatis exempla omnibus det. | Nevertheless, let it be granted him to stand after the Abbot, to give the blessing, and to say Mass, if so be that the Abbot bid him do so. Otherwise, let him presume to do nothing, knowing that he is subject to the discipline of the Rule; but rather let him give an example of humility to all. |

The integrity of the monastic life having been safeguarded by the measures which precede, St. Benedict now puts forward others which do honour to the priesthood; yet all is left to the judgement of the Abbot. He may give a priest (and probably St. Benedict means as soon as he enters) a higher position: " after the Abbot," perhaps even before the Prior and the deans of the monastery, if these be not priests; if there

---

[1] *Verba Seniorum: Vitæ Patrum*, V., xv., 9. ROSWEYD, p. 621.—ST. JOHN CLIMACUS also quotes the sentence *Amice, ad quid venisti ?* which a monk tempted with instability should say to himself (*Scala*, gradus iv. *P.G.*, LXXXVIII., 724).
[2] *Vita*, l. I., c. iv. *P.L.*, CLXXXV., 238.

are other older priests, the newcomer evidently takes his rank according to his age in the habit. " To give the blessing " (*benedicere*) means to give the regular blessings in the course of the office (or in the refectory for the meals and reading). *Missam* (or *Missas*) *tenere* means to celebrate Mass; according to Calmet, who has quite a little dissertation on this subject, it might also mean " to preside in choir or to recite the last Collect." In all else priests followed the régime of their brother novices: for without doubt they were not dispensed from the regular novitiate; and it should be noted that St. Benedict mentions only liturgical precedence. According to later monastic customs, when priests were also more numerous, priest novices were sometimes reduced to the position of laymen; when they were allowed, after profession, the privilege of saying Mass, it was not without a strict examination beforehand.

When the Abbot does not think fit, says St. Benedict, to sanction these exceptions, the priest must abide in the ranks, without attempting to exercise his sacred functions. He must remember that he is subject to the ordinary law; he who has so often, in the sacrifice of the altar, been face to face with the humility of God Himself, must possess the privilege of his priesthood in humility. It is a well-known fact that those who receive grace well, receive it after such a fashion that it emphasizes their nothingness. Every favour from God surprises them. When her divine motherhood raised Our Lady above all creatures, then did she recognize herself as nothing but the handmaid of the Lord. So everyone expects from priests an example of humility, rather than the sad spectacle of a ridiculous self-importance.

| Si forte ordinationis aut alicujus rei causa fuerit in monasterio, illum locum attendat, quando ingressus est in monasterium, non illum qui ei pro reverentia sacerdotii concessus est. | If there chance to be a question of an appointment, or other matter, in the monastery, let him expect the position due to him according to the time of his entrance, and not that which was granted to him out of reverence for the priesthood. |

This passage is somewhat puzzling and has been very variously interpreted. It may be understood in this way: if an important office in the monastery falls vacant, if there be question, for instance, of appointing or ordaining (in St. Benedict's use of the word) the Abbot, or Prior, the priest must not imagine that the position will come to him of right. Likewise, if any other important decision has to be taken in the monastery, or if Chapter deliberates upon a point proposed by the Abbot, the priest must not think himself indispensable, nor give his advice in a tone of authority, on the plea that he is better educated and more experienced than the others. St. Benedict stills these natural movements with a word: the priest must regard as his the rank which he would occupy according to the date of his entrance, and not the rank which the Abbot has freely granted him out of respect for his priesthood,

Of Priests who may wish to Dwell in the Monastery

and which he may always withdraw. Apart from such special arrangement he must keep the rank of monastic seniority. Our Holy Father repeats this almost in the same terms in Chapter LXII.: " Let him always keep the place due to him according to his entrance into the monastery, except with regard to the duties of the altar, and unless the choice of the community and the will of the Abbot should promote him for the merit of his life." The counsel has not lost its seasonableness: may we not say that to keep the rank of one's profession is almost a general rule of the spiritual life ? Throughout the whole course of our life, whatever may be the distinctions that come to us, we should put ourselves, before God, back into the place that is ours of right and which we know well: the last place, the place of nothingness.

Clericorum autem si quis eodem desiderio monasterio sociari voluerit, loco mediocri collocetur, et ipsum tamen, si promittit de observatione Regulæ, vel propria stabilitate.	If any cleric should desire in the same way to be admitted into the monastery, let him be placed in a middle rank: but this too only if he promise observance of the Rule and his own stability.

All that has just been said about priests applies, in due proportion, to other clerics. The Abbot may give them a middle rank—that is, one less exalted than that given to priests and in keeping with their ecclesiastical status. But St. Benedict again observes that the reception of clerics, as of priests, is conditional on their promise to observe the Rule and (*vel*) to be stable. We need not necessarily take this last sentence according to the too literal interpretation of Bernard of Monte Cassino; according to him, St. Benedict meant that a special place was granted to clerics only after their formal profession.

CHAPTER LXI

OF PILGRIM MONKS, HOW THEY ARE TO BE RECEIVED

DE MONACHIS PEREGRINIS, QUALITER SUSCIPIANTUR.—Si quis monachus peregrinus de longinquis provinciis supervenerit, si pro hospite voluerit habitare in monasterio, et contentus fuerit consuetudine loci quam invenerit, et non forte superfluitate sua perturbat monasterium, sed simpliciter contentus est quod invenerit, suscipiatur quanto tempore cupit.

If any pilgrim monk come from distant parts, and desire to dwell in the monastery as a guest, and if he be content with the custom of the place as he finds it, and do not trouble the monastery by any unreasonable wants, but be content simply with what he finds, let him be received for as long a time as he will.

HERE we have a new method of recruitment. To get the real meaning of this chapter we should remember what was the condition of religious in the West in our Holy Father's time. The monastic order, taken in its entirety, still resembled a nebula, unresolved and undifferentiated. There were monks, monasteries, and monastic customs, but no Congregation, such as Cluny formed later; no single rule governing many houses;[1] often, even, no other rule in a monastery than the will of the Abbot: it was thus that St. Romanus lived, as St. Gregory tells us, " under the rule of Abbot Deodatus." Even in the East, where true federations of monasteries with written rules had long existed, the religious life kept a somewhat private character, less strict and less official than that of later ages. A wide door was left open to instability: having obtained the blessing of his Abbot, a monk might freely set out on a long pilgrimage to some sanctuary, or monastic centre, to meet with holy folk; and it was open to him to settle there where the life suited his fervour or his laxity. The author of the *Monastic Constitutions* protests, if not against instability, at least against its abuses.[2]

The gyrovague and the sarabaite realized fully the ideal of instability. Probably it is not with them that our Holy Father deals in this chapter. They were people easily to be recognized and they were incorrigible; St. Benedict, on the very threshold of his Rule, draws their portrait in such indignant terms that the pilgrim monk (*monachus peregrinus*) whom he here receives with open arms cannot be a gyrovague by profession. Those he speaks of are monks coming " from distant parts ": not that the regulations which follow have only such in view and exclude religious coming from nearer monasteries; but because St. Benedict reserves to the end of the chapter his special reference to these, along with the counsel concerning them.

We do not think that the words of the text " as a guest " and, farther on, " during the time he was a guest " must be taken literally.

---

[1] *Cf.* CASS., *Inst.*, II., ii.   [2] Cap. vii. and viii. *P.G.*, XXXI., 1365–1370.

Of Pilgrim Monks, how they are to be Received

There is no reference whatever to the guest-house; on the contrary, St. Benedict says that the pilgrim is received "in the monastery," which seems decisive. Moreover, all the details which follow show clearly that the traveller was admitted into the intimate life of the monastery, where he could observe and be observed; and this was even indispensable if our Holy Father was to pursue prudently his merciful design of admitting him among those who were stable. We read in the Life of St. Benedict[1] that the monks of Abbot Servandus slept, when at Monte Cassino, in the same dwelling as the brethren. St. Pachomius, after having begun by allowing pilgrim monks into his community, changed his policy in order to prevent disorders.[2]

St. Benedict only requires of the monk thus received that he conform to the conditions of the new life to which God has led him: as regards the hour of rising, food, and work, he is treated as a brother but on condition that he acts amiably and simply, like a brother. If the pilgrim showed a desire for exceptional treatment and made unreasonable requests (*superfluitate sua*), he ceased to be anything but a nuisance: and St. Benedict tells us farther on how to behave towards him. But if he was reasonable and accommodating, he could be received into the monastery for as long a period as he wished.[3]

Si quæ tamen rationabiliter et cum humilitate caritatis reprehendit aut ostendit, tractet Abbas prudenter, ne forte eum propter hoc ipsum Dominus direxerit.	If, however, he censures or points out anything reasonably and with the humility of charity, let the Abbot treat the matter prudently, lest perchance God have sent him for this very end.

Here assuredly is one of those passages wherein is reflected most clearly the humble and discreet spirit of our Holy Father, his intellectual docility. One may be very holy and very clever, and yet have something to learn from others. Moses was certainly more elevated in grace and more gifted than Jethro; yet he received good counsel from him (Ex. xviii. 13 *sq.*)[4] and our souls should be all the more open to the ideas of others, the more we cease to be observant of the details of our own life. Those who come from outside, who have had other experience and do not bear our familiar yoke of custom, are more apt to discern our shortcomings.

But these criticisms to deserve a hearing must, says St. Benedict, be reasonable—*i.e.*, objectively justified—and courteous, without arrogance or excess. *Cum humilitate caritatis:* for it is under these forms that we are most likely to meet the Spirit of God. *Reprehendit* implies formal blame, the warning that a mode of action is unsuitable; *ostendit* implies a prudent suggestion that the superior should enquire into some matter or act in such and such a way. A discreet man will naturally

---

[1] S. Greg. M., *Dial.*, l. II., c. xxxv.
[2] *Vita S. Pachom., Acta SS.*, Maii, t. III., p. 307.
[3] It would seem that St. Benedict was much influenced by interrogation lxxxvii. (*Reg. contr.*) of St. Basil: *Concedi quidem ei convenit ingressum. . . . Interdum enim potest fieri, ut per tempus proficiat et delectetur sanctitate vitæ et permaneat in cœptis.*
[4] S. Aug., *De doctrina christ.*, præf., 7. *P.L.*, XXXIV., 18.

make such communications as these to the Abbot, and not to those who have not the authority necessary for correction or control. The Abbot must study the matter prudently and without prejudice; for it may be God Himself that has come in the guise of this pilgrim monk, so often does He hide in guests.

Si vero postea voluerit stabilitatem suam firmare, non renuatur talis voluntas, et maxime, quia tempore hospitalitatis potuit ejus vita dignosci. Quod si superfluus aut vitiosus inventus fuerit tempore hospitalitatis, non solum non debet sociari corpori monasterii,[1] verum etiam dicatur ei honeste ut discedat, ne ejus miseria etiam alii vitientur.

But if afterwards he wish to confirm his stability, let not such a purpose be denied, and especially since his manner of life could be well ascertained during the time he was a guest. But if, during that time, he was found exorbitant or prone to vice, not only should he not be admitted as a member of the community, but he should even be told courteously to depart, lest others should be corrupted by his wretchedness.

We may combine the first sentence of this section with the next extract and keep our commentary on it for that place.

His sojourn inside the monastery has given opportunity of ascertaining the traveller's dispositions. Just in proportion to the liberty allowed him of mingling with the brethren has his true temperament been disclosed. If he be exacting, hard to please, and always anxious to be somewhere else, then it is easy to foresee that as soon as he is affiliated to the monastery—if this be granted to him—he will repent of having vowed stability. Or he may be prone to vice: he may have not merely failings—who is without them?—but rooted habits, the obstinate nature of which would be burdensome to the community and dangerous for weak souls. A man often exercises an influence out of proportion to his moral worth; and it is their failings that men most readily communicate to others. The Abbot should then see that consideration for the general good prevails; he may not, in the hope of a very problematical cure, expose his subjects to real dangers. Therefore, when the stranger has exhausted our patience, he must be asked "courteously" to depart. St. Benedict would not have us use discourteous or rough methods towards him.

Quod si non fuerit talis qui mereatur projici, non solum si petierit suscipiatur congregationi sociandus, verum etiam suadeatur ut stet, ut ejus exemplo alii erudiantur, et quia in omni loco uni Domino servitur, et uni Regi militatur.

If, however, he is not such as to deserve to be cast forth, let him not merely on his own asking be received as a member of the community, but even be persuaded to stay, that others may be taught by his example, and because in every place we serve one Lord and fight under one King.

If, after having tried the rule of the monastery (see the previous extract), he shows a fixed determination to end his wanderings and asks

---

[1] A verbal reminiscence of ST. BASIL: . . . *Quem sociari voluerint corpori congregationis* (*Reg. contr.*, cxcii.).

Of Pilgrim Monks, how they are to be Received

for stability, such a purpose should not be opposed but considered: since, in St. Benedict's opinion, stability is for a monk the best of good things and the surest guarantee of spiritual progress. That he should ask for stability is already an excellent sign. And St. Benedict urges this course the more, because from the conduct of this monk while *de facto* a member of the community, it will be easy to estimate whether he deserves to belong to it by right.

But he goes farther. Supposing a good monk does not venture to ask, or does not give the matter a thought: he may be sweetly invited to remain. We should remember, in order to understand why our Holy Father inclines somewhat to commendation of his own monastery, that true stability existed nowhere else; that outside the Benedictine life there was as yet no solid bond between religious and their monastery; and that finally, in the particular case before us, the monk has already left his own. If he be virtuous, if he give promise, why should one not make advances? His monastery does not suffer, since he has left it and perhaps without promise of return; the monk gains by it, since he enters a life made more perfect by stability; the Benedictine monastery also gains, since it is increased by a good member in contact with whom the others will profit.[1] It will be pointed out to him that after all it is not contrary to his profession to stay there, since in every place we serve one and the same Lord and fight under the same King; he has not to change his master but to " fix " himself in surroundings where he will serve Him better.[2] We must be careful not to interpret these words in a sense hostile to stability: assuredly St. Benedict had no intention of saying that change was an indifferent matter. On the contrary, the remark is given as a motive for remaining.

A monk who decided to remain did not make a new novitiate, since monastic life was then one, and the question of the monastery accidental. Nor had he to make a new profession; he had only to promise stability. Paul the Deacon and Hildemar have preserved for us the form used in their day. The multiplication of religious Orders has introduced modifications of discipline on this point. Passage from one Order to another involves the repetition of novitiate and profession. And in the majority of cases the sanction of the Holy See is necessary.

Quem etiam si talem esse perspexerit Abbas, liceat eum in superiore aliquantulum constituere loco. Non solum autem monachum, sed etiam de supradictis gradibus sacerdotum vel	And if the Abbot perceive him to be a man of this kind, he may put him in a somewhat higher place. Not only a monk, but also any of the aforesaid priests or clerics, may be put

---

[1] We are led to translate thus by the symmetry between the two parts of the sentence: *ne ejus miseria etiam alii vitientur* and *ut ejus exemplo alii erudiantur*. Or else St. Benedict means that this achieving of stability is a lesson and an invitation to other wandering monks.

[2] Or, more simply, and without answering a tacit objection, he is told that there is no need for him to go seek the monastic life elsewhere, since he finds it just here, within his grasp.

clericorum, stabilire potest Abbas in majori quam ingreditur loco, si ejus talem prospexerit esse vitam.	by the Abbot in a higher place than according to the time of their entrance, if he sees that their lives are such [as we have said].

When the Abbot considers that the virtues of the newcomer justify an exception to the common rule and are such (this is St. Benedict's meaning) as we have said, he may, if he wish, raise him somewhat (*aliquantulum*) above the rank due to him by his entrance into the monastery.[1] The same shall hold for the priests and clerics spoken of a short while back. By this recommendation, the equivalent of which we find in Chapters LX., LXII., and LXIII., St. Benedict wished to reserve this power to the Abbot and to cut short all protestation and surprise, of a too natural sort, which might arise in the community: " These last have worked but one hour, and thou hast made them equal to us, who have borne the burden of the day and the heats " (Matt. xx. 12). However, this power of the Abbot is not arbitrarily exercised, and St. Benedict twice says that the precedence granted must be justified by a meritorious life.

Caveat autem Abbas, ne aliquando de alio noto monasterio monachum ad habitandum suscipiat, sine consensu Abbatis ejus, aut litteris commendatitiis: quia scriptum est: *Quod tibi non vis fieri, alteri ne feceris.*	But let the Abbot take care never to receive permanently a monk from any known monastery without his own Abbot's consent, and letters of recommendation; because it is written: " What thou wouldst not have done to thyself, do not thou to another."

Since the beginning of the chapter St. Benedict has been speaking about monks arriving from distant parts—from the East, it may be. In most cases of this kind the monastery which received him was forced to trust to the good faith of the visitor and to the impression which he gave of his character and habits; more than this could not often be asked from him. But St. Benedict is more exacting when it is a question of a monk coming from a neighbouring and known monastery. Since there was acquaintance, identity of language, and some intercourse, the respective Abbots could act in concert.

Such action was, in the first place, mere prudence on the part of the receiving Abbot. How had the monk come to leave his monastery? Was he a runaway, or had he the consent of his Abbot? St. Benedict was not a man to enrich himself by the loss of another, or even with his rejected subjects. It was also courteous and charitable; and St. Benedict bids the Abbot ask himself what he would think if a neighbour stole his monks: " What thou wouldst not have done to thyself, do not thou to another."[2] Finally, it was in obedience to monastic usage and to certain

---

[1] The first *Rule* of the HOLY FATHERS was more severe: *Ille vero monachus quantos fratres in alio monasterio invenerit, tantos se noverit habere priores. Nec attendendum est qui fuit antea, sed probandum est qualis esse cœperit* (xiii.).

[2] Read again the ninth instrument of good works and the end of Chapter LXX.

conciliar decrees of the period.[1] A pilgrim monk, therefore, shall not be received, unless it be established, by testimony which he bears, or by a letter addressed to the Abbot directly, or by some other method, that his superior has given him his *exeat*. Failing this special consent and formal attestation, *sine consensu Abbatis ejus*, the traveller must at least exhibit general letters of recommendation (*aut litteris commendatitiis*).[2] These documents—of which we have already said something in the chapter on guests—were drawn up sometimes under the form of letters from one Abbot to another, sometimes under a more general form, recommending to all ecclesiastical or monastic authorities a monk who had gone forth in regular fashion from his monastery, on a voyage of discovery, free to choose his new religious home.[3]

[1] The first *Rule* of the HOLY FATHERS said: *Nec tacendum est qualiter inter se monasteria pacem firmam obtineant. Non licebit de alio monasterio, sine voluntate ejus qui præest Patris, fratres recipere. Sed nec videre oportet, dicente Apostolo: quia qui primam fidem irritam fecit est infideli deterior.* (Note this witness in favour of stability, before St. Benedict.) *Quod si precatus fuerit ab eo qui præest Patre ut in alio monasterio ingrediatur, commendetur ab eo ei qui præest ubi esse desiderat, et sic suscipiatur*, etc. (xiii.). —The Council of Agde in 506 decreed: *Monachum nisi Abbatis sui aut permissu aut voluntate ad alterum monasterium commigrantem, nullus Abbas aut suscipere aut retinere præsumat* (Can. xxvii. MANSI, t. VIII., col. 329. See also the Council of Orleans of 511, Can. xix. MANSI, t. VIII., cols. 354–355).

[2] The Council of Agde of 506 forbids monks, as well as clerics, to travel without these Letters (Can. xxxviii. MANSI, t. VIII., col. 331).

[3] MARTÈNE cites several examples of these two sorts of letters, in his Commentary on this chapter. *Cf.* S. DESIDERII CADURCENSIS (+ 654 or 655), *Epist.* II. and IX. *P.L.*, LXXXVII., 249, 253.

CHAPTER LXII

OF THE PRIESTS OF THE MONASTERY

LET us not forget that the purpose of all this portion of the holy Rule is to describe the recruitment of the monastery, its composition, its internal good order, and the hierarchical organization which shall guarantee its peace. The commentary of this chapter should be connected with that on Chapter LX.

St. Epiphanius, enumerating the degrees of the Christian hierarchy, reserves the lowest for the married state; next comes widowhood consecrated to God; then the monastic life and virginity; and finally, as the crown of all and the source of all sanctity, the priesthood, recruited from among virgins—*i.e.*, monks and the chaste.[1] In the view of the author of the *Ecclesiastical Hierarchy* monks are perfect Christians; consequently they have their position at the summit of the passive part of the hierarchy, comprising purified, illuminated, and perfect souls; but they are quite distinct from the active part, which comprises those who purify, deacons; those who illuminate, priests; and those who complete and perfect, bishops. Yet there is no incompatibility, as we observed in the sixtieth chapter, between the priesthood and the monastic profession; quite the contrary, as says St. Denis, for " monks should form their lives on those of priests, with whom they have many points of affinity, and to whom they are nearer than are the members of the other degrees."[2] And those are more apt for priestly functions, who have been prepared for them by a holier life. Therefore the Church often, from the earliest times, entrusted monks with certain pastoral duties and even with the administration of dioceses. St. Athanasius made Egyptian solitaries bishops; St. Martin, St. Augustine, St. Eusebius of Vercellæ and others, themselves monks, recruited their clergy from among monks, or raised their clerics to the monastic life; Pope St. Siricius in his letter to Himerius of Tarragona (A.D. 385)[3] expresses his desire that exemplary monks should receive sacred Orders; St. Augustine of Canterbury and his brethren evangelized England. We have to speak at present only of monks ordained with a view to the spiritual interests of the community.[4]

The earliest ascetics attended the churches of their district. Anchorites most often regarded themselves as dispensed, and we know how our Holy Father, in his solitude at Subiaco, learnt that " it was Easter." To get a secular priest to come to the monastery to celebrate the holy mysteries and administer the sacraments was a method in use in some religious families, with St. Pachomius especially. But it was simpler

---

[1] *Adv. Hæreses*, l. III., t. ii.: *Expositio fidei*, xxi. P.G., XLII., 824–825.
[2] *De hierarch. eccles.*, c. vi.   [3] Cap. xiii. P.L., XIII., 1144.
[4] *Cf.*, with the Commentaries, HÆFTEN, l. III., tract. vii.

to supply your own needs and to institute a monastic clergy; which custom prevailed early both in East and West. So every monastery had its clerics, very few in number, as we said in Chapter LX.; sometimes a single priest sufficed, all the more that Mass was not celebrated every day. According to Palladius, in the monastery of Abbot Isidore, containing a thousand monks, the doorkeeper and two others of the brethren were priests.[1] The Abbot himself had not always this dignity, and it is conjectured that our Holy Father received only the diaconate.[2] In the ninth century Church discipline required the Abbot to be a priest (Council of Rome, A.D. 826):[3] and nothing could be more natural, especially when many ordinary religious had the honour of the priesthood. In the list of the monks of Saint-Denys, about the year 838, out of 123 monks, one is a bishop, 33 are priests, 17 deacons, 24 subdeacons and 7 acolytes.[4]

To assist the priests in their duties, they were given deacons, and St. Benedict speaks of the ordination " of a priest or a deacon." Why does he say nothing of the lower clergy ? Perhaps because simple monks could easily fulfil the liturgical functions reserved for these ministers in secular churches. Historians, such as Thomassin and Mabillon,[5] even think that monastic profession was often equivalent to the subdiaconate and took its place. But if such a custom did really exist for a time, it was neither general nor permanent; it is recorded, for instance, in the Life of St. Wandrille that St. Ouen conferred the subdiaconate on him.[6] St. Aurelian says in his Rule for monks:[7] " Let none receive the honour of the priesthood or diaconate except the Abbot wish a priest to be ordained, and a deacon and subdeacon. Let him have the power of ordaining (presenting ?) for these offices whomsoever he wishes and when he wishes." St. Benedict never dreamt of promoting his disciples to the episcopate. It was only much later that certain monasteries took care to have a bishop to ordain in the monastery; at one time this was the Abbot, as at Lobbes in Belgium or at St. Martin's of Tours, at another it was a simple monk, as sometimes happened at Saint-Denys.[8]

According to present-day discipline it is forbidden to receive as choir monks those who do not possess the qualifications requisite for sacred Orders. Pope Clement V. introduced this innovation in the Fifteenth Council at Vienne (A.D. 1311)[9] decreeing: " That all monks, there being

---

[1] *Hist. Laus.*, c. lxxi. (*Vitæ Patrum*, VIII. ROSWEYD, p. 759).
[2] Read the full dissertation of HÆFTEN, *Prolegom.*, xviii., pp. 33–35.—D. L'HUILLIER, *Le Patriarche S. Benoît*, pp. 267–270.
[3] Can. xxvii. MANSI, *ad ann.*, 853, t. XIV., col. 1007.
[4] LUC D'ACHERY, *Spicileg.*, t. IV., p. 229.
[5] THOMASSIN, *Ancienne et nouvelle discipline de l'Eglise*, P. II., l. I., chap. lxxxv. T. II., col. 547.—MABILLON, *Annales O.S.B.*, l. X., xx. T. I., p. 252.
[6] MABILLON, *Acta SS. O.S.B.*, Sæc. II., p. 507.
[7] Cap. xlvi.
[8] ARNOLD WION, in his *Lignum vitæ*, has essayed to draw up a list of monk-bishops.
[9] From the *Corpus juris:* Clement., l. III., t. X., c. i., *Ne in agro*.

no lawful excuse, should at the bidding of their Abbot have themselves promoted to all the sacred Orders "; and this, he said, was for the " amplification of divine worship ": a choir of priests and clerics offering God a more perfect praise than a choir of simple religious. The decree *Cum ad regularem* of Clement VIII. (March 19, 1603) laid further stress on the point. Canon Law permits only religious who have made their solemn vows to proceed to the major Orders.

DE SACERDOTIBUS MONASTERII.—
Si quis Abbas sibi presbyterum, vel diaconum ordinare petierit, de suis eligat qui dignus sit sacerdotio fungi.

If any Abbot seek to have a priest or deacon ordained for himself, let him choose from among his monks one who is worthy to fulfil the priestly office.

When the Abbot has need of a priest or a deacon for the service of his monastery (*sibi*), and when the method of recruitment provided in Chapter LX. is not applied or remains inadequate, he shall choose among his monks one who is worthy to fulfil the sacred duties (*sacerdotium* is here used by St. Benedict in a wide sense, as the words *de ordine sacerdotum* before); and he shall ask for his ordination—that is, present him for ordination. Quite a number of interesting conclusions may be drawn from these words.

And first: in our Holy Father's time not the local bishop, but the Abbot chose and presented. The point is of importance for the history of monastic exemption. When it was a matter of ordaining a monk for the external ministry and the service of the diocese, the bishop designated him at his pleasure; at the same time, Councils, such as that of Agde (A.D. 506),[1] remind him that he should ask the consent of the Abbot. Neither was it the community or the seniors who chose the candidates, as at Scete, though they were probably consulted.[2] Nor again was it the monk's business to ask for or presumptuously desire the honour and burden of the priesthood. On this point the fourteenth and fifteenth chapters of the eleventh book of Cassian's *Institutes* should be read. Still less does it become a religious to seek to avoid sacred Orders and to elude them by improper methods, as, for example, by cutting off an ear, as did the three fervent monks in the *Paradise of the Fathers*.[3] Cassian noted that such humility might very well be nothing but a variety of pride.[4] Everyone should put himself at the disposal of God and his Abbot.[5] St. Athanasius endeavoured to convince his friend, the monk Dracontius, that the episcopate does not

---

[1] Can. xxvii. MANSI, t. VIII., col. 329.
[2] *Verba Seniorum: Vitæ Patrum*, III., 22. ROSWEYD, pp. 499–500. *Cf.* MARTÈNE, *Comment. in h. l.*, p. 815.
[3] *P.G.*, LXV., 456.
[4] *Conlat.*, IV., xx.
[5] The ideal would be to make one's own principle of John of Lycopolis: *Neque fugiendum omnimodis dicimus clericatum vel sacerdotium, neque rursus omnimodis expetendum, sed danda opera est, ut vitia quidem a nobis depellantur, et virtutes animæ conquirantur. Dei autem judicio relinquendum est, quem velit, et si velit assumere sibi ad ministerium vel ad sacerdotium* (RUFIN., *Hist. monach.*, c. i. ROSWEYD, pp. 452–453).

necessarily constitute a state of perdition for a monk.[1] However, our Holy Father is careful to remind the monk ordained how he should behave in the community.

Ordinatus autem caveat elationem aut superbiam; nec quicquam præsumat, nisi quod ei ab Abbate præcipitur, sciens se multo magis disciplinæ regulari subditum. Nec occasione sacerdotii obliviscatur regulæ obedientiam et disciplinam, sed magis ac magis in Domino proficiat.	Let him that is ordained beware of arrogance and pride, and presume to do nothing that is not commanded him by the Abbot, knowing that he is now all the more subject to regular discipline. Let him not take occasion of his priesthood to forget the obedience and discipline of the Rule, but advance ever more and more in the Lord.

The special position occupied by a priest in an ancient monastery created dangers for the individual which St. Benedict enumerates. There was danger of vanity and of pride; danger of negligence or disobedience to the ordinances of Rule or Abbot, the priest imagining that he had a right to exceptional treatment, that he could do as he liked about such and such a monastic custom; danger of insubordination, because he sought to put himself forward in certain circumstances and laid claim to certain powers of initiative: *nec quidquam præsumat. . . .* It were a sad thing to take advantage of the priesthood in order to satisfy the petty designs of self-love. Such action would show a fundamental misunderstanding of the supernatural economy. "Noblesse oblige": the very fact that he is a priest binds a man to be a better monk; he must regard himself as subject to the regular discipline in a much greater degree than the rest.[2] The special law of his life is advancement, a continuous progress toward that example of obedience and humility which Our Lord gives him at the altar: *Sed magis ac magis in Domino proficiat.*[3]

Locum vero illum semper attendat, quo ingressus est monasterium, præter officium altaris, et si forte electio congregationis et voluntas Abbatis pro vitæ merito eum promovere voluerit: qui tamen regulam a decanis vel præpositis constitutam sibi servandam sciat; quod si aliter præsumpserit, non ut sacerdos, sed ut rebellis judicetur. Et sæpe admonitus si non correxerit, etiam episcopus adhibeatur in testimonium. Quod si nec sic emendaverit, clarescentibus culpis, projiciatur de	Let him always keep the place due to him according to his entrance into the monastery, except with regard to the duties of the altar, or unless the choice of the community and the will of the Abbot should wish to promote him for the merit of his life. Nevertheless, let him know that he must keep the rule given to him by the deans and priors. Should he presume to do otherwise he must be considered not as a priest, but as a rebel; and if after frequent admonition he do not

[1] *P.G.*, XXV., 531–534.
[2] Including the rod, if he deserves it, as Paul the Deacon and Hildemar note with some insistence. The true reading is probably *subdendum*.
[3] At the end of the *Sermo asceticus de renuntiatione sæculi*, inserted among the works of St. Basil, we read these words, which are in accord with those of our Holy Father: *Ne efferat te cleri gradus sed potius humiliet. Nam animæ profectus humilitatis profectus est. . . . Quanto ad majores sacerdotii gradus appropinquare te contigerit, tantum humilia teipsum . . .* (*P.G.*, XXXI., 647).

monasterio; si tamen talis fuerit ejus contumacia, ut subdi aut obedire regulæ nolit.

amend, let even the bishop be brought in as a witness. If even then he do not amend, and his guilt is manifest, let him be cast forth from the monastery; only, however, if his contumacy be such that he will not submit or obey the Rule.

We have already seen this advice addressed to all and especially to priests, that they should always keep to the order of their profession and seniority; exception is made only for priests or clerics who exercise sacred duties, and for those who receive a privileged rank on account of the merit of their lives. We have seen further that this precedence was in practice the ordinary lot of good priests, at least in liturgical functions, as soon as the Abbot granted it, whether on his own initiative, or, adds St. Benedict, at the suggestion of the community, as sometimes happened with the Prior. Some commentators think, in our opinion wrongly, that St. Benedict only alludes to their being chosen for the office of dean or Prior; in which case he says that a priest will not be dispensed from observing the rules laid down " for " deans and the Prior. It is true that the most authoritative manuscripts have not got the preposition *a* (by) before *decanis* (deans), a fact which would incline us to translate " for the deans." But even with this reading we may translate " by the deans." And it is certainly the more natural sense: a priest, though put above certain deans or above the Prior,[1] must accept and fulfil faithfully the orders of all his monastic superiors.

If, despite all these warnings of the Rule, a priest is insubordinate, measures will have to be taken against him. *Non ut sacerdos, sed ut rebellis judicetur.* He has two characters: henceforth we shall cease to honour his priesthood, which by his unworthy conduct he would seem to wish us to forget, and we shall regard him now as nothing but a rebel monk. As such shall he be treated. Some commentators give the word *judicetur* its formal signification of trial, legal process, and condemnation, an interpretation which scarcely alters the general sense of the passage. Whatever translation is adopted, and especially if the second is preferred: " He must be judged, not as a priest, but as a rebel," we may recognize in the logical distinction made by our Holy Father with regard to the person of the offender, a mark of his spirit of faith and of his respect for the priestly character. He would put the priesthood out of the case and not think of degrading it; the sole purpose of his action is to suppress rebellion. Moreover, the unruly priest is treated with consideration and tact. Numerous representations and loving exhortations shall be addressed to him, and there shall be much patience. St. Benedict does not add that he shall, if necessary, suffer corporal punishment and excommunication, which were the degrees of the regular discipline, and were inflicted even on the Prior if he proved incorrigible. Hildemar tells us that in his time, in French monasteries, disobedient priests were

[1] Some manuscripts have the singular *præposito.*—*Promovere* has the same sense as *prætulerit* in the next chapter.

flogged like ordinary monks, but that in Italy they were taken to the bishop, who judged and degraded them, if there were cause: after which the Abbot could chastise them.

This recourse to the bishop is put forward by our Holy Father as an extreme measure: "even the bishop" are his words. It would be difficult to prove by means of this "even" alone that recourse to episcopal authority was not obligatory; however, we should note that the bishop is called in only as "a witness": he is apprised and called as a witness of the scandalous conduct of the priest. St. Benedict does not tell us what the bishop's personal intervention meant for the offender: doubtless a more authoritative admonition, perhaps even judgement and sentence. However, it does not seem, from the words of the Rule, that it was he who pronounced definite sentence of expulsion. All these points concern the rights of monasteries with respect to bishops. Together with what is said briefly on the point in Chapter LXIV., this is the sole instance of our Holy Father's invoking episcopal authority. Freely chosen by the monks, often "ordained" by the bishop, and having, through this medium, received from God and the Church plenary jurisdiction over his family, the Abbot exercised this jurisdiction according to his conscience and good pleasure. When the Abbot wished to excommunicate or expel one of his monks, or even one of the officials of his house, we nowhere find the Rule prescribing that the bishop should be called in.

As early as the fourth century there are indications in certain ecclesiastical documents of what was subsequently known as monastic exemption. We may merely recall the fact that the Council of Chalcedon (A.D. 451), though subjecting monks, and especially those ordained by him, to the bishop of the diocese, at the same time wished that they should be undisturbed in their monastery—which is the chief purpose and most tangible benefit of exemption.[1] Subsequently, and this even in monasteries where the bishop only intervened to perform certain pontifical functions, there remained a canonical bond between him and the monks whom he had ordained: these latter depended on him in some manner, doubtless in what concerned the administration of the sacraments. The Third Council of Arles (between A.D. 455 and 460) which reasserted this, at the same time recognized that the Abbot of Lérins, Faustus (future Bishop of Riez), had the right to be sole master in his own house, and that the Bishop of Fréjus could not interfere in the government of "the whole multitude of the laity of the monastery."[2]

[1] *Monachos vero per unamquamque civitatem aut regionem subjectos esse episcopo, et quietem diligere, et intentos esse tantummodo jejunio et orationi, in locis in quibus renuntiaverunt sæculo, permanentes: nec ecclesiasticis vero, nec sæcularibus negotiis communicent, vel in aliquo sint molesti, propria monasteria deserentes, nisi forte his præcipiatur propter opus necessarium ab episcopo civitatis* (Can. iv. MANSI, t. VII., col. 374; *cf.* also Canons vi. and viii.). This same Council allows (Can. vi.) a priest or a deacon to be ordained *titulo monasterii*, the origin of the *titulus mensæ communis;* the *titulus paupertatis* came in only with the mendicant Orders.

[2] MANSI, t. VII., col. 908.—*Cf.* MABILLON, *Annales O.S.B.*, l. I., xxxix. T. I., pp. 15-17.

In Africa, exemption gained much strength from the decree of the Council of Carthage of A.D. 525: "Therefore, all monasteries whatsoever shall be as they have always been, free in every way from the conditions of the clergy, answerable only to themselves and God."[1] The same Council and that of A.D. 534 (or 536) sealed these monastic liberties; but the Council of A.D. 534 reserved to the diocesan the privilege of ordaining.[2] We shall say nothing of the letters of St. Gregory the Great, which, however, contain many interesting details on monastic exemption in Italy, shortly after St. Benedict.

We understand better now why our Holy Father, inspired doubtless by a discipline allied to that which we have just outlined, would have "even the bishop" intervene in the case of a rebellious monk, without, however, leaving to him the duty of expulsion, supposing this to be necessary. The two authorities, episcopal and abbatial, should work in concert. Then, if offences became glaring and scandalous, if the priest persisted in his refusal to obey and submit to the Rule, he should be expelled. Our Holy Father leaves it to be understood, in this last sentence, that so radical a measure should be adopted only if all other methods were really ineffective.

[1] MANSI, t. VIII., col. 656.
[2] *Oportet enim in nullo monasterio quemlibet episcopum cathedram collocare; aut qui forte habuerint, habere: nec aliquam ordinationem, quamvis levissimam facere, nisi clericorum, si voluerint habere; esse enim debent monachi in abbatum suorum potestate . . . Inter sacrificia vero ordinatos suos tantummodo idem episcopus plebium ubi monasteria sunt, recitet: hoc enim convenit paci* (MANSI, t. VIII., cols. 841–842.—MABILLON reads: . . . *ordinatores suos . . . episcopos plebium . . . recitent.* Annales O.S.B., l. II., xvii–xviii. T. I., p. 40).—On exemption, *cf.* CALMET, *Comment. sur la Règle*, t. I., Preface, xxii. *ff.*—S. CHAMARD, *De l'immunité ecclésiastique et monastique* (Rev. des quest. histor., 1877, T. XXII., pp. 428–464).—D. BESSE, *Le Monachisme africain*, chap. xii.; *Les Moines de l'Ancienne France, passim,* especially Bk. IV., chap. xvii.—CAM. DAUX, *La Protection apostolique au moyen âge* (Rev. des quest. histor., 1902, t. LXXII., pp. 5–60).—JULES VENDENNE, *L'Exemption de visite monastique*.—G. LETONNELIER, *L'Abbaye de Cluny et le privilège de l'exemption* (in *Millénaire de Cluny*, t. I., pp. 247–263).—AUG. HÜFNER, *Das Rechtsinstitut der klösterlichen Exemtion in der abendländischen Kirche* (Archiv. für Kath. Kirchenrecht, 1906, 1907).—*Dom Guéranger, Abbé de Solesmes*, par un Moine bénédictin de la Congrégation de France, chap. vii. T. I., pp. 216–217.

CHAPTER LXIII
OF THE ORDER OF THE COMMUNITY

THE previous chapters have enumerated the elements that compose a Benedictine family: young people, adults and old men, laymen and clerics, freemen and former slaves, educated and illiterate, dignitaries and simple monks. What place shall each hold in the community? For order is necessary both for the peace and the progress of a monastic house. St. Benedict's Rule does not countenance that haphazard system which some practise as an ordinance of humility. Order is the law of every group or collective body: it exists in nature, it is found among the angels, it is demanded by civil and religious society. And monastic society, being a liturgical choir whose business it is to answer the heavenly choir, does not escape this necessity, especially when its members are numerous. Now Monte Cassino was not a monastery of twelve monks like those at Subiaco, and many passages of the holy Rule—Chapter XXI., for example—in treating of the heads of the deaneries, presuppose a considerable community. At the hierarchical summit of all, and ruling the whole, is the Abbot, seconded at need by the Prior (Chapters LXIV. and LXV.); next come the deans and the various officials who form the staff. St. Benedict has already, in passing, given some rules of precedence, but he now wishes in a special chapter to arrange all expressly.

First of all he deals with the formal order of the community; then, from the words *Juniores ergo* . . . onwards, with the private relations of monks with one another, giving us quite a treatise on monastic courtesy and good manners.

DE ORDINE CONGREGATIONIS.—Ordines suos in monasterio ita conservent, ut conversionis tempus et vitæ meritum discernit, vel ut Abbas constituerit. Qui Abbas non conturbet gregem sibi commissum, nec quasi libera utens potestate, injuste disponat aliquid: sed cogitet semper, quia de omnibus judiciis et operibus suis redditurus est Deo rationem.

Let them so keep their order in the monastery, as the time of their conversion and the merit of their lives determine, or as the Abbot shall appoint. And let not the Abbot disturb the flock committed to him, nor by the use of arbitrary power ordain anything unjustly; but let him ever bear in mind that he will have to give an account to God of all his judgements and of all his deeds.

Three causes may operate in the determination of a monk's rank: the date of his conversion, the merit of his life, and the will of the Abbot. The first is the general rule, the two others being no more than exceptions. Given this law, all dispute about precedence is impossible. Moreover, it is founded on reason and is conformable to the dispositions of Providence. We shall explain farther on what our Holy Father means by the time of conversion (*tempus conversionis* or *conversationis*).

"Merit of life." Not certainly, as Calmet observes, that a special position might be given a monk merely because he was a saintly man, but rather because the perfection of his life recommends him for some office or for the priesthood. Is it necessary to say that no one should lay claim to distinction or office on the ground of his virtue? The initiative belongs to the superior.

The will of the Abbot and the date of conversion, these practically fix a monk's rank. So our Holy Father presently reduces all others to these two: "Therefore in that order which he shall have appointed, or which they hold of themselves (*i.e.*, by the date of their conversion)." However, he did right to distinguish here merit of life and the appointment of the Abbot; for the Abbot may promote a man for a motive other than his supernatural perfection, provided that he does not choose monks of rather inobservant or uncertain character. There may, for instance, be a monk who has not yet had time to give indubitable evidence of great virtue, but who could, it seems, be serviceable to the community and a credit to it, were he put into a position of authority. The Abbot is free to invite such a one to show his capacity. Or a young monk may be raised to the dignity of cantor in virtue of his possessing a good voice.

But the Rule, while leaving the Abbot free to create rights of precedence, warns him to use the power with reserve and for solid motives. It tells him again that his authority is paternal and not unrestricted, absolute but not arbitrary; the principle *Sic volo, sic jubeo, sit pro ratione voluntas* is never admissible in governing souls. The Abbot cannot upset the order of his community at his pleasure, as he might the pieces of a chessboard: he may not make a point of taking the youngest and putting him above his elders, and then tiring and taking another, to be rejected in his turn, and so disturb the whole flock that God has entrusted to him.[1] Monasteries need interior stability: the Abbot must choose his men after mature deliberation or he will always be changing. Yet, after all, he has the right, for instance, to choose as Prior one who has only been solemnly professed a fortnight, or as Novice Master a monk professed the day before. Our Holy Father is content to remind him that he is accountable to God for all his decisions and for all his deeds.

Ergo secundum ordines quos constituerit, vel quos habuerint ipsi fratres, sic accedant ad pacem, ad communionem, ad psalmum imponendum, in choro standum. Et in omnibus omnino locis ætas non discernatur in ordine, nec præjudicet; quia Samuel et Daniel pueri presbyteros judicaverunt.

Therefore in that order which he shall have appointed, or which they hold themselves, let the brethren approach to receive the kiss of peace, and to Communion, and in the same order intone psalms and stand in choir. And in all places whatsoever let not age decide the order or be prejudicial to it; for Samuel and Daniel when but children judged the elders.

---

[1] The *Rule of the Master* is less discreet in this matter than St. Benedict; read chap. xcii.

It will be noticed that St. Benedict specifies only liturgical occasions: these are the most important; in them the hierarchical order has need to be most scrupulously safeguarded. But the words " in all places whatsoever," purposely general, perhaps designate all the circumstances of monastic life, so that elsewhere too confusion did not reign, and the same principles of order were obeyed: thus, at the very end of the chapter, St. Benedict alludes to order in the refectory.[1] Therefore the monks shall " approach to receive the kiss of peace " in the prescribed order. In the time of our Holy Father, each individual went up to the altar and received the kiss of peace from the celebrant.[2] In the same order shall they go to Holy Communion, receiving it under both kinds;[3] so shall they take their places in choir, and give out psalms or antiphons, if they can fulfil this duty unto edification, as St. Benedict said in Chapter XLVII.: *Psalmos autem, vel antiphonas, post Abbatem, ordine suo, quibus jussum fuerit, imponant. Cantare autem aut legere non præsumat, nisi qui potest ipsum officium implere, ut ædificentur audientes.*

But, we might object, is age to confer no superiority? Is it not a reversal of natural law that the young should take precedence of the old, and that the government of men of years and experience should be entrusted to them? The Abbot will sometimes hear himself blamed for showing preference to "youngsters"; let him take comfort: for here the first law is to take the best wherever you find it, and often it is not possible to act otherwise; moreover, St. Benedict, in harmony with the oldest monastic tradition, is on the side of the Abbot. Just as it would be ludicrous to want none but the young, so it would be absurd to exclude them from office when they are capable. In the third chapter our Holy Father would have all professed monks, young as well as old, summoned to council: " Because it is often to the younger that the Lord reveals what is best." Here, he lays it down afresh that in no circumstance whatever shall a monk's age be a motive for precedence, still less an obstacle and a source of prejudice. And, that he might not have to cite his young oblates, Maurus and Placid, as examples, he takes his proofs from the Old Testament: Samuel was God's messenger to Heli and his sons (1 Kings iii.); Daniel confounded the two elders (Dan. xiii.).[4]

[1] Our Holy Father had in mind here the discipline of the monks of Tabennisi, described by St. Jerome in his preface to the translation of the *Rule* of St. Pachomius: *Quicumque autem monasterium primus ingreditur, primus sedet, primus ambulat, primus psalmum dicit, primus in mensa manum extendit, prior in ecclesia communicat: nec ætas inter eos quæritur sed professio.*
[2] On the monastic ceremonial for the kiss of peace read Martène, *De ant. monach. rit.*, l. II., c. iv., cols. 178–181.
[3] At Cluny Communion was still received under both kinds. *Cf.* Udalr., *Consuet. Clun.*, l. II., c. xxx.
[4] This is perhaps a reminiscence of St. Jerome: . . . *Neque vero eorum qui a me exemplaria acceperunt vel auctoritate vel ætate ducaris, quum et Daniel puer senes judicet, et Amos pastor caprarum in sacerdotum principes invehatur* (*Epist.* XXXVII., 4. P.L., XXII., 463).

Ergo exceptis iis, quos, ut diximus, altiori consilio Abbas prætulerit, vel degradaverit certis ex causis, reliqui omnes, ut convertuntur, ita sint, ut, verbi gratia, qui secunda diei hora venerit in monasterium, juniorem se noverit esse illo qui prima hora diei venit, cujuslibet ætatis aut dignitatis sit. Pueris vero per omnia ab omnibus disciplina teneatur.	Excepting, therefore, those whom (as we have said) the Abbot has promoted from higher motives, or degraded for solid reasons, let all the rest take the order of their conversion; so that, for example, he who enters the monastery at the second hour of the day must know that he is junior to him who came at the first hour, whatever may be his age and dignity. But children are to be kept under discipline in all matters and by everyone.

St. Benedict repeats once more that, apart from cases where the Abbot "promotes" for higher motives [1] or "degrades" for solid reasons, each must occupy the place which corresponds to the date of his conversion, of his "entry into the monastery."[2] And he explains his meaning by an example. Commentators, however, have wondered whether the date of conversion does not rather mean, in St. Benedict's intention, the date of profession: profession alone, they urge, is the definitive conversion and entry into the monastic life, and the Rule says in Chapter LVIII.: "From that day let him be counted as one of the community." It is certain that, according to monastic usage, almost universal and of long standing, every monk receives his rank in the community according to the date of his profession: but the text of the Rule, if read without prejudice, would seem to be clearly in favour of the date of entry into the monastery.[3] Generally, however, with rare exceptions, the first to enter makes his profession first.

"Whatever may be his age and dignity." Did children, therefore—*i.e.*, the young oblates—take rank according to the date of their offering, which was their profession, and so mingle with the other monks, taking precedence sometimes of mature and aged men ? The thought evidently occurred to St. Benedict, for he makes immediate allusion to the children, only to prevent the difficulties which would arise from such precocious precedence: "But children are to be kept under discipline in all matters and by everyone." They shall precede those who entered the monastery after them (for we must not forget that their oblate profession has the same juridical value as adult profession): nevertheless all their elders shall have the right to supervise, admonish, and correct them in all matters (*disciplina*).

St. Benedict explains his meaning more clearly still some lines farther on, when speaking of the relation of monks to one another: "Let young children and boys take their order in the oratory, or at table, with discipline. In other places also, wherever they may be, let them be under

---

[1] *Altiori consilio:* the expression occurs in SULP. SEVERUS, *Dial.* I., c. x. P.L., XX., 190.
[2] *Cf.* the passage before cited from the preface to the translation of the *Rule* of ST. PACHOMIUS.
[3] Read HÆFTEN, l. III., tract. iii., disq. vi.

custody and discipline, until they come to the age of understanding." To this passage should be joined that in Chapter LXX.: "However, with regard to children, until the fifteenth year of their age, let them be kept by all under diligent discipline and custody: yet this, too, with measure and discretion." Therefore very young children and those who are somewhat older must keep their rank: *ordines suos consequantur*. What order is meant? If we would translate in harmony with the whole context and make St. Benedict consistent, we must understand him to mean their order according to profession and years of monastic life (and not their order *among themselves* in the children's quarters). *Cum disciplina*, says St. Benedict in passing, which may be translated: without confusion, in good order; or rather, under the supervision and correction of the older brethren. Thus they must keep the order of profession, in oratory and refectory, without, however, escaping *disciplina;* but apart from those places, in all other places and circumstances (*foris autem vel ubiubi*), they shall have no precedence and shall simply remain under the guard and loving control of all. In the dormitory, for instance, care shall be taken that their beds are placed between those of their elders: *Adolescentiores fratres*, etc. (Chapter XXII.). This collective guardianship lasted until the children had attained their fifteenth year, and had reached mature intelligence and full discretion. In this matter St. Benedict parts with St. Basil, who separated the children absolutely from the rest of the monks, except in the oratory;[1] but we should remember that St. Basil's oblates were not professed.

After the time of our Holy Father, Western monastic custom also separated oblates more or less strictly from the rest. In choir and refectory they formed a separate group; they were under the control of special masters; even after their fifteenth year, if they were still too childish, they were closely watched.[2] Hildemar[3] tells us that children did not take the rank in the community which corresponded to their entry into the monastery until they ceased to be under tutelage. In course of time, in proportion as the system declined, not even this tardy honour was paid them. But, as Calmet maintains, primitive usage was as we have described it above, and several commentators have been misled by later customs.

Such is the prudent legislation which assures all monks their proper rank and dignity. It would be pitiful, however, and ridiculous, if questions of precedence should engender jealousy and quarrelling among religious.[4]

Juniores ergo priores suos honorent: priores vero juniores diligant.

Let the younger brethren, then, reverence their elders, and the elder love the younger.

Formal order, as fixed by St. Benedict in the first part of this chapter, while absolutely indispensable, is yet not sufficient by itself. We must add

---

[1] *Reg. fus.*, xv.
[2] *Cf.* UDALR., *Consuet. Clun.*, l. III., c. ix.
[3] Commentary on Chapter LXX.
[4] *Cf.* ST. BASIL., *Reg. contr.*, x.

to it mutual affection and regard, politeness and supernatural courtesy. We should not criticize worldly politeness too severely. Its most common defects are two: it is hollow, since it is not the expression of charity; it is false, since it easily changes its tune and in a moment decries without pity those whom it praised without conviction. Such as it is, however, it contains some self-denial; it often consists in voluntary self-effacement, in secret designs for another's honour or gratification. It is the business of God's children to restore this politeness to its integrity. Among them especially it shall be based on self-denial. We should note this point well, that we do not come into contact with our brethren by means of our interior virtues, but much rather on our external side; men scarcely know us else; and therefore are we bound, because of our common life, to get rid of our external faults. And monastic politeness should spring, not merely from education, refinement, and good taste, but above all from the spirit of faith and from charity. When Tobias, without disclosing his identity, presented himself before Raguel, the latter observed to his wife: "How like is this young man to my cousin!" And he began to love him on the strength of this likeness. Each of our brethren deserves the same honour: he is not only consecrated to God, but he has something of God in him: how shall we refuse him our respect and our affection? How shall we not treat him as one in whose company we are with God. Our conventual life is but an apprenticeship for our eternal intercourse with God in heaven.

St. Benedict first lays down an ordinance based on natural and supernatural law: that the young should honour their elders and that the old should love the young. (We recognize the sixty-eighth and sixty-ninth instruments of good works: *Seniores venerari, Juniores diligere*.) Without this mutual relation, the community will contain parties, which watch one another curiously, perhaps envy and decry one another. Old men may have their faults and their fads: but it is a pity to have eyes only for their eccentricities. Youth is often too exacting, too sure of itself, and full of reforming zeal. Age, on its side, is sometimes hard, anxious to see others perfect immediately: yet why not give novices and young monks time to eliminate the habits which they have brought from the world? *Juniores ergo* . . . this ordinance is the consequence and corollary of what St. Benedict decided before concerning the relative rights and duties of the young and those of greater natural or monastic age; at the same time it is the general principle inspiring the regulations which follow.

In ipsa autem appellatione nominum nulli liceat alium puro nomine appellare; sed priores juniores suos fratres nominent, juniores autem priores suos nonnos vocent, quod intelligitur paterna reverentia. Abbas autem, quia vices Christi agere videtur, Domnus et Abbas vocetur: non sua assumptione, sed honore et amore Christi.

In calling each other by name, let no one address another by his simple name; but let the elders call the younger brethren *Fratres*, and the younger call their elders *Nonni*, by which is conveyed the reverence due to a father. But let the Abbot, since he is considered to represent Christ, be called Lord and Abbot; not that

Ipse autem cogitet, et sic se exhibeat ut dignus sit tali honore.	he hath taken it on himself, but for honour and love of Christ. Let him reflect, and so act as to be worthy of such an honour.

Respect and mutual affection must be manifested exteriorly, first of all in the manner of address, for it is thus that we take contact with one another. Angels converse after a more simple method; but we men must employ an explicit form of speech. The holy Rule decides what it shall be.[1] It does so first negatively and by the method of exclusion: to designate a brother (whether we are addressing him or speaking about him) we must not employ his name simply and curtly, without any prefix.[2] Therefore we break the Rule if we use only Christian name or surname, if we designate a brother, and that habitually, by the mere name of his office in the monastery, by the name of his position in the world, by the name of his nationality, or, *a fortiori*, by a nickname. And we must eliminate from our vocabulary slang, schoolboy language, and all vulgar or too familiar modes of speech.

After this prohibition, St. Benedict indicates positively the monastic forms of address. Elders must call those younger than they (*juniores suos*) *fratres*, "brothers." The term is affectionate and pleasing; it emphasizes the united life of all religious of the same family;[3] the first Christians and first monks used it.[4] We must give up secular modes of address. The elders shall be called *Nonni*, conveying "paternal reverence" the word being equivalent to "Reverend Father" (a nun was called *Nonna*). Many derivations have been given for this word, of which the most probable is that it is of Egyptian origin, employed to express respect and reverence for an old and devout man; St. Jerome uses it several times in his letters.[5]

As for the Abbot, who represents Our Lord in the monastery and holds His place, he is to be called *Domnus*, "Dom" (a diminutive of *Dominus*, which is reserved to Our Lord). St. Benedict did not invent the term *Domnus*: the form *Domnus apostolicus* was already used in speaking of the Pope, and it was applied to great and saintly people: "They announce that Domnus Martinus has died," writes Sulpicius Severus.[6] The superior was also called "Abbot," a Syriac word meaning father. In the East this name was generally given to simple religious, venerable by age and virtue;[7] the superior was called by such names as προεστώς, præpositus, pater monasterii, archimandrite, hegoumenos, etc. St

---

[1] *Cf.* Hæften, l. III., tract. iv.

[2] The disciple and biographer of St. Fulgentius of Ruspe († 533) says of his hero: *Circa singulos ita mansuetus fuit et communis et facilis ut neminem fratrum puro nomine clamitaret* (*Vita S. Fulgent.*, c. xxvii. P.L., LXV., col. 144).

[3] *Bene fratres jussit appellari, quia uno sacro fonte baptismatis sunt renati, et uno Spiritu sanctificati, et unam professionem professi sunt, et unam remunerationem adipisci desiderant, et ab una matre, id est sancta Ecclesia, editi sunt. Et hoc notandum est, quia melior est ista fraternitas spiritualis, quam carnalis* (Paul the Deacon, *in h. l.*).

[4] *Cf.* S. Aug., *Enarrat. in Psalm.* cxxxii. P.L., XXXVII., 1729 sq.

[5] *Epist.* XXII., 16. P.L., XXII., 404; *Epist.* CXVII., 6. P.L., *ibid.*, 956.—Read Hæften, l. III., tract. iv., disq. iii.—Calmet, Comm. *in h. l.*

[6] *Epist.* II. P.L., XX., 179. [7] *Cf.* Cassian and the *Vitæ Patrum*, *passim*.

Benedict reserves the title of Abbot for him who is really the father of the family. And he reminds him that he receives this name in honour and for love of Christ, and not as a motive for pride. As in the second chapter, he bids him make his life and conduct conformable to all that is implied in such a name, and to show himself worthy of the honour conferred on him. Of course he does not mean that the Abbot has to be always " on stilts," or that he is obliged to be pontificating perpetually.

From the ninth century onwards the term *nonnus* was dropped in many monasteries. The Council of Aix-la-Chapelle (A.D. 817) recommends that the *Præpositi* (Priors or seniors?) should have this title; it survived in some parts, as for instance at Monte Cassino, where it is found at the end of the thirteenth century, in the writings of the commentator Bernard; and Citeaux preserved it down to our time. But the title *domnus* was more attractive: Smaragdus tells us that elders liked to be addressed thus. At Cluny, in the time of Udalric, every professed monk had a right to it.[1] Like the Benedictines of the Congregation of St. Vanne and the Maurists, we reserve it for the professed who are priests. Professed monks who are not priests are Reverends Pères (Reverend Fathers). Lay brothers, postulants, and novices, even if priests, are called brothers. In certain countries, Italy for instance, where secular priests are called " dom " or " don," novices also enjoy the title, and the style of "Reverend Father" is kept for professed monks who are priests. The name of " Abbot " (Abbé) itself has been usurped by the secular clergy in the Gallican Church, largely on account of the system of commendatory Abbots; it should be noted, however, that, since the sixth century, the title of Abbot (Abbé) was sometimes given, in France, to a secular priest charged with the government of an important church and the rule of the college of clerics who serve it.[2]

Ubicumque autem sibi obviant fratres, junior a priore benedictionem petat. Transeunte majore, junior surgat et det ei locum sedendi. Nec præsumat junior consedere, nisi ei præcipiat senior suus: ut fiat quod scriptum est: *Honore invicem prævenientes*.

Pueri parvuli vel adolescentes, in oratorio vel ad mensam, cum disciplina ordines suos consequantur. Foris autem vel ubiubi, custodiam habeant et disciplinam, usque dum ad intelligibilem ætatem perveniant.

Wherever the brethren meet one another, let the younger ask a blessing from the elder. And when the elder passes by, let the younger rise and give place to him to sit down. Nor let the younger presume to sit unless his senior bid him, that it may be as was written: "In honour anticipating one another."

Let young children and boys take their order in the oratory, or at table, with discipline. In other places also, wherever they may be, let them be under custody and discipline, until they come to the age of understanding.

We have seen how monks address one another; we have now to consider certain marks of courtesy which they owe one another, and first the salutation. In whatever place the brethren meet, the younger should

---

[1] UDALR., *Consuet. Clun.*, l. II., c. xx.
[2] *Cf.* S. GREG. TURON., *Liber Vitæ Patrum*, ii., 3-4. M.G.H.: *Script. rer. merov.*, t. I., pp. 670–671. *In gloria martyrum*, 60. M.G.H.: *ibid.*, p. 529.

ask the " blessing " of his elder. Our Holy Father has mentioned this blessing several times: in Chapter XXV. he said of the excommunicated monk: " Let none of those who pass by bless him "; in Chapter LIII. he told the brother who met a guest to salute him: " And asking their blessing, let him pass on "; in Chapter LXVI. he bids the porter: " As soon as anyone shall knock, or a poor man call to him, let him answer ' Deo gratias,' or bless him." The custom is of great antiquity. St. Paul (Heb. vii. 1 *ff*.) explains how Melchisedech " blessed " Abraham: " That which is less is blessed by the better." To bless also means to praise God on account of some thing or person: " And Simeon blessed them " (Luke ii. 34). At the Last Supper, Our Lord took bread and blessed: εὐλογήσας. The early Christians blessed each other when they met.[1] It is not a mere gesture, but a wish or an expression of gratitude towards God, something analogous to the *Dominus vobiscum* of the liturgy: God be blessed for this meeting! May God bless you!

According to the practice of the ancient monks both of East and West, you bowed before him whom you wished to honour and said: *Benedic Pater*, or *Benedicite*, recognizing thereby the presence of God in the guest or brother, and beseeching a blessing from God dwelling in him. We learn from the *Rule of the Master*, from Bernard of Monte Cassino, and from other sources, that the reply was: *Deus*, or *Dominus*;[2] but it was not always expressed, and Boherius says that he heard none at Subiaco and Monte Cassino: " I have not heard what the senior answers, nor do I find anything about his answer in the Rule, except he answers *Deo gratias*."[3] Our Holy Father does tell the porter to answer *Deo gratias;* but he adds: " or bless," which would lead us to suppose that the form of blessing was not *Deo gratias*. However this may be, *Deo gratias* is an ancient and beautiful formula of monastic salutation. The *circumcelliones* of St. Augustine's time blamed the monks for using it; we may see how the saintly Doctor censures them for this in his discourse on the hundred and thirty-second psalm.[4]

Blessing is asked and given, says Paul the Deacon, only in places and at times when speaking is allowed; in the regular places and during the privileged times of silence, salutation is confined to asking a blessing in the heart and a bow of the head. Peter the Venerable was compelled to prove to the Cistercians, who were shocked at it, that such a practice sufficed for the observance of the Rule on this point.[5] In the Declara-

---

[1] *Quod penes Deum bonitatis et benignitatis, omnis benedictio inter nos summum sit disciplinæ et conversationis sacramentum, " benedicat te Deus " tam facile pronuntias quam Cbristiano necesse est* (TERTULL., *De testim. animæ*, c. ii. P.L., I., 611).

[2] *Reg. Magistri*, xiii.—BERNARD. CASS., *in cap.* xxv.

[3] Commentary on this passage.

[4] *P.L.*, XXXVII., 1732: *Hi etiam insultare nobis audent quia fratres, cum vident homines, Deo gratias dicunt. Quid est, inquiunt, Deo gratias ? Itane surdus es ut nescias quid sit Deo gratias ? Qui dicit Deo gratias, gratias agit Deo. Vide si non debet frater Deo gratias agere, quando videt fratrem suum. Num enim non est locus gratulationis quando se invicem vident qui habitant in Cbristo ?*—And in Letter XLI., ST. AUGUSTINE says again: *Deo gratias ! nam quid melius et animo geramus et ore promamus, et calamo exprimamus quam Deo gratias ? Hoc nec dici brevius, nec audiri lætius, nec intelligi grandius ; nec agi fructuosius potest* (*P.L.*, XXXIII., 158).

[5] *Epist.*, l. I., *Ep.* XXVIII. P.L., CLXXXIX., 133-134.

tions for Sainte-Cécile, Dom Guéranger writes: " The younger sisters shall ask a blessing from their elders—that is to say, from the professed who have left the novitiate—saying: *Benedicite;* but, during the night silence they shall only bow to them. The senior shall receive this mark of honour in a humble and gracious manner; but those who were professed on the same day as the one who salutes them, shall answer: *Benedicite.*" We have not got this custom, and we must hold to what is established. But we are not dispensed from saluting a senior, and, in a general way, every brother we meet. It is by no means necessary to say a few pleasant words to him, to utter some joke or witticism; but it is always correct to uncover if we are wearing the hood, to look towards him and to bow. Even though the younger should forget to do it, the senior can certainly bow before his brother and before his brother's angel guardian.

St. Benedict provides finally for the case when a senior passes a junior who is seated: the latter must rise immediately; and if the senior is coming to sit in the spot or near the spot where the junior is, the latter ought to give place to him and not to sit down again until invited to do so. This is in accordance with the politeness of all countries and all times: Aristotle says:[1] " Honour should be paid to every elder in proportion to his age, both by rising and by giving place to him." Still we may note, with Paul the Deacon and Hildemar, that if the senior is merely passing, " the junior should rise a little, bow and ask a blessing "; that if the senior passes again and again, or if the junior is seated in a spot where many seniors come and go, he is dispensed from rising every time; that courtesy and charity make it a duty for the senior not to leave the junior standing before him. The Abbot, says Hildemar, shall bring up this last point at chapter, and if any senior transgresses it, he shall be punished; if he remains incorrigible, the Abbot shall put him down in the lowest place. It would, in fact, be somewhat ridiculous for a monk to be incessantly parading his seniority, and exacting haughtily all the honours that are due to him.

Let us never regard these ordinances of the Rule as out of date. To repeat, this politeness and these attentions are an index of our charity and supernatural refinement. Brethren should anticipate one another in honour (Rom. xii. 10); they should be zealous and should sometimes study to be kind, yet without affectation or obsequiousness. We should salute our seniors and let them pass before us; we should not be ashamed to speak to the Abbot kneeling. Commentators take occasion of what is said here about sitting to observe that a monk should never sit in the loose and lazy manner of the worldling.[2]

St. Benedict ends with instructions as to the attitude of the community towards the children: on these we have already commented.

[1] *Ethics*, l. IX., c. ii.—*Cf. Sermo asceticus de renuntiatione sæculi, inter* S. BASIL. *opp.* P.G., XXXI., 644.
[2] *Cum sedes, non superpones alteri cruri alterum crus tuum: siquidem istud facere, animi parum attenti atque aliud agentis indicium est (Sermo asceticus de renuntiat. sæc.,* 8. P.G., XXXI., 644).

CHAPTER LXIV
OF THE APPOINTMENT OF THE ABBOT

THE constant purpose of this portion of the Rule is to assure the good order, observance, and internal peace of the community. Consequently our Holy Father finds himself led to speak a second time about him whose mission it is to rule the whole monastic city and in whom resides the very fulness of authority. He does not consider that the second chapter and continual references to the Abbot's government throughout the Rule have exhausted so important a subject; and far from seeking to weaken and soften the austerity of the second chapter, as has been sometimes rather arbitrarily supposed, St. Benedict here completes it. He first establishes the procedure for the election and "ordination" of the Abbot, and then reminds us what spirit of wisdom and discretion should direct the Abbot in his dealings with souls.

DE ORDINANDO ABBATE.—In Abbatis ordinatione illa semper consideretur ratio, ut hic constituatur, quem sibi omnis concors congregatio, secundum timorem Dei, sive etiam pars quamvis parva congregationis saniori consilio elegerit.	In the appointment of an Abbot let this principle always be observed, that he be made Abbot who is chosen by the whole community unanimously in the fear of God, or even by a part, however small, with sounder counsel.

In the course of the centuries various methods have been employed in the appointment of abbots. Assuredly the method which from the eighth century onwards[1] allowed the king or lay lords, by right of foundation or patronage, to nominate to abbeys and priories was not the best of these. It even happened, in the hey-day of *commendam*, that these titular superiors were neither monks nor clerics; and the monasteries were governed for them, indifferently well, by men of their choice. The *mensa abbatialis* (Abbot's income) was distinct from the *mensa communis* (income of the community); and the whole function of the commendatory Abbot was to draw the revenues.[2] Abbeys were given to children at their birth or as wedding presents to princes and princesses. Thank God we no longer know the dearly bought splendours of the abbeys of the old régime; and in spite of the precarious and diminished character of our life, in spite of persecution and exile, we are at least free within our own walls.

The rights of the Sovereign Pontiff with respect to the appointment of an Abbot are incontestably more real than those of a king, though he be "the most Christian King." The Pope could, "out of the plenitude of his apostolic power," confer the dignity of Abbot and the government of a monastery on the candidate chosen by himself, just as he confers the episcopal dignity and the government of a diocese. In

---
[1] MABILLON, *Acta SS. O.S.B.*, Sæc. III., Præf., III.
[2] *Cf.* EMILE LESNE, *L'Origine des menses dans le temporel des Eglises et des monastères de France, au IXe siècle.*

practice Popes sometimes use this power, but only in special and extraordinary circumstances, as has for long been the case in the basilical monasteries of Rome. The Letters of St. Gregory the Great show us the Sovereign Pontiff appointing Abbots.[1] We shall presently describe the part ordinarily played by the Holy See in the election of an Abbot.

As regards bishops, Canon Law recognizes that they cannot of themselves, without delegation from the Pope, choose the superiors of regulars. Yet they did so more than once in the first centuries of monasticism,[2] whether in the capacity of founders and for the first occasion only, or as reformers,[3] or by abuse of their power. At the same time Councils, such as that of Carthage in A.D. 534,[4] strove to safeguard the liberties of monks. "And when abbots die, let those who are to succeed them be chosen by the judgement of the community; nor let the bishop claim or assume the function of making this choice." We find St. Aurelian obtaining from Pope Vigilius a confirmation of the right of monks to elect their own Abbot,[5] and St. Gregory the Great maintaining this ordinance of the Holy Rule.[6] What part bishops formerly played in this matter and what part they now play shall be made clear in the sequel.

So it is the privilege of monks to choose their Abbot; but, in actual practice, the exercise of this right has taken various forms. According to St. Basil's regulations, the superiors of the neighbouring communities chose the Abbot.[7] The fifteenth century saw the rise of great Benedictine congregations, some of which, while abandoning perpetual abbots, were wont to receive their superiors from the General Chapter or Diet. The Congregation, in the modern sense of that word, provided by the medium of its superiors for the maintenance of the officials. Under St. Pachomius, the superior of each monastery was nominated by the superior-general of the Congregation; and the latter himself designated his successor.[8]

Historically this last method was often employed. Theodoret[9] and Cassian[10] allude to it. For the West we have numerous pieces of evidence—as, for instance, in the *Lives of the Fathers of Jura*, in St. Gregory of Tours, etc. The *Rule of the Master*[11] describes at length the procedure to be followed when an Abbot wished to take to himself a coadjutor with right of succession; according to this Rule the monks had no say in the matter;[12] and if the Abbot departed without making provision for

---

[1] *Epist.*, l. IX., *Ep.* XCI. *P.L.*, LXXVII., 1018; M.G.H.: *Epist.*, t. II., p. 49.
[2] *Cf.* S. Isidori Pelus., *Epist.*, l. I., *Ep.* CCLXII. *P.G.*, LXXVIII., 339.
[3] *Cf. Vita S. Cæsarii*, l. I., 12. M.G.H.: *Script. rer. merov.*, t. III., p. 461.
[4] Mansi, t. VIII., col. 842.
[5] Mabillon, *Annales O.S.B.*, l. IX., xxviii. T. I., p. 231.
[6] *Epist.*, l. II., *Epp.* XLI. and XLII. *P.L.*, LXXVII., 578–580; M.G.H.: *Epist.*, t. I., pp. 348 and 346. [7] *Reg. fus.*, xliii.
[8] *Cf.* Ladeuze, *Etude sur le cénobitisme pakhomien pendant le IVe siècle et la première moitié du Ve*, pp. 286, 287, and 316.
[9] *Religiosa historia*, c. iv. *P.G.*, LXXXII., 1345.
[10] *Inst.*, IV., xxviii. [11] Cap. xciii. and xciv.
[12] ... *Ne cum unusquisque de suo judicio successionem præsumens, universos in seditionem exagitet, et studiosam partibus pugnam scandali domum pacis faciat in contentionem converti* (xciv.).

the future, the bishop and clergy of the district applied to a saintly neighbouring Abbot, and asked him to stay a month in the monastery that had lost its pastor, with power to choose the most worthy. At Cluny, whereas St. Odo and Blessed Aymard were elected by their brethren, St. Majolus and St. Odilo were designated by their predecessors, the community only intervening to approve of the choice. When St. Odilo, being now advanced in years, was asked to choose in his turn, he consented only to nominate some prudent monks to perform the election, which had then to be ratified by all: it was in this way that St. Hugh was chosen.[1] The method of election by "spiritual brethren," as Bernard of Cluny calls them, even passed into a custom.[2] If the Prior who presided at the meeting, or the first senior consulted, proposed a name which was acceptable to all, the election was accomplished.[3]

Nowadays still an Abbot has the right to concern himself about the future of his children, and to foresee, but with infinite discretion, who shall be the heir of his policy and the continuator of his work, if indeed he has had a policy and if he has endeavoured a work which deserves to last. For why should everything be periodically put into the melting-pot? The Abbot knows his family and knows what is good for it. He is going to appear before God; no man plays false at such a time, and human motives have little influence. It was at that moment that the Patriarchs became prophets, and, like Jacob or the dying Moses, traced the future history of their people. But it will be said that saints themselves have been deceived in their last choice. Are we sure that the responsibility for the failure that followed should be thrown on their choice? After all, you may make what use you will of the Abbot's advice; but, that he is free to leave such admits of no doubt. In this way do we compensate for the advantages of an actual hereditary succession, which has no place here. And it may be that it will help a community to realize that unanimity of which St. Benedict speaks: *Omnis consors congregatio.*

Consequently, under our Holy Father's arrangement, the members of the community alone have the duty of choosing their father. In most cases this is the safest and most equitable method, the monastic family being better informed and more directly concerned than anyone else. We may almost say that it is a point of natural law; and the Church recognizes it in the words of the Pontifical at the ordination of a priest: "All necessarily yield a more willing obedience to him to whose ordination they have given their consent." It is clear also from the context that the Rule expects monks to choose an Abbot from among themselves; but it is difficult to determine how this election was effected. St. Cæsarius is not more explicit than St. Benedict.[4] Nowadays, apart from the method of "compromise," the election is made by secret ballot, an oath being administered to each elector. As to the

---

[1] Read UDALRIC, *Consuet. Clun.*, l. III., c. i. [2] BERNARD., *Ordo Clun.*, P. I., c. i.
[3] *Constit. Hirsaug.*, l. II., c. i. [4] *Reg. ad vir.*, Recapitulatio, xii.

details of the election, each Congregation has its own rules of procedure.

St. Benedict supposes election to have three possible results: (1) The whole community, acting under the influence of the fear of God, is of one accord in choosing a good monk. (2) The whole community agrees in the choice of an unworthy candidate, one more or less a party to its irregularities; which case he examines farther on. (3) There is no unanimity and votes are divided: " Let him be made Abbot who is chosen . . . even by a part, however small, with sounder counsel." This passage is undeniably difficult.

According to the common interpretation, our Holy Father's meaning is as follows: supposing that there is on the one side a relative majority, or an absolute majority, or even practical unanimity, and on the other side a minority of some sort, however small it may be:[1] the one chosen by this minority shall be Abbot, if its choice is better and better inspired, *saniori consilio*. We see at once the dangers of such an arrangement: it is a proximate occasion of schism, an encouragement to turbulent and factious minorities: for no party will ever lack reasons for alleging that its opinion is the only wise one. For this reason the Church now requires a numerical majority. Did St. Benedict really cast this apple of discord among his monks and misunderstand human nature in this way? For voting would have no result, and it would be necessary continually to appeal to an outside authority which should give the casting vote and decide which is the better choice: the bishop, for instance, or the neighbouring abbots, whom St. Benedict mentions presently, or the Pope himself, says Calmet. Certainly matters happened so more than once in the course of the centuries; but the text of the Rule does not, for the case in point, provide for the intervention of the bishop or of another abbot: in the Rule the community is self-sufficient.

Another interpretation is proposed by the author of the *Explication ascétique et historique de la Règle de saint Benoît*. There are two methods of election: " either by the whole community unanimously " (several important manuscripts read *sive* instead of *sibi*); " or even by a part." The first is the more normal method; the second consists in entrusting the election of the Abbot to a portion, even a very small portion, of the community, but prudent and of " sounder counsel "; this method may be used in the ordinary course of events, or in exceptional cases, where the community foresees or has ascertained the ineffectiveness of a vote. The explanation is a good one. Yet, it would seem that our Holy Father distinguishes and contrasts in some way the case where the whole community is unanimous and that where, the community being divided, the choice of a minority, though small, deserves to prevail; but, according to the present explanation, practically, in spite of some delays required

---

[1] If only two monks choose a good abbot, and a hundred choose an unworthy one, say PAUL THE DEACON and HILDEMAR, the choice of the former should prevail.

for deliberation and the selection of the electoral committee, there is always unanimity in the election: opposition has vanished.

We must look for another solution of the difficulty. We may, for once, range ourselves on the side of the famous Caramuel, whose view was adopted also by Dom Mège. Take a case where several candidates receive votes. If there be an absolute majority, it settles the matter, though it be only a " part " in comparison with unanimity. If there be no absolute majority, but votes are scattered, St. Benedict does not desire a second voting: it would only cause some chance combination or a coalition of malcontents. In this hypothesis, then, the choice shall be determined by a simple relative majority. He shall be elected who has obtained the most votes. If this number be compared with the number of voters, it is only a part and a small part; it is in reality only a minority, if you add up the other minorities and compare the total with it. There remains to justify the words: " with sounder counsel." Caramuel has an answer for everything: " It is more numerous than the other parties, and therefore is to be presumed sounder." So says Caramuel and Dom Mège after him. Perhaps St. Benedict would suggest that in this case of an election accomplished by a relative majority, all have more reason to scrutinize the one elected, to verify his claims with more care, and to scrutinize also those who elected him. It was then that one might, at need, call in an arbiter from outside; but it would be an exceptional course and without danger to the independence of the community.

| Vitæ autem merito, et sapientiæ doctrina eligatur qui ordinandus est, etiam si ultimus fuerit in ordine congregationis. | Let him who is to be appointed be chosen for the merit of his life and the learning of his wisdom, even though he should be the last of the community. |

Whatever be the method of election, each monk should choose conscientiously, says St. Benedict, who now deals with the person of the elect. It would be a disgraceful thing if men who have taken a solemn oath to elect the most worthy should cast their votes in any direction at all, as chance passion may direct or the petty calculations of the moment. So would the government of souls be put into unstable or irresolute hands for twenty or thirty years, and that by the play of paltry passions. Here is one of those times when it is most important to put oneself in the presence of God and to stand before His judgement seat; the election must be performed, as our Holy Father has said already, " in the fear of God." A man must silence his prejudices and his dislikes, nay, even his likes and his enthusiasms: above all he must be intelligent and prudent.

St. Benedict indicates with precision the marks by which we shall recognize a suitable candidate. First, " merit of life." That a man has a great position in the world, a distinguished name and distinguished connections, a rich patrimony which inspires the hope that we shall live at our ease and be able to build, that he has financial and administrative capacity: all such considerations are banished. We shall examine whether there is merit and holiness of life, not necessarily absence of defects and failings, but a real worthiness of life and preoccupation with the things of God. Besides this[1] St. Benedict requires " the learning of wisdom." By which he does not mean knowledge simply: the higher mathematics, for instance, are not sufficient. Nor is it even ecclesiastical knowledge: for then a dry knowledge of theology, inspired by nothing better than curiosity, yet stamped with its doctor's degree, might suffice. Nor is it simply a theoretical or experimental knowledge of the mystical life. It is something much more comprehensive: it is a learning which comes of assiduous reading, reflection, practice, and prudence, and from the understanding of monastic institutions. We shall presently find St. Benedict reminding us that prudence, tact, and discretion are especially to be expected from an Abbot. And these are qualities which do not always accompany understanding, or virtue, or apostolic zeal. The ancient monks used to say: " Is he holy ? Let him pray for us. Is he learned ? Let him teach us. Is he prudent ? Let him rule us " (*Sanctus est? oret pro nobis. Doctus est? doceat nos. Prudens est? regat nos*).

When all these conditions are fulfilled, they ought to determine the vote of the community, even though the one chosen hold the lowest place in the monastery, and be therefore recently professed and even quite young in years. St. Placid did not do so badly, nor St. Hugh, who was Abbot at twenty-five. And then, if youth is a fault, it is one that is quickly and surely corrected. It is even a good principle to elect a young Abbot: there are works which he will undertake and which he will be able to pursue just because he is conscious of vigour and because he has the future before him. In a Benedictine community, life and activity come from the Abbot; and though other forms of the religious life, by their strong personnel, powerful organization, and minute regulations, maintain the unity and assure the development of their work, whatever be the changes of ruler: with us, on the contrary, everything depends on the person of the Abbot.[2]

Quod si etiam omnis congregatio vitiis suis (quod quidem absit) consentientem personam pari consilio elegerit, et vitia ipsa aliquatenus in notitiam episcopi, ad cujus diœcesim pertinet locus ipse, vel Abbatibus, aut christianis vicinis claruerint, prohibeant pravorum prævalere consensum, et

But even if all the community with one accord (which God forbid) should elect a person who condones their evil ways, and these somehow come to the knowledge of the bishop to whose diocese the place belongs, or of the Abbots or neighbouring Christians, let them prevent the agree-

---

[1] *Sancta quippe rusticitas solum sibi prodest; et quantum ædificat ex vitæ merito Ecclesiam Christi, tantum nocet si destruentibus non resistat. . . . Vides quantum inter se distent justa rusticitas et docta justitia* (S. HIERON., *Epist.* XLIII., 3. P.L., XXII., 542).

[2] Councils and popes long ago laid it down that an abbot should have the years and the dignity of the priesthood. The rule is embodied in the *Code*. To be validly elected an Abbot must be ten years professed and at least thirty years old. A Superior General must be forty years old. The same rules apply to Abbesses.

Of the Appointment of the Abbot

domui Dei dignum constituant dispensatorem; scientes pro hoc se recepturos mercedem bonam, si illud caste et zelo Dei faciant, sicut e contrario peccatum, si negligant.

ment of these wicked men prevailing, and appoint a worthy steward over the house of God, knowing that for this they shall receive a good reward, if they do it with a pure intention and for the love of God, as, on the other hand, they will sin if they neglect it.

St. Benedict considers, and that with horror: *Quod quidem absit!* a third result of an election: the case where the votes of the community unite to elect an unworthy man. A community never chooses an unworthy candidate except for its own pleasure and because it says to itself: " Look at his habits, look how he is involved in the same failings as ourselves; he is a monk who will not be troublesome: we may make him Abbot without fear." Calculations of this sort were not by any means impossible at a period when there were monks such as those of Vicovaro; if the monks could unite to poison the Abbot, they could also unite to provide him with a lamentable successor.[1]

When this misfortune happens, and the bishop of the place or the neighbouring abbots and influential layfolk have learnt with certainty, by whatever method, whether official or private, of the vicious proceedings of the community, they have a duty in conscience to intervene: if they do so, God will give them good recompense; if they take no notice, they shall sin and be punished. However, as St. Benedict quickly remarks, their intervention must be inspired by pure motives and by zeal for the glory of God, not by ambitious designs, by jealousy or unjustifiable preferences. It were wrong that the liberty of monastic life should be lessened under the pretext of vigilance, however devoted and affectionate, and that all the pious folk of the neighbourhood should go to war and take sides in a matter which concerns them not at all. Those to whom our Holy Father appeals shall have a double mission: first, to quash the evil or dubious election and frustrate the plans of the wicked; secondly, to provide a worthy ruler for God's house. What was the part played by each of the personages mentioned by St. Benedict? Everything would lead us to believe that they had to act in concert, under the guidance of the bishop, the abbots supporting him with their advice, and the Christians of the vicinity lending at need the help of the " secular arm." The proceedings probably took the form of an ecclesiastical enquiry.[2] And finally, how was the choice of the new Abbot determined? Our Holy Father is too laconic for us to be able to get answers to all these questions from his words alone.

---

[1] S. Greg. M., *Dial.*, l. II., c. iii.

[2] These dispositions of the Rule agree with those of the Council of Carthage of 536 (Mansi, t. VIII., col. 842): *Si qua vero contentio, quod non optamus, exorta fuerit, ut ista Abbatum aliorum concilio sive judicio finiatur; aut si scandalum perseveraverit, ad Primates uniuscujusque provinciæ universæ causæ monasteriorum judicandæ perducantur.* (*Cf.* Canon vii. of the Council of Tours [567] on the procedure to be followed in deposing an abbot. Mansi, t. IX., col. 793.)

Ordinatus autem Abbas cogitet semper quale onus suscepit, et cui redditurus est rationem villicationis suæ; sciatque sibi oportere prodesse magis quam præesse.

Let him that has been appointed Abbot always bear in mind what a burden he has undertaken, and to whom he will have to give an account of his stewardship; and let him know that it behoves him rather to profit his brethren than preside over them.

St. Benedict addresses some counsels to the Abbot elected and appointed[1] which often recall those of the second chapter and lead us also to repetition. Before descending to practical applications, he lays down the general principle which should regulate the whole conduct of the Abbot. He is required to bear in mind not so much the honour done him as the burden placed upon his shoulders: he is the Lord's steward and holds His place in regard to souls; he must think of this constantly, and must never forget to what Master of sovereign insight and equity he shall have to give an account of his stewardship.

The words which follow are weighty: the Abbot must know that it is his duty rather to serve than to command, to be useful to his children rather than to cut a great figure. Our Lord Himself said with the same apt assonance: " The Son of Man is not come to be ministered unto but to minister " (Matt. xx. 28). But our Holy Father's words are also a verbal reminiscence of St. Augustine, when speaking to the people on the anniversary of his episcopal consecration: " Help us, both by your prayers and by your docility, that we may delight to profit you rather than to preside over you "; and in another place: " That he may understand that he is not a bishop in order to delight in presiding and not in profiting."[2] And, in fact, how many ways there are in which an Abbot may regard his charge! " Behold," he might say to himself, " I have attained my goal; I have won my marshal's baton; I have nothing further to hope for; let me take my ease." By no means, for an Abbot is a man of toil. Or he might reason in this way: " I have numerous occupations, visits to make and receive, letters to write, connections to cultivate, material interests to safeguard: surely it is no longer possible for me to face the requirements of the Rule. They shall see me pontificating from time to time: as for all else, the monastic life shall go on without me." Of course the Abbot, because of his occupations and because of his work for the community, cannot be with it always and present at all observances; but does it not seem that an Abbot who should use his charge as an excuse for shirking the Rule—except it be

[1] In general, the confirmation of an abbatial election, the institution, or " ordination " of the Abbot, fell then by right to the bishop of the diocese, even in the case of monasteries which enjoyed much independence. From the sixth century onwards certain founders, and even bishops themselves, in Italy and in Gaul, reserved the protection of their monasteries and the confirmation of abbatial elections to the Sovereign Pontiff. But neither in Chapters LXIV. and LXV. of the Rule, nor in the Life of St. Benedict (S. GREG. M., *Dial.*, l. II., c. iii., xxii.), do we find sufficient data for deciding the manner of the *ordinatio Abbatis* at Subiaco and Monte Cassino.

[2] *Sermo* CCCXL. *P.L.*, XXXVIII., 1484. *De civitate Dei*, l. XIX., c. xix. *P.L.*, XLI., 647.

for sickness or old age—deprives himself of a great source of strength and defrauds his monks of a very good example? There is another danger: in the language of the Ceremonial an Abbot ranks next to a Bishop and possesses some of his external rights; *æquiparatus episcopis*. From a sense of his dignity, and for the good renown of his monastery, he may believe himself bound to multiply pontifical occasions both at home and abroad, to show himself at all ceremonies, ecclesiastical meetings, and congresses, and to claim privileges and honours. All this would be quite unworthy of an earnest man and very much against the words of the Rule. The Abbot is a monk, humble and simple; and his place is at home.

Oportet ergo eum esse doctum in lege divina, ut sciat unde proferat nova et vetera: castum, sobrium, misericordem; et semper superexaltet misericordiam judicio, ut idem ipse consequatur. Oderit vitia, diligat fratres.	He must, therefore, be learned in the law of God, that he may know whence to bring forth new things and old: he must be chaste, sober, merciful, and always exalt mercy above judgement, that he himself may obtain the same. Let him hate sin, and love the brethren.

The Abbot exists only for the good of his monks: "he must therefore (*oportet ergo*) be learned in the faith, in the spiritual life, and in the Sacred Scriptures?" This is the first precise counsel given to the Abbot, and we remember how our Holy Father insisted previously on this point. From a treasure already acquired and increased every day by study and prayer, the Abbot must draw, like a good householder, " new things and old " (Matth. xiii. 52; Cant. vii. 13): doctrine which does not change and application which changes from day to day, the eternal rules and the counsels appropriate to each individual nature. It is the father's duty to give light, as it is the duty of a son lovingly to let it penetrate his being: " And they shall all be taught of God " (John vi. 45). A monastery should be a school of supernatural learning. When men are not encouraged and sustained, daily nourished with intellectual food, they grow old before their time, and from day to day the number and compass of their ideas are reduced; they busy themselves with their health, with themselves, with a hundred nothings, which they magnify, and they become ungovernable. And if, unfortunately, the Abbot does not instruct at all, or confines himself to uttering futilities, he will never really be in touch with his monks, and will never know the greatest joys of life.

But besides theoretical instruction as to what we should think and believe, there is practical instruction as to what we must resolve and accomplish. With a view to this second kind of preaching St. Benedict marks out rapidly the virtues which shall give authority to the Abbot's words. He must be chaste and sober. To emphasize this point is unnecessary, for it would be simply monstrous if things were otherwise, and if the Abbot's life gave other example than this to his children. However, sobriety and chastity, as understood by the ancients, did not merely mean constraint and negation: they implied perfect moral delicacy, the spirit of detachment in the use of created goods, and that clinging to God which is the result of this sacrifice.

St. Benedict adds "merciful," because he is about to lead us to another topic, that of correction or active repression. Plato somewhere asks: "What is government?" and replies that it is to exchange enlightenment with the governed. The reply is a beautiful one and quite in conformity with the Socratic theory that no one does wrong but in his own despite: if the offender knew, he would not sin. Unhappily it is a principle too ideal for fallen beings; and authority must often resign itself to the duty of correction and punishment. Blessed be our Holy Father for giving us God's own method as our pattern and for exhorting the Abbot to it, not only because he is a father, but also on the ground of his own interest: "Blessed are the merciful, for they shall obtain mercy." St. Odilo used to say: "I would rather be condemned for mercifulness than for severity." If God, at the Last Judgement, reproaches us for excessive mercifulness, may we not kneel before Him and say with the greatest possible respect: "But what of Yourself, O Lord?" Therefore let the Abbot always exalt mercy above justice, when severity does not appear indispensable (Jas. ii. 13). He is not a minister of justice, but of mercy. Of course he must hate wrongdoing and dangerous tendencies: but at least let him love the brethren. This double principle must guide him in his correction.[1]

In ipsa autem correctione prudenter agat, et ne quid nimis; ne dum nimis eradere cupit æruginem, frangatur vas; suaque fragilitate semper suspectus sit, memineritque calamum quassatum non conterendum. In quibus non dicimus ut permittat nutriri vitia, sed prudenter et cum caritate ea amputet, prout viderit cuique expedire, sicut jam diximus; et studeat plus amari quam timeri.

And in his correction itself let him act prudently, and not go to excess, lest seeking too eagerly to scrape off the rust he break the vessel. Let him keep his own frailty ever before his eyes, and remember that the bruised reed must not be broken. By this we do not mean that he should suffer vices to grow up, but that he should cut them off prudently and with charity, according as he shall see that it is best for each, as we have said; and let him study rather to be loved than feared.

How then must correction be applied, when it has become necessary? With prudence and moderation, without ever going to excess: *ne quid nimis.*[2] In the first place, reprimands should be rare. When they fall

---

[1] It is borrowed from St. Augustine: *Dilige hominem, oderis vitium* (*Sermo* XLIX., 5. *P.L.*, XXXVIII., 323); *Oderit vitium, amet hominem* (*De civit. Dei.*, l. XIV., c. vi. *P.L.*, XLI., 409); *Cum dilectione hominum et odio vitiorum* (*Epist.* CCXI., 11. *P.L.*, XXXIII., 962).—S. Cæsar., *Reg. ad virg.*, xxii.: *Hoc facite cum dilectione sororum et odio vitiorum.*

[2] A reminiscence of St. Jerome or of St. Augustine. *Difficile est modum tenere in omnibus,* says St. Jerome, *et vere juxta philosophorum sententiam,* μεσότης ἡ ἀρετή, ὑπερβολὴ κακία *reputantur; quod nos una et brevi sententiola exprimere possumus: Ne quid nimis,* Terentius, *Andria,* I., i. 34 (*Epist.* CVIII., 20. *P.L.*, XXII., 898). Else-

thick and fast and frequently, men grow used to them and they cease to make an impression. Secondly, they should be really justified: some matters are of considerable moment and others less important; there may be some detail which an Abbot, from habit or temperament, does not like, and yet which he is not for that reason obliged to root out. Lastly, correction should be timely and adapted to the character and moral condition of the individual: some men are docile, others resent all interference; souls habitually submissive have moments of keen temptation, when it would be imprudent and perhaps even cruel to add to their burden. We must beware of exasperating souls: though we may have to scrape the rust off the kettle, we must not go so far as to break it. Our touch must be deft and delicate.

To induce the Abbot to be merciful St. Benedict gives him a double motive: he must consider his own state, and he must consider God. Ever bethinking himself of his own frailty, ever putting himself in the place of the one he corrects, he will be inclined to indulgence and compassion. Especially will this be so if, remaining united to the Lord and acting only in concert with Him, he remembers the terms in which Isaias (xlii. 3) and St. Matthew (xii. 20) describe the character of the Messias: "the bruised reed he shall not break." And while the Rule thus endeavours to restrain the Abbot from being prone to severity, it would be strange that any brother should think he has a mission to rebuke authority and spur it on, when it is not employed in correcting immediately all that he thinks intolerable. "Why does the Abbot not see that? It stares one in the face. Can it be that he is a party to it?" Have patience! It is bad taste thus to evoke the thunderbolt on all that is not in precise conformity with one's personal notions: "You know not of what spirit you are" (Luke ix. 55). Moreover, such indignant moods searcely come except to youth and inexperience; and those who are most impatient to have their brethren treated with severity are most easily taken aback when they themselves are reprimanded. Let us then leave the Abbot to intervene at his own time and in the way which he judges fit.

In quibus non dicimus . . . In this sentence we have, not an abatement of mercy, but a warning against a false interpretation of this virtue. The ideal of mercy is not the letting everyone do as he pleases; inobservance and laxity do not constitute the family spirit. And it is important that anxiety to show kindness to the individual should not make us forget to be kind to the community; for a monastery rapidly declines if the superior be too ready to forget, excuse, and pardon everything. St. Benedict would not have evil practices grow through such toleration. And his life shows us more than one occasion in which his fatherly love

---

where (*Epist.* CXXX., 11. *P.L.*, XXII., 1116) St. Jerome repeats the two quotations and attributes *Ne quid nimis* to one of the Seven Sages, adding: *Quod tam celebre factum est, ut comico quoque versu expressum sit.* In Letter LX., 7 (*P.L.*, XXII., 593) he asks Heliodorus to moderate his sorrow for the death of his nephew Nepotianus and quotes the *Ne quid nimis.*—On his part, ST. AUGUSTINE quotes and explains the same epigram (*Enarratio* IV. *in Ps.* cxviii., 1. *P.L.*, XXXVII., 1509).

was armed with holy severity: we have but to recall the story of the young monk who held the lamp; of him who could not remain at prayer but yielded to the solicitations of the little blackamoor; of the over-zealous cellarer who kept back the flask of oil. Faults undoubtedly have to be suppressed, but it must be done at the fitting moment, with skill and with charity.

Moreover, the Abbot is advised to aim at being loved rather than feared. St. Augustine gives the same counsel.[1] So the ancients knew not that superfine spirituality which would have us guard against a warm attachment to our superior, in order that we may obey with purer intention: which would make us distinguish carefully between the man and the superior, so as to fortify ourselves against a too natural affection for the former.[2] If our Holy Father bids the Abbot make himself loved and not feared, his first reason is that the Abbot holds the place of Our Lord and our relations with Our Lord are the same as our relations with the Abbot. His further reason is that the new dispensation is essentially and wholly a dispensation of love and not of fear: " You have not received the spirit of servitude again in fear." Finally, this affection itself is an indispensable help to virtue; it gives support and consolation to the heart of the Abbot. And, by means of it, he can lead them to God more effectively; for souls obey the better the more they love.

Non sit turbulentus et anxius, non sit nimius et obstinatus, non zelotypus et nimis suspiciosus, quia nunquam requiescet.	Let him not be violent and anxious, nor exacting and headstrong, nor jealous and too prone to suspicion, for he will never be at rest.

Having spoken of instruction and of correction, its necessary complement, our Holy Father now insists on that fundamental disposition which is called discretion. It should show itself first of all in the Abbot's character. A man's character is the moral form of his temperament. We might desire that he should have no temperament, or character, or personality: that he were wholly like to God, and that God's influence replaced self. But this is not always possible, and the Abbot and his monks must accept the fact. St. Benedict requires that the Abbot should at least strive not to be violent, anxious, exacting, headstrong, jealous, over-suspicious:[3] for, says he, there is no rest for such a one. How impossible is peacefulness in a house whose head is

---

[1] *Corripiat inquietas, consoletur pusillanimes, suscipiat infirmas, patiens sit ad omnes; disciplinam libens habeat, metuens imponat. Et quamvis utrumque sit necessarium, tamen plus a vobis amari appetat quam timeri, semper cogitans Deo se pro vobis redditurum esse rationem. Unde magis obediendo non solum vestri, verum etiam ipsius misereremini; quia inter vos quanto in loco superiore, tanto in periculo majore versatur* (Epist. CCXI., 15. P.L., XXXIII., 964-965).

[2] *Amastis enim ut veniretis: sed amastis, quid ? Si nos, et hoc bene; nam volumus amari a vobis, sed nolumus in nobis. Quia ergo in Christo vos amamus, in Christo nos redamate, et amor noster pro invicem gemat ad Deum: ipse enim gemitus columbæ est* (S. AUG., In Joannis Evang., tract. VI., 1. P.L., XXXV., 1425).

[3] Again a reminiscence of Isaias, who says of the Messias: *Non clamabit, neque accipiet personam. . . . Calamum quassatum non conteret. . . . Non erit tristis, neque turbulentus* (xlii. 2-4).

restless and passionate! Let us beware of passing lightly over these words and regarding them as so much padding. On the contrary, they seem to define once more, and by contrast, the general character of our life. Not instruction only, but peace as well, comes from above and is communicated to us through our superiors. A monastery should be the abode of peace; and we expect to see it radiate from the person of the Abbot. Let us repeat once more: St. Benedict does not recommend an Abbot to use the spur, to push, or to goad, in order to obtain the maximum of spiritual result in the minimum of time. Such violent methods may succeed: but they have a very good chance of failure; and even when they succeed they give the supernatural life a touch of anxiety and tension.

In ipsis imperiis suis sit providus et consideratus, sive secundum Deum, sive secundum sæculum sint. Opera quæ injungit, discernat ac temperet, cogitans discretionem sancti Jacob, dicentis: *Si greges meos plus in ambulando fecero laborare, morientur cuncti una die.*[1] Hæc ergo aliaque testimonia discretionis matris virtutis sumens, sic omnia temperet, ut sit quod et fortes cupiant, et infirmi non refugiant.

In his commands themselves, whether they concern God or the world, let him be prudent and considerate. Let him be discreet and moderate in the tasks which he imposes, bearing in mind the discretion of holy Jacob, who said: "If I cause my flocks to be overdriven, they will all die in one day." Taking, then, this and other examples of discretion, the mother of virtue, let him so temper all things, that the strong may have something to strive after, and the weak may not be dismayed.

The subject now is the Abbot's discretion, when he commands and imposes duties of obedience: for he may not abstain from giving orders, so as to avoid the faults that were pointed out to him a moment ago. But let him, "in his commands themselves," be careful and moderate, prudent and considerate, whether he be dealing with the things of God, such as the Divine Office and prayer, or with temporal matters, such as work and food. He should always divide his personality and in some sort live in the persons of the weak. When the Abbot is apportioning work, says St. Benedict, let him show discernment and moderation, adapting it carefully to the capacity and strength of the individual. God has given him no mission to crush His servants. He must remember the discretion of the holy Patriarch Jacob (Gen. xxxiii. 13), and in his reading make careful note of all the other examples of this discretion, the mother of virtues.[2]

Here again in these few words, and expressed positively, is the whole spirit of St. Benedict. Discretion is nothing else but a form of prudence, queen and mistress of the moral virtues, according to the exposition of

[1] Recent critical editions read: . . . *et consideratus; et sive secundum Deum, sive secundum sæculum sit opera quam injungit, discernat.*

[2] These are the very words of CASSIAN, in his 2nd *Conference* (chap iv.), which might well be re-read in its entirety: *Omnium namque virtutum generatrix, custos moderatrixque discretio est.*

the angelic Doctor.[1] Virtues should be deliberate and intelligent, and ever hold a mean: now it is the business of prudence to determine this virtuous mean, after careful consideration of the circumstances of action. Where prudence is, there also are the other moral virtues; just as all the theological virtues meet in charity. We might say of discretion that it is *prudentia regnativa*—that is to say, the virtue which, conscious of the end to be obtained and of the means at its disposal, ordains all acts to this desired end, sets itself to proportion all things and exceed in none, to measure the difficulty of a task both by its character and by the capacity of the individual. As a habit and a sustained quality of life, discretion is the wise moderation and exquisite tempering of action. It orders the virtues and powers of the soul harmoniously, in such sort that the lofty end of life, the contemplation of divine things, is attained.

" Let him so temper all things, that the strong may have something to strive after, and the weak may not be dismayed." There is our Holy Father's purpose, to rally all souls of goodwill to the perfect life and to lead them to union with God. But, that being so, one must be content not to require from everyone and at every moment the maximum of sustained effort. That would be to hurry towards inobservance under colour of perfection. How short a time such enthusiasms last! Lukewarmness is not a more serious danger than this. St. Benedict establishes a certain wise mean, easy of attainment, beyond which nothing shall be exacted. But a margin is left for personal sensitiveness and generosity. St. Benedict himself, in the last chapter of his Rule and in other passages, lays open vistas of greater perfection for the valiant. And prudence also would counsel a monk, who is desirous of attaining sanctity, not to slumber on the way, but to put his working ideal very high.

Et præcipue, ut præsentem Regulam in omnibus conservet; ut, dum bene ministraverit, audiat a Domino, quod servus bonus, qui erogavit triticum conservis suis in tempore suo: *Amen dico vobis*, ait, *super omnia bona sua constituet eum*.

And, especially, let him observe this present Rule in all things; so that, having ministered well, he may hear of the Lord what that good servant heard, who gave wheat to his fellow-servants in due season: "Amen, I say unto you, he shall place him over all his goods."

A last and weighty piece of advice is addressed to the Abbot: "And, especially, let him observe this present Rule in all things." All through this chapter he has heard scarcely of anything else than of mercy, discretion, and the adaptation of all things to the needs of his children. In order to avoid all misunderstanding, St. Benedict reminds him that he is by no means free to modify the Rule, to make it easier or harder, to substitute for it his own notions and his own extemporary arrangements. Till St. Benedict's time the will of the Abbot had often been the only rule of a monastery: but St. Benedict's cenobites require a written Rule, broadminded yet stable and precise. It is entrusted to

---

[1] *Summa*, II.–II., q. xlvii.

the Abbot's care. St. Benedict bids him preserve it intact—in spirit and in letter—to see to its observance, and, undoubtedly, to observe it also himself. The Abbot may not dispense with the Rule, which provides him instruction and restraint; nor is the Rule enough of itself without the Abbot, by reason of its abstract and general character. There should be a close union between the one and the other. And in this lies the very natural explanation of the difficulty created between a monk and his Abbot, when the monk begins to take liberties with the Rule. At the same moment and by the same act he separates himself from God, from the Rule, and from his Abbot; and, by remaining faithful to one or other of these three, a monk achieves fidelity to all, and happiness.

The last words of the chapter, which are meant for his encouragement, also tell the Abbot for the last time that he is the servant of the servants of God (*conservis suis*), that he is a steward whose business it is to distribute pure supernatural food to them, honestly and unselfishly. If he does his duty well, the Lord of the family will one day set him over all His goods (Matt. xxiv. 45 *sq.*).

CHAPTER LXV

OF THE PRIOR OF THE MONASTERY

THE Abbot may be assisted in his government by a second-in-command. Several ancient Rules[1] have no other title than "second" for this official; and St. Gregory tells us that St. Benedict at the time of the foundation of the monastery of Terracina appointed "a Father and one to second him" (*Patrem constituit et quis ei secundus esset*); while a little farther on he calls this "second" his prior: *Præpositus ejus*.[2] The title of "Præpositus," which is applied in a general way by Sacred Scripture and the Fathers to all those who exercise governing power, as for example to bishops, belonged also to the superiors of monastic communities; St. Basil calls the Abbot προεστώς. Cassian calls him "Præpositus;"[3] in the Rule of St. Pachomius, translated by St. Jerome, the "Præpositus domus" is the superior of a monastery. But in reserving this title for the Abbot's assistant, our Holy Father was no innovator; the Rule of St. Macarius[4] distinguished the Præpositus from the Abbot, and St. Cæsarius speaks of the Abbess, or Mother, and the Præposita.[5] As to the title "Prior" which now[6] takes the place of Præpositus or Provost, it designates in St. Benedict's Rule any superior whatever, an elder or one who presides.

Our actual legislation recognizes three kinds of Priors: conventual Priors, who have jurisdiction like Abbots; simple Priors, superiors of monasteries which are not yet canonically erected and are considered as forming a part of the mother house; claustral Priors, the only kind with which we shall presently have to deal. This Prior is called "claustral," says Lanfranc,[7] because he is specially charged with the supervision of the cloister and its surroundings—that is, with the region generally occupied by the monks. He was distinguished at Cluny and elsewhere from the one who was called Grand Prior, and was his vicar.[8] In actual fact, the duties of the Subprior of an abbey are in some degree

---

[1] S. Pach., *Reg.*, clxxxii., clxxxv.—Theodoreti, *Religiosa historia*, c. iv. P.G., LXXXII., 1348.—*Cf.* S. Basil., *Reg. fus.*, xlv.

[2] *Dial.*, l. II., c. xxii. [3] *Inst.*, V., xxvii.; *Conlat.*, XVIII., vii.

[4] Cap. xxvii. [5] *Reg. ad virg.*, xvi.

[6] Differing from the view of some commentators, we do not think that the term "Prior" had already acquired its narrower meaning in the letter of St. Gregory the Great *ad Victorem episcopum* (*Epist.*, l.V. Ep. VI. P.L., LXXVII., 727; M.G.H.: *Epist.*, t. I., p. 284): there, as in the interesting letter *ad Agnellum Abbatem* concerning the appointment of a "Præpositus" (*Epist.*, l. VII. Ep. X. P.L., ibid., 864; M.G.H.: ibid., p. 453), *locus Prioris* and *locus prioratus* refer to the superior; and St. Gregory always calls the Abbot's "second" *Præpositus* (*Epist.*, l. III., Ep. III. P.L., ibid., 605; M.G.H.: ibid., pp. 160 sq.). In order to find this personage with the name of "Prior," we have to come down to the *Statutes* of Lanfranc, the *Customs of Cluny*, the *Use of Cîteaux*, etc. (*Cf.* Hæften, l. III., tract. vi., disq. i.-iii.).

[7] *Statuta*, c. iii.

[8] Details as to their respective functions are to be found in Udalric, *Consuet. Clun.*, l. III., c. iv. and vi., in the *Ordo Cluniacensis* of Bernard, P. I., c. ii. and iii., and in the *Constitutions of Hirschau*, l. II., c. xvi., xvii., and xx.

Of the Prior of the Monastery

the same as those of the Cluniac Claustral Prior. In the Declarations or Constitutions of the Maurist Congregation mention is made only of one or several deans to help the superior and his " second " in the maintenance of discipline. The Subprior, or second Prior, existed in the Congregations of Bursfeld, Valladolid, etc.

The sixty-fifth chapter may be summarized as follows: The grave abuses that the appointment of a Prior may give rise to, especially if he is appointed by others and not by the Abbot. Is it possible to do without a Prior? Granted that it is not, how is he to be appointed? What should be the attitude of the Prior in the fulfilment of his duties? What is to be done should he conduct himself badly and prove incorrigible?

DE PRÆPOSITO MONASTERII. — Sæpius quidem contingit, ut per ordinationem præpositi scandala gravia in monasteriis oriantur, dum sint aliqui maligno spiritu superbiæ inflati, qui æstimantes se secundos Abbates esse, assumentes sibi tyrannidem, scandala nutriunt, dissensiones in congregatione faciunt, . . .

It happens very often that by the appointment of the Prior grave scandals arise in monasteries; since there are some who, puffed up by the evil spirit of pride, and deeming themselves to be second Abbots, take upon themselves a usurped power, and so foster scandals and cause dissensions in the Community, . . .

We cannot fail to be struck by the very severe tone which our Holy Father suddenly adopts, and by the extraordinary vigour with which he denounces the intrigues and scandals which he says very often follow the appointment of the Prior. He brands these intrigues with harsh and incisive words, such as we are not accustomed to expect from his pen. The sentences seem borne along in a torrent of holy indignation. And for a moment St. Benedict throws aside his wonted brevity, in order to analyze and describe the phases of the evil. We get the impression that he has met the thing at close quarters and speaks from an attentive and connected experience. But neither he nor history has told us of what precise facts he was thinking. After indicating the abuses in a general way, and without fixing the events which are their cause, our Holy Father draws attention to certain specially effective circumstances.

. . . et maxime in illis locis, ubi ab eodem sacerdote, vel ab eisdem Abbatibus qui Abbatem ordinant, ab ipsis etiam et præpositus ordinatur. Quod quam sit absurdum facile advertitur, quia ab ipso initio ordinationis materia ei datur superbiendi, dum ei suggeritur a cogitationibus suis, exutum eum esse a potestate Abbatis sui, quia ab ipsis est ordinatus a quibus et Abbas.

. . . and especially in those places where the Prior is appointed by the same Bishop or the same Abbots as appoint the Abbot himself. How foolish this custom is may easily be seen; for from his first entering upon office an incentive to pride is given to him, the thought suggesting itself that he is freed from the authority of his Abbot, since he has been appointed by the very same persons.

In the preceding chapter St. Benedict alluded to the extraordinary intervention of the bishop or of neighbouring abbots in the election of the Abbot. In this we learn that in certain places—St. Benedict does not say " everywhere "—the appointment or installation of the Abbot— he does not say " election "—belonged usually either to the bishop (*sacerdos*), or to a council of abbots, or rather to the bishop assisted by the neighbouring abbots. And it happened sometimes that the Prior received his appointment from the same persons as had appointed the Abbot, perhaps in the same ceremony.[1] " How foolish this custom is may easily be seen," St. Benedict boldly says. For the result is to furnish the Prior, from the very beginning, in the very act which sets him in power, with a proximate occasion of pride. We should not count too much on the virtue of men, and experience shows what happens when the Prior allows himself to be " puffed up with an evil spirit of pride."

Consider first of all the secret thoughts of the Prior; it is like the first act in a tragedy: " I am not the Abbot's man: he has not chosen me, I have been imposed on him. So I am independent; I hold the place of the superior authority, which has appointed me and to which alone I am accountable. Consequently it is my business to correct the Abbot and to control his activity."[2] The Abbot, however, from his own point of view, makes very similar reflections: " It will be no easy matter governing here. I have got a man by me to act as my supervisor, a man whose functions are very disagreeable to me—since he watches me in the name of the authority that has made him—and very easy for himself, since, with nothing positive to do, he is at full liberty to criticize." So opens the second act, and then the division begins to show itself externally. In fact, it is impossible to limit the operation of such causes, since they are organic and do not consist only in incompatibilities of temperament. In spite of precautions taken to save appearances the quarrel will break out and the whole house be invited to take sides.

Hinc suscitantur invidiæ, rixæ, detractiones, æmulationes, dissensiones, exordinationes; et dum contraria sibi invicem Abbas præpositusque sentiunt, et ipsorum necesse est sub hac dissensione animas periclitari; et ii qui sub ipsis sunt, dum adulantur partibus, eunt in perditionem. Cujus periculi malum illos respicit in capite, qui talibus in ordinatione se fecerunt auctores.

Hence are stirred up envy, quarrels, backbiting, dissensions, jealousy, and disorders. And while the Abbot and Prior are at variance with one another, it must needs be that their souls are endangered by reason of their disagreement; and those who are their subjects, while favouring one side or the other, run to destruction. The evil of this peril falls chiefly on those who by their appointment have originated such disorders.

The Prior regards himself and claims to be treated, not as the Abbot's second, but as a " second Abbot." He tries to draw all into his own hands, to seize a power which is then nothing else but usurpation and tyranny:

[1] *Mos erat eorum tunc*, observes SMARAGDUS, *ut quando Abbas ordinabatur, tunc et ab eodem episcopo et aliis coram adstantibus Abbatibus et præpositus ordinaretur.*
[2] The best manuscript reading is perhaps the very words, in " direct speech," which pride suggests to the soul: *Ab ipsis es et tu ordinatus a quibus et Abbas.*

assumentes sibi tyrannidem. He has his flatterers, his clients, his court. To attain his ends he encourages and foments scandals, sows tares, organizes conspiracies, and divides the community. And then all is hatred, altercation, backbiting, calumny, jealousy, envy, dissension, and disorder of every kind. The monks range themselves in one or other camp: for it is no longer permitted or possible to remain neutral. Those who love order and obedience take sides with the Abbot; those who profess to love reform and good sense and so on, these join the Prior.

Then there is an end of peace, of spirituality, of good example, of the monastery. The quarrel grows more bitter from day to day; sometimes the accursed heritage of these dissensions is passed on for a long period of years, and while all suffer from them, no one is willing to be cured. For all are thinking of revenge, of defence, or of attack, and they stand in an attitude of armed neutrality. With this lamentable result: those who have once tasted this bitter cup of fraternal discord can never again leave it alone; hostility enters into their temperament and distrust becomes incurable. Infallibly, says St. Benedict, the souls of the Prior and the Abbot himself are endangered; and those who espouse the side of one or the other run to perdition. For it is very hard then, even for the good, to preserve moderation and charity.

The responsibility for the evil which must result from such a dangerous state of affairs (*cujus periculi malum*) lies in the first place with those who, in appointing the Prior with the Abbot, have really made themselves the authors of such disorders.[1] This is a declaration as outspoken as the *quam sit absurdum* above. Yet this practice, in spite of all the anathemas of St. Benedict, was adopted in the seventeenth century by the Congregation of St. Vanne, in which General Chapter nominated the Claustral Priors or Subpriors. Among the Maurists and Cassinese the superior himself chose his assistant.

Ideoque nos prævidemus expedire, propter pacis caritatisque custodiam, in Abbatis pendere arbitrio ordinationem monasterii sui. Et si potest fieri, per decanos ordinetur (ut antea disposuimus) omnis utilitas monasterii, prout Abbas disposuerit: ut dum pluribus committitur, unus non superbiat.	We foresee, therefore, that it is expedient for the preservation of peace and charity, that the ordering of the monastery depend upon the will of the Abbot. If possible, let all the affairs of the monastery be attended to (as we have already arranged) by deans, as the Abbot shall appoint; so that, the same office being shared by many, no one may become proud.

St. Benedict here takes measures of a legislative character. Since the evil just described comes from alien interference in the appointment of officials, "we foresee," for the purpose of avoiding these scandals and in order to safeguard peace and charity—"we foresee" that it is expedient to leave to the Abbot full liberty to organize and rule his monastery (*ordinatio* has here its generic sense). This principle of the absolute power of the Abbot derives directly from the conception which

---

[1] Some manuscripts read *talius inordinationis.*

St. Benedict had of a monastic community; it is not merely suggested by emergency or given simply as an opportune safeguard.

In virtue of this principle the Abbot then shall choose his own Prior—if he think it necessary to choose one. For our Holy Father goes even farther. While his predecessors seemed to make no scruple of providing themselves with such an assistant, St. Benedict holds that it would be better to do without. He suspects, however, that this will not always be possible: *Et si potest fieri*. But it could be done; and especially since, according to the mind of St. Benedict, the Abbot should rarely be away and should consequently have less need of a substitute. By means of deans, according to his regulation in Chapter XXI., the Abbot shall secure all needful help and provide for the manifold necessities of the monastery.[1] St. Benedict does not mean that the deans, and they alone, should be given charge of the various offices, but rather that they should see to the maintenance of good discipline and fulfil the functions generally reserved to the Prior. In any case all will be done in conformity with the orders of the Abbot. And, thanks to this parcelling out of power among many, the individual will be less tempted to pride.

| Quod si aut locus expetit, aut congregatio petierit rationabiliter cum humilitate, et Abbas judicaverit expedire, quemcumque elegerit Abbas, cum consilio fratrum timentium Deum, ordinet ipse sibi præpositum. | But if the needs of the place require it, and the community ask for it reasonably and with humility, and the Abbot judge it expedient, let him himself appoint a Prior, whomsoever he shall choose with the counsel of brethren who fear God. |

Nevertheless, in wishing to guard himself against the ill-conduct of a Prior and the troubles which result, he must not leave the monastery without proper government. For if the house is large, if the Abbot is often absent or is overworked, it would seem difficult for the deans to maintain an identical policy and one absolutely according to the policy of the Abbot. The latter then, " if the needs of the place require it," may choose a Prior. He will do so all the more willingly because the community, it may be, asks him, humbly and for substantial reasons. But while he is recommended to confer in the matter with prudent and God-fearing brethren, the duty of estimating the suitability of the measure and deciding upon it is left to him.[2]

We shall observe how St. Benedict, in every phrase, sets himself to emphasize the entire freedom of the Abbot. He himself chooses whom he wishes (*quemcumque elegerit Abbas*) and when he wishes; he himself appoints his Prior (*ordinet ipse sibi præpositum*), and he is not the bishop's Prior nor the community's Prior; the Prior is his own, he is his man. And that is enough to determine the attitude and rôle of the Prior in the community.

[1] *Utilitas monasterii:* the same expression as in Chapter III.; it is found in CASSIAN, *Inst.*, VII., ix.
[2] See the old customaries, especially that of Cluny, for the manner of " ordination " of the Prior.

Of the Prior of the Monastery

Qui tamen præpositus illa agat cum reverentia quæ ab Abbate suo ei injuncta fuerint, nihil contra Abbatis voluntatem, aut ordinationem faciens: quia quantum prælatus est ceteris, tantum eum oportet sollicite observare præcepta regulæ.

Let the Prior, however, reverently do whatever is enjoined him by his Abbot, and nothing against his will or command; for the more he is raised above the rest, so much the more carefully ought he to observe the precepts of the Rule.

Qui tamen præpositus: we should notice the "however" (*tamen*), an adverb intended again to anticipate the encroachments of the official elected. He is Prior—that is to say, the one who comes immediately after the Abbot and who is after him the first authority in the monastery; to him in case of the absence, resignation, incapacity, or death of the Abbot falls the right of government; to him the Abbot leaves a large amount of activity and influence; but for all this the Prior is not to affect an arrogant and independent air. Since the Abbot has chosen him freely and not irreversibly, so that he may be his right arm and represent him among the brethren, the Prior would be disloyal if he strove to capture the affection of the monks, to dissuade them slyly from obeying the Abbot on this point or on that, and if he had no regard on his own part for orders or instructions that were given. "Let him do reverently," says St. Benedict, "whatever is enjoined by his Abbot, and *nothing* against his will or command."[1]

These words impel us to say something of the qualities of a Prior. God be blessed if he be a holy man, for he has need of virtue who has at once to command and to obey, to obey better and with a deeper docility, to obey a man whom he sees at closer quarters and whose failings he may know full well. It goes without saying that he must be intelligent and circumspect. He must be regular and a true monk, for his duty before all else is to maintain exact observance. And St. Benedict reminds him that in proportion as he is raised above others he must give an example of greater fidelity to the precepts of the Rule. That he should be devoted to his Abbot is only natural; and he shall force himself if necessary to draw near to him and to bring the brethren to him. And it follows that he must love these. It is almost desirable, too, that he should be of a somewhat different temperament from the Abbot, even in the interest of the Abbot himself, to whom, on occasion and respectfully, he will be able to give good advice; and also in the interest of the brethren, who will sometimes be able to find in the Prior certain qualities complementary to those of the Abbot; but to compare the Abbot to a father and the Prior to a mother is foolishness.[2]

Qui præpositus, si repertus fuerit vitiosus, aut elatione deceptus superbiæ, aut contemptor sanctæ regulæ fuerit comprobatus, admoneatur verbis

And if the Prior be found culpable or deceived by the haughtiness of pride, or be proved a contemner of the holy Rule, let him be admonished

---

[1] St. Pachomius likewise said of the local superior of each monastery: *Ipse autem præpositus nihil faciet, nisi quod Pater jusserit, maxime in re nova; nam quæ ex more descendit, servabit regulas monasterii* (clviii.).

[2] D. Mège, Comment., p. 750.

usque quater: si non emendaverit, adhibeatur ei correctio disciplinæ regularis. Quod si neque sic correxerit, tunc dejiciatur de ordine præpositurae, et alius qui dignus est, in loco ejus subrogetur. Quod si et postea in congregatione quietus et obediens non fuerit, etiam de monasterio expellatur. Cogitet tamen Abbas, se de omnibus judiciis Deo redditurum rationem, ne forte invidiæ aut zeli flamma urat animam.

by words until the fourth time; and then if he do not amend, let the correction of regular discipline be applied to him. But if even then he do not amend, let him be deposed from the office of Prior, and another, who is worthy, be substituted in his place. If afterwards he be not quiet and obedient in the community, let him be expelled from the monastery. Nevertheless let the Abbot bear in mind that he must give an account to God of all his judgements, lest perchance the flame of envy or jealousy be kindled in his soul.

We have to be prepared for all eventualities. If the Prior is presumptuous, if he be seduced and led away by pride, if he be convicted of contempt for the sacred monastic institutions,[1] if finally he be found vicious—then the Abbot is not to be helpless. Nevertheless he shall respect the office which he himself has given him and he shall not be in a hurry to discredit him in the esteem of the brethren. While the ordinary monks get two warnings and the deans three, the Prior is to be warned four times and secretly. If he do not amend then the severity of regular discipline must be applied; public reprimand, etc. (Chapter XXVIII.).

If all this leaves him incorrigible, then he must be degraded from his position of Prior, and another who is really worthy of the office put in his place. According to our actual discipline the deposition of a bad or doubtful Prior would not take so long; and the twofold ceremony of the deposition and renewal of officials which occurs every year provides a convenient opportunity for the Prior's disappearance, the more so as such a change of function carries no implication at all of degradation. However, if the monk should try in consequence, in a very human spirit of revenge, to foment discord in the community, and if he do not abide in his place, obedient and peaceable, then he must even be expelled from the monastery: *etiam de monasterio expellatur.*

But in a matter where the Abbot may go to excess, allowing himself to be led by jealousy, resentment, or passion, St. Benedict bids him remember that he shall have to render an account to God of all his decisions. There is nothing which will more effectively stifle in its origin every evil flame that may be kindled in his heart.

---

[1] D. CALMET gives five reasons to prove that our Holy Father could, without vanity or presumption, speak of the "holy Rule." As BOHERIUS observes, these words, although ill understood, are really insufficient ground for denying to St. Benedict the authorship of this chapter, or even of the whole Rule, as some writers have ventured to do.

CHAPTER LXVI

OF THE PORTER OF THE MONASTERY

THE internal order and peace of the monastery are only secure if its relations with the outside world are controlled and regulated with vigilance. So our Holy Father rounds off this portion of the Rule by devoting a few lines to the porter. The office has long been, and that almost everywhere, a most humble one, being handed over to lay brothers or servants: yet the ancients, as we shall see, viewed it in a very different way. The purpose of once more commending and safeguarding monastic enclosure and stability inspires also the second portion of this chapter, though it seems at first so disconnected. St. Benedict was led to make the connection by the very source from which he has drawn nearly all the points of this chapter: the seventeenth chapter of Rufinus's *History of Monks*.[1]

DE OSTIARIO MONASTERII.—Ad portam monasterii ponatur senex sapiens, qui sciat accipere responsum et reddere, cujus maturitas eum non sinat vagari. Qui portarius cellam debet habere juxta portam, ut venientes semper præsentem inveniant a quo responsum accipiant. Et mox ut aliquis pulsaverit aut pauper clamaverit, " Deo gratias " respondeat, aut benedicat; et cum omni mansuetudine timoris Dei reddat responsum festinanter, cum fervore caritatis. Qui portarius, si indiget solatio, juniorem fratrem accipiat.

At the gate of the monastery let there be placed a wise old man, who knows how to give and receive an answer, and whose ripeness of years suffers him not to wander. This porter ought to have his cell near the gate, so that they who come may always find someone at hand to give them an answer. As soon as anyone shall knock, or a poor man call to him, let him answer, " Deo gratias," or bid God bless him, and then with all gentleness of the fear of God, let him answer quickly in the fervour of charity. If the porter need solace, let him have with him one of the younger brethren.

We should notice that our Holy Father speaks of the gate of the monastery in the singular. It is in fact traditional[2] that one gate only

---

[1] Treating of the monastery of Abbot Isidore, in the Thebaid: *Intrinsecus putei plures, horti irrigui, omnium quoque pomorum arborumque paradisi, et quæcumque necessaria usibus erant sufficienter, immo et abundanter provisa; ab hoc ut nulli monachorum habitantium intrinsecus, necessitas ulla fieret exeundi foras ad aliquid requirendum. Senior quidam, vir gravis, et de primis electus, ad januam sedens, hoc habebat officii ut adventantes ea lege suscipiat, qua ingressi ultra non exeant.... Hic ergo senior in janua, ubi ipse commanet, adhærentem sibi habebat hospitalem cellulam, in qua adventantes hospitio recipiat et omni humanitate refoveat* (*Vitæ Patrum*, II., xvii. ROSWEYD, pp. 475-476). In chap. ii., RUFINUS had written: *Plantavit* (Hor) *hanc silvam, ut ibi fratres, quos inibi congregare cupiebat, non haberent necessitatem ligni gratia longius evagandi* (ROSWEYD, p. 457).

[2] The 133rd Novel of JUSTINIAN (c. i.: *Collatio* IX., tit. XVI.) legislated thus: *Volumus . . . non plurimos esse in monasterium ingressus sed unum, aut secundum forte; et adstare januæ viros senes et castos et testimonii boni ex omnibus, qui quidem neque reverendissimis monachis concedant sine abbatis voluntate exire monasterium. . . . Sitque cautissima maceria munitum monasterium, ut nullus exitus aliunde nisi per januas sit.*

—apart from another generally provided for domestic traffic—should give access to the monastery; and this to secure our enclosure. For the custody of this gate, the Rule institutes a porter. He is not a *concierge* (hall-porter), and should have neither his name nor his ways. St. Benedict would not have the first-comer appointed to the office. At three points does the monastery come into contact with the outside world: at guest-house, gate, and parlour. The monastic parlours are habitually used by no one except those brethren whose parents or friends live rather near the monastery and make frequent visits. Of the special dangers of the guest-master we spoke in commenting on Chapter LIII.; the same observations should be made again in reference to the porter, whose function also is a very delicate one.

He is the first to come into contact with guests. In ancient times he sometimes did duty for guest-master as well.[1] Many others besides guests present themselves at the gate-house: dependents of the monastery, tourists, penitents, pilgrims, and finally the poor; and the porter is often entrusted with the distribution of alms to the needy.[2] In a large monastery his office is never a sinecure, and provides abundant occasions for mortification and self-suppression. A happy disposition is not enough: a man must have supernatural virtue, in order to be affable always and always good-humoured, to know how to be silent and how to speak at the right time. If the porter has not got a real love of silence, his cell will be nothing but a place of idle gossip and tittle-tattle. All the news of the outside world will be reported there, and the monks, it may be, will come there to get it; from there, too, will be divulged certain details, more or less distorted, of the life within. God forbid that the porter should ever make himself an irregular intermediary between the monastery and the world. Moreover, he should not lack tact or discernment, so that he may know at once with whom he is dealing, and divine how he ought to treat individuals and give appropriate attention to all: he should be "a wise old man, who knows how to give and receive an answer." The word translated "answer" (*responsum*) often meant, in the language of the time, some business affair or message, a "commission," as we say commonly.[3]

The age of the porter is not unimportant. If he be too old, his task may easily become intolerable to him, and he may be tempted to get rid too summarily of those who interrupt his reading or quiet. If he be too young he does not command respect and consideration; he cannot well distinguish between those who should be received and those whom he should dismiss. Youthful impulsiveness may lead him abroad; he opens the gate for others and he may, if he be not over-conscientious,

---

[1] CASSIAN wrote of the postulant: *Deputatur seniori, qui seorsum haud longe a vestibulo monasterii commanens habet curam peregrinorum atque advenientium deputatam eisque omnem diligentiam susceptionis et humanitatis inpendit* (*Inst.*, IV., vii.).
[2] Such was the case at Cîteaux (according to chap. cxx. of the *Use*), at Bursfeld, etc.
[3] In Chapter LI. St. Benedict wrote: *Frater qui pro quovis responso proficiscitur*. . . . And ST. GREGORY THE GREAT: *Mos etenim cellæ fuit, ut quotiens ad responsum aliquod egrederentur fratres* . . . (*Dial.*, l. II., c. xii.).—*Cf.* DU CANGE, *Glossarium*.

open it for himself, and persuade himself that he needs a little excursion into the neighbouring country, whether for the enlargement of his life or even for the sake of his prayers. A taste for reading and prayer, combined with some small manual task, will help the porter to love perfect enclosure.[1] Very many visitors are able to judge the monastery only from the reception that they receive at the gate-house: which is a further reason why everything there should be worthy and edifying.

The commentators discuss whether our Holy Father really required an " old " man; the majority think so, and many pieces of historical evidence seem to support their view; especially as St. Benedict himself prescribes that the porter should be granted as assistant " a younger brother." But we may be content with simple maturity, of years and of prudence. Among the Fathers of the East, the porter was sometimes one of the few priests of the establishment. Everywhere, and for all the reasons which we have mentioned—the safety of the monastery, its good name, and the edification of strangers—this office was regarded as one of the principal ones; we should remember that the Church instituted a special order of clerics to guard the doors of her temples. The Council of Aix-la-Chapelle (A.D. 817) required well-instructed brethren to be chosen. And Calmet suggests that to leave this office to laymen is an indication of a lessening of the monastic sense. But this, perhaps, is rather severe. Peter the Venerable, in his controversy with Cîteaux, confessed that he did not see the good of fixing a monk at the gate-house. In a sense, he said, there were no gates at Cluny, for the gates of the monastery were almost always open to all comers. Sufficient, then, that an " honest servant " should guard them at the times when they should be closed.[2] The Cistercians placed a choir monk and a lay brother in this office. Let us desire to be able to do the same in our monasteries.

The porter should have his cell quite close to the gate: that is necessary. He is not fastened there with a chain, as was the practice of the Romans; but charity and prudence require that he should be faithful to his post, so that those who come may always find someone to answer them and with whom they may deal: *a quo responsum accipiant*. It is probable that, in St. Benedict's arrangement, the porter said certain parts of the Office and made his " sacred reading " in his cell; but, since the gate remained closed the whole night and even at certain times of the day—perhaps at meal-times, for instance—the porter was not completely excluded from conventual exercises.[3] Moreover, our Holy

---

[1] The *Regula cujusdam ad virgines* draws a beautiful portrait of nuns charged with the duty of guarding the door: . . . *Ætate senili; quibus mundus silet; quæ jam ex præsentibus pompis nihil desiderent; sed in toto cordis affectu Creatori inhærentes singulæ dicant: mihi autem adhærere Deo bonum est, ponere in Deo spem meam. . . . Sint mentis suæ statu firmissimæ, ut Domino cum Propheta orando dicant: Averte oculos nostros ne videant vanitatem. . . . Tale semper supervenientibus ostendant exemplum, ut et foris ab extraneis nomen Domini glorificetur, . . . et intus a consodalibus suis mercedis præparent lucra, dum omnium vice foris gerent curam* (iii.).

[2] *Epist.*, l. I., *Ep.* XXVIII. P.L., CLXXXIX., 134.

[3] *Cf. Reg Magistri*, xcv.

Father allows him as assistant a younger brother, who would do his behests and replace him at need, but without relieving him of responsibility, for he remains in charge.

The Rule enters next into some details with regard to the work of the porter. When anyone knocks, or when a poor man, seeking nothing else but an alms, cries out to announce his presence, the porter must, without the least delay, answer *Deo gratias* or bless him. We have said, in Chapter LXIII., what should be understood by this blessing. And we do not think there is reason to enquire, or that it is even possible to ascertain, whether the formula *Deo gratias* was reserved to the poor, while the blessing was kept for the rich, or *vice versa*.[1] But what should be noted is the counsel to " answer " with all possible sweetness, with all the gentleness that comes of the fear of God, and at the same time with all the zeal and holy fervour of charity. It is so natural for people who are harassed and hurried to be impatient, and, in the current phrase, to send everyone packing. That he may ever at need command the secret of this tranquil haste, the porter must remember that God Himself lies concealed in the person of the guest. And if there come one who is not expected, or who seems an intruder, he should receive the same loving welcome, in memory of St. Gregory's thirteenth pauper or St. Martin's beggar.

Monasterium autem si fieri potest, ita debet construi, ut omnia necessaria, id est, aqua, molendinum, hortus, pistrinum, vel artes diversæ intra monasterium exerceantur, ut non sit necessitas monachis vagandi foras; quia omnino non expedit animabus eorum.

The monastery, if it be possible, ought to be so constructed that all things necessary, such as water, a mill, a garden, a bakery, and the various crafts may be contained within it; so that there may be no need for the monks to go abroad, for this is altogether inexpedient for their souls.

We have pointed out the connection, over and above their common origin, between this ordinance and those which precede: St. Benedict's constant anxiety is to emphasize the separation of his monks from the world, and to guarantee their enclosure and stability. It is wholly unsuitable and dangerous for monks to roam here and there, to walk abroad, and in general to go out without permission, or with a permission which has been extorted and is then extended. The world is not a healthy place for us; our souls are ill at ease in it; we are no longer suited to sojourn there without danger. That a man should feel a need of distraction, of escaping observance and the common life, would be a very bad omen. And self-indulgence never lacks excuses; it can clothe itself in most edifying forms: it will allege work for souls, or sacred studies, or charity, or precious bodily health. But our Holy Father does not answer for the perseverance and sanctity of souls except they remain hidden in their monastery. He even desires that the monastery should be self-sufficing and so equipped that there is nothing wanting of the things necessary for life and work. Yet he recognizes that this is not

---

[1] Some manuscripts read *aut Benedic.*

always possible. The circumstances of a Mont St. Michel, for instance, do not lend themselves well to St. Benedict's intention; and the hills which, according to the old saying,[1] he loved so well, were not always, except by miracle, provided with a water-supply.[2]

The enumeration of things "necessary" does not, it is needless to say, pretend to be exhaustive; St. Benedict only mentions the essentials: water, a mill,[3] a garden, a bakery,[4] and finally the crafts and various works (see Chapter LVII.). We should note in passing that our Holy Father recommends occupations and enterprises in so far as they are necessary to the conventual life, and not as great commercial undertakings. It would seem, too, that he does not care to see his monks go to work far off, since he wishes to have the garden in the very enclosure.

Therefore the complete monastery resembles a city. This was the case with many of the monasteries of the Thebaid, where the different trades occupied each their own quarter. In the West, after St. Benedict's time, certain great abbeys were admirably organized, and trained a still greater variety of craftsmen and artists. But, under pain of extending the commentary immoderately, we must leave all these questions to the historian of monasticism.

| Hanc autem Regulam sæpius volumus in congregatione legi, ne quis fratrum de ignorantia se excuset. | And we wish this Rule to be frequently read in the community, that none of the brethren may excuse himself on the ground of ignorance. |

We may regard this sentence as the conclusion of a first redaction of the Rule; although, according to the view which tends to prevail, neither history, nor the intrinsic evidence of the manuscripts, really discloses the existence of two primitive and different texts. But it remains highly probable that the Rule was not composed in a single effort.

Our Holy Father enjoins that the code of the monastic life should be read very often in public, so that no one may excuse his laxity on the ground of ignorance or a treacherous memory. It is another example of St. Benedict's determination to have done with all the disorders produced in so many monasteries by the vagueness, or even the absence, of written rules. We are faithful to St. Benedict's precept, for his Rule is read several times to the novices, and is read to all, in Latin or in the vernacular, at Prime and at the evening meal.[5]

---

[1] *Bernardus valles, montes Benedictus amabat,*
   Oppida Franciscus, celebres Dominicus urbes.

[2] Read chap. v. of the Life of St. Benedict (S. GREG. M., *Dial.*, l. II.).

[3] D. CALMET has quite a little dissertation on mills.

[4] D. BUTLER's edition omits *pistrinum*. See the discussions of the commentators on the exact meaning of this word.

[5] This reading at Prime is already prescribed by the Council of Aix-la-Chapelle of 817 (cap. lxix.). The reading in the refectory is appointed in the *Rule of the Master* (xxiv.).

CHAPTER LXVII

OF BRETHREN WHO ARE SENT ON A JOURNEY

THERE is a connection between the sixty-sixth chapter and the first of those which careful critics regard as later additions. Our Holy Father foresees that it will sometimes be necessary for monks to leave their actual enclosure and go on a journey; but even then he would have them surrounded and protected by a spiritual enclosure, so that the monastery may, as it were, accompany them continually. That is the purpose which dictates all the arrangements of this chapter; their character and number show how much St. Benedict feared his sons going abroad, even though they did so in quite regular fashion. He has spoken already, in Chapters L. and LI., of monks on a journey, but briefly and only to remind us of their obligations in the matter of the Divine Office and of meals; in Chapter LV. their clothing was dealt with; but here the point of view is different. We should observe, finally, that the chapter deals with monks who are undertaking a real journey, and not with those who are absent only for a few hours.

DE FRATRIBUS IN VIA DIRECTIS.—Dirigendi fratres in via, omnium fratrum vel Abbatis orationi se commendent: et semper ad orationem ultimam operis Dei commemoratio omnium absentium fiat.

Let the brethren who are about to be sent on a journey commend themselves to the prayers of all the brethren and of the Abbot; and always, at the last prayer of the Work of God, let a commemoration be made of all the absent.

St. Benedict, therefore, admits that a monk may undertake a journey, without thereby violating his vow of stability. Yet he must be sent according to rule: *dirigendus*. The spiritual or financial interests of the monastery, the care of souls, messages to be taken to princes, bishops, or abbots, attendance at councils, and, in exceptional cases, a visit to one's family: these are some of the motives which may induce the Abbot to impose this hard obedience.[1] Even nowadays, when journeys are accomplished more rapidly, a man with the monastic spirit should never solicit, still less insistently claim, the favour of returning to his home—perhaps periodically—or of passing some weeks near a well-stocked library. But certain awkward situations should be laid before the Abbot as a matter of filial duty: his prudence shall decide.

Ordinarily, the Abbot gives the departing monk one or more companions: this is the best of safeguards, and thus community life is not wholly abandoned. Although St. Benedict says nothing of this custom (the plural "brethren" perhaps suggests it), it is probable that it existed in his monastery, as it did among the Fathers of the East.[2] The

---

[1] *Cf.* HÆFTEN, l. XI., tract. iv., *Itinerarium*.
[2] *Nullus solus foras mittatur ad aliquod negotium, nisi juncto ei altero* (S. PACH., *Reg.*, lvi.).—*Cf.* S. MACAR., *Reg.*, xxii.—S. BASIL., *Reg. fus.*, xxxix.—ST. GREGORY THE

Council of Aix-la-Chapelle (A.D. 817) prescribed that a monk on a journey should always have a companion.

Before going, the brethren recommended themselves to the prayers of all and of the Abbot. Some commentators (Bernard of Monte Cassino and Boherius) regard the particle *vel* in this place as disjunctive: St. Benedict, they say, foresees the case where a monk might have to quit the monastery without being able to appear before the assembled community, and then the prayer and blessing of the Abbot are to suffice.[1] The prayers of the community are asked in the oratory, at a fitting time.[2]

Thus armed and fortified they set out. As we said in Chapter L., they keep all the monastic observances that they can. Especially are they faithful to the Divine Office and to their reading.[3] The community, on its part, never fails to remember absent brethren at the end of each Hour. Several commentators think that St. Benedict means only the prayer at the end of the whole Office—that is, the one which ends Compline—since he does not mention all the canonical Hours expressly, as he does presently when dealing with the return. One may reply that in the latter passage St. Benedict uses the expression "the ending of the Work of God" for the conclusion of each Hour: *per omnes canonicas Horas, dum expletur Opus Dei;* why should he have given a different sense to a quite analogous phrase?—*et semper ad orationem ultimam Operis Dei.* However, general and ancient monastic usage is sufficient to justify our interpretation.[4] These touching prayers for absent brethren were formerly of some length. Those given by Smaragdus begin with the words: *Oremus pro fratribus nostris absentibus;* they comprise a series of short versicles with their responses, and then the fiftieth psalm. The Breviary of Paul V. selected a very much shortened formula, but one which is still attractive, and, if said with faith, sufficient.

GREAT sets down among the reasons which made him refuse to confirm the election of Abbot Constantius, that this monk had made a journey alone: *Epist.,* l. XII., *Ep.* XXIV. *P.L.*, LXXVII., 1233; M.G.H.: *Epist.,* t. II., p. 351.

[1] The Abbot's blessing was, moreover, necessary always, both on setting out and on returning: several passages in the Life of St. Benedict allude to it (S. GREG. M., *Dial.,* l. II.). See, for instance, chaps. xii., xxii., xxiv.: in this last passage is told the story of the young monk who loved his parents too much, and going to see them without having obtained a blessing, died that same day.

[2] The Gregorian Sacramentary has three special prayers for this occasion; they are quoted by HÆFTEN (l. XI., tract. iv., disq. iii.) along with those also which are given by Smaragdus. The one we recite occurs already in the *Customs of Cluny* (l. III., c. v.) and in the *Constitutions of Hirschau* (l. II., c. xviii.).

When travellers were to return the same day or after a few days, the blessing and short prayer of the superior usually sufficed (*cf.* HÆFTEN, *loc. cit.*). In actual fact, in our Congregation, we do not ask for prayers in the oratory unless the absence has to extend beyond a week; but, every time that we leave enclosure, we should, both going and returning, ask the superior's blessing and pray for a moment in the church.

[3] *Codiculum modicum cum aliquibus lectionibus de monasterio secum portet, ut quavis hora in via repausaverit, aliquantulum tamen legat,* etc. (*Reg. Magistri,* lvii.).

[4] We have recalled the fact before (p. 156), that the ancient services ordinarily ended with prayers for all the needs of the faithful.

Revertentes autem de via fratres, ipso die quo redeunt, per omnes canonicas Horas, dum expletur opus Dei, prostrati solo oratorii ab omnibus petant orationem propter excessus, ne quid forte subripuerit in via visus, aut auditus malæ rei, aut otiosi sermonis. Nec præsumat quisquam aliis referre quæcumque foris monasterium viderit aut audierit, quia plurima destructio est. Quod si quis præsumpserit, vindictæ regulari subjaceat.

Let the brethren that return from a journey, on the very day that they come back, lie prostrate on the floor of the oratory at all the canonical Hours at the ending of the Work of God, and beg the prayers of all on account of their transgressions, if perchance they should have seen or heard anything evil on their journey or have fallen into idle talk. And let no one presume to tell others what he may have seen or heard outside the monastery, for thence comes manifold destruction. If anyone shall so presume let him be subjected to the punishment of the Rule.

On the very day of their return, without any delay, the brethren must prostrate themselves on the floor of the oratory, at the end of each Hour, begging thus the prayers of all. The custom has been established of requiring this, once for all, at the end of the first canonical Hour that follows their return. The form used by us appears to be identical with that used at Cluny and Hirschau.[1] These prayers are a sort of sacramental, designed for the removal of all negligences and all faults into which eyes, ears, or tongue may have been surprised. Paul the Deacon and Hildemar note that we are dealing here chiefly and solely with those faults of surprise into which our weakness falls almost inevitably, and that such is the meaning suggested by the words *excessus* and *subripuerit;* graver faults, or faults of a different kind, would require, they say, to be confessed to the Abbot.[2] Our Holy Father's intention is to purify the spirit, heart, and senses of the monk from all the worldly impressions which he may have gathered in his own despite. As with the heavenly Jerusalem, no defilement may penetrate into the precincts of the monastic " Vision of Peace."

For the same reason, those who return from a journey shall spare their brethren what the Rule endeavours to deliver them from for themselves. St. Benedict does not forbid the recital of everything seen or heard: for why not tell of edifying matters,[3] or of certain harmless details ? What he requires is that a man should not relate at random and thoughtlessly all that he has observed: *quæcumque;* for, says he, " thence comes manifold destruction " (*destructio,* the opposite of *ædificatio*). Indiscreet or too circumstantial narratives might awaken memories here and there, might arouse interests, inspire regrets, suggest little romances, resuscitate

---

[1] *Constit. Hirsaug.,* l. II., c. xix.

[2] *Cf.* S. BASIL., *Reg. fus.,* xliv.: *Quibus permittendæ sint peregrinationes et quomodo, ubi redierint, sint interrogandi.*

[3] As is formally permitted by the *Regula Tarnatensis* (ii.).—St. Benedict is quoting ST. PACHOMIUS: *Et omnino quidquid foris gesserint et audierint, in monasterio narrare non poterunt. Si quis ambulaverit in via, vel navigaverit, aut operatus fuerit foris, non loquatur in monasterio quæ ibi geri viderit* (lvii., lxxxvi.).

matters to which we are dead, and which, by God's help, are dead to us: "The world is crucified unto me, and I unto the world." It is always better to keep on this side of what we think is the proper line, and to banish any matter which might be such as to trouble a soul, or even to disturb a brother's vocation.

St. Benedict lays down a severe penalty against such as dare to infringe this point of rule; they shall be subjected to the regular discipline.

Similiter, et qui præsumpserit claustra monasterii egredi, vel quocumque ire, vel quidpiam quamvis parvum sine Abbatis jussione facere.	He shall undergo a like penalty who presumes to leave the enclosure of the monastery and go anywhere or do anything, however small, without permission of the Abbot.

Nothing would be left of enclosure or stability if every individual had the right to weigh the reasons for and against his going out, for his turning this way or that in the course of a journey, or for undertaking any particular line of action. That is the reason why our Holy Father, in ending the chapter, reminds us that the Abbot's command or permission is designed for the prevention of all uncertainty, and is requisite so that the monk's conscience may rest in full security; moreover, the punishments of regular discipline are decreed against anyone who should leave the monastery without permission, turn his steps in any direction whatever, or do anything at all, though very trifling, outside the enclosure.[1] The parts of this sentence should be taken together, not disjunctively. Our Holy Father, always judicious and discreet, could not have threatened with so severe punishment a monk who should do anything irregularly, however trifling it might be, within the monastery; and how, too, could such an ordinance suit the context? Nor does the sentence concern one who should wander and go anywhere at all, without permission, in the monastery. Undoubtedly, as Smaragdus observed, St. Benedict seems in this place to have been inspired by one of St. Pachomius's rules[2] and by a passage in Cassian,[3] both of which imply the meaning which we reject (less the penalties); but our Holy Father sometimes modifies considerably the sources which he uses.

[1] St. Basil had asked: *An conveniat aliquo abire, moderatore non prius commonefacto?* (*Reg. brev.*, cxx.).
[2] *Nullus neque exeundi in agrum, neque ambulandi in monasterio, neque extra murum monasterii foras habeat facultatem, nisi interrogaverit præpositum et ille concesserit* (lxxxiv.).
[3] *Inst.*, IV., x.

CHAPTER LXVIII

IF A BROTHER BE COMMANDED TO DO IMPOSSIBILITIES

THERE is nothing in the Rule which does not deserve our greatest veneration: yet, these last pages, written by our Holy Father in the fulness of his years, of his knowledge of souls, and of his sanctity, resemble a spiritual testament, and have for us a savour of eternity. They are transfused with the brightness of God and impregnated with His sweetness.

Once more the subject is obedience. In the very Prologue our Holy Father defined the monastic life as a glorious labour of obedience: " That you may return by the labour of obedience to Him from whom you departed through the sloth of disobedience "; our spiritual armour, in all its parts, is called obedience: " Who renouncing your own will, do take up the strong and bright arms of obedience." The fifth chapter treats expressly of obedience and delineates it as above all else eager and joyous. The seventh chapter, in its first degrees of humility, perhaps even in all, really give us nothing but degrees of obedience. St. Benedict invokes obedience unceasingly, even as St. Francis of Assisi sang of poverty. And, confronted with this insistence, we are tempted to say: " Father, why always repeat the same thing?" Undoubtedly he would answer us with St. John: " Little children, it is the Lord's command, and, if it be done, all is done." We must have obedience always, obedience in all matters, obedience to all, and, when necessary, heroic obedience. St. Benedict has revealed his secret to us, has entrusted us with his ideal; he would have a monk to be not merely obedient, but a personification of obedience, like Him, by Him and in Him, who was " made obedient even unto death."

We may enquire, before commencing the commentary, whether any special motive led our Holy Father to treat this question of heroic obedience immediately after the sixty-seventh chapter rather than elsewhere. We believe that here again, as in the chapter on the porter, this order of treatment was suggested to him by the source which he utilized: the tenth chapter of the fourth book of Cassian's *Institutions*.[1]

Si fratri impossibilia injungan-   If on any brother there be laid
tur.—Si cui fratri aliqua forte gravia   commands that are hard and impos-

---

[1] *Post hæc tanta observantia obedientiæ regula custoditur, ut juniores absque præpositi sui scientia vel permissu non solum non audeant cella progredi, sed ne ipsi quidem communi ac naturali necessitati satisfacere sua auctoritate præsumant* (we recognize here the conclusion of our Chapter LXVII.; and here are words which resemble the succeeding chapter): *sicque universa complere, quæcumque fuerint ab eo præcepta, tamquam si ex Deo sint cælitus edita, sine ulla discussione festinant, ut nonnunquam etiam impossibilia sibimet imperata ea fide ac devotione suscipiant, ut tota virtute ac sine ulla cordis hæsitatione perficere ea et consummare nitantur et ne impossibilitatem quidem præcepti pro senioris reverentia metiantur.*—St. Benedict may have been thinking also of St. Basil, *Reg. contr.*, lxix, lxxxii.—*Cf. Reg. fus.*, xxviii.

aut impossibilia injunguntur, suscipiat quidem jubentis imperium cum omni mansuetudine et obedientia.	sible, let him receive the order of his superior with all meekness and obedience.

Commands that are hard and impossible? What becomes of the much-vaunted discretion of the Benedictine Rule? And what of St. Benedict's promise, in the Prologue, to enjoin nothing beyond ordinary human capacity: " we hope to order nothing that is harsh or rigorous"? No, he is not self-contradictory. He does not, we are sure, adopt those Eastern practices—though often venerable and suggestive—which aimed at breaking self-will by tasks of a violently paradoxical and contradictory character. Nothing in the Rule of St. Benedict, or in his life, permits us to assimilate the " *impossibilia* " of which he is thinking to the *impossibilia* mentioned by Cassian; the same expression often signifies very different realities. The miracle of St. Maurus walking on the water is assuredly an exceptional event; and perhaps, too, our Holy Father at first merely sent him to help the boy Placid: then his obedience provoked the miracle.

St. Benedict may be thinking of the case of a command which is scarcely to be fulfilled by ordinary methods, or even by merely human power; but he is especially concerned with the attitude of those people who, when they receive a command, are so ready to declare it impossible. The Abbot may reflect and contrive and calculate, yet this or that monk, to whom the office of cellarer, or infirmarian, or reader, is entrusted, will in all good faith allege his incapacity. So sweet is it to have no responsibility, to have no duties except one's prayers and studies. So pleasant is it to be a mere passenger on the ship, and not to be obliged to lend a hand in its working. Therefore, by a species of delusion which is only too natural, when authority with all kindliness makes certain brethren emerge from their quiet, and obliges them to undertake some task for the community, their first impulse is to entrench themselves in their incapacity. There is an exact parallel to their attitude in the amusing behaviour of the raven, when our Holy Father bade it carry off the poisoned loaf. " Then the raven, opening its mouth and stretching out its wings, began to flutter round about the loaf and to croak, as if it wished to express that it desired to obey and yet could not fulfil the command."[1]

In face of this state of trepidation St. Benedict's action is very fatherly; he says to his monk: " You are convinced that the command is hard, that it is impossible for you to fulfil it? That may be true, but I shall not discuss your estimate. Let it be agreed between us that the command is superhuman; perhaps it is something like that raising of the dead to life which the good peasant of Cassinum imposed on me one day.[2] But, after all, there are graces of state and graces of office:

---

[1] S. Greg. M., *Dial.*, l. II., c. viii.

[2] *Quid vultis onera nobis imponere, quæ non possumus portare?* exclaimed St. Benedict at first. But presently he worked the miracle, in all simplicity of faith (S. Greg. M., *Dial.*, l. II., c. xxxii.).

God helps us to carry that burden which He has Himself put upon us. Moreover, many things seem impossible only because we have not resolutely attempted them. Only try, and you will soon find your feet; if you do not try, you never will. Perhaps, too, your Abbot wishes to make you show your mettle and to compel you to develop by effort. Remember the calling of Moses, of Isaias, of Jonas, of Amos, and of St. John the Baptist."

Then, in the spirit of great gentleness and obedience (*cum omni mansuetudine et obedientia*), the religious shall accept the command. Thus does one learn to walk on the water, as did St. Maurus. How often does it not happen that God suddenly removes all difficulties, thanks to the joyous eagerness of our obedience! The women, who went to Our Lord's tomb, said doubtingly as they went: "Who shall roll us back the stone from the door of the sepulchre?" Yet they came there and the great stone was removed. "And looking they saw the stone rolled back; for it was very great."

| Quod si omnino virium suarum viderit pondus excedere, impossibilitatis suæ causas ei qui sibi præest patienter et opportune suggerat, non superbiendo, aut resistendo, vel contradicendo. | But if he sees that the burden altogether exceeds his strength, let him lay before his superior the reasons of his incapacity patiently and in due season, without showing pride, or resistance, or contradictoriness. |

But if, after a generous and loyal attempt, you find that you are certainly not equal to the task, do not sulk, or murmur, or complain to your brethren. Go, seek your Abbot, and gently, at the fitting time, lay before him the reasons of your failure, without pride, rebellion, or contentiousness. Endeavour to treat the matter as though it concerned another and not yourself, as a case for which you are merely supplying the details (*suggerat*). "In due season," adds St. Benedict; and in fact we must know how to wait for the proper time, when we are calm, when we know that our superior is so also; we must likewise choose a favourable place: nor is this diplomacy and deceit, but mere prudence and charity. And, in our entreaty itself, let us avoid all that savours of haughty demand, of passionateness, or of an unyielding obstinacy. Moreover, let us, on principle, never ask for a permission but with perfect liberty of spirit and that supernatural disinterestedness which is prepared to accept refusal. We belong wholly to obedience; obedience alone guarantees us against delusion; obedience is the guardian angel of our monastic life: "For what have I in heaven? And besides thee what do I desire upon earth? . . . Thou art the God of my heart, and the God that is my portion for ever" (Ps. lxxii. 25-26).

| Quod si post suggestionem suam in sua sententia prioris imperium perduraverit, sciat junior ita sibi expedire, et ex caritate confidens de adjutorio Dei, obediat. | If, however, after these representations, the superior still persist in his command, let the subject know that this is expedient for him, and let him obey out of love, trusting in the help of God. |

Though our representations may have been couched in the best terms possible and supported by the wisest of reasons, it may happen that the superior persists in his command. That is his business. His purpose may be to try or to constrain: he has a perfect right to do so, especially when it is a matter of imposing certain more difficult offices, such, for instance, as the government of a community. In such a case the monk must cease to consider the alleged insurmountable difficulties which he thinks he perceives; he must convince himself that it is proper for him to act thus, that it is good for him to obey even to the borders of absurdity. Souls, if they would mount high, have need to empty themselves thus. " Do you wish it, my Lord and my God? Then it is my wish also. Then all is simple, all is easy for me. I have put my hope in You: and You have promised Your grace to all those who trust in You." That is the disposition which our Holy Father St. Benedict ventures to require of us. It is not the disposition of the child who obeys for fear of the rod, nor of the man who resigns himself to something because he cannot do otherwise; but a tranquil, intelligent adhesion, submissiveness springing from love, a profound act of faith, hope, and charity: " Let him know that this is expedient for him, and let him obey in love, trusting in the help of God." If God's purpose is merely to prove the quality of our obedience, an angel will come at the right moment, as the angel came to Abraham. Without explaining his meaning further, our Holy Father bids us count on God.

And probably a miracle will not be necessary to relieve our trouble. For, as we may repeat, the incapacity of men often arises from sloth or pusillanimity. They too often forget the simple truth that if a thing is to get done we must do it. And when we have spent long hours in contemplating, in a spirit of false and foolish self-pity, the real or pretended difficulties of our duty, we have not changed the reality of things one whit: our duty is always our duty, and the will of God abides: we have only succeeded in weakening ourselves. " Fortune favours the brave ": in this case fortune is the grace of God.

CHAPTER LXIX
THAT MONKS PRESUME NOT TO DEFEND ONE ANOTHER

CHAPTERS LXVIII. to LXXI. seem to have a common purpose—viz., to destroy selfishness at the root, to pursue it into its most secret hiding-places, and therefore to regulate precisely our charity towards God and our brethren. They complete the fifth and seventh chapters. St. Benedict here signalizes some special circumstances of the monastic life wherein self is more tempted to assertion. A man may discuss the feasibility of commands (LXVIII.); he may without cause make himself the defender or the judge of his brethren (LXIX., LXX.); he may reject that obedience which, in varying degrees, each individual owes to all (LXXI.): all these tendencies originate in an exaggeration of the self.

UT IN MONASTERIO NON PRÆSUMAT ALTER ALTERUM DEFENDERE.—Summopere præcavendum est, ne quavis occasione præsumat alter alterum defendere monachum in monasterio, aut quasi tueri, etiamsi qualibet consanguinitatis propinquitate jungantur. Nec quolibet modo id a monachis præsumatur, quia exinde gravissima occasio scandalorum oriri potest. Quod si quis hæc transgressus fuerit, acrius coerceatur.

The greatest care must be taken that no one in the monastery presume for any reason to defend another, or to take his part, even though they be joined by some near tie of kinship. Let not the monks presume to do this in any way whatsoever, because the most grievous occasion of scandals may arise therefrom. If anyone transgress this rule, let him be very severely punished.

Here we have a thing which may occur in the best-regulated community. Suppose two brothers, or two cousins, or an uncle and nephew, are monks together; the ties of blood draw them to each other, and there is danger that natural affection, always blind, should close their eyes to very real defects and lead them to excuse each other. Superiors can never be careful enough in their treatment of those we love! The best-intentioned measures are blamed for severity and prejudice. The difficulty is more complex still if these measures are based on facts which are known only to the Abbot and which he may not divulge. So a man will defend his relative, either openly, or in a discreet and skilful manner; he makes himself a sort of officious guardian and claims a right of protection (*aut quasi tueri*).

Perhaps the most formidable relationships are not those of blood, but those of choice, those created by assiduous and exclusive attentions. "Particular friendships" should evidently be banished from a monastery. After having renounced the keenest and most legitimate natural affections we should not replace them with unreality and absurdity. This point does not need to be laboured, except for temperaments of a silly, frivolous, and rather foolish stamp. Monks should love as do the angels in heaven: " They shall be like the angels of God in heaven." The affection of the angels towards one another does not turn them from God, or diminish their submissiveness and obedience. It causes them neither trouble, nor anxiety, nor jealousy. They meet gladly; but they do not go in pursuit.

The danger emphasized by St. Benedict may exist also in little coteries, or particular friendships between a group, and even in certain gatherings of a regular character, as, for example, when several monks are continually together for some work in common. Hence the curious phenomenon that may sometimes be observed: these religious when together may agree or disagree. But whether they agree or not, they none the less form a distinct body, a State within a State. One cannot touch one of their number without touching all, and evoking discontent and murmuring. They share their grievances, and sometimes even invent a language, a special slang, in which to express and communicate them. They criticize the acts of authority and sympathize with the victims. From many observations made by our Holy Father we may infer that the monasteries of his time contained some meddlesome busybodies, thoughtless mischief-makers, or professional schemers, whether by temperament or inveterate habit. Such people unite the discontented and busy themselves with inflaming the petty wounds of self-love. All their strictures are wrapped in insinuation; they make hypocritical pretence of justifying authority, and abundant protestations of obedience; their sentences are punctuated with sighs, and so on. And, of course, there is always in this condolence some pretext of charity, or pity, or of " independence of character," even of piety itself. How easy is delusion in this matter !

In reality their action causes scandals and divisions in the community: *Exinde gravissima occasio scandalorum oriri potest.* At the same time they are doing the worst possible service to the brother whom they defend in this way. Who knows if our imprudent and thoughtless words may not sow the seeds of actual apostasy from the religious life ? Such action, too, often entails calumny and injustice towards the Abbot: for the Abbot cannot be justifying all the decisions that he takes, unless he would introduce the parliamentary system of government by debate. Finally, these little monastic cabals never lack a certain naïve self-sufficiency, since they appear to claim that government of which they judge the Abbot incapable.

We now understand the strong expressions employed by St. Benedict: " The greatest care must be taken . . . for any reason . . . in any way whatsoever ": whatever be the circumstances, whatever the methods employed; we understand also the " very severe " punishment decreed against those who infringe this rule.[1] Yet it is, of course, quite regular

---

[1] St. Benedict is not more severe than the ancient monastic legislators: *Qui consentit peccantibus et defendit alium delinquentem, maledictus erit apud Deum et homines, et corripietur increpatione severissima* (S. PACH., *Reg.*, clxxvi.—See also ST. BASIL, *Reg. contr.*, xxvi.

and very meritorious to help a brother to bear some punishment or difficult task. Moreover, it is charitable, both towards the Abbot and towards the brother, if we think that the punishment is out of proportion to the fault, if we know of extenuating circumstances, or if we are well informed as to the true state of the case, humbly to approach the Abbot himself and to enlighten him.

CHAPTER LXX
THAT NO ONE PRESUME RASHLY TO STRIKE OR EXCOMMUNICATE ANOTHER

IN the preceding chapter our Holy Father has warned us against that egoism which manifests itself in irregular sympathies on pretext of charity; he now denounces egoistic antipathies which betray themselves in correction, equally irregular, but coloured with the appearance of zeal. For this chapter deals only with those who presume to inflict what they regard as regular punishment, and not indiscriminately with all who permit themselves to indulge in rough conduct towards their brethren.

UT NON PRÆSUMAT QUISQUAM ALIQUEM PASSIM CÆDERE AUT EXCOMMUNICARE.—Ut vitetur in monasterio omnis præsumptionis occasio, ordinamus atque constituimus ut nulli liceat quemquam fratrum suorum excommunicare aut cædere, nisi cui potestas ab Abbate data fuerit. Peccantes autem coram omnibus arguantur, ut ceteri metum habeant.

In order that in the monastery every occasion of presumption may be avoided, we ordain and decree that it be lawful to no one to excommunicate or strike any of his brethren, except he be given power to do so by the Abbot. Those that sin before all shall be reproved, that the rest may have fear.

Authority is not to be usurped. It is unlawful and very imprudent to exercise so delicate a power as that of correction without any sort of right. Therefore no monk should of his own accord and without formal instructions from the Abbot inflict the punishment of excommunication or the rod on anyone whatsoever, and in a burst of " bitter zeal " come down upon all offenders. We must suppose that such abuses were to be met with in St. Benedict's days. And in our own time there are temperaments which seem predisposed towards the functions of the inquisitor or redresser of wrongs. Reprimand, denunciation, scolding, and a suspension of friendly relations which results in practical excommunication: all these methods are justified in their eyes, when they wish to have the Rule respected or to enforce unimportant customs that affect their vanity. " Such and such an abuse is glaring," they will say. But who compels you to notice it? Are *you* responsible? Why this morbid craving to interfere in other folks' business? Look to yourself. Be content to pray for the brother who annoys or scandalizes you. Give him good advice on occasion, and above all good example. And tell the proper authority. Turn to God: for experience shows that souls grow merciful in proportion to their nearness to Him. It is common knowledge, too, that the most intolerant and ill-advised critics are men without office, men who lack the grace of state and act only according to their character and the impulse of the moment. For the first danger to which this unseasonable correction is liable is the danger of striking too hard. The second is of achieving no result. No one can be a physician of the body off-hand, still less a physician of the soul.[1] But our Holy Father speaks explicitly only of the danger of pride, of arrogant rashness: *Ut vitetur[2] in monasterio omnis præsumptionis occasio*. To deal out the regular punishments of excommunication and the rod without authority and on any pretext, and to do this rashly (*passim*, as the title says), is to assume to oneself a strange importance; it is practically to usurp the powers of the lawful authority. It may even be an ambitious effort to win a reputation as a fervent and resolute man.[3]

Peccantes autem . . . This passage is a verbal quotation from St. Paul: "Them that sin reprove before all: that the rest also may have fear" (1. Tim. v. 20); but what is the exact meaning of our Holy Father, and what is the connection of this remark with the context? Various explanations have been given. "Those who sin against the foregoing regulations shall be corrected publicly." Such a development of the text is apt, but why did St. Benedict omit the few words needed to make the sentence clear, and say absolutely, without formal reference to what precedes: "those that sin"? Moreover, St. Benedict presently specifies the punishment which he reserves for those who correct without authority—viz., the degrees of the regular discipline; and the regular discipline implies something other than public rebuke—"Those who commit a fault shall be reprimanded publicly." When put in that general way the ordinance would seem to be at variance both with the Rule itself, which elsewhere prescribes secret admonition, and with morality; for to bring every fault, of whatever sort, before the whole community might be nothing short of defamation. The sense is rather this: transgressions of a public and scandalous character (*peccantes coram omnibus*) shall not remain unpunished; some authorized person must correct such faults, with vigour, publicly if necessary, and in such a way that the disorderly may be deterred.[4]

Infantibus vero usque ad quintum decimum annum ætatis, disciplinæ diligentia sit, et custodia adhibeatur ab omnibus: sed et hoc cum omni mensura et ratione.	Children, however, shall be kept by all under diligent and watchful discipline until their fifteenth year: yet this too with all measure and discretion.

[1] *Si enim objurgatio est animæ curatio, non est cujuslibet objurgare, sicut nec mederi, nisi si præfectus ipse, multo adhibito examine, id cuipiam permiserit* (S. BASIL., *Reg. fus.*, liii.).

[2] The most authoritative reading is: *Vetetur in monasterio . . . occasio, atque constituimus*.

[3] Is not this ST. BASIL's meaning also: *Si quis, non desiderio corrigendi fratres arguat eum qui delinquit, sed sui vitii explendi gratia, quomodo oportet hunc corrigi?* . . . *Iste velut suis commodis prospiciens et primatus desiderans notetur* . . . (*Reg. contr.*, cxciii.). In the answer to the next question, he points out that it lies with the superior to determine *vel quanto tempore vel quali modo corripi debeant*.

[4] The majority of the commentators connect the words *coram omnibus* with both *peccantes* and *arguantur*. SMARAGDUS recalls in this context the words of Leviticus: *Non oderis fratrem tuum in corde tuô, sed publice argue eum, ne habeas super eo peccatum* (xix. 17).—*Ipsa corripienda sunt coram omnibus, quæ peccantur coram omnibus; ipsa corripienda sunt secretius, quæ peccantur secretius* (S. AUG., *Sermo* LXXXII., 10. *P.L.*, XXXVIII., 511).—Another explanation is: no one should without authority inflict corporal or spiritual punishment (*excommunicare aut cædere*), but, in face of a public and scandalous fault, anyone may protest and reprove (*arguere*).

That no One Strike or Excommunicate Another

In stipulating that no one should usurp the right of punishing his brethren, St. Benedict did not wish to revoke the regulations which we have met already, and according to which children of less than fifteen years are subject to the supervision and correction of all their elders, whoever they may be. The children lived with the older monks, followed most of the exercises with them, and were trained by the influence of all. "This manner of bringing up the young was perhaps much better than that since used," says Calmet. "Experience shows that children brought up to think and speak seriously are capable of acquiring very early great maturity and rare wisdom, which we do not find in children educated among dissipated folk or with other children." But our Holy Father foresaw the danger. An older monk, who was rough and somewhat barbarous still in his ways, might get vexed with these little children—let us suppose they were frolicsome and had the bad taste too to be his elders by profession—and deal out his punishments with too liberal a hand. One cannot reason much with children, and St. Benedict was not unaware that early education is accomplished otherwise than through the intellect: yet he requires that correction should be exercised with all measure and discretion.

| Nam in fortiori ætate qui præsumpserit aliquatenus sine præcepto Abbatis, vel in ipsis infantibus sine discretione exarserit, disciplinæ regulari subjaceat, quia scriptum est: *Quod tibi non vis fieri, alii ne feceris.* | For if anyone presume, without leave of the Abbot, to chastise such as are above that age, or show undue severity even to the children, let him be subjected to the discipline of the Rule, for it is written: "Do not thou to another what thou wouldst not have done to thyself." |

St. Benedict sums up and concludes. Anyone who, without the Abbot's orders, has the temerity to punish adults in any way, or to punish children indiscreetly, shall be subjected to regular discipline; he shall experience on his own account, and for his future amendment, the wisdom of the divine counsel: "Do not thou to another, what thou wouldst not have done to thyself."[1]

The ordinances of this chapter are primarily addressed to those who have no authority to correct their brethren; they also concern all those who are invested by the monastic penal code, by lawful custom, or by special delegation, with ordinary or extraordinary right of correction, when they overstep the bounds of what is permitted by the Rule and by prudence. Speaking generally, all correction should fulfil the three following conditions: the corrector should have power to correct, the cause should be just and reasonably adequate, and the punishment should be proportioned to the fault. The effect of correction will be much jeopardized, if it is manifest that we are yielding to impatience, or to natural antipathy, or to irritability of temperament: let us keep our antipathies for our own faults.

[1] This is the ninth instrument of good works: see farther back, p. 67.

CHAPTER LXXI
THAT THE BRETHREN BE OBEDIENT ONE TO THE OTHER

NO one may correct his brethren without authority, but there are many with this authority; and it is far less important for a monk who is aiming at perfection to verify the credentials of the person who commands or punishes, than simply to obey all in all things. Therefore, far from exercising a disagreeable supervision over his brethren, or harassing them with tyrannical repression, each individual must study to subject himself to all.[1]

The chapter has two parts, the first telling us how to receive a brother's command or to do him a service; the second how to receive certain reprimands from superiors.

UT OBEDIENTES SINT SIBI INVICEM FRATRES.—Obedientiæ bonum non solum Abbati exhibendum est ab omnibus, sed etiam sibi invicem ita obediant fratres, scientes se per hanc obedientiæ viam ituros ad Deum. Præmisso ergo Abbatis, aut præpositorum qui ab eo constituuntur imperio (cui non permittimus privata imperia præponi), de cetero omnes juniores prioribus suis omni caritate et sollicitudine obediant. Quod si quis contentiosus reperitur, corripiatur.

Not only is the boon of obedience to be shown by all to the Abbot, but the brethren must also obey one another, knowing that by this path of obedience they shall go to God. The commands, therefore, of the Abbot or the superiors appointed by him (to which we allow no private orders to be preferred) having the first place, for the rest let all the younger brethren obey their elders with all charity and solicitude. But should anyone be found contentious, let him be corrected.

Obedientiæ bonum.[2] Obedience is not a wholly formal and external act, nor an alms disdainfully given, but a gift given gracefully, and gladly received by God: "acceptable to God and sweet to men" (Chapter V.). And it is also a benefit and a blessing for him who obeys: for each act of submission removes a portion of his self-love and gives him more of God. To draw near to God and to be united with Him is the end of all spiritual activity. And we know that the ancients viewed the Christian life as an uninterrupted march towards that blessed goal, union with the living God: "Father, I will that where I am there also my servant may be." We have been told, and our Lord and His Mother and the Saints have shown it to us in their lives, that obedience is the royal road by which we ascend to God. Our Holy Father St. Benedict is never weary of speaking of it; it is the alpha and omega of his Rule.

So, if we hasten to reach God, we shall seek occasions of obedience rather than ingenious ways of eluding it. With our eyes raised towards the heavenly Jerusalem, we shall journey light-heartedly, seeing now naught but God in all things, obeying God and every creature for the

---
[1] ST. BASIL has the same teaching: *Reg. contr.*, xiii., lxiv.
[2] The expression is CASSIAN'S, *Inst.*, IV., xxx.; XII., xxxi.

love of God, with our souls "lost," as the mystics say. Obedience to the Abbot, and to those who hold some measure of authority from him, will no longer suffice us: we shall bow as well, and for very similar motives, to the wishes of our seniors, and even to the wishes of our juniors, though St. Benedict does not require this explicitly; and there shall be among the brethren a sort of general eagerness to obey one another: *Sed etiam sibi invicem ita obediant fratres.* God forbid—we scarcely dare to make the supposition—that a monk should adopt a different view, maintaining that the monastic life means individualism and every man for himself, that each is isolated from the others and has no relations with them but those of juxtaposition. He will conclude that it is his duty to consider himself and no one else, to observe Chapter LXX. scrupulously, but, in return, to brook no interference.

The commentators observe that, even in a life where every moment is consecrated to some fixed work, where the laws of obedience and intercourse with others are determined by a written or living rule and by custom, there remain to the brethren plenty of opportunities for the exercise of mutual obedience. Are not courtesy, affability, and obligingness, so many engaging forms of obedience ? There are monks, very jealous of their time and very faithful to their studies, who yet seem always to be at one's service, and to have nothing else to do but to give themselves to all who seek them. *Omni caritate et sollicitudine obediant.* In that brief sentence the divine origin of our obedience, its character and its manner, are expressed. It is not a product of worldly politeness, but of charity. Let us not imagine that we are obeying as St. Benedict would have us obey when we consider that we are doing a favour; or when our obedience is accompanied by a bored and sceptical attitude; or, finally, when we put on a sad air and regard ourselves as martyrs. This is but a caricature of obedience.

There is always danger of delusion when we examine ourselves anxiously in order to see how we stand with God: "Are my sins forgotten ? Have I reached the illuminative way yet ? Or the unitive, perhaps ?" Though this be curiosity, yet after all it is a lawful curiosity, since our sole interest is to know whether we stand well with Him who alone counts. And God's answer never fails; but we do not usually listen where we should to hear it. Imagination, the senses, human understanding, the devils, delude us. We should not seek this dread secret even from God, even in prayer. Nor does our confessor know it. We must, in all humility and honesty, examine our obedience. If we find in fact that our soul has become pliable, profoundly and almost boundlessly docile, let us rejoice and let us thank God: for then He is very near. And it may be that the symbolical verses of St. John of the Cross echo softly in our hearts:

> My soul is occupied
> And all my substance in His service;
> Now I guard no flock,
> Nor have I any other employment:
> My sole occupation is love.

> If then on the common
> I am no longer seen or found,
> Say that I am lost;
> That, being enamoured,
> I lost myself, and yet I have been won.

St. Benedict observes that a certain order should be kept in this obedience which is due to all. The Abbot and deans shall of course be attended to first. When we ask for a permission or fulfil a command, we must avoid all conflict of jurisdictions, and certainly beware of provoking such maliciously. When authority properly so called has been obeyed first, says St. Benedict, or when it does not intervene, all shall receive with simplicity, humility, and good sense, the lawful orders, suggestions, and observations of the seniors. This is a counsel of perfection, but also, in some degree, a precept. And if there be found in the monastery a contentious person, one who is always eager to dispute, and always provided with excellent reasons for evading obedience, he shall be made to see that such a disposition is entirely incompatible with the religious life; and he shall be punished. St. Paul before him said: " But if any man seem to be contentious, we have no such custom, nor the Church of God " (1 Cor. xi. 16).

Si quis autem pro quavis minima causa, ab Abbate vel a quocumque priore suo corripiatur quolibet modo; vel si leviter senserit animum prioris cujuscumque contra se iratum vel commotum, quamvis modice, mox sine mora tamdiu prostratus in terra ante pedes ejus jaceat satisfaciens, usque dum benedictione sanetur illa commotio. Quod si quis contempserit facere, aut si contumax fuerit, de monasterio expellatur.	But if anyone be rebuked by the Abbot or by any superior in any way for however small a cause, or if he faintly perceive that the mind of any superior is angered or moved against him, however little, let him at once, without delay, cast himself on the ground at his feet, and there remain doing penance, until that feeling be appeased, as he gives him a blessing. But if anyone should disdain to do this, let him either be subjected to corporal chastisement, or, if he remain obdurate, be expelled from the monastery.

Each phrase of this passage is full of meaning, though its severity may astonish us. Yet it is in harmony with all the holy Rule and with the ancient rules;[1] and, certain details excepted, its ordinances have always been enforced. It would seem that the monk who is rebuked does not owe satisfaction in the case of every sort of reprimand, but only when the superior's words are emphasized by some feeling, by some animation of tone, and especially by indignation. The offender has not to wait for this extreme development; a slight display of feeling is enough: *quamvis modice*. Nor need it be manifest; it is enough that it be merely divined, faintly perceived: *vel si leviter senserit*. However trifling the cause of the rebuke may appear (*pro quavis minima causa*);

---

[1] *Frater qui pro qualibet culpa arguitur vel increpatur, patientiam habeat et non respondeat arguenti; sed humiliet se in omnibus* (S. Macar., Reg., xvi.).

whatever be the manner in which it is administered (*quolibet modo*); and whencesoever it comes (*ab Abbate vel a quocumque priore suo*): he must prostrate on the ground[1] at once without delay, without reflecting, or weighing the arguments for and against. And he shall remain in this humble posture until the superior blesses him and thereby shows that his irritation has passed. St. Benedict naturally takes it for granted that mercy will not lag behind repentance.

Our business, then, is not to justify ourselves, to prove that we meant no harm, to protest that our intentions were good; still less have we to launch out into irrelevancies. And, as we have said, this point of the Rule is not obsolete; there are occasions when the offender should ask pardon at once on his knees, or at least give excuses. The profit of this humble submission is twofold: the brother reprimanded finds an immediate and easy means of repairing his fault, and of becoming little again, and when prostrate he will no longer be tempted to dispute; the superior, on his part, is disposed to immediate forgiveness, and his feeling vanishes suddenly while his hand makes the sign of blessing: *usque dum benedictione sanetur illa commotio.* Both parties gain by the experience.

St. Benedict, in concluding, indicates the penalties reserved for those who refuse to make satisfaction. If a proud spirit resists, he shall be visited with the rod, or subjected probably to the graduated punishments detailed in the monastic penal code; and, finally, if he proves incorrigible, he shall be expelled from the community.[2] He shall be given back to the world, since by his spirit of contention he belongs to the world.

[1] Cass., *Inst.*, IV., xvi.
[2] According to the ancient commentators, if the monk be one who has been brought up in the monastery—that is, if he entered as an oblate—he shall not be sent back into the world of which he is ignorant, but shall be imprisoned.

CHAPTER LXXII

OF THE GOOD ZEAL WHICH MONKS OUGHT TO HAVE

DE ZELO BONO, QUEM DEBENT HABERE MONACHI.—Sicut est zelus amaritudinis malus, qui separat a Deo, et ducit ad infernum: ita est zelus bonus, qui separat a vitiis, et ducit ad Deum et ad vitam æternam. Hunc ergo zelum ferventissimo amore exerceant monachi. . . .

As there is an evil zeal of bitterness which separates from God and leads to hell, so there is a good zeal, which separates from vices and leads to God and to life everlasting. Let monks, therefore, practise this zeal with most fervent love. . . .

THIS chapter completes and summarizes the teaching of the four which precede it. We may even regard it as a synthesis of the entire Rule. St. Benedict condenses the whole science of monastic perfection into a few short and pithy sentences, which have the brightness and solidity of the diamond. Although the points of doctrine, and even the forms of their expression, are already partly known to us, their selection and grouping give them a new value.[1]

The idea is as old as Christianity, and very familiar to St. Benedict, that every human life has the choice between two directions or ways, and two only: the way of evil, of separation from God, of hell; and the way of good, of separation from vice, of union with God, of life everlasting. On these two roads two hostile armies are hastening, and between them are continual conflicts. Each has its chief and its standard, each its motto, its tactics, and its proper arms; in the one camp are pride and disobedience, and the *Non serviam* of Lucifer; in the other humility and obedience, and the *Quis ut Deus?* of St. Michael. Our Holy Father speaks to us here of two sorts of zeal, as St. Augustine spoke of two loves.[2]

Zeal is a secret ardour, a fermentation of the soul, its warmth and fervour. In Holy Scripture and the Fathers the word "zeal" most often means an evil tendency of the soul: jealousy, envy, greediness in the pursuit of some selfish satisfaction even at the expense of our neighbours. Cassian uses the word in this sense in the sixth chapter of his first Conference, and in the fifteenth and sixteenth chapters of his eighteenth Conference; in this sense, too, our Holy Father recommends us: "not to have zeal and envy" (Chapter IV.: sixty-fifth instrument), and warns the Abbot: "lest perchance the flame of envy or jealousy (*zelus*) be kindled in his soul" (Chapter LXV.). St. James was the first

---

[1] The chapter echoes the teaching of ST. BASIL: *Reg. contr.*, xii. sq. This is the way in which the ancients understood the contemplative life: *Quali affectu debet servire qui servit Deo? Affectum bonum vel animum illum esse arbitror ego, cum desiderium vehemens et inexplebile atque immobile inest nobis placendi Deo. Impletur autem iste affectus per theoriam (θεωρίαν), id est scientiam per quam intueri et perspicere possumus magnificentiam gloriæ Dei, et per cogitationes pias et puras, et per memoriam bonorum quæ nobis a Deo collata sunt; ex quorum recordatione venit animæ dilectio Domini Dei sui, ut eum diligat ex toto corde suo, et ex tota anima sua, et ex tota mente sua* (xiv.).

[2] *De civitate Dei*, l. XIV., c. xxviii. *P.L.*, XLI., 436.

to speak of "bitter zeal": " But if you have bitter zeal, and there be contentions in your hearts, glory not and be not liars against the truth. . . . For where zeal and contention is: there is inconstancy and every evil work" (Jas. iii. 14, 16). This evil zeal leads straight to death, as St. Clement of Rome had already written: τὸ εἰς θάνατον ἄγον ζῆλος (" zeal which leads to death ").[1] But there is also a good zeal, a holy ardour, " the zeal of God," which St. Benedict alluded to cursorily in the sixty-fourth chapter.[2] He tells us presently how this zeal manifests itself; here he merely notes its effect, which is to free souls from evil passions and lead them to God.[3]

So it is perfectly clear that the starting-point of all our moral activity is within; and it is to the interior, to the soul, that our Holy Father looks, and there that he wishes to evoke decisive action. The important point is to know what we have in our hearts. Perhaps we should have to answer: " I love myself much; scarcely anyone else counts. I possess a very keen self-assertiveness; I belong heart and soul to my own views— that is, to my delusions. And since I am not alone in the world, and there is a multitude of other selves around me who limit me and seek to check me, my zeal easily becomes impatience, anger, contentiousness, and rebellion: the evil zeal of bitterness." We are forbidden to remain neutral. Merely external correction has no value or lasting effect. If we assume an inert and frozen attitude, we have already chosen death. Let us rather allow the Spirit of God to enkindle in us the flame of that good zeal, whose name is charity. " Love and do what you will." The man who loves God is in some sort a law to himself. And when the fervour of faith and tenderness animates our deeds, all goes well. Evil habits, however inveterate, cannot resist this living and wholly divine flame. Such is the zeal, says St. Benedict, which monks should have and exercise " with most fervent love." Then he tells us in detail to what this holy rivalry is applied.

| . . . id est, ut honore se invicem præveniant. Infirmitates suas sive corporum sive morum patientissime tolerent; obedientiam sibi certatim impendant. Nullus quod sibi utile judicat sequatur, sed quod magis alii. Caritatem fraternitatis casto impendant amore. | . . . that is, in honour preventing one another. Let them most patiently endure one another's infirmities, whether of body or of character. Let them obey one another with rivalry. Let no one follow what he judges good for himself, but rather what seems good for another. Let them tender the charity of brotherhood with chaste love. |

---

[1] *Epist. ad Cor.*, ix. (FUNK, *Opera Patrum Apost.*, I., p. 72). Cited by D. BUTLER along with the " ancient Latin translation."

[2] *Cf.* CASS., *Conlat.*, II., xxvi.; VII., ii., xxvi., xxxi.; XII., i.; XIII., viii.; XVII., xxv.—S. BASIL., *Reg. contr.*, lxxviii.

[3] ST. JEROME, in his *Commentary on Ezechiel* (l. V., cap. xvi. *P.L.*, XXV., 156), cites as " from the Gospels " this sentence which is no longer to be found in them, but which recalls a passage in Ecclesiasticus (iv. 25): *Est confusio quæ ducit ad mortem, et est confusio quæ ducit ad vitam.* He quotes these words again in his letter LXVI., 6. *P.L.*, XXII., 642.—*Cf.* 2. Cor. vii. 10.

The subject is ever charity, and that fraternal charity: " by this shall all men know that you are my disciples, if you have love one for another " (John. xiii. 35). Charity is manifested in mutual regard and mutual kindnesses, and our Holy Father reminds us of the words of the Epistle to the Romans (xii. 10) already quoted in Chapter LXIII. Charity manifests itself also in loving toleration of the moral or corporal infirmities of our brethren;[1] and, we may add, in the peaceful acceptance of our own wretchedness. All things are common in a monastery, both good and evil. Perhaps even we may have to endure with tireless patience (*patientissime*), not only the infirmities of our neighbours but also their difference from ourselves. We all come from different provinces (*ex diversis provinciis*). This man comes from the fogs of the North; this other has matured under the strong suns of the south; such a one comes from Burgundy and has perhaps some drops of its wine in his veins, while another is a Breton and a Breton true to his race. Now God requires us to accommodate ourselves to diversities of temperament, and never to fret at an association which has been formed in Him and by means of His grace. Let us endure also our neighbour's superiority, and the love and confidence which are bestowed on him. God often allows us to suffer keenly on this point, in order to compel us to seek a higher affection where we may fear no rivalry: " Bear ye one another's burdens: and so you shall fulfil the law of Christ " (Gal. vi. 2).

Obey one another with rivalry, continues our Holy Father. Instead of pursuing his personal satisfaction, each one must seek every opportunity of obliging his brethren.[2] This is the great law of Christianity and the antithesis of animality; for the animal and the animal man order all things towards nothing but their own advantage. St. Paul with one stroke of his pen hits off a community which was not yet fully Christian: " All seek the things that are their own: not the things that are Jesus Christ's " (Phil. ii. 21); and, a few lines before, he draws the ideal of a Christian community: " Each one not considering the things that are his own, but those that are other men's " (*ibid.*, 4). And St. Benedict ends the series of counsels which ensure family peace by that most engaging one, again borrowed from St. Paul: that they pay their debt of chaste brotherly love (Rom. xii. 10; 1 Thess. iv. 9; Heb. xiii. 1. See also 1 Pet. i. 22 *sq.*). He emphasizes that character of supernatural purity which constitutes the charm and the enduring reality of monastic affection.

| Deum timeant; Abbatem suum sincera et humili caritate diligant; Christo omnino nihil præponant, qui | Let them fear God, and love their Abbot with sincere and humble affection. Let them prefer nothing |

---

[1] A reminiscence of CASSIAN: (*Lazarus*) *infirmitatem corporis patientissime toleravit* (*Conlat.*, VI., iii.). *Is vere et non ex parte perfectus est, qui et in eremo squalorem solitudinis et in cœnobio infirmitatem fratrum æquali magnanimitate sustentat* (*Conlat.*, XIX., ix.).

[2] *Sitque inter eos pax et concordia, et libenter majoribus subjiciantur, sedentes, ambulantes, ac stantes in ordine suo, et invicem de humilitate certantes* (S. PACH., *Reg.* clxxix.).

| nos pariter ad vitam æternam perducat. Amen. | whatever to Christ. And may He bring us all alike to life everlasting. Amen. |

Up to this point our Holy Father's counsels have chiefly concerned our relations towards our brethren and equals—what may be called our social co-ordination; now, it would seem, they concern our relations with those who are set over us—our social subordination: and a monastic family is bound together by the union of these two elements.

Deum timeant. They must fear God as dutiful servants, and as sons. We know this chaste fear well, a fear lasting for ever and ever: *timor castus permanens in sæculum sæculi;* it is the Benedictine spirit *par excellence.* We should have it always; it is the stimulus of our zeal, and the practical expression of our charity. And perhaps, too, the best attested reading is this: *Caritatem fraternitatis caste impendant. Amore Deum timeant* (Let them tender the charity of brotherhood chastely. Let them fear God in love). We find an identical expression in the Roman Pontifical in that admirable Preface for the Consecration of Virgins: *Amore te timeant* (Let them fear Thee in love).[1]

" Let them prefer nothing whatever to Christ." This is the twenty-first instrument of good works and a motto taken from St. Cyprian and St. Antony. It is easy, in days of sincerity and spiritual joy, to tell Our Lord that we prefer nothing whatever to Him: but it is easier still, alas! to unsay our words in the details of our life. And yet God loves us to repeat these elective words to Him. They are rich in faith, in hope, and in charity. God has pity on our desire, and contrives, little by little, that we become true: there is no longer aught but Him in us; we respond at last to that dateless, fathomless, boundless love which embraced us in our own despite.

And, as though to guarantee the Abbot's authority, as though to establish for the last time that it comes from God, and is a sacrament of the Lord in our midst, St. Benedict gives the Abbot a place between God the Father and His Christ. And again it is in charity that he seeks the sure norm of our relations towards the Abbot. *Abbatem suum*, he says, indicating that he is our own. We have elected him perhaps, or made our profession to him. We shall respect all prelates; but he who is the father of our monastic family and our soul's father, has a special title to our affection. It shall be "sincere": and by consequence steadfast under rebuke or severity. It shall be no fawning or foolish affection, but true, coming from the soul and from faith. St. Benedict would have it be "humble," a quality that we should understand. Doubtless it is right that our relations with him whose function it is, as our Holy Father noted before, to serve and not to domineer, should be distinguished by a holy and joyous liberty; but liberty is not unceremoniousness. The fabulist has described for us the impudence of the frogs towards their King Log:

[1] D. G. MORIN has made the same comparison: *Vers un texte définitif de la règle de S. Benoît: Revue Bénéd.*, October, 1912, pp. 408–409.

> Up came a crowd of them,
> Swarmed o'er the back of him,
> Made themselves quite at their ease;
> Respect was quite gone,
> Awe there was none,
> As they leapt on the neck of their king.

Humility consists in keeping one's proper place. Reverence might perhaps come more easy if authority held itself aloof, withdrew into splendid shadow, and played the prince; but that would not be St. Benedict's family, where the Abbot lives among his monks. Yet there is a degree of moderation, discretion, and filial respect, from which none should depart, and which is never lacking in a soul that is attached to Our Lord.

The chapter ends with a wish. May we by loving our brethren, by fearing God with the fear of love, by loving our Abbot, and clinging without reserve to Him who declared Himself "the way, the truth and the life"—may we all together, conventually, attain eternal life ![1]

---

[1] The *Amen* is not to be found in the best manuscripts nor in the most ancient commentators.

CHAPTER LXXIII

THAT THE WHOLE OBSERVANCE OF JUSTICE IS NOT SET DOWN IN THIS RULE

THIS chapter is a veritable storehouse of practical teaching. It even enlightens us anew on that question, so often discussed by the moralists and already answered by our Holy Father: What is the first directive principle of all our moral activity? We know the answer well: " Live conformably to what you are and you will grow." To progress, to go forward, to tend towards perfection, is our supreme law. Now two things are necessary for this: we need an interior stimulus, which is zeal, holy rivalry, and the fervent charity spoken of in the preceding chapter; but besides this, says St. Benedict, we need a field in which we may thus move and run: and of this he speaks now.

DE EO QUOD NON OMNIS OBSERVATIO JUSTITIÆ IN HAC SIT REGULA CONSTITUTA.—Regulam autem hanc descripsimus, ut eam observantes in monasteriis, aliquatenus vel honestatem morum, aut initium conversationis nos demonstremus habere.	We have written this Rule in order that, observing it in monasteries, we may show that in some measure we have goodness of manners and a beginning of religious life.

Here, he says, is the Rule promised at the end of the Prologue and the first chapter. It has been drawn up with care, to regulate observance in our monasteries of cenobites. If we remain faithful to it, that will be a sufficient proof that we have, if not extraordinary sanctity, at least a certain worthiness of life and a beginning,[1] or attempt, at a true monasticism: no one will now be tempted to confuse us with gyrovagues or sarabaites.

These words breathe a Christian simplicity, which of itself reveals the perfect sanctity of our Holy Father. Such candour and such moderation could only come from God. How different is human tendency! Men naturally regard their works as masterpieces. We claim, as though instinctively, to compass the whole world with our minds; what we do is always final and complete. Only the truly wise, only men of real artistic genius escape this fascination. Our Holy Father is of this number. The Rule appears to him as a modest sketch, as an introduction or initiation into a higher life. We know how the centuries have given the lie to this humble statement. And St. Benedict himself could not have altogether mistaken the true character and scope of his achievement. Having recommended the Abbot to " maintain every item of this Rule," having promulgated, as a guarantee of its observance, a complete and rigorous penal code, he could not have

---

[1] *Initium conversationis:* the same phrase occurs in CASSIAN, *Inst.*, IV., xxxix. See also *Verba seniorum: Vitæ Patrum*, V., xi., 29. ROSWEYD, p. 611.

intended to diminish our respect for that which he twice names " the holy Rule " (Chapters XXIII., LXV.). When we hear him bidding us have recourse to the teaching of Scripture and the Fathers, he does not mean that we should, according to the accident of devotion, introduce elements of all sorts drawn from very various sources into the form of life which he has given us. Did he not promise, at the end of the seventh chapter, that he who should scale the various degrees of humility would most surely attain to union with God ? Does not the teaching of his Rule aim at giving us in outline a complete code of monastic perfection ? Deep humility does not mean blindness, and " pious exaggeration " was not congenial to St. Benedict's temperament.

How, then, are we to justify his extreme modesty ? Let us remember in the first place that he wrote his Rule far less for perfect souls than for those who have resolved to become perfect. He sets himself to prepare them, to refine them, to lead them by an easy way to the very consummation of charity and the holy liberty of the children of God. The spiritual doctrine of the Rule is complete; but complete in the manner of a catechism, which condenses the whole of theology into the simple forms of its exposition, and really only needs to be developed. The observances of the Rule are discreet, chosen with care, proportioned to the average strength of human nature, without any leaning towards unsparing mortification: but souls which hunger for God will know well how to be generous, to go somewhat farther, under the guidance of obedience, to make their silence deeper, their prayers more assiduous, their liturgical duties more perfect; above all they can raise the interior principle of their actions almost to the power of infinity. All this is only virtually contained in the Rule; the Rule invites to it and suggests it: " this little Rule for beginners." Moreover, what rule is there that will not display its insufficiency when brought face to face with the boundless horizon of perfection laid open in the words of Our Lord: " Be ye therefore perfect, as also your heavenly Father is perfect " (Matt. v. 48) ? Our Holy Father finds his Rule mean and paltry in contrast with the splendours revealed by God to His saints, which he knew by experience: " To the soul that sees the Creator, every created thing is of small account."[1]

Ceterum ad perfectionem conversationis qui festinant, sunt doctrinæ sanctorum Patrum, quarum observatio perducit hominem ad celsitudinem perfectionis. Quæ enim pagina, aut quis sermo divinæ auctoritatis veteris ac novi Testamenti, non est rectissima norma vitæ humanæ ? Aut quis liber sanctorum catholicorum Patrum hoc non resonat, ut recto cursu perveniamus ad Creatorem nostrum ? Nec non

But for those who hasten to the perfection of the religious life, there are the teachings of the holy Fathers, the observance of which brings a man to the height of perfection. For what page or what word is there in the divinely inspired books of the Old and New Testaments, that is not a most accurate rule for human life ? Or what book of the holy Catholic Fathers does not loudly proclaim how we may

[1] S. Greg. M., *Dial.*, l. II., c. xxxv.

The whole Observance of Justice not in this Rule

et Collationes Patrum, et Instituta et Vita eorum; sed et Regula sancti Patris nostri Basilii, quid aliud sunt, nisi bene viventium et obedientium monachorum exempla, et instrumenta virtutum? Nobis autem desidiosis et male viventibus atque negligentibus, rubor confusionis est.

by a straight course reach our Creator? Moreover, the *Conferences of the Fathers*, their *Institutes* and their *Lives*, and the Rule of our holy Father Basil—what else are they but examples for well-living and obedient monks and instruments of virtue? But to us who are slothful and ill-living and negligent, they bring the blush of shame.

St. Benedict in a few words indicates to the soul that is eager to realize the monastic ideal[1] the sources from which it may complete its supernatural instruction. Let us note well the rôle given to the intellect. St. Benedict is concerned with the contemplative life; and this life develops according to laws of its own. We are not bidden walk and run in the apostolic and active life, but in the life wherein both night and day we scrutinize God and His works; wherein is revealed by way of illumination, love, and praise the mystery of God and of Christ. Nor would our Holy Father have us study the ancients merely in order to collect a variety of ascetical counsels, although he emphasizes on four occasions the practical moral benefit of this study: he is thinking of a profound doctrinal instruction, of an intellectual relish for divine things, which is all the more effectual in influencing our whole life because it is the fruit of a higher knowledge. However, men's minds differ, even as the stars: "For star differeth from star in glory" (1 Cor. xv. 41); all methods are good which reform the life and lead to God; but no one will wonder that the sons of St. Benedict remain faithful to the method of the early centuries, and that they find the guidance and nourishment of their souls in reading taken from "any page" of the Bible or the Fathers of the Church.

Here then, according to St. Benedict, is the matter of our contemplation: "the teachings of the holy Fathers." Perhaps this phrase embraces all our fathers in the faith, all those who have written on God and supernatural matters, beginning with the inspired writers; and St. Benedict goes on to enumerate three great classes of works. The first comprises the books of the Old and New Testaments that are recognized as of divine authority, and therefore excludes all apocryphal or doubtful books, which were still in circulation amongst the faithful. The Holy Bible is the monk's manual. But God grant that we may never treat these letters of our heavenly Father to His creatures—as St. Augustine[2] puts it—after the manner of rationalists or mere critics! Only if we regard Scripture with the same respect as the Eucharist, will each page or word become the surest moral rule for human life (*rectissima norma vitæ humanæ*).[3]

---

[1] *Ad perfectionem festinantibus* . . . (CASS., *Conlat.*, XXI., v.).
[2] *Enarrat. in Psalmum* lxiv. 2. P.L., XXXVI., 774.
[3] This is the whole theme of psalm cxviii.: *Lucerna pedibus meis verbum tuum, et lumen semitis meis.*

And since Scripture does not contain God's whole thought, we shall join to it the study of the Fathers (*sanctorum catholicorum Patrum*), those who are faithful mouthpieces of tradition, and whose works provide us with a continuous commentary on the Bible, the only commentary that we value. Neither heretics nor atheists are competent to explain the Scriptures to children of the Church: they are intruders; the Church was in possession before them; and the Church has from God the true meaning of the sacred books, even as Tertullian[1] long ago haughtily proclaimed. Is there one of the writings of the Fathers, continues St. Benedict, that does not call aloud upon us to mount by the straight path of the just (Isa. xxvi. 7) to our Creator?

Scripture and the Fathers belong to all the faithful; there are other books which are the special heritage of monks and bring us into communion with the spirit of all our saints. St. Benedict mentions the works which were best known in his time: the *Collationes*, in which John Cassian summarizes his admirable conferences with the Eastern monks; the *Instituta cœnobiorum* of the same author; the *Lives of the Fathers (Vitæ Patrum)*; and the Rule of one who was then regarded as the greatest monastic legislator: " our holy Father St. Basil." All these writings are nothing else than patterns, authentic models,[2] of a holy life and of monastic obedience; they are also "instruments of virtue": evidences and records of virtue, or rather, means and methods for the development of virtues in us.[3] They are at the same time an encouragement and a stimulus; and when we are weak, inobservant, and negligent,[4] their lessons will cause us to blush for shame. Our Holy Father's intention, we repeat, is not to depreciate his Rule, nor to confound souls that are satisfied with it; still less does he condone laxity. The most that he would say is this: that what we do is small, when compared with the austerity of the East. But perhaps he would rather, by depicting the perfection of former days, humble those who might be tempted to laxity, who might find in the very gentleness of their rule a pretext for evading it.

The whole of this paragraph of the Rule contains weighty teaching as to the chief interest of our monastic life, and as to the subject-matter of our reading and labour. Gossip, newspapers, reviews, criticism, or handbooks of devotion: none of these can lead a monk to the heights of

---

[1] *Ita non christiani nullum jus capiunt christianarum Litterarum; ad quos merito dicendum est: Qui estis ? quando et unde venistis ? quid in meo agitis, non mei ? quo denique, Marcion, jure silvam meam cædis ? qua licentia, Valentine, fontes meos transvertis ? qua potestate, Appeles, limites meos commoves ? quid hic ceteri ad voluntatem vestram seminatis et pascitis ? Mea est possessio, olim possideo. . . . Ego sum hæres apostolorum* . . . (*De præscriptione hæreticorum*, xxxvii. P.L., II., 51).

[2] The words *exempla et* are in the "received text" only.

[3] See the explanation of the word *instrumenta* which we gave at the beginning of Chapter IV.—TERTULLIAN, shortly after that passage from which we have just quoted, calls the Scriptures *instrumenta doctrinæ* (*De præscriptione hæreticorum*, xxxviii. P.L., II., 51).

[4] *A desidiosis ac neglegentibus* . . . (Cass., Conlat., XII., xvi.).

perfection: *ad celsitudinem perfectionis*.[1] They are broken cisterns that cannot hold or furnish the living water (Jer. ii. 13). As soon as monasticism abandons the wells of doctrine from which our fathers drew, it becomes enfeebled, and Esau's blessing of worldly prosperity cannot hide its insignificant triviality. Christian literature has been enriched since the times of St. Benedict; but his little library has not gone out of date. The Church herself in her official lessons scarcely knows any other books than those which our Holy Father recommends for their sovereign excellence.

Quisquis ergo ad patriam cælestem festinas, hanc minimam inchoationis Regulam descriptam, adjuvante Christo, perfice: et tunc demum ad majora, quæ supra commemoravimus, doctrinæ virtutumque culmina, Deo protegente, pervenies.

Whoever, therefore, you are who hasten towards your heavenly country, fulfil with the aid of Christ this little Rule for beginners which we have set forth; and then at length you shall arrive, under God's protection, at the lofty summits of doctrine and virtue of which we have spoken above.

Our Holy Father speaks too modestly of his Rule. Is there, apart from the Gospel, a book which has been able, as it has, to adapt itself to all the needs of Christian society from the sixth century to our own day, and which will, as God has revealed to certain of His saints, continue to do so until the coming of the Son of Man? Without adopting the arrogant claim that a Benedictine, in virtue of his Rule, is a man fit for any sphere, we should recognize for a last time that the Rule has lent itself with wonderful adaptability to works of extremely various kinds, that it has accommodated itself better than any other to times and circumstances, and that it has furnished a solid legislative framework to several founders of Orders or Congregations. To devise a Rule so wide as to embrace all, so strong as to contain all, so divinely simple as to be understood by the unlettered Goth and to charm St. Gregory the Great, so perfect as to deserve for ever the appellation of "the Rule," the monastic Rule *par excellence:* is not this a work of surpassing supernatural genius?

But St. Benedict is concerned with glory of a far different sort. Like the psalmist, his eyes are lifted up to the mountains. The Church has her giants of sanctity; there are lofty summits of wisdom and virtue,[2] towards which they have shown the road: perhaps Our Lord will give us the grace to attain them some day; but let us begin by observing in its entirety all that is taught us in the humble pages that we have just read. There is a heavenly country, a family sanctuary, where we are expected, where God and St. Benedict are waiting for us: let souls that hasten to reach it first achieve their novitiate for eternity.

[1] Cassian said: *scandere . . . culmina perfectionis* (*Inst.*, IV., viii.).
[2] *Dominicæ doctrinæ culmen ascendit* (Cass., *Conlat.*, XXI., xxxiv.). *Si ad culmen virtutum ejus volumus pervenire* . . . (*Conlat.*, XVIII., xv.). *Cf. Inst.*, IV., xxiii.; *Conlat.* XXII., vii.

Here we meet again that ardent and sweet invitation with which the Rule began. We meet again the profoundly Christian teaching of the Prologue, that we go to God only by the help of God and His Christ, by the divine strength given us by baptism and by faith. Above all we meet again that quiet yet confident assertion, that He who has loved us and called us will love us to the end and never betray our hopes. For the Rule ends on this blessed assurance: " You shall arrive " . . . you shall arrive even at the heart of God.

INDEX

The Index includes authors, proper names (with some necessary exclusions), Latin words and phrases explained in the Commentary, and subjects. The reference number covers the entire page, notes as well as text. It has not been attempted to give a verbal index to the text of the Rule, and the reader is recommended to consult the indexes in Abbot Butler's edition (published by Herder). Nor have quotations from Holy Scripture been indexed. It should be noted further that the majority of the references to authorities are to actual quotations, and not to mere citations of the authors specified.

ABANDONMENT of the monastery, 228–230, 405
abbas, 437
abbot, father of the monastery, 27, 37, 320; represents Christ, 36, 37, 437; physician and pastor of souls, 38–40, 54, 221, 223, 225–227, 300, 320, 453; master and teacher, 40–42, 45, 57, 95, 314, 449; his qualifications in detail, 35–55, 445–454; his paramount authority, 36–40, 56–60, 459, 479, to be exercised according to the law of God, 37, according to the Rule, 59, 454–455, according to constitutions, 60, 390, with the counsel of his monks, 56–60, 196, with prudence and equity, 42–46, with firmness and discretion, 45–51, 220–227, 357, 451–454, without arbitrariness, 431–432, and with a constant sense of his accountability, 38–40, 45, 50, 52, 54–55, 59, 356, 431, 443, 462; the officials of the monastery to be appointed by him and exercise their functions in entire obedience to him, 194–199, 235–236, 240, 303, 361–362, 378, 459–462; his permission constantly required, 245, 248, 320, 325, 343–346, 361, 471, 481; responsible for the choice of Lessons and Canticles, 150, 155, for furniture, tools, food, drink, and clothing, 200, 243, 272, 275, 347, 351, for signifying the Hours for the Office, 302, for the judgement of offences and their punishment, 211, 287, 289, 294–296, for studies, 308, for the observance of poverty, 245, 248, 343–346, 354–356, for the order of the monastery, 415, 422, 428, 431; chooses those to be ordained, 426; his functions at Matins, 155–156; duties towards sick, 258–262, and guests, 335–338, 358–360, towards postulants, 374, and novices, 377, 378, 386, 394, 397, 400; should listen to the criticisms of visiting monks, 419; should not take another Abbot's monks, 422–423; the manner of his appointment, 441–445; no term set to his rule, but deposition provided for, 447; monks going on a journey must commend themselves to his prayers, 468–469; entire obedience and submission to, 472–475, 484–485; to be loved with sincere and humble affection, 488–489

absent brethren, prayers for, 156, 468–469
abstinence, 319. See Fleshmeat
acus, 356
ad ipsum diem pertinentes, 165–167
address, modes of, to be used by monks, 437–438. See *Benedicite*
admission, of fugitive and expelled monks, 228–230, of postulants, 367–405, of oblates, 406–412, of priests and clerics, 413–417, of pilgrim monks, 418–423
adolescence, 231–232. See Children
Æsop, 309, 490
æterna clausura, 97
Agape, 138
Agape, Chionia and Irene, SS., *Acts* of, 114
Agde, Council of (A.D. 506), 152, 176, 389, 423, 426
agenda, 143, 163
agents of the monastery, 363
agricultural work of monks, 278, 312–313, 322
Aix-la-Chapelle, Councils of (A.D. 802, 817), 183, 358, 375, 384, 394, 410, 438, 465, 467, 469
Alberic, St., 351
alleluia, 147, 152, 153, 155, 158, 159, 160, 168–169
Ambrose, St., 146, 148, 312, 319
Ambrosian Liturgy, 138, 146, 147, 148, 155, 166, 177, 181, 182
ambrosianum, 148, 175
analogium, 151
anchorites, 28–30
Angela of Foligno, B., 191
angels, 1, 6, 89, 101, 102; guardian, 107, 108, 111, 112
ante-mass, 139, 149
antiphonal psalmody, 145–148
antiphons, at various Offices, 144–148, 152–157, 158–169, 175

Antony, St., 28, 70, 72, 276, 313, 373, 489
Apophthegmata patrum, 353
apostolate, the monastic, 137, 308, 340, 341–342, 360
apostolic activities, 82, 134, 308, 342, 424
Apostolic Constitutions, 62, 156
Aquinas. See Thomas Aquinas, St.
Arianism, 146, 334
Aristotle, 185
Arles, Council of (A.D. 456), 429
armour, the supernatural, 4
Arsenius, St., 415
artificers of the monastery, 361–366, 466–467
Asella, 406
astuteness in selling to be avoided, 364
Athanasius, St., 424, 426
Athos, Mt., 27
Augustine, St., 10, 16, 22, 23, 26, 32, 33, 53, 63, 68, 72, 105, 108, 110, 150, 178, 188, 195, 223, 226, 227, 236, 250, 304, 305, 306, 312, 313, 327, 345, 361, 363, 366, 382, 388, 424, 439, 448, 450, 451, 452, 480, 486, 493
Augustine of Canterbury, St., 424
Aurelian, St., 148, 151, 375, 425, 442
austerity, great, not the aim of St. Benedict, 19, 251, 270, 317, 492
authority, comes from God, 36; to be exercised for God, 37–38; relation to liberty, 39; a dangerous thing in the hands of a man, 155; not to be usurped, 479. See also Abbot
avarice, to be avoided by the cellarer, 237–238, by monks, 363–364
Aymard, B., 443

bakery of the monastery, 466, 467
Bartholomew, St., 21
Basil, St., his Rule recommended by St. Benedict, 493, 494; quoted, 38, 46, 93, 97, 102, 113, 115, 120, 159, 172, 187, 204, 224, 238, 246, 259, 276, 291, 293, 304, 323, 333, 351, 357, 380, 395, 407, 408, 419, 420, 427, 435, 440, 442, 470, 471, 480, 486, 494
baths, 259–262
Bäumer, Dom, 159, 161, 170
Bavarian Congregation of the Holy Angels, 385
Bec, 411
bedding, 354–355
Bede, Venerable, 412
bells, 302
benedicere, benedictio, 150, 156, 176, 416
benedicite, 93, 217, 341, 439, 465–466; canticle, 159, 161
Benedict, St., ix; begins his Rule with a loving address, a master and father, 1, 220, 226, 229; requires docility, 2, and obedience, 3; conceives our life as a journey to God, 3; continual insistence on obedience, 1–5, 78, 83–91, 114–119, 472–475, 482–485, on stability, 24, 81–82, 388–389, on the love of Christ, 69–70, 81, 84, 488–489, who is to be recognized in the Abbot, 36, 37, 437, in the sick, 258, in guests, 330; calls the monastery a school of His service, 19, 23, 136; insists on the thought of God's presence, 74–75, 104–109, 110–112, 185–186; urges the thought of eternity and judgement, 6, 7, 9, 16–17, 24, 72–74, 105–110, 112, 128, 130, 185, 489; gentleness and discretion of, 19, 205, 251, 263, 275, 346, 453, 473; prefers the cenobitical life, 27–34, 87; regards the Abbot as the keystone of the monastery, 35, see also Abbot; specially severe on murmuring, 90, 206, 253, 277, 279, 351; borrows largely from Cassian, 102–103, 129, etc.; gives paramount importance to the Work of God, 136, 286; borrows his cursus from many sources, 138; his own contributions, 145, 159, 161, 162, 172; humble about his arrangement of the psalms, but wishes the entire psalter to be said in a week, 183; recognizes three chief monastic occupations: the Work of God, sacred reading, manual labour, 304; his master thought that we should seek God, 305; displays the genius of a Roman, 396; was perhaps a deacon, 425; *montes amabat*, 467; his modesty about his Rule, ix, 491–492, 495; the vogue and influence of his Rule, ix, 495. For detail of his teaching and regulations see the index, *passim*
Benedict Labre, St., 18
Benedictine mission, 134–135. See Apostolate
Benedictine piety, 379. See Prayer
Benedictus (Canticle), 159, 162
benedictus es, 257
Bernard, St., 52, 93, 104, 123, 351, 411, 415, 467
Bernard, Claude, 2
Bernard of Cluny, 443
Bernard of Monte Cassino, 322, 336, 390, 417, 438, 439
Bethlehem, monastery at, 171
biberes, 256
bishops, relations of monks with, 426, 429–430, 442, 447–448, 458
blessing. See *Benedicere*
Boherius, 439, 462
Bonaventure, St., 26
books, for Lent, 314–315, 318; for the Office, 142, 150, 157, 166, 323–324
boots, 350
Bossuet, 96, 119, 310

Index

boys, how to be corrected, 231–232. See also Children, Oblates
bracile, 201, 356
breakfast, not provided by the Rule, 256
breve, 244
breviary, a late invention, 323; the Roman, 161. See Roman Liturgy; quoted, 24, 74, 75, 75, 81, 173, 242
brevity in prayer, 192
Bruno, St., 26
buffoonery, 97, 125–126
Bursfeld Congregation, 201, 366, 386, 456, 457, 464
Butler, Dom, 5, 62, 133, 143, 155, 228, 304, 367

cabals, monastic, 477
Cabrol, Dom, 139
cædere, 209
Cæsaria, Abbess, 403
Cæsarius, St., 24, 147, 151, 157, 159, 165, 167, 188, 199, 222, 244, 261, 262, 265, 291, 314, 352, 355, 375, 383, 384, 389, 403, 407, 450, 456
Cagin, Dom, 146
Cajetan, St., 248
Calends, meaning of, in the Rule, 139, 311, 313
caligæ, 350
Callinicus, 172
Calmet, Dom, 19, 139, 142, 151, 159, 160, 165, 166, 184, 202, 206, 209, 256, 262, 265, 272, 280, 415, 432, 435, 462, 465, 481
Camaldolese, 28, 201, 366
Canons Regular, 390
Canticles, at Matins, 155; at Lauds, 158–159, 161–162; at Vespers, 159, 175
cantors, 303
capitale, 355
Cappadocian monks, 146, 265
Capuchins, 248
Caramuel, 445
Carmelites, 390
carnes, 274
Carthage, Councils of, 430, 442, 447
Carthusians, 28, 29, 142, 201, 250, 362, 366, 390
Cassian, his *Conferences* and *Institutes* recommended by St. Benedict, 283, 493–494; freely used by St. Benedict, 103 and *passim*; quoted, 5, 22, 26–27, 29, 31, 53, 61, 76, 93, 95, 96, 102–103, 104, 112, 120, 121, 124, 129, 141, 142, 143, 145, 147, 150, 163, 171, 172, 174, 176, 191, 193, 195, 246, 249, 254, 255, 256, 257, 267, 268, 281, 283, 284, 286, 290, 292, 298, 299, 325, 329, 336, 348, 350, 352, 354, 355, 363, 369, 371, 377, 405, 409, 426, 453, 464, 472, 488, 494, 495

Cassinese Congregation, 300, 366, 459
Cassinum, 473. See Monte Cassino
Cassiodorus, 14, 261
Cato, 352
Celestine III., Pope, 411
cellarer, appointment of, 233; qualifications and duties, 233–242
cenobite, 25–34
ceremonies, of choir, 187; of profession, 393–402
Chalcedon, Council of (A.D. 451), 389, 410, 429
chanting, manner of, 187. See Psalmody
Chapman, Dom, 228
chapter, conventual, 56–60; of faults, 299; for novices, 384, 386
charity, love of God and neighbour, 28, 63–71, 78–80, 163, 488
Charlemagne, 157, 209, 272
Chasles, M. Raymond, 364–365
chastity, 79, 245
Chezal-Benoît, *Constitutions* of, 379, 384
children (*pueri parvuli vel adolescentes*) admitted into the monastery, 406–412; discipline, 231–232, 297, 298, 434–435, 438, 480–481; indulgence towards, 263–264; food of, 273
choir, ceremonies of, 187; mistakes in, 297–298
choir-monks, a distinction not made by St. Benedict, 365; must now be qualified to receive Orders, 425
Christ, see Jesus Christ
Church, an organ of worship, 133; divine authority of, 310–311; regulates and approves vows, 388; the church of the monastery, 327–329
circatores, 197, 202, 315
Cistercians. See Cîteaux
Cîteaux, 52, 93, 98, 122, 209, 250, 300, 323, 336, 349, 350, 351, 353, 366, 375, 438, 439, 464, 465
civil death, the system of, 248
Clement III., Pope, 411
Clement V., Pope, 425
Clement VIII., Pope, 375, 376, 426, 443
Clement of Alexandria, 170
Clement of Rome, St., 487
clocks, ancient substitutes for, 141
clothing, for night, 202; in general, 346–357; Abbot's duty with regard to, 351–355
clothing in the monastic habit, postulants, 374–375, novices, 375; professed monks, 375, 399–400, 405
Cluny, 93, 98, 151, 176, 197, 201, 209, 229, 255, 257, 271, 273, 276, 300, 323, 331, 338, 339, 350, 351, 353, 355, 356, 358, 365–366, 374, 375, 384, 393, 394, 404, 411, 418, 433, 438, 443, 456, 465, 470
collect, 156 193

32*

colour of habit, 351
Columbanus, St., 140, 209
Columella, 81, 194, 244, 348
commendam, 60, 441
Communion, Holy, 10, 23, 66, 176, 213, 257, 266, 269, 402, 433
community, to be consulted by the Abbot, 56–60; chooses the Abbot, 442–443; order of, 431–440
Compline, 148, 172, 175, 182; silence after, 281–285; institution of, attributed to St. Benedict, 172
compunction, 77–78, 191, 318
concupiscence, 77–79, 111
Conferences, of Cassian, recommended by St. Benedict, 283, 493. See Cassian
confession of faults and temptations, 76, 120–121, 300–301
confinement, solitary, 209, 215, 227, 405
congregational system not known to St. Benedict, 418
constitutam annonam, 241
Constitutiones monasticæ, 246
Constitutions, vows taken according to, 390. See under names of various Congregations
contemplation, 307
contemplative life, qualifications required for, 370–371; trials of, 21–22, 382
contempt of the Rule, 207, 391
contentiousness, 79, 484
contumacia, 206
conversatio, 29, 491
conversation, 93–98, 76, 125, 316
conversio, 29, 245, 367, 389, 431
conversion of manners, vow of, 245, 389–390
Conybeare, F. C., 127
corporal punishment. See Punishment
correction, necessity of, 48–50; ordinary procedure for, 207–208, 213, 225–227; Abbot's duty regarding, 450–452; of priests, 428–430; of prior, 462; irregular, 479–481. See also Children.
council, of the whole community, 56–60; of seniors, 59, 60, 196; Abbot's relation to, 58–60, 196
courtesy, 435–440, 483
cowl, 347–349, 352, 353
crafts. See Artificers
critical spirit, 38, 94–95, 310. See Murmuring
cuculla, 348
cultellus, 201, 356
Curé d'Ars, 412
Cyprian, St., 70, 163, 227, 489

David, King, 47
Day Hours, 170–182; unpunctuality at, 289–290. See under names of Hours
deacons of the monastery, 424

deans, 194–199
death, the thought of, 73–74
decanus, 194–195
delusion, 32, 110
De Meester, Dom Placid, 156
Denis the Areopagite, 26, 396, 424
denunciation, the practice of, 300
Deo gratias, 439, 465–466
Deodatus, Abbot, 418
desideria carnis, 107
desolation, spiritual, 21–22, 128, 382
despair, 80–81
Deus in adjutorium, 144, 158, 174, 177, 257, 290
devil, the, 5, 7, 13, 14, 28, 73, 103, 106, 121, 126, 193, 216, 218, 334, 486
devotio, 190
Didache, 62, 67, 162, 170
directanee, in directum, 148
direction of conscience, 96–97
dirigatur oratio mea, 181
disciplina, 45, 189, 208–209, 211, 434–435
Disciplina Farfensis, 260
discipline, the, 208–209
discretion, 453–454. See Abbot; Benedict, St.; Rule
disobedience, 39–40, 206. See Obedience
distinction of persons in the monastery, 43–45, 365. See Order
docility required by St. Benedict, 2. See Obedience
dom, domnus, 437–438
domestici fidei, 332
Domine labia mea aperies, 267
Dominic, St., 26, 467
Dominic Loricatus, St., 184
Dominicans, 142, 390
Domitian, 49
Donatus, St., 355
dormitory, 201–204
Dracontius, 426
drink, the measure of, 275–277
duality in moral life, 10

Eastern monks, 26–27, 144, 145, 146, 147, 148, 151, 197, 333, 407, 467, 468
eating between meals forbidden, 292
education, function of punishment in, 49
Egyptian monks, 144, 147, 192, 254
election of Abbot, 443–445
enclosure, 81–82, 322, 466–467, 468, 471
English Benedictine Congregation, 349, 399, 400, 402
Ephrem, St., 29, 332, 360
Epicurus, 75
Epiphanius, St., 424
equality, absolute, not aimed at by St. Benedict, 252
Equitius, St., 351
Erasmus, 343
eremita, 28

eremitical life, 28–30
Essenes, 70
eternity, the desire of, 70. See Benedict, St.
Eucharist, the Holy. See Mass; Communion
eulogia, 343–344
εὐτραπελία, 94, 125
examination of conscience, 15, 301
excess in eating and drinking, 273
excommunicated monks, improper communication with, 218–219; Abbot must be solicitous for, 220–224, 226; reconciliation of, 221–224, 294–296
excommunication, monastic, 205–227, 325, 479–481
exemption, monastic, 426, 429–430, 442, 447–448, 458
Exhortatio de panoplia ad monachos, 4
experientia magistra, 31
Explication ascétique et historique de la Règle, 444
expulsion of incorrigible monks, 227; readmission of, 228–230
Eusebius of Vercellæ, St., 424
Euthymius, St., 176
Eutychius, 408
Evagrius of Pontus, 395

Faber, Father, 32, 307, 321
Farfa, 260, 411
fast, ecclesiastical, 271, 279–280, 282, 284, 314, 336, see also Lent; eucharistic, 257, 269; monastic, 271, 279, 280, 282, 284, 313–314, 336, 359; summer, 278–279, 284
fastidiousness to be avoided, 122
fasting, a mortification, 68, 319–320; a punishment, 208, 214, 217, 225, 231–232
Fathers of the Church, appropriate reading for Benedictines, 306–310; recommended by St. Benedict, 493–494
faults, chapter of, 299; confession of, 76, 120, 300–301; correction of, 205–230, 286–301
Faustus of Lérins, 429
Faustus of Rhegium, 395, 399
fear of God, 105–112, 489. See God
feast-days. See Saints'-days
femoralia, 352–353
ferias, Office on. See Matins; Lauds; etc.
Ferreolus, St., 375, 384
fervor novitius, 29
fields, Office in the, 323. See Agricultural work
flesh meat, forbidden by St. Benedict, 274; except for the sick and infirm, 260, 262, 274; may it be given to guests? 336
Florence, Council of, 37

food, provided by the cellarer, 240–241; measure and kinds of, 270–274, 275–277; for the sick, 260, 262, 274; for old men and children, 263–264; for guests, 336
footgear, 350
forgetfulness to be shunned, 106–108
fowls regarded as fasting fare, 274
Francis of Assisi, St., 26, 467, 472
Francis de Sales, St., 11, 98
Franciscans, 142, 248, 349
François, Dom Philip, 118
Frankfort, Council of (A.D. 794), 209
Fratres sobrii estote, 175
French Benedictine Congregation, *Constitutions* of, 192, 249, 272, 366, 379, 384, 385, 390
friendships, particular, 476–477
Fructuosus, St., 209, 353, 355, 375, 384, 395
Fulgentius, St., 437

gaiety, 77, 94, 97, 126
garden of the monastery, 466, 467
gate of the monastery, 463–464
Gelasius, Pope, 150
Gertrude, St., 412
Girone, Council of (A.D. 517), 162
Gloria Patri, 144, 145, 174
gluttony, 273, 275–276
God, the fatherhood of, 1, 6; we must be docile and attentive to, 2; will require an account, 3, 39–40, 42, 51, 54, 59, 357, see also Abbot; life a journey to, in obedience, 3; necessity of His grace, 5–6, 15, 102, 496; fear of, 7, 9, 72–73, 105–110, 112, 128, 130, 185, 489; His call, 10, 12, 23, 368; all good to be ascribed to, 15, 72; the patience of, 17; trust in, 18, 53, 80–81, 301, 412, 475; the lover and purifier of souls, 21, 22, 117, 382; union with, 23, 24, 173, 301, 482; all authority from, 36–38; no respecter of persons, 43; discretion of His Providence, 46; blesses fervent monasteries, 52–53; reflected in good souls, 55; actively interested in the affairs of a monastic house, 57; the love of, and of our neighbour for Him, 28, 63–65, 65–71, 173, 301; sees us always, 74–75, 107–109, 111–112, 128, 185–186; His purpose in creation, 83–84; rejoices in our obedience, 85, 87, 89; wins all His victories by obedience, 88; loves a cheerful giver, 91; silence of, 97; requires humility, 101; His rights absolute, 106, 238, 244, 249; requires us to obey others, 114, and gives us His graces in and through our social state, 216; liturgical worship of, 131–136; gave us the psalter, 183; reverence

in prayer to, 189–193, 327–328; generous to those who sacrifice themselves for the Community, 237; nothing to be put before His Work, 286–287; the object of our study, 306; vocation comes from, 368; novice must seek, 379–380; the end of our lives, 482, 495–496. See also Jesus Christ; Trinity
Gospel at Matins, 155
grace, necessity of, 5–6, 15, 102, 496
grace at meals, 290–291
Gradual Psalms, 173, 180, 183
graphium, 356
Gratian, *Decree* of, 97
Greek monks, 151. See Eastern monks
Gregory the Great, St., 24, 48, 120, 165, 191, 193, 213, 248, 250, 302, 308, 329, 339, 348, 351, 418, 419, 442, 456, 464, 465, 473, 495
Gregory II., St., 410
Gregory of Tours, St., 141, 407
grumbling. See Murmuring
guardian angels, 107, 108, 111, 112
guest-house, 331, 338–340
guest-master, 340
guests, reception of, 330–342, 418–423; cellarer's duty towards, 237; relations of community with, 341; separate refectory for, 358–360
gyrovague, 27, 33–34, 388, 418

habit, the Benedictine, 346–357; colour of, 351; significance of, 400; not to be taken away by a monk who leaves, 405; taking of the, see Clothing
hæc complens, 17
Haeften, Dom, 35
hardships of monastic life, 381–382
hegoumenos, 437
hemina, 272, 275
Heli, 48
hermits, 28–30
Herwegen, Dom, 205
Hilarion, St., 28, 353
Hildegarde, St., 30, 92
Hildemar, 96, 139, 353, 398, 408, 414, 421, 427, 435, 470
Hirschau, 366, 470
Holy Spirit, the, 133, 135
Horace, 211, 228
hospitality, 330–331, 340, 360. See Guest
hour, for Offices, signifying of, 302–303; of rising, see Rising
hours, division of, by the ancients and St. Benedict, 139–140
hours of the Office. See under Matins; Lauds; etc.
Hugh of Cluny, St., 443
humanitas, 335
humility, 100–130; relation to obedience, 83; in prayer, 190

humiliations, novice to be eager for, 380; fictitious, 118–119, 380
hymns, of Matins, 145, 148–149; of Lauds, 159, 162; of Prime, 174; of Little Hours, 175, 179–180; of Vespers, 175, 181; of Compline, 175
Hypatius, St., 172

Idleness, the enemy of the soul, 304
Imitation of Christ, 67, 76, 96, 191, 259
imponere, 148
impossibilities, if a monk be commanded, 472–475
inattentiveness, spiritual, 106–108
infirmarian, 261
infirmary, 260
ingenuus, 45
Inscriptionum latinarum . . . collectio (Orelli-Henzen), 383
Institutes, of Cassian, recommended by St. Benedict, 493. See Cassian
instruments of good works, 61–82
instrumentum, 61
intentio cordis, 329
introspection, dangers of, 11, 15, 116
Invitatory, 145
Isaias, Abbot, 338
Isidore, St., 28, 227, 231, 355, 395
Isidore, Abbot, 425, 463
Ivo of Chartres, St., 29

Jacob, 101, 443, 453
Jephte, 406
Jerome, St., 26, 34, 35, 45, 78, 102, 127, 194, 263, 279, 291, 316, 331, 364, 407, 413, 433, 446, 450, 487
jesting, 97, 125–126
Jesuits, 142, 394
Jesus Christ, the monk a soldier of, 3–5; must follow Him in obedience, 5, 83–85, 112–113, 114–115, in patience, 23–24, in self-denial, 67–68; must cast down temptations before Him, 13–14, 75–76; and prefer nothing to Him, 69–70, 83–85, 488–489; the perfect monk lives by His love, 129–130; the Abbot represents Him, 35–38, 437; to be seen in all our brethren, and especially in the sick, 258–259, in guests, 330, 335, 340, in the poor, 332–333, 337; the monastery a school of His service, 18–19, 23; must suffer with Him, 24; teaches humility, 36–37, 100; desire of, 13, 73; priesthood of, 133; used the psalms, 183; bids us avoid wordiness in prayer, 191, and intemperance, 273; *Imitation of Christ*, see *Imitation*
Jethro, 195, 419
Jews, psalmody of, 146, 149, 170
Job, 22, 89
John, St., on charity, 66–67

Index

John the Baptist, St., 28, 164, 165, 406, 474
John Chrysostom, St., 89
John Climacus, St., 415
John of the Cross, St., 97, 306, 483–484
John of Gorze, B., 151
John of Lycopolis, 426
Jonas, 474
Joseph, St., 183
Josephus, 70
journeys, 322–326, 468–471; how the Office is to be said on, 322–324; clothes for, 353; prayers before and after, 468–470; things seen and heard on, 470–471
Judgement, the Last, 73
juniors, 203–204, 435–440
Justinian, 231, 248, 375, 463
juxta considerationem rationis, 140

Kitchens of the monastery, 338
Kitchen servers, 254–257
Kyrie eleison, 152, 156, 159, 174, 175, 176

labour, manual, 304–316
ladder of humility, 101–102
Ladeuze, Mgr., 384
læna, 355
La Fontaine, 490
Lanfranc, *Statutes* of, 386, 394, 456
Last Things, the, 72–74
Lauds, on Sundays and feast-days, 158–159, 164; on ferias, 160–163; antiquity of, 170; to begin at daybreak, 143; interval between Matins and Lauds, 141–143, between Lauds and Prime, 171; *Paternoster* at, 162–163
laughter, 125–126
laus perennis, 173
lay brothers, 364–366; not distinguished from choir monks by St. Benedict, 365
Lawrence, St., 18, 383
lectio divina, 142, 192, 201, 304, 306. See Reading
lectiones cum responsoriis suis, 151. See Lessons
lectisternia, 200
Lent, observance of, 317–321; silence in, 93, 319–320; hours of meals in, 279–280; special books for, 314–315, 318
Leo the Great, St., 318, 319
Lérins, 201, 429
Le Roy, William, 118–119
Lessons, of the Office, at Matins on ferias, 149–151, 152, 153, on Sundays, 154–155, on Saints'-days, 150, 164–167; length of, 151, 157; to be shortened if the monks rise late, 157
Lessons (short) at Lauds, 159, 162; at Little Hours, 175, 179–180; at Vespers, 175, 181; at Compline, 175
letters of monks, 343–345

libra, 271–272
library of the monastery, 314, 355
lighting of dormitory, 202
litaniæ, 152, 156, 159, 162
litteræ commendatitiæ, formatæ, 212, 334, 423
Little Hours, the, 148. See also Terce; Sext; None
liturgy, idea of, 131–133; the *Opus Dei*, 133; the special province of religious, 134; the main Benedictine work, 134–137; apostolic value of, 137; sources of St. Benedict's, 138–139; Matins most ancient part of, 138–139; books for, 142, 150, 157, 166, 323–324; care in performance of, 186–187. See also under the names of the parts and elements of the liturgy
Lives of the Fathers, recommended by St. Benedict, 283, 493. See *Vitæ Patrum*
Lobbes, 425
Lombards, 272
love of God and neighbour. See Charity
lucernarium, 171, 172, 181
Lucifer, 486. See Devil
lying, in word and deed, 10

Mabillon, 119, 395, 425
Macarius, St., 206, 211, 268, 287, 314, 337, 373, 383, 403, 484, 456
Macon, Council of, 407
Magnificat, 159, 175
Maistre, Count de, 123
Majolus, St., 443
Mandatum, 256, 337, 339
manifestation of conscience, 75, 76, 120–121, 300–301
manual labour, 304–316
manufactures suitable to monks, 362–363
mappula, 356
Martène, 119, 122, 141, 165, 180, 323, 358, 360, 377, 384, 404
Martin, St., 77, 89, 165, 201, 337, 353, 424, 425, 465
Mary, B.V.M., 13, 106, 183, 190, 416
Mary Magdalene, St., 223
Mass, the, 133, 156, 176, 213, 257, 266, 269, 314, 400, 401–402, 416
Matins, on ferias, 138–153, 168; on Sundays, 154, 157, 169; on Saints'-days, 164–167; the psalms of, 182; most ancient part of the Office, 138–139; the time of, 139–141, 143; probably began with *Domine labia mea aperies*, 144; interval before Lauds, 142–143, 156–157; no interval between the nocturns, 152. See also under names of various elements
matta, 355
Matutinorum solemnitas, 158. See Lauds
Maundy, the, 337

Maurus, St., 57, 91, 408, 412, 433, 473, 474
meals, reading at, 265; silence at, 267–268; hours of, 278–280; eating between, forbidden, 292; away from the monastery, 322–326. See also Fast; Food; Drink
meat. See Flesh meat
meditari, 142
meditation, 142–143, 307
Mège, Dom, 104, 119, 140, 165, 337, 445
Melania the Elder, 395
melota, 348, 349
Ménard, Dom, 126, 142, 145, 263–264, 285
mental prayer, 142–143, 192, 306–307, 493
mercy, works of, 68–69
Michael, St., 486
Milan, Liturgy of. See Ambrosian Liturgy
mill of the monastery, 466, 467
minutio, 261
miscens temporibus tempora, 46
Miserere, 158–159
missæ sint, fiant, 156, 174
Missal, the Roman, 23, 402
missam, missas tenere, 413
mixtum, 269
Molesmes, 353
monastery, a school of the Lord's service, 18, 19, 23, 319; a family, 27, 51, 252; the house of God, 36, 57; prosperity of, 48, 52–53; property of sacred, 238, 244; to be self-sufficing, 466–467
monastic life, a counsel, 7; hardships of, 381–383; distinct from priestly, 413. See Vocation and *passim*
Monica, St., 305
monk, meaning of the word, 25, 26; kinds of, 25–34; varying temperament and character, 41–42, 46–48, 51; for duties see Index, *passim*
Mont St. Michel, 467
Monte Cassino, 57, 144, 147, 160, 165, 197, 257, 269, 272, 276, 328, 335, 346, 352, 353, 355, 365, 401, 418, 431, 439
mortification, 19–20, 68, 317, 319, 320–321
Moses, 50, 195, 419, 443, 474
murmuring, 71, 90–91, 206, 253, 256, 277, 279, 338

Nathan, 47
necessaries to be provided for all alike, 251–253
negligence to be avoided, 122, 354
Nerva, 39
Night Office, unpunctuality at, 287–289. See also Matins
night silence, 204, 281–285
Nilus, St., 29, 395
Nitria, 333, 338

nobles, sons of, who are offered, 406–412
nocturns, of ferial Office, 149, 152; of Sunday Office, 154–155; of festal Office, 165
None, 148, 168–169, 170, 175, 179–180, 314
nonnus, 437
novices, 367–405; separated from the professed, 376; studies of, 379; chapter of, 384, 386; admitted to profession by vote of the Community, 386
novice-master, 377–379
novitiate, tests and training of, 379–383; stages and length of, 383–384; one novitiate for a Congregation, 377, 378
nulla regula approbati, 31

obedience, 3–5, 32, 34, 83–91, 472; for love of Our Lord, 83–85, 115; as a part of humility, 114–115; in spite of difficulties, 115–118, 472–475; vow of, 390; novice to be zealous for, 377, 380; of monks one to another, 482–485, 487–488; the best index of spiritual progress, 483
obedientiæ bonum, 482
oblates, adult, 365, 412; children, 406–412, 434–435. See Children
obligation of the Rule, 391–393
oblivio, 106
Odilo, St., 443, 450
Odo of Cluny, St., 443, 446
Office, the Divine, the *Opus Dei*, 133; its meaning and place in Benedictine life, 131–137; terminations of, 152, 156, 162; excessive multiplication of Offices, 173; beginning of, 177; how to be said, 185–193; the Night Office, 138–157, 164–167, 182; the Day Offices, 158–163, 170–182; nothing to be put before it, 287; the sign for, 302; how to be said away from the monastery, 322–324; novices to be zealous for, 380
Office of the Dead, 173
officials of the monastery hold their offices *ad nutum Abbatis*, 198. See also Cellarer, etc.
officiousness, 479–480
old monks, 263
Optatus, St., 114
opus Dei, 133
opus peculiare, 355
Orange, Council of, 5, 72
oratory of the monastery, 327–329
order of the Community, 431–440; not to be determined by age, 433; generally fixed by date of "conversion," 434; special ordinances for priests and clerics, 415–417, 422, 428, and for pilgrim monks, 422
Ordericus Vitalis, 353

Orleans, Councils of, 219, 407, 423
Ouen, St., 425
Ovid, 76

Pachomius, 22, 85, 93, 98, 193, 206, 229, 243, 281, 288, 291, 299, 316, 323, 332, 333, 343, 371, 373, 379, 384, 395, 405, 414, 419, 424, 442, 456, 461, 468, 470, 471, 477, 488
Palestine, psalmody of, 147
Palladius, *Lausiac History*, 221, 335, 425
Palladius, *De re rustica*, 348
Paphnutius, Abbot, 369
Paradise of the Fathers, 426
Pardon, humble asking for, 484–485. See also Confession
Pargoire, Père, 171
pastoral work, 424. See also Apostolic activities
Paternoster, 162–163
patria potestas, 37, 60, 411
Paul, St., 18, 123. Quoted, *passim*
Paul the Deacon, 338, 353, 358, 404, 408, 409, 414, 421, 427, 437, 440, 470
Paul Orosius, 26
Paul the Simple, St., 28, 373
Paula, St., 302
Paulinus of Nola, St., 4, 344
Paulinus (biographer of St. Ambrose), 146
Pax, the Benedictine motto, 11
pedules, 201, 350
Pelagianism, 5, 72, 163
penances, for faults in general, 205–217, 299–301; for the incorrigible, 225–227; for boys, 231–232, 298; for unpunctuality, 286–293; for the excommunicated, 294–296; for mistakes in choir, 297–298
Penitential psalms, 173
Peregrinatio Eucheriæ, 156, 164–165, 166
Perpetua and Felicity, SS., 102
Peter Damian, St., 184
Peter the Venerable, 93, 230, 323, 337, 351, 358, 384, 439, 465
Petit, Mgr., 146
Petition, the Profession, 385
Petronax, 272
pigmentum, 276
pilgrim monks, 418–423. See also Guests
Pius X., Pope, 161, 183
Placid, St., 57, 408, 412, 433, 446, 473
Plato, 42, 72, 75, 450
Pliny, 138–139
politeness, 435–440, 483
Pontifical, the Roman, 413, 443, 489
poor, sons of, who are offered, 406–412. See also Guests
Porcarius, 287
Porphyry, 72
porter of the monastery, 463–467
postulants, 371–375

poverty, monastic, 245–253; vow of, 247, 345; Abbot sees to observance of, 355–356. See Clothes, etc.
præpositus, 437, 456
prayer, necessity of, 5–6; qualities of, 77, 97, 189–193; remote preparation for, 186–187; private prayer, 192–193, 318–319, 327–329. See also Meditation; Mental Prayer; Liturgy
preces feriales, 152
presence of God, the thought of the, 74–75, 107–109, 111–112, 128, 185–186
presents to monks, 343–345.
pride, 72, 100–101, 206, 266–267, 361. See Self-complacency
priesthood, relation of, to monastic life, 413–414, 424
priests in the monastery, 413–417, 424–430
Prime, 168–169, 171, 172, 174, 178–179; interval between Lauds and, 171; night silence ends at, 285; work begins after, 312
prior (*præpositus*) of the monastery, 197, 456–462; St. Benedict severe about, 457–459; to be appointed by the Abbot, 459–460; to be in all things submissive to the Abbot, 461; to be punished if refractory, 462
prior, signifies in the Rule the Abbot, a superior, a senior, 96, 117, 162, 192, 267, 275, 292, 333, 335, 336, 435, 436, 438, 474, 482, 484
pro modo conversationis, 200, 204
προεστώς, 437, 456
profession, admission of novices to, 386; character and consequences of, 392–398; a second baptism, 399; ceremonial of, 393–402; schedule of, 385, 397–398
Prometheus, 21
promptitude in rising, 203, 204
property, private, 245–250; arrangements concerning, before Profession, 402–404, 409–410. See also Poverty
psalms, at Matins on ferial days, 144–153, 182, on Sundays, 154–157, 182, on Saints'-days, 164–167; at Lauds on ferial days, 160–163, on Sundays, 158–159, on Saints'-days, 164–167; at Prime, 174, 178–179; at Little Hours, 175, 179–180; at Vespers, 175, 180–181; at Compline, 175, 182; probably said standing, 151; study of, 142; the principle of St. Benedict's distribution of, 165, 167, 183; does not regard his distribution of, as final, 183; the authentic Divine prayer, 183
psalmody, kinds of, 145–148; essential part of the Office, 149
psalmus responsorius, 146
pueritia, 231

pulmentarium, 270
punctuality, in rising from sleep, 203, 204; at Community exercises, 286–293; law allowed at different Offices, 288–290; penances for faults in, 288–291; Abbot to be responsible for, 302–303
punishment, ground of, 220; not to be inflicted without authority, 479–481; corporal, 49–50, 207–210, 225, 231, 298, 485. See also Correction; Penances
puritatis devotio, 190
purity of prayer, 190

Quintilian, 49
Quintus Curtius, 8

Racine, 218
Raguel, 436
Rancé, Abbot de, 118–119, 300
reader, the weekly, 265–269; of Lessons, 142, 303
reading, at meals, 265–268; after supper or Vespers, 283–284; sacred, 77, 142, 306–308, 314–316, 318–319, 493–495
reception of brethren into religion, 367–405. See Admission; Guests
recollection, 2, 173, 281, 301; before sleep, 204
recreation, 94. See Conversation
recruitment of the monastery, 52, 340, 360, 371–373. See Admission
refectory, servers in, 254–257; reading in, 265–268; penances in, 300; for the sick, 260; for guests, 338–340; the Abbot's, 358–360
Regula S. Antonii, 72
Regula cujusdam ad virgines, 465
Regula Magistri, 33, 141, 142, 196, 209, 269, 331, 338, 404, 442, 469
Regula Orientalis, 207
Regula SS. Patrum I., 46, 211, 234, 237, 244, 268, 303, 341, 359, 371, 422, 423
Regula SS. Patrum II., 321
Regulus, 228
relationships, in the monastery, 476
religion, meaning of, 131–137
religious, what is a? 134; religious life the perfection of the Christian life, 387
Responses, at Matins, 148, 151, 153, 155, 157, 165; at Lauds, 159, 162; at Vespers, 175, 181
responsorial psalmody, 146
responsum, 325, 464
reverence in prayer, 189–193
Ring of Pope Xystus, 127
rising, time of, 139–141, 143, 154, 157; promptitude in, 203, 204
Robert, St., 353
Roman Liturgy, 138, 149, 150, 152, 155, 161, 166, 177, 181, 182

Romanus, St., 302, 347, 418
Rome, Council of (A.D. 826), 425
Rufinus, 34, 68, 101, 126–127, 176, 191, 267, 330, 333, 334, 336, 426, 463
Rule of St. Basil, recommended by St. Benedict, 493. See also Basil, St.
Rule of St. Benedict, manuscripts, sources, commentaries, x–xii; moderation of, 19, 251, 473, 492; stability an essential element of, 24; titles of the chapters, 25; to be observed by all, 58–59, 454; called "holy" by St. Benedict himself, 206, 461, 462; its master thought the seeking of God, 305; to be read to the novices frequently, 383–384, and to the whole Community, 384, 467; one of those approved by the Church, 388; vows to be taken according to, 390; the obligation of, 390–391; the closing chapters especially venerable, 472; obedience its alpha and omega, 482; Chapter LXXII. a synthesis of, 486; St. Benedict's modest opinion of, 491–496; adaptability of, 495. Textual notes, 3, 5, 12, 17, 18, 25, 31, 33, 38, 40, 59, 63, 91, 96, 104, 109, 112, 113, 127, 143, 155, 202, 205, 221, 223, 228, 229, 241, 270, 282, 284, 299, 301, 323, 367, 428, 453, 466, 467, 480
Rule of SS. Paul and Stephen, 80
Rule. See also Regula
Rutilius Namatianus, 25

Sacred reading. See Reading
sagum, 355
Saint-Denys, 425
St. Maur, Congregation of, 260, 310, 366, 374, 377, 379, 384, 385, 394, 398, 399, 401, 438, 459
St. Vanne, Congregation of, 366, 438, 459
SS. Vitonus and Hydulphus, Congregation of, 300
Saints, cultus of, in monastic churches, 164–165
Saints'-days, Office on, 150, 164–167
Salmanticenses, 94
salutation, modes of, between monks, 439. See *Benedicite*
Samuel, 57, 433
sanatorium, 260
sanctity, kinds of, 354
sapientiæ doctrina, 197
Sarabaites, 31–33, 418
Satan. See Devil
scapular, 202, 349–350
Scete, 333, 426
Schenoudi of Atripé, 395
schola dominici servitii, 19
scriptorium, 201

Index

Scripture, use of, in the *Rule*, 8, 9; sacramental value of, 226; to be read to guests, 335; recommended by St. Benedict, 492-495. See also Lessons; Reading
self-assertion, 124
self-complacency, 15, 72, 78, 321. See Pride
self-love, 68, 100-101, 476
self-will, 21, 109-110, 113
selling of the produce of the monastery, 363-364
Seneca, 75
seniores, 202, 204
seniors, relations of, with juniors, 435-440; council of, 59-60, 196
Sens, Council of, 105
Sentences of Sextus, 62, 126
Serapion Sindonita, 221
Sermo asceticus de renuntiatione sæculi, 440
Servandus, Abbot, 419
servers in the kitchen and at meals, 254-257
seven Offices of the day, 172-173
Sext, 148, 168-169, 170, 171, 175, 179-180, 312
Sextus, Sentences of, 62, 126
shoes, 349-350
sic stemus ad psallendum, 151
sick monks, 258-262; cellarer's duty towards, 237
sicut erat . . ., 145
Sidonius Apollinaris, 348
siesta, 143, 312, 314
signs, use of, at meals, 267-268; for Hours of the Office, 302, 314
silence, the spirit of, 92-99; a part of humility, 115-116, 125-126; how far enjoined by St. Benedict, 76, 93, 125, 316; material silence, 98; interior, 98-99; at meals, 267-268; after Compline, 204, 281-285; in Lent, 319; in the oratory, 328
silent obedience, 116
simple vows distinguished from solemn, 247, 388
simplicity of heart, 10, 71
sincerity, 10, 71
singularity, to be avoided, 124
Siricius, Pope St., 424
sleep, manner and measure of, 200-204; time of rising from, 139-141, 143, 154, 157; promptitude in rising from, 203, 204; recollection before, 204. See Siesta
Smaragdus, 59, 150, 267, 350, 438, 458, 469, 471, 480
solemn vows distinguished from simple, 247, 388
solemnitas, 158
Solesmes, 374, 394

solitude, dangers of, 28, 30
somnolentorum excusationes, 204
Spiritual Life and Prayer, 382
spiritual reading, 77, 142, 306-308, 314-316, 318-319, 493-495
stability, essential element in the Rule, 24, 27, 34, 82; meaning of, 389; vow of, 388-389; to be promised by pilgrim monk, 421; St. Benedict anxious for, 466-467
statio, 187
Stephen, St., 123
Stobæus, 78
stockings, 350, 352
Stoics, 117, 211
study, of psalter and lessons, 142; matter and method of, 306-311; studies of novices, 379. See also Reading
Subiaco, 195, 298, 348, 424, 431, 439
sufferings, 20-24; of obedience, 115-118; of monastic life, 381-383
Sulpicius Severus, 58, 77, 88, 437
Sunday, occupations of, 316; the Office of, 154-159, 168-169
super statutam annonam, 256
superfluitas, 259, 419
supplicatio litaniæ, 156
Surin, Père, 126
sympæçta, 221

Tabennisi, 433
tabulæ, 356
tacita conscientia, 116
Tacitus, 39, 69
taciturnitas, 92
talkativeness, 95-97, 125
talking. See Conversation; Silence
Te decet laus, 156
Te Deum, 155
tears, gift of, 191, 328, 329
temptations, to be cast down before Our Lord, 14, 75, 76; manifestation of, 75, 76, 120-121, 300-301
Terce, 148, 168-169, 170-171, 175, 179-180; in the fields, 312, 314
Terence, 450
Teresa, St., 22, 104, 204, 259
Terracina, 195, 339, 346, 356
Tertullian, 7, 130, 189, 334, 347, 439, 494
Tertullus, 408, 412
Thebaid, 467
Thelema, 35
Theodemar, 348, 349, 353
Theodore of Canterbury, St., 394
Theodoret, 442
Theophilus of Alexandria, 102
therapeutæ, 26
Thomas Aquinas, St., 1, 11, 26, 30, 43, 64, 76, 79, 94, 103, 131, 132, 134, 135, 192, 249, 370, 372, 387, 391, 399, 453
Thomassin, 407, 425

time, how computed by St. Benedict, 139–141. See Meals; Office; Sleep; Year
Tobias, 436
tokens (*eulogiæ*), 343–345
Toledo, Council of (A.D. 633), 410, 411
tolerance, mutual, 488
tonsure, 30, 375, 395
tools of the monastery, 243–244
Trappists, 122, 362
Trent, Council of, 384, 404, 406, 443, 446
Trinity, the Blessed, 37, 130, 131, 133, 216
tunic, 350, 352, 353
Turrecremata, 336
typus, 241

Udalric, 151, 438
University of Paris, 26
unpunctuality, in rising, 203–204; at Community exercises, 286–293
unworldliness, 69, 326
ut prævalet, 48

Vaison, Council of (A.D. 529), 145, 152
valetudinarianism, 259
Valladolid, Congregation of, 457
Vallombrosan Order, 336
Vannes, Council of (A.D. 465), 29
Varro, 244
vel, 27, 469
Verba Seniorum, 3, 28, 33, 125, 184, 236, 276, 354, 415
Versicles, at Matins, 150, 154, 155, 157; at Lauds, 162; at Prime, 174; at Little Hours, 175, 179–180; at Vespers, 175, 181; at Compline, 175
versus = grace at meals, 291
Vespers, 169, 170, 171, 172, 175, 180–181; Paternoster at, 162; hour of, 279–280; reading after, 283–284
Vicovaro, 32, 67, 447
Vienne, Council of (A.D. 1311), 425
Vigilantius, 168
vigiliæ, 140
Vigilius, Pope, 442
Vigils. See Matins

Virgil, 189, 381
Vitæ Patrum, 72, 93, 184, 494. See also *Verba Seniorum*
Vitry, Jacques de, 93
Vivarium, 261
vocation, 368–370; requirements of Benedictine, 370–373
voluptas habet pœnam, 113
vows of religion, 386–392; theological basis of, 386–388; distinction between simple and solemn vows, 388; vow of stability, 388–389, of conversion of manners, 389–390, of obedience, 390; taken according to Rule and Constitutions, 390; obligation of, 390–393; vow of poverty, 247; formula of, 385, 397–398, to be kept in the monastery, 405; vows of Oblates, 406–408. See also Profession

Wandrille, St., 425
washing of the feet. See Maundy
water-supply of monastery, 466, 467
weapons of obedience, 4
will, renunciation of, 4; perversity of, the root of serious faults, 206–207. See also Self-will.
wine, allowed by St. Benedict, 275–277
wit, pleasantness of (εὐτραπελία), 94, 125
work, value of, 304–305; kinds of, for monks, 361–366. See also Manual labour; Study
Work of God, the Divine Office, 133. See Office
world, relations of monks with, 340–342, 343, 371, 466. See Enclosure
worldliness, 69, 326
Worms, Council of (A.D. 868), 410

Year, variously divided by St. Benedict, 311

Zachary, Pope, 272
zeal for the Work of God, 287, 380; the good zeal which monks ought to have, 486–490

Printed in England

Printed in Great Britain
by Amazon